EXAM SHELF

Cracking the

SAT®

2017 Edition

The Staff of The Princeton Review

PrincetonReview.com

Penguin
Random
House

The Princeton Review
555 W. 18th Street
New York, NY 10011
E-mail: editorialsupport@review.com

ISBN: 978-1-101-92047-3
eBook ISBN: 978-1-101-92064-0
ISSN: 1934-239X

Editor: Colleen Day
Production Editors: Lee Elder and Harmony Quiroz
Production Artist: Deborah A. Silvestrini

2017 Edition

Acknowledgments

An SAT course is much more than clever techniques and powerful computer score reports. The reason our results are great is that our teachers care so much about their students. Many teachers have gone out of their way to improve the course, often going so far as to write their own materials, some of which we have incorporated into our course manuals as well as into this book. The list of these teachers could fill this page.

Special thanks to Jonathan Chiu and all those who contributed to this year's edition: Cat Healey, Amy Minster, Sara Soriano, and Elizabeth Owens.

Thanks to Brian Becker, Joelle Cotham, Julia Ayles, Lori DesRochers, Bobby Hood, Aaron Lindh, Garrison Pierzynski, Nicole-Henriette Pirnie, Ed Carroll, Pete Stajk, David Stoll, and Curtis Retherford for their work on previous iterations of this title.

Special thanks to Adam Robinson, who conceived of and perfected the Joe Bloggs approach to standardized tests and many of the other successful techniques used by The Princeton Review.

Finally, we would like to thank the people who truly have taught us everything we know about the SAT: our students.

Contents

Foreword

Welcome to *Cracking the SAT!* The SAT is not a test of aptitude, how good of a person you are, or how successful you will be in life. The SAT simply tests how well you take the SAT. And performing well on the SAT is a skill, one that can be learned like any other. The Princeton Review was founded more than 30 years ago on this very simple idea, and—as our students' test scores show—our approach is the one that works.

Sure, you want to do well on the SAT, but you don't need to let the test intimidate you. As you prepare, remember two important things about the SAT:

- **It doesn't measure the stuff that matters.** It measures neither intelligence nor the depth and breadth of what you're learning in high school. It doesn't predict college grades as well as your high school grades do. Colleges know there is more to you as a student—and as a person—than what you do in a single 3-hour test administered on a random Saturday morning.

- **It underpredicts the college performance of women, minorities, and disadvantaged students.** Historically, women have done better than men in college but worse on the SAT. For a test that is used to help predict performance in college, that's a pretty poor record.

Your preparation for the SAT starts here. We at The Princeton Review spend millions of dollars every year improving our methods and materials so that students are always ready for the SAT, and we'll get you ready too.

However, there is no magic pill: Just buying this book isn't going to improve your scores. Solid score improvement takes commitment and effort from you. If you read this book carefully and work through the problems and practice tests included in the book, not only will you be well-versed in the format of the SAT and the concepts it tests, you will also have a sound overall strategy and a powerful arsenal of test-taking strategies that you can apply to whatever you encounter on test day.

In addition to the comprehensive review in *Cracking the SAT*, we've included additional practice online, accessible through our website—**PrincetonReview. com**—to make it even more efficient at helping you to improve your scores. Before doing anything else, be sure to register your book at **PrincetonReview. com/cracking.** When you do, you'll gain access to the most up-to-date information on the SAT, as well as more SAT and college admissions resources.

The more you take advantage of the resources we've included in this book and the online student tools that go with it, the better you'll do on the test. Read the book carefully and learn our strategies. Take the full-length practice tests under actual timed conditions. Analyze your performance and focus your efforts where you need improvement. Perhaps even study with a friend to stay motivated. Attend a free event at The Princeton Review to learn more about the SAT and how it is used in the college admissions process. Search our website for an event that will take place near you!

This test is challenging, but you're on the right track. We'll be with you all the way.

Good luck!

The Staff of The Princeton Review

Register Your

1 Go to **PrincetonReview.com/cracking**

2 You'll see a welcome page where you can register your book using the following ISBN: 9781101920473

3 After placing this free order, you'll either be asked to log in or to answer a few simple questions in order to set up a new Princeton Review account.

4 Finally, click on the "Student Tools" tab located at the top of the screen. It may take an hour or two for your registration to go through, but after that, you're good to go.

If you are experiencing book problems (potential content errors), please contact EditorialSupport@review.com with the full title of the book, its ISBN number (located above), and the page number of the error. Experiencing technical issues? Please e-mail TPRStudentTech@review.com with the following information:

- your full name
- e-mail address used to register the book
- full book title and ISBN
- your computer OS (Mac or PC) and Internet browser (Firefox, Safari, Chrome, etc.)
- description of technical issue

Book Online!

Once you've registered, you can...

- Access and print out an additional full-length practice test (Practice Test 4) as well as the corresponding answers and explanations

- Find any late-breaking information released about the SAT

- Check out articles with valuable advice about the college application process

- Sort colleges by whatever you're looking for (such as Best Theater or Dorm), learn more about your top choices, and see how they all rank according to *The Best 381 Colleges*

- Download printable resources such as score conversion tables, extra bubble sheets, and essay answer forms for the practice tests

- Check to see if there have been any corrections or updates to this edition

Look For These Icons Throughout The Book

 Online Articles   Applied Strategies

 Online Practice Tests   Study Break

 Proven Techniques   More Great Books

The
Princeton
Review®

Part I
Orientation

LET'S GET THIS PARTY STARTED!

You are about to unlock a vast repertoire of powerful strategies that have one and only one purpose: to help you get a better score on the SAT. This book contains the collected wisdom of The Princeton Review, which has spent more than 35 years helping students achieve higher scores on standardized tests. We've devoted millions of dollars and years of our lives to cracking the SAT. It's what we do (twisted as it may be), and we want you to benefit from our expertise.

WHAT IS THE PRINCETON REVIEW?

The Princeton Review is the leader in test prep. Our goal is to help students everywhere crack the SAT and a bunch of other standardized tests, including the PSAT and ACT as well as graduate-level exams like the GRE and GMAT. Starting from humble beginnings in 1981, The Princeton Review is now the nation's largest SAT preparation company. We offer courses in more than 500 locations in 20 different countries, as well as online; we also publish best-selling books, like the one you're holding, and online resources to get students ready for this test.

Our techniques work. We developed them after spending countless hours scrutinizing real SATs, analyzing them with computers, and proving our theories in the classroom.

The Princeton Review Way

This book will show you how to crack the SAT by teaching you to:

- extract important information from tricky test questions
- take full advantage of the limited time allowed
- systematically answer questions—even if you don't fully understand them
- avoid the traps that the SAT has laid for you (and use those traps to your advantage)

Study!
If you were getting ready to take a biology test, you'd study biology. If you were preparing for a basketball game, you'd practice basketball. So, if you're preparing for the SAT, you need to study and practice for the SAT. The exam can't test everything you learn in school (in fact, it tests very little), so concentrate on learning what it *does* test.

The test is written by Educational Testing Service (ETS) and administered by the College Board, and they know that our techniques work. For years, the test writers claimed that the SAT couldn't be coached. But we've proven that view wrong, and they in turn have struggled to find ways of changing the SAT so that The Princeton Review won't be able to crack it—in effect, acknowledging what our students have known all along: that our techniques really do work. (In fact, ETS has recently admitted that students can and should prepare for the SAT. So there!) The SAT has remained highly vulnerable to our techniques. And the current version of the SAT is even more susceptible to our methods. Read this book, work through the drills, take the practice tests, and you'll see what we mean.

Chapter 1
The SAT, The Princeton Review, and You

Welcome! Our job is to help you get the best possible score on the SAT. This chapter tells you what to expect from the SAT as well as some specifics about the test. It will also explain how to make the most of all your Princeton Review materials.

GENERAL INFORMATION ABOUT THE SAT

You may have bought this book because you know nothing about the SAT, or perhaps you took the test once and want to raise your score. Either way, it's important to know about the test and the people who write it. Let's take a second to discuss some SAT facts: Some of them may surprise you.

What Does the SAT Test?

Just because the SAT features math, reading, and writing questions doesn't mean that it reflects what you learned in school. You can ace calculus or write like Faulkner and still struggle with the SAT. The test writers claim that the test predicts how well you will do in college by measuring "reasoning ability," but all the SAT really measures is how well you take the SAT. It does *not* reveal how smart—or how good of—a person you are.

Who Writes the SAT?

Wait, *Who* Writes This Test?
You may be surprised to learn that the people who write SAT test questions are NOT necessarily teachers or college professors. The people who write the SAT are professional test writers, not superhuman geniuses, so you can beat them at their own game.

Even though colleges and universities make wide use of the SAT, they're not the ones who write the test. That's the job of Educational Testing Service (ETS), a nonprofit company that writes tests for college and graduate school admissions on behalf of the College Board, the organization that decides how the tests will be administered and used. ETS also writes tests for groups as diverse as butchers and professional golfers (who knew?).

ETS and the College Board are often criticized for the SAT. Many educators have argued that the test does not measure the skills you really need for college. This led them in 2005 to overhaul the entire test, only to revise it all over again in early 2016. The important takeaway here is that the people who write the SAT are professional test writers, and, with some practice, it's possible to beat them at their own game.

What's on the SAT?

Key Takeaway
What really matters to you as a test-taker is how the test is divided up and what YOU need to know to crack it!

The SAT is 3 hours long, or 3 hours and 50 minutes long if you choose to take the "optional" 50-minute essay. (Note: The essay is optional for colleges, but many schools require it. Be sure to research and determine if you need to take the essay for the schools you're applying to!). The exam consists of the following:

- 1 multiple-choice Reading Test (52 questions, 65 minutes)
- 1 multiple-choice Writing and Language Test (44 questions, 35 minutes)
- 1 Math Test, consisting of a No Calculator section (20 questions, 25 minutes) and a Calculator section (38 questions, 55 minutes)
- the optional Essay (50 minutes)

Both sections of the Math Test contain some student-produced-response questions, called Grid-Ins, but all other questions on the exam are multiple choice. All multiple-choice sections on the SAT have four possible answer choices.

Each part of this book covers these tests in detail, but here's a brief rundown of what you can expect.

Reading Test

Your scores on the Reading Test and the Writing and Language Test (see below) together comprise your Evidence-Based Reading and Writing score on the SAT. The Reading Test is 65 minutes long and consists of 52 questions, all of which are passage-based and multiple choice. Passages may be paired with informational graphics, such as charts or graphs, and there will also be a series of questions based on a pair of passages. The selected passages will be from previously published works in the areas of world literature, history/social studies, and science. Questions based on science passages may ask you to analyze data or hypotheses, while questions about literature passages will concentrate more on literary concepts like theme, mood, and characterization. The main goal is to measure your ability to both understand words in context and find and analyze evidence.

Want More?
For even more practice, check out *6 Practice Tests for the SAT.*

Writing and Language Test

The Writing and Language Test is 35 minutes long and consists of 44 questions, which are also multiple choice and based on several passages. However, instead of asking you to analyze a passage, questions will ask you to proofread and edit the passage. That means you'll have to correct grammar and word choice and make larger changes to the organization or content of the passage.

Math Test

You'll have a total of 80 minutes to complete the Math Test, which, as mentioned earlier, is divided into two sections: No Calculator (Section 3; 25 minutes, 20 questions) and Calculator (Section 4; 55 minutes, 38 questions). Most questions are multiple choice, but there are also a handful of student-produced response questions, which are also known as Grid-Ins. (Instead of choosing from four answer choices, you'll have to work through a problem and then enter your answer on your answer sheet by bubbling in the appropriate numbers. We'll discuss this in more detail in Chapter 17.) Exactly 13 of the 58 math questions will be Grid-Ins.

The Math Test covers four main content areas, which the test developers have named the following: (1) Heart of Algebra, (2) Problem Solving and Data Analysis, (3) Passport to Advanced Math, and (4) Additional Topics in Math. This last section includes topics in geometry and trigonometry. Part IV of this book covers each of these content areas in depth.

Optional Essay

As of March 2016, the Essay section of the SAT is "optional." This word is in quotes because many schools may require the essay portion of the SAT, so be sure to do your research and determine if you need to take this part of the test! This essay requires you to read a short passage and explain how the author effectively builds his or her argument. The test writers want to see how you comprehend a text and demonstrate that understanding in writing, using evidence from the text.

Scoring on the SAT

The SAT is scored on a scale of 400–1600, which is a combination of your scores for Evidence-Based Reading and Writing (a combination of your Reading and W & L scores; scored from 200 to 800) and Math (also scored from 200 to 800). The exam also has detailed scoring system that includes cross-test scores and subscores based on your performance on each of the three tests. Your score report for the SAT will feature scores for each of the following:

A Note on Essay Scoring

If you choose to write the essay, you will be graded by two readers in three areas: Reading, Writing, and Analysis. Your total essay score will be on a 2- to 8-point scale for each of the three areas. See Part V for more on the essay and how it is scored.

- **Total score (1):** The sum of the two section scores (Evidence-Based Reading and Writing and Math), ranging from 400 to 1600
- **Section scores (2):** Evidence-Based Reading and Writing, ranging from 200–800; Math, also ranging from 200 to 800
- **Test scores (3):** Reading Test, Writing and Language Test, Math Test, each of which is scored on a scale from 10 to 40
- **Cross-test scores (2):** Each is scored on a scale from 10 to 40 and based on selected questions from the three tests (Reading, Writing and Language, Math):
  1. Analysis in History/Social Studies
  2. Analysis in Science
- **Subscores (7):** Each of the following receives a score from 1 to 15:
  1. Command of Evidence (Reading; Writing and Language)
  2. Words in Context (Reading; Writing and Language)
  3. Expression of Ideas (Writing and Language)
  4. Standard English Conventions (Writing and Language)
  5. Heart of Algebra (Math)
  6. Problem Solving and Data Analysis (Math)
  7. Passport to Advanced Math (Math)

This scoring structure was designed to help provide a more holistic profile of students' skills and knowledge, as well as readiness for college.

WHEN IS THE SAT GIVEN?

The SAT schedule for the school year is posted on the College Board website at www.collegeboard.org. There are two ways to sign up for the test. You can either sign up online by going to www.collegeboard.org and clicking on the SAT hyperlink, or sign up through the mail with an SAT registration booklet, which may be available at your school guidance counselor's office.

Try to sign up for the SAT as soon as you know when you'll be taking the test. If you wait until the last minute to sign up, there may not be any open spots in the testing centers.

If you require any special accommodations while taking the test (including, but not limited to, extra time or assistance), www.collegeboard.org has information about applying for those accommodations. Make sure to apply early; we recommend applying six months before you plan to take the test.

Stay on Schedule
Although you may take the SAT any time starting freshman year, most students take it for the first time in the spring of their junior year and possibly retake it in the fall of their senior year. In addition, you may also need to take SAT subject tests (many competitive colleges require them), so don't leave everything to the last minute. You can't take SAT and SAT Subject Tests on the same day. Sit down and plan a schedule.

HOW TO USE THIS BOOK

This book is organized to provide as much—or as little—support as you need, so you can use it in whatever way will be helpful to improving your score on the SAT. But before you can decide how to use this book, you should take a practice test to determine your strengths and weaknesses and figure out how to make an effective study plan. If you're feeling test-phobic, remind yourself that a practice test is a tool for diagnosing yourself—it's not how well you do that matters, but how you use the information gleaned from your performance to guide your preparation.

So, before you read any further, take **Practice Test 1** that starts on page 481 of Part VII. Be sure to take it in one sitting so as to mimic the real test-taking experience, and remember to follow the instructions that appear at the beginning of each section of the exam.

After you take the test, check your answers against the Answers and Explanations that start on page 547, reflect on your performance, and determine the areas in which you need to improve. Which sections or types of questions presented the most difficulty to you? Which sections or types of questions did you feel most confident about? Based on your performance on each of the sections, should you focus your study more on math, reading, or writing?

How you answer those questions will affect how you engage with **Part II** (How to Crack the Reading Test), **Part III** (How to Crack the Writing and Language Test), **Part IV** (How to Crack the Math Test), and **Part V** (How to Crack the Essay) of this book. Each of these parts is designed to give a comprehensive review of the content tested on the SAT, including the level of detail you need to know and how the content is tested. At the end of each of these chapters, you'll have the opportunity to assess your mastery of the content covered through targeted drills that reflect the types of questions and level of difficulty you'll see on the actual exam.

Scoring Your Practice Tests
At the end of each Answers and Explanations chapter, we've provided a table and step-by-step equation to help you score your practice test and determine how your performance would translate to the actual SAT. You can also generate a detailed online score report in your Student Tools. Follow the steps on the Register Your Book Online! page to access this awesome feature.

In addition to content review, this book also provides essential test-taking strategies that will help you avoid traps and manage your time in order to maximize the number of points available to you. Strategies are discussed in every content chapter, but you can also find a helpful overview in **Chapter 2** of the ones that come up frequently throughout the book. This chapter will help you think about your approach to the various question types on the exam.

You'll have the chance to apply these strategies in **Part VII**, which contains the remaining practice tests. If you need additional practice, you can download Practice Test 4 online by registering your book on our website and following the steps to access your online resources. (See "Register Your Book Online!" on page x.) You do not have to take every practice test available to you, but doing so will allow you to continually gauge your performance, address your deficiencies, and improve.

And remember, your prep should not end with this book. There are a host of resources available to you online, including the online tools accompanying this book (see "Register Your Book Online!") as well as the College Board website, **www.collegeboard.org.**

Get More Online

If you need more practice, head over to our website to register your book and download Practice Test 4. Follow the directions on the Register Your Book Online! page to access this content and more!

Chapter 2
Cracking the SAT: Basic Principles

The first step to cracking the SAT is knowing how best to approach the test. The SAT is not like the tests you've taken in school, so you need to learn to look at it in a different way. This chapter will show test-taking strategies that immediately improve your score. Make sure you fully understand these concepts before moving on to Part II. Good luck!

BASIC PRINCIPLES OF CRACKING THE TEST

What ETS Does Well

The folks at ETS have been writing standardized tests for more than 80 years, and they write tests for all sorts of programs. They have administered the SAT so many times that they know exactly how you will approach it. They know how you'll attack certain questions, what sort of mistakes you'll probably make, and even what answer you'll be most likely to pick. Freaky, isn't it?

However, ETS's strength is also a weakness. Because the test is standardized, the SAT has to ask the same type of questions over and over again. Sure, the numbers or the words might change, but the basics don't. With enough practice, you can learn to think like the test writers. But try to use your powers for good, okay?

The SAT Isn't School

Our job isn't to teach you math or English—leave that to your supersmart school teachers. Instead, we're going to teach you what the SAT is and how to crack the SAT. You'll soon see that the SAT involves a very different skill set.

> **No More Wrong-Answer Penalty!**
> You will NOT be penalized on the SAT for any wrong answers. This means you should always guess, even if this means choosing an answer at random.

Be warned that some of the approaches we're going to show you may seem counterintuitive or unnatural. Some of these strategies may be very different from the way you learned to approach similar questions in school, but trust us! Try tackling the problems using our techniques, and keep practicing until they become easier. You'll see a real improvement in your score.

Let's take a look at the questions.

Cracking Multiple-Choice Questions

What's the capital of Azerbaijan?

Give up?

Unless you spend your spare time studying an atlas, you may not even know that Azerbaijan is a real country, much less what its capital is. If this question came up on a test, you'd have to skip it, wouldn't you? Well, maybe not. Let's turn this question into a multiple-choice question—just like all the questions on the SAT Reading Test and Writing and Language Test, and the majority of questions you'll find on the SAT Math Test—and see if you can figure out the answer anyway.

The capital of Azerbaijan is

A) Washington, D.C.

B) Paris.

C) London.

D) Baku.

The question doesn't seem that hard anymore, does it? Of course, we made our example extremely easy. (By the way, there won't actually be any questions about geography on the SAT.) But you'd be surprised by how many people give up on SAT questions that aren't much more difficult than this one just because they don't know the correct answer right off the top of their heads. "Capital of Azerbaijan? Oh, no! I've never heard of Azerbaijan!"

These students don't stop to think that they might be able to find the correct answer simply by eliminating all of the answer choices they know are wrong.

You Already Know Almost All of the Answers

All but a handful of the questions on the SAT are multiple-choice questions, and every multiple-choice question has four answer choices. One of those choices, and only one, will be the correct answer to the question. You don't have to come up with the answer from scratch. You just have to identify it.

How will you do that?

Look for the Wrong Answers Instead of the Right Ones

Why? Because wrong answers are usually easier to find than the right ones. After all, there are more of them! Remember the question about Azerbaijan? Even though you didn't know the answer off the top of your head, you easily figured it out by eliminating the three obviously incorrect choices. You looked for wrong answers first.

In other words, you used the Process of Elimination, which we'll call POE for short. This is an extremely important concept, one we'll come back to again and again. It's one of the keys to improving your SAT score. When you finish reading this book, you will be able to use POE to answer many questions that you may not understand.

It's Not About Circling the Right Answer

Physically marking in your test booklet what you think of certain answers can help you narrow down choices, take the best possible guess, and save time! Try using the following notations:

- ✔ Put a check mark next to an answer you like.
- ~ Put a squiggle next to an answer you kind of like.
- ? Put a question mark next to an answer you don't understand.
- A̶ Cross out the letter of any answer choice you KNOW is wrong.

You can always come up with your own system. Just make sure you are consistent.

The great artist Michelangelo once said that when he looked at a block of marble, he could see a statue inside. All he had to do to make a sculpture was to chip away everything that wasn't part of it. You should approach difficult SAT multiple-choice questions in the same way, by chipping away everything that's not correct. By first eliminating the most obviously incorrect choices on difficult questions, you will be able to focus your attention on the few choices that remain.

PROCESS OF ELIMINATION (POE)

There won't be many questions on the SAT in which incorrect choices will be as easy to eliminate as they were on the Azerbaijan question. But if you read this book carefully, you'll learn how to eliminate at least one choice on almost any SAT multiple-choice question, if not two or even three choices.

What good is it to eliminate just one or two choices on a four-choice SAT question?

Plenty. In fact, for most students, it's an important key to earning higher scores. Here's another example:

2

The capital of Qatar is

A) Paris.

B) Dukhan.

C) Tokyo.

D) Doha.

On this question you'll almost certainly be able to eliminate two of the four choices by using POE. That means you're still not sure of the answer. You know that the capital of Qatar has to be either Doha or Dukhan, but you don't know which.

Should you skip the question and go on? Or should you guess?

Close Your Eyes and Point

There is no guessing penalty on the SAT, so you should bubble something for every question. If you get down to two answers, just pick one of them. There's no harm in doing so.

You're going to hear a lot of mixed opinions about what you should bubble or whether you should bubble at all. Let's clear up a few misconceptions about guessing.

FALSE: Don't answer a question unless you're absolutely sure of the answer.

You will almost certainly have teachers and guidance counselors who tell you this. Don't listen to them! The SAT does not penalize you for wrong answers. Put something down for every question: You might get a freebie.

FALSE: If you have to guess, guess (C).

This is a weird misconception, and obviously it's not true. As a general rule, if someone says something really weird-sounding about the SAT, it's usually safest not to believe that person.

FALSE: Always pick the [fill in the blank].

Be careful with directives that tell you that this or that answer or type of answer is always right. It's much safer to learn the rules and to have a solid guessing strategy in place.

As far as guessing is concerned, we do have a small piece of advice. First and foremost, make sure of one thing:

Answer every question on the SAT. There's no penalty.

LETTER OF THE DAY (LOTD)

Sometimes you won't be able to eliminate any answers, and other times there are questions that you won't have time to look at. For those, we have a simple solution. Pick a "letter of the day," or LOTD (from A to D) and use that letter for all the questions from which you weren't able to eliminate any choices.

This is a quick and easy way to make sure that you've bubbled everything. It also has some potential statistical advantages. If all the answers show up about a fourth of the time and you guess the same answer every time you have to guess, you're likely to get a couple of freebies.

LOTD should absolutely be an afterthought; it's far more important and helpful to your score to eliminate answer choices. But for those questions you don't know at all, LOTD is better than full-on random guessing or no strategy at all.

Are You Ready?
Check out *Are You Ready for the SAT and ACT?* to brush up on essential skills for these exams and beyond.

PACE YOURSELF

LOTD should remind us about something very important: There's a very good chance that you won't answer every question on the test.

Think about it this way. There are 5 passages and 52 questions on the Reading Test. You've got 65 minutes to complete those questions. Now, everyone knows that the Reading Test is super long and boring, and 52 questions in 65 minutes probably sounds like a ton. The great news is that you don't have to work all 52 of these questions. After all, do you think you read most effectively when you're in a huge rush? You might do better if you worked only four of the passages and LOTD'd the rest. There's nothing in the test booklet that says that you can't work at your own pace.

Let's say you do all 52 Reading questions and get half of them right. What raw score do you get from that? That's right: 26.

Now, let's say you do only three of the 10-question Reading passages and get all of them right. It's conceivable that you could because you've now got all this extra time. What kind of score would you get from this method? You bet: 30—and maybe even a little higher because you'll get a few freebies from your Letter of the Day.

In this case, and on the SAT as a whole, slowing down can get you more points. Unless you're currently scoring in the 650+ range on the two sections, you shouldn't be working all the questions. We'll go into this in more detail in the later chapters, but for now remember this:

> Slow down, score more. You're not scored on *how many questions you do*. You're scored on *how many questions you answer correctly*. Doing fewer questions can mean more correct answers overall!

EMBRACE YOUR POOD

Embrace your what now? POOD! It stands for "Personal Order of Difficulty." One of the things that SAT has dispensed with altogether is a strict Order of Difficulty—in other words, an arrangement of problems that puts easy ones earlier in the test than hard ones. In the absence of this Order of Difficulty (OOD), you need to be particularly vigilant about applying your *Personal* Order of Difficulty (POOD).

Think about it this way. There's someone writing the words that you're reading right now. So what happens if you are asked, *Who is the author of Cracking the SAT?* Do you know the answer to that question? Maybe not. Do we know the answer to that question? Absolutely.

So you can't exactly say that that question is "difficult," but you can say that certain people would have an easier time answering it.

As we've begun to suggest with our Pacing, POE, and Letter of the Day strategies, The Princeton Review's strategies are all about making the test your own, to whatever extent that is possible. We call this idea POOD because we believe it is essential that you identify the questions that you find easy or hard and that you work the test in a way most suitable to your goals and strengths.

As you familiarize yourself with the rest of our strategies, keep all of this in mind. You may be surprised to find out how you perform on particular question types and sections. This test may be standardized, but the biggest improvements are usually reserved for those who can treat the test in a personalized, un-standardized way.

Summary

o When you don't know the right answer to a multiple-choice question, look for wrong answers instead. They're usually easier to find.

o When you find a wrong answer choice, eliminate it. In other words, use POE, the Process of Elimination.

o There's no more guessing penalty on the SAT, so there's no reason NOT to guess.

o There's bound to be at least a few questions you simply don't get to or where you're finding it difficult to eliminate even one answer choice. When this happens, use the LOTD (letter of the day) strategy.

o Pace yourself. Remember: You're not scored on how many questions you answer, but on how many questions you answer correctly. Take it slow and steady.

o Make the test your own. When you can work the test to suit your strengths (and use our strategies to overcome any weaknesses), you'll be on your way to a higher score.

Part II
How to Crack
the Reading Test

Chapter 3
The SAT
Reading Test:
Basic Approach

Half of your Evidence-Based Reading and Writing score comes from the Reading Test, a 65-minute test that requires you to answer 52 questions spread out over five passages. The questions will ask you to do everything from determining the meaning of words in context to deciding an author's purpose for a detail to finding the main idea of a whole passage to pinpointing information on a graph. Each passage ranges from 500 to 750 words and has 10 or 11 questions. Time will be tight on this test. The purpose of this chapter is to introduce you to a basic approach that will streamline how you take the test and allow you to focus on only what you need to get your points.

SAT READING: CRACKING THE PASSAGES

You read every day. From street signs to novels to the back of the cereal box, you spend a good part of your day recognizing written words. So this test should be pretty easy, right?

Unfortunately, "SAT Reading" is different from "real life reading." In real life, you read *passively*. Your eyes go over the words, the words go into your brain, and some stick and some don't. On the SAT, you have to read *actively*, which means trying to find specific information to answer specific questions. Once you've found the information you need, you have to understand what it's actually saying.

Another problem is that SAT Reading can be very different from the reading you do in school. Often, in an English class, you are asked to give your own opinion, supported by the text. You might have to explain how Scout Finch and Boo Radley in *To Kill a Mockingbird* are, metaphorically speaking, mockingbirds. Or explain who is actually responsible for the tragedies in *Romeo and Juliet*. On the SAT, however, there is no opinion. You don't have the opportunity to justify why your answer is the right one. That means there is *only* one right answer, so your job is to find it. It's the weirdest scavenger hunt ever.

Your Mission:

Read five passages and answer 10 or 11 questions for each passage (or set of passages). Get as many points as you can.

Okay, so how do you get those points? Let's start with the instructions for the Reading Test.

DIRECTIONS

Each passage or pair of passages below is followed by a number of questions. After reading each passage or pair, choose the best answer to each question based on what is stated or implied in the passage or passages and in any accompanying graphics (such as a table or graph).

Great news! This is an open-book test. Notice the directions say, "based on what is stated or implied in the passage." This means that you are NOT being tested on whether you have read, studied, and become an expert on the Constitution, *The Great Gatsby*, or your biology textbook. All the test writers care about is whether or not you can read a text and understand it well enough to correctly answer some questions about it. Unlike the Math or Writing and Language Tests, there are no formulas to memorize or comma rules to learn in the Reading Test. You just need to know how to approach the text and the questions/answers in order to maximize accuracy and efficiency. It's all about the text! (No thinking!)

Another awesome thing about an open-book test is that you don't have to waste time reading every single word of the passage and trying to become an expert on whatever the topic is. You have the passage right there in front of you. So, move back and forth between the passage and the questions, focusing only on what you need instead of getting mired down in all the little details.

Your POOD and Your Reading Test

You will get all five of the reading passages at the same time, so use that to your advantage. Take a quick look through the whole section and figure out the best order for you to do the passages. Depending on your target score, you may be able to skip an entire passage or two, so figure out which passages are likely to get you the most points.

Consider:

- **Type of passage**: You'll have one literature passage and two each of science and history/social studies. If you like to read novels and short stories, the literature passage may be a good place to start. If you prefer nonfiction, you might consider doing the science and history/social studies first.
- **Topic of passage:** The blurb will give you some basic information about the passage that may help you decide whether to do the passage or skip it.
- **Types of questions**: Do the questions have a good number of Line References and Lead Words? Will you be able to find what you're looking for relatively quickly, or will you have to spend more time wading through the passage to find what you want?

Don't forget: On any questions or passages that you skip, always fill in your LOTD!

Basic Approach for the Reading Test

Follow these steps for every Reading passage. We'll go over these in greater detail in the next few pages.

Where the Money Is

A reporter once asked notorious thief Willie Sutton why he robbed banks. Legend has it that his answer was, "Because that's where the money is." While reading comprehension is safer and slightly more productive than larceny, the same principle applies: Concentrate on the questions and answer choices because that's where the points are. The passage is just a place for the test writers to stash facts and details. You'll find them when you need to. What's the point of memorizing all 67 pesky details about plankton if you're asked about only 12?

1. **Read the Blurb.** The little italicized bit at the beginning of each passage may not contain a lot of information, but it can be helpful for identifying the type of passage.

2. **Select and Understand a Question.** For the most part, do the questions in order, saving the general questions for last and using your LOTD on any questions or passages you want to skip.

3. **Read What You Need.** Don't read the whole passage! Use Line References and Lead Words to find the reference for the question, and then carefully read a window of about 10–12 lines (usually about 5 or 6 lines above and below the Line Reference/Lead Word) to find the answer to the question.

4. **Predict the Correct Answer.** Your prediction should come straight from the text. Don't analyze or paraphrase. Often, you'll be able to find something in the text that you can actually underline to predict the answer.

5. **POE.** Eliminate anything that isn't consistent with your prediction. Don't necessarily try to find the right answer immediately, because there is a good chance you won't see anything that you like. If you can eliminate answers that you know are wrong, though, you'll be closer to the right answer. If you can't eliminate three answers with your prediction, use the POE criteria (which we'll talk about in a few pages.)

Let's see these steps in action!

A sample passage and questions appear on the next few pages. Don't start working the passage right away. In fact…you can't! The answer choices are missing. Just go ahead to page 26, where we will begin going through the steps of the Basic Approach, using the upcoming passage and questions.

SAMPLE PASSAGE AND QUESTIONS

Here is an example of what a reading comprehension passage and questions look like. We will use this passage to illustrate the reading Basic Approach throughout this chapter. You don't need to do the questions now, but you might want to paperclip this page so it's easy to flip back to later.

Questions 11-21 are based on the following passage.

This passage is adapted from Linton Weeks's "The Windshield-Pitting Mystery of 1954." © 2015 by NPR History Dept.

The nationwide weirdness that was the Windshield-Pitting Mystery began in the spring of 1954. Looking back at the events today may give us a window—OK, a windshield—on the makeup and
[Line] 5 the mindset of mid-20th-century America.

The epidemic's epicenter, according to HistoryLink—an online compendium of Washington state history— was the town of Bellingham, where "tiny holes, pits, and dings ...
10 seemingly appeared in the windshields of cars at an unprecedented rate" in late March.

"Panicked residents," the website reports, suspected "everything from cosmic rays to sand-flea eggs to fallout from H-bomb tests."
15 In Canton, Ohio, some 1,000 residents notified police that their windshields had been "blemished in a mysterious manner," the *Daily Mail* of Hagerstown, MD reported on April 17. And United Press in New York noted on April 20
20 that "new reports of mysterious windshield pittings came in today almost as fast as theories about what causes them." A Canadian scientist posited that the marks were made by the skeletons of minute marine creatures that had been propelled into
25 the air by hydrogen bomb testing in the Pacific Ocean. In Utah, someone suggested that acid from flying bugs might be the source of the windshield-denting, but a Brigham Young University biologist disproved the theory, the Provo *Daily Herald*
30 reported on June 27. As summer rolled on, reports of pitting decreased everywhere and the country moved on to building backyard fallout shelters.

But the question remains: What about those pitted windshields?
35 For guidance, we turn to Missouri State University sociologist David Rohall, who has taught courses in social movements and collective behavior for more than a decade. "Much of what

happens in society is a numbers game," Rohall
40 says. "If you have more people, any phenomenon starts to appear more common if you focus on any one event or behavior. Even something that is very infrequent may start to appear to be a trend, he says, "when you aggregate those events. There are
45 millions of cars in Washington state but thousands of cases of pitting. While thousands sounds like a huge phenomenon, it represents less than 1 percent of cars. If everyone is looking for and reporting it, it would appear to be a conspiracy of some sort."
50 Windshield-pitting, Rohall says, "may be more like crop circles in which there is physical evidence that 'something' happened but no one is certain of the cause. Of course, we have since found evidence that, in some cases, people utilize special
55 equipment to make those crop circles. The cause of the pitting is different because it would be very difficult to capture someone creating them."

"Most people in the field no longer believe in mass hysteria as a cause of large-group behavior,"
60 Rohall says. "The idea came from Gustave Le Bon, a French theorist trying to explain the strange behavior of large groups during the French Revolution, in which average citizens began killing large numbers of people via the guillotine. What
65 would cause them to do such a heinous thing?"

Even if the theory were true, Rohall says, "it is designed to be applied to situations of heightened emotional arousal—for example: large crowds. While the ideas about pitting may have 'caught
70 on' among people in the region, I doubt it was an emotional contagion that drove them to act in a particular way."

"*War of the Worlds* is a wonderful example of how the media emphasizes the few 'real cases' of
75 hysteria without recognizing that the vast majority of people knew that the radio program was fictional and did nothing," Rohall adds. "Like crop circles, we know that some of them are man-made, so might these pits. However, the media may have
80 had people start noticing the pits that had already been there."

He likens the experience to this: "It is very common for people to believe that they have contracted an illness when they hear a doctor
85 describe a medical problem and the symptoms associated with that problem. I suspect that most people already had these pits all along and only attributed it to the mysterious cause when they heard other people doing it. Still others may have
90 resulted from vandalism or new cases from simple accidents—debris from the roads. Is this hysteria or simply logical thinking utilizing information from the media and their own situation—a pitted car? Some research about supposed 'hysteria' really
95 shows that people are not hysterical at all."

These are the questions for the passage. We've removed the answer choices because, for now, we just want you to see the different question types the SAT will ask. Don't worry about answering these here; we'll walk you through some of them in the rest of this chapter.

11

The central claim of the passage is that

12

The author most likely mentions the Canadian scientist (line 22) and the Utah resident (line 26) in order to

13

The author's statement that the "country moved on to building backyard fallout shelters" (lines 31-32) implies that Americans

14

As used in line 41, "common" most nearly means

15

The passage indicates that an effect of aggregating events is

16

According to the passage, what percent of cars in Washington suffered damage?

17

Which choice provides the best evidence for the answer to the previous question?

18

The author most likely mentions *War of the Worlds* in line 73 in order to

19

The quotation marks around the word "hysteria" in line 94 most likely indicate

20

Based on the passage, the author most likely agrees that "pitting" is

21

Which choice provides the best evidence for the answer to the previous question?

The Strategy
1. Read the Blurb

Step 1: The Blurb

You should always begin by reading the blurb (the introductory material above the passage). The blurb gives you the title of the piece, as well as the author and the publication date. Typically the blurb won't have much more information than that, but it'll be enough to let you know whether the passage is literature, history/social studies, or science. It will also give you a sense of what the passage will be about and can help you make a POOD (personal order of difficulty) decision about when to do the passage.

Read the blurb at the beginning of the passage on page 23. Based on the blurb, is the passage literature, history/social studies, or science? What will the passage be about?

_____

_____

The Strategy
1. Read the Blurb
2. Select and Understand
   a Question

Step 2: Select and Understand a Question

Select…

Notice that the steps of the Basic Approach have you jumping straight from the blurb to the questions. There is no "Read the Passage" step. You get points for answering questions, not for reading the passage, so we're going to go straight to the questions.

On a test you take in school, you probably do the questions in order. That seems logical and straightforward. However, doing the questions in order on a Reading passage can set you up for a serious time issue. According to ETS and the College Board, the order of the questions "is also as natural as possible, with general questions about central ideas, themes, point of view, overall text structure, and the like coming early in the sequence, followed by more localized questions about details, words in context, evidence, and the like." So to sum it up: The general questions come first, followed by the specific questions.

That question structure works great in an English class, when you have plenty of time to read and digest the text on your own. When you're trying to get through five passages in just over an hour, you don't have time for that. Instead of starting with the general questions and then answering the specific questions, we're going to flip that and do the specific questions first.

Look back at the questions on page 25.

What does the first question ask you about?

In order to answer that question, you'd have to read what part of the passage?

And what we don't want to do is read the whole passage! So skip that first question. You'll come back to it, but not until you've done the specific questions. Once you go through and answer all (or most) of the specific questions, you'll have a really good idea what the test writers think is important. You'll also have read most of the passage, so answering the general questions will be easy.

Remember we mentioned earlier that the questions are in chronological order? Look at the Line References in the specific questions. What do you notice about them?

Yep! They're in order through the passage! So work through them as they're given, and you'll work through the passage from beginning to end. Do not get stuck on a hard question, though. If you find yourself stumped, use your LOTD and move on to the next question. You can always come back if you have time.

Based on that logic, let's skip the first question and move on to the second question.

…and Understand

Once you've selected a question, you need to make sure you understand what it's asking. Reading questions are often not in question format. Instead, they will make statements such as, "The author's primary reason for mentioning the gadfly is to," and then the answer choices will follow. Make sure that you understand the question by turning it into a question—that is, back into a sentence that ends with a question mark and begins with Who/What/Why.

The author most likely mentions the Canadian scientist (line 22) and the Utah resident (line 26) in order to

Rephrase the Question...

...so that it asks:
Who?
What?
Why?

What is this question asking?

Notice the phrase "in order to" at the end of the question. That phrase lets you know the question can be rephrased as a "why" question. So for this particular question, you want to figure out "Why does the author mention the Canadian scientist and the Utah resident?"

Step 3: Read What You Need

Line Reference and Lead Words

Many questions will refer you to a specific set of lines or to a particular paragraph, so you won't need to read the entire passage to answer those questions. Those are Line References. Other questions may not give you a Line Reference, but may ask about specific names, quotes, or phrases that are easy to spot in the text. We'll call those Lead Words. It's important to remember that the Line Reference or Lead Word shows you where the *question* is in the passage, but you'll have to read more than that single line in order to find the *answer* in the passage.

If you read a window of about five lines above and five lines below each Line Reference or Lead Word, you should find the information you need. It's important to note that while you do not need to read more than these 10–12 lines of text, you usually cannot get away with reading less. If you read only the lines from the Line Reference, you will very likely not find the information you need to answer the question. Read carefully! You should be able to put your finger on the particular phrase, sentence, or set of lines that answers your question. If you save the general questions that relate to the passage as a whole for last, then by the time you begin those questions, you'll have a greater understanding of the passage even if you haven't read it from beginning to end.

> Read a window of about 5 lines above and 5 lines below
> your Line Reference to get the context for the question.

The Strategy
1. Read the Blurb
2. Select and Understand a Question
3. Read What You Need

5 Above, 5 Below
5 is the magic number when it comes to Line Reference questions. Read 5 lines above the Line Reference and then 5 lines below it to get all of the information you need in order to answer the question correctly.

The author most likely mentions the Canadian
scientist (line 22) and the Utah resident (line 26)
in order to

What are the Line References in this question?

What lines will you need to read to find the answer?

Once you underline the Line References and find your window, draw a bracket around it so you can find it easily. The more you can get out of your brain and onto the page, the better off you'll be. Because the Line References are line 22 and line 26, you'll want to read lines 17–31. In this case, that paragraph would be a good window.

Now it's time to read. Even though you're only reading a small chunk of the text, make sure you read it carefully.

Step 4: Predict Your Answer

The test writers do their best to distract you by creating tempting but nevertheless wrong answers. However, if you know what you're looking for in advance, you will be less likely to fall for a trap answer. Before you even glance at the answer choices, take the time to think about what specific, stated information in your window supplies the answer to the question. Be careful not to paraphrase too far from the text or try to analyze what you're reading. Remember: What might be a good "English class" answer may lead you in the wrong direction on the SAT! Stick with the text.

As you read the window, look for specific lines or phrases that answer the question. Often what you're looking for will be in a sentence before or after the Line Reference or Lead Word, so it's crucial that you read the full window.

Once you've found text to answer the question, underline it if you can! Otherwise, jot down a prediction for the answer, sticking as close to the text as possible.

Let's take a look at question 12 again, this time with the window.

The Strategy
1. Read the Blurb
2. Select and Understand a Question
3. Read What You Need
4. Predict Your Answer

> **12**
>
> The author most likely mentions the Canadian scientist (line 22) and the Utah resident (line 26) in order to

Here's your window from the passage. See if you can read it and find something that answers the question. Underline your prediction if you can.

> In Canton, Ohio, some 1,000 residents notified police that their windshields had been "blemished in a mysterious manner," the Daily Mail of Hagerstown, MD, reported on April 17. And United Press in New York noted on April 20 that "new reports of mysterious windshield pittings came in today almost as fast as theories about what causes them." A Canadian scientist posited that the marks were made by the skeletons of minute marine creatures that had been propelled into the air by hydrogen bomb testing in the Pacific Ocean. In Utah, someone suggested that acid from flying bugs might be the source of the windshield-denting, but a Brigham Young University biologist disproved the theory, the Provo Daily Herald reported on June 27.

Did you underline the phrase *new reports of mysterious windshield pittings came in today almost as fast as theories about what causes them*? The passage gives you clear evidence that the Canadian scientist and Utah resident are mentioned in order to give examples of some of the theories about the causes of pitting that were zipping in.

Step 5: Process of Elimination

A multiple-choice test is a cool thing because you have all the right answers on the page in front of you. All you have to do is eliminate anything that isn't right. Sometimes, especially on Reading, it's easier to find wrong answers that aren't supported by the passage rather than trying to find the right answer that might not look the way you think it should.

Process of Elimination, or POE, involves two steps. The first step will be the question, "What can I eliminate that doesn't match––or is inconsistent with––my prediction?" For many of the easy and medium questions, this step will be enough to get down to the right answer.

12

The author most likely mentions the Canadian scientist (line 22) and the Utah resident (line 26) in order to

Remember, on the previous page, you used the text to predict that the Canadian scientist and Utah resident are mentioned in order to give examples of some of the theories about the causes of pitting that were zipping in. Eliminate anything that has nothing to do with that prediction.

	Keep?	Eliminate?
A) provide support for a previous statement.		
B) dispute claims made by experts.		
C) prove a theory about an occurrence.		
D) show the unprecedented nature of a phenomenon		

Did you eliminate everything except (A)? None of the other answers have anything to do with the prediction you made. Additionally, once you're down to an answer that seems to support your prediction, use the text to make sure you can prove it. What's the previous statement? Theories coming in quickly. What's the support? Examples from Canada and Utah.

The Strategy
1. Read the Blurb
2. Select and Understand a Question
3. Read What You Need
4. Predict Your Answer
5. Process of Elimination

POE Criteria

On most of the Easy and Medium questions, you'll be able to eliminate three of the four answers simply by using your prediction. On other questions, usually the Hard questions, your prediction will help you get rid of one or two answers, and then you'll need to consider the remaining answers a little more carefully. If you're down to two answers, and they both seem to make sense, you're probably down to the right answer and the trap answer. Luckily, there are some common traps that the test writers will set for you, so knowing them can help you figure out which is the trap answer and which is the right answer. These traps include:

- **Mostly Right/Slightly Wrong**: These answers look just about perfect except for a word or two that doesn't match what's in the text.
- **Could Be True**: These answers might initially look good because they make sense or seem logical. You might be able to support these answers in an English class, but they lack the concrete support from the text to make them correct SAT answers.
- **Deceptive Language**: You'll be given answer choices with words that look exactly like what you saw in the passage, but the words are put together in such a way that they don't actually say what you need them to say. Make sure you're reading carefully and not just matching words.

Predictions and POE
Use these criteria after you have eliminated anything that doesn't match your prediction.

USING THE BASIC APPROACH

Now that you know the steps of the Basic Approach, let's practice them on some different question types.

Infer/Imply/Suggest

When you see a question that contains the word *infer*, *imply*, or *suggest*, be extra careful. In real life, those words often signify a question asking your opinion. You may think that the test writers want you to do some English-class-level reading between the lines. In actuality, though, they don't. It's still just a straight reading comprehension question. There may be a tiny bit of reading between the lines, so far as the answer will not be directly stated in the text as it will with a detail question, but there will still be plenty of evidence in the text to support the correct answer.

13

The author's statement that the "country moved on to building backyard fallout shelters" (lines 31-32) implies that Americans

A) were aware that the threat from bombs was more imminent than that from windshield pitting.

B) had lost interest in the windshield pitting phenomenon.

C) needed a place to be protected from nuclear fallout.

D) did not yet have fallout shelters in their backyards.

Here's How to Crack It

First you need to go back to the text and find the Line Reference. Underline it. Then mark and read your window. Make sure you know what the question is asking. In this case, you want to figure out what the Line Reference tells you about Americans. When you carefully read your window you see that "as summer rolled on, reports of pitting decreased everywhere" and the "country moved on." They are leaving the mystery of pitting behind. Once you have your prediction, use POE to work through your answers. Choice (A) doesn't match the idea of Americans moving on, so eliminate it. Choice (B) looks pretty good, so hang on to it. Choice (C) might look good initially because we did see something earlier about nuclear fallout, but it has nothing to do with moving on from the pitting phenomenon, so you can eliminate it. Choice (D) might make sense—if they are building the shelters, they probably don't have them already—but it has nothing to do with

Line Reference Questions

On any Line Reference question, you need to go back to the passage and find the Line Reference, mark it, and then read your window.

our prediction. That leaves (B), which answers the question and matches the prediction from the text!

Vocabulary-in-Context

Another way that your reading comprehension will be tested is with Vocabulary-in-Context (VIC) questions. The most important thing to remember is that these are **IN CONTEXT!** Gone are the days of "SAT Vocabulary" when you had to memorize lists of obscure words like *impecunious* and *perspicacious*. Now the focus is on whether you can understand what a word means based on the context of the text. You'll see words that look familiar, but are often used in ways that are a little less familiar. Do not try to answer these questions simply by defining the word in your head and looking for that definition. You have to go back to the text and look at the context for the word.

14

As used in line 41, "common" most nearly means

A) tasteless.

B) popular.

C) frequent.

D) inferior.

Here's How to Crack It

With VIC questions, you don't need to read a full 10–12 line window. Typically a few lines before and a few lines after will give you what you need. Go to line 41 and find the word *common*. Underline it. When you read before and after the word, the text talks about a "numbers game" and "more people." The next sentence says that something "infrequent may start to appear to be a trend…" Use those context clues to predict something that refers to "numbers game," "more people," and something that would be the opposite of "infrequent." Put in something like *often* and then use POE to eliminate (A), (B), and (D).

Be careful with VIC questions. As with the other questions, you have to rely heavily on the text, not your own opinions. You might be able to rather convincingly talk yourself into the idea that if something is common, it's popular, because if it's common, it's everywhere, and if it's everywhere, that must mean a lot of people like it… It can be easy to talk yourself into a tangle if you use your brain. Try to avoid that, and instead focus on what the text actually says. In this case, we only have evidence for *common* having something to do with numbers and frequency, not how the general public feels about something.

Try another question:

15

The passage indicates that an effect of aggregating events is

A) patterns seem to emerge more frequently.

B) the truth about a conspiracy is easier to find.

C) a tiny percent of the events are similar.

D) connections between unrelated events can be reported.

Here's How to Crack It

This question doesn't have a Line Reference, but notice that both the question before it and the question after it do. Since question 14 references line 41, and question 18 references line 73, question 17 should fall somewhere between those lines. Look through those lines for the Lead Words *aggregating events* and use that phrase to find your window. Carefully read the window, looking for the answer to the question, "What is an effect of aggregating events?" Within the window, you find …*something that is very infrequent may start to appear to be a trend* and *[i]f everyone is looking for and reporting it, it would appear to be a conspiracy of some sort.* Go through your answers and eliminate anything that has nothing to do with appearing to be a trend or conspiracy.

Choice (A) definitely seems to match an *appearing trend*, so hang on to it.

Choice (B) mentions finding a conspiracy, which might seem to match.

Choice (C) doesn't match at all, so eliminate it.

Choice (D) might be true, but doesn't match our prediction, so eliminate it.

Based on our first pass through the answer choices, we are now down to (A) and (B). Remember the POE criteria? Let's take a closer look at these two answers.

Choice (A): *patterns seem to emerge more frequently* is almost an exact paraphrase of *something…may start to appear to be a trend*, so this one still looks pretty good.

Choice (B): Although we see the word *conspiracy* in both the text and the answer choice, don't forget that you need to read carefully. The text says that it would *appear to be a conspiracy*, which is much different from finding the *truth about a conspiracy*. Don't be deceived by deceptive language! Match content, not just words. Choice (B) is out, leaving (A) as the correct answer.

Let's try one more.

○

The author most likely mentions *War of the Worlds* in line 73 in order to

A) argue some cases of mass hysteria are legitimate.

B) prove the media was responsible for people's reactions.

C) point out that most people were not upset by the broadcast.

D) criticize the media for failing to recognize the program was fictional.

Here's How to Crack It

Find your window and carefully read it, looking for the answer to the question, "Why does the author mention *War of the Worlds*?" When you read your window, you find that the author says *War of the Worlds is a wonderful example of how the media emphasizes the few 'real cases' of hysteria without recognizing that the vast majority of people knew that the radio program was fictional and did nothing*. We are looking for an answer choice that has something to do with the media overplaying the hysteria and not acknowledging the majority of people who did nothing.

Choice (A): This doesn't match our prediction. Also, don't be deceived by Deceptive Language! Noticed that in the text, "real cases" is in quotation marks. This indicates the author doesn't agree with the phrase, so it's the opposite of what we're looking for.

Choice (B): Doesn't match our prediction.

Choice (C): That almost exactly matches the second part of our prediction, so hang on to it.

Choice (D): Doesn't match our prediction. It was people who didn't know the program was fictional, not the media.

That leaves (C) as the correct answer!

○

So you can see that by following the Basic Approach on every question, you'll be in good shape to answer a majority of the Reading questions! You'll use your time more efficiently, focusing on the pieces of the test that will get you points, and your accuracy will be much higher. There are a few other question types which we'll look at in the next chapter.

Summary

o The Reading Test on the SAT makes up 50 percent of your score on the Evidence-Based Reading and Writing section.

o Reading questions are *not* presented in order of difficulty, but they are in chronological order. Don't be afraid to skip a hard question, and don't worry if you can't answer every question.

o Use your POOD to pick up the points you can get, and don't forget LOTD on the rest!

o Reading is an open-book test! Use that to your advantage by focusing only on the text you need to get each point.

o Translate each question back into a *what* or *why* question before you start reading your window.

o Use Line References, Lead Words, and chronology to help you find the answer in the passage. Always start reading a few lines above the Line Reference or the Lead Words and read until you have the answer.

o Use the text to predict your answer to the question before you look at the answer choices.

o Use POE to eliminate answers that don't match your prediction.

o If you have more than one answer left after you eliminate anything that doesn't match your prediction, compare your remaining answers and see if any of them:

• Are Mostly Right/Slightly Wrong
• Could Be True
• Contain Deceptive Language

Chapter 4
More Question Types

In this chapter we'll take a look at some of the remaining question types on the Reading Test, including general questions, paired questions, and quantitative questions. For the most part, these questions will still follow the Basic Approach, but the general paired questions and quantitative questions will look a little different.

MORE QUESTION TYPES ON THE READING TEST

In this chapter, we'll look at other question types you'll see on the SAT Reading Test, including paired questions, main idea questions, general questions, questions featuring charts and graphs, and questions based on dual passage sets.

Remember the Windshield-Pitting passage from the last chapter? We'll continue to use it for the questions in this chapter, too.

Questions 11-21 are based on the following passage.

This passage is adapted from Linton Weeks's "The Windshield-Pitting Mystery of 1954." © 2015 by NPR History Dept.

The nationwide weirdness that was the Windshield-Pitting Mystery began in the spring of 1954. Looking back at the events today may give us
Line a window—OK, a windshield—on the makeup and
5 the mindset of mid-20th-century America.

The epidemic's epicenter, according to HistoryLink—an online compendium of Washington state history— was the town of Bellingham, where "tiny holes, pits, and dings ...
10 seemingly appeared in the windshields of cars at an unprecedented rate" in late March.

"Panicked residents," the website reports, suspected "everything from cosmic rays to sand-flea eggs to fallout from H-bomb tests."
15 In Canton, Ohio, some 1,000 residents notified police that their windshields had been "blemished in a mysterious manner," the *Daily Mail* of Hagerstown, MD reported on April 17. And United Press in New York noted on April 20
20 that "new reports of mysterious windshield pittings came in today almost as fast as theories about what causes them." A Canadian scientist posited that the marks were made by the skeletons of minute marine creatures that had been propelled into
25 the air by hydrogen bomb testing in the Pacific Ocean. In Utah, someone suggested that acid from flying bugs might be the source of the windshield-denting, but a Brigham Young University biologist disproved the theory, the Provo *Daily Herald*
30 reported on June 27. As summer rolled on, reports of pitting decreased everywhere and the country moved on to building backyard fallout shelters.

But the question remains: What about those pitted windshields?
35 For guidance, we turn to Missouri State University sociologist David Rohall, who has taught courses in social movements and collective behavior for more than a decade. "Much of what happens in society is a numbers game," Rohall
40 says. "If you have more people, any phenomenon starts to appear more common if you focus on any one event or behavior. Even something that is very infrequent may start to appear to be a trend, he says, "when you aggregate those events. There are
45 millions of cars in Washington state but thousands

of cases of pitting. While thousands sounds like a huge phenomenon, it represents less than 1 percent of cars. If everyone is looking for and reporting it, it would appear to be a conspiracy of some sort."
50 Windshield-pitting, Rohall says, "may be more like crop circles in which there is physical evidence that 'something' happened but no one is certain of the cause. Of course, we have since found evidence that, in some cases, people utilize special
55 equipment to make those crop circles. The cause of the pitting is different because it would be very difficult to capture someone creating them."

"Most people in the field no longer believe in mass hysteria as a cause of large-group behavior,"
60 Rohall says. "The idea came from Gustave Le Bon, a French theorist trying to explain the strange behavior of large groups during the French Revolution, in which average citizens began killing large numbers of people via the guillotine. What
65 would cause them to do such a heinous thing?"

Even if the theory were true, Rohall says, "it is designed to be applied to situations of heightened emotional arousal—for example: large crowds. While the ideas about pitting may have 'caught
70 on' among people in the region, I doubt it was an emotional contagion that drove them to act in a particular way."

"*War of the Worlds* is a wonderful example of how the media emphasizes the few 'real cases' of
75 hysteria without recognizing that the vast majority of people knew that the radio program was fictional and did nothing," Rohall adds. "Like crop circles, we know that some of them are man-made, so might these pits. However, the media may have
80 had people start noticing the pits that had already been there."

He likens the experience to this: "It is very common for people to believe that they have contracted an illness when they hear a doctor
85 describe a medical problem and the symptoms associated with that problem. I suspect that most people already had these pits all along and only attributed it to the mysterious cause when they heard other people doing it. Still others may have
90 resulted from vandalism or new cases from simple accidents—debris from the roads. Is this hysteria or simply logical thinking utilizing information from the media and their own situation—a pitted car? Some research about supposed 'hysteria' really
95 shows that people are not hysterical at all."

Paired Questions

You will notice on every passage, there is at least one set of questions that are paired together. The first question looks and sounds just like a regular question. It may ask about a detail, it may be an inference question, or it may be a main idea question. The second question in the pair will always ask, "Which choice provides the best evidence for the answer to the previous question?" There are two types of paired questions: specific and general.

Specific Paired Questions

The specific paired questions are a fabulous two-for-one deal. If you're following all the steps of the Basic Approach, you'll find when you get to the "best evidence" question of a specific paired set, you've already answered it. This is because you've already found the best evidence when you carefully read your window and underlined your prediction. Let's take a look at a set.

16

According to the passage, what percent of cars in Washington suffered damage?

A) About 20%

B) Approximately 10%

C) Between 5% and 6%

D) Less than 1%

17

Which choice provides the best evidence for the answer to the previous question?

A) Lines 6-11 ("The epidemic's . . . March.")

B) Lines 15-18 ("In Canton . . . April 17.")

C) Lines 44-48 ("There are . . . cars.")

D) Lines 55-57 ("The cause . . . them.")

Start with the first question. This question is very straightforward to answer by itself. All you need to do is find out what percent of the cars in Washington were damaged. Although there isn't a given line reference, you can still skim through the text looking for the lead words *Washington* and *percent*. You'll find these in the sixth paragraph, around lines 35–49. The text clearly states that less than 1% of cars suffered damage. Underline that line and choose (D) for question 16. Then, because you already have the "best evidence" underlined, when you get to question 17, you've already answered it. Just find your line reference in the answers, bubble it in, and move on.

General Paired Sets and Parallel POE

Not all sets of paired questions will be as easy as specific paired sets, but they'll still be approachable. If you have a question that is a main idea/general question or a question without a clear Line Reference or Lead Word, Parallel POE is a very useful strategy.

Using Parallel POE, you'll be able to work through the questions at the same time! When you find yourself faced with a set of paired questions, you can start with the second question (the "best evidence" question) if (1) you aren't sure where to look for the answer or (2) the first question is a general question about the passage. Because the second question in the pair asks which lines provide the *best evidence* for the previous question, you can use those lines to help work through the answers for the previous question. Let's take a look.

Best Evidence
Not sure where to find the answer? Let the "best evidence" lines help!

20

Based on the passage, the author most likely agrees that "pitting" is

A) a coincidence based on group observations.

B) the result of cosmic rays and nuclear fallout.

C) an example of mass hysteria similar to the Salem Witch trials.

D) the result of a streak of vandalism in the spring of 1954.

21

Which choice provides the best evidence for the answer to the previous question?

A) Lines 12-14 ("Panicked residents . . . tests.")

B) Lines 30-32 ("As summer . . . shelters.")

C) Lines 60-64 ("The idea . . . guillotine.")

D) Lines 86-89 ("I suspect . . . it.")

When you read question 20, you might have an initial feeling of, "Well, that could be from anywhere in the passage." Sure could. Now you're potentially faced with the *worst* scavenger hunt ever. Instead of wading through the entire passage, though, and trying to find something you think answers the question and then hope it's included in the "best evidence" question, go to the "best evidence" first! This is the Parallel POE strategy.

What's great about Parallel POE is that, in the first instance, the original question does not even matter. Think for a moment about how paired questions operate. The correct answer to the first question *must* be supported by an answer to the evidence question, and the correct answer to the evidence question *must* support an answer to the first question. In other words, if there is an evidence answer that doesn't support an answer to the first question, it is wrong. Period. Likewise, if there is an answer to the first question that isn't supported by an evidence answer, it too is wrong. Period.

Let's use this to our advantage! Rather than worry about what the first question is asking and what the answer might be, just start making connections between the two answer sets. If an evidence answer supports a first question answer, literally draw a line connecting them. You should not expect to have four connections. If you are lucky, you will have only one connection, and you will therefore have your answer pair. Otherwise, you might have two or three connections and will then (and only then) worry about the first question. The important thing to remember is that any answer choice in the first question that isn't physically connected to an evidence answer—and any evidence answer that isn't connected to an answer in the first question—must be eliminated.

Let's take a look at how this first Parallel POE pass would look. (The paired questions have been arranged in two columns to help understand this, and the lines have been written out for your convenience. This does not represent what you will see on the official test.)

20. Based on the passage, the author most likely agrees that "pitting" is	21. Which choice provides the best evidence for the answer to the previous question?
A) a coincidence based on group observations.	A) "Panicked residents" suspected "everything from cosmic rays to sand-flea eggs to fallout from H-bomb tests."
B) the result of cosmic rays and nuclear fallout.	B) As summer rolled on, reports of pitting decreased everywhere and the country moved on to building backyard fallout shelters.
C) an example of mass hysteria similar to the Salem Witch trials.	C) "The idea came from Gustave Le Bon, a French theorist trying to explain the strange behavior of large groups during the French Revolution, in which average citizens began killing large numbers of people via the guillotine."
D) the result of a streak of vandalism in the spring of 1954.	D) "I suspect that most people already had these pits all along and only attributed it to the mysterious cause when they heard other people doing it."

Don't worry about the question itself yet. Go straight to the "best evidence" lines.

- 21 (A) says *"Panicked residents" suspected "everything from cosmic rays to sand-flea eggs to fallout from H-bomb tests."* Read through all four answer choices for question 20. Do you see any answers that those lines support? Notice 20 (B) pretty much says the same thing? Draw a line connecting 21 (A) with 20 (B). Nothing else from question 20 matches with 21 (A), so let's move on to 21 (B).

- 21 (B) says *As summer rolled on, reports of pitting decreased everywhere and the country moved on to building backyard fallout shelters.* Looking through the answers for question 20, there's nothing that is supported by these lines, so we can eliminate 21 (B). It doesn't matter what the question asks; if there's no support, the answer cannot be right.
- 21 (C) says *"The idea came from Gustave Le Bon, a French theorist trying to explain the strange behavior of large groups during the French Revolution, in which average citizens began killing large numbers of people via the guillotine."* As with 21 (B), there are no answers in the first question that are supported by these lines, so 21 (C) is gone.
- 21 (D) says *"I suspect that most people already had these pits all along and only attributed it to the mysterious cause when they heard other people doing it"* which seems to pretty clearly support 20 (A). Draw a line physically connecting 21 (D) with 20 (A).

Now, notice that (C) and (D) in question 20 have no support? Regardless of the question or what you read in the text, if the answers have no support from the "best evidence" question, they cannot be right. Eliminate those two.

Your question should look something like this at this point:

20. Based on the passage, the author most likely agrees that "pitting" is	21. Which choice provides the best evidence for the answer to the previous question?
A) a coincidence based on group observations.	A) "Panicked residents" suspected "everything from cosmic rays to sand-flea eggs to fallout from H-bomb tests."
B) the result of cosmic rays and nuclear fallout.	B) As summer rolled on, reports of pitting decreased everywhere and the country moved on to building backyard fallout shelters.
C) an example of mass hysteria similar to the Salem Witch trials.	C) "The idea came from Gustave Le Bon, a French theorist trying to explain the strange behavior of large groups during the French Revolution, in which average citizens began killing large numbers of people via the guillotine."
D) the result of a streak of vandalism in the spring of 1954.	D) "I suspect that most people already had these pits all along and only attributed it to the mysterious cause when they heard other people doing it."

Now you're down to a very nice 50/50 split. Go back to the question. Of the two pairs, which one best describes pitting in a way the *author would most likely agree with*? The author definitely did not believe the pitting was caused by cosmic rays or nuclear fallout, so you can eliminate the 20 (B)/21 (A) pair, leaving you with the correct answer of 20 (A)/21 (D).

Parallel POE

Since you can't draw a full table on the actual exam, try making notations as shown in question 21; that is, create a column to the left of the "best evidence" answer choices listing out the choices to the previous question.

On the official test, it would be too complicated to draw a full table, so all you need to do is create a column to the left of the "best evidence" choices for the answers to the previous question. It should look something like this:

Q20   21. Which choice provides the best evidence for the answer to the previous question?

A   A) Lines 12-14 ("Panicked residents . . . tests.")

B   B) Lines 30-32 ("As summer . . . shelters.")

C   C) Lines 60-64 ("The idea . . . guillotine.")

D   D) Lines 86-89 ("I suspect . . . it.")

Main Idea/General Questions

For many of the Reading passages, the very first question will ask a general question about the passage. It might ask about the main idea or purpose of the passage, the narrative point of view, or a shift that occurs through the passage. Remember the Select a Question step? Those general questions are not good to do first because you haven't read the passage yet, but once you've done most of the other questions, you have a really good idea of the overall themes of the text.

Let's take a look at the first question from the windshield passage:

11

The central claim of the passage is that

Because this question asks about the *central claim* of the passage, there's no one place you can look. General questions don't have line references or lead words, so there's no way to use the text to predict an answer. It's okay, though: You've answered almost all of the questions about the passage, so you know what the main idea of the passage is. Not only that, but you also have a good sense of what the test writers found most interesting about the passage. While having this knowledge does not always help, it sure can sometimes. If there are answer choices that have nothing to do with either the questions or the answers you've seen repeatedly, you can probably eliminate them and instead choose the one that is consistent with those questions and answers.

Let's take a look at the answers:

A) windshield pitting was a major source of concern for most drivers in 1954.

B) windshield pitting turned out to be nothing but a prank.

C) widespread focus on a specific event can make random occurrences seem significant.

D) lack of consensus for an event's explanation can cause hysteria.

Remember: If it's a *central claim*, it's a main point of the text. What can you eliminate?

Choice (A) might look good initially because it has the words "windshield pitting," "drivers," and "1954," but this is definitely not a *central claim* of the passage.

Choice (B) can be eliminated because the only mention of a prank was as a possible theory put forward by someone else.

Choice (C) looks pretty good. You've already answered several specific questions dealing with this idea.

Choice (D) might look pretty good at first, too. When you go back to the text, though, you see that the author's *central claim* is not about the lack of consensus causing the hysteria. That's a part of it, but it's not a complete answer.

Choice (C) is best supported by the text and all the other questions you've answered.

Charts and Graphs

Charts, graphs, and diagrams are no longer limited to the Math Test! You will now see a variety of graphics in the Reading Test and even in the Writing and Language Test! (More on the Writing and Language test later.) The good news is that the graphics you'll be dealing with in the Reading Test are very straightforward and do not require any computations. All you need to do is make sure you can put your pencil on the place on the graphic that proves a reason to keep or eliminate an answer choice. Let's take a look at an example.

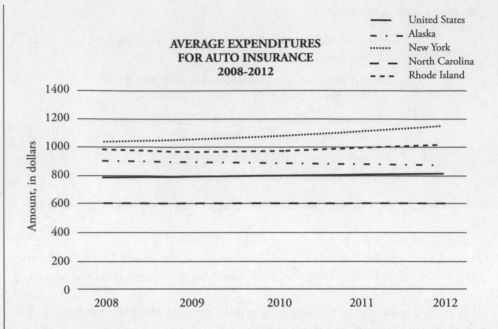

**AVERAGE EXPENDITURES
FOR AUTO INSURANCE
2008-2012**

Legend:
— United States
— · — Alaska
······ New York
— — North Carolina
- - - Rhode Island

Amount, in dollars (vertical axis): 0, 200, 400, 600, 800, 1000, 1200, 1400

Years (horizontal axis): 2008, 2009, 2010, 2011, 2012

Data collected by Insurance Information Institute, http://www.iii.org/fact-statistic/auto-insurance.

Step 1: Read the graphic. Carefully look at the title, axis labels, and legend. Notice on this graph we're looking at *Average Expenditures for Auto Insurance* from 2008–2012. The years are listed across the horizontal axis, and the amount, in dollars, is listed on the vertical axis. According to the legend, we are comparing the entire country to Alaska, New York, North Carolina, and Rhode Island.

Step 2: Read your question.

30

According to the graph, which of the following statements is most consistent with the data?

Since the question asks you which is consistent with the data, see if you can find specific reasons to eliminate three answer that are NOT consistent with the data. Another possibility for Charts and Graphs questions is to simply find the data point that answers the question.

Step 3: Read your answers.

A) Auto insurance expenditures have increased in all states from 2008–2012.

B) Of all the states shown on the graph, New York had the greatest total increase in auto insurance expenditures.

C) The states shown on the graph all have auto insurance expenditures higher than the United States' average.

D) North Carolina drivers are better than New York drivers.

Let's take another look at the graph, this time looking for specific reasons to keep or eliminate answers.

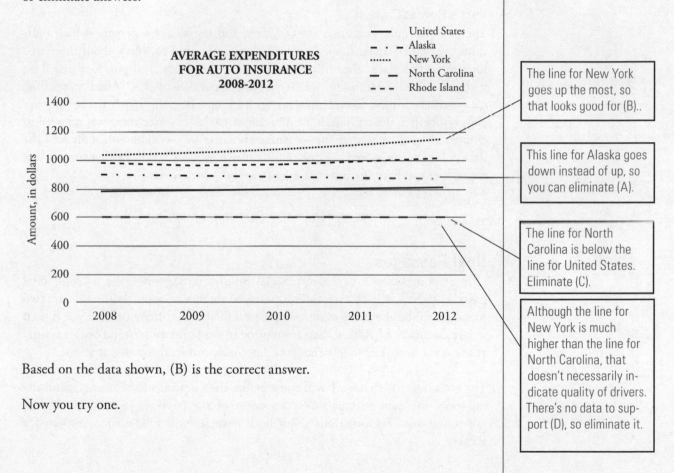

The line for New York goes up the most, so that looks good for (B)..

This line for Alaska goes down instead of up, so you can eliminate (A).

The line for North Carolina is below the line for United States. Eliminate (C).

Although the line for New York is much higher than the line for North Carolina, that doesn't necessarily indicate quality of drivers. There's no data to support (D), so eliminate it.

Based on the data shown, (B) is the correct answer.

Now you try one.

31

Data in the graph indicate that Rhode Island's average expenditure for auto insurance was closest to the national average in which year?

A) 2009

B) 2010

C) 2011

D) 2012

Here's How to Crack It

The question only asks about *Rhode Island* and the *national average* (which indicates the United States line). That means you only need to worry about those two lines. Find the place where those two lines are the closest and put your pencil on it. Notice the Rhode Island line is just about parallel to the United States line, except where it dips down before it goes back up? That dip is where the lines are closest together, which is in 2009. Your answer is (A)! Notice there was no need to eliminate the three wrong answer choices because we were able to simply find the data point that answered the question? Sometimes it really will be that simple. Just make sure you have the information to support your answer.

Dual Passages

One of your Science or History/Social Studies passages will be a set of dual passages. There will be two shorter passages about one topic. Although the two passages will be about the same topic, there will also be differences that you'll need to pay attention to. Rather than attempting to read and understand both passages at the same time, just follow the Basic Approach and focus on one at a time.

The questions for Passage 1 will come before the questions for Passage 2, and the questions for each passage follow the order of the passage, just like single-passage questions. The questions about both passages will follow the questions for Passage 2.

Two-Passage Questions

For questions asking to compare or contrast both passages, it's helpful to consider one passage at a time rather than trying to juggle both passages at the same time. First, find the answer for the first passage (or the second passage if that one is easier) and use POE to narrow down the answer choices. Then find the answer in the other passage and use POE to arrive at the correct answer. This will save time and keep you from confusing the two passages when you're evaluating the answer choices. Always keep in mind that the same POE criteria apply, no matter how two-passage questions are presented.

- If a question is about what is supported by both passages, make sure that you find specific support in both passages, and be wary of all the usual trap answers.

- If a question is about an issue on which the authors of the two passages disagree or on how the passages relate to one another, make sure you find support in each passage for the author's particular opinion.

- If the question asks how one author would respond to the other passage, find out what was said in that other passage, and then find out exactly what the author you are asked about said on that exact topic.

The bottom line is that if you are organized and remember your basic reading comprehension strategy, you'll see that two-passage questions are no harder than single-passage questions! In the following drill, you'll have a chance to try a set of dual passages. Answers and explanations can be found at the end of the chapter.

Dual-Passage Drill

Questions 12-22 are based on the following passage.

Passage 1 is adapted from Louisa Twining, "Workhouses and Women's Work" © 1857 by The National Association for the Promotion of Social Science. Passage 2 is adapted from Florence Nightingale and William Rathbone, "Workhouse Nursing, the Story of a Successful Experiment" © 1867 by Macmillan and Co.

Passage 1

The evils of the employment of pauper nurses is dwelt upon by all who have considered the subject of workhouse management. When we
Line consider the persons to whom such extensive
5   power and responsibility are entrusted, in the care of 50,000 sick persons in the London workhouses alone, we can hardly wonder at what is told of the results of the system. The only way in which an employment of the inmates could
10 be successfully carried out, would be under the constant supervision of superior persons; but in the present system that is an impossibility. Efficient nurses, who could gain a living in any of our hospitals, would not be likely to offer
15 themselves for a post in which it is nearly all work of the hardest kind, and no pay. One of these pauper nurses boldly stated that she had been sixteen times in the House of Correction, and she was not ashamed of it. Of course such labor
20 is cheap, and it is desirable, if possible, to employ those who must be maintained at the cost of the parish; but in no case should they be left with the sole charge and responsibility of sick wards, as they continually are at present, without any other
25 control than the occasional visit of the matron, bestowed at the utmost once a day, in some cases only once a week.

    Seeing how careful boards of guardians are in all matters of expense, it would have been well if
30 the recommendation of the poor law with regard to the employment of at least one paid nurse had been a law; as it is, many workhouses are without one. That such a person would always be all we could desire for so important a post we could
35 hardly hope, from what we know of the paid nurses in hospitals, but at any rate there would be a better chance of efficiency and character than in the present plan.

Passage 2

    But on the 18th of May, 1865, a Lady
40 Superintendent who had received a thorough training at Kaiserswerth and St. Thomas's, twelve Nightingale nurses from St. Thomas's, eighteen probationers, and fifty-two of the old pauper nurses were placed in charge of the patients in the
45 male wards of the Workhouse Infirmary.

    With the exception of the failure of the nurses taken from the pauper class, the first year's trial was sufficiently successful to induce a continuance of the experiment. It was impossible,
50 however, to judge the result by statistics. None that were available could be considered as an evidence of success or failure, for several reasons. The season was very unhealthy, and to relieve the pressure on the space and resources of the
55 hospital, steps were taken to treat slight cases outside.

    The endeavor to limit the admissions to serious cases would of course affect the returns, both as regards the time taken in curing, and the
60 proportion of deaths. Even had there been no exceptional disturbing element, there is a defect in the statistics of workhouse hospitals which affects all inferences from them, in the absence of any careful classified list of cases kept by the
65 medical officers, such as might fairly enable one to form a judgment from mere statistical tables. These, then, are not reliable as means of judgment, unless extending over a long period. The character of seasons, and nature of cases
70 admitted, varies so much from year to year as to invalidate any deductions, unless founded on minutely kept medical records. The following extracts, however, from the reports of the Governor, and the surgical and medical officers of
75 the Workhouse, bear decisive witness to the value of the "new system," especially as contrasted with the "old system," which in 1865-66 still prevailed in the female wards. All these reports bear

emphatic testimony to the merits and devotion
80 of the Lady Superintendent and her staff. The
medical men, it is noteworthy, speak strongly of
the better discipline and far greater obedience to
their orders observable where the trained nurses
are employed—a point the more important
85 because it is that on which, before experience has
reassured them, medical and other authorities
have often been most doubtful.

12

The primary purpose of Passage 1 is to

A) praise an effective structure.

B) criticize a social group.

C) examine the finances of a system.

D) advocate for a necessary change.

13

Which choice provides the best evidence for the
answer to the previous question?

A) Lines 13-16 ("Efficient nurses . . . pay")

B) Lines 16-19 ("One of . . . it")

C) Lines 22-27 ("but in . . . week")

D) Lines 28-32 ("Seeing how . . . law")

14

As used in lines 21, "maintained" most nearly
means

A) provided for.

B) affirmed.

C) healed.

D) fixed.

15

The phrase in lines 34-35 ("we could hardly
hope") most directly suggests that

A) an ideal candidate should be found for a
position.

B) people who go to hospitals should be critical
of nurses.

C) allowances should be made, since no person
is perfect.

D) an improvement is still likely to have some
flaws.

16

Which choice provides the best evidence for the
answer to the previous question?

A) Lines 13-16 ("Efficient nurses . . . pay")

B) Lines 19-22 ("Of course . . . parish")

C) Lines 29-32 ("it would . . . law")

D) Lines 35-38 ("from what . . . plan")

17

The final sentence of Passage 1 has which effect?

A) It emphasizes that the current situation is
unpleasant.

B) It shares the author's despair over the
circumstances.

C) It casts an entirely optimistic light on a
proposal.

D) It evokes the generally low opinion held for a
certain group.

18

It can be most directly inferred from the second paragraph of Passage 2 (lines 46-56) that the first year of the experiment described in the passage was unusual in

A) having weather that caused an uncharacteristic amount of illness.

B) the overall number of people who required medical treatment.

C) that effective medical treatment exceeded statistical expectations.

D) the number of people who died from disease.

19

The author of Passage 2 references a "careful classified list of cases" (line 64) in order to

A) specify what will be required of all workhouses in the future, if the experiment continues.

B) explain a missing element that would have ensured an outcome.

C) reveal an inconsistency which made more accurate analysis impossible.

D) detail the extent to which records can be kept over a long period.

20

As used in line 69, the phrase "character of seasons" most nearly means

A) changes in morality.

B) weather patterns.

C) the overall health during a period.

D) the unpredictable nature of human behavior.

21

The author of Passage 1 would most likely respond to the phrase in lines 46-47 ("With the exception . . . class") of Passage 2 by

A) expressing surprise at an unexpected result that is inconsistent with prior observations.

B) acknowledging that an ideal situation may not be practical to attain.

C) noting that intervention earlier in life may have changed an outcome.

D) suggesting that the data may not be entirely representative.

22

Which choice best describes the relationship between the two passages?

A) Passage 2 describes a scenario that addresses some elements of the situation shown in Passage 1.

B) Passage 2 discusses potential results of the overall problem reviewed in Passage 1.

C) Passage 2 underscores the futility of attempts to resolve the concerns of Passage 1.

D) Passage 2 resolves the issues brought to light in Passage 1.

DUAL-PASSAGE DRILL ANSWERS AND EXPLANATIONS

12. **D** Because this is a general question followed by a "best evidence" question, Parallel POE lets you use the answer choices for the next question to help with this one. Remember: You can look at the lines given in the "best evidence" question to see if they support any of these answer choices. None of the choices for the next question seem to support (A), so you can eliminate (A). Choice (B) might initially seem to be supported by (B) from the next question, so keep that pair. Choice (C) might have a connection with (D) from the next question, as it mentions *matters of expense,* so keep that pair as well. Choice (D) is supported by (C) from the next question. Now consider your remaining pairs. The passage discusses *the evils of the employment of pauper nurses,* and that *in no case should they be left with the sole charge and responsibility of sick* [patients], *as they continually are at present;* the passage is primarily concerned with describing a system that needs to be changed. The passage is not criticizing a social group or focusing specifically on financial matters. This leaves (D) as the correct answer, automatically making (C) the correct answer for the "best evidence" question.

13. **C** Because this is a "best evidence" question following a general question, Parallel POE lets you use the answer choices for this question to help with the previous one. Remember: You can look at the lines given in the "best evidence" question to see if they support any of the answer choices for the previous question. Choice (A) does not support any of the answer choices from the previous question, so you can eliminate (A). Choice (B) in this question seems to support (B) in the previous question, since the lines refer to a woman who's proud of being in jail, so keep that pair. Choice (C) in this question supports (D) in the previous question, as the lines show a problem that clearly needs to be changed. Choice (D) in this question seems to support (C) from the previous question, as it mentions *matters of expense* and *finances of a system.* Now you're down to three pairs, so go back to the question, which asks about the *primary purpose* of the passage. The passage discusses *the evils of the employment of pauper nurses,* and that *in no case should they be left with the sole charge and responsibility of sick* [patients], *as they continually are at present,* the passage is primarily concerned with describing a system that needs to be changed. The passage does not criticize a social group or focus specifically on financial matters. This leaves (D) as the correct answer to question 12, automatically making (C) the right answer for this "best evidence" question.

14. **A** Careful reading is necessary in order to dissect the context of the word *maintained* in the passage. The passage draws a contrast between *pauper* and *efficient* nurses. *Those* refers to *pauper nurses,* since *in no case should they be left with the sole charge…of sick* [people], which the passage indicates immediately after referring to the *evils of the employment of pauper nurses.* Since a *pauper* is "one who relies on charity," *pauper nurses* can be inferred to rely on charity. Thus, since these *pauper nurses* must be *maintained at the cost of the parish, maintained* can be inferred to mean at least "given assistance with basic needs." Choice (A) is correct because it matches the predicted answer. Choice (B) is a secondary meaning of *maintained,* but it does not match the predicted answer; eliminate it. Choice (C) is tempting, as the passage discusses *nurses,* but it's still incorrect because it does not match the predicted answer. Choice (D) also doesn't match the predicted answer, so eliminate (D).

15.   **D**   The phrase *we could hardly hope* refers to whether *a paid nurse* would be *all* [the author] *could desire for so important a post*, indicating that the author does not believe a paid nurse would do a perfect job. The author continues to say that the reason for this judgment is *what we know of the paid nurses in hospitals*, implying that paid nurses are known to have flaws. Finally, the author states that *at any rate there would be a better chance* of an effective system with a paid nurse. Thus, the correct answer should indicate that while a paid nurse would be an improvement, the author still expects there to be problems. Choice (A) is incorrect, as *ideal* is the opposite of the predicted answer. Choice (B) is incorrect because the author discusses *paid nurses in hospitals* in order to make a point about what could be expected from a paid nurse in general, not about hospitals themselves, and *critical* is too extreme. Choice (C) is incorrect because it does not match that there is evidence of a problem with *paid nurses in hospitals*, and the phrase *we could hardly hope* does not indicate that all people have flaws. Choice (D) is correct because it matches the prediction.

16.   **D**   When you made your prediction for the previous question, you should have underlined *that such a person would be…all we desire…we could hardly hope, from what we know of the paid nurses in hospitals…but better chance of efficiency and character than present plan.* Therefore, (D) is correct.

17.   **A**   In the final sentence of Passage 1, the author acknowledges that a solution has flaws but is nonetheless a preferable solution. By using the phrasing *we could hardly hope*, and *at any rate…better… than…the present plan*, the author attempts to gain sympathy for the perspective that the current situation is so negative that even a flawed solution is an improvement. Choice (A) is correct because it matches the prediction. Choice (B) is incorrect because the author is providing a potential solution, which doesn't match *despair*. Choice (C) is also incorrect, since *optimistic* is the opposite of the predicted answer, and *entirely* is extreme language. Choice (D) is incorrect because the author is not trying to criticize *a certain group* but rather show that the overall circumstances require even a flawed solution.

18.   **B**   The second paragraph of Passage 2 indicates that *the season was very unhealthy*, which means that more people than usual became sick during a particular period. Eliminate (A), as the *weather* is not supported as the cause of sickness. Choice (B) matches the prediction, so keep it. Eliminate (C) because the passage indicates that *it was impossible…to judge the result by statistics*. Choice (D) may be true, but it is still incorrect because the third paragraph of Passage 2 implies only that the *proportion of deaths* may have been unusually high, not the *number of people who required medical treatment*. Choice (B) is the answer.

19.   **C**   The author of Passage 2 states that *It was impossible…to judge the result by statistics*, and that *even had there been no exceptional disturbing element, there is a defect in the statistics of workhouse hospitals*. Thus, the author indicates that there were other reasons statistical results could not be drawn, but that even without those other reasons, workhouse hospitals lack a *careful classified list of cases*, which would be necessary for statistical analysis. Choices (A) and (D) are incorrect because they do not match the prediction. Choice (B) is also incorrect; the passage states that there were *several reasons* for the lack of *evidence of success or failure*, and the *season* [being] *very unhealthy* may still

have made analysis impossible. Choice (C) is correct: While the author states that there were other reasons that the results could not be judged by statistics, *a defect in the statistics…affects all inferences from them.*

20. **C** Passage 2 refers to a *season* as *very unhealthy* as part of the reason that statistics couldn't be judged accurately. The reference to the *character of seasons* in the third paragraph of Passage 2 serves a similar purpose by listing reasons that statistical judgments are difficult to make in general. When compared with the earlier reference to an unhealthy season, the *character of seasons* refers most clearly to the health of the population during a certain period of time. Eliminate (A) and (B), which do not match the prediction. Choice (D) is incorrect because the predicted answer refers to the *health* of people, not their *behavior;* eliminate (D). Choice (C) matches the prediction and is the correct answer.

21. **B** The phrase *with the exception of the failure of the nurses taken from the pauper class* very briefly indicates that the pauper nurses included in the experiment made in Passage 2 were not *successful.* The author of Passage 1 states that *it is desirable, if possible, to employ* [the pauper nurses], and that *the only way…* [such] *employment…could be* [successful]*…would be under the constant supervision* or trained nurses. The qualifying phrase, *if possible*, indicates that the author of Passage 2 would prefer that the pauper nurses be involved in a new system but is not certain this would be possible. Choice (A) is incorrect because the author of Passage 1 indicated *prior observations*, which were negative toward the pauper nurses. Choice (B) is correct because it matches the prediction. Choice (C) is incorrect; while it could be true, it is not directly supported by the information in Passage 1. Choice (D) is incorrect because it is not supported by Passage 1 and relies on the unrelated surrounding information in Passage 2.

22. **A** Passage 1 describes an overall problem, and Passage 2 describes a specific attempt to solve the problem. Choice (A) is correct because it matches the prediction. Choice (B) is incorrect because it does not match the prediction, and (C) is wrong because *futility* is too extreme. Choice (D) can be eliminated because *resolves* is extreme as well.

Summary

o   For Paired Sets, make sure you're following the right strategy.
  •   Specific Paired Questions simply require you to follow the Basic Approach, making sure you've underlined the evidence for your prediction in the text.
  •   General Paired Questions will be much more straightforward if you use Parallel POE to consider the "best evidence" in tandem with the previous question.

o   For Dual Passages, do questions about the first passage first, questions about the second passage second, and dual questions last. Remember that even with dual questions, you must find support in the passages.

o   Save Main Idea or General Questions until the end of the passage. POE will be much more efficient once you've done all of the other questions.

o   Don't get bogged down by hard or time-consuming questions! If you find yourself stuck or running short on time, use LOTD and move on!

Chapter 5
Reading Drills

Use your new reading comprehension and test-taking skills on these two Reading drills, which contain passages on science and literature topics. Then, check your responses against the answers and explanations provided at the end of the chapter.

Reading Drill 1

This passage is adapted from Charles Anderson, "Conflict Minerals from the Democratic Republic of the Congo – Tin Processing Plants, a Critical Part of the Tin Supply Chain" © 2015 by U.S. Geological Survey

Tin is a metal often found in nature in its oxidized form, as the mineral called cassiterite. Cassiterite has been the primary source of tin throughout history, and remains the primary
5 source of tin today. Small amounts of tin are also recovered from sulphide minerals such as stannite. Cassiterite is found in alluvial deposits and can also be found in lode deposits in association with other metallic minerals.
10 Cassiterite is mined by the dredging of alluvial deposits, where the ore is broken up by either high-pressure water or an excavator, or hard-rock mining methods, usually from underground mines. Crushed ore is concentrated, usually
15 in co-location with the mine, through a combination of flotation, gravity, and magnetic processes to produce a cassiterite concentrate containing 70–77 percent tin. Tin concentrate is then smelted by heating it in the presence of
20 carbon to 1,200–1,300 degrees Celsius, reducing the cassiterite to tin metal, and releasing carbon dioxide. Following the smelting process to produce tin metal, the remaining impurities are removed through a refining process, usually at a
25 facility co-located with the smelter. Refining tin involves heating it to temperatures just past the tin melting point, allowing impurities to drop out as solids, and then skimming off the pure liquid tin. Refining is done by either heat treatment
30 or electrolytic processes. Heat treatment uses carbon-based fuel as a main heat source, usually in a reverberatory furnace. Heat treatment is more widely used than electrolytic processes, but produces only 99.85 percent tin. Electrolytic
35 processing involves inserting the smelted tin in an ionic solution and running an electrical current through it. The smelted tin is the anode, and the cathode collects the pure tin metal. Electrolytic processing is more expensive, but provides up to
40 99.9999 percent tin.

Tin is often found in everyday life. It is the primary component of solder. Solder is used to combine two pieces of metal, allowing an electrical charge to flow across the connection.
45 Solder is used on every electronic circuit board, and it is difficult or expensive to replace. There are some substitutes available for tin, with lead being the most viable alternative. Solder has been made from lead and tin, but since the Safe
50 Drinking Water Act, tin has become the primary metal in solder. Tin is also a primary component in food grade tin cans manufactured from tinplate. Tinplate is made by annealing molten tin onto a steel sheet. The resulting metal, formed
55 into cans, is then used in canning food, where the tin prevents corrosion and leaching of steel into the food product. Tinplate accounts for about 25 percent of domestic tin consumption. Because tin is not harmful to humans, it is a preferred
60 method of canning and preserving food for long-term storage. Substitutes for tinplate include aluminum, plastic, and organic-coated steel. Tin is also used in chemicals and accounts for 35 percent of domestic consumption.
65 The tin supply chain is complex and, often, opaque. Companies usually report products that they supply to the market place; however, they may not describe which of their plants use which starting materials or processes. As a result, plants
70 reported for some multi-plant corporations may or may not consume or produce all of the tin materials reported. Some large companies have multiple plants, which may or may not have been described in sufficient detail to identify their
75 location or the tin material that was processed. For example, information was not available on all tin producing companies, and many companies that were reported to have been tin suppliers could not be confirmed as such. Companies
80 changed names, were referred to imprecisely, changed ownership, or went out of business.

1

Based on the passage, the author would most likely consider tin to be

A) expensive.

B) practical.

C) complicated.

D) synthetic.

2

Which choice provides the best evidence for the answer to the previous question?

A) Lines 14-18 ("Crushed . . . tin")

B) Lines 38-40 ("Electrolytic . . . tin")

C) Lines 58-61 ("Because tin . . . storage")

D) Lines 65-66 ("The tin . . . opaque")

3

The overall structure of the passage could best be described as

A) a complete analysis of a naturally occurring element.

B) an overview of the steps and results of a process.

C) an introduction written for a geology course.

D) an explanation of the solution to a problem.

4

The most likely application of tin produced by means of electrolytic processing would be

A) plating for commonly produced canned goods, to be widely distributed.

B) miniature figurines designed to be painted and displayed.

C) small amounts of material intended for scientific analysis.

D) solder sold worldwide as part of a campaign to market lead-free products.

5

Between the first and second paragraphs, the focus shifts from

A) meticulous attention to detail to broad, assumptive generalizations.

B) scientific analysis of the properties and uses of a material to industrial processes.

C) detailed description of a series of steps to implementation of a result.

D) overview of a specific cycle to its role in the mining industry.

6

What can most reasonably be inferred about the Safe Drinking Water Act from the passage?

A) It specified the nature and percentage of the components of solder.

B) It may have impacted what elements a company chose to use in making solder.

C) It promoted tin over lead for all applications.

D) It prompted shifts in the manufacture and distribution of canned goods.

7

The author indicates that the demand for tin in part exists because

A) tin can be found in nature.

B) tin of nearly 100% purity can be produced.

C) tin is the best conductor of electricity.

D) of tin's impact on an individual's health.

8

Which choice provides the best evidence for the answer to the previous question?

A) Lines 1-2 ("Tin is . . . cassiterite")

B) Lines 38-40 ("Electrolytic . . . tin")

C) Lines 42-44 ("Solder . . . connection")

D) Lines 58-61 ("Because tin . . . storage")

9

As used in line 66, "opaque" most nearly means

A) dark.

B) wide.

C) impenetrable

D) dense.

10

The sentence in lines 79-81 ("Companies changed . . . business") primarily serves to

A) indicate a continuation of an existing chain.

B) describe the many uses for a product.

C) show the sole difficulty in answering a question.

D) support an earlier statement through an example.

Reading Drill 2

Questions 1-11 are based on the following passage.

This passage is excerpted from the 1854 book *Walden* by Henry David Thoreau, which details Thoreau's experiences living in a cabin alone for two years.

I think that I love society as much as most, and am ready enough to fasten myself like a bloodsucker for the time to any full-blooded man that comes in my way. I am naturally no hermit, but might possibly sit out the sturdiest frequenter of the bar-room, if my business called me thither.

I had three chairs in my house; one for solitude, two for friendship, three for society. When visitors came in larger and unexpected numbers there was but the third chair for them all, but they generally economized the room by standing up. It is surprising how many great men and women a small house will contain. I have had twenty-five or thirty souls, with their bodies, at once under my roof, and yet we often parted without being aware that we had come very near to one another.

One inconvenience I sometimes experienced in so small a house, the difficulty of getting to a sufficient distance from my guest when we began to utter the big thoughts in big words. You want room for your thoughts to get into sailing trim and run a course or two before they make their port. The bullet of your thought must have overcome its lateral and ricochet motion and fallen into its last and steady course before it reaches the ear of the hearer, else it may plow out again through the side of his head. Also, our sentences wanted room to unfold and form their columns in the interval. Individuals, like nations, must have suitable broad and natural boundaries, even a considerable neutral ground, between them. I have found it a singular luxury to talk across the pond to a companion on the opposite side. In my house we were so near that we could not begin to hear—we could not speak low enough to be heard; as when you throw two stones into calm water so near that they break each other's undulations. As the conversation began to assume a loftier and grander tone, we gradually shoved our chairs farther apart till they touched the wall in opposite corners, and then commonly there was not room enough.

My "best" room, however, my withdrawing room, always ready for company, on whose carpet the sun rarely fell, was the pine wood behind my house. Thither in summer days, when distinguished guests came, I took them, and a priceless domestic swept the floor and dusted the furniture and kept the things in order.

If one guest came he sometimes partook of my frugal meal, and it was no interruption to conversation to be stirring a hasty-pudding, or watching the rising and maturing of a loaf of bread in the ashes, in the meanwhile. But if twenty came and sat in my house there was nothing said about dinner, though there might be bread enough for two, more than if eating were a forsaken habit; but we naturally practised abstinence; and this was never felt to be an offence against hospitality, but the most proper and considerate course. The waste and decay of physical life, which so often needs repair, seemed miraculously retarded in such a case, and the vital vigor stood its ground. I could entertain thus a thousand as well as twenty; and if any ever went away disappointed or hungry from my house when they found me at home, they may depend upon it that I sympathized with them at least. So easy is it, though many housekeepers doubt it, to establish new and better customs in the place of the old. You need not rest your reputation on the dinners you give.

As for men, they will hardly fail one anywhere. I had more visitors while I lived in the woods than at any other period in my life; I mean that I had some. I met several there under more favorable circumstances than I could anywhere else. But fewer came to see me on trivial business. In this respect, my company was winnowed by my mere distance from town. I had withdrawn so far within the great ocean of solitude, into which the rivers of society empty, that for the most part, so far as my needs were concerned, only the finest sediment was deposited around me.

1

The main narrative point of view of the passage is of

A) a man adjusting to life in a big city after growing up on a farm.

B) a discussion of visitors to a small house away from city life.

C) a sailor discussing the pond on which he grew up and how it affected his friendships.

D) a man discussing the potential of big thoughts and their need to be expressed.

2

The passage suggested which of the following about the author?

A) He enjoyed living in the country near a pond.

B) He had more visitors to his home in the country than at any other time in his life.

C) He felt that having more than three people in his house was too many.

D) He needed to throw dinner parties to entice guests to come from town to his home.

3

Which choice provides the best evidence for the answer to the previous answer?

A) Lines 7-11 ("I had three . . . for them all")

B) Lines 33-35 ("I have found . . . opposite side")

C) Lines 72-73 ("You need . . . you give")

D) Lines 75-76 ("I had more...in my life")

4

As used in line 11, "economized" most nearly means

A) wasted.

B) used efficiently.

C) squandered.

D) purchased.

5

It can be inferred from the passage that "big thoughts" (line 21) must

A) become violent before settling down.

B) bounce around and break out of one's head.

C) be mulled over and formulated before being heard.

D) have time to move around before being heard.

6

In the context of the passage, the phrase "as when you throw two stones into calm water so near that they break each other's undulations" (lines 37-39) is best described as

A) a reference to the author's childhood days when he threw stones into a lake.

B) an analogy used to elaborate on a previous statement.

C) a way to expand on the reasons national boundaries are always changing.

D) a reason that the author and his companion had to continually move their chairs to be heard.

7

As used in line 27, "plow" most nearly means

A) push.

B) furrow.

C) cultivate.

D) walk.

8

What happens when the author does not have enough food for his guests?

A) He shares.

B) He turns them away.

C) He buys more food.

D) They refrain from eating.

The passage suggests that housekeepers most likely

A) are stuck in their ways and unable to change.

B) feel that traditions should not change.

C) believe there is a certain protocol that must be followed when hosting guests.

D) feel that pudding and bread are not a suitable meal.

What does the author mean when he said that "only the finest sediment was deposited" (lines 84-85) on him?

A) He was living far from town and his visitors were of a higher caliber.

B) He was covered in a fine dust while living in the woods.

C) The pond near his home frequently flooded, leaving sediment in his "best" room.

D) Many people came to see him about the dirty business of trivial matters.

What choice provides the best evidence for the answer to the previous question?

A) Lines 48–50 ("a priceless . . . order")

B) Lines 75-77 ("I had more . . . some")

C) Lines 70–72 ("though many . . . old")

D) Line 79 ("But fewer . . . business")

READING DRILL ANSWERS AND EXPLANATIONS

Reading Drill 1

1. **B** Because this is a general question followed by a "best evidence" question, Parallel POE lets you use the answer choices for the next question to help with this one. Remember: You can look at the lines given in the "best evidence" question and see if they support any of these answer choices. Choice (A) initially looks like it could be supported by (B) from the next question, so keep that pair as well. Choice (B) in this question is supported by (C) in the next question, so keep that pair. Neither (C) nor (D) in this question has support in the "best evidence" question, so eliminate those two. When you consider your remaining pairs of choices more carefully, you see that the author refers to the process of *electrolytic processing* as *expensive*, not the tin itself. Therefore, you can eliminate (A), which also eliminates (B) from the next question. The answer here is (B).

2. **C** Because this is a "best evidence" question following a general question, Parallel POE lets you use the answer choices for this question to help with the previous one. Remember: You can look at the lines given in the "best evidence" question to see if they support any of these answer choices. Choice (A) does not support any of the answer choices in the previous question, so you can eliminate (A). Choice (B) initially looks like it could support (A) in the previous question, so keep that pair. Choice (C) supports (B) in the previous question, so keep that pair as well. Choice (D) does not support any of the answers to the previous question, so you can eliminate (D). When you consider your remaining pairs of choices more carefully, you see that the author refers to the process of *electrolytic processing* as *expensive*, not the tin itself. Therefore, you can eliminate (B), which also eliminates (A) from the previous question. Choice (C) is correct.

3. **B** The passage discusses the nature of tin, the procedures of mining for tin, the uses of tin, and the supply chain of tin. While the nature of tin is discussed in extreme detail, the supply chain is described as *complex*, and the passage provides only a broad overview of some of the obstacles in determining the exact chain. Thus, the passage reviews several elements of tin in varying degrees of detail. Choice (A) is incorrect because the *analysis* of the supply chain is not *complete*. Choice (B) matches the prediction and is therefore correct. Choice (C) is also incorrect: While the passage could be used for a *geology course*, it does not provide any information to describe the passage. Choice (D) can be eliminated because it does not match the prediction.

4. **C** According to the passage, *electrolytic processing is more expensive, but produces up to 99.9999 percent tin*, which indicates that tin produced in this fashion would be less common (since it is more expensive), and appeals most to those who required a purer form of tin. Choice (A) is incorrect because *commonly produced* items do not match the predicted answer. Choice (B) can be eliminated because there is no indication that the *figurines* would benefit from a purer form of tin. Choice (C) is correct because it matches both the small quantity and the appeal of a purer form of tin. Choice (D) is incorrect; an item *sold worldwide* does not match the predicted answer.

5. **C** The first paragraph discusses how tin is found in nature, mined, and processed into an industrial form. The second paragraph discusses the uses of tin. Choice (A) is incorrect because *assumptive generalizations* do not match the specific numbers provided in the second paragraph. Choice (B) can be eliminated because *industrial processes* would be a better fit for the discussion in the first paragraph about *refining tin;* the second paragraph mainly details the uses for tin. Choice (C) may be vague, but it matches the prediction and is therefore the correct answer. Choice (D) is is incorrect because it does not match the prediction.

6. **B** The passage states that *Solder has been made from lead and tin, but since the Safe Drinking Water Act, tin has become the primary metal in solder.* This suggests that the Safe Drinking Water Act may have caused the change from solder being made with both lead and tin to primarily tin. Choice (A) is incorrect because *specified* is extreme. Similarly, eliminate (C) because *all applications* is too extreme. Choice (D) does not match the prediction, so it is incorrect. Choice (B) is the correct answer, as it matches the prediction.

7. **D** According to the passage, *Because tin is not harmful to humans, it is a preferred method of canning and preserving food.* Choices (A) and (B) can be eliminated because they do not match the predicted answer. Choice (C) is tempting, as the passage indicates a demand for tin in solder, but *the best* is extreme and unsupported by the passage. Choice (D) is the correct answer because the *impact on an individual's health* can be *not harmful.*

8. **D** Based on the previous question, tin has a high demand because it is *not harmful to humans.* Choices (A), (B), and (C) are incorrect because they do not match the previous answer's prediction. Only (D) matches the predicted answer.

9. **C** According to the passage, *companies...may not describe which of their plants use which starting materials, plants...may or may not consume and (or) produce all of the tin materials reported,* and *companies that were reported to have been tin suppliers could not be confirmed as such,* among other descriptions of what results in an extremely difficult—if not impossible—trail to follow. Therefore, a phrase to use in place of *opaque* is "very difficult to understand." Choices (A), (B), and (D) are incorrect because they do not match the prediction. Only (C) matches the predicted answer, as *impenetrable* can mean "inaccessible to knowledge" or something that can't be known.

10. **D** The final paragraph discusses the *complex* nature of the tin supply chain and lists a number of reasons why the tin supply chain is difficult—if not impossible—to follow. The sentence *companies changed names, were referred to imprecisely, changed ownership, or went out of business* provides another example to support the idea that the tin supply chain is complex. Choices (A) and (B) do not match the prediction and are therefore incorrect. Choice (C) may be tempting, but *sole* is too extreme; eliminate (C). Choice (D) matches the predicted answer because the *earlier statement* is that the *tin supply chain is complex.* The answer is (D).

Reading Drill 2

1. **B** The main narrative point of view in this passage is from a man who is living in a house next to a pond (*I have found it a singular luxury to talk across the pond*), which is near the woods (*the pine wood behind my house*). Choice (A) is incorrect because the narrator is not in the city. Choice (C) is incorrect because there is no evidence that the author was a sailor. Choice (D) is also incorrect: Although the author does discuss thoughts in the third paragraph, it is not the main subject of the passage. Therefore, (B) is the correct answer.

2. **B** Because this is a general paired question, you can use the answer choices in the next question to help with this question. Remember, the correct answer for question 3 must support the correct answer for this question. Use the choices from question 3 to see which of these answer choices you can keep or eliminate. Choice (A) in question 3 might initially seem to support (C) for this question, so connect those two answer choices. Choice (B) in question 3 can connect to (A) here, so draw that line. Choice (C) in question 3 does not support any of the choices in this question, so you can eliminate (C). Choice (D) in question 3 supports (B) in this question. Because this question's (D) had no support from question 3, you can eliminate (D). Now go back and reread the question to make further POE decisions. The 2(A)-3(B) set does not address the author's enjoyment of living near the pond, so eliminate it. The 2(C)-3(A) pair does not answer the question, so eliminate that one as well. The remaining set of 2(B) and 3(D) answers the question, so those are your correct answers.

3. **D** When solving general paired questions, match the line references to the answer choices available in the previous question. In this case, there are several possible matches. Choice (A) in this question seems to relate to (C) in question 2, but on further inspection, this line reference does not support this choice in a way that answers the previous question, so it can be eliminated. Choice (B) seems to relate to question 2's (A), but it does not address the author's enjoyment of living near the pond, so eliminate it. Choice (C) refers to the food that the author prepares but does not support the reference in question 2's (D) and is therefore incorrect. Choice (D) does support question 2's (B) and is the correct answer.

4. **B** The author notes that if there are more than three people in the room, they *economized the space by standing,* showing that they were making the most of the room available by using a method that allows more people to exist in the same amount of space. He further notes, *I have had twenty-five or thirty souls, with their bodies, at once under my roof, and yet we often parted without being aware that we had come very near to one another.* This again shows that there were many people in a small space. Choices (A), (C), and (D) do not match the prediction and can be eliminated, making (B) correct.

5. **D** The author says that big thoughts must have room to move around before being heard. He says that he enjoys talking across the pond because there is enough room for thoughts *to be heard.* There is no evidence in the passage that the big thoughts need to be violent, so eliminate (A). Eliminate (B) because the author does not state that big thoughts *need* to break out of the receiver's head, only

that they could if they are not given enough time to develop. Choice (C) is incorrect because it is not supported by the text; the author is not literally saying that thoughts need more time to reach the hearer. Choice (D) matches the text most closely and is the correct answer.

6. **B** The phrase in the question is used to provide a common experience by which the author can give more detail to his explanation of what happens when speaking inside his house. Words do not literally bump into one another. The author has made no reference to his childhood in this passage, so eliminate (A). While national boundaries are mentioned in this paragraph, they are just another analogy by which the author is describing his experience; therefore, (C) is incorrect. The reason that the author moves his chair is due to the conversation, not the analogy by which the author is trying to bring clarity to his ideas; thus, (D) is incorrect. Choice (B) most closely matches the prediction from the text, so it is correct.

7. **A** The author notes that the ideas need to bounce around and settle, or they will plow and push their way out of the listener's head. Choice (A) is the correct answer because it matches the prediction from the text; the other answer choices do not.

8. **D** The author states that when more than a few guests are present, they treat eating as a *forsaken habit* and practice abstinence. Choice (A) is incorrect because the author shares his food only when there is enough to feed each guest adequately. Choice (B) is incorrect because there is no mention of the author ever turning away a guest, and (C) is incorrect because there is no mention of the author purchasing food in this passage. Choice (D) best matches the prediction from the text and is therefore the correct answer.

9. **B** The passage mentions that the author was unable to feed large groups of visitors to his home, and that in such cases all guests, including the author, refrained from eating. He mentions the ease by which he has established a new custom. He also states that housekeepers may doubt the ease by which the social convention was changed. This prediction most closely matches (B), so it is the correct answer. Choice (A) is incorrect because the author makes no such statement about housekeepers. Choice (C) is incorrect because the author does not state that the housekeepers have a certain way in which to serve guests, only that they would doubt establishing *new and better customs in place of the old*. Choice (D) is incorrect because although the author is preparing pudding and bread for a guest, there is no mention of what the housekeepers would think of the meal.

10. **A** The author mentions that because his house was located far from the town, he had fewer visitors coming to discuss trivial matters; therefore, (D) is incorrect. The sentence that discusses sediment is figurative, so any literal reference to dirt or dust can be eliminated: get rid of (B) and (C). Choice (A) best matches the information in the last paragraph of the passage, in which the author addresses the number of visitors he has received and how fewer guests came to see him about trivial business. Therefore, (A) is the correct answer.

11. **D** Remember, with specific paired questions, as long as you use the text to support your answer for the first question, you have an actual two-for-one deal. You used the reference *But fewer came to see me on trivial business,* to answer question 10, so you know the answer to this question is (D)! Done.

Part III
How to Crack the Writing and Language Test

Chapter 6
Introduction
to Writing and
Language Strategy

The Writing and Language Test consists of 44 multiple-choice questions that you'll have 35 minutes to complete. The questions are designed to test your knowledge of grammatical and stylistic topics. In this chapter, we'll introduce you to the format of Writing and Language Test, the types of questions and passages you'll encounter, and the overall strategies you need to ace this section.

CAN YOU REALLY TEST WRITING ON A MULTIPLE-CHOICE EXAM?

We'd say no, but ETS and the College Board seem to think the answer is yes. To that end, you will have 35 minutes to answer 44 multiple-choice questions that ask about a variety of grammatical and stylistic topics. If you like to read and/or write, the SAT may frustrate you a bit because it may seem to boil writing down to a couple of dull rules. But as you will see, we will use the next few chapters to suggest a method that keeps things simple for pro- and antigrammarians alike.

WHERE DID ALL THE QUESTIONS GO?

One thing that can seem a little strange about the Writing and Language Test of the SAT is that many of the questions don't have, well, questions. Instead, many of the questions look something like this:

The history of language although it may sound like a boring subject, is a treasure trove of historical, cultural, and psychological insights.

1

A) NO CHANGE

B) language, although it may sound like a boring subject

C) language, although it may sound, like a boring subject,

D) language, although it may sound like a boring subject,

How are you supposed to pick an answer when there's no question?

Well, actually, what you'll find throughout this chapter and the next two chapters is that you're given a *lot* of information in this list of answer choices.

Look at these pairs, and you'll see just what we mean. As you read through these pairs of answer choices, think about what each question is probably testing.

i.   A) could of
       B) could have

ii.   A) tall, dark, and handsome
       B) tall, dark and handsome

iii.   A) let them in
       B) let Sister Susie and Brother John in

iv.   A) We arrived in Paris on a Sunday. Then we took the train to Nantes. Then we took the train to Bordeaux.
       B) We arrived in Paris on a Sunday. Then we took the train to Bordeaux. Then we took the train to Nantes.

If you were able to see the differences in these answer choices, you're already more than halfway there. Now, notice how the differences in these answers can reveal the question that is lurking in the heart of each list of answer choices.

i. The difference between the word "of" and "have" means that this question is asking, *Is the correct form "could of" or "could have"?*

ii. The difference between having a comma after the word "dark" and not having one there means that this question is asking, *How many commas does this sentence need, and where do they belong?*

iii. The difference between "them" and "Sister and Susie and Brother John" means that this question is asking, *Is "them" adequately specific, or do you need to refer to people by name?*

iv. The difference between the order of these sentences asks, *What order should the sentences be in?*

Therefore, what we have noticed in these pairs of answer choices is something that may seem fairly simple but which is essential to success on the SAT.

THE ANSWER CHOICES ASK THE QUESTIONS

At some point, you've almost certainly had to do the English-class exercise called "peer editing." In this exercise, you are tasked with "editing" the work of one of your fellow students. But this can be really tough, because what exactly does it mean to "edit" an entire essay or paper when you aren't given any directions? It's *especially* tough when you start getting into the subtleties between whether things are *wrong* or whether they could merely be improved.

Look, for example, at these two sentences:

> *It was a beautiful day outside birds were singing cheerful songs.*

> *It was a beautiful day outside; birds were singing cheerful songs.*

You'd have to pick the second one in this case because the first has a grammatical error: it's a run-on sentence. Or for the non-grammarians out there, you have to break that thing up.

Now, look at these next two sentences:

> *The weather was just right, so I decided to play soccer.*

> *Just right was how I would describe the weather, so a decision of soccer-playing was made by me.*

In this case, the first sentence is obviously better than the second, but the second technically doesn't have any grammatical errors in it. The first may be *better*, but the second isn't exactly *wrong*.

What made each of these pairs of sentences relatively easy to deal with, though, was the fact that you could compare the sentences to one another. In doing so, you noted the differences between those sentences, and you picked the *better* answer accordingly.

Let's see how this looks in a real SAT situation.

Language is a living [2] document shows how people think and communicate.

2
A) NO CHANGE
B) document it shows
C) document that shows
D) document, which showing

Here's How to to Crack It

First, look at what's changing in the answer choices. The word "document" remains the same in each, but what comes after it changes each time. This question, then, seems to be asking, *Which words will best link the two ideas in the sentence?*

Choices (A) and (D) make the sentence incomplete, so those should be eliminated. Choice (B) creates a run-on sentence, so that should also be eliminated. It looks like only (C) appropriately links the ideas without adding new errors.

Notice that the entire process started with asking, "What's changing in the answer choices?" With that question, we figured out what was being tested, and we used POE to do the rest.

Let's try another.

A community's very soul, we might say, is communicated through [3] their language.

3
A) NO CHANGE
B) they're language.
C) their languages.
D) its language.

Here's How to Crack It

As always, start with what is changing in the answer choices. It looks like the main change is between the words "their," "they're," and "its," with a minor change between the words "language" and "languages." As such, this question seems to be asking, *What is the appropriate pronoun to use in this context, and just how many "languages" are we talking about?*

Start wherever is easiest. In this case, it can be a little bit difficult to say for sure whether we are talking about one language or about a bunch of languages. Instead, let's work with the pronoun. What does it refer back to? In this sentence, it seems that the pronoun refers back to "a community," which is a singular noun (even though it describes a lot of people). Therefore, the only possible answer that could work is (D), which contains the singular pronoun "its."

Notice how we made the question irrelevant as to whether we were talking about one language or many languages. Sometimes fixing one problem will make others irrelevant!

LEARN FROM THE ANSWER CHOICES

Let's think about the previous question a bit more. If someone said to you, *A community's very soul, we might say, is communicated through their language*, you might not necessarily hear that as wrong. That's because the way we speak is often very different from the way we write. On this test, the test writers are more concerned with how we write and with the stricter set of rules that go along with writing.

As such, the answer choices can not only tell us what a particular question is testing, but can also reveal mistakes that we might not have otherwise seen (in the original sentence) or heard (in our heads). In the previous question, we might not have noted the mistake at all if we hadn't looked at what was changing in the answer choices.

Let's see another.

---

4 For all intensive purposes, any social, cultural, or historical study *must* start with an analysis of language.

4

A) NO CHANGE
B) For all intents and purposes,
C) For all intent's and purpose's,
D) For all intensive purpose's,

Here's How to Crack It

First, as always, check what's changing in the answer choices. In this case, that step is especially important because you can't really hear the error. People misuse this idiom all the time because they so rarely see it written, and all four of the answer choices sound basically the same. So, having checked the answer choices in this case *reveals* an error that you might not have otherwise seen.

Then, start Process of Elimination. There's no good reason to have apostrophes anywhere (there are neither contractions nor possessions), so eliminate (C) and (D). Then, if you're not sure, take a guess. The correct form of the saying here is (B).

Notice, though, that looking at the answer choices revealed the problem that you might not have otherwise been able to see or hear. Then, POE took you the rest of the way.

POE DOES THE BIG WORK

Once you have a sense of what the question is testing, POE can get you closer and closer to the answer. POE is especially helpful when you're dealing with sentences that have lots of issues, like this one:

It may seem that how people speak is distinct from how **5** they are acting; however, there's something that most historians will tell you is wrong.

5

A) NO CHANGE

B) they act, however, there's something

C) they are acting, however, that's something

D) they act; however, that's something

Here's How to Crack It

First, as always, check what's changing in the answer choices. In this case, there are three things changing: the difference between *act* and *are acting*, the difference between *that's* and *there's*, and the difference between a period and a semicolon. While this may seem like a lot, this is actually a huge POE opportunity! Start with the one you find easiest, and work backwards from there.

Because the semicolon is not commonly used, let's save the punctuation part for last. Hopefully we can get the right answer without having to deal with the punctuation at all. Let's start with the difference between *that's* and *there's*. The sentence doesn't contain any mention of place, so the sentence can't contain *there's*, eliminating (A) and (B). Then, to choose between the last two, *they act* is more concise and more consistent with the rest of the sentence than is *they are acting*, which makes (D) better than (C). In this instance, we got to the correct answer without having to deal with all the messiness in the question!

ALL OF THE QUESTIONS CAN'T BE WRONG ALL OF THE TIME

Now that our strategy is basically set, let's look at a more difficult question.

---

[6] Your knowledge of grammar and vocabulary may be shaky, but you can learn a lot from some basic tenets of linguistics.

6

A) NO CHANGE

B) You're knowledge of grammar or vocabulary might be shaky,

C) Your knowledge of grammar and vocabulary might be shakily,

D) You're knowledge of grammar and vocabulary might be shaky,

Here's How to Crack It

As always, check the answers first. In this case, here's what's changing: The answers are switching between *your* and *you're*, between *and* and *or*, and between *shaky* and *shakily*. Let's do the easy parts first!

First of all, there's no reason to insert the word *shakily* here. You can't say that someone has *shakily knowledge* of something, so eliminate (C). Then, the *knowledge* belongs to *you*, so it is *your knowledge*, not *you are knowledge*, thus eliminating (B) and (D). This leaves us with only (A).

Remember, NO CHANGE is right sometimes! Some people pick it too much. Some people don't pick it enough, but if you've done the other steps in the process and have eliminated all the other choices, go ahead and pick (A)!

HOW TO ACE THE WRITING AND LANGUAGE TEST: A STRATEGY

- Check what's changing in the answer choices.
- Figure out what the question is testing and let the differences reveal potential errors.
- Use Process of Elimination.
- If you haven't eliminated three answers, pick the shortest one that is most consistent with the rest of the sentence.

In the next few chapters, we'll get in to some of the more technical issues in Writing and Language, but we'll be using this strategy throughout. Try the drill on the next page to get some of the basics down.

Writing and Language Drill 1

The purpose of this drill is to get a basic idea of what each question is testing from only the answer choices. Check your answers on page 84.

1

A) NO CHANGE

B) babies' favorite bottles

C) baby's favorite bottle's

D) babies' favorite bottles'

What's changing in the answer choices?

_____

What is this question testing?

_____

2

A) NO CHANGE

B) did

C) does

D) have done

What's changing in the answer choices?

_____

What is this question testing?

_____

3

A) NO CHANGE

B) Although

C) While

D) Because

What's changing in the answer choices?

_____

What is this question testing?

_____

4

A) NO CHANGE

B) was notable for their

C) were notable for its

D) were notable for their

What's changing in the answer choices?

_____

What is this question testing?

_____

5

A) NO CHANGE

B) beautiful, as in super pretty.

C) beautiful, like easy on the eyes.

D) beautiful.

What's changing in the answer choices?

_____

What is this question testing?

_____

WRITING AND LANGUAGE DRILL 1 ANSWER KEY

1. Apostrophes; apostrophes and where they go
2. Verbs; verb tense and number
3. Words; transition words (direction)
4. Was/were and their/its; verb number and pronoun number
5. Number of words; conciseness

Summary

o   The Writing and Language Test on the SAT is 35 minutes long and contains 44 questions.

o   Many of the "questions" on the W & L Test aren't exactly questions; instead, you'll be presented with a series of passages with different portions of it underlined, and you need to determine whether the underlined portion is correct or if it should be replaced with one of the given choices.

o   Check what's changing in the answer choices. The answer choices not only tell you what a particular question is testing, but also reveal mistakes that you might not have otherwise seen.

o   Use POE to get rid of the incorrect answers. If you can't eliminate three choices, pick the shortest one that is most consistent with the rest of the sentence.

Chapter 7
Punctuation

Punctuation is the focus of many questions on the Writing and Language Test. But how do you know when to use the different punctuation marks that are being tested? This chapter will answer that question as well as highlight some of the SAT's rules for using punctuation and the strategies you can use to outsmart the test writers.

WAIT, THE SAT WANTS ME TO KNOW HOW TO USE A SEMICOLON?

Kurt Vonnegut once wrote, "Here is a lesson in creative writing. First rule: Do not use semicolons… All they do is show you've been to college." Unfortunately, this does not apply to the SAT. For the SAT, you'll need to know how to use the semicolon and a few other types of weird punctuation. In this chapter, we're going to talk about the variety of punctuation you need to know how to use on the SAT. Learn these few simple rules, and you'll be all set on the punctuation questions.

First and foremost, stick to the strategy!

> Start by asking, "What's changing in the answer choices?"

If you see punctuation marks—commas, periods, apostrophes, semicolons, colons—changing, then the question is testing punctuation. Then, as you work the problem, make sure to ask the big question:

> Does this punctuation need to be here?

The particular punctuation mark you are using—no matter what it is—must have a specific role within the sentence. You wouldn't use a question mark without a question, would you? Nope! Well, all punctuation works that way, and in what follows, we'll give you seven basic instances in which you would use some type of punctuation. Otherwise, let the words do their thing unobstructed!

STOP, GO, AND THE VERTICAL LINE TEST

Let's get the weird ones out of the way first. Everyone knows that a period ends a sentence, but once things get more complicated, even a particularly nerdy grammarian can get lost. Because of this confusion, we've come up with a basic chart that summarizes the different times you might use what the SAT calls "end-of-sentence" and "middle-of-sentence" punctuation.

When you are linking ideas, you must use one of the following:

STOP
- Period
- Semicolon
- Comma + FANBOYS
- Question mark
- Exclamation Mark

HALF-STOP
- Colon
- Long dash

GO
- Comma
- No punctuation

FANBOYS stands for **F**or, **A**nd, **N**or, **B**ut, **O**r, **Y**et, and **S**o.

> STOP punctuation can link *only* complete ideas.
>
> HALF-STOP punctuation must be *preceded* by a complete idea.
>
> GO punctuation can link anything *except* two complete ideas.

Let's see how these work. Here is a complete idea:

Samantha studied for the SAT.

Notice that we've already used one form of STOP punctuation at the end of this sentence: a period.

Now, if we want to add a second complete idea, we'll keep the period.

Samantha studied for the SAT. She ended up doing really well on the test.

In this case, the period is linking these two complete ideas. But the nice thing about STOP punctuation is that you can really use any of the punctuation in the list to do the same thing, so we could also say this:

Samantha studied for the SAT; she ended up doing really well on the test.

What the list of STOP punctuation shows us is that essentially, a period and a semicolon are the same thing. We could say the same for the use of a comma plus one of the FANBOYS.

Samantha studied for the SAT, and she ended up doing really well on the test.

You can also use HALF-STOP punctuation to separate two complete ideas, so you could say

Samantha studied for the SAT: she ended up doing really well on the test.

or

Samantha studied for the SAT—she ended up doing really well on the test.

There's a subtle difference, however, between STOP and HALF-STOP punctuation: for STOP punctuation, both ideas have to be complete, but for HALF-STOP punctuation, only the first one does.

Let's see what this looks like. If we want to link a complete idea and an incomplete idea, we can use HALF-STOP punctuation as long as the complete idea comes first. For example,

Samantha studied for the SAT: all three sections of it.

or

Samantha studied for the SAT: the silliest test in all the land.

When you use HALF-STOP punctuation, there has to be a complete idea before the punctuation. So, these examples wouldn't be correct:

Samantha studied for: the SAT, the ACT, and every AP test in between.

The SAT—Samantha studied for it and was glad she did.

When you are not linking two complete ideas, you can use GO punctuation. So you could say, for instance,

Samantha studied for the SAT, the ACT, and every AP test in between.

or

Samantha studied for the SAT, all three sections of it.

These are the three types of mid-sentence or end-of-sentence punctuation: STOP, HALF-STOP, and GO. You'll notice that there is a bit of overlap between the concepts, but the SAT couldn't possibly make you get into the minutia of choosing between, say, a period and a semicolon. If you can figure out which of the big three (STOP, HALF-STOP, and GO) categories you'll need, that's all you need to be able to do.

So let's see what this looks like in context.

Jonah studied every day for the big **1** test he was taking the SAT that Saturday.

1

A) NO CHANGE
B) test, he was taking
C) test, he was taking,
D) test; he was taking

Here's How to Crack It

As always, check what's changing in the answer choices. In this case, the words all stay the same. All that changes is the punctuation, and notice the types of punctuation that are changing: STOP and GO.

Now, when you see STOP punctuation changing in the answer choices, you can do a little something we like to call the Vertical Line Test.

Draw a line where you see the punctuation changing—in this case, between the words *test* and *he*. Then, read up to the vertical line: *Jonah studied every day for the big test.* That's complete. Now, read after the vertical line: *he was taking the SAT that Saturday.* That's also complete.

So let's think; we've got two complete ideas here. What kind of punctuation do we need? STOP or HALF-STOP. It looks like STOP is the only one available, so let's choose (D).

Let's try another.

It was very important for him to do **2** well. High scores in all the subjects.

2

A) NO CHANGE
B) well; high
C) well: high
D) well, he wanted high

Here's How to Crack It

Check the answer choices. What's changing? It looks like the punctuation is changing, and some of that punctuation is STOP. Let's use the Vertical Line Test. Draw a vertical line where you see the punctuation: between *well* and *high* or *well* and *he*.

What's before the vertical line? *It was very important for him to do well* is complete. Then, *high scores in all the subjects* is not. Therefore, because we have one complete idea (the first) and one incomplete idea (the second), we can't use STOP punctuation, thus eliminating (A) and (B).

Now, what's different between the last two? Choice (C) contains HALF-STOP punctuation, which can work, so we'll keep that. Choice (D) adds some words, with which the second idea becomes *he wanted high scores in all the subjects*, which is complete. That makes two complete ideas separated by a comma, but what do we need when we're separating two complete ideas? STOP punctuation! Eliminate (D)! Only (C) is left.

———————◯———————

Let's see one more.

———————◯———————

Whenever Jonah had a free

3 moment—he was studying.

3

A) NO CHANGE

B) moment; he

C) moment, he,

D) moment, he

Here's How to Crack It

The punctuation is changing in the answer choices, and there's some STOP punctuation, so let's use the Vertical Line Test. Put the line between *moment* and *he*. The first idea, *Whenever Jonah had a free moment*, is incomplete, and the second idea, *he was studying*, is complete. Therefore, we can't use STOP (which needs two complete ideas) or HALF-STOP (which needs a complete idea before the punctuation), thus eliminating (A) and (B). Then, because there is no good reason to put a comma after the word *he*, the correct answer must be (D).

———————◯———————

A SLIGHT PAUSE FOR COMMAS

Commas can be a little tricky. In question 3, we got down to two answer choices, (C) and (D), after having completed the Vertical Line Test. But then how do you decide whether to keep a comma in or not? It seems a little arbitrary to say that you use a comma "every time you want to pause," so let's reverse that and make it a little more concrete.

> If you can't cite a reason to use a comma, *don't use one.*
>
> On the SAT, there are only four reasons to use a comma:
> - in STOP punctuation, with one of the FANBOYS
> - in GO punctuation, to separate incomplete ideas from other ideas
> - in a list of three or more things
> - in a sentence containing unnecessary information

We've already seen the first two concepts, so let's look at the other two.

Try this one.

His top-choice schools were

4 Harvard, Yale and Princeton.

4
A) NO CHANGE
B) Harvard, Yale, and Princeton.
C) Harvard, Yale, and, Princeton.
D) Harvard Yale and Princeton.

Here's How to Crack It

First, check what's changing in the answer choices. It looks like the commas in this list are changing. Because there's not any obvious STOP or HALF-STOP punctuation, the Vertical Line Test won't do us much good.

Then, it will help to know that the rule on the SAT is to place a comma after every item in a series. Think of it this way. There's a potential misunderstanding in this sentence:

I went to the park with my parents, my cat Violet and my dog Stuart.

Without a comma, it sure sounds like this guy has some interesting parents. If there's no comma, how do we know that this sentence isn't supposed to say his parents are *my cat Violet and my dog Stuart?* The only way to remove the ambiguity would be to add a comma like this:

I went to the park with my parents, my cat Violet, and my dog Stuart.

Keep that in mind as we try to crack number 4. In this problem, *Harvard, Yale, and Princeton* form a list, so they should be set off by commas as they are in (B).

———————————○———————————

Let's try another.

———————————○———————————

5 Jonah, everyone seemed

fairly certain, was going to get into one

of those schools.

5
A) NO CHANGE
B) Jonah everyone seemed fairly certain
C) Jonah, everyone seemed fairly certain
D) Jonah everyone seemed fairly certain,

Here's How to Crack It

First, check what's changing in the answer choices. Just commas. And those commas seem to be circling around the words *everyone seemed fairly certain*. When you've got a few commas circling around a word, phrase, or clause like this, the question is usually testing necessary vs. unnecessary information.

A good way to test whether the idea is necessary to the meaning of the sentence is to take it out. Read the original sentence again. Now read this one: *Jonah was going to get into one of those schools.*

Is the sentence still complete? Yes. Has the meaning of the sentence changed? No, we just lost a little extra thing. Therefore, the idea is *unnecessary* to the meaning of the sentence and should be set off with commas as it is in (A).

———————————○———————————

Let's try a few more. Try to figure out whether the word or idea in italics is necessary to the meaning of the sentence, and whether or not commas need to surround the italics. The answers are on page 98.

i.   The student *with the best GPA* will be admitted to the best college.
ii. Edward wants to go to Pomona College *which is a really good school.*
iii. The car *that was painted red* drove off at a hundred miles an hour.
iv. Charles Chesnutt *who wrote a lot of great stories* was also a lawyer.
v.   Philadelphia Flyers goalie *Steve Mason* is an underappreciated player.

Now let's put it all together in this question.

Everyone [6] hoped, he would get in, after his brother and two sisters had gone to their first-choice schools.

6

A) NO CHANGE

B) hoped, he would get in, after his brother, and two sisters had

C) hoped, he would get in after his brother, and, two sisters had

D) hoped he would get in after his brother and two sisters had

Here's How to Crack It

Check what's changing in the answer choices. There are varying numbers of commas in varying places. Remember, the rule of thumb with commas is that if you can't cite a reason to use a comma, *don't use one.*

It looks like *he would get in* is being set off by commas. Let's see whether it's necessary or unnecessary information. Read the original sentence; then read the sentence again without that piece of information: *Everyone hoped after his brother and two sisters had gone to their first-choice schools.* It looks like the sentence has changed meaning and is not really complete anymore. Therefore, that bit of information is necessary to the meaning of the sentence, so it doesn't need commas. Then, there are no good reasons to put commas around or in the phrase *after his brother and two sisters.*

In the end, there aren't reasons to put commas anywhere in this sentence. The correct answer is (D). Sometimes SAT will test "unnecessary punctuation" explicitly, so make sure you have a good reason to use commas when you use them!

YOUR GOING TO BE TESTED ON APOSTROPHE'S (AND INTERNET SPELLING IS A TERRIBLE GUIDE!)

As with commas, apostrophes have only a very limited set of applications. Apostrophes are a little trickier, though, because you can't really hear them in speech, so people misuse them all the time. Think about the header of this section. The apostrophes are wrong there. Here's the correct way of punctuating it: *You're going to be tested on apostrophes*. Can you hear the difference? Neither can we.

Therefore, as with commas, if you can't cite a reason to use an apostrophe, don't use one. There are only two reasons to use apostrophes on the SAT:

> - Possessive nouns (NOT pronouns)
> - Contractions

Let's see some examples.

Some of those very **7** selective schools' require really high score's.

7

A) NO CHANGE
B) selective school's require really high scores'.
C) selective schools require really high score's.
D) selective schools require really high scores.

Here's How to Crack It

Check what's changing in the answer choices. In this case, the words are all staying the same, but the apostrophes are changing. Remember, we don't want to use apostrophes at all if we can't cite a good reason to do so.

Does anything belong to *schools* or *score*? No! Are they forming contractions like *school is* or *score is*? No! Therefore, there's no reason to use apostrophes, and the only possible answer is (D), which dispenses with the apostrophes altogether.

As in the previous question, there's no need for any punctuation, and in a question like this, you're being tested on whether you can spot unnecessary punctuation.

But sometimes the apostrophes will be necessary. Let's have a look at another.

———————○———————

8 It's tough to get in to you're

top-choice schools.

8

A) NO CHANGE

B) Its tough to get in to your

C) Its tough to get in to you're

D) It's tough to get in to your

Here's How to Crack It

Check what's changing in the answer choices. The main changes have to do with apostrophes, particularly on the words *its/it's* and *your/you're*.

The first word, *its/it's*, needs an apostrophe: It creates the contraction *it is*. Therefore, because this one needs an apostrophe, get rid of (B) and (C). As for the other, this word is possessive (as in, the *top-choice schools* belonging to *you*), but remember: Possessive *nouns* need an apostrophe, but possessive *pronouns* don't. Therefore, because *you* is a pronoun, this word should be spelled *your*, as it is in (D).

———————○———————

Phew! These apostrophes can get a little tricky, so let's try a few more. On these (as on many parts of the SAT), you'll find that using your ear and sounding things out doesn't really help all that much.

Circle the option that works. The big question is, apostrophes or no apostrophes? You can find the answers on page 98.

i. *Tinas/Tina's* boss said *shes/she's* allowed to take the next few *days/day's* off.

ii. If *your/you're* not coming to my party, *its/it's* really fine with me.

iii. *There/they're* are really no good *reasons/reason's* for *your/you're* bad attitude.

iv. *Well/we'll* get back to you as soon as *your/you're* application is received.

v. *Its/it's his/his'* guacamole, and he said we *cant/can't* have any because *its/it's* not *ours/our's*.

CONCLUSION

In sum, we've looked at all the punctuation you'd ever need on the SAT. It's really not that much, and you probably knew a lot of it already. In general, checking what's changing in the answer choices can help reveal mistakes that you may not have heard, and POE can help you narrow those answers down.

Punctuation rules are easy to learn, as is the biggest rule of all about punctuation.

> Know why you are using punctuation, whether that punctuation is STOP, HALF-STOP, GO, commas, or apostrophes. If you can't cite reasons to use these punctuation marks, don't use them!

Try out these skills on the drill on the next page.

Answers to Questions on Page 95:

i. NECESSARY to the meaning of the sentence (no commas). If you remove the italicized part, the sentence is not adequately specific.

ii. UNNECESSARY to the meaning of the sentence (commas). If you remove the italicized part, the sentence is still complete and does not change meaning.

iii. NECESSARY to the meaning of the sentence (no commas). If you remove the italicized part, the sentence is not adequately specific.

iv. UNNECESSARY to the meaning of the sentence (commas). If you remove the italicized part, the sentence is still complete and does not change meaning.

v. NECESSARY to the meaning of the sentence (no commas). If you remove the italicized part, the sentence is no longer complete.

Answers to Questions on Page 97:

i. Tina's, she's, days
ii. you're, it's
iii. There, reasons, your
iv. We'll, your
v. It's, his, can't, it's, ours

Writing and Language Drill 2

Use what you've learned in this chapter in the drill questions that follow. Answers can be found on page 103.

Time: 7–8 minutes

More and more of our lives are mechanized, and at some point, we have to start wondering, what's the limit of that mechanization? Many factory workers in the 19th century thought their jobs **1** were safe but we know now that they were wrong. Many people **2** in today's world believe there jobs are safe, but how safe are those jobs really?

Studies abound that ask whether man or machine is better at particular tasks, and the results are not always so obvious. Sure, a machine is obviously **3** better at say, welding huge pieces of steel together, but what would you say if someone told you people are more likely to open up to a machine than to a psychologist? Or that a machine could write a quicker, more efficient news story than an experienced reporter could?

1

A) NO CHANGE
B) were safe, but we know
C) were safe; but we know
D) were safe. But we know

2

A) NO CHANGE
B) in todays world believe their jobs
C) in todays world believe they're jobs
D) in today's world believe their jobs

3

A) NO CHANGE
B) better at, say welding
C) better at, say, welding
D) better at say welding

These questions may seem overly pessimistic (or overly optimistic depending on [4] your point of view); however, some recent studies have been truly remarkable. Take Ellie, a computer program used primarily to diagnose patients with [5] depression, PTSD and other mood disorders. Many patients found it easier to talk to "Ellie" than [6] to a real person: she didn't react in some of those seemingly judgmental ways that a person would, and her voice [7] never broke on top of that she could help psychologists to diagnose mental illnesses better than human observation could. She could detect facial movements or voice tones that a person might have not heard or ignored.

4

A) NO CHANGE
B) your point of view), however,
C) you're point of view), however,
D) you're point of view); however,

5

A) NO CHANGE
B) depression, PTSD, and other
C) depression, PTSD, and, other
D) depression, PTSD, and other,

6

A) NO CHANGE
B) to a real person, she
C) to a real person; but she
D) to a real person she

7

A) NO CHANGE
B) never broke, on top of that,
C) never broke. On top of that,
D) never broke; on top, of that,

Whether Ellie is the way of the future is yet to be determined. We can't know right now, but there is no question that she raises some interesting questions, not only about **8** the work of psychologists', but also about all of what we think are definitively human activities.

On the other side of the discussion, however, there's some evidence that humans may have the upper hand. In some of the more basic **9** tasks those learned before the age of about 10 humans have a huge upper hand. Computers can do the complex thinking, but one thing with which they have a lot of trouble is, paradoxically, simplicity. Sure, a computer **10** can tell your washer's and dryer's what a perfect washing and drying cycle is, but can it fold your laundry? Your GPS can tell you the fastest route to the next state, but can it tell you the prettiest way to go or the best restaurants along the way? Not without humans!

8

A) NO CHANGE

B) psychologists work

C) the work of psychologists

D) the work of psychologist's

9

A) NO CHANGE

B) tasks those learned before the age of about 10, humans

C) tasks, those learned before the age of about 10 humans

D) tasks, those learned before the age of about 10, humans

10

A) NO CHANGE

B) can tell your washer and dryer what

C) can tell you're washers and dryers

D) can tell you're washer and dryer

While the battle of man against machine rages **11** on. The questions will persist. No matter who wins, though, humans will almost assuredly find ways to adapt: that's something we've been doing for thousands of years, which is something that no computer can say.

11

A) NO CHANGE

B) on; the

C) on—the

D) on, the

WRITING AND LANGUAGE DRILL 2: ANSWERS AND EXPLANATIONS

1. **B** The first change in the answer choices is the punctuation after the word *safe*. The idea *Many factory workers in the 19th century thought their jobs were safe* is a complete idea. The idea that follows, *we know now that they were wrong,* is also a complete idea. Two complete ideas must be separated by STOP punctuation. Choice (A) uses no punctuation between the ideas; eliminate (A). Choices (C) and (D) use STOP punctuation followed by the conjunction *but,* which makes the second part of the sentence an incomplete idea. Choice (B) uses the combination of a comma and the conjunction *but,* which together function as STOP punctuation. Choice (B) is the correct answer.

2. **D** The first change in the answer choices is the removal of the apostrophe in the word *today's,* so the question is testing possession. To determine whether the word is possessive and requires an apostrophe, consider the word that follows, *world.* Because the passage discusses the world of today, *today's* is possessive, and the form with the apostrophe is correct. Eliminate (B) and (C). The next decision to be made is between *there* and *their.* Because the word refers to the jobs belonging to the people, the possessive pronoun *their* is consistent with the meaning of the sentence. Therefore, (D) is the correct answer.

3. **C** Notice that the placement of commas is changing in the answer choices. This indicates that the question is testing comma rules. In the sentence, the word *say* has a meaning similar to "for example." This makes the word *say* unnecessary information. To make the commas consistent with this meaning, commas before and after the word are necessary. Choice (C) is correct.

4. **A** The first change in the answer choices is between *your* and *you're. Your* is a possessive pronoun, while *you're* is a contraction for the *you are.* The sentence requires the possessive form of the word, not the contraction. Eliminate (C) and (D). The next change is the punctuation after the close of the parentheses. Since parentheses indicate unnecessary information, you should check the punctuation by reading the sentence without the parenthetical information. The phrases *These questions may seem overly pessimistic* and *However, some recent studies have been truly remarkable* are both complete ideas. STOP punctuation is necessary, so eliminate (B). Choice (A) is the correct answer.

5. **B** Notice that the placement of commas is changing in the answer choices. Therefore, this question is testing comma rules. The underlined portion is part of a list. The rule for comma use in a list is to have a comma after every item in the list. The items in the list here are *depression, PTSD,* and *other mood disorders.* Therefore, a comma is needed after *depression* and after *PTSD,* but not after *other* or *and.* The correct answer is (B).

6. **A** The first change in the answer choices is the punctuation after *person.* The idea preceding the punctuation is complete, and the idea that follows is also complete. The answer must have punctuation that is consistent with two complete ideas. Choice (D) has no punctuation; eliminate (D). A comma without one of the FANBOYS is not STOP punctuation; eliminate (B). Choice (C) uses STOP punctuation followed by the conjunction *but,* which makes the second part of the sentence an incomplete idea. Eliminate (C). Choice (A) is the correct answer.

7. **C** Notice the punctuation changing in the answer choices. The idea ending with *broke* is a complete idea. The idea that follows, beginning with *on top of that,* is also a complete idea. Look for answer choices with STOP punctuation. Choice (A) has no punctuation; eliminate (A). Choice (B) has a comma, but a comma without one of the FANBOYS is not able to separate complete ideas; eliminate (B). Choice (C) has a period, and (D) has a semicolon, which are both acceptable forms of punctuation for separating complete ideas. However, (D) includes an unnecessary comma after *top,* so eliminate (D). The correct answer is (C).

8. **C** Notice the wording and the use of an apostrophe changing in the answer choices, which indicates that the question is testing possession. When using the phrase *the work of,* possession is already accounted for, and an apostrophe is not needed in *psychologists.* Eliminate (A) and (D). When using the phrase *psychologists work,* the apostrophe is necessary; eliminate (B). Choice (C) is the correct answer.

9. **D** Notice the placement of commas changing in the answer choices; this question is testing comma rules. The commas in the answer choices are placed after the word *tasks* and/or after the number 10. The phrase *those learned before the age of about 10* is unnecessary information. The answer choice consistent with unnecessary information must have commas before and after the phrase. Therefore, (D) is the correct answer.

10. **B** The first change in the answer choices is between *your* and *you're,* so the question is testing possession. *Your* is a possessive pronoun, while *you're* is a contraction for *you are.* The possessive form is consistent with the meaning of the sentence. Eliminate (C) and (D). Choice (A) includes apostrophes on the words *washers* and *dryers,* which implies possession. This is not consistent with the meaning of the sentence. Eliminate (A). Choice (B) is correct.

11. **D** Notice the punctuation changing in the answer choices. The idea preceding the punctuation change, *While the battle of man against machine rages on,* is not a complete idea. Therefore, eliminate any answer choices using punctuation consistent with complete ideas. Eliminate (A) and (B). A dash must follow a complete idea, so eliminate (C). Choice (D) is the correct answer.

Summary

○ Remember STOP, HALF-STOP, and GO punctuation.
- STOP punctuation can link *only* complete ideas.
- HALF-STOP punctuation must be *preceded* by a complete idea.
- GO punctuation can link anything *except* two complete ideas.

○ When you see STOP punctuation changing in the answer choices, use the Vertical Line Test.

○ On the SAT, there are only four reasons to use a comma:
- STOP punctuation (with one of the FANBOYS)
- GO punctuation
- after every item in a list
- to set off unnecessary information

○ On the SAT, there are only two reasons to use an apostrophe:
- possessive nouns (NOT pronouns)
- contractions

○ Know why you are using punctuation, whether that punctuation is STOP, HALF-STOP, GO, commas, or apostrophes. If you can't cite reasons to use these punctuation marks, don't use them!

Chapter 8
Words

In addition to testing punctuation, the Writing and Language Test will focus on words—mainly nouns, pronouns, and verbs. While we will discuss a few of these grammatical concepts along the way, this chapter will boil these many concepts down to three main terms: Consistency, Precision, and Concision. With less minutia to remember, you will be able to work through Words questions with confidence and ease.

THE WORDS CHANGE, BUT THE SONG REMAINS THE SAME

In the last chapter, we looked at what to do when the SAT is testing punctuation. In this chapter, we're going to look at what to do when the SAT is testing words—mainly verbs, nouns, and pronouns.

Our basic strategy, however, has remained the same. As we saw in the previous two chapters, when faced with an SAT Writing and Language question, we should always

> Check what's changing in the answer choices and use POE.

As you will notice, throughout this chapter, we talk a lot about certain parts of speech, but we don't really use a lot of grammar terms. That's because we find that on the SAT, the correct answers across a lot of different parts of speech can be summed up more succinctly with three basic terms: Consistency, Precision, and Concision.

You don't need to know a ton of grammar if you can remember these three basic rules.

> **CONSISTENCY:** Correct answers are consistent with the rest of the sentence and the passage.
>
> **PRECISION:** Correct answers are as precise as possible.
>
> **CONCISION:** Barring other errors, correct answers are as concise as possible.

Let's look at some examples of each.

Achieve Grammar Greatness
While you don't need to be a grammar expert to do well on the W & L Test, you may want to brush up on your grammar terms, especially if you're feeling a bit rusty. Pick up a copy of *Grammar Smart* for a quick refresher!

Consistency

The speakers of what has come to be known as **1** Appalachian English has used a form of English that few can explain.

1

A) NO CHANGE
B) Appalachian English uses
C) Appalachian English use
D) Appalachian English using

Here's How to Crack It

First, as always, check what's changing in the answer choices. In this case, *Appalachian English* stays the same, but the forms of the verb *to use* change. Therefore, because the verbs change, we know that the question is testing verbs.

When you see verbs changing in the answer choices, the first thing to check is the subject of the sentence. Is the verb consistent with the subject? In this case, it's not. The subject of this sentence is *speakers*, which is plural. Therefore, (A) and (B) have to be eliminated, and (D) creates an incomplete idea. Only (C) can work in the context.

Thus, when you see verbs changing in the answer choices, check the subject first. Subjects and verbs need to be consistent with each other.

Let's have a look at another.

Many scholars believe Appalachian pronunciation comes from Scots-Irish immigration, but **2** some theorizes that this dialect of English may be closer to what Londoners spoke in Elizabethan times.

2

A) NO CHANGE
B) some theorized
C) some have theorized
D) some theorize

Here's How to Crack It

Check what's changing in the answer choices. The word *some* remains consistent, but the verbs are changing. Remember from the first question that whenever you see verbs changing, make sure the verb is consistent with the subject. Because the subject of this sentence is *some*, you can eliminate (A), which isn't consistent.

Then, because all the others are consistent with the subject, make sure they are consistent with the other verbs. It looks like all the other verbs in this sentence—*believe, comes, may be*—are in the present tense, so the underlined verb should be as well, as it is in (D). Choices (B) and (C) could work in some contexts, but not this one!

As you can see, verbs are all about consistency.

───────────○───────────

When you see verbs changing in the answer choices, make sure those verbs are

- CONSISTENT with their subjects
- CONSISTENT with other verbs in the sentence and surrounding sentences

Let's try one that has a little bit of everything.

───────────○───────────

Trying to understand these changes **3** demonstrate that although we all technically speak English, we speak very different languages indeed.

3

A) NO CHANGE

B) demonstrate that although we all technically spoke English, we speak

C) demonstrates that although we all technically speak English, we might have been speaking

D) demonstrates that although we all technically speak English, we speak

Here's How to Crack It

Check what's changing in the answer choices. It looks like lots of verbs!

Let's start with the first. See which one, *demonstrate* or *demonstrates*, is consistent with the subject. That subject is *Trying*, which is singular, thus eliminating (A) and (B).

Then, we have to choose between *speak* and *might have been speaking*. Since both of these are consistent with the subject *we*, let's try to pick the one that is most consistent with other verbs. The only other verbs are *demonstrates* and *speak*, both of which are in the present tense and don't use the odd *might have been* form. Therefore, if we have to choose between (C) and (D), (D) is definitely better.

―――――――――――◯―――――――――――

Consistency applies across the test. Let's see another question in which the idea of Consistency might help us.

―――――――――――◯―――――――――――

Appalachian-English speakers and [4] their family communicate in a way that shows just how influential diversity can be on the language we speak.

4
A) NO CHANGE
B) they're families communicate
C) their families communicate
D) their family communicates

Here's How to Crack It

Check the answer choices first. It looks like pretty much everything is changing here: *they're/their*, *families/family*, and *communicate/communicates*. Let's look at the ones we have done already.

We can't cite a good reason to use an apostrophe, so let's get rid of (B). Then, the verb changes, so let's check the subject. That subject is *Appalachian-English speakers and their family/families*, which is plural regardless of the word *family* or *families*. Keep the verb consistent with the plural subject and eliminate (D).

Then, we have to choose between *family* and *families*, two nouns. As with verbs, nouns are all about consistency. When you see nouns changing in the answer choices, make sure they are consistent with the other nouns in the sentence. In this case, we are talking about *Appalachian-English speakers*, all of them, so we must be talking about all of their *families* as well. Many speakers must mean many families, as (C) suggests.

―――――――――――◯―――――――――――

Noun consistency can show up in other ways as well. Let's have a look at question 5.

The language of the West Virginians in Applachia is almost nothing like [5] New Yorkers or even other West Virginians.

5

A) NO CHANGE

B) the language of New Yorker's or even other West Virginian's.

C) that of New Yorkers or even other West Virginians.

D) people from New York or from West Virginia.

Here's How to Crack It

Look at what's changing in the answer choices. It looks like the main change is between the nouns—*New Yorkers or even other West Virginians* and *the language*. We saw in the last problem that when nouns are changing in the answer choices, we want to make sure those nouns are consistent with other nouns in the sentence.

In this case, the nouns are being compared. The language of Appalachia is being compared with the language of New Yorkers and West Virginians. Choices (A) and (D) suggest that the *language* is being compared with the *people*, so those are inconsistent. Then, (B) contains some unnecessary apostrophes, so only (C) is left.

The SAT calls this concept "faulty comparison," but we don't have to know that name. Instead, we can just remember that *nouns have to be consistent with other nouns*. When the answer choices show a change in nouns, look for the sentence's other nouns. They'll provide the clue!

Scholars today are not sure whether to call it a purely European dialect or [6] a uniquely American one.

6

A) NO CHANGE

B) uniquely American.

C) a unique one.

D) American.

Here's How to Crack It

Check what's changing in the answer choices. There's a fairly significant change between *American* and *American one*. As in the previous sentence, let's make sure this is consistent. The part of the sentence right before the underlined portion refers to a *European dialect*, so we should make our part of the sentence consistent: an *American dialect*, not merely *American*, as in (B) and (D).

Then, we are down to (A) and (C). The difference here comes between the words *unique* and *uniquely American*. While we do want to be concise when possible, we need to make sure first and foremost that we are being *precise*. Choice (A) is more precise than (C) in that it has a clearer relation to the *European dialect* with which it is being contrasted. Therefore, (A) is the correct answer in that it is the most *consistent* with the rest of the sentence and the most *precise* of the remaining possible answers.

Consistency

- When the verbs are changing in the answer choices, make sure those verbs are consistent with their subjects and with other verbs.

- When the nouns are changing in the answer choices, make sure those nouns are consistent with the other nouns in the sentence and the paragraph.

Precision

Consistency is probably the most important thing on the SAT, but precision is a close second. Once you've made sure that the underlined portion is consistent with the rest of the sentence, then make sure that the underlined portion is as precise as possible. Perfect grammar is one thing, but it won't matter much if no one knows what the writer is talking about!

Let's hear that one more time.

Once you are sure that a word or phrase is consistent with the non-underlined portion of the sentence, make that word or phrase as precise as you can.

Really, [7] most are collections of many influences, but the Appalachian dialect seems unique.

7

A) NO CHANGE

B) most of them

C) most Americans

D) most American dialects

Here's How to Crack It

Check what's changing in the answer choices. The changes could be summed up with the question "*most* what?" We've got four different options, so let's use our main guiding principles of consistency and precision.

First of all, there's a comparison in this sentence between different kinds of *dialects*, so (C) can be eliminated because that explicitly changes the comparison to something else inconsistent.

Then, let's be as precise as possible. Choices (A) and (B) are very similar in that they say *most*, but they don't specify *what* that *most* refers to. Even though these are grammatically consistent with the rest of the sentence, they're not quite precise enough, which makes (D) a lot better.

As question 7 shows, pronouns can be a bit of a challenge. They can appear in otherwise grammatically correct sentences. Still, precision is key when you're dealing with pronouns. See what you can do with these sentences. Circle the potentially imprecise pronouns and rewrite the sentences. Answers can be found on page 119.

i. Certain dialects have obvious sources, but that doesn't make it any easier to understand.

ii. Each of us speaks with an accent because of where they are from.

iii. Word choice and pronunciation it's usually easy to hear in someone's accent.

iv. Everyone uses some kind of dialect words in their everyday speech.

v. Movies, TV, the internet: it may be destroying differentiated dialects in the modern world.

Precision can show up in some other ways as well. Have a look at this question.

The Appalachian region's **8** isolation has led to some hypotheses from major urban centers that its dialect has remained intact from the days of its earliest settlers.

8

A) NO CHANGE

B) isolation has led to some hypotheses that its dialect from major urban centers has remained intact

C) isolation from major urban centers has led to some hypotheses that its dialect has remained intact

D) isolation has led to some hypotheses that its dialect has remained intact from major urban centers

Here's How to Crack It

Check what's changing in the answer choices. This step is crucial here because there are no obvious grammatical errors, so the answer choices are essential to figuring out exactly what the question is asking you to do.

In the end, the only difference among the answer choices is that the phrase *from major urban centers* is in different places. In the end, we will just need to put that phrase in the most precise place, hopefully right next to whatever it is modifying.

In this case, we can choose from among *hypotheses*, *dialect*, *isolation*, and *intact*. Which of these would have the most precise need for the phrase *from major urban centers*? Because *urban centers* seems to have something to do with place, we should eliminate (A), *hypotheses*, and (D), *intact*, which don't have anything to do with place. Then, because the passage as a whole has talked about the remoteness of the Appalachian dialect, we can say for sure that it is not a *dialect from major urban centers*, eliminating (B). All that remains, then, is (C), which completes the phrase *isolation from major urban centers*, which is the most precise answer.

Let's have a look at some more of these modifiers. Rewrite the sentence so the modifier makes the *precise* sense that it should. Check your answers against those on page 119.

i.   With all its ins and outs, many people find language a tough thing to study.

_____

_____

ii. Dialects are really fascinating to anyone who wants to study them of a particular language.

_____

_____

iii. Once opened up, you can find endless mysteries in the study of language.

_____

_____

iv. I first learned about the Appalachian dialect from a professor in college at age 19.

_____

_____

v.   Frankly pretty boring, Donald didn't pay much attention in his linguistics class.

_____

_____

Concision

This is not to say, however, that more words always mean more precision. In fact, a lot of the time less is more. If you were to ask for directions, which answer would you rather receive?

> *Turn right at Main Street and walk four blocks.*

or

> *Since this street, Elm Street, is facing in a northerly direction, and your destination is due north east, go east when you arrive at the intersection of Elm and Main. Going east will entail making a right turn in quite that easterly direction. After having made this turn and arrived on the perpendicular street…*

The first one, obviously.

And that's because concision is key when you want to communicate meaning. Really, as long as everything else is in order—as long as the grammar and punctuation are good to go—the correct answer will almost always be the shortest.

Let's see an example.

It is precisely this isolation that has led many scholars to believe that Appalachian English is alike and similar to the English spoken in Shakespeare's time.

9

A) NO CHANGE

B) similar

C) likely similar

D) similarly alike

Here's How to Crack It

Check what's changing in the answer choices. In this case, the word *similar* appears in all the answer choices, and in some it is paired with the word *alike*. Typically, if you see a list of answer choices wherein one answer is short and the rest mean the same thing but are longer, the question is testing conciseness.

What, after all, is the difference between the words *similar* and *alike*? There really isn't one, so there's no use in saying both of them, as in (A), or pairing them awkwardly, as in (D). In fact, the shortest answer choice, (B), does everything the other choices do, but it does so in the fewest words. Therefore, (B) is the correct answer.

Let's see one more.

---○---

10 Whatever the case may be, Appalachian is a fascinating dialect, and we can only hope that it persists against the onslaught of mass media.

10

A) NO CHANGE
B) Whoop-de-doo, Appalachian
C) All things considered, Appalachian
D) Appalachian

Here's How to Crack It

As always, check what's changing in the answer choices. The changes could be summed up like this: There's a bunch of stuff before the word *Appalachian*. Does any of that stuff contribute in a significant way to the sentence? No. Does the word *Appalachian* alone help the sentence to fulfill its basic purpose? Yes. Therefore, the correct answer is (D).

---○---

As we have seen in this chapter, when SAT is testing *words* (any time the words are changing in the answer choices), make sure that those words are

- **Consistent.** Verbs, nouns, and pronouns should agree within sentences and passages.
- **Precise.** The writing should communicate specific ideas and events.
- **Concise.** When everything else is correct, the shortest answer choice is correct.

Answers to Questions on Page 114:

i.   *it* is the problem. *Certain dialects have obvious sources, but that doesn't make those dialects any easier to understand.*

ii.   *they* is the problem. *Each of us speaks with an accent because of where he or she is from.*

iii. *it's* is the problem. Change *it's* to *are*! *Word-choice and pronunciation are usually easy to hear in someone's accent.*

iv.   *their* is the problem. *Everyone uses some kind of dialect words in his or her everyday speech.*

v.   *it* is the problem. *Movies, TV, the internet: all three may be destroying differentiated dialects in the modern world.*

Answers to Questions on Page 116:

i.   Many people find language a tough thing to study because of all its ins and outs.

ii.   Dialects of a particular language are really fascinating to anyone who wants to study them.

iii. Once opened up, the mysteries of a language can be endless.

iv.   I first learned about the Appalachian dialect from a college professor when I was 19 years old.

v.   Donald didn't pay much attention in his linguistics class, which he found, frankly, pretty boring.

Writing and Language Drill 3

Answers can be found on page 124.

Time: 7–8 minutes

War and Peace (1869) is **1** <u>well-known and famous</u> mainly for its length. Not many readers, especially in the modern day, **2** <u>has</u> the time or the patience to work through Leo Tolstoy's 1,400 pages, countless characters, and plot twists. **3** <u>They are</u> missing a major opportunity, not only because the novel is more fun than its page count suggests, but also because it marks the end of a particular moment in history.

1

A) NO CHANGE
B) famous and well-known
C) famously well-known
D) well-known

2

A) NO CHANGE
B) have
C) are having
D) do have

3

A) NO CHANGE
B) Those readers
C) Many of them
D) Some

Czech novelist Milan Kundera cited Tolstoy as the last novelist who could [4] be possessing the sum of his era's human knowledge. This may seem like an odd claim. Some people may be very intelligent, others may be know-it-alls, but is it really possible to know everything? A book like *War and Peace* makes the case that it is possible to know it all, or at least that it *was* possible, [5] alongside Tolstoy's other great novels and non-fiction writings. Shakespeare [6] seemed to have an emotional vocabulary that was advanced for his age, but Tolstoy lived in [7] an era of facts and discoveries, and his novels show the fruits of his vast study. It is frankly conceivable that a man with Tolstoy's leisure, intelligence, and curiosity [8] learns about his age's most current findings in literature, politics, religion, and science.

4

A) NO CHANGE
B) of had
C) possess
D) possessed

5

If the punctuation were adjusted accordingly, the best placement for the underlined portion would be
A) where it is now.
B) at the beginning of the sentence.
C) after the word *that*.
D) after the word *least*.

6

A) NO CHANGE
B) seems having
C) has
D) seemingly has

7

A) NO CHANGE
B) an era,
C) a historical time period,
D) one,

8

A) NO CHANGE
B) had been learning
C) could have learned
D) are learning

The very fact that such an achievement is impossible now shows us just how much things have changed since Tolstoy's death in 1910. **9** This was the year, in fact, that Virginia Woolf cited in her oft-quoted remark, "On or about 1910 human character changed." If we at least entertain the idea that she is correct, we can begin to see why she would be willing to make such a grandiose remark. After 1910, the twentieth century started in earnest. Knowledge became more complex as it became more specialized, and although airplanes seemed to make the world a smaller place, the differences among all the places in that small world truly emerged.

9

The writer is considering deleting the phrase *since Tolstoy's death in 1910* and ending the sentence with a period after the word *changed*. Should the phrase be kept or deleted?

A) Kept, because it contributes to the essay's biographical sketch of the author of *War and Peace*.

B) Kept, because it introduces a topic of discussion that is continued throughout the paragraph.

C) Deleted, because the remainder of the paragraph describes the insignificance of Tolstoy's death.

D) Deleted, because the paragraph as a whole is focused on the achievements of another author.

War and Peace is the great document of that pre-1910 era, of a moment when the great scientists were also 10 into philosophy and when the great mathematicians were also the great theologians. A great discovery in one field could also be 11 another. Although it was certainly remarkable, it was also possible for a man like Tolstoy to have a fundamental grasp of all that united the many branches of knowledge. Tolstoy's achievement is impossible today, but it is a wonderful reminder of the value of intellectual curiosity and cosmopolitanism. No matter how brilliant and refined we may become, we can always stand to be reminded that there is a world outside of our immediate circle.

10

A) NO CHANGE
B) fascinated with philosophical inquiry
C) interested in philosophy
D) the great philosophers

11

A) NO CHANGE
B) another field.
C) a great discovery for another.
D) the same thing elsewhere.

WRITING AND LANGUAGE DRILL 3: ANSWERS AND EXPLANATIONS

1. **D** Notice that the length of the phrase is changing in the answer choices. Some of the answer choices have extra words, which indicates that the question is testing concision. Because the words *famous* and *well-known* are synonyms, it would be redundant to use both. Choose the most concise answer, which eliminates this redundancy. Choice (D) is correct.

2. **B** Since the verb is changing in the answer choices, the question is testing subject-verb agreement. First, find the subject. *Readers* is the subject of the sentence, which is plural. The verb will need to be consistent with that subject. Eliminate (A). The remaining options are all plural, but only (B) is concise and consistent with the meaning of the sentence, which makes it the correct answer.

3. **B** When the use of pronouns changes in the answer choices, the question is usually testing precision. It is unclear who *many of them, they,* and *some* are. Only (B) precisely identifies readers as the subject. Choice (B) is the correct answer.

4. **C** Notice that verb tense is changing in the answer choices. The word *could* precedes the underlined portion, so in order to be consistent with the sentence, the verb should be in its base form. Eliminate (A) and (D). Otherwise, *could* can be followed by *have*, not *of*. Eliminate (B). Choice (C) is the correct answer.

5. **B** The question asks for the best placement of the underlined portion, which is a reference to Tolstoy's *other novels* and writings. Therefore, its best placement is next to the mention of one of his novels: *War and Peace*. Of the answer choices, (B) does this the best. Choice (B) is the correct answer.

6. **A** Notice that verb tense changing in the answer choices. The subject of the sentence is *Shakespeare*, a playwright from the past. Therefore, to remain consistent with the sentence, use past tense. Eliminate (B), (C), and (D) because they use verbs in the present tense. Choice (A) is correct.

7. **A** The description of Tolstoy's time is changing in the answer choices. The sentence refers to Tolstoy's *vast study*. The only answer choice that is consistent with the idea of a *vast study* is (A), which is the correct answer.

8. **C** Again, notice that verb tense changing in the answer choices. The sentence here refers to Tolstoy, a writer from the past. Therefore, to remain consistent with the sentence, use past tense. Eliminate (A) and (D). Because the sentence is remarking on Tolstoy's ability to learn so much, the use of the word *could* is most consistent with the meaning of the sentence. Choice (C) is the correct answer.

9. **B** The question asks whether the phrase *since Tolstoy's death* should be deleted. The phrase is consistent with the content of the paragraph and precisely identifies the time period in question. The phrase should be kept. Eliminate (C) and (D). The phrase does more to introduce the time period as a topic of discussion than to describe Tolstoy himself, so eliminate (A). The correct answer is (B).

10. **D** Notice the wording changing in the answer choices. The *great scientists were also the great philosophers* is the only choice that is consistent with the second half of the sentence, which says *the great mathematicians were also the great theologians.* Choice (D) is the correct answer.

11. **C** Again, notice the wording changing in the answer choices. In the sentence, it is not clear what the underlined portion, the pronoun *another,* is referring back to. Choice (C) clarifies this confusion and is consistent with the idea in the previous sentence that scientists were also philosophers and mathematicians were also theologians. The correct answer is (C).

Summary

o   When faced with a Writing and Language question, always check what's changing in the answer choices and use POE.

o   The correct answers across a lot of different parts of speech can be summed up succinctly with three basic terms: Consistency, Precision, and Concision. You don't need to know a ton of grammar if you can remember these three basic rules:
   - Consistency: Correct answers are consistent with the rest of the sentence and the passage.
   - Precision: Correct answers are as precise as possible.
   - Concision: Barring other errors, correct answers are as concise as possible.

o   When you see verbs changing in the answer choices, make sure those verbs are consistent with their subjects as well as with other verbs in the sentence and surrounding sentences.

o   When the nouns are changing in the answer choices, make sure those nouns are consistent with the other nouns in the sentence and the paragraph.

o   Once you are sure that a word or phrase is consistent with the non-underlined portion of the sentence, make that word or phrase as precise as you can.

o   Concision is key when you want to communicate meaning. As long as the grammar and punctuation are good to go, the correct answer will almost always be the shortest.

Chapter 9
Questions

In the previous chapters, we've seen "questions" that don't have questions at all. In this chapter, we will deal with those questions that actually do contain questions and some of the strategies that can help to simplify them.

AND THEN SAT WAS LIKE, "HEY, CAN I ASK YOU A QUESTION?"

In the previous two chapters, we saw most of the concepts that will be tested on the Writing and Language Test. In this chapter, we're not going to learn a lot of new stuff in the way of grammar. Instead, we'll look at some of the questions you'll see in this section.

As we've seen, a lot of the questions on the Writing and Language Test aren't questions at all. They're just lists of answer choices, and we start the process of answering them by asking a question of our own: "What's changing in the answer choices?"

Because you need to move quickly through this test, you may fall into the habit of not checking for questions. Even when you do read the questions, you may read them hastily or vaguely. Well, we are here to tell you that neither of these approaches will work.

> The most important thing about Writing and Language questions is that you *notice* those questions and then *answer* those questions.

This may seem like just about the most obvious advice you've ever been given, but you'd be surprised how much less precise your brain is when you're working quickly.

Here's an example. Do these next 10 questions as quickly as you can.

1. $2 + 1 =$

2. $1 + 2 =$

3. $3 + 1 =$

4. $3 + 2 \neq$

5. $1 + 2 =$

6. $2 - 1 <$

7. $2 \pm 2 =$

8. $3 + 1 =$

9. $3 + 2 =$

10. $3 + 3 \neq$

Now check your answers.

1.   3

2.   3

3.   4

4.   Anything but 5

5.   3

6.   Any number greater than 1 (but not 1!)

7.   0 or 4

8.   4

9.   5

10. Anything but 6

Now, it's very possible that you got at least one of those questions wrong. What happened? It's not that the questions are hard. In fact, the questions are about as easy as can be. So why did you get some of them wrong? You were probably moving too quickly to notice that the signs changed a few times.

This is a lot like the Writing and Language Test. You might miss some of the easiest points on the whole test by not reading carefully enough.

As we will see throughout this chapter, most of the questions will test concepts with which we are already familiar.

WORDS AND PUNCTUATION IN REVERSE

Many of the concepts we saw in the chapters on punctuation and words show up explicitly with questions, but usually there's some kind of twist.

Here's an example.

Most people are familiar with the idea of a gender pay **1** gap. What most people don't realize is just how persistent that pay gap has been.

1

Which of the following alternatives to the underlined portion would NOT be acceptable?

A) gap; what

B) gap: what

C) gap, however,

D) gap, but

Here's How to Crack It

First and foremost, it's important to notice the question. This one is asking for the alternative that would NOT be acceptable, so we'll need to find an answer that doesn't work.

In the meantime, let's go through the steps. What's changing in the answer choices? STOP, HALF-STOP, and GO punctuation. Use the Vertical Line Test between the words *gap* and *what*. The idea before the line, *Most people are familiar with the idea of a gender pay gap*, is complete. The idea after the line, *what most people don't realize is just how persistent that pay gap has been*, is also complete. Therefore, we need either STOP or HALF-STOP punctuation.

Choices (A) and (B) definitely provide the punctuation we want. Choice (D) doesn't look like it does, but remember! *But* is one of the FANBOYS, and comma + FANBOYS is one of the forms of STOP punctuation! Therefore, the only choice that doesn't work in the context is (C), so it is the alternative that would NOT be acceptable.

Notice how important that word NOT was in this question. If you missed it, you might have thought the question had three correct answers!

Let's try another.

The **2** size of the gap may have narrowed, but we still have a long way to go.

2

Which of the following substitutions would be LEAST acceptable?

A) magnitude

B) proportion

C) vastness

D) immensity

Here's How to Crack It

Again, the question asks for the LEAST acceptable, so find and eliminate answers that work. In this case, we need something similar in meaning to the word *size* as it is used in this sentence. All four words mean something similar to *size* in different contexts, but we want something that refers to just how *large* the gap is, so (A), (C), and (D) would work.

Choice (B) does give a synonym for the word *size*, but it means something more like "dimensions" than "largeness," so it is the LEAST acceptable of the substitutions.

Let's look at another that deals with some of the topics we've seen earlier.

The problem has certainly gained a good deal of traction in public debates. The fact that it has gained such traction makes us wonder why isn't there more significant action to combat the gender pay gap. **3**

3

Which of the following gives the best way to combine these two sentences?

A) The problem has certainly gained a good deal of traction in public debates; the fact that it has gained such traction makes us wonder why isn't there more significant action to combat the gender pay gap.

B) The problem has certainly gained a good deal of traction in public debates, which raises the question of why more isn't being done to combat the gap.

C) The problem has certainly gained a good deal of traction in public debates: this fact of more public attention raises a serious question of why more isn't being done to close that gap.

D) The problem has certainly gained a good deal of traction in public debates. Why isn't more being done to combat the gap?

Here's How to Crack It

The question asks us to combine the two sentences. Your eyes were probably drawn immediately to (D), which is the most concise of the choices. There's just one problem: (D) doesn't answer the question! The question asks to *combine* the sentences, and while (D) shortens them, it doesn't combine them.

Therefore, (B) is the answer. It combines the sentences and shortens them a bit, unlike (A) and (C), which combine the sentences, but don't really do much beyond changing the punctuation.

Questions like question 3 are why…

> The most important thing about Writing and Language questions is that you *notice* those questions and then *answer* those questions.

PRECISION QUESTIONS

Not all questions will be just applications of punctuation and words. Some questions will ask you to do more specific things. Remember the three terms we kept repeating in the Words chapter: Consistency, Precision, and Concision. We'll start with the Precision-related questions. Even when Precision is not asked about directly, or when it is mixed with Consistency or Concision, remember this:

> Answer the question in the most precise way possible. Read literally!

Let's try one.

The question of unequal pay for women draws on many other broader social issues. [4]

[4]

The writer is considering deleting the phrase *of unequal pay for women* from the preceding sentence. Should this phrase be kept or deleted?

A) Kept, because removing it would remove a crucial piece of information from this part of the sentence.

B) Kept, because it reminds the reader of social injustice in the modern world.

C) Deleted, because it wrongly implies that there is a disparity between what women and men are paid.

D) Deleted, because it gives information that has no bearing on this particular text.

Here's How to Crack It

This question asks whether we should keep or delete the phrase *of unequal pay for women*. Without that phrase, the sentence reads, *The question draws on many other broader social issues*. Because nothing in this sentence or any of the previous ones specifies what this *question* might be, we should keep the phrase. We want to be as precise as possible!

And, as (A) says, we want to keep the phrase because it is crucial to clarifying precisely what *the question* is. Choice (B) is a little too grandiose a reason to keep the phrase, especially when the whole passage is about the particular injustice of the gender pay gap. Choice (A) is the correct answer.

Let's try another.

The gender disparities persist in areas other than pay. It is a kind of open secret, for instance, that women have had the right to vote in the United States for less than a century. **5** There is a long history of misogyny written into the very cultural and social fabric of the United States.

5

At this point, the writer is considering adding the following true statement:

> The year that women's suffrage became legal in the United States was also the year that the American Football League was formed under the leadership of Jim Thorpe.

Should the writer make this addition here?

A) Yes, because it gives a broader context to the achievement of women's suffrage.

B) Yes, because it helps to ease some of the political rhetoric in the rest of the passage.

C) No, because it does not contribute in a significant way to the discussion of the gender pay gap.

D) No, because the question of gender pay is irrelevant when all football players are men.

Here's How to Crack It

The proposed sentence does contain an interesting bit of information, but that piece of information has no clear place either in these few sentences or in the passage as a whole. Therefore, it should not be added, thus eliminating (A) and (B).

Then, because it does not play a significant role in the passage, the sentence should not be added for the reason stated in (C). While (D) may be true in a way, it does not reflect anything clearly relating to the role the sentence might play in the passage as a whole. Read literally, and answer as literally and precisely as you can.

CONSISTENCY QUESTIONS

Just as questions should be answered as *precisely* as possible, they should also be answered with information that is *consistent* with what's in the passage.

When answering consistency questions, keep this general rule in mind:

> Writing and Language passages should be judged on what they *do* say, not on what they *could* say. When dealing with Style, Tone, and Focus, make sure to work with the words and phrases the passage has already used.

Let's look at two questions that deal with the idea of consistency.

[1] One need look no further than to the idea of the "traditional" family. [2] The shift, however, has yet to produce a substantive increase in how women, who are now nearly as likely to work as men, are paid. [3] In this idea, the father of the family earns the family wage **6** and gives the children his last name. [4] With such an idea bolstering what many consider to be the goal inherent in the "American dream," it is no wonder that women in the workplace should have a somewhat degraded position. [5] Shifting social and economic roles, however, have begun to change how people think about gender roles within the family. **7**

6

Which of the following choices would best complete the distinction described in this sentence and the paragraph as a whole?

A) NO CHANGE

B) while the mother tends to the children and the home.

C) though his interest in masculine things like sports may vary.

D) but will only be able to achieve a wage commensurate with his skills and education.

7

The best placement for sentence 2 would be

A) where it is now.

B) before sentence 1.

C) after sentence 4.

D) after sentence 5.

Here's How to Crack It

Let's look at question 6 first. In this case, the question tells us exactly what to look for: something that would *complete the distinction* in the sentence, a distinction made between what is expected of a man and a woman in a "traditional" family. Choices (A), (C), and (D) may be true in some definitions of what that "traditional" family is, but none of those answers fulfills the basic demands of the question. Only (B) does so by describing what is expected of a *mother* in contrast to what is expected of a *father*, as described earlier in the sentence.

Now, as for question 7, we need to find some very literal way to make Sentence 2 consistent with the rest of the paragraph. Look for words and phrases that will link Sentence 2 to other sentences. Remember, it's not what the passage *could* say; it's what the passage *does* say. Sentence 2, we should note, starts with *the shift*, thus clearly referring to a shift that has been mentioned before it. As such, Sentence 2 belongs after Sentence 5, which discusses *shifting social and economic roles*.

As we have seen, these questions are not difficult, but they do require very specific things. Make sure you read the questions carefully and that you answer those questions as precisely and consistently as you can.

The same goes for charts and graphs on the Writing and Language Test. Don't let the strangeness of the charts throw you off! Just read the graphs with as much precision as you can and choose the most precise answers possible.

Let's have a look at one.

Even as women's roles in high-level positions, such as Congress, have increased almost five-fold since 1981, **8** the pay that women receive relative to men has increased by only approximately 33%.

8

Which of the following choices gives information consistent with the graph?

A) NO CHANGE

B) women's wages have increased by over 80%.

C) the wages of women in Congress have decreased.

D) the efforts of women in Congress to raise wages have failed.

Women in Congress and Women's Pay

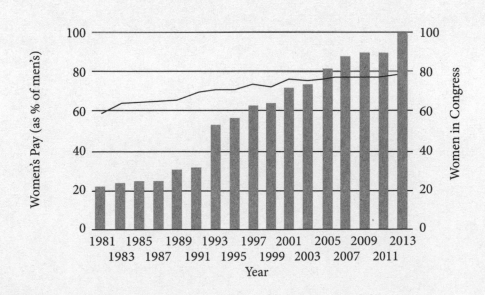

Here's How to Crack It

This question is asking for what agrees with the graph. From what we have seen, these questions are usually pretty straightforward. You don't have to do anything overly complex with the graphs, and that is certainly the case here.

It looks like "Women in Congress" goes up significantly where "Women's Pay" remains relatively consistent. The only choice that reflects that trend is (A). Choice (B) misreads the graph, and (C) and (D) can't be supported one way or the other. Choice (A) is therefore the correct answer.

In general, graphs on the SAT Reading and Writing and Language Tests are very straightforward, and the fundamental question they ask is, "Can you read a graph?" These are easy points as long as you read the graphs carefully and use POE.

CONCLUSION

As we have seen in this chapter, the SAT can ask a lot of different kinds of questions, but you're not going to have anything really crazy thrown at you. The biggest things to remember, aside from the punctuation rules, are CONSISTENCY and PRECISION. If you pick answers that are precise and consistent with other information in the passage, you should be good to go. Just make sure to answer the question!

Writing and Language Drill 4

Answers can be found on page 144.

Time: 7–8 minutes

[1]

 Genre in Hollywood movies is a constant but inconstant thing. Horror, Western, and Sci-Fi movies are made every year, but the number of movies produced in each genre fluctuates annually. For example, as the number of Westerns has stayed at or below about 25 per year since the 1960s, the number of Zombie and Vampire films **2** has risen, with Zombie films increasing nearly six-fold.

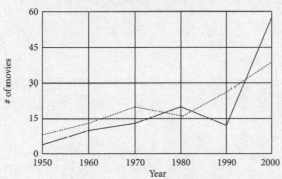

Zombie vs. Vampire Films Over Time

— Zombie Films (Maximum in a single year)

····· Vampire Films (Maximum in a single year)

1

Which of the following choices would best introduce the essay by pointing to the variability in interest in different types of movies?

A) NO CHANGE

B) While many movie genres are staples in Hollywood, the popularity of these genres has changed over time.

C) Everyone knows that the highest form of Hollywood film is the drama.

D) There's a lot that you may not know about how films are made in Hollywood.

2

Which of the following gives information consistent with the graph?

A) NO CHANGE

B) has risen, with Vampire films increasing nearly six-fold.

C) has declined, with Zombie film production decreasing by a sixth.

D) has declined, with Vampire film production decreasing by a sixth.

[2]

While the saying goes that there's "no accounting for the public's taste," **3** lots of people like lots of different things. Why should the number of Westerns have remained relatively low while the number of Zombie films has skyrocketed? Maybe we should ask the question another way: what do people today get from Zombie films that they don't from Westerns?

Which of the following choices would offer the most effective transition between the previous paragraph and the current one?

A) NO CHANGE

B) these trends nonetheless invite us to try.

C) a lot of people don't even care about Zombie movies.

D) science has not yet shown that zombies exist.

[3]

Westerns dominated the 1920s. Zombie films have dominated the 1990s and 2000s. Beginning with these facts alone, we can start to see why these films might have been popular in different eras. `4` The 1920s, for instance, was an American moment of crusade. `5` Only a tough sheriff, the kind one might get in an old-west town, could find the perfect balance between justice and `6` brutality. Thus, if the world could not be contained by law and order, at least here was an imaginary space that could be in the West.

`4`

The writer is considering deleting the phrase *in different eras* and ending the sentence with a period after the word *popular*. Should the phrase be kept or deleted?

A) Kept, because the meaning of the sentence changes without the phrase.

B) Kept, because it is interesting to think about history and film together.

C) Deleted, because the essay is more concerned with the genres' popularity across time periods.

D) Deleted, because the essay is already dull and could stand to have some words removed.

`5`

At this point, the writer wants to insert an idea that will support the idea given in the previous sentence ("The 1920s...crusade"). Which of the following true statements would offer that support?

A) These were crusades altogether distinct from those conducted by the Catholic Church starting in 1095.

B) The U.S. is still interested in crusade today, so it's hard to see why they don't make as many Westerns anymore.

C) Led by Woodrow Wilson's plan for a U.S.-led League of Nations, the world, reeling from World War I, wanted justice among the outlaws.

D) The stock market wouldn't crash for another nine years, at which point people would really freak out.

`6`

Which of the following alternatives to the underlined portion would NOT be acceptable?

A) brutality, and if

B) brutality: if

C) brutality; thus, if

D) brutality, thus, if

[4]

It may seem that genre conventions never change. Because they never change, it probably seems like a Western today follows the same set of rules as a Western from 100 years ago. **7** What the rise in Zombie films shows, however, is that the genres themselves change, and they provide different things to different eras. **8** This is not to say that one genre is better than the other—that it's better, for instance, to watch a tough cowboy fight off a gang of cattle rustlers—but it is to say that these genres hold a lot more than their mere entertainment value.

7

Which of the following gives the most effective way to combine the previous two sentences, reproduced below?

It may seem that genre conventions never change. Because they never change, it probably seems like a Western today follows the same set of rules as a Western from 100 years ago.

A) (keep the sentences as they are)

B) It may seem that genre conventions never change; because of it, it could be argued that a Western today follows the same set of rules as a Western from 100 years ago.

C) It may seem that genre conventions never change: a Western today follows the same set of rules as a Western from 100 years ago.

D) Because Westerns today follow the same set of rules as they did 100 years ago, it seems to most outside observers that genre conventions never change.

8

At this point, the author is considering adding the following true statement:

For what it's worth, my personal favorite is Jacques Tourneur's *I Married a Zombie*, which is based loosely on *Jane Eyre*.

Should the writer make this addition here?

A) Yes, because the essay as a whole is filled with these kinds of examples and personal preferences.

B) Yes, because the author's quirky choice shows that he has an off-beat perspective.

C) No, because the author's strange choice disqualifies him from discussing popular taste.

D) No, because the essay as a whole is not primarily focused on the author's personal preferences.

[5]

The 1990s and 2000s, dominated as they are by Zombie films, show that contemporary conflicts are not so far away. Although we now have the world at the click of a button, Zombie films show that we are not all that interested in that world. Instead, we are interested in and suspicious of the people around us. Whether coworkers or fellow students, the people around us, especially when **9** viewed as a mass, can seem almost "dead." And the reasons for this are fairly obvious: our private or online personalities have become so robust that the "real world" outside cannot help but seem dull or claustrophobic by comparison. **10**

9

Which of the following alternatives to the underlined portion would be LEAST acceptable?

A) taken

B) espied

C) seen

D) regarded

10

The writer is considering replacing the word *robust* in the preceding sentence with the word *healthy*. Should the writer make the change or keep the sentence as it is?

A) Make the change, because the word *robust* is not familiar to many readers.

B) Make the change, because the word *healthy* provides a more accurate representation of people's medical conditions.

C) Keep the sentence as it is, because the word *healthy* changes the meaning in a way inconsistent with the passage as a whole.

D) Keep the sentence as it is, because the word *robust* keeps the level of vocabulary within the passage at an appropriately high level.

11

The best placement for paragraph 5 would be

A) where it is now.

B) before paragraph 1.

C) after paragraph 2.

D) after paragraph 3.

WRITING AND LANGUAGE DRILL 4: ANSWERS AND EXPLANATIONS

1. **B** The question asks for the choice that points out the potential confusion in how to understand the role of genre. Choice (A) implies that a paradox might exist but does not point it out; eliminate (A). Choices (C) and (D) do not discuss genre and are therefore unrelated, so eliminate (C) and (D). Choice (B) is the correct answer.

2. **B** Here you need to find the answer choice that is consistent with the graph. The graph shows how the numbers of vampire and zombie films have increased since 1950. Choices (C) and (D) are not consistent with this information; eliminate them. Zombie films have increased dramatically, from about 10 in 1960 to about 55 in 2000, while vampire movies went from about 15 to about 40. Because vampire movies did not increase nearly six-fold, eliminate (A). Choice (B) is the correct answer.

3. **B** The question asks you to identify the correct transition between the paragraph about trends involving Western, zombie, and vampire movies and the current paragraph. Choice (A) does not address either paragraph, so eliminate (A). Choice (C) mentions zombie movies, but not in relation to the trends, so eliminate (C). Choice (D) mentions zombies but not in relation to movies; get rid of (D). Choice (B) mentions the trends and introduces a discussion, and is therefore the correct answer.

4. **A** The question asks about deleting the phrase *in different eras*. The topic of the paragraph is why different genres dominated in different time periods, so the phrase is necessary to keep this sentence consistent with the paragraph. Eliminate (C) and (D). The phrase is important to the meaning of the sentence. Choice (A) is correct.

5. **C** Here you're looking for the statement that supports the idea of American crusade. Choice (A) contains an unrelated reference to the Catholic Church; eliminate (A). Choice (B) relates the information to today, which is not the time period in question, so eliminate (B). Choice (D) contains unrelated information about the stock market crash that happened years later, so eliminate (D). Choice (C) mentions the postwar *crusade* mentioned in the previous sentence and is the correct answer.

6. **D** You're looking for an alternate form of punctuation that would not be acceptable. Since the original underlined portion contains a period, the ideas before and after the punctuation must be complete. Therefore, replacing a period with a comma-conjunction pair or with a semicolon would be acceptable. Eliminate (A) and (C). Choice (B) makes use of the colon, which can be used between two complete ideas. Choice (B) is acceptable, so eliminate (B). Choice (D) uses a comma without one of the FANBOYS in place of stop punctuation, so this is incorrect. Choice (D) is the correct answer.

7. **C** The question asks for the most effective way to combine the sentences. Because (A) repeats the phrase *never change,* eliminate (A), as it is not concise. Choice (B) includes the phrase *because of it,* but the use of the ambiguous pronoun *it* nullifies this choice as well. Choice (D) adds the phrase *to outside observers,* which is neither necessary nor concise. Thus, (C) is the most concise option and is the correct answer.

8. **D** This question asks whether a statement about the author's personal favorite zombie movie should be included in the paragraph. The essay is about the overall trends and changes regarding movie genres, not someone's personal preferences. Because it is not consistent with the topic of the passage, do not add the sentence. Eliminate (A) and (B). The reason for not adding the sentence is not related to the choice of movie but, rather, to the unrelated focus on personal preference. The correct answer is (D).

9. **B** Here you're looking for the option that is least acceptable when used in place of *viewed* in the phrase *viewed as a mass. Taken, seen,* and *regarded* would all have a meaning consistent with the intended meaning in the sentence. *Espied,* while related to the verbs *view* and *see,* has a different meaning. *Espy* means "to spot" or "to catch sight of" something, which is not consistent with the meaning of the other verbs here. Eliminate (A), (C), and (D). Choice (B) is the correct answer.

10. **C** The question asks if *robust* should be changed to *healthy* to describe online personalities. The sentence describes the excitement of online personalities as the reason people feel real life is dull. *Healthy* would not make the same point, and the meaning would not be consistent with the rest of the paragraph. Keep *robust*. Eliminate (A) and (B). The reason for keeping the original word has nothing to do with the level of difficulty of the vocabulary, just the consistent meaning of the passage. Eliminate (D). Choice (C) is correct.

11. **D** This questions asks about the placement of the paragraph, which discusses how contemporary conflicts of the 1990s and 2000s relate to the popularity of particular genres. This is similar to paragraph 3, which discusses how the American crusade related to the popularity of Westerns in the 1920s. Therefore, paragraph 5 should be placed after paragraph 3. Choice (D) is the correct answer.

Summary

o The most important thing about Writing and Language questions is that you *notice* those questions and then *answer* those questions. Don't miss out on some of the easiest points on the whole test by not reading carefully enough.

o As we saw in the Words chapter, answer questions in the most precise way possible.

o When answering consistency questions, keep this general rule in mind: Writing and Language passages should be judged on what they *do* say, not on what they *could* say. When dealing with Style, Tone, and Focus, make sure to work with the words and phrases the passage has already used.

o There will be charts or graphs on the Writing and Language Test, but don't let that throw you off. Just read the graphs with as much precision as you would a passage and choose the most precise answers possible.

Part IV
How to Crack the Math Test

A FEW WORDS ABOUT SAT MATH

As we've mentioned before, the SAT isn't your normal school test. The same is true of the Math sections of the SAT. There are two types of questions that you'll run into: multiple-choice and student-produced response questions. We've talked before about multiple-choice, so let's talk about these strange questions known as student-produced response questions. These questions are the only non-multiple-choice questions on the SAT, other than the essay; instead of selecting the correct answer from among several choices, you will have to find the answer on your own and mark it in a grid, which is why we call them Grid-Ins. The Grid-In questions on your test will be drawn from arithmetic, algebra, and geometry, just like the multiple-choice SAT Math questions. However, the format has special characteristics, so we will treat them a bit differently. You'll learn more about them later in this book.

What Does the SAT Math Test Measure?

ETS and the College Board say that the Math Test covers "all mathematical practices," with a strong focus on problem solving, using tools appropriately, and using structure to manipulate expressions. Fortunately for you, there is no way one test can cover all mathematical concepts. The SAT Math Test is actually a brief test of arithmetic, algebra, and a bit of geometry—when we say a "bit," we mean it. There are only 6 geometry questions at most on the test. We'll show you which geometry concepts are important. We will also give you the tools you need and the skills to use them appropriately.

Order of Difficulty

The questions in the two parts of the Math Test (No Calculator and Calculator) are arranged in a loose order of difficulty. The earlier questions are generally easier and the last few are harder, but the difficulty may jump around a little. Also, "hard" on the SAT means that more people get it wrong, often due to careless errors or lack of time. In addition, the questions within the Grid-In part of each section will also be arranged in a rough order of difficulty. Because difficulty levels can go up and down a bit, don't worry too much about how hard the test writers think a question is. Focus on the questions that are easiest for you, and do your best to get those right before moving on to the tougher ones, no matter where they appear.

You Don't Have to Finish

We've all been taught in school that when you take a test, you have to finish it. If you answered only two-thirds of the questions on a high school math test, you probably wouldn't get a very good grade. But as we've already seen, the SAT is not at all like the tests you take in school. Most students don't know about the difference, so they make the mistake of doing all of the problems on both Math sections of the SAT.

Because they have only a limited amount of time to answer all the questions, most students rush through the questions they think are easy to get to the harder ones as soon as possible. At first, it seems reasonable to save more time for the more challenging questions, but think about how the test is scored for a minute. All correct answers are worth the same amount, no matter how difficult they are or how long they take to answer. So when students rush through a Math Test, they're actually spending less time on the easier questions (which they have a good chance of getting right), just so they can spend more time on the harder questions (which they have very little chance of getting right). Does this make sense? Of course not.

Here is the secret: On the Math Test, you don't have to answer every question in each section. In fact, unless you are aiming for a top score, you should intentionally skip some harder questions in each section. Most students can raise their Math scores by concentrating on correctly answering all of the questions that they find easy and medium. In other words…

Slow Down!

Most students do considerably better on the Math Test when they slow down and spend less time worrying about the more complex questions (and more time working carefully on the more straightforward ones). Haste causes careless errors, and careless errors can ruin your score. In most cases, you can actually raise your score by answering fewer questions. That doesn't sound like a bad idea, does it? If you're shooting for an 800, you'll have to answer every question correctly. But if your target is 550, you should ignore the hardest questions in each section and use your limited time wisely.

Quick Note
Remember, this is not a math test in school! It is not scored on the same scale your math teacher uses. You don't need to get all the questions right to get an above-average score.

Calculators

Calculators are permitted (but not required) on Section 4 of the SAT. You should definitely take a calculator to the test. It will be extremely helpful to you on many questions, as long as you know how and when to use it and don't get carried away. In this book, questions that would likely appear in the Calculator section will have a calculator symbol next to them. If there is no symbol by a question, it is more likely to be found in the No Calculator section of the test. We'll tell you more about calculators as we go along, and teach you how to manage without it on Section 3.

The Princeton Review Approach

We're going to give you the tools you need to handle the easier questions on the Math section, along with several great techniques to help you crack some of the more difficult ones. But you must concentrate first on getting the easier questions correct. Don't worry about the questions you find difficult on the Math sections until you've learned to work carefully and accurately on the easier questions.

When it does come time to look at some of the harder questions, use Process of Elimination to help you avoid trap answers and to narrow your choices if you have to guess. Just as you did in the other sections of the test, you'll learn to use POE to improve your odds of finding the answer by getting rid of answer choices that can't possibly be correct.

Generally speaking, each chapter in the Math section of this book begins with the basics and then gradually moves into more advanced principles and techniques. If you find yourself getting lost toward the end of the chapter, don't worry. Concentrate your efforts on principles that are easier to understand but that you still need to master.

Chapter 10
SAT Math: The Big Picture

In this chapter, we'll see a few ways you can eliminate bad answer choices, avoid traps, improve the odds if you have to guess, and maximize your Math score. We'll also teach you how to best make use of your calculator, when it is permitted, and how to get along without it.

THE BIG PICTURE

In the Reading section of this book, you learned about various ways to eliminate wrong answers on hard questions. Well, that idea comes into play in the Math sections of the SAT, too. This chapter provides an overview of the strategies you should know to maximize your Math score, as well as some tips on how to use your calculator wisely (and how to work without it!).

Ballparking

One way to eliminate answers on the Math Test is by looking for ones that are the wrong size, or that are not "in the ballpark." Although you can use your calculator on the following question, you can eliminate without doing any calculations.

25

Joy plants three rows of corn in her garden. The row on the south edge of the garden receives more sunlight than the row on the north edge of the garden. Therefore, the corn on the north edge of the garden is 30% shorter than that on the south. If the corn on the south edge of the garden is 50 inches tall, how tall is the corn on the north edge of the garden, in inches?

A) 30

B) 33

C) 35

D) 65

Here's How to Crack It

The question states that the corn on the north edge is shorter than the corn on the south edge, which is 50 inches tall. You are asked to find the height of the corn on the north edge, so the correct answer must be less than 50. Eliminate (D), which is too large. Often, one or more of the bad answers on these questions is the result you would get if you applied the percentage to the wrong value. To find the right answer, take 30% of 50 by multiplying 0.3 by 50 to get 15, then subtract that from 50. The corn on the north edge would be 35 inches tall, which is (C).

Read the Full Question

You never know what ETS is going to decide to ask for, so make sure to always read the full question before solving. Underline what you are actually solving for and any key words you think you might forget about as you solve the question. Then, try to Ballpark before you solve.

7

If $16x - 2 = 30$, what is the value of $8x - 4$?

A) 12

B) 15

C) 16

D) 28

Here's How to Crack It

First, see if you can eliminate answers by Ballparking, which can also work on algebra questions. To go from $16x$ to $8x$, you would just divide by 2. Dividing 30 by 2 gives you 15, so 28 is way too big. Eliminate it. The correct answer is not likely to be 15, either, because that ignores the −2 and the −4 in the question.

To solve this one, add 2 to each side of the equation to get $16x = 32$. Divide both sides by 2, which gives you $8x = 16$. But don't stop there! The full question asks for $8x - 4$, so (C) is a trap answer. You have to take the last step and subtract 4 from both sides to find that $8x - 4 = 12$, which is (A).

One Piece at a Time

When dealing with complicated math problems, make sure to take it one little piece at a time. We call this strategy "bite-sized pieces." If you try to do more than one step at a time, especially if you do it in your head, you are likely to make mistakes or fall for trap answers. After each step, see if you can eliminate any answer choices.

Let's give it a try.

9

A paper airplane is thrown from the top of a hill and travels horizontally at 9 feet per second. If the plane descends 1 foot for every 3 feet travelled horizontally, how many feet has the plane descended after 5 seconds of travel?

A) 3

B) 10

C) 15

D) 20

Here's How to Crack It

There are a few things going on here. The plane is traveling horizontally, and it is also descending. Start by figuring out how far it travels horizontally. It moves in that direction at 9 feet per second for 5 seconds, so it moves horizontally $9 \times 5 = 45$ feet. It descends 1 foot for every 3 traveled horizontally. If it goes 45 feet horizontally, it will descend more than 3 feet, so eliminate (A). Now see how many "3 feet" are in 45 feet—for each one of them, the plane will descend 1 foot. $45 \div 3 = 15$, so the plane descends 15 feet, (C).

You may also have noticed that all the numbers in the question are odd. This makes it unlikely that the answer would be 10 or 20, which are even. If you see things like that, use them as opportunities to eliminate.

Here's another example.

6

$$(5jk^2 + 5j^2 - 2j^2k) - (jk^2 + 2j^2k + 5j^2)$$

Which of the following is equivalent to the expression above?

A) $4jk^2$

B) $4jk^2 - 4j^2k$

C) $5j^2k^4 - 10j^4k$

D) $8j^2k^3 + 7j^2k - 5j^2$

Here's How to Crack It

Start with one tiny piece of this ugly looking question. The first set of parentheses starts with a term containing jk^2. Check in the second set of parentheses for the same combination of variables and exponents. The first term there matches, so the first tiny step to take is $5jk^2 - jk^2 = 4jk^2$. There are no other terms with jk^2, so the correct answer must contain $4jk^2$. Eliminate (C) and (D). Now you have a fifty-fifty chance of getting it right, so you could guess and go. Or you could do one more step to determine if the answer is (A) or (B). The difference between the two answers is the $-4j^2k$ term, so focus on the terms in the expression that contain j^2k. In the first set of parentheses, you have $-2j^2k$, and then you subtract the $2j^2k$ term in the second set of parentheses. $-2j^2k - 2j^2k = -4j^2k$, so the correct answer is (B).

Write Stuff Down

As you solve questions in small pieces, write down the steps. Don't keep track of things in your head—your test booklet is there for your notes. If a figure is given, write the information from the question right on it.

Here's an example.

12

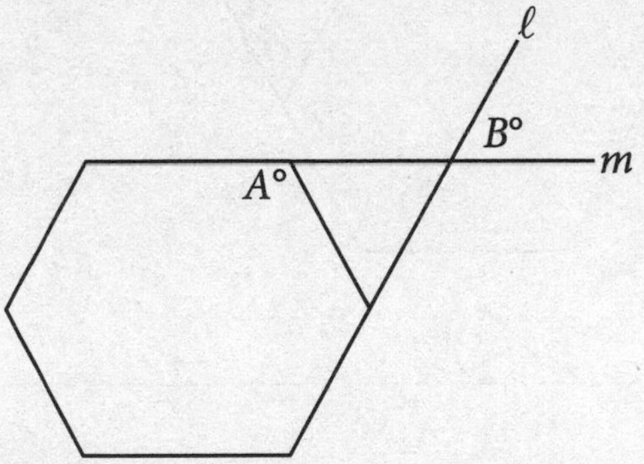

Lines l and m extend from two sides of the regular hexagon as shown above. If $A = 120$, what is the value of B, in degrees?

A) 30

B) 60

C) 90

D) 140

Here's How to Crack It

Sometimes, Ballparking can even help on geometry questions. Not all pictures are drawn to scale, so don't assume the figure is exact. You can, however, use what the question tells you about the figure to estimate angles, line lengths, areas, and points on graphs in the *xy*-plane.

If this picture is drawn to scale, the angle with measurement *B* looks to be acute, making (A) or (B) a good bet. The question says the hexagon is "regular," which means that all the interior angles have the same measure, and the drawing looks like this is the case. Start by marking the angle that is *A*° as 120° on the figure. This angle looks like 120°, so *B* can't possibly equal 90° or 140°. Eliminate (C) and (D). To find the exact value of *B*, you need to find the measure of the angle opposite it, which is one of the angles from the triangle. The angle of the upper left corner of the triangle is formed by drawing a straight line from the angle that is *A*°, or 120°. There are 180° in a straight line, so the upper left corner of the triangle measures 180 − 120 = 60°. Label that on the figure as well. The fact that the hexagon is a regular one means that all the interior angles are 120°, so label the one next to the bottom corner of the triangle. Since this corner of the triangle is formed in the same way as the upper left corner, the bottom corner also measures 60°. Label that. There are 180° in a triangle, so the upper right angle is also 60°. The angle measuring *B*° is opposite this, so *B* is 60° and (B) is correct.

By the time you're done, your figure should look like this:

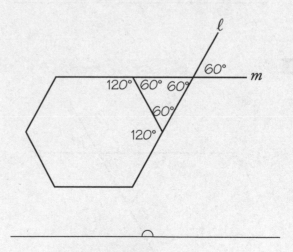

THE CALCULATOR

As you already know, the Math Test is divided into a shorter section in which calculator use is not permitted and a longer section in which it is permitted. This affects the way you do the questions in each of these sections. The No Calculator section will lean more toward "fluency" and "understanding" of mathematical concepts, but that doesn't mean you won't have to calculate anything. On the Calculator section, using the calculator is not always helpful. In this book, if you see a calculator symbol next to a question, it means you may use your calculator as needed to arrive at the answer. If there is no calculator symbol by a question, leave that calculator alone! The rest of this chapter will give you general information about how to use your calculator when you can and what to do when you can't. Other Math chapters will give you specific information about using your calculator in particular situations.

You'll need to take your own calculator when you take the SAT. Even if you now use a calculator regularly in your math class at school, you should still read this chapter and the other Math chapters carefully and practice the techniques we describe. Make sure that your calculator is either a scientific or a graphing calculator. It must perform the order of operations correctly. To test your calculator, try this problem. Type it in to your calculator exactly as written without hitting the ENTER or "=" key until the end: $3 + 4 \times 6 =$. The calculator should give you 27. If it gives you 42, it's not a good calculator to use.

Many students already own a graphing calculator. If you have one, great; if you don't, don't sweat it. Graphing calculators are not necessary on the SAT. However, if you have one, it may simplify certain graphing problems on the SAT.

If you do decide to use a graphing calculator, keep in mind that it *cannot* have a QWERTY-style keyboard (like the TI-95). Most of the graphing calculators have typing capabilities, but because they don't have typewriter-style keyboards, they are perfectly legal.

Also, you *cannot* use the calculator on your phone. In fact, on test day, you will have to turn your phone off and put it underneath your seat.

The only danger in using a calculator on the SAT is that you may be tempted to use it in situations in which it won't help you. The average student thinks using his or her calculator will solve many difficulties he or she has with math. It won't.

This type of thinking may even occasionally cause students to miss a problem they might have otherwise answered correctly on their own. Remember: Your calculator is only as smart as you are. But if you practice and use a little caution, you will find that your calculator will help you a great deal.

What a Calculator Is Good at Doing

Here is a complete list of what a calculator is good at on the SAT.

- arithmetic
- decimals
- fractions
- square roots
- percentages
- graphs (if it is a graphing calculator)

We'll discuss the calculator's role in most of these areas in the next few chapters.

Calculator Arithmetic

Calculators Don't Think for You
A calculator crunches numbers and often saves you a great deal of time and effort, but it is not a substitute for your problem-solving skills.

Adding, subtracting, multiplying, and dividing integers and decimals is easy on a calculator. But, you need to be careful when you key in the numbers. A calculator will only give you an incorrect answer to an arithmetic calculation if you press the wrong keys.

The main thing to remember about a calculator is that it can't help you find the answer to a question you don't understand. If you wouldn't know how to solve a particular problem using pencil and paper, you won't know how to solve it using a calculator either. Your calculator will help you, but it won't take the place of a solid understanding of basic SAT mathematics.

Use Your Paper First

Write Things Down
You paid for the test booklet, so make the most of it. Keep track of your progress through each problem by writing down each step.

Whether or not calculator use is permitted, the first step should be to set up the problem or equation on paper; this will keep you from getting lost or confused. This is especially important when solving the problem involves a number of separate steps. The basic idea is to use the extra space in your test booklet to make a plan, and then use your calculator to execute it.

Working on scratch paper first will also give you a record of what you have done if you change your mind, run into trouble, or lose your place. If you suddenly find that you need to try a different approach to a problem, you may not have to go all the way back to the beginning. This will also make it easier for you to check your work, if you have time to do so.

Don't use the memory function on your calculator (if it has one). Because you can use your test booklet as scratch paper, you don't need to juggle numbers within the calculator itself. Instead of storing the result of a calculation in the calculator, write it on your scratch paper, clear your calculator, and move to the next step of the problem. A calculator's memory is fleeting; scratch paper is forever.

Order of Operations

In the next chapter, we will discuss the proper order of operations when solving equations that require several operations to be performed. Be sure you understand this information, because it applies to calculators as much as it does to pencil-and-paper computations. You may remember PEMDAS from school. PEMDAS is the order of operations. You'll learn more about it and see how questions on the SAT require you to know the order of operations. You must always perform calculations in the proper order.

Fractions

Most scientific calculators have buttons that will automatically simplify fractions or convert fractions from decimals. (For instance, on the TI-81, TI-83, and TI-84, hitting "Math" and then selecting the first option, "Answer → Fraction," will give you the last answer calculated as a fraction in the lowest terms.) Find out if your calculator has this function! If it does, you can use it to simplify messy fractions on the Calculator section. This function is also very useful when you get an answer as a decimal, but the answer choices given are all fractions. For the No Calculator section, you will have to be able to do these things by hand, so practice these skills in the next chapter. (For Grid-In questions, it is not necessary to reduce a fraction to its simplest form if it fits in the grid, and the decimal equivalent will also be accepted as a correct answer.)

Batteries

Change the batteries on your calculator a week before the SAT so that you know your calculator won't run out of power halfway through the test. You can also bring extra batteries with you, just in case. Although it isn't very likely that the batteries will run out on your calculator on the day of the test, it could happen—so you want to be prepared.

FINAL WORDS ON THE CALCULATOR

Remember that the test writers are trying to test your ability to use your calculator wisely. They know you have one. They also know that they have created many questions in which the calculator is worthless (there are questions that are so wordy and deceptive that reading carefully is a much more important skill than properly using a calculator). So be sure to Read the Full Question—there may be some serious surprises in there. Finally, use your calculator wisely, and remember that on one section, you won't be able to use it at all. Practice your math skills, so you can solve questions with or without your calculator.

Summary

o   Look for ways to eliminate answer choices that are too big or too small. Ballparking can help you find the right answer without extensive paper-and-pencil calculations when calculator use is not allowed. Even when you can use your calculator, Ballparking can help you avoid trap answers and improve your chances of getting the question right if you have to guess.

o   When Ballparking answers on geometry questions, use a bit of caution. The figures are not always drawn to scale. Use the given information to determine if you can trust your figure before using it to eliminate answers.

o   After you've set up the problem on the page, you should definitely use the calculator when allowed to avoid careless mistakes from doing math in your head.

o   Take your own calculator when you take the test. You don't need a fancy one. Make sure your calculator doesn't beep or have a typewriter-style keyboard.

o   Even if you already use a calculator regularly, you should still practice with it before the test.

o   Be careful when you key in numbers on your calculator. Check each number on the display as you key it in. Clear your work after you finish each problem or after each separate step.

o   A calculator can't help you find the answer to a question you don't understand. (It's only as smart as you are!) Be sure to use your calculator as a tool, not a crutch.

o   Set up the problem or equation on paper first. By doing so, you will eliminate the possibility of getting lost or confused.

o   Don't use the memory function on your calculator (if it has one). Scratch paper works better.

o   Whether you are using your calculator or paper and pencil, you must always perform calculations in the proper order.

o   If your calculator runs on batteries, make sure it has fresh ones at test time! Change them a week before.

o   Make sure your math skills are solid so you can tackle questions in the No Calculator section with confidence.

Chapter 11
Fun with Fundamentals

Although we'll show you which mathematical concepts are most important to know for the SAT, this book relies on your knowledge of basic math concepts. If you're a little rusty, though, this chapter is for you. Read on for a quick review of the math fundamentals you'll need to know before you continue.

THE BUILDING BLOCKS

As you go through this book, you might discover that you're having trouble with stuff you thought you already knew—like fractions or square roots. If this happens, it's probably a good idea to review the fundamentals. That's where this chapter comes in. Our drills and examples will refresh your memory if you've gotten rusty. Always keep in mind that the math tested on the SAT is different from the math taught in school. If you want to raise your score, don't waste time studying math that the SAT never tests.

Let's talk first about what you should expect to see on the test.

THE MATH BREAKDOWN

The SAT includes two scored Math sections: Section 3 and Section 4. Section 3, which does not allow the use of a calculator, is 25 minutes long and includes 20 questions. Section 4, which allows the use of a calculator, is 55 minutes long and includes 38 questions.

According to ETS and the College Board, the Math questions on the SAT fall into the following cleverly named categories:

1. Heart of Algebra
2. Passport to Advanced Math
3. Problem Solving and Data Analysis
4. Additional Topics

The first three will give you some of your test subscores, but the names of all four categories don't really mean anything. This is what will really be tested:

1. Algebra I and II
2. Arithmetic/Probability/Data Analysis
3. Plane Geometry/Coordinate Geometry/Trigonometry

That's it! Of these categories, Algebra makes up the largest part of the test, accounting for more than half of the questions. Plane Geometry and Trigonometry make up the smallest part—there will only be a maximum of 6 questions from that category on the SAT.

The Math questions on your SAT will appear in two different formats:

1. Regular multiple-choice questions
2. Grid-Ins

The Grid-Ins will appear at the end of each Math section: 5 questions in Section 3, and 8 questions in Section 4. (See Chapter 17 for more on the Grid-In questions.)

No Need to Know
Here are a few things you won't need to know to answer SAT math questions: calculus, logarithms, matrices, and geometric proofs. Essentially, the SAT tests a whole lot of algebra and some arithmetic, statistics, and geometry.

THE INSTRUCTIONS

Both of the Math sections on the SAT will begin with the same set of instructions. We've reprinted these instructions, just as they appear on the SAT, in the Math sections of the practice tests in this book. These instructions include a few formulas and other information that you may need to know in order to answer some of the questions. You should learn these formulas ahead of time so you don't have to waste valuable time flipping back to them during the test.

Still, if you do suddenly blank out on one of the formulas while taking the test, you can always refresh your memory by glancing back at the instructions. Be sure to familiarize yourself with them thoroughly ahead of time, so you'll know which formulas are there.

STANDARD SYMBOLS

The following standard symbols are used frequently on the SAT:

SYMBOL	MEANING
$=$	is equal to
$\neq$	is not equal to
$<$	is less than
$>$	is greater than
$\leq$	is less than or equal to
$\geq$	is greater than or equal to

THERE ARE ONLY SIX OPERATIONS

There are only six arithmetic operations that you will ever need to perform on the SAT:

1. Addition ($3 + 3$)
2. Subtraction ($3 - 3$)
3. Multiplication (3×3 or $3 \cdot 3$)
4. Division ($3 \div 3$ or $3/3$)
5. Raising to a power (3^3)
6. Finding a square root ($\sqrt{3}$)

If you're like most students, you probably haven't paid much serious attention to these topics since junior high school. You'll need to learn about them again if you want to do well on the SAT. By the time you take the test, using them should be automatic. All the arithmetic concepts are fairly basic, but you'll have to know them cold. You'll also have to know when and how to use your calculator, which will be quite helpful.

What Do You Get?

You should know the following arithmetic terms:

- The result of addition is a *sum* or *total*.
- The result of subtraction is a *difference*.
- The result of multiplication is a *product*.
- The result of division is a *quotient*.
- In the expression 5^2, the 2 is called an *exponent*.

Do It Yourself
Some calculators automatically take order of operations into account, and some don't. Either way, you can very easily go wrong if you are in the habit of punching in long lines of arithmetic operations. The safe, smart way is to clear the calculator after every individual operation, performing PEMDAS yourself. When calculator use is not allowed, make sure to write out all the steps on your paper to avoid careless errors.

The Six Operations Must Be Performed in the Proper Order

Very often, solving an equation on the SAT will require you to perform several different operations, one after another. These operations must be performed in the proper order. In general, the problems are written in such a way that you won't have trouble deciding what comes first. In cases in which you are uncertain, you need to remember only the following sentence:

Please Excuse My Dear Aunt Sally;
she limps from *left* to *right*.

That's **PEMDAS**, for short. It stands for Parentheses, Exponents, Multiplication, Division, Addition, and Subtraction. First, do any calculations inside the parentheses; then take care of the exponents; then perform all multiplication and division, from *left* to *right*, followed by addition and subtraction, from *left* to *right*.

The following drill will help you learn the order in which to perform the six operations. First, set up the equations on paper. Then, use your calculator for the arithmetic. Make sure you perform the operations in the correct order.

DRILL 1

Solve each of the following problems by performing the indicated operations in the proper order. Answers can be found on page 192.

1. $107 + (109 - 107) = $ _____

2. $(7 \times 5) + 3 = $ _____

3. $6 - 3(6 - 3) = $ _____

4. $2 \times [7 - (6 \div 3)] = $ _____

5. $10 - (9 - 8 - 6) = $ _____

Parentheses Can Help You Solve Equations

Using parentheses to regroup information in SAT arithmetic problems can be very helpful. In order to do this, you need to understand a basic law that you have probably forgotten since the days when you last took arithmetic—*the distributive law*. You don't need to remember the name of the law, but you do need to know how to use it to help you solve problems.

The Distributive Law

If you're multiplying the sum of two numbers by a third number, you can multiply each number in your sum individually. This comes in handy when you have to multiply the sum of two variables.

If a problem gives you information in "factored form"—$a(b + c)$—then you should distribute the first variable before you do anything else. If you are given information that has already been distributed—$(ab + ac)$—then you should factor out the common term, putting the information back in factored form. Very often on the SAT, simply doing this will enable you to spot the answer.

Here are some examples:

Distributive: $6(53) + 6(47) = 6(53 + 47) = 6(100) = 600$

Multiplication first: $6(53) + 6(47) = 318 + 282 = 600$

You get the same answer each way, so why get involved with ugly arithmetic? If you use the distributive law for this problem, you don't even need to use your calculator.

The drill on the following page illustrates the distributive law.

Whichever Comes First
For addition and subtraction, solve from left to right. The same is true of multiplication and division. And remember: If you don't solve in order from left to right, you could end up with the wrong answer! Example:
$24 \div 4 \times 6 = 24 \div 24 = 1$ wrong
$24 \div 4 \times 6 = 6 \times 6 = 36$ right

DRILL 2

Rewrite each problem by either distributing or factoring (Hint: For questions 1, 2, 4, and 5, try factoring) and then solve. Questions 3, 4, and 5 have no numbers in them; therefore, they can't be solved with a calculator. Answers can be found on page 192.

1. $(6 \times 57) + (6 \times 13) =$ _____

2. $51(48) + 51(50) + 51(52) =$ _____

3. $a(b + c - d) =$ _____

4. $xy - xz =$ _____

5. $abc + xyc =$ _____

Fractions and Your Calculator

When calculator use is not allowed, be sure to write out all the steps on your paper to avoid careless errors. When calculator use is allowed, you can use your calculator to solve fraction problems. When you do, ALWAYS put each of your fractions in a set of parentheses. This will ensure that your calculator knows that they are fractions. Otherwise, the order of operations will get confused. On a scientific calculator, you can write the fraction in two different ways:

1. You will have a fraction key, which looks similar to "$a^b/_c$." If you wanted to write $\frac{5}{6}$, you'd type "5 $a^b/_c$ 6."

2. You can also use the division key, because a fraction bar is the same as "divided by." Be aware that your answer will be a decimal for this second way, so we recommend the first.

On a graphing calculator, you'll use the division bar to create fractions. Keep in mind that, whatever calculator you are using, you can always turn your fractions into decimals before you perform calculations with them. Just be aware that the answer won't always be exact.

FRACTIONS

A Fraction Is Just Another Way of Expressing Division

The expression $\frac{x}{y}$ is exactly the same thing as $x \div y$. The expression $\frac{1}{2}$ means nothing more than $1 \div 2$. In the fraction $\frac{x}{y}$, x is known as the numerator (hereafter referred to as "the top") and y is known as the denominator (hereafter referred to as "the bottom").

Adding and Subtracting Fractions with the Same Bottom

To add two or more fractions that all have the same bottom, simply add the tops and put the sum over the common bottom. Consider the following example:

$$\frac{1}{100} + \frac{4}{100} = \frac{1+4}{100} = \frac{5}{100}$$

Subtraction works exactly the same way:

$$\frac{4}{100} - \frac{1}{100} = \frac{4-1}{100} = \frac{3}{100}$$

Adding and Subtracting Fractions with Different Bottoms

In school you were taught to add and subtract fractions with different bottoms, or denominators, by finding a common bottom. To do this, you have to multiply each fraction by a number that makes all the bottoms the same. Most students find this process annoying.

Fortunately, we have an approach to adding and subtracting fractions with different bottoms that simplifies the entire process. Use the example below as a model. Just multiply in the direction of each arrow, and then either add or subtract across the top. Lastly, multiply across the bottom.

$$\frac{1}{3} + \frac{1}{2} =$$

$$2 \qquad\qquad 3$$

$$\frac{1}{3} \times \frac{1}{2} \quad 6$$

$$\frac{2+3}{6} = \frac{5}{6}$$

We call this procedure the *Bowtie* because the arrows make it look like a bowtie. Use the Bowtie to add or subtract any pair of fractions without thinking about the common bottom, just by following the steps above.

Calculating Fractions

Let's say you wanted to find $\frac{1}{3} + \frac{1}{2} =$ using your calculator. For a scientific calculator, you'd type in "(1 $a\frac{b}{c}$ 3) + (1 $a\frac{b}{c}$ 2) –." The answer will come up looking like something similar to 5⌐6, which means 5/6. On a graphing calculator, you'd type in (1/3) + (1/2) [ENTER]. This gives you the repeating decimal .833333. Now hit the [MATH] button and hit the [>FRAC] button and press [ENTER]. The calculator will now show "5/6." The shortcut to turn a decimal into a fraction on a TI-80 series graphic calculator is [MATH][ENTER][ENTER]. Remember those parentheses for all fraction calculations!

Multiplying All Fractions

Multiplying fractions is easy. Just multiply across the top; then multiply across the bottom.

Here's an example:

$$\frac{4}{5} \times \frac{5}{6} = \frac{20}{30}$$

When you multiply fractions, all you are really doing is performing one multiplication problem on top of another.

You should never multiply two fractions before looking to see if you can reduce either or both. If you reduce first, your final answer will be in the form that the test writers are looking for. Here's another way to express this rule: Simplify before you multiply.

$$\frac{63}{6} \times \frac{48}{7} = \frac{\overset{9}{\cancel{63}}}{6} \times \frac{48}{\underset{1}{\cancel{7}}} = \frac{\overset{9}{\cancel{63}}}{\underset{1}{\cancel{6}}} \times \frac{\overset{8}{\cancel{48}}}{\underset{1}{\cancel{7}}} =$$

$$\frac{9}{1} \times \frac{8}{1}$$

$$\frac{72}{1} = 72$$

Dividing All Fractions

To divide one fraction by another, flip over (or invert) the second fraction and multiply.

Here's an example:

$$\frac{2}{3} \div \frac{4}{3} =$$

$$\frac{2}{3} \times \frac{3}{4} = \frac{6}{12} = \frac{1}{2}$$

Just Flip It
Dividing by a fraction is the same thing as multiplying by the reciprocal of that fraction. So just flip over the fraction you are dividing by and multiply instead.

Be careful not to cancel or reduce until after you flip the second fraction. You can even do the same thing with fractions whose tops and/or bottoms are fractions. These problems look quite frightening but they're actually easy if you keep your cool.

Here's an example:

$$\frac{\frac{4}{4}}{3} =$$

$$\frac{4}{1} \div \frac{4}{3} =$$

$$\frac{4}{1} \times \frac{3}{4} =$$

$$\frac{\cancel{4}}{1} \times \frac{3}{\cancel{4}} =$$

$$\frac{3}{1} = 3$$

Reducing Fractions

When you add or multiply fractions, you will very often end up with a big fraction that is hard to work with. You can almost always reduce such a fraction into one that is easier to handle.

To reduce a fraction, divide both the top and the bottom by the largest number that is a factor of both. For example, to reduce $\frac{12}{60}$, divide both the top and the bottom by 12, which is the largest number that is a factor of both. Dividing 12 by 12 yields 1; dividing 60 by 12 yields 5. The reduced fraction is $\frac{1}{5}$.

If you can't immediately find the largest number that is a factor of both, find any number that is a factor of both and divide both the top and bottom by that number. Your calculations will take a little longer, but you'll end up in the same place. In the previous example, even if you don't see that 12 is a factor of both 12 and 60, you can no doubt see that 6 is a factor of both. Dividing top and bottom by 6 yields $\frac{2}{10}$. Now divide by 2. Doing so yields $\frac{1}{5}$. Once again, you have arrived at the answer.

Start Small
It is not easy to see that 26 and 286 have a common factor of 13, but it's pretty clear that they're both divisible by 2. So start from there.

Fast Reduction
When calculator use is allowed, reducing fractions can be pretty easy. To reduce fractions in your scientific calculator, just type in the fraction and hit the equals key. If you are using a graphing calculator, type in the fraction, find the [>FRAC] function, and hit ENTER.

Converting Mixed Numbers to Fractions

A mixed number is a number such as $2\frac{3}{4}$. It is the sum of an integer and a fraction. When you see mixed numbers on the SAT, you should usually convert them to ordinary fractions.

> Here's a quick and easy way to convert mixed numbers.
>
> - Multiply the integer by the bottom of the fraction.
> - Add this product to the top of the fraction.
> - Place this sum over the bottom of the fraction.

For practice, let's convert $2\frac{3}{4}$ to a fraction. Multiply 2 (the integer part of the mixed number) by 4 (the bottom of the fraction). That gives you 8. Add that to the 3 (the top of the fraction) to get 11. Place 11 over 4 to get $\frac{11}{4}$.

The mixed number $2\frac{3}{4}$ is exactly the same as the fraction $\frac{11}{4}$. We converted the mixed number to a fraction because fractions are easier to work with than mixed numbers.

DRILL 3

Try converting the following mixed numbers. Answers can be found on page 192.

1. $8\dfrac{1}{3}$

2. $2\dfrac{3}{7}$

3. $5\dfrac{4}{9}$

4. $2\dfrac{1}{2}$

5. $6\dfrac{2}{3}$

Just Don't Mix
For some reason, the test writers think it's okay to give you mixed numbers as answer choices. On Grid-Ins, however, if you use a mixed number, you won't get credit. You can see why. In your Grid-In box, $3\frac{1}{4}$ will be gridded in as 3 1 / 4, which looks like $\dfrac{31}{4}$.

Fractions Behave in Peculiar Ways

Fractions don't always behave the way you might want them to. For example, because 4 is obviously greater than 2, it's easy to forget that $\dfrac{1}{4}$ is less than $\dfrac{1}{2}$. It's particularly confusing when the numerator is something other than 1. For example, $\dfrac{2}{7}$ is less than $\dfrac{2}{5}$. Finally, you should keep in mind that when you multiply one fraction by another, you'll get a fraction that is smaller than either of the first two. Study the following example:

$$\frac{1}{2}\times\frac{1}{4}=\frac{1}{8}$$

$$\frac{1}{8}<\frac{1}{2}$$

$$\frac{1}{8}<\frac{1}{4}$$

A Final Word About Fractions and Calculators

Throughout this section, we've given you some hints about your calculator and fractions. Of course, you still need to understand how to work with fractions the old-fashioned way for the No Calculator section. On the section in which its use is allowed, your calculator can be a tremendous help if you know how to use it properly. Make sure that you practice with your calculator so that working with fractions on it becomes second nature before the test.

DRILL 4

Work these problems with the techniques you've read about in this chapter so far. Then check your answers by solving them with your calculator. If you have any problems, go back and review the information just outlined. Answers can be found on page 192.

1. Reduce $\dfrac{18}{6}$. _____

2. Convert $6\dfrac{1}{5}$ to a fraction. _____

3. $2\dfrac{1}{3} - 3\dfrac{3}{5} =$ _____

4. $\dfrac{5}{18} \times \dfrac{6}{25} =$ _____

5. $\dfrac{3}{4} \div \dfrac{7}{8} =$ _____

6. $\dfrac{\dfrac{2}{5}}{5} =$ _____

7. $\dfrac{\dfrac{1}{3}}{\dfrac{3}{4}} =$ _____

DECIMALS

A Decimal Is Just Another Way of Expressing a Fraction

Fractions can be expressed as decimals. To find a fraction's decimal equivalent, simply divide the top by the bottom. (You can do this easily with your calculator.)

$$\frac{3}{5} =$$

$$3 \div 5 = 0.6$$

Adding, Subtracting, Multiplying, and Dividing Decimals

Manipulating decimals is easy with a calculator. Simply punch in the numbers—being especially careful to get the decimal point in the right place every single time—and read the result from the display. A calculator makes these operations easy. In fact, working with decimals is one area on the SAT where your calculator will prevent you from making careless errors. You won't have to line up decimal points or remember what happens when you divide. The calculator will keep track of everything for you, as long as you punch in the correct numbers to begin with. Just be sure to practice carefully before test day.

What can you do when the math decimals get ugly on the No Calculator section? Never fear—you can still answer these questions. Just round the awkward numbers to ones that are easier to work with. As long as you aren't rounding things too far, like rounding 33 to 50, the answers are likely to be spread far enough apart that only one or maybe two will be close to your estimated answer.

DRILL 5

Calculate each of the answers to the following questions on paper with your pencil, rounding any awkward numbers to make the math easier to handle. Then check your answers with your calculator. Answers can be found on page 192.

1. $0.43 \times 0.87 = $ _____

2. $\dfrac{43 + 0.731}{0.03} = $ _____

3. $3.72 \div 0.02 = $ _____

4. $0.71 - 3.6 = $ _____

Place Value

Compare decimals
place by place, going
from left to right.

Comparing Decimals

Some SAT problems will ask you to determine whether one decimal is larger or smaller than another. Many students have trouble doing this. It isn't difficult, though, and you will do fine as long as you remember to line up the decimal points and fill in missing zeros.

Here's an example:

Problem: Which is larger, 0.0099 or 0.01?

Solution: Simply place one decimal over the other with the decimal points lined up, like this:

$$0.0099$$
$$0.01$$

To make the solution seem clearer, you can add two zeros to the right of 0.01. (You can always add zeros to the right of a decimal without changing its value.) Now you have this:

$$0.0099$$
$$0.0100$$

Which decimal is larger? Clearly, 0.0100 is, just as 100 is larger than 99. Remember that $0.0099 = \dfrac{99}{10,000}$, while $0.0100 = \dfrac{100}{10,000}$.

Analysis

Watch out for problems like this with decimals in the answers. Any time you encounter a problem involving the comparison of decimals, be sure to stop and ask yourself whether you are about to make a careless mistake.

EXPONENTS AND SQUARE ROOTS

Exponents Are a Kind of Shorthand

Many numbers are the product of the same factor multiplied over and over again. For example, $32 = 2 \times 2 \times 2 \times 2 \times 2$. Another way to write this would be $32 = 2^5$, or "thirty-two equals two to the fifth power." The little number, or *exponent*, denotes the number of times that 2 is to be used as a factor. In the same way, $10^3 = 10 \times 10 \times 10$, or 1,000, or "ten to the third power," or "ten cubed." In this example, the 10 is called the *base* and the 3 is called the *exponent*. (You won't need to know these terms on the SAT, but you will need to know them to follow our explanations.)

> **Exponents and Your Calculator**
>
> Raising a number to a power is shown in two different ways on your calculator, depending on the type of calculator you have. A scientific calculator will use the y^x button. You'll have to type in your base number first, then hit the y^x key, and then type the exponent. So 4^3 will be typed in as "4 y^x 3 =" and you'll get 64. If you have a calculator from the TI-80 series, your button will be a ^ sign. You'll enter the same problem as "4^3 [ENTER]." Think of these two keys as the "to the" button, because you say "4 to the 3rd power."

Multiplying Numbers with Exponents

When you multiply two numbers with the same base, you simply add the exponents. For example, $2^3 \times 2^5 = 2^{3+5} = 2^8$.

Dividing Numbers with Exponents

When you divide two numbers with the same base, you simply subtract the exponents. For example, $\dfrac{2^5}{2^3} = 2^{5-3} = 2^2$.

Raising a Power to a Power

When you raise a power to a power, you multiply the exponents. For example, $(2^3)^4 = 2^{3 \times 4} = 2^{12}$.

Warning
The rules for multiplying and dividing exponents do not apply to addition or subtraction:
$2^2 + 2^3 = 12$
$(2 \times 2) + (2 \times 2 \times 2) = 12$
It does not equal 2^5 or 32.

Warning
Parentheses are very important with exponents, because you must remember to distribute powers to everything within them. For example, $(3x)^2 = 9x^2$, not $3x^2$.
Similarly, $\left(\dfrac{3}{2}\right)^2 = \dfrac{3^2}{2^2}$, not $\dfrac{9}{2}$. But the distribution rule applies only when you multiply or divide. $(x + y)^2 = x^2 + 2xy + y^2$, not $x^2 + y^2$.

MADSPM

To remember the exponent rules, all you need to do is remember the acronym MADSPM. Here's what it stands for:

- Multiply → Add
- Divide → Subtract
- Power → Multiply

Whenever you see an exponent problem, you should think MADSPM. The three MADSPM rules are the only rules that apply to exponents.

Here's a typical SAT exponent problem:

14

For the equations $\dfrac{a^x}{a^y} = a^{10}$ and $(a^y)^3 = a^x$, if $a > 1$,

what is the value of x?

A) 5

B) 10

C) 15

D) 20

Here's How to Crack It

This problem looks pretty intimidating with all those variables. In fact, you might be about to cry "POOD" and go on to the next problem. That might not be a bad idea but before you skip the question, pull out those MADSPM rules.

For the first equation, you can use the Divide-Subtract rule: $\dfrac{a^x}{a^y} = a^{x-y} = a^{10}$. In other words, the first equation tells you that $x - y = 10$.

For the second equation, you can use the Power-Multiply rule: $\left(a^y\right)^3 = a^{3y} = a^x$. So, that means that $3y = x$.

Now, it's time to substitute: $x - y = 3y - y = 10$. So, $2y = 10$ and $y = 5$. Be careful, though! Don't choose (A). That's the value of y, but the question wants to know the value of x. Since $x = 3y$, $x = 3(5) = 15$, which is (C).

If calculator use was allowed on this one, you could also do this question by plugging in the answer choices, or PITA, which will be discussed in more detail later in this book. Of course, you still need to know the MADSPM rules to do the question that way.

The Peculiar Behavior of Exponents

Raising a number to a power can have quite peculiar and unexpected results, depending on what sort of number you start out with. Here are some examples.

- If you square or cube a number greater than 1, it becomes larger.
  For example, $2^3 = 8$.
- If you square or cube a positive fraction smaller than one, it becomes smaller.
  For example, $\left(\dfrac{1}{2}\right)^3 = \dfrac{1}{8}$.

- A negative number raised to an even power becomes positive.
  For example, $(-2)^2 = 4$.
- A negative number raised to an odd power remains negative.
  For example, $(-2)^3 = -8$.

See the Trap
The test writers may hope you won't know these strange facts about exponents and throw them in as trap answers. Knowing the peculiar behavior of exponents will help you avoid these tricky pitfalls in a question.

You should also have a feel for relative sizes of exponential numbers without calculating them. For example, 2^{10} is much larger than 10^2. ($2^{10} = 1,024$; $10^2 = 100$.) To take another example, 2^5 is twice as large as 2^4, even though 5 seems only a bit larger than 4.

Square Roots

The radical sign ($\sqrt{}$) indicates the square root of a number. For example, $\sqrt{25} = 5$. Note that square roots cannot be negative. If the test writers want you to think about a negative solution, they'll say $x^2 = 25$ because then $x = 5$ or $x = -5$.

The Only Rules You Need to Know

Here are the only rules regarding square roots that you need to know for the SAT:

1. $\sqrt{x}\sqrt{y} = \sqrt{xy}$. For example, $\sqrt{3}\sqrt{12} = \sqrt{36} = 6$.

2. $\sqrt{\dfrac{x}{y}} = \dfrac{\sqrt{x}}{\sqrt{y}}$. For example, $\sqrt{\dfrac{5}{4}} = \dfrac{\sqrt{5}}{\sqrt{4}} = \dfrac{\sqrt{5}}{2}$.

3. $\sqrt{x}$ = positive root only. For example, $\sqrt{16} = 4$.

Note that rule 1 works in reverse: $\sqrt{50} = \sqrt{25} \times \sqrt{2} = 5\sqrt{2}$. This is really a kind of factoring. You are using rule 1 to factor a large, clumsy radical into numbers that are easier to work with. Rule 2 works in reverse as well. $\sqrt{75}$ divided by $\sqrt{3}$ looks ugly, but $\sqrt{\dfrac{75}{3}} = \sqrt{25} = 5$. And remember that radicals are just fractional exponents, so the same rules of distribution apply.

Roots and Your Calculator

Another important key is the root key. On a scientific calculator it is often the same button as y^x, but you'll have to hit shift first. The symbol is $\sqrt[x]{y}$. So "the 4th root of 81" would be "81 $\sqrt[x]{y}$ 4 = ." Sometimes the calculator will have y^x or $\sqrt[x]{y}$ as x^y or $\sqrt[y]{x}$. They mean the same thing. Just know which number you're supposed to type in first.

The root key in the TI-80 graphing calculator series varies, but the most common symbol is the square root sign, which you can get to by pressing "[SHIFT] x^2." In case you want to find the 3rd, 4th, or other root of a number, there is a button in the [MATH] directory for $\sqrt[3]{}$ or $\sqrt[x]{}$. In the case of the $\sqrt[x]{}$, you have to type in the root you want, then hit [MATH] and $\sqrt[x]{}$, and finally hit your base number. For example, if you wanted to find the 4th root of 81, you'd type "4 [MATH]," then select $\sqrt[x]{}$, then type 81 and press [ENTER]. If you look at it on the screen, it will appear as "4 $\sqrt[x]{}$ 81," which is similar to how you'd write it. You can also use the ^ symbol if you remember that a root is the same as the bottom part of a fractional exponent. So the fourth root of 81 would be written as "81 ^ (1/4)" on your calculator.

Careless Errors

Don't make careless mistakes. Remember that the square root of a number between 0 and 1 is *larger* than the original number. For example, $\sqrt{\dfrac{1}{4}} = \dfrac{1}{2}$, and $\dfrac{1}{2} > \dfrac{1}{4}$.

Negative and Fractional Exponents

So far we've dealt with only positive integers for exponents, but they can be negative integers as well as fractions. The same concepts and rules apply, but the numbers just look a little weirder. Keep these concepts in mind:

- Negative exponents are a fancy way of writing reciprocals:

$$x^{-n} = \frac{1}{x^n}$$

- Fractional exponents are a fancy way of taking roots and powers:

$$x^{\frac{y}{z}} = \sqrt[z]{x^y}$$

Here's an example:

———————○———————

14

If $x > 0$, which of the following is equivalent to $\sqrt{x^3}$?

I. $\quad x + x^{\frac{1}{2}}$

II. $\quad \left(x^{\frac{1}{2}} \right)^3$

III. $\quad \left(x^2 \right) \left(x^{-\frac{1}{2}} \right)$

A) None
B) I and II only
C) II and III only
D) I, II, and III

Here's How to Crack It

This problem really tests your knowledge of exponents. First, convert $\sqrt{x^3}$ into an exponent, since all of the Roman numerals contain expressions with exponents. (Plus, exponents are easier to work with because they have those nice MADSPM rules.) So, using the definition of a fractional exponent, $\sqrt{x^3} = x^{\frac{3}{2}}$. You want the items in the Roman numerals to equal $x^{\frac{3}{2}}$.

Now, it's time to start working with the Roman numerals. In (I), the test writers are trying to be tricky. (There's a surprise.) There's no exponent rule for adding exponent expressions with like bases. So, $x + x^{\frac{1}{2}}$ does *not* equal $x^{\frac{3}{2}}$. (If you want to be sure, you could try a number for x: If $x = 4$, then $\sqrt{4^3} = 8$, but $4 + 4^{\frac{1}{2}} = 4 + 2 = 6$.) So, cross off any answer that includes (I): (B) and (D) are gone.

Now, since you are down to either (A) or (C), all you really need to do is try either (II) or (III). If either one works, the answer is (C). So, try (II). Use the power-multiply rule: $\left(x^{\frac{1}{2}} \right)^3 = x^{\left(\frac{1}{2} \right)(3)} = x^{\frac{3}{2}}$. So, since (II) works, (C) is the correct answer.

Notice that you didn't even need to check (III). Using good POE on a Roman numeral question often means that you don't need to check all the Roman numerals.

HOW TO READ CHARTS AND GRAPHS

Another basic math skill you will need for the SAT is the ability to interpret data from charts, graphs, tables, and more. This section will cover the basics of reading these figures. We will discuss how to answer questions related to charts and other figures in detail in Chapter 14.

What's Up with All These Figures?

The SAT now includes charts, graphs, and tables throughout the test (not just in the Math sections) to present data for students to analyze. ETS and the College Board believe this will better reflect what students learn in school and need to understand in the real world. The situations will typically include real-life applications, such as finance and business situations, social science issues, and scientific matter.

Since you'll be seeing graphics throughout the test, let's look at the types you may encounter and the skills you'll need to be familiar with when you work with charts and graphs.

Types of Graphics

The Scatterplot

A scatterplot is a graph with distinct data points, each representing one piece of information. On the scatterplot below, each dot represents the number of televisions sold at a certain price point.

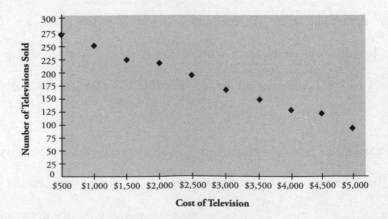

Here's How to Read It

To find the cost of a television when 225 televisions are sold, start at 225 on the vertical axis and draw a horizontal line to the right until you hit a data point. Use the edge of your answer sheet as a straight-edge if you have trouble drawing your own straight lines. Once you hit a point, draw a straight line down from it to the horizontal axis and read the number the line hits, which should be $1,500. To determine the number of televisions sold when they cost a certain amount, reverse the steps—start at the bottom, draw up until you hit a point, then move left until you intersect the vertical axis.

Try the question now.

9

A certain store sells televisions ranging in price from $500 to $5,000 in increments of $500. The graph above shows the total number of televisions sold at each price during the last 12 months. Approximately how much more revenue did the store collect from the televisions it sold priced at $3,500 than it did from the televisions it sold priced at $1,000 ?

A) $175,000

B) $250,000

C) $275,000

D) $350,000

Here's How to Crack It

The revenue is the *cost of television* × *number of televisions sold*. We need the information from the graph only for the television that costs $3,500 and for the television that costs $1,000 in order to determine how much more revenue the $3,500 television produced. There were 150 of the $3,500 televisions sold, for a revenue of $525,000. There were 250 of the $1,000 televisions sold, for a revenue of $250,000. The difference between the two is $525,000 – $250,000 = $275,000, as seen in (C).

A question may ask you to draw a "line of best fit" on a scatterplot diagram. This is the line that best represents the data. You can use the edge of your answer sheet as a ruler to help you draw a line that goes through most of the data.

The Line Graph

A line graph is similar to a scatterplot in that it shows different data points that relate the two variables. The difference with a line graph, though, is that the points have been connected to create a continuous line.

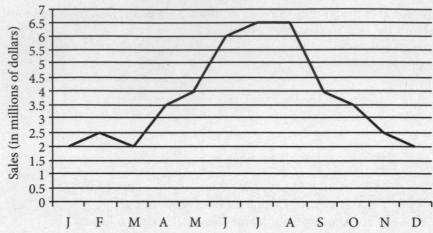

Monthly Sales of Always Sunny Sunscreen

Here's How to Read It

Reading a line graph is very similar to reading a scatterplot. Start at the axis that represents the data given, and draw a straight line up or to the right until you intersect the graph line. Then move left or down until you hit the other axis. For example, in February, indicated by an F on the horizontal axis, Always Sunny sunscreen had 2.5 million in sales. Make sure to notice the units on each axis. If February sales were only $2.50, rather than $2.5 million, then this company wouldn't be doing very well!

Let's look at a question about this line graph.

———————————○———————————

2

The forecasted monthly sales of Always Sunny Sunscreen are presented in the figure above. For which period are the forecasted monthly sales figures strictly decreasing then strictly increasing?

A) January to March

B) February to April

C) June to August

D) September to November

Here's How to Crack It

Look up the values for each period in question and use Process of Elimination to get rid of those that don't fit. For (A), January sales are forecasted to be $2 million, February $2.5 million, and March $2 million. This is an increase then a decrease, not the other way around, so eliminate (A). For (B), you already know sales decreased from February to March, so check for a following increase in April. The figure for April is $3.5 million, which is an increase over the March figure, so (B) is correct.

The Bar Graph (or Histogram)

Instead of showing a variety of different data points, a bar graph will show how many items belong to a particular category. If the variable at the bottom is given in ranges, instead of distinct items, the graph is called a histogram, but you read it the same way.

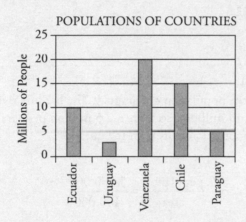

Here's How to Read It

The height of each bar corresponds to a value on the vertical axis. In this case, the bar above Chile hits the line that intersects with 15 on the vertical axis, so there are 15 million people in Chile. Again, watch the units to make sure you know what the numbers on the axes represent. On this graph, horizontal lines are drawn at 5 unit intervals, making the graph easier to read. If these lines do not appear on a bar graph, use your answer sheet to determine the height of a given bar.

A bar chart question might look like this:

14

The populations of five countries are shown in the graph above. If population density is defined as $\dfrac{\text{population}}{\text{area}}$, and the area of Paraguay is 400,000 square kilometers, what is the population density of Paraguay, in people per square kilometer?

A) 0.08

B) 0.8

C) 1.25

D) 12.5

Here's How to Crack It

Start by determining the population of Paraguay. The bar hits right at the horizontal line for 5, which is in millions, so there are 5 million people in Paraguay. Now use the definition of population density in the question.

$$\frac{\text{population}}{\text{area}} = \frac{5,000,000}{400,000}$$

Be very careful with the number of zeroes you put in the fraction—the answer choices are pairs that vary by a factor of 10, meaning the test writers expect you to miss a zero. The answer must be greater than 1, since your numerator is bigger than your denominator, so eliminate (A) and (B). Choice (C) also seems too small, but check the math on your calculator (carefully). You should get 12.5 people per square kilometer, so (D) is correct.

The Two-Way Table

A two-way table is another way to represent data without actually graphing it. Instead of having the variables represented on the vertical and horizontal axes, the data will be arranged in rows and columns. The top row will give the headings for each column, and the left-most column will give the headings for each row. The numbers in each box indicate the data for the category represented by the row and the column the box is in.

Computer Production		
	Morning Shift	Afternoon Shift
Monday	200	375
Tuesday	245	330
Wednesday	255	340
Thursday	250	315
Friday	225	360

Here's How to Read It

If you want to find the number of computers produced on Tuesday morning, you can start in the Morning Shift column and look down until you find the number in the row that says "Tuesday," or you can start in the row for Tuesday and look to the right until you find the Morning Shift column. Either way, the result is 245. Some tables will give you totals in the bottom row and/or the right-most column, but sometimes you will need to find the totals yourself by adding up all the numbers in each row or in each column. More complicated tables will have more categories listed in rows and/or columns, or the tables may even contain extraneous information.

Give this one a try.

3

Computer production at a factory occurs during two shifts, as shown in the chart above. If computers are produced only during the morning and afternoon shifts, on which of the following pairs of days is the greatest total number of computers produced?

A) Monday and Thursday

B) Tuesday and Thursday

C) Wednesday and Friday

D) Tuesday and Friday

Here's How to Crack It

This is a perfect calculator question. Just add the morning shift and the afternoon shift for each day and see which total is the greatest. Write each total down next to the day on the chart, so you don't have to keep track of it all in your head. Monday is 200 + 375 = 575, Tuesday is 245 + 330 = 575, Wednesday is 255 + 340 = 595, Thursday is 250 + 315 = 565, and Friday is 225 + 360 = 585. According to these calculations, Wednesday and Friday have the two greatest totals, so the greatest number of computers is produced on those two days together, making (C) the right answer.

Figure Facts

Every time you encounter a figure or graphic on the SAT, you should make sure you understand how to read it by checking the following things:

- What are the variables for each axis or the headings for the table?
- What units are used for each variable?
- Are there any key pieces of information (numbers, for example) in the legend of the chart that you should note?
- What type of relationship is shown by the data in the chart? For instance, if the chart includes curves that show an upward slope, then the graph shows a *positive association*, while curves that show a downward slope show a *negative association*.
- You can use the edge of your answer sheet as a ruler to help you make sure you are locating the correct data in the graph or to draw a line of best fit if necessary.

Fundamentals Drill 1: No Calculator Section

Work these Fundamentals questions without your calculator using the skills you've learned so far. Answers and explanations can be found on page 193.

1

Which of the following represents the statement "the sum of the squares of x and y is equal to the square root of the difference of x and y"?

A) $x^2 + y^2 = \sqrt{x - y}$

B) $x^2 - y^2 = \sqrt{x + y}$

C) $(x + y)^2 = \sqrt{x} - \sqrt{y}$

D) $\sqrt{x + y} = (x - y)^2$

4

If $a = -2$, then $a + a^2 - a^3 + a^4 - a^5 =$

A) -22

B) -18

C) 32

D) 58

6

If $9^{-2} = \left(\dfrac{1}{3}\right)^x$, what is the value of x?

A) 1

B) 2

C) 4

D) 6

7

$$\frac{1}{8} + \frac{1}{10} = \frac{a}{b}$$

In the equation above, if a and b are positive integers and $\dfrac{a}{b}$ is in its simplest reduced form, what is the value of a?

A) 2

B) 9

C) 18

D) 40

Fundamentals Drill 2: Calculator-Permitted Section

These Fundamentals questions are likely to appear in the section in which calculator use is allowed. Make sure to use it when you need to in order to avoid careless calculation errors. Don't forget, though, that using it may slow you down when doing the math on paper would be faster. Answers and explanations can be found on page 193.

1

If 7 times a number is 84, what is 4 times the number?

A) 16

B) 28

C) 48

D) 56

4

If $3x = 12$, what is the value of $\dfrac{24}{x}$?

A) $\dfrac{1}{6}$

B) $\dfrac{2}{3}$

C) 4

D) 6

6

Which of the following graphs shows a strong positive association between x and y?

A)

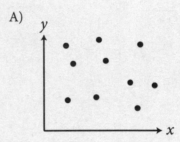

B)

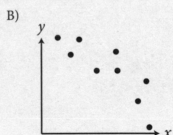

C)

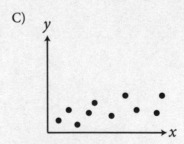

D)

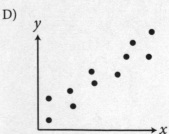

If $\sqrt{x} + 22 = 38$, what is the value of x ?

A) 4

B) 16

C) 32

D) 256

If each number in the following sum were increased by t, the new sum would be 4.22. What is the value of t ?

$$
\begin{array}{r}
0.65 \\
0.85 \\
0.38 \\
+\,0.86 \\
\hline
2.74
\end{array}
$$

A) 0.24

B) 0.29

C) 0.33

D) 0.37

If $4^x \cdot n^2 = 4^{x+1} \cdot n$ and x and n are both positive integers, what is the value of n ?

A) 2

B) 4

C) 6

D) 8

CHAPTER DRILL ANSWERS AND EXPLANATIONS

Drill 1

1. 109

2. 38

3. −3

4. 10

5. 15

Drill 2

1. $6(57 + 13) = 6 \times 70 = 420$

2. $51(48 + 50 + 52) = 51(150)$
   $= 7{,}650$

3. $ab + ac - ad$

4. $x(y - z)$

5. $c(ab + xy)$

Drill 3

1. $\dfrac{25}{3}$

2. $\dfrac{17}{7}$

3. $\dfrac{49}{9}$

4. $\dfrac{5}{2}$

5. $\dfrac{20}{3}$

Drill 4

1. 3

2. $\dfrac{31}{5}$

3. $-1\dfrac{4}{15}$ or $-\dfrac{19}{15}$

4. $\dfrac{1}{15}$

5. $\dfrac{6}{7}$

6. $\dfrac{2}{25}$

7. $\dfrac{4}{9}$

Drill 5

	Estimated Answer	Calculator Answer
1.	$0.4 \times 0.9 = 0.36$	0.3741
2.	$44 \div 0.03 = 1{,}466$	1,457.7
3.	$3.7 \div 0.02 = 185$	186
4.	$0.7 - 3.6 = -2.9$	−2.89

Fundamentals Drill 1: No Calculator Section

1. **A** Take it one phrase at a time. The "sum" means you will add two things. The "squares of x and y" means to square x and square y, or x^2 and y^2. Add these to get $x^2 + y^2$. Cross out any choice that does not have $x^2 + y^2$ as the first part of the equation. You're left with (A), which is the correct answer.

4. **D** Plug in the number given for a in the expression to find the value: $-2 + (-2)^2 - (-2)^3 + (-2)^4 - (-2)^5$. Remember PEMDAS, the order of operations: The first thing to do here is deal with the **E**xponents, then we can take care of the **A**ddition and **S**ubtraction: $-2 + 4 - (-8) + 16 - (-32)$, which simplifies to $-2 + 4 + 8 + 16 + 32 = 58$, (D).

6. **C** Negative exponents mean to take the reciprocal and apply the positive exponent. So $9^{-2} = \left(\dfrac{1}{9}\right)^2 = \dfrac{1}{81}$. Now find what power of $\dfrac{1}{3}$ equals $\dfrac{1}{81}$. Because $3^4 = 81$, $\left(\dfrac{1}{3}\right)^4 = \dfrac{1}{81}$, and x must be 4. The correct answer is (C).

7. **B** The lowest number that both 8 and 10 are factors of is 40. Convert the fractions to a denominator of 40: $\dfrac{5}{40} + \dfrac{4}{40} = \dfrac{9}{40}$. There is no factor that 9 and 40 have in common, so the fraction cannot be reduced. The number in place of a in $\dfrac{a}{b}$ is 9, so the answer is (B). Be careful not to choose (D), which contains the value of b.

Fundamentals Drill 2: Calculator-Permitted Section

1. **C** Translate the words into math: $7 \times n = 84$, and we want to know the value of $4n$. $7n = 84$, so $n = 12$, and $4n = 48$, (C).

4. **D** First, solve for x. Divide both sides of the equation by 3, and you get $x = 4$. Then divide 24 by 4, which gives you 6, which is (D).

6. **D** A "strong positive association" means that as one variable increases, the other one increases. This will be shown as a line that angles through the graph from the lower left to the upper right. These scatterplots don't have any lines of best fit drawn on them, so imagine the line that would go through most of the points on each graph. In (A), the points are all over the place, so no line of best fit can even be drawn. Eliminate (A). In (B), the line that hits most of the points would go from the upper left to the lower right. This is a negative association, not a positive one, so eliminate (B). In (C), the line would go straight across, parallel to the x-axis. This is not a positive association, so eliminate (C). The correct answer is (D).

9. **D** To solve this equation, get $\sqrt{x}$ by itself. $\sqrt{x} = 16$, so square both sides: $(\sqrt{x})^2 = 16^2$, so $x = 256$. Choice (D) is correct.

14. **D** To figure out how much you need to add to 2.74 to get to 4.22, take 4.22 − 2.74 on your calculator. The difference between the two numbers is 1.48. This increase reflects the same number, t, added to each of the four numbers on the list. Divide 1.48 by 4 to find that $t = 0.37$, which is (D).

20. **B** First simplify the equation $4^x \cdot n^2 = 4^{x+1} \cdot n$ to $4^x \cdot n = 4^{x+1}$, and then try an easy number for x. If $x = 2$, then $4^2 \cdot n = 4^{2+1}$. Since $16n = 4^3$, then $16n = 64$ and $n = 4$. The correct answer is (B).

Summary

○   There are only six arithmetic operations tested on the SAT: addition, subtraction, multiplication, division, exponents, and square roots.

○   These operations must be performed in the proper order (PEMDAS), beginning with operations inside parentheses.

○   Apply the distributive law whenever possible. This is usually enough to find the answer.

○   A fraction is just another way of expressing division.

○   You must know how to add, subtract, multiply, and divide fractions. Don't forget that you can also use your calculator in the section where it is permitted.

○   If any problems involving large or confusing fractions appear, try to reduce the fractions first. Before you multiply two fractions, for example, see if it's possible to reduce either or both of the fractions.

○   If you know how to work out fractions on your calculator, use it when it is allowed to help you with questions that involve fractions. If you intend to use your calculator for fractions, make sure you practice. You should also know how to work with fractions the old-fashioned way.

○   A decimal is just another way of expressing a fraction.

○   When a calculator is permitted, use it to add, subtract, multiply, and divide decimals. When the calculator is not allowed, try rounding and estimating before doing the math with your pencil and paper.

○   Exponents are a kind of shorthand for expressing numbers that are the product of the same factor multiplied over and over again.

○   To multiply two exponential expressions with the same base, add the exponents.

○   To divide two exponential expressions with the same base, subtract the exponents.

o   To raise one exponential expression to another power, multiply the exponents.

o   To remember the exponent rules, think MADSPM.

o   When you raise a positive number greater than 1 to a power greater than 1, the result is larger. When you raise a positive fraction less than 1 to an exponent greater than 1, the result is smaller. A negative number raised to an even power becomes positive. A negative number raised to an odd power remains negative.

o   When you're asked for the square root of any number, $\sqrt{x}$, you're being asked for the positive root only.

o   Here are the only rules regarding square roots that you need to know for the SAT:

$$\sqrt{x} \times \sqrt{y} = \sqrt{xy}$$

$$\sqrt{\frac{x}{y}} = \frac{\sqrt{x}}{\sqrt{y}}$$

o   The rule for fractional exponents is this:
$$x^{\frac{y}{z}} = \sqrt[z]{x^y}$$

o   The rule for negative exponents is this:

$$x^{-n} = \frac{1}{x^n}$$

o   When you encounter charts, carefully check the chart for information you should note, and remember that you can use your answer sheet as a ruler to help you locate information or to draw a line of best fit.

Chapter 12
Algebra: Cracking the System

In the last chapter we reviewed some fundamental math concepts featured on the SAT. Many questions on the SAT combine simple arithmetic concepts with more complex algebraic concepts. This is one way the test writers raise the difficulty level of a question—they replace numbers with variables, or letters that stand for unknown quantities. In this chapter you will learn multiple ways to answer these algebraic questions.

SAT ALGEBRA: CRACKING THE SYSTEM

The SAT generally tests algebra concepts that you likely learned in eighth or ninth grade. So, you are probably pretty familiar with the level of algebra on the test. However, the test writers are fairly adept at wording algebra questions in a way that is confusing or distracting in order to make the questions harder than the mathematical concepts that are being tested.

In that fashion, the SAT Math sections are testing not only your math skills, but also, and possibly even more important to your score improvement, your reading skills. It is imperative that you read the questions carefully and translate the words in the problem into mathematical symbols.

ENGLISH	MATH EQUIVALENTS
is, are, were, did, does, costs	=
what (or any unknown value)	*any variable (x, y, k, b)*
more, sum	+
less, difference	−
of, times, product	× *(multiply)*
ratio, quotient, out of, per	÷

BASIC PRINCIPLES: FUNDAMENTALS OF SAT ALGEBRA

Many problems on the SAT require you to work with variables and equations. In algebra class you learned to solve equations by "solving for x" or "solving for y." To do this, you isolate x or y on one side of the equal sign and put everything else on the other side. The good thing about equations is that to isolate the variable you can do anything you want to them—add, subtract, multiply, divide, square—provided you perform the same operation to all the numbers in the equation.

Thus, the golden rule of equations:

> Whatever you do to the items on one side of the equal sign, you must do to the items on the other side of it as well.

Let's look at a simple example of this rule, without the distraction of answer choices.

If $2x - 15 = 35$, what is the value of x?

Here's How to Crack It
You want to isolate the variable. First, add 15 to each side of the equation. Now you have the following:

$$2x = 50$$

Divide each side of the equation by 2. Thus, x equals 25.

The skills for algebraic manipulation work just as well for more complex equations. The following question is another example of the way the SAT may ask you to manipulate equations. Don't panic when you see a question like this; just use the skills you already have and work carefully so you don't make an avoidable mistake in your algebra.

A Little Terminology
Here are some words that you will need to know to understand the explanations in this chapter. These words may even show up in the text of a question, so make sure you are familiar with them.

Term: An equation is like a sentence, and a term is the equivalent of a word. It can be just a number, just a variable, or a number multiplied by a variable. For example, 18, $-2x$, and $5y$ are the terms in the equation $18 - 2x = 5y$.

Expression: If an equation is like a sentence, then an expression is like a phrase or a clause. An expression is a combination of terms and mathematical operations with no equal or inequality sign. For example, $9 \times 2 + 3x$ is an expression.

Polynomial: A polynomial is any expression containing two or more terms. Binomials and trinomials are both examples of polynomials.

Suppose the evaporation rate of water in a lake is given by the equation $E = \dfrac{\dfrac{T_a - T_d}{700} - \dfrac{V}{T_w}}{h^4}$, where E

is the evaporation rate in gallons/day, T_a is the air

temperature, T_d is the dew point temperature, V

is the volume of water in the lake, T_w is the water

temperature, and h is the number of hours the water

is exposed to sunlight. Which of the following

expresses T_w in terms of T_a, T_d, V, E, and h ?

A) $T_w = \dfrac{Eh^4}{(T_a - T_d)V}$

B) $T_w = \dfrac{700}{(T_a - T_d - Eh^4)V}$

C) $T_w = \dfrac{V^4(T_a - T_d)}{Eh^4}$

D) $T_w = \dfrac{V}{\dfrac{T_a - T_d}{700} - Eh^4}$

Cut the Fat
Word problems on the SAT often contain unnecessary information. If you find the unnecessary information distracting, you can lightly strike through it. In this question, the explanation of the variables is not necessary, so you can cross out everything after the equation to "…the water is exposed to sunlight" without removing any information necessary to answering the question.

Here's How to Crack It

The goal is to get T_w by itself. Anything you do to one side of the equation, you must also do to the other side of the equation. Start by multiplying both sides by h^4 to get rid of the denominator on the right side of the equation.

The equation becomes

$$Eh^4 = \frac{T_a - T_d}{700} - \frac{V}{T_w}$$

To get the fraction with T_w alone on the right side, subtract the other fraction from both sides to get

$$Eh^4 - \frac{T_a - T_d}{700} = -\frac{V}{T_w}$$

Multiply both sides by T_w to get that variable out of the denominator.

$$T_w\left(Eh^4 - \frac{T_a - T_d}{700}\right) = -V$$

Now divide the whole expression by the entire thing inside the parentheses.

$$T_w = -\frac{V}{\left(Eh^4 - \dfrac{T_a - T_d}{700}\right)}$$

This doesn't match any of the answers exactly, but it looks a lot like (D). To make it match exactly, multiply the fractional part by $\dfrac{-1}{-1}$, which won't change the value of the fraction, to get

$$T_w = \frac{V}{\left(-Eh^4 + \dfrac{T_a - T_d}{700}\right)}$$

Then, just swap the positions of the two parts of the denominator to get (D).

Solving Radical Equations

Radical equations are just what the name suggests: an equation with a radical ($\sqrt{}$) in it. Not to worry, just remember to get rid of the radical first by raising both sides to that power.

Here's an example:

───────○───────

7

If $7\sqrt{x} - 24 = 11$, what is the value of x?

A) $\sqrt{5}$

B) $\sqrt{7}$

C) 5

D) 25

Here's How to Crack It

Start by adding 24 to both sides to get $7\sqrt{x} = 35$. Now, divide both sides by 7 to find that $\sqrt{x} = 5$. Finally, square both sides to find that $x = 25$, which is (D).

───────○───────

Solving Rational Equations

Since you are not always allowed to use your calculator on the SAT, there will be some instances in which you will need to solve an equation algebraically. Even on the sections in which calculator use is permitted, you may find it faster and more effective to use your mathematical skills to efficiently answer a question. Another way ETS may make your calculator less effective is by asking you to solve for an expression. A lot of the time, algebraic manipulation will be the means by which you can solve that problem.

Here is an example:

─────────────────○─────────────────

5

If $\dfrac{18}{r+10} = \dfrac{3}{r}$, what is the value of $\dfrac{r}{3}$?

A) $\dfrac{2}{3}$

B) $\dfrac{3}{2}$

C) 2

D) 3

Here's How to Crack It

This question appears in the No Calculator section, so you must use your math skills to solve for r. You can cross multiply to get $18r = 3(r + 10)$ or $18r = 3r + 30$. Subtracting $3r$ from both sides gives you $15r = 30$, so $r = 2$. Finally, $\dfrac{r}{3} = \dfrac{2}{3}$, which is (A).

─────────────────○─────────────────

Extraneous Solutions

Sometimes solving a rational or radical expression makes funny things happen. Let's look at an example.

$$\frac{1}{z+2} + \frac{1}{z-2} = \frac{4}{(z+2)(z-2)}$$

Given the equation above, what is the value of z ?

Here's How to Crack It

Use the Bowtie method to get a common denominator for the fractions on the left side of the equation. The numerator of the fraction on the left becomes $(z - 2)$ and the numerator of the fraction on the right becomes $(z + 2)$. The numerators are added together, and the new denominator is the product of the old ones. The equation becomes

$$\frac{(z-2)+(z+2)}{(z+2)(z-2)} = \frac{4}{(z+2)(z-2)}$$

Since the denominators are equal, the numerators are equal. This gives you

$$(z-2) + (z+2) = 4$$

When you simplify the left side, you get $2z = 4$, so $z = 2$. Sounds great, right? However, you need to plug this solution back into the original equation to make sure that it works. You get

$$\frac{1}{2+2} + \frac{1}{2-2} = \frac{4}{(2+2)(2-2)}$$

Once simplified, two of the three denominators become zero. That is not allowed, so the solution you found isn't really a solution at all. It is referred to as an "extraneous solution." That term refers to any answer you get to an algebraic equation that results in a false statement when plugged back in to the original equation.

Here's another example.

29

$$\sqrt{t+4} = t-2$$

In the equation above, what is the value of the extraneous solution, if one exists?

A) 0

B) 4

C) 5

D) There are no extraneous solutions.

Extra Answers
Any time you are solving for a variable, make sure your solutions actually work. If they do not, they are "extraneous," or extra.

Here's How to Crack It

Start by squaring both sides of the equation to get rid of the radical. The equation becomes

$$t + 4 = (t - 2)^2$$

Use FOIL to multiply the right side of the equation to get $t^2 - 2t - 2t + 4$ or $t^2 - 4t + 4$. Now the equation is

$$t + 4 = t^2 - 4t + 4$$

Subtract t and 4 from both sides to get

$$0 = t^2 - 5t$$

The right side factors to $t(t - 5)$, so $t = 0$ or 5. Eliminate (B), since 4 is not a solution at all, extraneous or otherwise. Now plug 0 and 5 back into the original equation to see if they work. If both do, the answer is (D). If one of them does not, that one is the extraneous solution.

$\underline{t = 0}$

$$\sqrt{0+4} = 0-2$$

$$\sqrt{4} = -2$$

$$2 \neq -2$$

$\underline{t = 5}$

$$\sqrt{5+4} = 5-2$$

$$\sqrt{9} = 3$$

$$3 = 3$$

Since the equation is false when $t = 0$, then 0 is the extraneous solution. The correct answer is (A).

Solving for Expressions

Some SAT algebra problems ask you to find the value of an expression rather than the value of a variable. In most cases, you can find the value of the expression without finding the value of the variable.

5

If $4x + 2 = 4$, what is the value $4x - 6$?

A) −6

B) −4

C) 4

D) 8

Math Class Solution:

In math class, you would find the value of x and then plug that value into the provided expression. So, subtract 2 from both sides to find that $4x = 2$. Then divide both sides by 4 to find that $x = \dfrac{1}{2}$. Then, $4x - 6 = 4\left(\dfrac{1}{2}\right) - 6 = -4$.

So, the answer is (B).

Here's How to Crack It

Since you're being asked for the value of an expression $(4x - 6)$ rather than the value of x, you correctly suspect that there might be a shortcut. So, you look for a way to turn $4x + 2$ into $4x - 6$ and realize that subtracting 8 from both sides of the equation will do just that.

So, you just do $(4x + 2) - 8 = 4 - 8 = -4$ and you've got (B).

The Princeton Review solution will save you time—provided that you see it quickly. So, while you practice, you should train yourself to look for these sorts of direct solutions whenever you are asked to solve for the value of an expression.

However, don't worry too much if you don't always see the faster way to solve a problem like this one. The math class way will certainly get you the right answer.

Here's another example:

9

If $\sqrt{5} = x - 2$, what is the value of $(x-2)^2$?

A) $\sqrt{5}$

B) $\sqrt{7}$

C) 5

D) 25

Here's How to Crack It

If you were to attempt the math class way, you'd find that $x = \sqrt{5} + 2$ and then you'd have to substitute that into the provided expression. There's got to be an easier way!

The problem is much easier if you look for a direct solution. Then, you notice that all the problem wants you to do is to square the expression on the right of the equal sign. Well, if you square the expression on the right, then you'd better square the expression on the left, too. So, $\left(\sqrt{5}\right)^2 = 5 = (x-2)^2$ and the answer is (C). That was pretty painless by comparison.

Solving Simultaneous Equations

Some SAT problems will give you two or more equations involving two or more variables and ask for the value of an expression or one of the variables. These problems are very similar to the problems containing one variable. ETS would like you to spend extra time trying to solve for the value of each variable, but that is not always necessary.

Learn Them, Love Them
Don't get bogged down looking for a direct solution. Always ask yourself if there is a simple way to find the answer. If you train yourself to think in terms of shortcuts, you won't waste a lot of time. However, if you don't see a quick solution, get to work. Something may come to you as you labor away.

Here's an example:

If $4x + y = 14$ and $3x + 2y = 13$, then $x - y = ?$

Here's How to Crack It

You've been given two equations here. But instead of being asked to solve for a variable (x or y), you've been asked to solve for an expression ($x - y$). Why? Because there must be a direct solution.

In math class, you're taught to solve one equation for one variable in terms of a second variable and to substitute that value into the second equation to solve for the first variable.

Forget it. These methods are far too time consuming to use on the SAT, and they put you at risk of making mistakes. There's a better way. Just stack them on top of each other, and then add or subtract the two equations; either addition or subtraction will often produce an easy answer. Let's try it.

Adding the two equations gives you this:

$$
\begin{array}{r}
4x + y = 14 \\
+ 3x + 2y = 13 \\
\hline
7x + 3y = 27
\end{array}
$$

Unfortunately, that doesn't get us anywhere. So, try subtracting:

$$
\begin{array}{r}
4x + y = 14 \\
(3x + 2y = 13)
\end{array}
$$

When you subtract equations, just change the signs of the second equation and add. So the equation above becomes

$$
\begin{array}{r}
4x + y = 14 \\
+(-3x - 2y = -13) \\
\hline
x - y = 1
\end{array}
$$

The value of ($x - y$) is precisely what you are looking for, so the answer is 1.

You can also use this method to solve problems in which you are asked to solve for an expression and gives you fewer equations than variables. If you have dealt with simultaneous equations in your math classes you may know that that puts you in a bind since it may be impossible to solve for each individual variable.

Here is an example:

$$3a - 7b = 4d - 9$$
$$-4c + 10a = 6b + 7$$
$$-2a + 3c - 4d = 10$$

Given the system of equations above, what is the value of $-10a - 2b + 2c$?

Here's How to Crack It

Notice that the test writers have made this problem harder by mixing up the variables. Your first step is to line up the variables on the left side of the equation and arrange them in alphabetical order; move the constants to the right side of the equation. Combine like terms in each equation, and use a place holder for any variables that are missing in each equation.

Step 1:

$$3a - 7b + 0c - 4d = -9$$
$$10a - 6b - 4c + 0d = 7$$
$$-2a + 0b + 3c - 4d = 10$$

Once you have the variables aligned, complete this problem just like the previous problem by adding and subtracting the equations until you get something that looks like the expression in the question.

IF YOU ADD:

$$3a - 7b + 0c - 4d = -9$$
$$+ (10a - 6b - 4c + 0d = 7)$$
$$+ \underline{(-2a + 0b + 3c - 4d = 10)}$$
$$11a - 13b - 1c - 8d = 8$$

IF YOU SUBTRACT:

$$3a - 7b + 0c - 4d = -9$$
$$+ (-10a + 6b + 4c - 0d = -7)$$
$$+ \underline{(2a - 0b - 3c + 4d = -10)}$$
$$-5a - 1b + 1c + 0d = -26$$

Neither of these answers appears to be what the test writers are asking for, but on closer inspection, the equation that resulted from subtraction can be multiplied by 2 to get the expression in the question.

$$2(-5a - 1b + 1c) = 2(-26)$$

$$-10a - 2b + 2c = -52$$

Solving for Variables in Simultaneous Equations

Shortcuts are awesome, so take them whenever you can on the SAT. But occasionally, you won't have the option of using a short-cut with simultaneous equations, so knowing how to solve for a variable is imperative.

Here's an example:

If $3x + 2y = 17$ and $5x - 4y = 21$, what is the value of y ?

Here's How to Crack It

In this case, the stack and solve method doesn't bring us an immediate answer:

IF YOU ADD:	IF YOU SUBTRACT:
$3x + 2y = 17$	$3x + 2y = \ \ \ 17$
$\underline{+\ 5x - 4y = 21}$	$\underline{+\ (-5x + 4y = -21)}$
$8x - 2y = 38$	$-2x + 6y = \ \ -4$

Neither of these methods gives you the value of y. The best way to approach this question is to try to eliminate one variable. To do this, multiply one or both of the equations by a number that will cause the other variable to have a coefficient of 0 when the equations are added or subtracted.

In this case, the question is asking us to solve for y, so try to make the x terms disappear. You want to make the coefficient of x zero, so you can quickly find the value of y. Here's how:

Use the coefficient of x in the second equation, 5, to multiply the first equation:

$$5(3x + 2y) = 5(17)$$

$$15x + 10y = 85$$

Then use the original coefficient of x in the first equation to multiply the second equation:

$$3(5x - 4y) = 3(21)$$
$$15x - 12y = 63$$

Now stack your equations and subtract (or flip the signs and add, which is less likely to lead to a mistake.)

$$\begin{array}{r} 15x + 10y = 85 \\ + (-15x + 12y = -63) \\ \hline 0x + 22y = 22 \end{array}$$

Simplify your equation and you have your answer.

$$22y = 22$$
$$y = 1$$

Solving Inequalities

In an equation, one side equals the other. In an inequality, one side does not equal the other. The following symbols are used in inequalities:

$\neq$	is not equal to
$>$	is greater than
$<$	is less than
$\geq$	is greater than or equal to; at least
$\leq$	is less than or equal to; no more than

Solving inequalities is pretty similar to solving equations. You can collect like terms, and you can simplify by doing the same thing to both sides. All you have to remember is that if you multiply or divide both sides of an inequality by a negative number, the direction of the inequality symbol changes. For example, here's a simple inequality:

$$x > y$$

Now, just as you can with an equation, you can multiply both sides of this inequality by the same number. But if the number you multiply by is negative, you have to change the direction of the symbol in the result. For example, if you multiply both sides of the inequality above by -2, you end up with the following:

$$-2x < -2y$$

Hungry Gator
Think of the inequality sign as the mouth of a hungry alligator. The alligator eats the bigger number.

Remember: When you multiply or divide an inequality by a negative number, you must reverse the inequality sign.

Here's an example of how an inequality question may be framed on the test:

―――――――――○―――――――――

8

If $-3x + 6 \geq 18$, which of the following must be true?

A) $x \leq -4$

B) $x \leq 8$

C) $x \geq -4$

D) $x \geq -8$

Here's How to Crack It

Simplify the inequality like any other equation:

$$-3x + 6 \geq 18$$

$$-3x \geq 12$$

Remember to change the direction of the inequality sign!

$$x \leq -4$$

So (A) is the correct answer.

―――――――――○―――――――――

A Range of Values

Another skill ETS may test is solving inequalities for a range of values. In these instances, you can simplify the process by initially treating the inequality as two separate problems.

Here's an example:

If $-8 < -\dfrac{3}{5}m + 1 \le -\dfrac{16}{5}$, what is one possible value of m?

Here's How to Crack It

First work on the left side of the equation: $-8 < -\dfrac{3}{5}m + 1$.

$$5(-8) < 5\left(-\dfrac{3}{5}m + 1\right)$$

$$-40 < -3m + 5$$

$$-40 - 5 < -3m + 5 - 5$$

$$-45 < -3m$$

$$\dfrac{-45}{-3} > \dfrac{-3m}{-3}$$

$$15 > m$$

Then work on the right side of the equation: $-\dfrac{3}{5}m + 1 \le -\dfrac{16}{5}$

$$-\dfrac{3}{5}m + 1 - 1 \le -\dfrac{16}{5} - 1$$

$$-\dfrac{3}{5}m \le -\dfrac{21}{5}$$

$$5\left(-\dfrac{3}{5}m\right) \le 5\left(-\dfrac{21}{5}\right)$$

$$-3m \le -21$$

$$\dfrac{-3m}{-3} \ge \dfrac{-21}{-3}$$

$$m \ge 7$$

Once you have both pieces of the inequality simplified, you just need to put them back together.

If $15 > m$ and $m \geq 7$, then $15 > m \geq 7$, but this inequality doesn't make logical sense. Generally, inequalities are written with the smaller number on the left and the larger number on the right, so when you solve an inequality like this, you may need to rearrange the equation. This isn't difficult, just make sure the "arrows" are still pointing at the same numbers when you change the order.

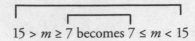

$15 > m \geq 7$ becomes $7 \leq m < 15$

So a correct answer to this question would be any number between 7 and 15, which includes 7, but does NOT include 15.

Writing Your Own System of Equations

Sometimes you'll be asked to take a word problem and create a system of equations or inequalities from that information. Usually they will not ask you to solve this system of equations/inequalities, so if you are able to locate and translate the information in the problem, you have a good shot at getting the correct answer. Always start with the most straightforward piece of information. What is the most straightforward piece of information? Well, that's up to you to decide. Consider the problem on the next page.

9

Aubrie, Bera, and Kea are running a lemonade and snack stand to earn money. They are selling lemonade for $1.07 a cup and chocolate chip cookies for $0.78 each. Their customers arrive on foot or by car. During a three-hour period, they had 47 customers each buying only one item and made $45.94. Aubrie, Bera, and Kea need to determine if they have enough supplies for tomorrow. Solving which of the following system of equations will let them know how many cups of lemonade, x, and how many cookies, y, they sold today?

A) $\begin{cases} x + y = 45.94 \\ 1.07x + 0.78y = 47 \end{cases}$

B) $\begin{cases} x + y = 47 \\ 1.07x + 0.78y = 45.94 \end{cases}$

C) $\begin{cases} x + y = 47 \\ 0.78x + 1.07y = 45.94 \end{cases}$

D) $\begin{cases} x + y = 47 \\ 107x + 78y = 45.94 \end{cases}$

Here's How to Crack It

For some people, the most straightforward piece of information deals with the number of items being sold. For others, it may be the price of the items being sold. Whichever piece of information you choose, use the math to English translations in this chapter to help you identify the mathematical operations you will need to write your equation.

Let's work through the previous problem.

You may have noticed that at least some of this word problem is just providing background information that isn't really necessary to solve the problem. Lightly striking through the information will make the problem look less intimidating, as shown on the next page.

~~Aubrie, Bera, and Kea are running a lemonade and snack stand to earn money.~~ They are selling lemonade for $1.07 a cup and chocolate chip cookies for $0.78 each. ~~Their customers arrive on foot or by car. During a three-hour period~~ they had 47 customers each buying only one item and they made $45.94. ~~Aubrie, Bera, and Kea need to determine if they have enough supplies for tomorrow.~~ Solving which of the following system of equations will let them know how many cups of lemonade, x, and how many cookies, y, they sold today?

The shortened problem makes it a lot easier to recognize important information. Start by identifying a straightforward piece of information, so you can start writing your own equations.

They are selling lemonade for $1.07 a cup and chocolate chip cookies for $0.78 each.

This is a fairly straightforward piece of information. Once you identify which variable represents lemonade and which one represents cookies, you can begin to write your equation. In this problem, the very last sentence gives us the needed information.

...how many glasses of lemonade, x, and how many cookies, y...

Now you know that the number of cups of lemonade they sold, multiplied by $1.07 per cup, will give you the amount of money they made selling lemonade, and the number of cookies they sold, multiplied by $0.78, will give you the amount of money they made selling cookies. Since the problem also gives you the total amount of money they made, $45.94, and states that customers were "each buying only one item" you can use the information above to write your first equation.

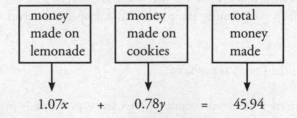

Once you have your first equation, go to your answer choices to determine which answers you can eliminate. You'll quickly see that (A), (C), and (D) are all wrong, so you can select (B) without even having to construct the second equation.

Now try one on your own!

7

To save on helium costs, a balloon is inflated with both helium and nitrogen gas. Between the two gases, the balloon can be inflated up to 8 liters in volume. The density of helium is 0.20 grams per liter, and the density of nitrogen is 1.30 grams per liter. The balloon must be filled so that the volumetric average density of the balloon is lower than that of air, which has a density of 1.20 grams per liter. Which of the following system of inequalities best describes how the balloon will be filled, if x represents the number of liters of helium and y represents the number of liters of nitrogen?

A. $\begin{cases} x + y > 8 \\ 20x + 130y > 120 \end{cases}$

B. $\begin{cases} x + y = 8 \\ \dfrac{0.2x + 1.30y}{2} < 1.20 \end{cases}$

C. $\begin{cases} x + y \le 8 \\ 0.20\left(\dfrac{x}{x+y}\right) + 1.30\left(\dfrac{y}{x+y}\right) < 1.20 \end{cases}$

D. $\begin{cases} x + y \le 8 \\ 0.20x + 1.30y < 1.20 \end{cases}$

Here's How to Crack It

Start with the most straightforward piece of information and translate that. In this case, it is probably the information about the total volume of the balloon. "Between the two gases" would indicate addition, and the gases are represented as x and y, so you need $x + y$ in the correct answer. They all have that, so go to the next piece. Together, x and y can be "up to 8 liters." This translates to "less than or equal to 8," because the balloon's volume can't be greater than 8, but it could be 8 or less. Therefore, one equation must be $x + y \le 8$. You can eliminate (A) and (B), as those answers have different equations related to $x + y$. The next part may be hard to translate, so pick some numbers and try them out. Make $x = 2$ and $y = 2$. The second equation in (D) is easier to work with, so see if these numbers make that equation true. $0.2(2) + 1.30(2) = 0.4 + 2.60 = 3$. This is not less than 1.20, so eliminate (D) and choose (C).

―――――――――――――――○―――――――――――――――

Simplifying Expressions

Something to Hide
Because factoring or expanding is usually the key to finding the answer on such problems, learn to recognize expressions that could be either factored or expanded. This will earn you more points. The test writers will try to hide the answer by factoring or expanding the result.

If a problem contains an expression that can be factored, it is very likely that you will need to factor it to solve the problem. So, you should always be on the look-out for opportunities to factor. For example, if a problem contains the expression $2x + 2y$, you should see if factoring it to produce the expression $2(x + y)$ will help you to solve the problem.

If a problem contains an expression that is already factored, you should consider using the distributive law to expand it. For example, if a problem contains the expression $2(x + y)$, you should see if expanding it to $2x + 2y$ will help.

Here are five examples that we've worked out:

1. $4x + 24 = 4(x) + 4(6) = 4(x + 6)$

2. $\dfrac{10x - 60}{2} = \dfrac{10(x) - 10(6)}{2} = \dfrac{10(x - 6)}{2} = 5(x - 6) = 5x - 30$

3. $\dfrac{x + y}{y} = \dfrac{x}{y} + \dfrac{y}{y} = \dfrac{x}{y} + 1$

4. $2(x + y) + 3(x + y) = (2 + 3)(x + y) = 5(x + y)$

5. $p(r + s) + q(r + s) = (p + q)(r + s)$

Here's how this might be tested on the SAT.

10 ▮▮▮▮▮▮▮▮▮▮▮▮▮▮▮▮▮▮▮▮▮▮▮

Which of the following is equivalent to $\dfrac{f^2}{g} + f$?

A) $\dfrac{f}{g}(f+g)$

B) $f\left(\dfrac{f}{g}+f\right)$

C) $f^2\left(\dfrac{1}{g}-\dfrac{1}{f}\right)$

D) $f^2\left(\dfrac{1}{g}+1\right)$

Here's How to Crack It

Depending on what you see when you approach this problem, you may choose to solve with distribution or factoring. You may notice that there is an f in each term of the expression. In this case, you may choose to factor the expression to $f\left(\dfrac{f}{g}+1\right)$, but that doesn't give you a possible answer; however, you can eliminate (B), since $f\left(\dfrac{f}{g}+f\right)$ is not equivalent to your expression. Now you are left with an expression you may find hard to manipulate. Let's go back and look at the mathematics behind our initial factorization so the next step in the process will make more sense.

When you factor an f out of the expression, what you are really doing is this:

Multiply the expression by 1 so that you do not change the expression.

$$\frac{f}{f}\left(\frac{f^2}{g}+f\right)$$

$$f \times \frac{1}{f}\left(\frac{f^2}{g}+f\right)$$

Distribute the $\dfrac{1}{f}$.

$$f\left(\dfrac{f^2}{g}\times\dfrac{1}{f}+f\times\dfrac{1}{f}\right)$$

Cancel where possible.

$$f\left(\dfrac{f}{g}+1\right)$$

We can follow the exact same steps to factor an $\dfrac{f}{g}$ like you see in (A).

$$\dfrac{\dfrac{f}{g}}{\dfrac{f}{g}}\left(\dfrac{f^2}{g}+f\right)$$

$$\dfrac{f}{g}\times\dfrac{g}{f}\left(\dfrac{f^2}{g}+f\right)$$

$$\dfrac{f}{g}\left(\dfrac{f^2}{g}\times\dfrac{g}{f}+f\times\dfrac{g}{f}\right)$$

$$\dfrac{f}{g}(f+g)$$

This leaves you with the same expression as (A).

If you notice that the answers are all expressions themselves, you may choose to distribute the variable in front of the parentheses instead of trying to factor the expression.

Start with (A): $\dfrac{f}{g}\overparen{\left(f+g\right)}$

Distribute to each term within the binomial: $f\times\dfrac{f}{g}+g\times\dfrac{f}{g}$

Cancel where you can: $\dfrac{f^2}{g}+f$

Both methods give you the same answer; however, this type of algebra leaves you open to making mistakes. In the next chapter, you will discover a third way to approach this problem that you may find even easier than the methods above.

Multiplying Binomials

Multiplying binomials is easy. Just be sure to use FOIL (First, Outer, Inner, Last).

$$(x + 2)(x + 4) = (x + 2)(x + 4)$$
$$= (x \times x) + (x \times 4) + (2 \times x) + (2 \times 4)$$
$$\text{FIRST} \quad \text{OUTER} \quad \text{INNER} \quad \text{LAST}$$
$$= x^2 + 4x + 2x + 8$$
$$= x^2 + 6x + 8$$

Combine Similar Terms First

When manipulating long, complicated algebraic expressions, combine all similar terms before doing anything else. In other words, if one of the terms is $5x$ and another is $-3x$, simply combine them into $2x$. Then you won't have as many terms to work with. Here's an example:

$$(3x^2 + 3x + 4) + (2 - x) - (6 + 2x) =$$
$$3x^2 + 3x + 4 + 2 - x - 6 - 2x =$$
$$3x^2 + (3x - x - 2x) + (4 + 2 - 6) =$$
$$3x^2$$

TERMinology
Remember: A *term* is a number, variable, or a number *and* variable that are combined by multiplication or division. So in the expression $6x + 10 = y$, $6x$, 10, and y are all terms. $6x + 10$, however, is not a term because a term includes only variables and their coefficients.

Evaluating Expressions

Sometimes you will be given the value of one of the variables in an algebraic expression and asked to find the value of the entire expression. All you have to do is plug in the given value and see what you come up with.

Here is an example:

Problem: If $2x = -1$, then $(2x - 3)^2 = ?$

Solution: Don't solve for x; simply plug in -1 for $2x$, like this:

$$(2x - 3)^2 = (-1 - 3)^2$$
$$= (-4)^2$$
$$= 16$$

Solving Quadratic Equations

To solve quadratic equations, remember everything you've learned so far: Look for direct solutions and either factor or expand when possible.

Here's an example:

If $(x + 3)^2 = (x - 2)^2$, what is the value of x ?

Here's How to Crack It

Expand both sides of the equation using FOIL:

$$(x + 3)(x + 3) = x^2 + 6x + 9$$

$$(x - 2)(x - 2) = x^2 - 4x + 4$$

$$x^2 + 6x + 9 = x^2 - 4x + 4$$

Now you can simplify. Eliminate the x^2 terms, because they are on both sides of the equal sign. Now you have $6x + 9 = -4x + 4$, which simplifies to

$$10x = -5$$
$$x = -\frac{1}{2}$$

Factoring Quadratics

To solve a quadratic, you might also have to factor the equation. Factoring a quadratic basically involves doing a reverse form of FOIL.

For example, suppose you needed to know the factors of $x^2 + 7x + 12$. Here's what you would do:

1. Write down 2 sets of parentheses and put an x in each one because the product of the first terms is x^2.

    $$x^2 + 7x + 12 = (x \quad)(x \quad)$$

2. Look at the number at the end of the expression you are trying to factor. Write down its factors. In this case, the factors of 12 are 1 and 12, 2 and 6, and 3 and 4.

Factoring
When factoring an equation like $x^2 + bx + c$, think "**A.M.**" Find two numbers that **A**dd up to the middle term (b) and **M**ultiply to give the last term (c).

3. To determine which set of factors to put in the parentheses, look at the coefficient of the middle term of the quadratic expression. In this case, the coefficient is 7. So, the correct factors will also either add or subtract to get 7. Write the correct factors in the parentheses.

$$x^2 + 7x + 12 = (x \underline{} 3)(x \underline{} 4)$$

4. Finally, determine the signs for the factors. To get a positive 12, the 3 and the 4 are either both positive or both negative. But, since 7 is also positive, the signs must both be positive.

$$x^2 + 7x + 12 = (x + 3)(x + 4)$$

You can always check that you have factored correctly by FOILing the factors to see if you get the original quadratic expression.

Now, try this one:

16

In the expression $x^2 + kx + 12$, k is a negative integer. Which of the following is a possible value of k ?

A) −13

B) −12

C) −6

D) 7

Here's How to Crack It

Since the question told you that k is a negative integer, you can immediately eliminate (D) because it is a positive integer. To solve the question, you need to factor. This question is just a twist on the example used above. Don't worry that we don't know the value of k. The question said that k was an integer, so you need to consider only the integer factors of 12. The possible factors of 12 are 1 and 12, 2 and 6, and 3 and 4. Since 12 is positive and k is negative, then you'll need subtraction signs in both factors.

The possibilities are as follows:

$$x^2 + kx + 12 = (x - 1)(x - 12)$$

$$x^2 + kx + 12 = (x - 2)(x - 6)$$

$$x^2 + kx + 12 = (x - 3)(x - 4)$$

If you FOIL each of these sets of factors, you'll get the following expressions:

$$(x - 1)(x - 12) = x^2 - 13x + 12$$

$$(x - 2)(x - 6) = x^2 - 8x + 12$$

$$(x - 3)(x - 4) = x^2 - 7x + 12$$

The correct answer is (A), as –13 is the only value from above included in the answers. Of course, you didn't need to write them all out if you started with 1 and 12 as your factors.

SAT Favorites

The test writers play favorites when it comes to quadratic equations. There are three equations that they use all the time. You should memorize these and be on the lookout for them. Whenever you see a quadratic that contains two variables, it is almost certain to be one of these three.

$$(x + y)(x - y) = x^2 - y^2$$

$$(x + y)^2 = x^2 + 2xy + y^2$$

$$(x - y)^2 = x^2 - 2xy + y^2$$

Here's an example of how these equations will likely be tested on the SAT. Try it:

11

If $2x - 3y = 5$, what is the value of $4x^2 - 12xy + 9y^2$?

A) $\sqrt{5}$

B) 12

C) 25

D) 100

Here's How to Crack It

We are given a quadratic equation that contains two variables.

In this case, work with $2x - 3y = 5$. If you square the left side of the equations, you get

$$(2x - 3y)^2 = 4x^2 - 12xy + 9y^2$$

That's precisely the expression for which you need to find the value. It's also the third of the equations from the box. Now, since you squared the left side, all you need to do is square the 5 on the right side of the equation to discover that the expression equals 25, (C).

Did you notice that this question was just another version of being asked to solve for the value of an expression rather than for a variable? Quadratics are one of ETS's favorite ways to do that.

Solving Quadratics Set to Zero

Before factoring most quadratics, you need to set the equation equal to zero. Why? Well, if $ab = 0$, what do you know about a and b? At least one of them must equal 0, right? That's the key fact you need to solve most quadratics.

Here's an example:

9

If $3 - \dfrac{3}{x} = x + 7$, and $x \neq 0$, which of the following is a possible value for x?

A) -7
B) -1
C) 1
D) 3

Here's How to Crack It

The test writers have tried to hide that the equation is actually a quadratic. Start by multiplying both sides of the equation by x to get rid of the fraction.

$$x\left(3 - \frac{3}{x}\right) = x(x+7)$$

$$3x - 3 = x^2 + 7x$$

Now, just rearrange the terms to set the quadratic equal to 0. You'll get $x^2 + 4x + 3 = 0$. Now, it's time to factor:

$$x^2 + 4x + 3 = (x+1)(x+3) = 0$$

So, at least one of the factors must equal 0. If $x + 1 = 0$, then $x = -1$. If $x + 3 = 0$, then $x = -3$. Since -1 is (B), that's the one you want.

In addition to your knowing how to solve easily factorable quadratics, the test writers would also like to see you demonstrate your understanding of the quadratic formula. I know what you are thinking: "Not that thing AGAIN! Can't I just solve it with that nifty program I have on my graphing calculator?" Why yes, yes you can, but only if the problem appears in the calculator-permitted section of the test. Trust us on this one—the test writers are not always going to put these types of problems in the calculator section. Knowing the quadratic formula is an easy way to gain points on a question the test writers intend to be "hard."

> For a quadratic equation in the form $y = ax^2 + bx + c$, the quadratic formula is:
>
> $$x = \frac{-b \pm \sqrt{b^2 - 4ac}}{2a}$$

To find the roots of a quadratic, or the points where $y = 0$, simply plug your values for a, b, and c into the quadratic formula.

Here's an example:

$$7x^2 - 5x - 17 = 0$$

So $a = 7$, $b = -5$, and $c = -17$. Plugging the constants into the quadratic equation you get

$$x = \frac{5 \pm \sqrt{(-5)^2 - 4(7)(-17)}}{2(7)}$$

$$x = \frac{5 \pm \sqrt{25 + 476}}{14}$$

$$x = \frac{5 \pm \sqrt{501}}{14}$$

$$x = \frac{5}{14} + \frac{\sqrt{501}}{14} \text{ and } x = \frac{5}{14} - \frac{\sqrt{501}}{14}$$

Let's put your quadratic skills to work with a problem you may see on the SAT.

12

What is the product of all the solutions to the equation $3z^2 - 12z + 6 = 0$?

A) $\sqrt{2}$

B) 2

C) 4

D) $4\sqrt{2}$

The Signs They Are a Changin'
The quadratic formula works for quadratics in the form $y = ax^2 + bx + c$. There is only addition in that form, so be careful when your quadratic has negative signs in it.

Here's How to Crack It

Using the quadratic formula $x = \dfrac{-b \pm \sqrt{b^2 - 4ac}}{2a}$ you would do the following:

$$x = \frac{12 \pm \sqrt{(-12)^2 - 4(3)(6)}}{2(3)}$$

$$x = \frac{12 \pm \sqrt{72}}{6} = \frac{12 \pm \sqrt{36 \times 2}}{6}$$

$$x = \frac{12 \pm 6\sqrt{2}}{6}$$

$$x = \frac{2 \pm 1\sqrt{2}}{1}$$

$$x = 2 \pm 1\sqrt{2}$$

So $x = 2 + \sqrt{2}$ or $2 - \sqrt{2}$. "Product" means to multiply, so use FOIL to multiply $\left(2 + \sqrt{2}\right) \times \left(2 - \sqrt{2}\right)$ to get $4 - 2\sqrt{2} + 2\sqrt{2} - \left(\sqrt{2}\right)^2 = 4 - 2 = 2$, which is (B).

Wow, that was a lot of work! Wouldn't it be great if there were a shortcut? Actually, there is! When a quadratic is in the form $y = ax^2 + bx + c$, the product of the roots is equal to the value of c divided by the value of a. In this case, that's $6 \div 3 = 2$! It's the same answer for a lot less work. (See the inset "The Root of the Problems" for this and another handy trick—they're worth memorizing.)

IMAGINARY AND COMPLEX NUMBERS

So far you have been working with real numbers, which are any numbers that you can place on a number line. The SAT will also ask you to do mathematical operations with imaginary or complex numbers.

The Root of the Problems

Sometimes you'll be asked to solve for the sum or the product of the roots of a quadratic equation. You can use the quadratic formula and then add or multiply the results, but it's quicker to just memorize these two expressions.

sum of the roots: $-\dfrac{b}{a}$

product of the roots: $\dfrac{c}{a}$

Imaginary Numbers

An imaginary number, very simply, is the square root of a negative number. Since there is no way to have a real number that is the square root of a negative number, mathematicians needed to come up with a way to represent this concept when writing equations. They use an italicized lowercase "I" to do that: $i = \sqrt{-1}$, and the SAT will likely tell you that in any problem involving imaginary numbers.

Another common piece of information you will need to know about i is how it behaves when it is raised to a power. Here is i raised to the powers 1 through 8. Can you complete the next four values of i in the series?

$$i = \sqrt{-1} \qquad\qquad i^5 = \sqrt{-1} \qquad\qquad i^9 = ?$$

$$i^2 = -1 \qquad\qquad i^6 = -1 \qquad\qquad i^{10} = ?$$

$$i^3 = -\sqrt{-1} = -i \qquad\qquad i^7 = -\sqrt{-1} = -i \qquad\qquad i^{11} = ?$$

$$i^4 = 1 \qquad\qquad i^8 = 1 \qquad\qquad i^{12} = ?$$

Did you notice anything about the answer? If you said that there is a repeating pattern, then you are correct. This pattern will be helpful in answering questions containing imaginary and complex numbers.

Complex Numbers

Complex numbers are another way in which the SAT may test the concept of imaginary numbers. A complex number is one that has a real component and an imaginary component connected by addition or subtraction. $8 + 7i$ and $3 - 4i$ are two examples of complex numbers.

Complex numbers might be tested in a variety of ways. You may be asked to add or subtract the complex numbers. When you are completing these operations, you can treat i as a variable. Just combine the like terms in these expressions and then simplify (don't forget to distribute the subtraction sign).

Here's an example:

○

<table>
<tr><td>2</td></tr>
</table>

For $i = \sqrt{-1}$, what is the result of subtracting $(2 + 4i)$ from $(-5 + 6i)$?

A) $-7 + 2i$

B) $-3 - 10i$

C) $3 + 2i$

D) $7 - 10i$

Here's How to Crack It

Set up the subtraction necessary.

$$(-5 + 6i) - (2 + 4i)$$

Distribute the negative sign to both terms in the second set of parentheses to get

$$-5 + 6i - 2 - 4i$$

Combine like terms to get $-7 + 2i$, which is (A).

Since you never ended up with an i^2 term, you never even needed to worry about the fact that $i = \sqrt{-1}$. You just treat i as a regular variable.

○

The SAT may also test your ability to multiply complex numbers. Again you can treat i as a variable as you work through the multiplication as if you were multiplying binominals. In other words, use FOIL to work through the problem. The only difference is that you substitute -1 for i^2.

$$
\begin{array}{cccc}
\text{F} & \text{O} & \text{I} & \text{L} \\
\downarrow & \downarrow & \downarrow & \downarrow
\end{array}
$$
$$(4 + 8i) \times (3 - 2i) = 12 - 8i + 24i - 16i^2 = 12 + 16i - 16(-1) = 12 + 16i + 16 = 28 + 16i$$

Finally, you may be asked about fractions with complex numbers in the denominator. Don't worry—you won't need polynomial or synthetic division for this. You just need to rationalize the denominator, which is much easier than it may sound.

To rationalize the denominator of a fraction containing complex numbers, you need to multiply the numerator and denominator by the conjugate. To create the conjugate of a complex number, you simply need to switch the addition or subtraction sign connecting the real and imaginary parts of the number for its opposite.

For example, the conjugate of $8 + 7i$ is $8 - 7i$, and the conjugate of $3 - 4i$ is $3 + 4i$.

Just like when you expand the expression $(x + y)(x - y)$ to get $x^2 - y^2$, you can do the same with a complex number and its conjugate. The Outer and Inner terms will cancel out, giving you $(x + yi)(x - yi) = (x^2 - i^2y^2) = (x^2 + y^2)$.

$(8 + 7i) \times (8 - 7i) = 8^2 - 7^2i^2$, and substituting $i^2 = -1$ gives you $8^2 + 7^2 = 113$.

Here's an example of how the SAT will use complex numbers in a fraction.

3

If $i - \sqrt{-1}$, which of the following is equivalent to

$$\frac{14}{2 - \sqrt{10}i} ?$$

A) $2 + \sqrt{10}i$

B) $2 - \dfrac{\sqrt{10}}{14}i$

C) $\dfrac{2 - \sqrt{10}i}{14}$

D) $28 - 14\sqrt{10}i$

Here's How to Crack It
None of the answer choices have i in the denominator, if they have a denominator at all, so you need to get rid of that i. Roots in denominators are generally not accepted, either. To get rid of both things, you need to multiply the whole fraction by the conjugate of the denominator. This means keep the same terms, but switch the sign between them. Be very careful to not make a sign error as you work through the problem. The expression becomes

$$\left(\frac{14}{2 - \sqrt{10}i}\right)\left(\frac{2 + \sqrt{10}i}{2 + \sqrt{10}i}\right)$$

Multiplying by One (in Disguise)
In order to keep a fraction the same, you must multiply by 1. If you multiply the numerator of a fraction by the conjugate, you must do that same operation to the denominator or you have changed the fraction:
$$\frac{18}{8 + 7i} \times \left(\frac{8 - 7i}{8 - 7i}\right)$$
is the same thing as
multiplying $\dfrac{18}{8 + 7i} \times 1$.

Multiply the two fractions, using FOIL on the denominators to get

$$\frac{28+14\sqrt{10}i}{4+2\sqrt{10}i-2\sqrt{10}i-10i^2}$$

Combine like terms in the denominator, and the expression becomes

$$\frac{28+14\sqrt{10}i}{4-10i^2}$$

There is still an i in the denominator, but you can get rid of it. Since $i=\sqrt{-1}$, $i^2=-1$, so substitute that into the fraction to get

$$\frac{28+14\sqrt{10}i}{4-10(-1)}=\frac{28+14\sqrt{10}i}{4+10}=\frac{28+14\sqrt{10}i}{14}$$

Reducing the fraction gives you $2+\sqrt{10}i$, which is (A).

When Values Are Absolute

Absolute value is just a measure of the distance between a number and 0. Since distances are always positive, the absolute value of a number is also always positive. The absolute value of a number is written as $|x|$.

When solving for the value of a variable inside the absolute value bars, it is important to remember that variable could be either positive or negative. For example, if $|x|=2$, then $x=2$ or $x=-2$ since both 2 and –2 are a distance of 2 from 0.

SAT Smoke and Mirrors
When you're asked to solve an equation involving an absolute value, it is very likely that the correct answer will be the negative result. Why? Because the test writers know that you are less likely to think about the negative result! Another way to avoid mistakes is to do all the math inside the absolute value symbols first, and then make the result positive.

Here's an example:

9

$$|x + 3| = 6$$
$$|y - 2| = 7$$

For the equations shown above, which of the
following is a possible value of $x - y$?

A) −14

B) −4

C) −2

D) 14

Here's How to Crack It

To solve the first equation, set $x + 3 = 6$ and set $x + 3 = -6$. If $x + 3 = -6$, then the
absolute value would still be 6. So, x can be either 3 or −9. Now, do the same thing
to solve for y. Either $y = 9$ or $y = -5$.

To get the credited answer, you need to try the different combinations. One
combination is $x = -9$ and $y = -5$. So, $x - y = -9 - (-5) = -4$, which is (B).

Algebra Drill 1: No Calculator Section

Work these questions without your calculator using the skills you've learned so far. Answers and explanations can be found on page 238.

Answers and explanations can be found on page 238.

5

$$y = 3x - 1$$

$$\frac{1}{2}y + x = 1$$

In the system of equations above, if (x, y) is the solution to the system, what is the value of $\dfrac{x}{y}$?

A) $\dfrac{3}{8}$

B) $\dfrac{2}{5}$

C) $\dfrac{3}{4}$

D) $\dfrac{4}{3}$

8

For the equation $\sqrt{mx - 5} = x + 3$, the value of m is –3. What is the solution set for the equation?

A) $\{-3, 3\}$

B) $\{-2\}$

C) $\{-2, -7\}$

D) $\{3, 6\}$

11

If $i = \sqrt{-1}$, what is the product of $(4 + 7i)$ and $\left(\dfrac{1}{2} - 2i\right)$?

A) $16 - \dfrac{9}{2}i$

B) $14 + \dfrac{9}{2}i$

C) $2 - 8i - 14i^2$

D) $i\left(8 + \dfrac{9}{2}\right)$

$$rx^2 = \frac{1}{s}x + 3$$

A quadratic equation is provided above, where r and s are constants. What are the solutions for x ?

A) $x = \dfrac{1}{2sr} \pm \dfrac{\sqrt{\dfrac{1}{s^2} + 12r}}{2r}$

B) $x = \dfrac{1}{2sr} \pm \dfrac{\sqrt{-\dfrac{1}{s^2} - 12r}}{2sr}$

C) $x = \dfrac{s}{2r} \pm \dfrac{\sqrt{\dfrac{1}{s^2} - 12r}}{2r}$

D) $x = \dfrac{s}{2r} \pm \dfrac{\sqrt{s^2 - 12sr}}{2sr}$

Algebra Drill 2: Calculator-Permitted Section

Work these questions using your calculator as needed and applying the skills you've learned so far. Answers and explanations can be found on page 240.

4

If $x + 6 > 0$ and $1 - 2x > -1$, then x could equal each of the following EXCEPT

A) –6

B) –4

C) 0

D) $\dfrac{1}{2}$

7

If $\dfrac{2x}{x^2+1} = \dfrac{2}{x+2}$, what is the value of x?

A) $-\dfrac{1}{4}$

B) $\dfrac{1}{2}$

C) 0

D) 2

10

If the product of x and y is 76, and x is twice the square of y, which of the following pairs of equations could be used to determine the values of x and y?

A) $xy = 76$

   $x = 2y^2$

B) $xy = 76$

   $x = (2y)^2$

C) $x + y = 76$

   $x = 4y^2$

D) $xy = 76$

   $x = 2y$

12

If $-6 < -4r + 10 \leq 2$, what is the least possible value of $4r + 3$?

A) 2

B) 5

C) 8

D) 11

How many solutions exist to the equation $|x| = |2x - 1|$?

A) 0

B) 1

C) 2

D) 3

The sum of three numbers, a, b, and c, is 400. One of the numbers, a, is 40 percent less than the sum of b and c. What is the value of $b + c$?

A) 40

B) 60

C) 150

D) 250

CHAPTER DRILL ANSWERS AND EXPLANATIONS

Algebra Drill 1: No Calculator Section

5. **C**   Start by multiplying the second equation by 2 to clear the fractions. The equation becomes $y + 2x = 2$.

    To get it into the same form as the other equations, subtract $2x$ from both sides to get $y = -2x + 2$.

    Set the two x expressions equal to get $3x - 1 = -2x + 2$. Add $2x$ and 1 to both sides, so the equa-

    tion becomes $5x = 3$, then divide by 5 to find that $x = \dfrac{3}{5}$. Plug this value into the $y = 3x - 1$ to get

    $y = 3\left(\dfrac{3}{5}\right) - 1 = \dfrac{9}{5} - 1 = \dfrac{9}{5} - \dfrac{5}{5} = \dfrac{4}{5}$. Finally, find the value of $\dfrac{x}{y}$: $\dfrac{\frac{3}{5}}{\frac{4}{5}} = \dfrac{3}{5} \times \dfrac{5}{4} = \dfrac{3}{4}$, which is (C).

8. **B**   Since the question gives the value of m, the first step is to plug that value into the original equa-

    tion to get $\sqrt{-3x - 5} = x + 3$. Now square both sides of the equation to remove the square root:

    $\left(\sqrt{-3x - 5}\right)^2 = (x + 3)^2$ or $-3x - 5 = x^2 + 6x + 9$. Now combine like terms. If you combine the

    terms on the right side of the equation, you can avoid having a negative x^2 term. The equation

    becomes $0 = x^2 + 9x + 14$. Factor the equation to find the roots: $0 = (x + 2)(x + 7)$. The possible

    solutions to the quadratic are -2 and -7. Don't forget to plug these numbers back into the original

    equation to check for extraneous solutions. Begin by checking $x = -2$. When you do this, you get

    $\sqrt{(-3)(-2) - 5} = (-2) + 3$, or $\sqrt{6 - 5} = 1$, or $\sqrt{1} = 1$, which is true. Now, check $x = -7$. Set it up

    as $\sqrt{(-3)(-7) - 5} = (-7) + 3$, and start simplifying to get $\sqrt{21 - 5} = -4$. You can technically stop

    simplifying here, as there is a negative number on the right-hand side of the equal sign. Remember,

    when taking a square root with a radical provided, it will yield the positive root only. So -7 cannot

    be part of the solution set. Be very careful of trap answer (C), and choose (B).

11. **A**   Use FOIL to multiply the two binomials together. The expression becomes $4\left(\dfrac{1}{2}\right) - 8i + 7i\left(\dfrac{1}{2}\right)$

    $- 14i^2$. Simplify the result by multiplying through where you can to get $2 - 8i + \dfrac{7}{2}i - 14i^2$. To

    combine the i terms, multiply 8 by $\dfrac{2}{2}$ to get $\dfrac{16}{2}$. Now the expression is $2 - \dfrac{16}{2}i + \dfrac{7}{2}i - 14i^2$,

    which can be further simplified to $2 - \dfrac{9}{2}i - 14i^2$. Substitute -1 for i^2 and combine like terms:

    $2 - \dfrac{9}{2}i + 14 = 16 - \dfrac{9}{2}i$, which is (A).

14.   **A**   The first step to answering this question is to get the equation into the standard form of a qua-

dratic equation by moving all the terms to the left or right side of the equation and setting it

equal to zero, like this: $rx^2 - \dfrac{1}{s}x - 3 = 0$. Now that you have the equation in standard form, you

can begin to solve for the roots. Since you are given variables instead of numbers, factoring this

quadratic would require higher-level math, if it were even possible. You may have noticed the

familiar form of the answer choices. They are in a form similar to the quadratic equation. Re-

member that a quadratic in standard form is represented by the equation $ax^2 + bx + c = 0$, and the

quadratic formula is $x = \dfrac{-b \pm \sqrt{b^2 - 4ac}}{2a}$. In this equation, $a = r$, $b = -\dfrac{1}{s}$, and $c = -3$. Therefore,

$x = \dfrac{\dfrac{1}{s} \pm \sqrt{\left(-\dfrac{1}{s}\right)^2 - 4r(-3)}}{2r} = \dfrac{\dfrac{1}{s} \pm \sqrt{\dfrac{1}{s^2} + 12r}}{2r}$. This exact format is not present in the answer choices,

but the root part only matches the one in (A), so that is likely the answer. You will have to do a

little more manipulation before you can get the equations to match exactly. The fractions need to

be split up, so rewrite the equation as $x = \dfrac{\dfrac{1}{s}}{2r} \pm \dfrac{\sqrt{\dfrac{1}{s^2} + 12r}}{2r}$ or $x = \dfrac{1}{2sr} \pm \dfrac{\sqrt{\dfrac{1}{s^2} + 12r}}{2r}$.

Algebra Drill 2: Calculator-Permitted Section

4. **A** Solve the first inequality by subtracting 6 from each side so that $x > -6$. You are looking for values that won't work for x, and x cannot equal -6. Therefore, the answer must be (A). Just to be sure, solve the next inequality by subtracting 1 from each side to get $-2x > -2$. Divide by -2, remembering to switch the sign because you are dividing by a negative number, to get $x < 1$. The values in (B), (C), and (D) fit this requirement as well, so they are values for x and not the correct answer.

7. **B** To solve this equation, use cross multiplication to get $(2x)(x + 2) = (x^2 + 1)(2)$. Expand the equation to get $2x^2 + 4x = 2x^2 + 2$. Once you combine like terms, the result is $2x^2 - 2x^2 + 4x = 2$ or $4x = 2$. Solve for x by dividing both sides by 4 to get $x = \dfrac{1}{2}$, which is (B).

10. **A** Translate each statement, piece by piece. The first part tells us that "the product of x and y is 76." Since *product* means multiplication, the first equation must be $xy = 76$, so you can eliminate (C). The second part says that "x is twice the square of y," which translates to $x = 2y^2$, so eliminate (B) and (D), and (A) is the only choice left. Notice that only the y needs to be squared, which is why (B) is wrong. The second equation for (B) would be written as "the square of twice y," which is not what the problem states.

12. **D** Notice that this question is asking for an expression instead of a variable, so manipulate the inequality to so that you get $4r + 3$ in the inequality. Treat each side of the inequality separately to avoid confusion. Starting with the $-6 < -4r + 10$ part, multiply both sides of the inequality by -1, remembering to switch the sign, to get $6 > 4r - 10$. Add 13 to each side to get $19 > 4r + 3$. Then solve the right side of the inequality. Again, multiply both sides of the inequality by -1, switching the sign to get $4r - 10 \geq -2$. Now add 13 to each side of the equation: $4r + 3 \geq 11$. Finally, combine the equations to get the range for $4r + 3$. Since the question asks for the least possible value of the expression, 11, (D), is the correct answer to the question. If you see the answer before the last step above, you don't need to combine the equations.

16. **C** If $|x| = |2x - 1|$, either $x = 2x - 1$ or $-x = 2x - 1$. The solutions to these equations are 1 and $\dfrac{1}{3}$, respectively. However, the only thing you need to recognize is that the equation has two different solutions to establish that the correct answer is (C).

25. **D** This is a system of equations question in disguise. First, locate a piece of information in this question that you can work with. "The sum of three numbers, *a, b,* and *c,* is 400," seems very straightforward. Write the equation $a + b + c = 400$. Now the question tells you that "one of the numbers, *a,* is 40 percent less than the sum of *b* and *c.*" Translate this piece by piece to get $a = (1 - 0.4)(b + c)$, or $a = 0.6(b + c)$. Distribute the 0.6 to get $a = 0.6b + 0.6c$. Arrange these variables so they line up with those in the first equation as $a - 0.6b - 0.6c = 0$. To solve for $b + c$, stack the equations and multiply the second equation by –1:

$$a + b + c = 400$$
$$-1(a - 0.6b - 0.6c) = 0(-1)$$

Now solve:

$$a + b + c = 400$$
$$\underline{-a + 0.6b + 0.6c = 0}$$
$$1.6b + 1.6c = 400$$

Simplify by dividing both sides by 1.6 to get $b + c = 250$. The correct answer is (D).

Summary

- Don't "solve for x" or "solve for y" unless you absolutely have to. (Don't worry; your math teacher won't find out.) Instead, look for direct solutions to SAT problems. ETS rarely uses problems that necessarily require time-consuming computations or endless fiddling with big numbers. There's almost always a trick—if you can spot it.

- If a problem contains an expression that can be factored, factor it. If it contains an expression that already has been factored, unfactor it.

- To solve simultaneous equations, simply add or subtract the equations. If you don't have the answer, look for multiples of your solutions. When the simultaneous equation question asks for a single variable and addition and subtraction don't work, try to make something disappear. Multiply the equations to make the coefficient(s) of the variable(s) you don't want go to zero when the equations are added or subtracted.

- Some SAT problems require algebraic manipulation. Use tricks when you can, but if you have to manipulate the equation, take your time and work carefully to avoid unnecessary mistakes. You don't get partial credit on the SAT for getting the problem mostly correct.

- When working with inequalities don't forget to flip the sign when you multiply and divide by negative numbers.

- When working with inequalities over a range of values, treat each side of the inequality as a separate problem. Then combine the problems in a logical order, making sure the "arrows" are pointing to the correct numbers.

- When writing a system of equations, start with the most straightforward piece of information. You can also use the equations in the answer choices to help you narrow down the possibilities for your equations. Eliminate any answers in which an equation doesn't match your equation.

- When a question asks for an extraneous solution, first solve your equation, and then plug the answers back into the equation. If the equation is not true when solved with the solution, then that solution is extraneous.

o   When solving quadratic equations, you may need to FOIL or factor to get the equation into the easiest form for the question task. Don't forget about the common equations that ETS uses when writing questions about quadratics.

o   To solve for the roots of a quadratic equation, set it equal to zero by moving all the terms to the left side of the equation, or use the quadratic formula:

$$x = \frac{-b \pm \sqrt{b^2 - 4ac}}{2a}$$

When solving for the sum or product of the roots, you can also use these formulas:

sum of the roots: $-\dfrac{b}{a}$

product of the roots: $\dfrac{c}{a}$

o   The imaginary number $i = \sqrt{-1}$, and there is a repeating pattern when you raise i to a power: i, -1, $-i$, 1. When doing algebra with i, treat it as a variable, unless you are able to substitute -1 for i^2 when appropriate.

o   A complex number is a number with a real and an imaginary component joined by addition or subtraction. In order to rationalize a complex number, you need to multiply it by its conjugate, or the same complex number with the addition or subtraction sign switched to the opposite sign.

o   The absolute value of a number is its distance from zero; distances are always positive. When working inside the ||, remember to consider both the positive and the negative values of the expression. Also remember that | | work like ( ); you need to complete all the operations inside the | | before you can make the value positive.

Chapter 13
Other Algebra
Strategies

Now that you're familiar with the basics of algebra, it's time to learn how to avoid using algebra on the SAT. Yes, you read that correctly. Algebra problems on the SAT are filled with traps carefully laid by the test writers, so you need to know how to work around them. This chapter gives you the strategies you need to turn tricky algebra problems into simple arithmetic.

PRINCETON REVIEW ALGEBRA, OR HOW TO AVOID ALGEBRA ON THE SAT

Now that you've reviewed some basic algebra, it's time for some Princeton Review algebra. At The Princeton Review, we like to avoid algebra whenever possible, and we're going to show you how to avoid doing algebra on the SAT. Now, before you start crying and complaining that you love algebra and couldn't possibly give it up, just take a second to hear us out. We have nothing against algebra—it's very helpful when solving problems, and it impresses your friends—but on the SAT, using algebra can actually hurt your score. And we don't want that.

We know it's difficult to come to terms with this. But if you use algebra on the SAT, you're doing exactly what the test writers want you to do. You see, when the test writers design the problems on the SAT, they expect the students to use algebra to solve them. Many SAT problems have built-in traps meant to take advantage of common mistakes that students make when using algebra. But if you don't use algebra, there's no way you can fall into those traps.

Plus, when you avoid algebra, you add one other powerful tool to your tool belt: If you are on Section 4, you can use your calculator! Even if you have a super-fancy calculator that plays games and doubles as a global positioning system, chances are it doesn't do algebra. Arithmetic, on the other hand, is easy for your calculator. It's why calculators were invented. Our goal, then, is to turn all the algebra on the SAT into arithmetic. We do that using something we call Plugging In.

PLUGGING IN THE ANSWERS (PITA)

Algebra uses letters to stand for numbers. You don't go to the grocery store to buy x eggs or y gallons of milk. Most people think about math in terms of numbers, not letters that stand for numbers.

You should think in terms of numbers on the SAT as much as possible. On many SAT algebra problems, even very difficult ones, you will be able to find ETS's answer without using any algebra at all. You will do this by working backward from the answer choices instead of trying to solve the problem using your standard math-class methods.

Plugging In The Answers is a technique for solving word problems in which the answer choices are all numbers. Using this powerful technique can solve many algebra problems on the SAT simply and quickly.

In algebra class at school, you solve word problems by using equations. Then, you check your solution by plugging in your answer to see if it works. Why not skip the equations entirely by simply checking the four possible solutions ETS offers on the multiple-choice questions? One of these must be the correct answer. You don't have to do any algebra, you will seldom have to try more than two choices, and you will never have to try all four. Note that you can use this technique only for questions that ask for a specific amount.

Here's an example:

9

Zoë won the raffle at a fair. She will receive the prize money in 5 monthly payments. If each payment is half as much as the previous month's payment and the total of the payments is $496, what is the amount of the first payment?

A) $256

B) $96

C) $84

D) $16

Here's How to Crack It
ETS would like you to go through all of the effort of setting up this equation:

$$p + \frac{1}{2}p + \frac{1}{4}p + \frac{1}{8}p + \frac{1}{16}p = 496$$

Then, of course, they want you to solve the equation. But, look at all those fractions! There are plenty of opportunities to make a mistake and you can bet that ETS has figured most of them out so they can have a trap answer waiting. So, let's work with the answers instead.

To work with the answer choices, first you need to know what they represent so that you can label them. In this case, the question asks for the first payment, so write something like "first payment" over the answers.

Now, it's time to start working the steps of the problem. But first, notice that the answer choices are in numerically descending order. ETS likes to keep their problems organized so they will always put the answers in order. You can use that to your advantage by starting with one of the middle answer choices. Let's try (C).

Grab (C) and ask yourself, "If the first payment is $84, what's the next thing I can figure out?" In this case, you could figure out the second payment.

Representation
Make sure you know what the numbers in the answer choices represent. Be sure to label them!

So, make a chart and write down 42 (half of 84) next to the 84. Keep doing that to find the values of the third, fourth, and fifth payments. When you have worked all the steps, your problem should look like this:

9

Zoë won the raffle at a fair. She will receive the prize money in 5 monthly payments. If each payment is half as much as the previous month's payment and the total of the payments is $496, what is the amount of the first payment?

	1st PMT	2nd PMT	3rd PMT	4th PMT	5th PMT
(A)	$256				
(B)	$96				
(C)	$84	42	21	10.50	5.25
(D)	$16				

You need to determine if that was the correct answer. The problem says that the total is supposed to be $496, so add up the payments: 84 + 42 + 21 + 10.50 + 5.25 = 162.75, which is much smaller than 496. So, cross off (C) and (D).

Now, all you need to do is try (B). If (B) works, then you're done. And, if (B) doesn't work, you're still done because the answer must be (A). That's putting your POE to good use! If the first payment is $96, then the payments are 96 + 48 + 24 + 12 + 6 = 186, which is still too small. That means the answer must be (A), and you don't really need to check it.

Here are the steps for solving a problem using the PITA approach:

> To solve a problem by Plugging In The Answers:
>
> 1. Label the answer choices.
> 2. Starting with one of the middle answer choices, work the steps of the problem. Be sure to write down a label for each new step.
> 3. Look for something in the problem that tells you what must happen for the answer to be correct.
> 4. When you find the correct answer, STOP.

6

$$2x + y = 6$$
$$7x + 2y = 27$$

The system of equations above is satisfied by which of the following ordered pairs (x, y) ?

A) $(-5, 4)$

B) $(4, -2)$

C) $(5, 4)$

D) $(5, -4)$

Which Way?
Sometimes, it's hard to tell if you need a larger number or a smaller number if the first answer you tried didn't work. Don't fret. Just pick a direction and go! Spend your time trying answers rather than worrying about going in the wrong direction.

Here's How to Crack It

When you feel the urge to do a whole lot of algebra, it is a good time to check whether it would be possible to just plug in the answers instead. In this case, trying your answer choices will be not only effective but also incredibly fast.

It doesn't seem like we will be able to tell whether to move up or down this time, as the ordered pairs don't really have an ascending or descending order, but let's start in the middle anyway. Even if you end up trying all four, you will be saving time by plugging in the answers instead of solving.

Starting with (B) gives you 4 for x and -2 for y. Try that out in the first equation: $2(4) + (-2) = 6$. That matches the first equation, so this is a possibility. Let's try it out in the second equation: $7(4) + 2(-2) = 24$. That does not match the second equation, so you can eliminate (B).

Let's try out (C) next. If $x = 5$ and $y = 4$, then $2(5) + 4 = 14$, and you wanted it to be 6, so you can eliminate this answer choice, too.

Let's move on to (D). That would give you 2(5) + (–4) = 6. So far so good! Let's try the second equation to see if this choice satisfies both: 7(5) + 2(–4) = 27. Since (D) satisfies both equations, this is your answer!

———————◯———————

You may recall that we covered questions like this in the last chapter. It is important to know how to solve these, in case a question like this comes up in the Grid-In part of a Math section. When you have answers available to you, though, don't be afraid to use them!

One last thing about PITA: Here's how you spot that you should use this approach to solve the problem.

> Three ways to know that it's time for PITA:
>
> 1. There are numbers in the answer choices.
> 2. The question asks for a specific amount such as "what was the first payment."
> 3. You have the urge to write an algebraic equation to solve the problem.

Plugging In the Answers: Advanced Principles

Plugging In the Answers works the same way on difficult problems as it does on easy and medium ones. You just have to watch your step and make certain you don't make any careless mistakes.

Here's one example:

———————◯———————

12

A bakery sold exactly 85% of the cupcakes it baked on Tuesday. Which of the following could be the total number of cupcakes baked on Tuesday?

A) 150

B) 145

C) 140

D) 130

Here's How to Crack It

Is your first reaction that there isn't nearly enough information here to start on this problem? That makes it a great opportunity to plug in the answers! Let's start with one of the middle answer choices and test it out. Sometimes, even if you can't see how a problem works ahead of time, it starts to make a lot more sense once you plug real numbers into it.

Choice (B) is 145, but 145 what? Read the question very carefully. The question asks for the total number of cupcakes baked on Tuesday, so label the column of answer choices "Total."

Next, work your way through the problem. If 145 is the total number of cupcakes baked on Tuesday, the number the bakery sold on Tuesday is 85% of 145, or 123.25. Have you ever bought 0.25 cupcakes at a bakery? It would be really weird for a bakery to sell fractions of cupcakes, so this answer could not be the total number baked on Tuesday.

In this particular question, it is hard to tell whether you should try bigger or smaller numbers next, but you have learned two things from your first attempt: You can get rid of (B), and the correct answer will be the one that gives you a whole number of cupcakes. Instead of spending time trying to predict which direction to go for the answer, let's just get to work on the other answer choices.

We'll try (C) next. If the bakery baked 140 cupcakes on Tuesday, they sold 85% of 140, or 119. Is there anything wrong with selling 119 cupcakes? No! Since the bakery sold only whole cupcakes, you can select (C).

———————◯———————

Here's another example:

———————◯———————

7

For what value of x is $|2x + 3| + 5 = 0$?

A) -4

B) 0

C) 4

D) There is no such value of x.

Here's How to Crack It

Although we covered it in the last chapter, solving algebraically on an absolute value question can be treacherous: There are so many ways to go wrong with those signs! Luckily, this absolute value question comes complete with answer choices, so we can simply plug in the answers to get a solution.

Let's start with (C). When you put 4 in for x, you get $|2(4) + 3| + 5 = 0$, or $16 = 0$. This is clearly not true, so cross off (C) and move on to (B). If x is 0, then the original equation says $|2(0) + 3| + 5 = 0$ or $8 = 0$, so you can eliminate (B), too. Let's try (A). $|2(-4) + 3| + 5 = 0$ could be rewritten as $|-8 + 3| + 5 = 0$, or $|-5| + 5 = 0$. As long as you remember that the absolute value of a number is always positive, it is clear that this gives you $5 + 5 = 0$. Since this is also clearly untrue, eliminate (A), and choose (D). Apparently, there is no such value of x!

Solving Rational Equations

A rational equation is basically an equation in which one (or more) of the terms is a fractional one. Rational equations look scary, but there are very simple ways of solving them. One way is to factor out like terms and then cancel. All in all, the test writers can't get too messy here, so they will keep the math nice and tidy.

Try one:

18

If $\dfrac{x^2 + 6x - 16}{x^2 - 5x + 6} = \dfrac{-6}{x^2 - 2x - 3}$, then which of the following could be a value of x ?

A) −7

B) −5

C) 0

D) 6

Here's How to Crack It

Hate factoring? PITA! Start with (C) and plug in 0 for x. Does everything work out? In this case, it doesn't. Keep trying other answer choices until you find one that works. Choice (A) does, so that's the correct answer choice. See? These are all bark and no bite.

Solving Radical Equations

We covered this topic in the previous chapter, but here's another example of solving radical equations using the PITA approach.

> **11**
>
> $$\sqrt{2x-k} = 3-x$$
>
> If $k = 3$, what is the solution set of the equation above?
>
> A) $\{-2\}$
>
> B) $\{2\}$
>
> C) $\{2, 6\}$
>
> D) $\{6\}$

Here's How to Crack It

In the last chapter, we showed you how to solve these—a necessary skill if there are no answer choices to plug In. Here, PITA is definitely the way to go. Start by plugging in the value given for k, which is 3. The equation becomes $\sqrt{2x-3} = 3-x$.

Now pick a value for x from the answer choices and plug it into the equation to see if it works. Rather than starting with a specific answer choice, start with a number that appears more than once in the answers, such as $x = 2$. The equation becomes $\sqrt{2(2)-3} = 3-2$, then $\sqrt{4-3} = 1$, and $1 = 1$. That's true, so eliminate (A) and (D), which don't include 2.

Try it again with $x = 6$ to see if the correct answer is (B) or (C). You get $\sqrt{2(6)-3} = 3-6$ or $\sqrt{12-3} = -3$. This doesn't work, so eliminate (C) and choose (B).

PLUGGING IN YOUR OWN NUMBERS

Plugging In the Answers enables you to find the answer to problems whose answer choices are all numbers. What about problems that have answer choices containing variables? On these problems, you will usually be able to find the answer by Plugging In your own numbers.

Plugging In is easy. It has three steps:

1. Pick numbers for the variables in the problem.
2. Use your numbers to find an answer to the problem. Circle your answer.
3. Plug your numbers from Step 1 into the answer choices to see which choice equals the answer you found in Step 2.

The Basics of Plugging In Your Own Numbers

This sort of Plugging In is simple to understand. Here's an example:

13

Which of the following is equivalent to the expression $\dfrac{7x-4}{x+9}$?

A) $7 - \dfrac{4}{x+9}$

B) $7 - \dfrac{67}{x+9}$

C) $7 - \dfrac{4}{9}$

D) $\dfrac{7-4}{9}$

Here's How to Crack It

First, pick a number for x. Pick something easy to work with, like 2. In your test booklet, write $x = 2$, so you won't forget. If $x = 2$, then $7x - 4 = 10$, and $x + 9 = 11$.

So, when $x = 2$, the expression in the problem equals $\dfrac{10}{11}$. Circle it! That is your target answer. When you find the answer choice that also gives you $\dfrac{10}{11}$ when you plug in $x = 2$, you will know you have found an equivalent expression.

Start with the easier answer choices: (C) and (D). For (C), does $7 - \dfrac{4}{9} = \dfrac{10}{11}$? No! Eliminate it and move on to (D): $\dfrac{7-4}{9}$ also does not equal your target answer, so it cannot be an equivalent expression.

Let's try (B): When you put in 2 for x, you get $7 - \dfrac{67}{2+9} = 7 - \dfrac{67}{11} = \dfrac{77}{11} - \dfrac{67}{11} = \dfrac{10}{11}$. This is the number that you are looking for. Unlike PITA, when you plug in your own numbers, you must check all four answer choices, just in case more than one works. Go ahead and try the last answer just to make sure that you're right. Choice (A) does not give you your target answer, so you know that (B) is the one!

———○———

Here's another example:

———○———

19

During a special sale at a furniture store, Erica bought a floor lamp at a 10% discount. She paid a total of t dollars, which included the discounted price of the floor lamp and a 6% sales tax on the discounted price. In terms of t, what was the original price of the floor lamp?

A) $\dfrac{t}{0.96}$

B) $(0.9)(1.06)\, t$

C) $\dfrac{t}{(0.9)(1.06)}$

D) $0.96t$

Get Real
Trying to imagine how numbers behave in the abstract is a waste of time. So, if the problem says that Tina is x years old, why not plug in your own age? That's real enough. You don't have to change your name to Tina.

Here's How to Crack It

This could be a pretty tricky algebra question, but if you read the question carefully and plug in easy numbers, it will be a breeze.

Let's start at the beginning. When Erica bought that floor lamp on sale, what did you really wish you knew? It would be very helpful to start this problem knowing the original price of the floor lamp. So, let's start plugging in there. Plug in something you know how to take a percentage of, say 100. Write down "original = 100" on your scratch paper and move on the next step of the problem. Erica got a 10% discount, so take 10% of the original price. That means she got a $10 discount, and the discounted price of her floor lamp was $90. Write that down and move on to the sales tax. If you read carefully, it is clear that the sales tax is 6% of the discounted price. So, you need to take 6% of the $90 discounted price, or $5.40. To get her total, add the $5.40 of tax to the $90 for the discounted floor lamp, and you get $95.40. This is where the careful reading comes in. The variable t in this problem is supposed to be the total amount she paid, so make sure that you label this on your scratch paper "$t = 95.40."

Next, read the last sentence of the question again, to be sure you know which of the answers is your target answer. The question asks for the original price of the floor lamp, so circle the number you plugged in for the original price. Your target answer is 100.

On to the answer choices! When you put $95.40 in for t in (A), you get 99.375. This is not your target answer, so you can eliminate (A). Choice (B) gives you 91.0116, so that will not work, either. Plugging in $95.40 into (C) yields the target of 100, so hang on to it while you check (D) just in case. When you plug in for (D), you get 91.584. Since that does not match your target, you can eliminate (D) and choose (C)!

Which Numbers?

Although you can plug in any number, you can make your life much easier by plugging in "good" numbers—numbers that are simple to work with or that make the problem easier to manipulate. Picking a small number, such as 2, will usually make finding the answer easier. If the problem asks for a percentage, plug in 100. If the problem has to do with minutes, try 30 or 120.

Except in special cases, you should avoid plugging in 0 and 1; these numbers have weird properties. Using them may allow you to eliminate only one or two choices at a time. You should also avoid plugging in any number that appears in the question or in any of the answer choices. Using those numbers could make more than one answer match your target. If more than one answer choice matches your target, plug in a new number and check those answer choices. You may have to plug in more than once to eliminate all three incorrect answers.

Be Good
"Good" numbers make a problem less confusing by simplifying the arithmetic. This is your chance to make the SAT easier for you.

Many times you'll find that there is an advantage to picking a particular number, even a very large one, because it makes solving the problem more straightforward.

Here's an example.

14

If 60 equally priced downloads cost x dollars, then how much do 9 downloads cost?

A) $\dfrac{20}{3x}$

B) $\dfrac{20x}{3}$

C) $60x + 9$

D) $\dfrac{3x}{20}$

Here's How to Crack It

Should you plug in 2 for x? You could, but plugging in 120 would make the problem easier. After all, if 60 downloads cost a total of $120, then each download costs $2. Write $x = 120$ in your test booklet.

If each download costs $2, then 9 downloads cost $18. Write an 18 in your test booklet and circle it. You are looking for the answer choice that works out to 18 when you plug in $120 for x. Let's try each choice:

A) $\dfrac{20}{3(120)} \neq 18$

B) $\dfrac{20(120)}{3} \neq 18$

C) $60(120) + 9 \neq 18$

D) $\dfrac{3(120)}{20} = 18$ Here's your answer.

Let's try another example.

20

A watch loses x minutes every y hours. At this rate, how many <u>hours</u> will the watch lose in one week?

A) $7xy$

B) $\dfrac{5y}{2x}$

C) $\dfrac{14y}{5x}$

D) $\dfrac{14x}{5y}$

Here's How to Crack It

This is an extremely difficult problem for students who try to solve it using math-class algebra. You'll be able to find the answer easily, though, if you plug in carefully.

What numbers should you plug in? As always, you can plug in anything. However, if you think just a little bit before choosing the numbers, you can make the problem easier to understand. There are three units of time—minutes, hours, and weeks—and that's a big part of the reason this problem is hard to understand. If you choose units of time that are easy to think about, you'll make the problem easier to handle.

Start by choosing a value for x, which represents the number of minutes that the watch loses. You might be tempted to choose $x = 60$ and that would make the math pretty easy. However, it's usually not a good idea to choose a conversion factor such as 60, the conversion factor between minutes and hours, when plugging in. When dealing with time, 30 is usually a safer choice. So, write down $x = 30$.

Next, you need a number for y, which represents the number of hours. Again, you might be tempted to use $y = 24$ but that's the conversion factor between hours and days. So, $y = 12$ is a safer choice. Write down $y = 12$.

Now, it's time to solve the problem to come up with a target. If the watch loses 30 minutes every 12 hours, then it loses 60 minutes every 24 hours. Put another way, the watch loses an hour each day. In one week, the watch will lose 7 hours. That's your target so be sure to circle it.

Now, you just need to check the answer choices to see which one gives you 7 when $x = 30$ and $y = 12$.

A) $7xy = 7(30)(12) =$ Something too big! Cross it off.

B) $\dfrac{5y}{2x} = \dfrac{5(12)}{2(30)} = \dfrac{60}{60} = 1$. Also wrong.

C) $\dfrac{14y}{5x} = \dfrac{14(12)}{5(30)} = \dfrac{168}{150} = \dfrac{28}{25}$ Cross it off.

D) $\dfrac{14x}{5y} = \dfrac{14(30)}{5(12)} = \dfrac{420}{60} = 7$. Choose it!

Inequalities

Plugging In works on problems containing inequalities, but you will have to follow some different rules. Plugging in one number is often not enough; let's look at an example where this is the case.

6

Mammoth Printing Company charges a fee of $28 to print an oversized poster, and $7 for each color of ink used in the poster. Colossal Printing charges a fee of $34 to print an oversized poster and $5.50 for each color of ink used. If x represents the number of colors of ink used to print a poster, what are all the values of x for which Mammoth Printing Company would charge more to print the poster than Colossal Printing?

A) $x < 4$

B) $2 \le x \le 4$

C) $4 \le x \le 7$

D) $x > 4$

Here's How to Crack It

Since you are looking for an amount that would make the Mammoth Printing Company's price *greater than* Colossal Printing's price, you have an inequality.

Plugging In on an inequality question means selecting a value for x that answers the question, and then comparing it to the inequalities in the answer choices. Remember, you may have to try more than one number with inequality questions, since the number you try first may satisfy the inequality in more than one answer choice!

Let's start out by trying something small, like $x = 2$. Since x is the number of colors of ink used, Mammoth Printing Company would charge $28 to print the poster, plus $7 for each of the 2 colors, for a total of $42. Colossal Printing would charge $34 to print the poster, plus $5.50 for each of the 2 colors, or $45 total. That means that when $x = 2$, Mammoth Printing Company would charge less than Colossal Printing, and 2 is not a number that works as a solution to this problem.

Let's try something bigger, say $x = 5$. If the poster had 5 colors, Mammoth Printing Company would charge $28 to print the poster, plus $7 for each of the 5 colors, for a total of $63. Colossal Printing would charge $34 to print the poster, plus $5.50 for each of the 5 colors, or $61.50 total. That means that when $x = 5$, the price Mammoth charges would be more than Colossal's price, so this is a possible value for x.

Once you have a value for x that satisfies the question, it's time to move to the answer choices. You should eliminate (A) and (B), because $x = 5$ does not satisfy either of those inequalities. Choices (C) and (D) are satisfied when $x = 5$, so they are still possible.

Next, you need to find a number that will satisfy the inequality in one of the remaining answer choices but not the other, so you can determine whether (C) or (D) is your final answer. Looking at our answer choices, we can see that we will have to think about plugging in something that will eliminate one answer choice but not the other. Let's try out $x = 4$, because it satisfies (C) but not (D). Mammoth Printing Company would charge $56 for a 4-color poster.

$$\$28 + \$7(4) = \$56$$

Colossal Printing would also charge $56 for a 4-color poster.

$$\$34 + \$5.50(4) = \$56$$

Since Mammoth would not charge more to print the poster than Colossal, you can eliminate (C) and choose (D).

Using different integers got you down to one answer choice on that question. Sometimes, to find the answer, you may have to plug in several numbers, including weird numbers like -1, 0, 1, $\frac{1}{2}$, and $-\frac{1}{2}$.

The five numbers just mentioned all have special properties. Negatives, fractions, 0, and 1 all behave in peculiar ways when, for example, they are squared. Don't forget about them!

Plugging In: Advanced Principles

If there are variables in the answer choices, you should definitely consider Plugging In. However, sometimes a question will be a Plug In question that doesn't have variables in the answer choices. It is, instead, a hidden Plug In question. It will refer to some unknown amount, but never actually give you a number. So, you're going to have to make up your own number.

Here's an example.

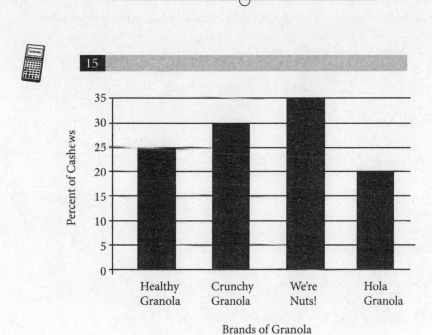

15

Brands of Granola

Vik is deciding which brand of granola to buy. He prefers granola with a lot of cashews, so he has made a chart (above) showing the cashew content, as a percentage of the total weight of the granola, of each of the 4 leading brands of bulk granola. If Healthy Granola costs $4 a pound, Crunchy Granola costs $5.40 a pound, We're Nuts! Granola costs $7.00 a pound, and Hola Granola costs $5 a pound, which brand of granola would offer Vik the greatest amount of cashews per dollar?

A) Healthy Granola

B) Crunchy Granola

C) We're Nuts!

D) Hola Granola

Here's How to Crack It

This is one of those questions that has so much information in it, it is almost impossible to know where to start. It doesn't help that all the amounts are percentages, and you don't even know the total amount of granola Vik is going to buy. That feeling that you wish you had some real amount to start with tells you that this is a great opportunity to plug in, even though there are no variables in the answer choices. This is a Hidden Plug In.

You have already realized that the most helpful thing to know here would be how much granola Vik will buy, so start by plugging in for that amount. The easiest number to plug in when you will be using percentages is 100, so even though it is a pretty ridiculous amount of granola for one guy, let's find out what happens if Vik buys 100 pounds of granola. Write down "total = 100 pounds" in your test booklet, and start to work the problem one piece at a time.

Once you have a 100 pound total, it is relatively simple to come up with the amount of cashews in each granola. Keep track of them in your test booklet:

100 lbs Healthy Granola = 25 lbs of cashews

100 lbs Crunchy Granola = 30 lbs of cashews

100 lbs We're Nuts! = 35 lbs of cashews

100 lbs Hola Granola = 20 lbs of cashews

The next piece is price. Add the price of 100 pounds of each granola to your scratch paper:

100 lbs Healthy Granola = 25 lbs of cashews = $400 total

100 lbs Crunchy Granola = 30 lbs of cashews = $540 total

100 lbs We're Nuts! = 35 lbs of cashews = $700 total

100 lbs Hola Granola = 20 lbs of cashews = $500 total

With this information, you can start to figure out how much Vik is paying per pound of cashews.

Healthy Granola contains 25 lbs of cashews for $400. If you do the math, that is $400 ÷ 25 lbs cashews or $16 per pound of cashews. Crunchy Granola costs $540 for 30 lbs of cashews or $540 ÷ 30 lbs cashews = $18/lb cashews. Since this is more expensive, you can eliminate (B). This is not how Vik is going to get the greatest amount of cashews per dollar. We're Nuts!, besides having a great name, also has a really high percentage of cashews. You might think that would be Vik's best buy, but when you do the math, $700 for 35 lbs of cashews is $700 ÷ 35 lbs cashews or $20/lb cashews. This is less cashew per dollar than (A), so eliminate (C). Hola Granola costs $500 for 20 lbs of cashews, and $500 ÷ 20 lbs cashews is going to come out to a whopping $25/lb cashews. That is definitely not the best deal on cashews, so eliminate (D).

Apparently, nothing is going to beat Healthy Granola in terms of the cashew content per dollar! You can choose (A), and leave Vik to figure out what he is going to do with all that granola.

———————○———————

Meaning in Context

Some questions, instead of asking you to come up with an equation, just want you to recognize what a part of the equation stands for. It sounds like a simple enough task, but when you look at the equation, they have made it really hard to see what is going on. For this reason, Meaning in Context questions are a great opportunity to plug in real numbers and start to see how the equation really works!

First things first, though, you want to think about your POOD: Does this question fit into your pacing goals? It might take a bit of legwork to get an answer, and you may need that time to go collect points on easier, quicker questions.

If this question does fit into your pacing plan, you should read carefully, label everything you can in the equation, and POE to get rid of any answer choices that are clearly on the wrong track. Then, it's time to plug some of your own numbers in to see what is going on in there.

Here's an example:

———————○———————

7

$$n = 1,273 - 4p$$

The equation above was used by the cafeteria in a large public high school to model the relationship between the number of slices of pizza, n, sold daily and the price of a slice of pizza, p, in dollars. What does the number 4 represent in this equation?

A) For every $4 the price of pizza decreases, the cafeteria sells 1 more slice of pizza.

B) For every dollar the price of pizza decreases, the cafeteria sells 4 more slices of pizza.

C) For every $4 the price of pizza increases, the cafeteria sells 1 more slice of pizza.

D) For every dollar the price of pizza increases, the cafeteria sells 4 more slices of pizza.

Here's How to Crack It

First, read the question very carefully, and use your pencil to label the variables. You know that p is the price of pizza, and n is the number of slices, so you can add that information to the equation. If you can, eliminate answer choices that don't make sense. But what if you can't eliminate anything, or you can eliminate only an answer choice or two?

Even with everything labeled, this equation is difficult to decode, so it's time to plug in! Try a few of your own numbers in the equation, and you will get a much better understanding of what is happening.

Let's try it out with $p = 2$. When you put 2 in for p, $n = 1{,}273 - 4(2)$ or $1{,}265$.

So, when $p = 2$, $n = 1{,}265$. In other words, at $2 a slice, the cafeteria sells 1,265 slices.

When $p = 3$, $n = 1{,}261$, so at $3 a slice, the cafeteria sells 1,261 slices.

When $p = 4$, $n = 1{,}257$, so at $4 a slice, the cafeteria sells 1,257 slices.

So now, let's use POE. First of all, is the cafeteria selling more pizza as the price goes up? No, as the price of pizza goes up, the cafeteria sells fewer slices of pizza. That means you can eliminate (C) and (D).

Choice (A) says that for every $4 the price goes down, the cafeteria sells 1 more slice of pizza. Does your plugging in back that up? No. The cafeteria sells 8 more slices of pizza when the price drops from $4 to $2, so (A) is no good.

Now, let's take a look at (B). Does the cafeteria sell 4 more slices of pizza for every dollar the price drops? Yes! Choice (B) is the correct answer.

———————◯———————

Here are the steps for using Plugging In to solve Meaning in Context questions:

Meaning In Context

1. Read the question carefully. Make sure you know which part of the equation you are being asked to identify.
2. Use your pencil to label the parts of the equation you can identify.
3. Eliminate any answer choices that clearly describe the wrong part of the equation, or go against what you have labeled.
4. Plug in! Use your own numbers to start seeing what is happening in the equation.
5. Use POE again, using the information you learned from plugging in real numbers, until you can get it down to one answer choice. Or, get it down to as few choices as you can, and guess.

Let's look at a slightly different one now.

10

$$7x + y = 133$$

Jeffrey has set a monthly budget for purchasing frozen blended mocha drinks from his local SpendBucks coffee shop. The equation above can be used to model the amount of his budget, y, in dollars that remains after buying coffee for x days in a month. What does it mean that (19, 0) is a solution to this equation?

A) Jeffrey starts the month with a budget of $19.

B) Jeffrey spends $19 on coffee every day.

C) It takes 19 days for Jeffrey to drink 133 cups of coffee.

D) It takes 19 days for Jeffrey to run out of money in his budget for purchasing coffee.

Here's How to Crack It

Start by labeling the x and the y in the equation to keep track of what they stand for. Use your pencil to write "days" above the x and "budget" above the y. So $7 \times$ days + budget = 133. Hmm, still not very clear, is it? One way to approach this is to plug in the point. If x = days = 19 when y = budget = 0, then Jeffrey will have no budget left after 19 days. This matches (D).

If you have trouble seeing this, you can use the answer choices to help you plug in. If (A) is true, the budget at the start of the month, when days = 0, is $19. Plug these values into the equation to see if it is true. Is $7 \times 0 + 19 = 133$? Not at all, so eliminate (A). If (B) is true, Jeffrey drinks a lot of coffee! Let's try some numbers and see if it works. For $x = 1$, the equation becomes $7(1) + y = 133$ or $y = 126$, and for $x = 2$, it is $7(2) + y = 133$ or $y = 119$. The difference in y, the budget remaining, is $126 - 119 = 7$, so that's not $19 per day. Eliminate (B) so only (C) and (D) remain. These both have 19 for the number of days, and the point (19, 0) would indicate that 19 is the x value, or days. If you saw that right away—great! That would allow you to skip right to testing (C) and (D).

For (C), you can plug in 19 for days in the equation to get $7 \times 19 +$ budget = 133, or budget = 0. Does that tell you how many cups of coffee Jeffrey drank? You have no information about the cost of a single cup of coffee, so the answer can't be (C). It does tell you, however, that after 19 days, Jeffrey has no budget left, so (D) is not only the one remaining answer, but it is also the correct one!

Algebra Strategies Drill 1: No Calculator Section

Work these algebra questions, without your calculator, using Plugging In or Plugging In the Answers. Answers and explanations can be found on page 269.

5

The length of a certain rectangle is twice the width. If the area of the rectangle is 128, what is the length of the rectangle?

A) 4

B) 8

C) 16

D) $21\frac{1}{3}$

10

If $xy < 0$, which of the following must be true?

I. $x + y = 0$

II. $2y - 2x < 0$

III. $x^2 + y^2 > 0$

A) I only

B) III only

C) I and III

D) II and III

13

If $\dfrac{\sqrt{x}}{2} = 2\sqrt{2}$, what is the value of x ?

A) 4

B) 16

C) $16\sqrt{2}$

D) 32

15

If $y = 3^x$ and x and y are both integers, which of the following is equivalent to $9^x + 3^{x+1}$?

A) y^3

B) $3y + 3$

C) $y(y + 3)$

D) $y^2 + 3$

Algebra Strategies Drill 2: Calculator-Permitted Section

Feel free to use your calculator as needed to apply the Plugging In skills you've learned so far. Answers and explanations can be found on page 269.

8

If Alex can fold 12 napkins in x minutes, how many napkins can he fold in y hours?

A) $\dfrac{720}{xy}$

B) $\dfrac{xy}{720}$

C) $\dfrac{720y}{x}$

D) $\dfrac{720x}{y}$

12

Nails are sold in 8-ounce and 20-ounce boxes. If 50 boxes of nails were sold and the total weight of the nails sold was less than 600 ounces, what is the greatest possible number of 20-ounce boxes that could have been sold?

A) 33

B) 25

C) 17

D) 16

18

If a is 63% of x and c is $\dfrac{3}{8}$ of x, which of the following is the closest equivalent of the ratio of a to c ?

A) 0.236

B) 0.381

C) 0.595

D) 1.680

21

If $c = \dfrac{1}{x} + \dfrac{1}{y}$ and $x > y > 0$, then which of the following is equal to $\dfrac{1}{c}$?

A) $x + y$

B) $x - y$

C) $\dfrac{x + y}{xy}$

D) $\dfrac{xy}{x + y}$

A gas station sells regular gasoline for $2.39 per gallon and premium gasoline for $2.79 per gallon. If the gas station sold a total of 550 gallons of both types of gasoline in one day for a total of $1,344.50, how many gallons of premium gasoline were sold?

A) 25

B) 75

C) 175

D) 475

There are k gallons of gasoline available to fill a tank. After d gallons have been pumped, in terms of k and d, what percent of the gasoline has been pumped?

A) $\dfrac{100d}{k}\%$

B) $\dfrac{k}{100d}\%$

C) $\dfrac{100k}{d}\%$

D) $\dfrac{100(k-d)}{k}\%$

CHAPTER DRILL ANSWERS AND EXPLANATIONS

Algebra Strategies Drill 1: No Calculator Section

5.   **C**   Plug in the answers. If you start with (B), the length is 8, and the width is half that, or 4. Area is length × width. The area of this rectangle is 8 × 4, which is nowhere near 128. Eliminate (A) and (B), as both are too small. Try (C): If the length is 16, the width is 8. So, does 128 = 16 × 8? You could write it all out, since you can't use your calculator, but you can also estimate. 16 × 10 = 160, so 16 × 8 would be about 130. The number in (D) is too large and will give a weird fraction, so (C) is correct. Alternatively, write an equation. The equation is area = w × $2w$. So, 128 = $2w^2$. Divide by 2 to get 64 = w^2. Take the square root of both sides to find w = 8. The length is twice this width, so length = 2 × 8 = 16, and the answer is (C).

10.   **B**   A question with unknown variables indicates a good place to plug in. You need numbers for x and y that will give you a negative product. Try x = 1 and y = –2. If you plug these into the statements in the Roman numerals, you find that (I) is false, but (II) and (III) are true. You can eliminate any answer choice that contains (I). This leaves (B) and (D). Now try different numbers to see if you can eliminate another choice. If you try x = –1 and y = 2, you find that (II) is false and (III) is still true. This leaves you with (B), which is correct.

13.   **D**   Plug in the answers, starting with (B). If x = 16, the left side of the equation is $\frac{\sqrt{16}}{2} = \frac{4}{2} = 2$. Does that equal $2\sqrt{2}$? No—it's too small. Choice (C) is ugly to work with, so try (D) next. If it is too big, (C) is your answer. For (D), x = 32, and the left side of the equation becomes $\frac{\sqrt{32}}{2} = \frac{\sqrt{16 \times 2}}{2} = \frac{4\sqrt{2}}{2} = 2\sqrt{2}$. It's a match, so (D) is correct. You could also solve this algebraically. Multiply both sides by 2 to get $\sqrt{x} = 4\sqrt{2}$. Square both sides to get x = 16 × 2 = 32. Choice (D) is correct.

15.   **C**   We've got variables in the answer choices, which means this is a perfect Plug In problem. Since we can't use calculators, let's make up an easy value for x, such as 2. $9^x + 3^{x+1}$ then becomes $9^2 + 3^{2+1} = 81 + 27 = 108$. We plugged in x = 2, so let's use that to find y: $y = 3^x$, so $y = 3^2 = 9$. Now plug in y = 9 to each answer choice to see which one gives you 108. Choice (C) is $y(y + 3)$, which is 9(12) = 108, which is the correct answer.

Algebra Strategies Drill 2: Calculator-Permitted Section

8. **C** Two variables tells you this is a great place to plug in. Let's pick numbers that make the math easy. You can try $x = 30$ and $y = 2$. So in 2 hours there are 4 periods of 30 minutes each: $12 \times 4 = 48$. Alex can fold 48 napkins in 2 hours. 48 is your target. Plugging into your answer choices gives you (C).

12. **D** This is a perfect question for PITA. The question asks for the greatest possible number of 20-ounce boxes. Start with (B). If there are twenty-five 20-ounce boxes, then there are twenty-five 8-ounce boxes because a total of 50 boxes was purchased. In this case, the twenty-five 20-ounce boxes weigh 500 ounces, and the twenty-five 8-ounce boxes weigh 200 ounces; the total is 700 ounces. This is too big because the question says the total weight was less than 600. If (B) is too big, (A) must also be too big; eliminate both answers. If you try (C), the total weight is 604 ounces, which is still too big. Thus, the answer is (D).

18. **D** Since you are never told what x is, and there is no way to find it, plug in for x. Say that $x = 100$. 63% of 100 is 63, and $\frac{3}{8}$ of 100 is 37.5. The ratio of a to c is $\frac{a}{c}$. So, $\frac{63}{37.5} = 1.68$. To save time, you can Ballpark the answer, since $a > c$ and (D) is the only choice greater than 1.

21. **D** Here's yet another chance to plug in because of the variables in the answer choices. In this case, you have several variables. You should start by plugging in values for x and y, and then work out c. Because $x > y > 0$, let's say $x = 6$ and $y = 3$. Therefore, $c = \frac{1}{6} + \frac{1}{3} = \frac{1}{6} + \frac{2}{6} = \frac{3}{6} = \frac{1}{2}$. The question asks for the value of $\frac{1}{c}$, which is the reciprocal of $\frac{1}{2}$, or 2. This is your target answer. If you plug $x = 6$ and $y = 3$ into all of the answer choices, you'll find that only (D) equals 2.

24. **B** When asked for a specific value, try Plugging In the Answers. Label them as gallons of premium and start with the value in (B). If 75 gallons of premium were sold, the station would make $75(\$2.79) = \$209.25$ for those sales. A total of 550 gallons was sold, so the station would have sold $550 - 75 = 475$ gallons of regular gasoline. The sales for the regular gasoline would be $475(\$2.39) = \$1,135.25$. The total sales for both types of gasoline would be $\$209.25 + \$1,135.25 = \$1,344.50$. That matches the information in the question, so (B) is correct.

25. **A** Variables in the answer choices? Plug in! This is a percent question, so make $k = 100$ and $d = 40$. If 40 out of the 100 gallons have been pumped, that equals 40%. So 40% is your target answer. When you plug $k = 100$ and $d = 40$ into the answers, only (A) gives you 40. Remember, Plugging In can turn a difficult question into a much more straightforward one.

Summary

o   When an algebra question has numbers in the answer choices, plug each of the numbers in the answer choices into the problem until you find one that works.

o   If you start with one of the middle numbers, you may be able to cut your work. The answer choices will be in order, so if your number is too high or too low, you'll know what to eliminate.

o   When the question has variables in the answer choices, you can often plug in your own amounts for the unknowns and do arithmetic instead of algebra.

o   When you plug in, use "good" numbers—ones that are simple to work with and that make the problem easier to manipulate: 2, 5, 10, or 100 are generally easy numbers to use.

o   Plugging In works on problems containing inequalities, but you will have to be careful and follow some different rules. Plugging in one number is often not enough; to find the answer, you may have to plug in several numbers.

o   Not every Plug In question has variables in the answer choices. For some problems, there will be some unknown amount: in that case, try making up a number.

o   Plugging In can also be used on Meaning In Context questions. If a question asks you to identify a part of an equation, plug your own amounts into the equation so you can start to see what is going on.

Chapter 14
Advanced
Arithmetic

Now that we have reviewed some mathematical fundamentals and some algebra, it is time to jump into our
review of the more advanced arithmetic concepts you
will find on the SAT. Many questions on the Math Test
test concepts you learned in junior high school, such as
averages and proportions. Some difficult questions
build on these basic concepts by requiring you to use
charts and data to obtain your numbers or combine
multiple techniques. In this chapter, we will review
the arithmetic concepts you'll need to know for the
SAT and show you how to apply these concepts when
working with charts and data. *All of the questions in this
chapter represent the kinds of questions that appear in the
Calculator section of the test.*

RATIOS AND PROPORTIONS

A Ratio Is a Comparison

Many students get extremely nervous when they are asked to work with ratios. But there's no need to be nervous. A ratio is a comparison between the quantities of ingredients you have in a mixture, be it a class full of people or a bowl of cake batter. Ratios can be written to look like fractions—don't get them confused.

The ratio of x to y can be expressed in the following three ways:

1. $\dfrac{x}{y}$

2. the ratio of x to y

3. $x{:}y$

Part, Part, Whole

Ratios vs. Fractions
Keep in mind that a ratio compares part of something to another part. A fraction compares part of something to the whole thing.

Ratio: $\dfrac{part}{part}$

Fraction: $\dfrac{part}{whole}$

Ratios are a lot like fractions. In fact, anything you can do to a fraction (convert it to a decimal or percentage, reduce it, and so on), you can do to a ratio. The difference is that a fraction gives you a part (the top number) over a whole (the bottom number), while a ratio typically gives you two parts (boys to girls, CDs to cassettes, sugar to flour), and it is your job to come up with the whole. For example, if there is one cup of sugar for every two cups of flour in a recipe, that's three cups of stuff. The ratio of sugar to flour is 1:2. Add the parts to get the whole.

Ratio to Real

If a class contains 3 students and the ratio of boys to girls in that class is 2:1, how many boys and how many girls are there in the class? Of course: There are 2 boys and 1 girl.

Now, suppose a class contains 24 students and the ratio of boys to girls is still 2:1. How many boys and how many girls are there in the class? This is a little harder, but the answer is easy to find if you think about it. There are 16 boys and 8 girls.

How did we get the answer? We added up the number of "parts" in the ratio (2 parts boys plus 1 part girls, or 3 parts all together) and divided it into the total number of students. In other words, we divided 24 by 3. This told us that the class contained 3 equal parts of 8 students each. From the given ratio (2:1), we knew that two of these parts consisted of boys and one of them consisted of girls.

An easy way to keep track of all this is to use a tool we call the *Ratio Box*.

Here's how it works:

Let's go back to our class containing 24 students, in which the ratio of boys to girls is 2:1. Quickly sketch a table that has columns and rows, like this:

	Boys	Girls	Whole
Ratio (parts)	2	1	3
Multiply By			
Actual Number			24

This is the information you have been given. The ratio is 2:1, so you have 2 parts boys and 1 part girls, for a total of 3 parts. You also know that the actual number of students in the whole class is 24. You start by writing these numbers in the proper spaces in your box.

Your goal is to fill in the two empty spaces in the bottom row. To do that, you will multiply each number in the *parts* row by the same number. To find that number, look in the last column. What number would you multiply by 3 to get 24? You should see easily that you would multiply by 8. Therefore, write an 8 in all three blanks in the *Multiply By* row. (The spaces in this row will always contain the same number, although of course it won't always be an 8.) Here's what your Ratio Box should look like now:

	Boys	Girls	Whole
Ratio (parts)	2	1	3
Multiply By	8	8	8
Actual Number			24

The next step is to fill in the empty spaces in the bottom row. You do that the same way you did in the last column, by multiplying. First, multiply the numbers in the boys column (2 × 8 = 16). Then multiply the numbers in the girls column (1 × 8 = 8).

Here's what your box should look like now:

	Boys	Girls	Whole
Ratio (parts)	2	1	3
Multiply By	8	8	8
Actual Number	16	8	24

Now you have enough information to answer any question you might be asked. Here are some examples:

- What is the ratio of boys to girls? You can see easily from the ratio (parts) row of the box that the ratio is 2:1.
- What is the ratio of girls to boys? You can see easily from the ratio (parts) row of the box that the ratio is 1:2.
- What is the total number of boys in the class? You can see easily from the bottom row of the box that it is 16.
- What is the total number of girls in the class? You can see easily from the bottom row of the box that it is 8.
- What fractional part of the class is boys? There are 16 boys in a class of 24, so the fraction representing the boys is $\frac{16}{24}$, which can be reduced to $\frac{2}{3}$.

As you can see, the Ratio Box is an easy way to find, organize, and keep track of information on ratio problems. And it works the same no matter what information you are given. Just remember that all the boxes in the *Multiply By* row will always contain the same number.

Here's another example:

12

An acidic solution is mixed so that the mass ratio of nitric acid to water is 2:7. If a total of 270 grams of acid solution is mixed, how many more grams of water are there than the nitric acid?

A) 60

B) 110

C) 150

D) 210

Here's How to Crack It

For this question, your Ratio Box should look like this:

	Nitric Acid	Water	Total
Ratio	2	7	9
Multiply By			
Actual Number			270

Now find the multiplier. What do you multiply 9 by to get 270? That number is 30, so write 30 in each box in the *Multiply By* row.

	Nitric Acid	Water	Total
Ratio	2	7	9
Multiply By	30	30	30
Actual Number			270

The question asks how many more grams of water are in the solution than there are grams of nitric acid, so multiply both columns to find the actual numbers.

	Nitric Acid	Water	Total
Ratio	2	7	9
Multiply By	30	30	30
Actual Number	60	210	270

To find the difference between the number of grams of nitric acid and water, subtract: $210 - 60 = 150$. The correct answer is (C).

———————————◯———————————

Don't forget that you can use more than one technique to solve a problem. There's no reason why you can't combine the Ratio Box with some form of Plugging In. In fact, if one technique makes the problem easy, two techniques might make it downright simple!

Here's a problem for which combining techniques is just the ticket:

———————————◯———————————

17

In Miss Hoover's class, the ratio of boys to girls is x to y. If the total number of children in the class is five times the number of boys in the class, and x and y are integers, which of the following could be the sum of x and y?

A) 9

B) 10

C) 11

D) 12

Here's How to Crack It

Since the problem uses the word *ratio,* you can use the Ratio Box. However, the Ratio Box works best with numbers rather than variables. What to do? Plug in, of course! It's difficult to plug in for x and y, because the ratio will depend on the number of boys in the class. Start with that number and say there are 4 boys in the class. The total number of students is therefore 20, or five times 4. Now, it's time to draw the Ratio Box and fill in what you know:

	Boys	Girls	Total
Ratio (parts)			
Multiply By			
Actual Number	4		20

Now use the box to find the ratio, which will give you your x and y values. If there are 4 boys, there are 16 girls. Plug in a simple multiplier, like 2. Work backwards to find the parts of the ratio. If there are 4 actual boys and the multiplier is 2, the boys part of the ratio is 2. The girls part of the ratio is 8. Here's what your filled-in box should look like:

	Boys	Girls	Total
Ratio (parts)	2	8	10
Multiply By	2	2	2
Actual Number	4	16	20

In this example, $x = 2$ and $y = 8$, so the sum is 10, which happens to be one of our numbers: (B). We got lucky with the numbers we picked and got exactly what we wanted. Sometimes, you may need to plug in a few times to see if there is a pattern. Regardless of where you start, the sum of the ratio parts in this class will always be a multiple of 5.

———————————○———————————

Proportions Are Equal Ratios

Some SAT math problems will contain two proportional, or equal, ratios from which one piece of information is missing.

Here's an example:

───────────────────○───────────────────

5

If 2 packages contain a total of 12 doughnuts, how many doughnuts are there in 5 packages?

A) 24

B) 30

C) 36

D) 60

Here's How to Crack It

This problem simply describes two equal ratios, one of which is missing a single piece of information. Here's the given information represented as two equal ratios:

$$\frac{2 \text{ (packages)}}{12 \text{ (doughnuts)}} = \frac{5 \text{ (packages)}}{x \text{ (doughnuts)}}$$

Because ratios can be written so they look like fractions, we can treat them exactly like fractions. To find the answer, all you have to do is figure out what you could plug in for x that would make $\frac{2}{12} = \frac{5}{x}$. Now cross-multiply:

$$\frac{2}{12} \diagup\!\!\!\!\diagdown \frac{5}{x}$$

so, $2x = 60$

$x = 30$

The answer is (B).

───────────────────○───────────────────

Many proportion questions will also involve unit conversion. Make sure to pay attentions to the units and have the same units in both numerators and the same units in both denominators.

Let's look at an example.

21

Gary is using a 3D printer to create a miniature version of himself. The scale of the miniature is 0.4 inches to 1 foot of Gary's actual height. If Gary is 5 feet and 9 inches tall, what will be the height of his 3D-printed miniature? (12 inches = 1 foot)

A) 2.0 inches

B) 2.3 inches

C) 2.6 inches

D) 2.9 inches

Here's How to Crack It

The scale of the 3D printer is in inches and feet—0.4 inches on the miniature for every 1 foot in real life. Start by converting every measurement to inches. There are 12 inches in each foot, so the scale will be 0.4 inches = 12 inches in real life. Now convert Gary's height into inches. Begin by setting up a proportion to find out how many inches are in 5 feet.

$$\frac{12 \text{ inches}}{1 \text{ foot}} = \frac{x \text{ inches}}{5 \text{ feet}}$$

Cross-multiply to find that 5 feet equals 60 inches. Gary is 5 feet and 9 inches tall, so he is 60 + 9 = 69 inches tall. Now set up a proportion with the scale of the miniature and Gary's height in inches.

$$\frac{0.4 \text{ inches}}{12 \text{ inches}} = \frac{x \text{ inches}}{69 \text{ inches}}$$

Cross-multiply to get $12x = 27.6$, and then divide both sides by 12 to find that $x = 2.3$ inches. The answer is (B).

Direct and Inverse Variation

Problems dealing with direct variation (a fancy term for *proportion*) are exactly what you've just seen: If one quantity grows or decreases by a certain amount (a factor), the other quantity grows or decreases by the same amount. Inverse variations (also known as *inverse proportions*) are just the opposite of that. As one quantity grows or decreases, the other quantity decreases or grows by the same factor.

What's in a Name?
When you see *variation*, think *proportion*.

> The main formula you want to remember for inverse proportions is
>
> $$x_1 y_1 = x_2 y_2$$

Try one:

15

The amount of time it takes to consume a buffalo carcass is inversely proportional to the number of vultures. If it takes 12 vultures 3 days to consume a buffalo, how many fewer hours will it take if there are 4 more vultures?

A) $\frac{1}{4}$

B) $\frac{3}{4}$

C) 18

D) 54

Translate!
Direct means divide. Since *inverse* is the opposite, inverse means multiply.

Here's How to Crack It

For inverse proportions, follow the formula. First, convert the days: 3 days is equal to 72 hours. Now set up the equation: (12 vultures)(72 hours) = (16 vultures)(*x*). We solve to get *x* = 54, which is 18 fewer hours. The answer is (C).

Since ratios and proportions are related concepts, you might be wondering how you can tell when you should set the problem up as a proportion and when you should use a Ratio Box. Here are some guidelines to help you decide.

- If the question gives you a *ratio* and an *actual number*, use a Ratio Box.
- If the question compares items that have *different units* (like feet and seconds), set up a proportion.
- If you don't need the total column in the Ratio Box, then you can also do the question by setting up a proportion.

PERCENTAGES

Percentages Are Fractions

There should be nothing frightening about a percentage. It's just a convenient way of expressing a fraction whose bottom is 100.

Percent means "per 100" or "out of 100." If there are 100 questions on your math test and you answer 50 of them, you will have answered 50 out of 100, or $\frac{50}{100}$, or 50 percent. To think of it another way:

$$\frac{\text{part}}{\text{whole}} = \frac{x}{100} = x \text{ percent}$$

Memorize These Percentage-Decimal-Fraction Equivalents

These show up all the time, so go ahead and memorize them.

$$0.01 = \frac{1}{100} = 1 \text{ percent} \qquad 0.25 = \frac{1}{4} = 25 \text{ percent}$$

$$0.1 = \frac{1}{10} = 10 \text{ percent} \qquad 0.5 = \frac{1}{2} = 50 \text{ percent}$$

$$0.2 = \frac{1}{5} = 20 \text{ percent} \qquad 0.75 = \frac{3}{4} = 75 \text{ percent}$$

Converting Percentages to Fractions

To convert a percentage to a fraction, simply put the percentage over 100 and reduce:

$$80 \text{ percent} = \frac{80}{100} = \frac{8}{10} = \frac{4}{5}$$

Converting Fractions to Percentages

Because a percentage is just another way to express a fraction, you shouldn't be surprised to see how easy it is to convert a fraction to a percentage. To do so, simply use your calculator to divide the top of the fraction by the bottom of the fraction, and then multiply the result by 100. Here's an example:

Problem: Express $\frac{3}{4}$ as a percentage.

Solution: $\frac{3}{4} = 0.75 \times 100 = 75$ percent.

Converting fractions to percentages is easy with your calculator.

Converting Percentages to Decimals

To convert a percentage to a decimal, simply move the decimal point *two places to the left*. For example, 25 percent can be expressed as the decimal 0.25; 50 percent is the same as 0.50 or 0.5; 100 percent is the same as 1.00 or 1.

Converting Decimals to Percentages

To convert a decimal to a percentage, just do the opposite of what you did in the preceding section. All you have to do is move the decimal point *two places to the right*. Thus, 0.5 = 50 percent; 0.375 = 37.5 percent; 2 = 200 percent.

The following drill will give you practice working with fractions, decimals, and percentages.

Another Way
You can also convert fractions to percentages by cross-multiplying.
$$\frac{3}{4} = \frac{x}{100}$$
$$4x = 3(100)$$
$$x = \frac{3(100)}{4}$$
$$x = 75$$

FRACTIONS, DECIMALS, AND PERCENTS DRILL

Fill in the missing information in the following table. Answers can be found on page 318.

	Fraction	Decimal	Percent
	$\frac{1}{5}$	.2	20%
1.	$\frac{1}{2}$		
2.		3.0	
3.			0.5%
4.	$\frac{1}{3}$		

Translation, Please!

On the SAT Math Test, we can convert (or translate) words into arithmetic symbols. Here are some of the most common:

Word	Symbol
is, are, costs	=
greater than, more than	+
fewer than, less than	−
of	× (multiply)
percent	÷ 100
what	n (variable)

Do You Speak Math?

Problem: What number is 5 more than 10 percent of 20?

Students often make careless errors on questions like this because they aren't sure how to turn the words they are reading into math. You won't make mistakes if you take the words slowly and translate each one into a mathematical symbol. Let's use the chart on the previous page to write this question in math. *What number* means "variable" so we can write that as n (or x or whatever letter works for you!). *Is* means "equals," so now we have $n = 5$. *More than* translates to +, and *10 percent* is $\frac{10}{100}$. That gives us $n = 5 + \frac{10}{100}$. Finally, *of 20* means multiply by 20, so we've got our equation:

$$n = 5 + \frac{10}{100}(20)$$

$$n = 5 + 2$$

$$n = 7$$

You will see the words *of, is, product, sum,* and *what* pop up a lot in the Math sections of the SAT. Don't let these words fool you because they all translate into simple math functions. Memorize all of these terms and their math equivalents. It will save you time on the test and make your life with the SAT much nicer.

What Percent of What Percent of What?

On harder SAT questions, you may be asked to determine the effect of a series of percentage increases or decreases. The key point to remember on such problems is that each successive increase or decrease is performed on the result of the previous one.

Here's an example:

Bite-Size Pieces
Always handle
percentage problems in
bite-size pieces:
one piece at a time.

15

A business paid $300 to rent a piece of office equipment for one year. The rent was then increased by 10% each year thereafter. How much will the company pay for the first three years it rents the equipment?

A) $920

B) $960

C) $990

D) $993

Here's How to Crack It

This problem is a great place to use bite-sized pieces. You know that the business paid $300 to rent the piece of office equipment for the first year. Then, you were told that the rent increases by 10 percent for each year thereafter. That's a sure sign that you're going to need the rent for the second year, so go ahead and calculate it. For the second year, the rent is $300 + \left(\dfrac{10}{100} \times 300 \right) = 330$.

Now, the problem tells you that the business rents the equipment for three years. So, you need to do the calculation one more time. At this point, you might want to set up a chart to help keep track of the information.

Year 1: $300

Year 2: $330 = 300 + \left(\dfrac{10}{100} \times 300 \right)$

Year 3: $363 = 330 + \left(\dfrac{10}{100} \times 330 \right)$

To find the answer, all you need to do is add up the costs for each of the three years.

Year 1: $300
Year 2: $330
Year 3:   <u>$363</u>
          $993

The correct answer is (D), $993.

What Percent of What Percent of . . . Yikes!

Sometimes you may find successive percentage problems in which you aren't given actual numbers to work with. In such cases, you need to plug in some numbers.

Here's an example:

17

A number is increased by 25 percent and then decreased by 20 percent. The result is what percent of the original number?

A) 80

B) 100

C) 105

D) 120

Careful!
Number 17 is a tricky question. Beware of percentage change problems in the later questions. The answers to these problems almost always defy common sense. Unless you are careful, you may fall for a trap answer.

Here's How to Crack It

You aren't given a particular number to work with in this problem—just "a number." Rather than trying to deal with the problem in the abstract, you should immediately plug in a number to work with. What number would be easiest to work with in a percentage problem? Why, 100, of course.

1. 25 percent of 100 is 25, so 100 increased by 25 percent is 125.
2. Now you have to decrease 125 by 20 percent; 20 percent of 125 is 25, so 125 decreased by 20 percent is 100.
3. 100 (our result) is 100 percent of 100 (the number you plugged in), so the answer, once again, is (B).

Remember: Never try to solve a percentage problem by writing an equation if you can plug in numbers instead. Plugging in on percentage problems is faster, easier, and more accurate. Why work through long, arduous equations if you don't have to?

Percent Change

There's one more fundamental concept that you should know about percents. Some problems will ask for a percent increase or decrease. For these problems, use the following formula.

$$\% \ change = \frac{Difference}{Original} \times 100$$

Most of the time that you use the formula, it will be pretty clear which number you should use for the original. However, if you're not sure, remember that you should use the *smaller* number for the original if you are finding a percent *increase*. You should use the *larger* number for the original if you are finding a percent *decrease*.

Here's an example of how to use the formula:

8

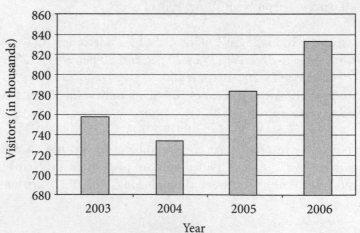

VISITATION AT ARCHES NATIONAL PARK 2003–2006

The chart shown above shows the number of visits, in thousands, at Arches National Park for the years 2003 to 2006. Which of the following is the closest approximation of the percent increase in the number of visits from 2004 to 2006?

A) 5%

B) 15%

C) 20%

D) 115%

Here's How to Crack It

First, you need to get the data from the chart. In 2004, the chart shows that there were approximately 730,000 visitors to Arches. In 2006, the chart shows that there were about 830,000 visitors to the park. Now, it's time to use the percent change formula. The difference is about 100,000 and the original is the 730,000 visitors in 2004:

$$\% \text{ increase} = \frac{100,000}{730,000} \times 100 \approx 15\%$$

The correct answer is (B).

Percentages: Advanced Principles

Another aspect of percent questions may relate to things that increase or decrease by a certain percent over time. This is known as "growth and decay." Real world examples include population growth, radioactive decay, and credit payments, to name a few. While Plugging In can help on these, it is also useful to know the growth and decay formula.

> When the growth or decay rate is a percent of the total population:
>
> $$\textit{final amount} = \textit{original amount } (1 \pm \textit{rate})^{\textit{number of changes}}$$

Let's see how this formula can make quick work of an otherwise tedious question.

23

Becca deposits $100 into a bank account that earns an annual interest rate of 4%. If she does not make any additional deposits and makes no withdrawals, how long will it take her, in years, to increase the value of her account by at least 60% ?

A) 12

B) 15

C) 25

D) 30

Here's How to Crack It

You could add 4% to the account over and over again until you get to the desired amount, but that would take a long time. Knowing the formula will make it a lot easier. First, set up the equation with the things you know. 100 is the original amount, and the rate is 4%, or 0.04. The account is increasing, so you add the rate, and you can put in "years" for the number of changes. The formula becomes

$$\textit{final amount} = 100(1 + 0.04)^{\textit{years}}$$

Now you need to figure out what you want the final amount to be. Translate the English to math: the value of her account (100) will increase (+) by 60 percent (0.6) of the current value (×100). This becomes $100 + (0.6)(100) = 100 + 60 = 160$. Now the formula is

$$160 = 100(1.04)^{\textit{years}}$$

The answer choices represent the number of years Becca keeps her money in the account. Now you are all set to easily plug in the answers. Start with (B), so *years* = 15. Is $100(1.04)^{15} = 160$? Use your calculator to check, making sure to follow PEMDAS rules and do the exponent before you multiply by 100. The result is $180.09. That is a bit too much money, so the answer will likely be (A), but let's just check it. $100(1.04)^{12} = \$160.10$, which is at least $160.

A final note on growth and decay: Sometimes the population is tripling or halving instead of changing by a certain percent. In that case, the formula changes to

$$\textit{final amount} = \textit{original amount} \, (\textit{multiplier})^{\textit{number of changes}}$$

Two more topics related to percentages may be tested. You may be given a sample of a population that fits a certain requirement and asked to determine how many members of the general population will also be expected to fit that requirement. You may also be given the results of a study or poll and told that there is a margin of error of a certain percentage.

Let's look at an example that tests both of these advanced ideas.

29

A summer beach volleyball league has 750 players in it. At the start of the season, 150 of the players are randomly chosen and polled on whether games will be played while it is raining, or if the games should be cancelled. The results of the poll show that 42 of the polled players would prefer to play in the rain. The margin of error on the poll is ±4%. What is the range of players in the entire league that would be expected to prefer to play volleyball in the rain rather than cancel the game?

A) 24–32

B) 39–48

C) 150–195

D) 180–240

Here's How to Crack It

The first step is to determine the percent of polled players that wanted to play in the rain.

$$\frac{42}{150} = 0.28 \text{ or } 28\%$$

Now apply this percent to the entire population of the league. Since 28% of the polled players wanted to play in the rain, 28% of all players should want to play in the rain.

$$\frac{28}{100} \times 750 = 210$$

The only range that contains this value is (D), so that is the correct answer. To actually calculate the margin of error, add and subtract 4% to the actual percent of 28% to get a range of 24–32% of the total.

$$24\% \text{ of } 750 = 180$$

$$32\% \text{ of } 750 = 240$$

Therefore, the entire range is 180 to 240.

AVERAGES

What Is an Average?

The average (also called the *arithmetic mean*) of a set of *n* numbers is simply the sum of all the numbers divided by *n*. In other words, if you want to find the average of three numbers, add them up and divide by 3. For example, the average of 3, 7, and 8 is $\frac{(3+7+8)}{3}$, which equals $\frac{18}{3}$, or 6.

That was an easy example, but average questions on the SAT won't always have clear solutions. That is, you won't always be given the information for averages in a way that is easy to work with. For that reason, we have a visual aid, like the Ratio Box for ratios, that helps you organize the information on average questions and find the answer.

We call it the *Average Pie*. Here's what it looks like:

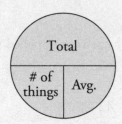

The *total* is the sum of all the numbers you're averaging, and the *number of things* is the number of elements you're averaging. Here's what the Average Pie looks like using the simple average example we just gave you.

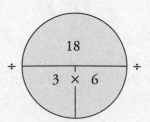

Here's how the Average Pie works mathematically. The horizontal line in the middle means *divide*. If you know the total and the number of things, just divide to get the average (18 ÷ 3 = 6). If you know the total and the average, just divide to get the number of things (18 ÷ 6 = 3). If you know the average and the number of things, simply multiply to get the total (6 × 3 = 18). The key to most average questions is finding the total.

Here's another simple example:

Problem: If the average of three test scores is 70, what is the total of all three test scores?

Solution: Just put the number of things (3 tests) and the average (70) in the pie. Then multiply to find the total, which is 210.

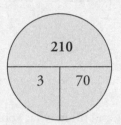

Total
When calculating averages and means, always find the total. It's the one piece of information that ETS loves to withhold.

Averages: Advanced Principles

To solve most difficult average problems, all you have to do is fill out one or more Average Pies. Most of the time you will use them to find the total of the number being averaged. Here's an example:

Mark It!
Make sure you're drawing a new Average Pie each time you see the word *average* in a question.

10

Maria has taken four chemistry tests and has an average (arithmetic mean) score of 80. If she scores a 90 on her fifth chemistry test, what is her average for these five tests?

A) 80

B) 81

C) 82

D) 84

Here's How to Crack It

Start by drawing an average pie and filling in what you know. You can put 4 in for the number of things and 80 for the average. You can calculate that Maria has gotten 320 total points on her first four tests. Your pie should look like this:

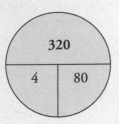

Now, draw another average pie and fill in what you know. This time, there are five tests. The question wants to know the average, so you also need to fill the total. The total for all five tests is the total from the first four tests plus the score from the fifth test: 320 + 90 = 410. Put that on the pie and divide to find the average:

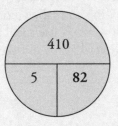

The answer is (C), 82.

Averages, and many other arithmetic topics, may be tested using charts and data. To find the numbers to average, look them up on the graphic provided and watch out for mismatched units.

Charge No.	Battery Life
1	1:11
2	1:05
3	0:59
4	0:55
5	0:55
6	0:54
7	0:54

A toy drone is opened and charged to full battery life. The table above shows the duration of the battery life in hours and minutes between charges. What is the average battery life for the first five charges?

A) 55 minutes

B) 58 minutes

C) 1 hour and 1 minute

D) 1 hour and 5 minutes

Here's How to Crack It

To find the average, add up the battery life values for the first 5 charges and divide by 5. Make sure that you convert the battery charge time for Charge 1 and 2 into minutes before calculating: 1:11 = 60 + 11 = 71 minutes, and 1:05 = 60 + 5 = 65 minutes. The average is equal to $\frac{71+65+59+55+55}{5} = \frac{305}{5} = 61$ minutes, which is equal to 1 hour and 1 minute. Therefore, (C) is the correct answer.

Don't forget that you can also plug in when using the Average Pie.

_____◯_____

The average (arithmetic mean) of a list of 5 numbers is *n*. When an additional number is added to the list, the average of all 6 numbers is *n* + 3. Which of the following is the value, in terms of *n*, of the number added to the list?

A) 6*n* + 18

B) 5*n*

C) *n* + 18

D) *n* + 6

Here's How to Crack It

Plug in for the value of *n*. If *n* = 20, then you can use the Average Pie to find the total of the five numbers on the list.

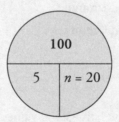

As shown on the Average Pie above, the total of the 5 numbers is 100. Now, it's time for another Average Pie. For this pie, you know that there are 6 numbers and that their average is 20 + 3 = 23.

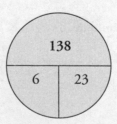

Using the Average Pie as shown above, the total of the six numbers is 138. Since the difference in the two totals was caused by the addition of the sixth number, the sixth number must be 138 − 100 = 38. That's the target, so be sure to circle it. Only (C) is 38 when *n* = 20.

_____◯_____

On the SAT, you'll also need to know three other statistical topics related to averages: *median*, *mode*, and *range*. These topics have pretty straightforward definitions. One way the SAT will complicate the issue is by presenting the data in a chart or graph, making it harder to see the numbers you are working with.

What Is a *Median*?

The median of a list of numbers is the number that is exactly in the middle of the list when the list is arranged from smallest to largest, as on a number line. For example, in the group 3, 6, 6, 6, 6, 7, 8, 9, 10, 10, 11, the median is 7. Five numbers come before 7 in the list, and 5 come after. Remember it this way: Median sounds like *middle*.

Let's see how this idea might be tested:

Missing the Middle?
To find the median of a set containing an even number of items, take the average of the two middle numbers.

23

Milligrams of Gold					
	1	**2**	**3**	**4**	**5**
Limestone	0.45	0.58	0.55	0.42	0.41
Granite	0.94	0.87	0.82	0.55	0.73
Gneiss	0.38	0.60	0.37	0.40	0.34

Five samples of each of three different rock types were collected on a hiking trip in Colorado. Each sample was analyzed for its gold content. The milligrams of gold found in each sample are presented in the table above. How much larger is the median of the amount of gold in the granite samples than that of the limestone samples?

A) 0.00

B) 0.37

C) 0.45

D) 0.55

Here's How to Crack It

Start by putting the gold weights for limestone in order to get:

$$0.41, 0.42, 0.45, 0.55, 0.58$$

The median for limestone is the middle number: 0.45 mg.

Next, place the gold weights for granite in order to get:

$$0.55, 0.73, 0.82, 0.87, 0.94$$

The median for granite is 0.82.

Therefore, the difference between the median amount of gold in the granite and limestone samples is $0.82 - 0.45 = 0.37$, and the correct answer is (B).

What Is a *Mode*?

The mode of a group of numbers is the number in the list that appears most often. In the list 3, 4, 4, 5, 7, 7, 8, 8, 8, 9, 10, the mode is 8, because it appears three times while no other number in the group appears more than twice. Remember it this way: Mode sounds like *most*.

Mode is often tested with bar graphs or points on a scatterplot. Look for the tallest bar on the bar graph or the row or column with the most points in a scatterplot to find the mode.

6

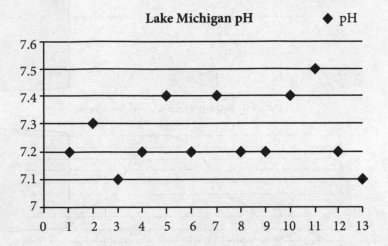

The pH of the water in Lake Michigan was tested at 13 locations along the Illinois shoreline. The data is presented in the scatterplot above. Which answer choice best represents the mode of the pH in the collected data?

A) 7.2

B) 7.3

C) 7.4

D) 7.5

Here's How to Crack It

The mode is the data point that occurs most frequently. Each diamond is a data point, so look for the line with the most diamonds on it. That line is 7.2, which means that when the lake was tested, the pH level most often read 7.2. The correct answer is (A).

What Is a *Range*?

The range of a list of numbers is the difference between the greatest number on the list and the least number on the list. For the list 4, 5, 5, 6, 7, 8, 9, 10, 20, the greatest number is 20 and the least is 4, so the range is 20 − 4 = 16.

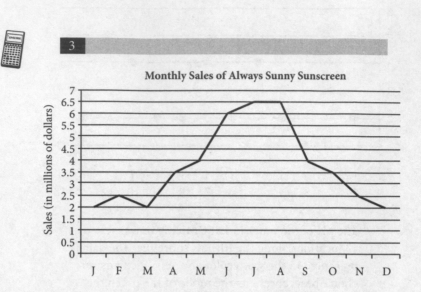

3

Monthly Sales of Always Sunny Sunscreen

The forecasted monthly sales of Always Sunny Sunscreen are presented in the figure above. Which of the following best describes the range of monthly sales, in millions of dollars, throughout the year shown?

A) 2.5

B) 3.5

C) 4.0

D) 4.5

Here's How to Crack It

The range of a set of values is the difference between the greatest and the smallest value. Looking at the chart, the lowest monthly sales number for Always Sunny can be found where the line dips closest to the bottom of the graph. This happens in both January and March, when the forecasted sales are 2 million. Make sure to read the units carefully. The highest point is where the line goes closest to the top of the graph. This happens in July and August, when the forecasted monthly sales are 6.5 million. Therefore, the range is 6.5 million − 2 million = 4.5 million. The correct answer is (D).

By the way, you may recognize this graph from Chapter 11. On the SAT, the same chart or figure may be used for two different questions. We'll talk more about sets of questions later in this chapter.

———————————◯———————————

The SAT might even have a question that tests more than one of these statistical concepts at the same time. Take it one step at a time and use Process of Elimination when you can.

———————————◯———————————

23

Precious Metals in Catalytic Converters, in grams					
1	2	2	3	4	6
6	6	9	9	10	10
11	13	14	14	15	17

The grams of precious metals in recycled catalytic converters were measured for a variety of automobiles. The data is presented in the table above. If the lowest data point, 1 gram, and highest data point, 17 grams, are removed from the set, which of the following quantities would change the most?

A) Mode

B) Mean

C) Range

D) Median

Here's How to Crack It

Start by evaluating the easier answer choices and save mean for last. The mode of the current list is 6, and removing 1 and 17 from the list won't change that. Eliminate (A). The range is the difference between the smallest number and the largest number on the list. Right now, the range is $17 - 1 = 16$. If those extremes are removed from the list, the new range is $15 - 2 = 13$, and the range changed by 3 units. Keep (C) for now. The median is the middle number in the list, or the average of the middle two numbers. Currently, both middle numbers are 9, so the median is 9. This won't change if 1 and 17 are removed, so eliminate (D). The mean of a list is not likely to change dramatically with the removal of the numbers at the extremes, so (C) is likely correct. To actually evaluate the mean, you need to add up all the numbers on the list and divide by the number of items in the list. For the current list, the total is 152 for the 18 items, so the average is $8.\overline{44}$. To find the new total if 1 and 17 are removed, don't re-add everything; just subtract 18 from the previous total. The new list will have only 16 items, so the new average is 8.375. This is only slightly different than the previous mean, so eliminate (B) and choose (C).

RATES

Rate is a concept related to averages. Cars travel at an average speed. Work gets done at an average rate. Because the ideas are similar, you can also use a pie to organize your information on rate questions.

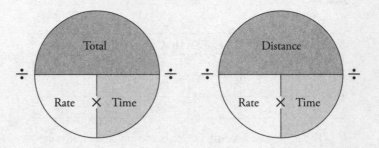

Here's a simple example:

Problem: If a fisherman can tie 9 flies for fly fishing in an hour and a half, how long does it take him to tie one fly, in minutes?

Solution: First, convert the hour and a half to 90 minutes, so your units are consistent. Then fill in the top of the pie with the amount (9 flies) and the lower right part with the time (90 minutes). Divide 9 by 90 to get the rate, $\frac{1}{10}$, or one fly every 10 minutes.

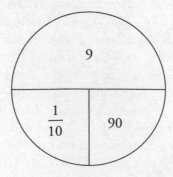

Rates: Advanced Principles

Just as with complicated average questions, harder rate questions will also require more than one pie to solve. Here's an example:

25

Brian plans to complete a 100-mile bike race for charity. According to his registration materials, he will need to ride at an average speed of 12.5 miles per hour if he wants to complete the course before it closes. On a practice ride the week before the race, Brian rides 60 miles and tracks his speed. For the first 30 miles, his average speed is 16 miles per hour, and for the next 30 miles, his average speed is 15 miles per hour. If Brian can match these speeds for the first 60 miles of the charity race, then he rests for a total of 1 hour after that, what approximate speed must he maintain for the last 40 miles in order to complete the ride on time?

A) 8 miles per hour

B) 10 miles per hour

C) 13 miles per hour

D) 14 miles per hour

Here's How to Crack It

Draw a Rate Pie, filling in the numbers for the entire ride. You can put in 100 in for the total miles and 12.5 in for the rate. Dividing 100 by 12.5 tells you that Brian has 8 hours to complete the ride. Your pie will look like this:

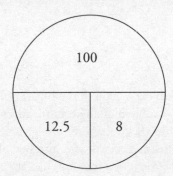

Now draw two more pies to determine how much time he would use for the first 60 miles. He rides at 16 miles an hour for the first 30 miles and 15 miles per hour for miles 31–60. Again, divide the number of miles by the rate to get the time for each portion, which is 1.875 hours for the first part and 2 hours for the second part.

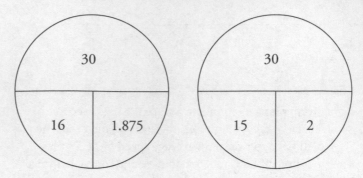

Therefore, the first 60 miles took Brian 1.875 + 2 = 3.875 hours to complete. After resting for an hour, he's used up 4.875 of his 8 hours, so he has 3.125 hours left. He needs to go 40 miles in that time, so draw one more pie with 40 at the top and 3.125 in the lower right for time. Divide 40 by 3.125 to get 12.8 or 13 miles per hour (it is okay to round, since you are looking for the approximate speed).

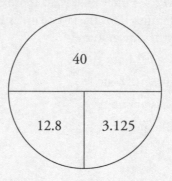

The correct answer is (C).

PROBABILITY

Probability is a mathematical expression of the likelihood of an event. The basis of probability is simple. The likelihood of any event is discussed in terms of all of the possible outcomes. To express the probability of a given event, x, you would count the number of possible outcomes, count the number of outcomes that give you what you want, and arrange them in a fraction, like this:

$$\text{Probability of } x = \frac{\text{number of outcomes that are } x}{\text{total number of possible outcomes}}$$

Every probability is a fraction. The largest a probability can be is 1; a probability of 1 indicates total certainty. The smallest a probability can be is 0, meaning that it's something that cannot happen. Furthermore, you can find the probability that something WILL NOT happen by subtracting the probability that it WILL happen from 1. For example, if the weatherman tells you that there is a 0.3 probability of rain today, then there must be a 0.7 probability that it won't rain, because $1 - 0.3 = 0.7$. Figuring out the probability of any single event is usually simple. When you flip a coin, there are only two possible outcomes, heads and tails; the probability of getting heads is therefore 1 out of 2, or $\frac{1}{2}$. When you roll a die, there are six possible outcomes, 1 through 6; the odds of getting a 6 is therefore $\frac{1}{6}$. The odds of getting an even result when rolling a die are $\frac{1}{2}$ because there are 3 even results in 6 possible outcomes.

Here's an example of a probability question:

2

A bag contains 7 blue marbles and 14 marbles that are not blue. If one marble is drawn at random from the bag, what is the probability that the marble is blue?

A) $\frac{1}{3}$

B) $\frac{1}{2}$

C) $\frac{2}{3}$

D) $\frac{3}{7}$

Here's How to Crack It
Here, there are 21 marbles in the bag, 7 of which are blue. The probability that a marble chosen at random would be blue is therefore $\frac{7}{21}$, or $\frac{1}{3}$. The correct answer is (A).

Some probability questions might include variables. Not to worry. Plugging in will save the day!

Here's an example:

17

A jar contains only red marbles and white marbles. If the probability of selecting a red marble is $\dfrac{r}{y}$, which of the following expressions gives the probability of selecting a white marble in terms of r and y ?

A) $\dfrac{r-y}{y}$

B) $\dfrac{y-r}{y}$

C) $\dfrac{r}{y}$

D) $\dfrac{y}{r}$

Here's How to Crack It

Plug in! You could make the probability of choosing a red marble be $\dfrac{2}{3}$. Then $\dfrac{r}{y} = \dfrac{2}{3}$, which means that $r = 2$ and $y = 3$.

Now, to get the numerical answer, you need to remember that the probabilities of all the things that can happen always add up to 1. Since there are only red marbles and white marbles in the jar, choosing a red marble or choosing a white marble are the only things that can happen. So, the probability of selecting a white marble can be found by subtracting the probability of getting a red marble from 1: Probability of white = $1 - \dfrac{2}{3} = \dfrac{1}{3}$. That's your target, so circle it.

Now, go find the answer that gives you $\dfrac{1}{3}$ when $r = 2$ and $y = 3$. Choice (B) is $\dfrac{y-r}{y} = \dfrac{3-2}{3} = \dfrac{1}{3}$. Since no other answer works out to $\dfrac{1}{3}$, (B) is the answer.

Finally, let's look at a probability question based on a chart. Again, getting to the correct answer involves reading the chart carefully to find to right numbers to use.

26

Size of College Manhattan High Students Plan to Attend

	Small (Fewer than 5,000 students)	Medium (From 5,000 to 10,000 students)	Large (More than 10,000 students)	Total
Manhattan High East	25	155	75	255
Manhattan High West	39	112	98	249
Total	64	267	173	504

At two high schools, those planning to attend college after graduation were polled. The sizes of the colleges they planned to attend based on student body sizes were tabulated in the table above. The 255 polled students from Manhattan High East had an average SAT score above 1100, and the 249 polled students from Manhattan High West had an average SAT score below 1100. If a poll respondent were chosen at random from those planning to attend a college with at least 5,000 students, what is the probability that the respondent would be enrolled at Manhattan High West?

A) $\dfrac{210}{249}$

B) $\dfrac{210}{440}$

C) $\dfrac{230}{440}$

D) $\dfrac{440}{504}$

Here's How to Crack It

Probability is defined as the number of things that fit the requirements divided by the total number of possible outcomes. Read the graph carefully to figure out how many respondents fit into each of these categories. The respondent is chosen from among those planning to attend colleges with "at least 5,000 students." That means that the total number of possible outcomes includes the 267 respondents who plan to attend medium schools and the 173 who plan to attend large schools, for 440 total. That is the denominator of the probability fraction, and the answer choices aren't reduced, so the answer must be (B) or (C). To find the number from among these 440 respondents who are enrolled at Manhattan High West, look in that row and add the 112 from the medium column to the 98 from the large column to get 210 for the numerator. The correct answer is (B).

Did the average SAT scores of the students at these two schools affect the answer at all? No! Watch out for extraneous information on the SAT. The test writers may include it to distract you.

SETS OF QUESTIONS

Sometimes, two questions will refer to the same information. These will usually be found in the calculator-permitted section, where there will be one set in the grid-in part and about three sets in the multiple-choice part of that section. Often, these sets are about arithmetic concepts, but they can also cover things like functions or exponential growth.

Try an arithmetic set on the next page.

Grade	Activity	Price per item	Funds Raised from Activity
9th	Car Wash	$5.00 per car	$255.00
10th	Bake Sale	$2.00 per cookie	$360.00
11th	Magazine Sales	$2.50 per magazine	$337.50
12th	Bake Sale	$1.50 per cookie	$180.00

4

How many cars did the 9th grade class wash during the car wash?

A) 5

B) 51

C) 122

D) 180

Here's How to Crack It

Look up the numbers you need on the chart, ignoring all the extraneous informa-

tion. To find out how many cars the 9th graders washed, take the *Funds Raised*

and divide by the *Price per item* in the row for the 9th graders. $\frac{\$255.00}{\$5.00} = 51$,

which is (B).

5

How many more cookies were sold by the 10th grade than were sold by the 12th grade?

A) 60

B) 90

C) 120

D) 150

Here's How to Crack It

First find the number of cookies sold by 10th graders, again dividing *Funds Raised* by *Price per item*. $\frac{\$360.00}{\$2.00} = 180$. Now find the number of cookies sold by 12th graders: $\frac{\$180.00}{\$1.50} = 120$. Now subtract to find out how many more cookies the 10th graders sold: $180 - 120 = 60$, which is (A).

ANALYSIS IN SCIENCE

If some of these questions are reminding you of science class, you're not crazy. One of the "Cross-Test scores" the SAT aims to measure is called Analysis in Science. This means that questions on science-based ideas will show up in Reading and Writing passages and also in Math questions. That's part of the reason for all these charts and graphs. Many times, you will be asked if a conclusion can be reached based on the chart. In those cases, just do as you have been throughout this chapter—carefully look up the numbers in question, do the required calculations, and eliminate answers that aren't true.

You may also be asked to graph the data presented in a table. Your knowledge of positive and negative relationships from Chapter 11 will help—you can eliminate things with the wrong relationship.

See the next page for an example.

7

Temperature in °F	Number of Customers
10	4
20	9
30	37
40	66
50	100

A coffee shop noticed that the outside temperature affected the number of customers who came to the shop that day, as shown in the table above. Which of the following graphs best represents the relationship between the outside temperature and the number of customers, as indicated by the table?

A) Number of Customers

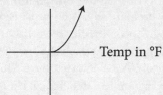

B) Number of Customers

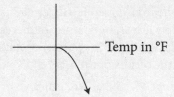

C) Number of Customers

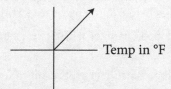

D) Number of Customers

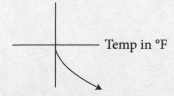

Here's How to Crack It

Notice that the number of customers increases as the temperature increases. The line of best fit will go up as you follow the graph from left to right, so eliminate (B) and (D). To determine if the correct graph is the one in (A) or in (C), try roughly plotting the data points, and then look at your graph. Notice that the number of customers does not increase by the same number for each 10-degree temperature increase. This is an exponential increase, not a linear increase. So, the graph will be curved. Eliminate (C). Only (A) fits the data in the chart.

———————○———————

Sometimes you will be asked to draw conclusions without much data at all. The following question from the calculator section has only one number in it, making the calculator pretty useless. Just stick to the facts of the study and make sure not to take a conclusion too far.

———————○———————

14

When trees become iron deficient, their leaves will turn yellow prematurely. A botanist is testing iron-doped fertilizers on maple trees with iron deficiencies. The botanist has selected 200 maple trees in the state of Wisconsin that have been identified as having an iron deficiency. Half of the trees are randomly chosen to receive the iron-doped fertilizer, while the other half are given a fertilizer without iron. The results from the test show that trees administered the iron-doped fertilizer had fewer premature yellow leaves, indicating an increase in their iron levels. Which of the following statements best describes the results of the test?

A) The iron-doped fertilizer will improve iron levels in any tree.

B) The iron-doped fertilizer reduces premature yellow leaves better than any other fertilizer.

C) The iron-doped fertilizer will cause a significant increase in iron levels.

D) The iron-doped fertilizer will result in fewer premature yellow leaves in maple trees in Wisconsin.

Here's How to Crack It

For this type of question, underline key words about how the study was conducted and what the study found. In this case, the study was on 200 maples trees with iron deficiencies in Wisconsin, and the conclusion is "The results from the test show that trees administered the iron-doped fertilizer had fewer premature yellow leaves, indicating an increase in their iron levels." Eliminate answers that don't hit this mark or go too far. In (A), it says that this treatment will help "any tree." We are told only about "200 maples trees in the state of Wisconsin," so we can't draw conclusions about other trees. Eliminate (A). In (B), the fertilizer used is compared to other fertilizers, which we also don't know about. Choice (C) sounds good, but it is hard to say what qualifies as "a significant increase in iron levels." The statement in (D) matches the key words you underlined perfectly without taking any aspect too far.

Advanced Arithmetic Drill: Calculator-Permitted Section

Work these problems using the advanced arithmetic techniques and tips we've covered in this chapter. These would all be found in section 4 of the test, on which calculator use is allowed. Answers and explanations can be found on page 318.

5

$$20 - 2x$$
$$20 - x$$
$$20$$
$$20 + x$$
$$20 + 2x$$

What is the average (arithmetic mean) of the list of numbers above?

A) 20

B) 100

C) $20 + \dfrac{x}{5}$

D) $\dfrac{100}{x}$

8

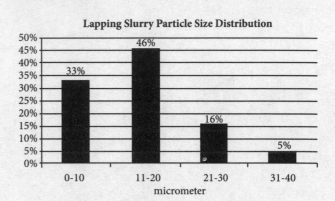

Lapping Slurry Particle Size Distribution

A lapping slurry contains microbeads suspended in a solution and is used to polish a silicon wafer by abrasion of the surface. The distribution of the particle size, in micrometers, is shown above. If the particle size distribution ranges were changed to 0-20 micrometers and 21-40 micrometers, which of the following is the closest to the ratio of the number of 0-20 micrometer microbeads to the number of 21-40 micrometer microbeads?

A) 3 : 1

B) 4 : 1

C) 5 : 2

D) 9 : 1

Steve ran a 12-mile race at an average speed of 8 miles per hour. If Adam ran the same race at an average speed of 6 miles per hour, how many minutes longer did Adam take to complete the race than did Steve?

A) 12

B) 16

C) 24

D) 30

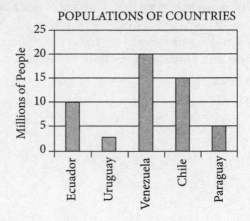

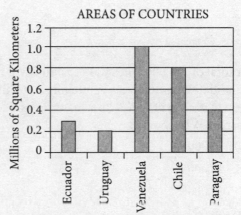

The populations and areas of five countries are shown in the graphs above. If population density is defined as $\dfrac{\text{population}}{\text{area}}$, which of the five countries has the highest population density?

A) Ecuador

B) Uruguay

C) Venezuela

D) Chile

The amount of time that Amy walks is directly proportional to the distance that she walks. If she walks a distance of 2.5 miles in 50 minutes, how many miles will she walk in 2 hours?

A) 4.5

B) 5

C) 6

D) 6.5

A total of 140,000 votes were cast for two candidates, Skinner and Whitehouse. If Skinner won by a ratio of 4 to 3, how many votes were cast for Whitehouse?

A) 30,000

B) 40,000

C) 60,000

D) 80,000

SPICE PRICES OF DISTRIBUTOR D	
Spice	Price Per Pound
Cinnamon	$8.00
Nutmeg	$9.00
Ginger	$7.00
Cloves	$10.00

The owner of a spice store buys 3 pounds each of cinnamon, nutmeg, ginger, and cloves from distributor D. She then sells all of the spices at $2.00 per ounce. What is her total profit, in dollars?

(1 pound = 16 ounces)

A) $192

B) $282

C) $384

D) $486

Milligrams of Gold					
	1	**2**	**3**	**4**	**5**
Limestone	0.45	0.58	0.55	0.42	0.41
Granite	0.94	0.87	0.82	0.55	0.73
Gneiss	0.38	0.60	0.37	0.40	0.34

Five samples of each of three different rock types were collected on a hiking trip in Colorado. Each sample was analyzed for its gold content. The milligrams of gold found in each sample are presented in the table above. What is the percent difference of the average gold content in the granite samples when compared to the average gold content of the gneiss samples?

A) The gold content in the gneiss samples is 62% higher than the gold content in the granite samples.

B) The gold content in the granite samples is 62% higher than the gold content in the gneiss samples.

C) The gold content in the gneiss samples is 87% higher than the gold content in the granite samples.

D) The gold content in the granite samples is 87% higher than the gold content in the gneiss samples.

Of all the houses in a certain neighborhood, 80% have garages. Of those houses with garages, 60% have two-car garages. If there are 56 houses with garages that are <u>not</u> two-car garages, how many houses are there in the neighborhood?

A) 93

B) 117

C) 156

D) 175

28

On Tuesday, a watchmaker made 4 more watches than he made during the previous day. If he made 16% more watches on Tuesday than on Monday, how many watches did he make on Tuesday?

A) 20

B) 21

C) 25

D) 29

CHAPTER DRILL ANSWERS AND EXPLANATIONS

Fractions, Decimals, and Percents Drill

1. $\dfrac{1}{2}$ 0.5 50

2. $\dfrac{3}{1}$ 3.0 300

3. $\dfrac{1}{200}$ 0.005 0.5

4. $\dfrac{1}{3}$ $0.333\overline{3}$ $33\dfrac{1}{3}$

Advanced Arithmetic Drill: Calculator-Permitted Section

5. **A** Variables in the answers? Plug in! Make up a value for *x*. Let's say that *x* is 3. The list of numbers then becomes 20 − 2(3), 20 − 3, 20, 20 + 3, 20 + 2(3), so the list is 14, 17, 20, 23, and 26. To find the average, make an average pie: We know the number of things (5) and the total (14 + 17 + 20 + 23 + 26 = 100), so the average is 100 ÷ 5 = 20, which is (A).

8. **B** In the new groupings, 79% of the particles are in the 0–20 micrometer grouping (33% + 46% = 79%) and 21% of the particles are in the 21–40 micrometer grouping (16% + 5%) = 21%. That is a ratio of 79:21. Because the question is asking for the closest ratio, round the numbers to get a ratio of 80:20, or 4:1. The correct answer is (B).

11. **D** Use a Rate Pie to calculate the time for each runner. Steve runs 12 miles at 8 miles per hour, so his pie looks like this:

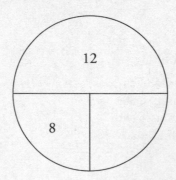

To find his time, divide his distance by his rate, which means that he runs for $1\frac{1}{2}$ hours (or 1.5 if you're using your calculator). Adam runs the same 12 miles at 6 miles per hour, so this is his Rate Pie:

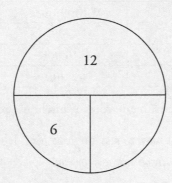

This means that Adam runs for 2 hours. Adam takes half an hour longer to complete the race, and half an hour is 30 minutes: (D).

15. **A** The top graph is of the countries' populations, and the bottom graph is of the countries' areas. Find the population density, $\frac{population}{area}$, for each country by taking its number from the top graph and dividing that by its number from the bottom graph:

$$\text{Ecuador} = \frac{10}{0.3}, \text{ which equals } 33.33$$

$$\text{Uruguay} = \frac{2.5}{0.2}, \text{ which equals } 12.5$$

$$\text{Venezuela} = \frac{20}{1.0}, \text{ which equals } 20$$

$$\text{Chile} = \frac{15}{0.8}, \text{ which equals } 18.75$$

The highest value among the countries is that of Ecuador, which is (A).

19. **C** Since we know the time that Amy walked and the distance she walked are directly proportional, we can set up a proportion to show her distance ÷ time. We want to know how many miles she'll walk in two hours, so put 120 (60 × 2) minutes in the second half of the ratio: $\frac{2.5}{50} = \frac{x}{120}$. To solve, cross-multiply, and you'll get $50x = 2.5 \times 120$; $50x = 300$; $x = 6$ miles, which is (C).

20. **C** Since this is a ratio question, let's draw a Ratio Box. We know the ratio for the votes for Skinner and Whitehouse, and the total number of votes cast. Fill in the total by adding the ratio (4 + 3 = 7), and then find the multiplier by seeing how many times 7 goes into 140,000 (140,000 ÷ 7 = 20,000).

Skinner	Whitehouse	Total
4	3	7
× 20,000	× 20,000	× 20,000
80,000	60,000	140,000

The question wants to know how many votes Whitehouse received, which is 60,000, (C).

23. **B** This is a hard question, so you have to stay on your toes. If the owner buys 3 pounds of each spice, that means she pays the following amounts for each spice:

$$\begin{aligned}
\text{cinnamon:} &\quad \$8 \times 3 = \$24 \\
\text{nutmeg:} &\quad \$9 \times 3 = \$27 \\
\text{ginger:} &\quad \$7 \times 3 = \$21 \\
\text{cloves:} &\quad \$10 \times 3 = \$30
\end{aligned}$$

So she pays a total of 24 + 27 + 21 + 30, or $102 for 12 pounds of spices. She then sells the spices per *ounce*, so you have to figure out first how many ounces of spices she has. If 1 pound is 16 ounces, then 12 pounds is 12 × 16, or 192 ounces. She sells all the spices at $2 per ounce, so she makes 192 × $2, or $384. To figure out her profit, subtract the amount she paid for the spices from the amount she made selling them: $384 − $102 = $282, (B).

25. **D** The average gold content in the granite samples can be calculated as follows:

$$\frac{0.94 + 0.87 + 0.82 + 0.55 + 0.73}{5} = 0.782$$

The average gold content in the gneiss samples can be calculated as

$$\frac{0.38 + 0.60 + 0.37 + 0.40 + 0.34}{5} = 0.418$$

Because the average gold content in the granite samples is higher, you can eliminate (A) and (C). Ballpark to find the right answer. 0.782 is almost twice as much as 0.418. Therefore, granite contains, on average, almost 100% more gold than gneiss does. The correct answer is (D).

26.   **D**   Start by figuring out what percent of the houses do not have two-car garages. Since 60% of the houses with garages have two-car garages, 40% of the houses with garages do not have two-car garages. In other words, 40% of 80% of the houses do not have two-car garages. Translate that into math to get $\frac{40}{100} \times \frac{80}{100} = 0.32$, or 32% of the houses. The problem tells us that 56 houses do not have two-car garages, which means 32% of the houses equals 56. Translating into math gives us $\frac{32}{100} \times x = 56$. Solve for x, and you'll get 175, which is (D).

28.   **D**   Let's try out the answers and see which one works. Start with (B). If the watchmaker made 21 watches on Tuesday, then he must have made 17 watches on Monday. We know that he should have made 16% more watches on Tuesday than on Monday, so let's use the percent change formula $\left(\frac{difference}{original} \times 100 \right)$ to see if we get 16% : $\frac{4}{17} \approx 23.5\%$, which is too big. Eliminate (B). We want the 4 watches to be a smaller percent of the total, so we need a bigger total. Try a bigger answer choice, like (D). If he made 29 watches on Tuesday, then he made 25 watches on Monday. Now the percent change is $\frac{4}{25} = 0.16 = 16\%$, which is exactly what we wanted. Therefore, (D) is the correct answer.

Summary

- A ratio can be expressed as a fraction, but ratios are not fractions. A ratio compares parts to parts; a fraction compares a part to the whole.

- You can use a Ratio Box to solve most ratio questions.

- Direct proportion is $\frac{x_1}{y_1} = \frac{x_2}{y_2}$. Indirect proportion is $x_1 y_1 = x_2 y_2$.

- A percentage is just a convenient way of expressing a fraction whose bottom is 100.

- To convert a percentage to a fraction, put the percentage over 100 and reduce.

- To convert a fraction to a percentage, use your calculator to divide the top of the fraction by the bottom of the fraction. Then multiply the result by 100.

- To convert a percentage to a decimal, move the decimal point two places to the left. To convert a decimal to a percentage, move the decimal point two places to the right.

- In problems that require you to find a series of percentage increases or decreases, remember that each successive increase or decrease is performed on the result of the previous one.

- If you need to find the percent increase or decrease use % change $= \frac{difference}{original} \times 100$.

- To find the average (arithmetic mean) of several values, add up the values and divide the total by the number of values.

- Use the Average Pie to solve problems involving averages. The key to most average problems is finding the total.

- The median of a group of numbers is the number that is exactly in the middle of the group when the group is arranged from smallest to largest, as on a number line. If there is an even number of numbers, the median is the average of the two middle numbers.

o   The mode of a group of numbers is the number in the group that appears most often.

o   The range of a group of numbers is the difference between the greatest number in the group and the least number.

o   On questions about rates, use the Rate, or Work, Pie. Be careful with the units—the SAT will often require you to do a unit conversion such as minutes to hours or inches to feet.

o   Probability is expressed as a fraction:

$$\text{Probability of } x = \frac{\text{number of outcomes that are } x}{\text{total number of possible outcomes}}$$

Chapter 15
Functions and Graphs

In the last chapter, we looked at a lot of charts and graphs. Another way data can be represented is with a graph in the xy-plane. This chapter will give you the tools you need to understand these graphs and other representations of functions.

FUNCTION FUNDAMENTALS

Think of a function as just a machine for producing ordered pairs. You put in one number and the machine spits out another. The most common function is an $f(x)$ function. You've probably dealt with it in your algebra class.

Let's look at a problem.

――――――◯――――――

3

If $f(x) = x^3 - 4x + 8$, then $f(5) =$

A) 67

B) 97

C) 113

D) 147

Here's How to Crack It

Any time you see a number inside the parentheses, such as $f(5)$, plug in that number for x. The question is actually telling you to plug in! Let's do it:

$$f(5) = 5^3 - 4(5) + 8$$
$$f(5) = 125 - 20 + 8$$
$$f(5) = 113$$

That's (C).

Try this next one:

――――――◯――――――

14

If $f(x) = x^2 + 2$, which of the following could be a value of $f(x)$?

A) −1

B) 0

C) 1

D) 2

What's This?
Anytime you see the notation $f(x)$, know that f isn't a variable. It's the name of the function. When you say it out loud it's "f of x." Though $f(x)$ is the most common way to show that an equation is a mathematic function, any letter can be used. So you may see $g(x)$ or $h(d)$. Know that you're still dealing with a function.

Here's How to Crack It

Note that the problem is asking which of the answers could be equal to $f(x)$—in other words, the problem is asking which of these values could be spit out of the $f(x)$ machine. Think about what is going in: No matter what you put in as a value for x, the value of x^2 has to be positive or zero. So, the lowest possible value of $x^2 + 2$ is 2, which is (D).

Note that you could also approach this question by Plugging In the Answers. If you plugged in 1 for $f(x)$, for instance, you would get $1 = x^2 + 2$, which becomes $x^2 = -1$, which is impossible.

○

Sometimes you'll get more complicated questions. As long as you know that when you put in x, your function will spit out another number, you'll be fine. Try this next one:

○

 20

Let the function g be defined by $g(x) = 5x + 2$. If

$$\sqrt{g\left(\frac{a}{2}\right)} = 6, \text{ what is the value of } a ?$$

A) $\dfrac{1}{\sqrt{6}}$

B) $\dfrac{1}{\sqrt{2}}$

C) $\dfrac{34}{5}$

D) $\dfrac{68}{5}$

Here's How to Crack It

This may look complicated, but just follow the directions. You know that

$g(x) = 5x + 2$. You also know that $\sqrt{g\left(\dfrac{a}{2}\right)} = 6$. First, get rid of the square root by

squaring both sides. Now you have $g\left(\dfrac{a}{2}\right) = 36$. Usually there's an x inside the

parentheses. Treat this the same. This statement says that g of some number equals

6. We also know that g of some number is the same as $5x + 2$. So $5x + 2 = 36$.

PITA!
Don't forget that you can often plug in the answer choices on function questions! Noticing a pattern yet? Just a few easy tricks can unlock a lot of easy points.

Simplify and you get $\dfrac{34}{5}$. Careful, you're not done. You now know that $\dfrac{a}{2} = \dfrac{34}{5}$, so $a = \dfrac{68}{5}$, or (D).

Another way the SAT can make functions more complicated is to give you two functions to deal with together. If you approach these problems one piece at a time, they will be easier to handle.

Here's an example:

15

If $f(g(a)) = 6$, $f(x) = \dfrac{x}{2} + 2$, and $g(x) = |x^2 - 10|$, which

of the following is a possible value of a ?

A) $\sqrt{2}$

B) 2

C) 6

D) 18

Here's How to Crack It
This is a great opportunity to plug in the answers! Take one of the middle answer choices and plug it in for a, then work the problem one step at a time to see if $f(g(a)) = 6$. Try (B): If $a = 2$, then $g(a) = |(2)^2 - 10| = |4 - 10| = |-6| = 6$. So, $f(g(a)) = f(g(2)) = f(6) = \dfrac{6}{2} + 2 = 3 + 2 = 5$. Since the problem states that $f(g(a))$ is supposed to equal 6, (B) is not correct.

If you don't know which way to go next, just pick a direction. Try (A): If $a = \sqrt{2}$, then $g(a) = |(\sqrt{2})^2 - 10| = |2 - 10| = |-8| = 8$. So, $f(g(a)) = f(g(\sqrt{2})) = f(8) = \dfrac{8}{2} + 2 = 4 + 2 = 6$. Choice (A) is correct.

Sometimes the SAT will use a word problem to describe a function, and then ask you to "build a function" that describes the real-world situation.

Try one of those:

15

Rock climbing routes are rated on a numbered scale with the highest number representing the most difficult route. Sally tried a range of shoe sizes on each of several routes of varying difficulty and found that when she wore smaller shoes, she could climb routes of greater difficulty. If D represents the difficulty rating of a route Sally successfully climbed and s represents the size of the shoes she wore on such a route, then which of the following could express D as a function of s ?

A) $D(s) = s^2$

B) $D(s) = \sqrt{s}$

C) $D(s) = s - 3.5$

D) $D(s) = \dfrac{45}{s}$

Here's How to Crack It

Start by thinking about the relationship described in the question: the smaller the shoes, the greater the difficulty. This is an inverse relationship. So, look for an inverse function. Only (D) is an inverse function.

If you aren't sure, try plugging in numbers to try it out. Plug in $s = 8$ then $s = 10$ to see if the result for D is smaller when you use a larger shoe size. Since only (D) results in a smaller difficulty for a larger shoe size, the correct response is (D).

WHAT'S THE POINT?

Why did math folks come up with functions? To graph them of course! When you put in a value for *x*, and your machine (or function) spits out another number, that's your *y*. You now have an ordered pair. Functions are just another way to express graphs. Knowing the connection between functions and graphs is useful, because you will most likely see questions involving graphs on the SAT.

The Coordinate Plane

A coordinate plane, or the "*xy*-plane," is made up of two number lines that intersect at a right angle. The horizontal number line is called the *x*-axis, and the vertical number line is the *y*-axis.

The four areas formed by the intersection of the axes are called *quadrants*. The location of any point can be described with a pair of numbers (*x*, *y*), just the way you would point on a map: (0, 0) are the coordinates of the intersection of the two axes (also called the *origin*); (1, 2) are the coordinates of the point one space to the right and two spaces up; (–1, 5) are the coordinates of the point one space to the left and five spaces up; (–4, –2) are the coordinates of the point four spaces to the left and two spaces down. All these points are located on the diagram below.

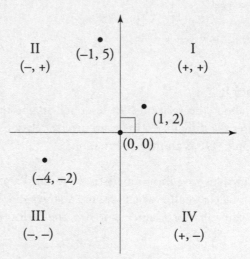

Some of the questions on the SAT may require you to know certain properties of lines on the *xy*-plane. Let's talk about them.

Quadrants
A coordinate plane has four distinct areas known as quadrants. The quadrants are numbered counterclockwise, starting from the top right. They help determine generally whether *x* and *y* are positive or negative. Sometimes knowing what quadrant a point is in and what that means is all you need to find the answer.

Points on a Line

You may be asked if a point is on a line or on the graph of any other equation. Just plug the coordinates of the point into the equation of the line to determine if that point makes the equation a true statement.

3

In the xy-plane, which of the following ordered pairs is a point on the line $y = 2x - 6$?

A) $(6, 7)$

B) $(7, 7)$

C) $(7, 8)$

D) $(8, 7)$

Ways to Remember
Having trouble remembering that the x-coordinate comes before the y-coordinate in an ordered pair? Just remember the phrase "x before y, walk before you fly." The letter x comes before y in the dictionary.

Here's How to Crack It

Plug in the answers, starting with (B). The (x, y) point is $(7, 7)$, so plug in 7 for x and 7 for y. The equation becomes $7 = 2(7) - 6$ or $7 = 8$. This isn't true, so eliminate (B). The result was very close to a true statement, and the point in (C) has the same x-coordinate and a larger y-coordinate, so try that next. Because $8 = 2(7) - 6$, (C) is the correct answer.

Slope

You always read a graph from left to right. As you read the graph, how much the line goes up or down is known as the slope. Slope is the rate of change of a line and is commonly known as "rise over run." It's denoted by the letter m. Essentially, it's the change in the y-coordinates over the change in x-coordinates and can be found with the following formula:

$$m = \frac{(y_2 - y_1)}{(x_2 - x_1)}$$

This formula uses the points (x_1, y_1) and (x_2, y_2).

Let's do an example. If you have the points (2, 3) and (7, 4), the slope of the line created by these points would be

$$m = \frac{(4-3)}{(7-2)}$$

So the slope of a line with points (2, 3) and (7, 4) would be $\frac{1}{5}$, which means that every time you go up 1 unit, you travel to the right 5 units.

Equation of a Line—Slope-Intercept Form

The equation of a line can take multiple forms. The most common of these is known as the slope-intercept form. If you know the slope and the y-intercept, you can create the equation of a given line. A slope-intercept equation takes the form $y = mx + b$, where m is the slope and b is the y-intercept.

Let's say that we know that a certain line has a slope of 5 (which is the same as $\frac{5}{1}$) and a y-intercept of 3. The equation of the line would be $y = 5x + 3$. You could graph this line simply by looking at this form of the equation. First, draw the y-intercept, (0, 3). Next, plug in a number for x and solve for y to get a coordinate pair of a point on the line. Now connect the point you just found with the y-intercept you already drew, and voilà, you have a line. If you want more points, you can create a table such as this one:

x	y
−2	−7
−1	−2
0	3
1	8

Take a look at the finished product:

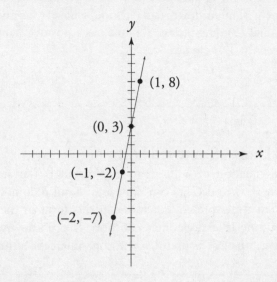

One way the SAT can test your understanding of lines is to show you a graph and ask you which equation describes that graph.

Here's an example:

◯ ───────────────────

4

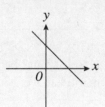

Which of the following could be the equation of the line represented in the graph above?

A) $y = 2x + 4$

B) $y = 2x - 4$

C) $y = -2x - 1$

D) $y = -2x + 4$

Here's How to Crack It

Remember that the equation of a line is $y = mx + b$, where m is the slope and b is the y-intercept. Look at the graph and think about what the equation should look like. Since the line is sloping downward, it should have a negative slope, so you can eliminate (A) and (B). Next, since the line has a positive y-intercept, you can eliminate (C), and only (D) remains.

Equation of a Line—Standard Form

Another way the equation of a line can be written is the standard form of $Ax + By = C$, where A, B, and C are constants and A and B do not equal zero. The test writers will sometimes present equations in this form in the hopes that you will waste time putting it in slope-intercept form. If you know what to look for, the standard form can be just as useful as the slope-intercept form.

> In standard form $Ax + By = C$:
>
> The slope of the line is $-\dfrac{A}{B}$.
>
> The y-intercept of the line is $\dfrac{C}{B}$.
>
> The x-intercept of the line is $\dfrac{C}{A}$.

The equation in the previous example would be $-5x + y = 3$ when written in the standard form. Using the information above, you can see that

$$\text{slope} = -\left(\frac{-5}{1}\right) = 5$$

$$y\text{-intercept} = \frac{3}{1} = 3$$

$$x\text{-intercept} = \frac{3}{-5} = -\frac{3}{5}$$

The answers for the slope and the y-intercept were the same as when the slope-intercept form was used. Depending on the form of the equation in the question or in the answers, knowing these line equation facts can help save time on the test.

Let's look at how this may be tested.

15

The graph of which of the following equations is parallel to the line with equation $y = -3x - 6$?

A) $x - 3y = 3$

B) $x - \dfrac{1}{3}y = 2$

C) $x + \dfrac{1}{6}y = 4$

D) $x + \dfrac{1}{3}y = 5$

Here's How to Crack It

The question asks for the equation of a line that has a slope parallel to the slope of the line given in the problem. In the form $y = mx + b$, m represents the slope. So, the slope of the equation given in the problem, $y = -3x - 6$, is -3. All you need to do now is find which choice also has a slope of -3.

One way to do that would be to rewrite each answer into the $y = mx + b$ form.

However, if you notice that each equation is presented in the $Ax + By = C$ form, you know that the slope in that form is equal to $-\dfrac{A}{B}$. So, check each answer choice: the slope of (A) is $-\dfrac{1}{-3}$, or $\dfrac{1}{3}$; the slope of (B) is $-\left(\dfrac{1}{-\dfrac{1}{3}}\right)$ or 3; the slope of (C) is $-\left(\dfrac{1}{\dfrac{1}{6}}\right)$, or -6; and the slope of (D) is $-\left(\dfrac{1}{\dfrac{1}{3}}\right)$, which equals -3 . So, (D) is the correct answer.

Parallel and Perpendicular Lines

So now we know that parallel lines have the same slope. Whenever the SAT brings up *perpendicular* lines, just remember that a perpendicular line has a slope that is the *negative reciprocal* of the other line's slope. For instance, if the slope of a line is 3, then the slope of a line perpendicular to it would be $-\dfrac{1}{3}$. Combine this with the skills you've already learned to attack a problem about perpendicular lines.

Here's an example:

18

Which of the following is the graph of a line perpendicular to the line defined by the equation $2x + 5y = 10$?

A)

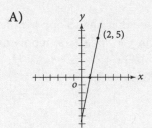

B)

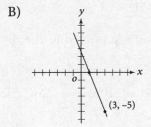

C)

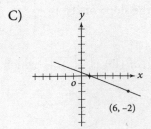

D)

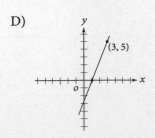

Here's How to Crack It

Since the question asks for a line perpendicular to the line $2x + 5y = 10$, you need

to find the slope of the line, and then take the negative reciprocal to find the slope.

You could convert the equation into the $y = mx + b$ format in order to find the slope,

or simply remember that when an equation is presented in the form $Ax + By = C$,

the slope is equal to $-\dfrac{A}{B}$. So the slope of this line is $-\dfrac{2}{5}$, and the slope of a per-

pendicular line would be $\dfrac{5}{2}$.

Look at the answer choices for one with a positive (upward) slope. Choices (B) and (C) slope downward, so eliminate them. Next, use points in the graph to find the slope of each answer. Eliminate (A); it has points at (1, 0) and (2, 5), for a slope of 5—too steep. The only remaining choice is (D), which is the correct answer.

Two Equations with Infinitely Many Solutions

In the chapters on algebra, we talked about equations with one or multiple solutions. Now imagine an equation in which any value of x would create a viable solution to the equation.

$$x + 3 = x + 3$$

In this case, it is fairly obvious that any number you choose to put in for x will create a true equation. But what does it mean when two lines have infinitely many solutions? Let's look at an example.

20

$$gx - hy = 78$$
$$4x + 3y = 13$$

In the system of equations above, g and h are constants. If the system has infinitely many solutions, what is the value of gh ?

A) -432

B) -6

C) 6

D) 432

To Infinity…and Beyond!
When given two equations with infinitely many solutions, find a way to make them equal. The equations represent the same line.

Here's How to Crack It

This question may have you scratching your head and moving on to the next question, but let's explore what you can do to solve this before you decide it's not worth your time. You may be surprised by how easy it is to solve a problem like this.

When they say that these equations have infinitely many solutions, what they are really saying is that these are the same equation, or that one equation is a multiple of the other equation. In other words, these two equations represent the same line. With that in mind, try to determine what needs to be done to make these equations equal. Since the right side of the equation is dealing with only a constant, first determine what you would need to do to make 13 equal to 78.

In this case, you need to multiply 13 by 6. Since we are working with equations, we need to do the same thing to both sides of the equation in order for the equation to remain equal.

$$6(4x + 3y) = 6 \times 13$$

$$24x + 18y = 78$$

Since both equations are now equal to 78, you can set them equal to one another, giving you this equation:

$$24x + 18y = gx - hy$$

You may know that when you have equations with the same variables on each side the coefficients on those variables must be equal, so you can deduce that $g = 24$ and $h = -18$. (Be cautious when you evaluate this equation. The test writers are being sneaky by using addition in one equation and subtraction in another.) Therefore, gh equals $24 \times -18 = -432$. Choice (A) is correct.

Two Equations with No Solutions

You saw above that a system of equations can have infinitely many solutions. When solving equations, you likely assume, as most people do, that there will be at least one solution to the equation, but that is not always the case. Look at the example below.

$$3x - 6 = 3x + 7$$

If we solve this equation we find that $-6 = 7$. Since -6 can never equal 7, there is no value of x that can be put into this equation to make it true. In this case, the equation has no solutions.

What does it mean if two equations of lines have no solutions? Here's one to try.

---○---

There's Just No Solution
When given two equations with no solutions, find a way to compare slopes. The equations represent parallel lines.

15

Which of the following accurately represents the set of solutions for the lines $6x + 12y = -24$ and $y = -\frac{1}{2}x + 2$?

A) $(0, -4)$

B) $(0, 4)$

C) There are no solutions.

D) There are infinitely many solutions.

Here's How to Crack It

Start by putting the first line into $y = mx + b$ form: $12y = -6x - 24$. Divide the whole equation by 12, so $y = -\frac{1}{2}x - 2$. Since these lines have the same slope but different y-intercepts, the lines are parallel, and they will never intersect. Therefore, (C) is the correct answer.

If two lines had different slopes, the lines would intersect at a single point such as (A) or (B). If the equations were identical, then they would be the same line and therefore have infinitely many solutions.

---○---

Points of Intersection

In the chapters on algebra, we talked about how to find the solution to a system of equations. There are several options, including stacking up the equations and adding or subtracting, setting them equal, or even Plugging In the Answers. The SAT may also ask about the intersection of two graphs in the xy-plane, which is a similar idea.

Let's try one:

14

In the *xy*-plane, which of the following is a point of intersection between the graphs of $y = x + 2$ and $y = x^2 + x - 2$?

A) $(0, -2)$

B) $(0, 2)$

C) $(1, 0)$

D) $(2, 4)$

Here's How to Crack It

Think about what the question is asking: A *point of intersection* means a point that is on the graphs of both equations. Therefore, the point would actually work if plugged into the equation of the line and the equation of the parabola.

So, use PITA by testing the answer choices: Start with one of the answers in the middle and plug in the point to each equation to see if it is true. The correct point of intersection will work in both functions. Try (C) in the first equation: Does $0 = (1) + 2$? No. So, (C) is not the answer. Try (D) in the first equation: Does $4 = (2) + 2$? Yes. So, try (D) in the second equation: Does $4 = (2)2 + 2 - 2$? Yes. Because (D) works in both equations, it is the correct answer.

Other Things You Can Do to a Line

The **midpoint** formula gives the midpoint of *ST,* with points $S\ (x_1, y_1)$ and $T\ (x_2, y_2)$. It's simply the average of the *x*-coordinates and the *y*-coordinates. In our example, the midpoint would be $\left(\dfrac{x_1 + x_2}{2}, \dfrac{y_1 + y_2}{2} \right)$.

Let's see an example of a midpoint problem.

In the xy-plane, what is the midpoint of the line segment with endpoints at (3, 4) and (0, 0) ?

A) (1.5, 2)

B) (5, 0)

C) (2.5, 0)

D) (3.5, 3.5)

Here's How to Crack It

You can use the formula for the midpoint of a line segment: $\left(\dfrac{x_1 + x_2}{2}, \dfrac{y_1 + y_2}{2} \right)$. If you forget it, try to remember that you are just taking the average of the x-coordinates of the two points to get the x-coordinate of the midpoint, and doing the same for the y-coordinates. For the x-coordinates, the average of 3 and 0 is $(3 + 0) \div 2 = 1.5$. Only one answer has this for the x-coordinate: (A). Don't waste time calculating the y-coordinate if you don't have to!

The **distance** formula looks quite complicated. The easiest way to solve the distance between two points is to connect them and form a triangle. Then use the Pythagorean Theorem. Many times, the triangle formed is one of the common Pythagorean triplets (3-4-5 or 5-12-13).

Let's try a distance formula question.

3

Which of the following points lies the greatest distance from the origin in the xy-plane?

A) $\left(-\dfrac{3}{2}, -\dfrac{3}{2}\right)$

B) $(-1, -1)$

C) $\left(-\dfrac{1}{2}, 0\right)$

D) $(0, 1)$

Here's How to Crack It

Draw the line between the origin and the point in each answer choice and use the technique described above to see which has the longest hypotenuse. Choice (A) would look like this:

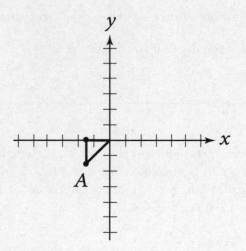

This creates a triangle with legs of 1.5 and 1.5; the hypotenuse (the distance from the origin) would then be $\sqrt{1.5^2 + 1.5^2}$, or about 2.12. Do the same with (B), (C), and (D). The distance of (B) would be $\sqrt{2}$, or about 1.4. Choices (C) and (D) lie in a straight line left and up from the origin, respectively, so the distance of (C) is 0.5, and the distance of (D) is 1. The distance farthest from the origin is about 2.12, which is (A).

Roots, Solutions, and *x*-intercepts

We've talked about *y*-intercepts in the discussion of the slope-intercept form of a line, and we talked about solutions when we covered systems of equations. But what about *x*-intercepts, or the solution for just one equation? A "solution," sometimes called a "root," is simply any point where a line or curve intersects the *x*-axis. Similarly, just as the *y*-intercept was the point where a line crossed the *y*-axis, an "*x*-intercept" is a point where a line or curve intersects the *x*-axis.

Keep these terms straight and you'll be in great shape!

Let's try a question that requires knowledge of intercepts and distance in the *xy*-plane.

15

What is the distance between the *x*-intercept and the *y*-intercept of the line $y = \dfrac{2}{3}x - 6$?

A) 9

B) 15

C) $\sqrt{89}$ (approximately 9.43)

D) $\sqrt{117}$ (approximately 10.82)

Here's How to Crack It

Start by finding the *x*- and *y*-intercepts of the line. When an equation is in $y = mx + b$ form, the *y*-intercept is *b*. So, the *y*-intercept is at the point (0, −6).

To find the *x*-intercept, you need a point where the *y* value is 0, just like how the *y*-intercept has an *x* value of 0. So, plug in 0 for *y* in the equation: $0 = \dfrac{2}{3}x - 6$, so $\dfrac{2}{3}x = 6$, and $x = 6\left(\dfrac{3}{2}\right) = 9$. The *x*-intercept, then, is (9, 0).

Now draw a right triangle and use the Pythagorean Theorem to calculate the distance: $6^2 + 9^2 = c^2$, so $c^2 = 117$, and the distance is $\sqrt{117}$, which is (D).

$y = f(x)$

Sometimes, instead of seeing the typical $y = mx + b$ equation, or something similar, you'll see $f(x) = mx + b$. Look familiar? Graphs are just another way to show information from a function. Functions show information algebraically and graphs show functions geometrically (as pictures).

Here's an example. The function $f(x) = 3x - 2$ is shown graphically as the following:

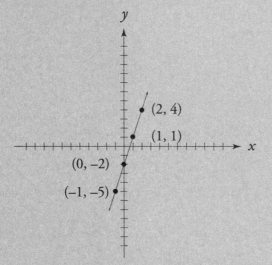

The reason the SAT includes function questions is to test whether you can figure out the relationship between a function and its graph. To tackle these questions, you need to know that the independent variable, the x, is on the x-axis, and the dependent variable, the $f(x)$, is on the y-axis. For example, if you see a function of $f(x) = 7$, then you need to understand that this is a graph of a horizontal line where $y = 7$.

Graphing Functions

One type of function question you might be asked is how the graph of a function would shift if you added a value to it.

Here is a quick guide (c is a constant) for the graph of $f(x) = x^2$:

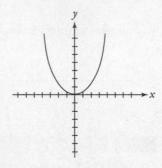

For $f(x) + c$, the graph will shift up c units, as shown in the diagram below:

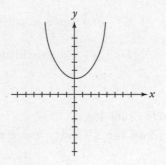

Conversely, $f(x) - c$ will shift the graph down by c units:

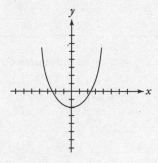

For $f(x + c)$, the graph will shift c units to the left:

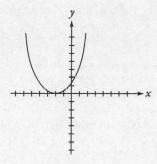

For $f(x - c)$, the graph will shift to the right by c units:

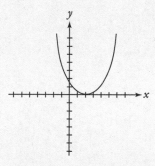

You may have realized how easy these problems would become if you simply put them into your graphing calculator. If calculator use is allowed, type in the function; if not, remember the four simple rules for transforming graphs.

You could also plug in points to find the correct graph.

Forms of Equations

The SAT will ask questions using two different forms of the equation for a parabola.

> The standard form of a parabola equation is:
>
> $$y = ax^2 + bx + c$$

In the standard form of a parabola, the value of a tells whether a parabola opens upwards or downwards (if a is positive, the parabola opens upwards, and if a is negative, the parabola opens downwards).

> The vertex form of a parabola equation is:
>
> $$y = a(x - h)^2 + k$$
>
> In the vertex form, the point (h, k) is the vertex of the parabola.

Simply knowing what the vertex form looks like may help you answer a question, like the following example.

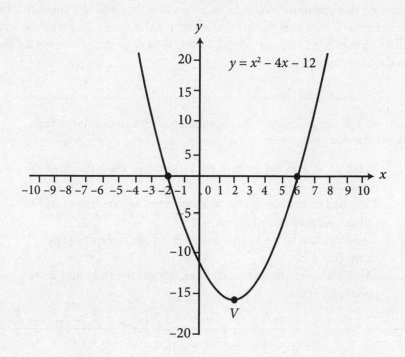

$y = x^2 - 4x - 12$

29

Which of the following is an equivalent form of the equation of the graph shown in the *xy*-plane above, from which the coordinates of vertex *V* can be identified from constants in the equation?

A) $y = (x - 2)^2 - 16$

B) $y = x(x - 4) - 12$

C) $y = (x - 6)(x + 2)$

D) $y = (x + 6)(x - 2)$

Here's How to Crack It

Looking at the graph tells you that the vertex of the parabola is at about (2, –16). Only (A) has the numbers 2 and 16 in it, so it must be the correct answer. If more than one choice had these constants, you could use your knowledge of the vertex form. If you recognize that the question is asking for the vertex form of the equation of the parabola, you can simply select (A), the only choice that actually uses that form. Finally, if you forget the form, you can multiply out the answers to see which of them match the original equation. Of course, the test writers have written the answers such that all but (D) are equivalent, so you would still have to guess from among the remaining three answer choices.

Knowing the vertex of a parabola can help you more easily answer questions about the minimum or maximum value a parabolic function will reach or the x-value that results in that minimum or maximum y-value. Say the last question was a grid-in on the No Calculator section that asked for the x-coordinate of the vertex. You couldn't graph it to find the vertex, so you'd have to get it into vertex form. Here are the steps to do that.

> To convert a parabola equation in the standard form to the vertex form, complete the square.
>
> 1. Make $y = 0$, and move any constants over to the left side of the equation.
> 2. Take half of the coefficient on the x-term, square it, and add it to both sides of the equation.
> 3. Convert the x terms and the number on the right to square form: $(x - h)^2$.
> 4. Move the constant on the left back over to the right and set it equal to y again.

For the equation in the last question, you would make it $0 = x^2 - 4x - 12$, then $12 = x^2 - 4x$. You'd add 4 to both sides to get $16 = x^2 - 4x + 4$, then convert the right side to the square form to get $16 = (x - 2)^2$. Finally, you'd move the 16 back over and set it equal to y to get $y = (x - 2)^2 - 16$.

The SAT will also ask questions about the equation of a circle in the xy-plane.

> The equation of a circle is:
>
> $$(x - h)^2 + (y - k)^2 = r^2$$
>
> In the circle equation, the center of the circle is the point (h, k), and the radius of the circle is r.

Let's look at a question that tests the use of the circle equation.

26

Which of the following is the equation of a circle with center (2, 0) and a radius with endpoint $\left(5, \sqrt{7}\right)$?

A) $(x - 2)^2 + y^2 = 4$

B) $(x + 2)^2 + y^2 = 4$

C) $(x - 2)^2 + y^2 = 16$

D) $(x + 2)^2 + y^2 = 16$

Here's How to Crack It

Start by building what you know of the circle formula: If the center is at point (2, 0), then the circle equation will be $(x - 2)^2 + (y - 0)^2 = r^2$, or more simply, $(x - 2)^2 + y^2 = r^2$. Choices (B) and (D) do not match, so eliminate them.

Now calculate the radius of the circle. Find the distance between points (2, 0) and $(5, \sqrt{7})$ by drawing a right triangle. The base of the right triangle will be the difference between the x values of 5 and 2, so the base of the right triangle is 3. The height of the right triangle will be the difference between the y values, which is $\sqrt{7}$. Use the Pythagorean Theorem to find the hypotenuse of the triangle, which will be the distance between the points (and, therefore, the length of the radius). So, $r^2 = 3^2 + \left(\sqrt{7}\right)^2 = 9 + 7 = 16$. Since you have the value of r^2, which is 16, use POE to eliminate (A) and select (C).

Just as you may be given a parabola in standard form and expected to convert it into vertex form, you may also be given an equation for a circle that is not in the form $(x - h)^2 + (y - k)^2 = r^2$ and expect you to figure out the radius or center. To do so, you just need to complete the square as you did above with the equation of a parabola. You will need to do it twice, though—once for the x-terms and again for the y-terms.

Functions and Graphs Drill 1: No Calculator Section

Use your new knowledge of functions and graphs to complete these questions, but don't use your calculator! Answers and explanations can be found on page 354.

3

Let the function f be defined such that $f(x) = x^2 - c$, where c is a constant. If $f(-2) = 6$, what is the value of c ?

A) -10

B) -2

C) 0

D) 2

7

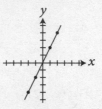

The graph above shows $y = 2x$. Which of the following graphs represents $y = |2x|$?

A)
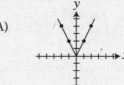

B)

C)

D)
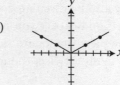

The graph of line l in the xy-plane passes through the points (2, 5) and (4, 11). The graph of line m has a slope of –2 and an x-intercept of 2. If point (x, y) is the point of intersection of lines l and m, what is the value of y ?

A) $\dfrac{3}{5}$

B) $\dfrac{4}{5}$

C) 1

D) 2

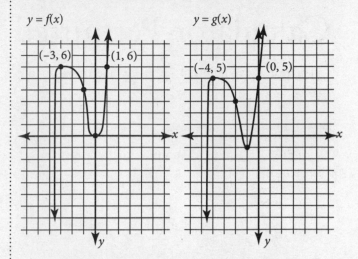

The figures above show the graphs of the functions f and g. The function f is defined by $f(x) = 2x^3 + 5x^2 - x$. The function g is defined by $g(x) = f(x - h) - k$, where h and k are constants. What is the value of hk ?

A) –2

B) –1

C) 0

D) 1

Functions and Graphs Drill 2: Calculator-Permitted Section

Calculator use is allowed on these questions, so use it wisely. Answers and explanations can be found on page 355.

6

If $f(x) = \sqrt{3x - 2}$, what is the smallest possible value of $f(x)$?

A) 0

B) $\dfrac{2}{3}$

C) 1

D) 2

10

x	y
−3	−7
−1	−3
2	3

Based on the chart above, which of the following could express the relationship between x and y?

A) $y = x - 4$

B) $y = 2x - 1$

C) $y = 2x + 2$

D) $y = 3x - 3$

13

Line l contains points (3, 2) and (4, 5). If line m is perpendicular to line l, then which of the following could be the equation of line m?

A) $x + 5y = 15$

B) $x + 3y = 15$

C) $3x + y = 5$

D) $-5x + y = \dfrac{1}{3}$

18

If $f(x) = 2x^2 + 4$ for all real numbers x, which of the following is equal to $f(3) + f(5)$?

A) $f(4)$

B) $f(6)$

C) $f(10)$

D) $f(15)$

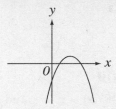

The graph of $y = g(x)$ is shown in the figure above. If $g(x) = ax^2 + bx + c$ for constants a, b, and c, and if $abc \neq 0$, then which of the following must be true?

A) $ac > 1$

B) $c > 1$

C) $ac > 0$

D) $a > 0$

Carlos and Katherine are estimating acceleration by rolling a ball from rest down a ramp. At 1 second, the ball is moving at 5 meters per second (m/s); at 2 seconds, the ball is moving at 10 m/s; at 3 seconds, the ball is moving at 15 m/s; and at 4 seconds, it is moving at 20 m/s. When graphed on an xy-plane, which equation best describes the ball's estimated acceleration where y expresses speed and x expresses time?

A) $y = 5x + 5$

B) $y = 25x$

C) $y = 5x$

D) $y = (4x + 1)^2 + 5$

CHAPTER DRILL ANSWERS AND EXPLANATIONS

Functions and Graphs Drill 1: No Calculator Section

3. **B** Start by plugging in what you know into the function given. If $f(x) = x^2 - c$, and $f(-2) = 6$, then plug in -2 for x in the function: $f(-2) = (-2)^2 - c$. Solve and replace $f(-2)$ with 6: $6 = 4 - c$; $2 = -c$; and $c = -2$. If you picked (A), you forgot that $(-2)^2$ is positive 4.

7. **A** Try plugging in some values for x and see if the graphs include that point. If $x = 0$, then $y = 0$, so $(0, 0)$ should be a point on the graph. Unfortunately this doesn't eliminate anything. If $x = 1$, then $y = 2$, so $(1, 2)$ should be a point on the graph. Eliminate (B), (C), and (D). The correct answer is (A).

10. **D** First, find the slope of line l by using the slope formula: $\dfrac{y_2 - y_1}{x_2 - x_1} = \dfrac{11 - 5}{4 - 2} = \dfrac{6}{2} = 3$. Plug this slope and one of the points on line l into the slope-intercept form $y = mx + b$ to solve for b, giving you the full equation of the line. If you use the point $(2, 5)$, you get $5 = 3(2) + b$ or $5 = 6 + b$, so $b = -1$. Therefore, the equation for line l is $y = 3x - 1$. For line m, the slope is given as -2, and the x-intercept is 2. Be very careful not to jump to the conclusion that the equation of line m is $y = -2x + 2$! In the form $y = mx + b$, the b is the y-intercept, not the x-intercept. The x-intercept is where $y = 0$, so you know that $(2, 0)$ is a point on line m. Use this point and the slope to find the equation of line m in the same way you did for line l. $0 = -2(2) + b$, so $b = 4$ and the equation is $y = -2x + 4$. Now set the x parts of the equations equal to find the point of intersection. If $3x - 1 = -2x + 4$, then $5x = 5$ and $x = 1$. Again, be careful! The question asked for the value of y! Plug $x = 1$ into one of the line equations to find y. For line l, the equation becomes $y = 3(1) - 1 = 3 - 1 = 2$, which is (D).

15. **B** The second graph moves down 1 and to the left 1. Remember that when a graph moves to the left, it is represented by $(x + h)$, which would be the same as $x - (-1)$. So $h = -1$. Because a negative k represents moving down, $k = 1$. Therefore, $hk = (-1) \times (1) = -1$, and the correct answer is (B).

Functions and Graphs Drill 2: Calculator-Permitted Section

6. **A** On this question you can use Plugging In the Answers. The numbers in the answer choices replace the $f(x)$ portion of the equation, so you can just write out the rest of it, $\sqrt{3x-2}$, next to each to see if it can be true. Start with (A) since you are looking for the smallest value of $f(x)$. If $0 = \sqrt{3x-2}$, then $0 = 3x - 2$ when you square both sides. Add 2 to both sides to get $2 = 3x$, and then divide both sides by 3. You get $x = \dfrac{2}{3}$. Since this is a real value, the equation works, so the smallest value of $f(x)$ is 0. Choice (A) is correct.

10. **B** Plug in the values from the chart! Use the pair $(-3, -7)$ from the top of the chart and eliminate answers that are not true: Choice (A) becomes $-7 = -3 - 4$, which is true. Keep it. Keep (B): $-7 = 2(-3) - 1$ is true. Get rid of (C), which becomes $-7 = 2(-3) + 2$: -7 does not equal -4. Get rid of (D): $-7 = 3(-3) - 3$. -7 does not equal -12. Now use another pair just to test (A) and (B). Using $(-1, -3)$, (A) gives $-3 = -1 - 4$, which is not true, so eliminate it, leaving only (B). The values $(-1, -3)$ work: $-3 = 2(-1) - 1$.

13. **B** First, find the slope of line l by using the slope formula: $\dfrac{y_2 - y_1}{x_2 - x_1} = \dfrac{5-2}{4-3} = \dfrac{3}{1}$. A line perpendicular to line l must have a slope that is the negative reciprocal of l's slope. So, its slope should be $-\dfrac{1}{3}$. In the standard form of a line $Ax + By = C$, the slope is $-\dfrac{A}{B}$. Only (B) has a slope of $-\dfrac{1}{3}$. If you didn't remember the rule about the slope of perpendicular lines in standard form, you could have converted the answers to slope-intercept form and sketched out each of the lines to look for the answer that looked perpendicular to l.

18. **B** To find the value of $f(3) + f(5)$, find the values of $f(3)$ and $f(5)$ separately: $f(3) = 2(3)^2 + 4 = 22$ and $f(5) = 2(5)^2 + 4 = 54$. So $f(3) + f(5) = 76$. You can tell that $f(4)$ will be between 22 and 54, so you can cross out (A). If you Ballpark (C) and (D), putting 10 or 15 in the function will give you a number bigger than 100, and you're looking for 76, so (C) and (D) are too big. That means the answer is (B) by POE.

21. **C** Remember your transformation rules. Whenever a parabola faces down, the quadratic equation has a negative sign in front of x^2 term. It always helps to plug in! Let's take an example. If your original equation was $(x-2)^2$, putting a negative sign in front would make the parabola open downward, so you'll have $-(x-2)^2$. If you expand it out, you get $-x^2 + 4x - 4$. Notice that the value of a in this equation is -1. Also notice that the value of c is -4. This allows you to eliminate (B) and

(D). Now you must plug in differently to distinguish between (A) and (C). Be warned: You must use fractions to help discern which is correct. Let's say the x-intercepts take place at $x = \dfrac{1}{2}$ and $x = \dfrac{3}{4}$. Rewriting those two expressions means that the factors are $\left(x - \dfrac{1}{2} \right)$ and $\left(x - \dfrac{3}{4} \right)$. If you FOIL out the terms, you end up with $x^2 - \dfrac{5}{4}x + \dfrac{3}{8}$. Remember, the parabola opens downward, so you must multiply by -1 to each term to yield $-x^2 + \dfrac{5}{4}x - \dfrac{3}{8}$. Your values of a and c are now -1 and $-\dfrac{3}{8}$, respectively. Multiply the two values and you get $\dfrac{3}{8}$, which allows you to eliminate (A) and confidently choose (C). (And that was worth only 1 point! Embrace the POOD!)

26. **C**   Figure out the points that will be on the graph from the data given: (0, 0), (1, 5), (2, 10), (3, 15), (4, 20). Draw a line through or close to these points to get an idea of what the graph will look like. Then use POE. The line is linear, not quadratic, so you can eliminate (D). It is also clear that the line begins at the origin, so the y-intercept will be 0. This will eliminate (A). A slope of 25 is far too big—Ballpark—so you can eliminate (B), leaving (C).

Summary

o   Given a function, you put an x value in and get an $f(x)$ or y value out.

o   Look for ways to use Plugging In and PITA on function questions.

o   For questions about the graphs of functions, remember that $f(x) = y$.

o   If the graph contains a labeled point or the question gives you a point, plug it into the equations in the answers and eliminate any that aren't true.

o   The equation of a line can take two forms. In either form, (x, y) is a point on the line.
   •   In slope-intercept form, $y = mx + b$, the slope is m, and the y-intercept is b.
   •   In standard form, $Ax + By = C$, the slope is $-\dfrac{A}{B}$, and the y-intercept is $\dfrac{C}{B}$.

o   Given two points on a line, (x_1, y_1) and (x_2, y_2), the slope is $\dfrac{(y_2 - y_1)}{(x_2 - x_1)}$.

o   Two linear equations with infinitely many solutions actually represent the same line.

o   Parallel lines have the same slopes and no points of intersection.

o   Perpendicular lines have slopes that are negative reciprocals and intersect at a right angle.

o   To find a point of intersection, plug the point into both equations to see if it works or graph the lines on your calculator when it is allowed.

o   To find the midpoint between two points, average the x-coordinates and average the y-coordinates.

o   To find the distance between two points, make them the endpoints of the hypotenuse of a right triangle and use Pythagorean Theorem.

o   The roots of a function, also known as solutions, zeroes, or x-intercepts, are the points where the graph crosses the x-axis and where $y = 0$.

- Graphs of functions can be moved up or down if a number is added to or subtracted from the function, respectively. They can move left if a number is added inside the parentheses of the function or move right if a number is subtracted inside the parentheses.

- The vertex form of a parabola equation is $y = a(x - h)^2 + k$, where (h, k) is the vertex. To get a parabola in the standard form into vertex form, complete the square.

- The standard form of a circle equation is $(x - h)^2 + (y - k)^2 = r^2$, where (h, k) is the center and r is the radius. To get a circle equation into the standard form, complete the square for both the x-terms and the y-terms.

Chapter 16
Geometry

Now that you've had some review and practice in coordinate geometry, it's time to learn a few more geometry rules. The SAT Math Test contains five or six questions that test your basic geometry knowledge on topics like lines and angles, triangles, and circles. This chapter covers each of these topics and more and provides a step-by-step walk-through for each type of problem.

GEOMETRY ON THE SAT

We covered coordinate geometry in Chapter 15. But in addition to coordinate geometry questions, there will be five or six questions on the SAT that test your knowledge of basic geometry rules. Well, kinda. At the beginning of each Math section, you are provided with the following:

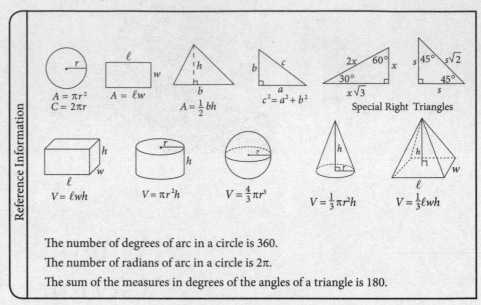

The number of degrees of arc in a circle is 360.

The number of radians of arc in a circle is 2π.

The sum of the measures in degrees of the angles of a triangle is 180.

This box of information contains *some* of what you'll need to tackle geometry on the SAT. In this chapter, we'll cover how to approach geometry questions and what else you will need to know to handle geometry questions on the SAT.

Geometry: Basic Approach

For the handful of non-coordinate geometry questions that appear on the SAT, The Princeton Review recommends this step-by-step approach:

1. **Draw a figure** if a figure is not provided. Also, if there is a figure provided, but the question has a "<u>Note</u>: figure not drawn to scale" by the figure, you might also want to redraw the figure using the information in the question.
2. **Label the figure** with any information given in the text of the question. Sometimes, you can plug in for parts of the figure as well.
3. **Write down formulas** that you might need for the question.
4. **Ballpark** if you're stuck or running short on time.

These four steps, combined with the techniques you've learned in the rest of this book and the geometry concepts this chapter will cover, will enable you to tackle any geometry question you might run across on the SAT.

Before we dive in to the nitty-gritty, let's try a problem using the approach.

25

In $\triangle ABC$ (not shown), $\angle ABC = 60°$ and $AC \perp BC$. If $AB = x$, then what is the area of $\triangle ABC$, in terms of x ?

A) $\dfrac{x^2 \sqrt{3}}{8}$

B) $\dfrac{x^2 \sqrt{3}}{4}$

C) $\dfrac{x^2 \sqrt{3}}{2}$

D) $x^2 \sqrt{3}$

Here's How to Crack It

Follow the geometry approach steps. Start by drawing the figure. If $AC \perp BC$, then $\triangle ABC$ is a right triangle with the right angle at point C:

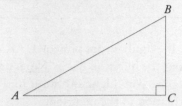

The next step is to label what you know. $\angle ABC = 60°$ can go right into the diagram. Because $AB = x$, you can plug in for x; make $x = 4$. Label this information into the diagram:

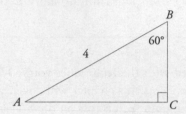

Next, figure out what else you know. Because there are 180° in a triangle, $\angle BAC = 180 - 90 - 60 = 30°$. This is a 30°-60°-90° special right triangle, information about which is given in the box of information at the start of the section. Based on the figure given in the box, the hypotenuse is equal to $2x$. (Note that this is a different x than what you plugged in for, because the test writers are trying to confuse you.) So, if the hypotenuse is 4, then $x = \dfrac{4}{2} = 2$; this is the side opposite the 30° angle, BC. The remaining side, AC, is $x\sqrt{3}$, which is $2\sqrt{3}$. Label this information in your diagram:

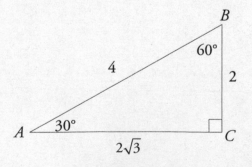

Now write down the formula you need. The question is asking for the area, so use the area of a triangle formula from the box: $A = \dfrac{1}{2}bh$. Fill in what you know; because this is a right triangle, you can use the two legs of the triangle as the base and the height. Make $b = 2\sqrt{3}$ and $h = 2$ in the equation and solve: $A = \frac{1}{2}(2\sqrt{3})(2) = 2\sqrt{3}$. This is your target; circle it. Now, plug in $x = 4$ (that's the x from the problem, NOT the x from the information in the box!) into each answer choice and eliminate what doesn't equal $2\sqrt{3}$. The only choice that works is (A).

Now that we've covered the approach to geometry questions, let's look more closely at some of the geometry concepts you'll need for these problems.

Lines and Angles

Here are the basic rules you need to know for questions about lines and angles on the SAT.

1. **A circle contains 360 degrees.**

    Every circle contains 360 degrees. Each degree is $\frac{1}{360}$ of the total distance around the outside of the circle. It doesn't matter whether the circle is large or small; it still has exactly 360 degrees.

2. **When you think about angles, remember circles.**
    An angle is formed when two line segments extend from a common point. If you think of the point as the center of a circle, the measure of the angle is the number of degrees enclosed by the lines when they pass through the edge of the circle. Once again, the size of the circle doesn't matter; neither does the length of the lines.

    Please refer to the figure below for clarification.

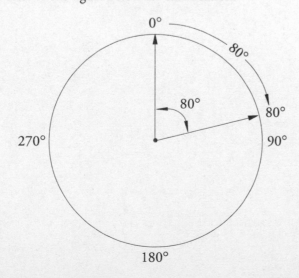

3. **A line is a 180-degree angle.**
   You probably don't think of a line as an angle, but it is one.
   Think of it as a flat angle. The following drawings should help:

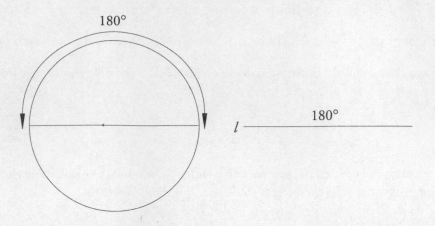

4. **When two lines intersect, four angles are formed.**
   The following diagram should make this clear. The four angles are indicated by letters.

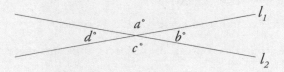

5. **When two lines intersect, the angles opposite each other will have the same measures.**
   Such angles are called *vertical angles*. In the following diagram, angles *a* and *c* are equal; so are angles *b* and *d*.

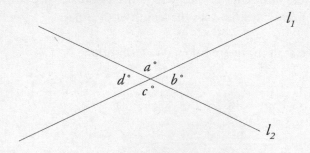

$$a + b + c + d = 360°$$
$$a = c, \ b = d$$

The measures of these four angles add up to 360 degrees. (Remember the circle.)

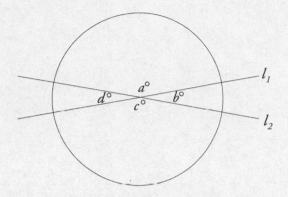

$$a + b + c + d = 360°$$

It doesn't matter how many lines you intersect through a single point. The total measure of all the angles formed will still be 360 degrees.

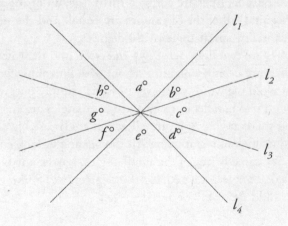

$$a + b + c + d + e + f + g + h = 360°$$
$$a = e, \, b = f, \, c = g, \, d = h$$

6. If two lines are perpendicular to each other, each of the four angles formed is 90 degrees. A 90-degree angle is called a *right angle*.

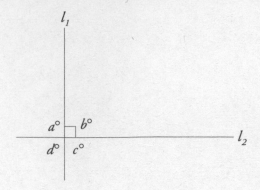

Flip and Negate
If two lines are perpen-
dicular, then their slopes
are negative reciprocals;
i.e., if l_1 has a slope of
2 and l_2 is perpendicular
to l_1, then l_2 must have a
slope of $-\frac{1}{2}$.

Angles *a*, *b*, *c*, and *d* all equal 90 degrees.

The little box at the intersection of the two lines is the symbol for a right angle. If the lines are not perpendicular to each other, then none of the angles will be right angles. Don't assume that an angle is a right angle unless you are specifically told that it is a right angle, either in the problem or with the 90° symbol.

Parallel Lines
Parallel lines have
the same slope.

7. When two parallel lines are cut by a third line, all of the small angles are equal, all of the big angles are equal, and the sum of any big angle and any small angle is 180 degrees.
    Parallel lines are two lines that never intersect, and the rules about parallel lines are usually taught in school with lots of big words. But we like to avoid big words whenever possible. Simply put, when a line cuts through two parallel lines, two kinds of angles are created: big angles and small angles. You can tell which angles are big and which are small just by looking at them. All the big angles look equal, and they are. The same is true of the small angles. Lastly, any big angle plus any small angle always equals 180 degrees. (ETS likes rules about angles that add up to 180 or 360 degrees.)

In any geometry problem, never assume that two lines are parallel unless the question or diagram specifically tells you so. In the following diagram, angle *a* is a big angle, and it has the same measure as angles *c, e,* and *g,* which are also big angles. Angle *b* is a small angle, and it has the same measure as angles *d, f,* and *h,* which are also small angles.

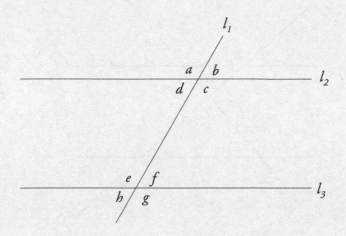

$$a = c = e = g$$
$$b = d = f = h$$
$$l_2 = l_3$$

You should be able to see that the degree measures of angles *a, b, c,* and *d* add up to 360 degrees. So do those of angles *e, f, g,* and *h.* If you have trouble seeing it, draw a circle around the angles. What is the degree measure of a circle? Also, the sum of any small angle (such as *d*) and any big angle (such as *g*) is 180°.

Let's see how these concepts might be tested on the SAT.

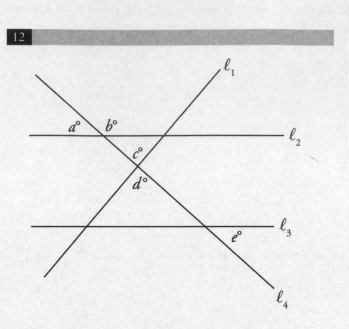

12

Note: Figure not drawn to scale.

In the figure above, $l_2 \parallel l_3$. Which of the following *could* be false?

A) $a = e$

B) $b + e = 180$

C) $l_1 \perp l_4$

D) $c = d$

Here's How to Crack It

Start by marking l_2 and l_3 as parallel lines. Next, because you're looking for what could be false, consider each answer choice and use POE. For (A), if l_2 and l_3 are parallel, then l_4 transects both lines and creates sets of equal angles. All small angles around l_4 which are formed by l_2 or l_3 are equal, so a must be equal to e; eliminate (A). Choice (B) is based on the same set of intersecting lines; because l_2 and l_3 are parallel and l_4 transects both lines, then any big angle plus any small angle equals 180°. Therefore, (B) must be true; eliminate it. For (C), you don't know the value of any angles, so you cannot determine if these lines are perpendicular. Since (C) could be false, choose (C). Choice (D) must be true because opposite angles created by two lines are always equal.

Converting Degrees to Radians

Some geometry questions will ask you to convert an angle measurement from degrees to radians. While this may sound scary, doing this conversion requires only that you remember that 180 degrees = π radians. Use this relationship to set up a proportion (see Chapter 14) and convert the units.

─────────────────○─────────────────

27

$\dfrac{54}{7}\pi$ radians is approximately equal to how many degrees?

A) 8°

B) 694°

C) 1,389°

D) 2,777°

Here's How to Crack It

Use the relationship between radians and degrees to set up a proportion. If 180 degrees = π radians, then the proportion will look like the following:

$$\frac{180\,\text{degrees}}{\pi\,\text{radians}} = \frac{x\,\text{degrees}}{\dfrac{54}{7}\pi\,\text{radians}}$$

Cross-multiply to get $180 \times \dfrac{54}{7}\pi = \pi x$. Divide both sides by π: $180 \times \dfrac{54}{7} = x$.

Finally, use your calculator, and you find that x is approximately 1,389, which

is (C).

─────────────────○─────────────────

Triangles

Here are some basic triangle rules you'll need to know for the SAT.

1. **Every triangle contains 180 degrees.**
   The word *triangle* means "three angles," and every triangle contains three interior angles. The measure of these three angles always adds up to exactly 180 degrees. You don't need to know why this is true or how to prove it. You just need to know it. And we mean *know* it.

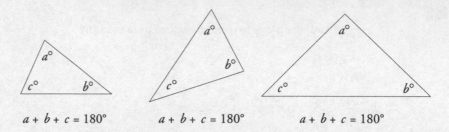

$a + b + c = 180°$ $a + b + c = 180°$ $a + b + c = 180°$

Your Friend the Triangle
If ever you are stumped by a geometry problem that deals with a quadrilateral, hexagon, or other polygon, look for the triangles that you can form by drawing lines through the figure.

2. **An isosceles triangle is one in which two of the sides are equal in length.**
   The angles opposite those equal sides are also equal because angles opposite equal sides are also equal.

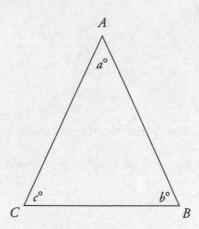

$$AB = AC \quad AB \neq BC$$
$$c = b \quad c \neq a$$

3. **An equilateral triangle is one in which all three sides are equal in length.**

Because the angles opposite equal sides are also equal, all three angles in an equilateral triangle are equal too. (Their measures are always 60 degrees each.)

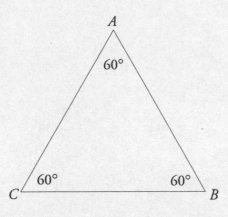

$$AB = BC = AC$$

Equilateral Triangles
An equilateral triangle is also isoceles.

4. **A right triangle is a triangle in which one of the angles is a right angle (90 degrees).**

The longest side of a right triangle, which is always opposite the 90-degree angle, is called the *hypotenuse*.

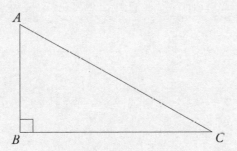

AC is the hypotenuse.

Some right triangles are also *isosceles*. The angles in an isosceles right triangle always measure 45°, 45°, and 90°.

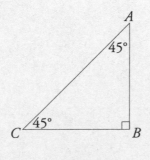

$$AB = BC$$

5. The perimeter of a triangle is the sum of the lengths of its sides.

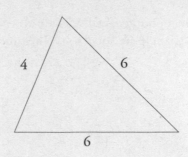

perimeter = 4 + 6 + 6 = 16

In or Out
The height can be found with a line dropped inside or outside the triangle—just as long as it's perpendicular to the base.

6. The area of a triangle is $\frac{1}{2}$ (base × height).

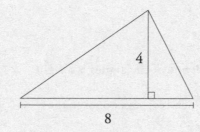 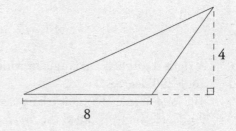

area = $\frac{1}{2}$ (8 × 4) = 16   area = $\frac{1}{2}$ (8 × 4) = 16

Try a question testing some of these concepts:

3

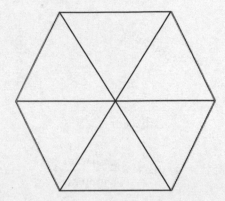

The regular hexagon shown above is divided into six congruent equilateral triangles. What is the measure, in degrees, of one of the interior angles of the hexagon?

A) 60°

B) 120°

C) 180°

D) 360°

Here's How to Crack It

First, you can Ballpark and eliminate (C) and (D); (C) would be a straight line, and (D) is all the way around a circle, so neither of those can be the interior angle of this figure. Next, label what you know. If each of the triangles in the figure is equilateral, then all of the angles within the triangles are equal to 60°. The interior angles of the hexagon are comprised of two angles of the triangles, so the interior angles of the hexagon must be 2 × 60 = 120°, which is (B).

SOHCAHTOA

Trigonometry will likely appear on your SAT. But fear not! Many trigonometry questions you will see mostly require you to know the basic definitions of the three main trigonometric functions. SOHCAHTOA is a way to remember the three functions:

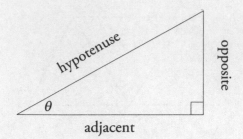

$$\text{sine } \theta = \frac{\text{opposite}}{\text{hypotenuse}} \qquad \text{cosine } \theta = \frac{\text{adjacent}}{\text{hypotenuse}} \qquad \text{tangent } \theta = \frac{\text{opposite}}{\text{adjacent}}$$

Let's see an example:

11

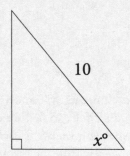

In the triangle above, sin $x = 0.8$ and cos $x = 0.6$. What is the area of the triangle?

A) 0.48

B) 4.8

C) 24

D) 48

Here's How to Crack It

Use the definitions of sine and cosine to find the two legs of the triangle. Sine is $\dfrac{opposite}{hypotenuse}$, so if sin x = 0.8, then $0.8 = \dfrac{opposite}{10}$. Multiply both sides by 10 and you find the side opposite the angle with measure $x°$ is 8. Similarly, cosine is $\dfrac{adjacent}{hypotenuse}$, so if cos x = 0.6, then $0.6 = \dfrac{adjacent}{10}$. Multiply both sides by 10 to determine the side adjacent to the angle with measure $x°$ is 6. With those two sides, find the area. The formula for area is $A = \dfrac{1}{2}bh$, so $A = \dfrac{1}{2}(6)(8) = 24$, which is (C).

Pythagorean Theorem

The Pythagorean Theorem states that in a right triangle, the square of the hypotenuse equals the sum of the squares of the other two sides. As we told you earlier, the hypotenuse is the longest side of a right triangle; it's the side opposite the right angle. The square of the hypotenuse is its length squared. Applying the Pythagorean Theorem to the following drawing, we find that $c^2 = a^2 + b^2$.

Pythagorean Theorem
$a^2 + b^2 = c^2$, where c is the hypotenuse of a right triangle. Learn it; love it.

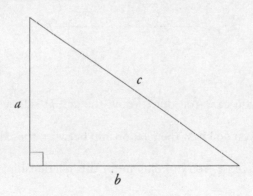

If you forget the Pythagorean Theorem, you can always look it up in the box at the beginning of the Math sections.

ETS loves to test the Pythagorean Theorem along with SOHCAHTOA. See the following sample question.

In $\triangle ABC$ (not shown), $AC \perp BC$ and $\cos \angle ABC = \dfrac{12}{13}$. What is the value of $\tan \angle ABC$?

A) $\dfrac{5}{13}$

B) $\dfrac{5}{12}$

C) $\dfrac{12}{13}$

D) $\dfrac{12}{5}$

Here's How to Crack It

Start by drawing triangle ABC.

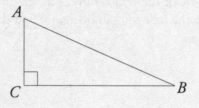

Next, label what you can. You don't know the actual side lengths, but because $\cos \angle ABC = \dfrac{12}{13}$, you do know the relationship between the side adjacent to angle ABC and the hypotenuse. You can plug in for this relationship: Make BC (the side adjacent to the angle) 12 and AB (the hypotenuse) 13:

You need to find tan $\angle ABC$, which means you need $\frac{opposite}{adjacent}$. You already know the adjacent side is 12, but you still need the side opposite, AC. Use the Pythagorean Theorem to find the missing side:

$$a^2 + b^2 = c^2$$
$$12^2 + b^2 = 13^2$$
$$144 + b^2 = 169$$
$$b^2 = 25$$
$$b = 5$$

Therefore, $AC = 5$, and tan $\angle ABC = \frac{5}{12}$, which is (B).

Special Right Triangles

Both of the previous questions you worked also used special right triangles. While in the last question we used the Pythagorean Theorem to find the missing side, if you memorize these special triangles you can avoid using the Pythagorean Theorem in a lot of cases.

ETS writes very predictable geometry questions involving right triangles, reusing certain relationships. In these questions the triangles being used have particular ratios. There are two different types of special right triangles. The first involves the ratio of sides and the second involves the ratio of angles.

The most common special right triangles with side ratios are known as Pythagorean triplets. Here are ETS's favorites:

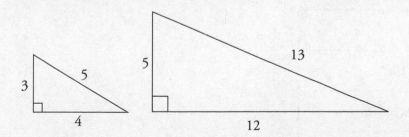

If you memorize these two sets of Pythagorean triplets (3-4-5 and 5-12-13), you'll often be able to find the answer without using the Pythagorean Theorem. If you're given a triangle with a side of 3 and a hypotenuse of 5, you know right away that the other side has to be 4. Likewise, if you see a right triangle with sides of 5 and 12, you know the hypotenuse must be 13.

Your Friend the Rectangle
Be on the lookout for problems in which the application of the Pythagorean Theorem is not obvious. For example, every rectangle contains two right triangles. That means that if you know the length and width of the rectangle, you also know the length of the diagonal, which is the hypotenuse of both triangles.

Relax; It's Just a Ratio
A 3-4-5 triangle may be hiding, disguised as 6-8-10 or 18-24-30. It's all the same ratio though, so be on the lookout.

ETS also likes to use right triangles with sides that are simply multiples of the common Pythagorean triplets. For example, you might see a 6-8-10 or a 10-24-26 triangle. These sides are simply the sides of the 3-4-5 and 5-12-13 triangles multiplied by 2.

There are two types of special right triangles that have a specific ratio of angles. They are the 30°-60°-90° triangle and the 45°-45°-90° triangle. The sides of these triangles always have the same fixed ratio to each other. The ratios are as follows:

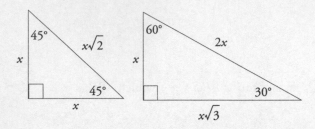

Let's talk about a 45°-45°-90° triangle first. Did you notice that this is also an isosceles right triangle? The sides will always be the same. And the hypotenuse will always be the side times $\sqrt{2}$. Its ratio of side to side to hypotenuse is always $1{:}1{:}\sqrt{2}$. For example, if you have a 45°-45°-90° triangle with a side of 3, then the second side will also be 3 and the hypotenuse will be $3\sqrt{2}$.

Now let's talk about a 30°-60°-90° triangle. The ratio of shorter side to longer side to hypotenuse is always $1{:}\sqrt{3}{:}2$. For example, if the shorter side of a 30°-60°-90° triangle is 5, then the longer side would be $5\sqrt{3}$ and the hypotenuse would be 10.

Symbols

Things aren't always written out on the SAT. Here's a list of symbols you might see, along with a translation of each one into English:

Symbol	Meaning
$\triangle ABC$	triangle ABC
$\overline{AB}$	line segment AB
AB	the length of line segment AB

Learn these symbols and keep an eye out for them!

Similar Triangles

Similar triangles have the same shape, but they are not necessarily the same size. Having the same shape means that the angles of the triangles are identical and that the corresponding sides have the same ratio. Look at the following two similar triangles:

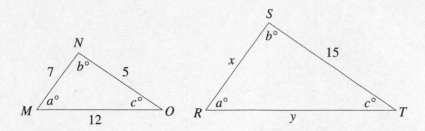

These two triangles both have the same set of angles, but they aren't the same size. Whenever this is true, the sides of one triangle are proportional to those of the other. Notice that sides NO and ST are both opposite the angle that is $a°$. These are called corresponding sides, because they correspond to the same angle. So the lengths of $\overline{NO}$ and $\overline{ST}$ are proportional to each other. In order to figure out the lengths of the other sides we set up a proportion: $\dfrac{MN}{RS} = \dfrac{NO}{ST}$. Now fill in the information that you know: $\dfrac{7}{x} = \dfrac{5}{15}$. Cross-multiply and you find that $x = 21$. You could also figure out the length of y: $\dfrac{NO}{ST} = \dfrac{MO}{RT}$. So, $\dfrac{5}{15} = \dfrac{12}{y}$, and $y = 36$. Whenever you have to deal with sides of similar triangles, just set up a proportion.

Finally, there's a special relationship between similar triangles and trigonometry. Side lengths in similar triangles are proportional, and the trigonometric functions give the proportions of the sides of a triangle. Therefore, if two triangles are similar, the corresponding trigonometric functions are equal! Let's look at how this might work in a problem.

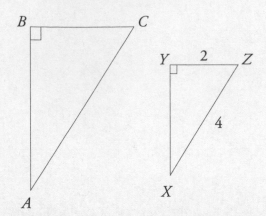

16

In the figure above, $\triangle ABC$ is similar to $\triangle XYZ$. What is the value of cos A?

A) $\dfrac{1}{2}$

B) $\dfrac{\sqrt{3}}{2}$

C) $\sqrt{3}$

D) 2

Here's How to Crack It

Because the two triangles are similar, the value of corresponding trigonometric functions will be equal. Therefore, cos A = cos X. The value of cos X is $\dfrac{adjacent}{hypotenuse}$ or $\dfrac{XY}{XZ}$. You could use the Pythagorean Theorem to find XY, but it's easier to use the special right triangle discussed earlier. Because the hypotenuse is twice one of the legs, you know this is a 30°-60°-90° triangle. YZ is the shortest side (x), so XY is $x\sqrt{3}$ or $2\sqrt{3}$. Therefore, $\cos X = \dfrac{2\sqrt{3}}{4}$, which reduces to $\dfrac{\sqrt{3}}{2}$. Because $\cos X = \cos A$, cos A also equals $\dfrac{\sqrt{3}}{2}$, which is (B).

Circles

Here are the rules you'll need to tackle circle questions on the SAT.

1. **The circumference of a circle is $2\pi r$ or πd, where r is the radius of the circle and d is the diameter.**

   You'll be given this information in your test booklet, so don't stress over memorizing these formulas. You will always be able to refer to your test booklet if you forget them. Just keep in mind that the diameter is always twice the length of the radius (and that the radius is half the diameter).

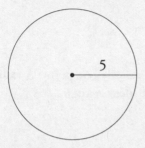

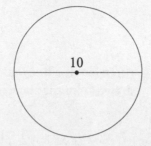

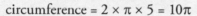

circumference = $2 \times \pi \times 5 = 10\pi$ circumference = 10π

In math class you probably learned that $\pi = 3.14$ (or even 3.14159). On the SAT, $\pi = 3^+$ (a little more than 3) is a good enough approximation. Even with a calculator, using $\pi = 3$ will give you all the information you need to solve difficult SAT multiple-choice geometry questions.

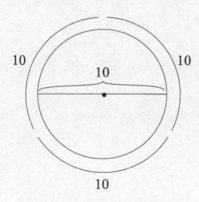

circumference = about 30

A Few Formulas
Area = πr^2
Circumference = $2\pi r$ or πd
Diameter = $2r$

Leave That π Alone!
Most of the time, you won't multiply π out in circle problems. Because the answer choices will usually be in terms of π (6π instead of 18.849...), you can save yourself some trouble by leaving your work in terms of π.

2. The area of a circle is πr^2, where r is the radius of the circle.

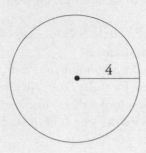

area = $\pi 4^2 = 16\pi$

Circles Have Names?

If a question refers to Circle R, it means that the center of the circle is point R.

3. A tangent is a line that touches a circle at exactly one point. A radius drawn from that tangent point forms a 90-degree angle.

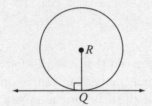

Let's see how these rules can show up on the SAT.

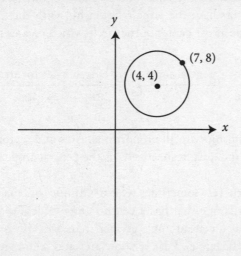

22

The circle defined by the equation $(x - 4)^2 + (y - 4)^2 = 25$ has its center at point $(4, 4)$ and includes point $(7, 8)$ on the circle. This is shown in the figure above. What is the area of the circle shown?

A) 5π

B) 10π

C) 16π

D) 25π

Here's How to Crack It

You want the area, so write down the formula for area of a circle: $A = \pi r^2$. That means you need to determine the radius of the circle. If you remember the circle formula from the previous chapter, you simply need to recall that $r^2 = 25$ and just multiply by π to find the area. If not, you can find the distance between $(4, 4)$ and $(7, 8)$ by drawing a right triangle. The triangle is a 3-4-5 right triangle, so the distance between $(4, 4)$ and $(7, 8)$ (and thus the radius) is 5. If the radius is 5, then the area is $\pi(5)^2$, or 25π. The answer is (D).

Arcs and Sectors

Many circle questions on the SAT will not ask about the whole circle. Rather, you'll be asked about arcs or sectors. Both arcs and sectors are portions of a circle: arcs are portions of the circumference, and sectors are portions of the area. Luckily, both arcs and sectors have the same relationship with the circle, based on the central angle (the angle at the center of the circle which creates the arc or sector):

$$\frac{\text{part}}{\text{whole}} = \frac{\text{central angle}}{360°} = \frac{\text{arc length}}{2\pi r} = \frac{\text{sector area}}{\pi r^2}$$

Note that these relationships are all proportions. Arcs and sectors are proportional to the circumference and area, respectively, as the central angle is to 360°.

Questions on the Math Test sometimes refer to "minor" or "major" arcs or sectors. A minor arc or sector is one that has a central angle of less than 180°, whereas a major arc or sector has a central angle greater than 180° (in other words, it goes the long way around the circle). Let's see how arcs and sectors might show up in a problem.

15

Points *A* and *B* lie on circle *O* (not shown). *AO* = 3 and ∠*AOB* = 120°. What is the area of minor sector *AOB*?

A) $\dfrac{\pi}{3}$

B) π

C) 3π

D) 9π

Here's How to Crack It

Because *O* is the name of the circle, it's also the center of the circle, so *AO* is the radius. ∠*AOB* is the central angle of sector *AOB*, so you have all the pieces you need to find the sector. Put them into a proportion:

$$\frac{120°}{360°} = \frac{x}{\pi (3)^2}$$

Cross-multiply to get 360*x* = 1,080π (remember to not multiply out π). Divide both sides by 360 and you get *x* = 3π, which is (C).

Relationship Between Arc and Angle in Radians

Sometimes you'll be asked for an arc length, but you'll be given the angle in radians instead of degrees. Fear not! Rather than making the problem more complicated, the test writers have actually given you a gift! All you need to do is memorize this formula:

$$s = r\theta$$

In this formula, s is the arc length, r is the radius, and θ is the central angle in radians. If you know this formula, these questions will be a snap!

Rectangles and Squares

Here are some rules you'll need to know about rectangles and squares:

1. **The perimeter of a rectangle is the sum of the lengths of its sides.**
    Just add them up.

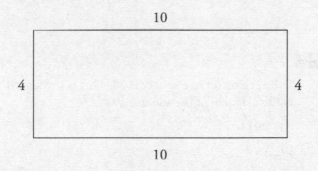

perimeter = 10 + 4 + 10 + 4 = 28

2. **The area of a rectangle is length × width.**
    The area of the preceding rectangle, therefore, is 10 × 4, or 40.

Little Boxes
Here's a progression of quadrilaterals from least specific to most specific: quadrilateral is any 4-sided figure
↓
parallelogram is a quadrilateral in which opposite sides are parallel
↓
rectangle is a parallelogram in which all angles = 90 degrees
↓
square is a rectangle in which all sides are equal

3. **A square is a rectangle whose four sides are all equal in length.**
The perimeter of a square, therefore, is four times the length of any side. The area is the length of any side squared.

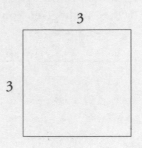

$$\text{perimeter} = 4(3) = 12$$
$$\text{area} = 3^2 = 9$$

4. **In rectangles and squares all angles are 90-degree angles.**
It can't be a square or a rectangle unless all angles are 90 degrees.

Let's check out an example.

6

If the perimeter of a square is 28, what is the length of the diagonal of the square?

A) $2\sqrt{14}$

B) $7\sqrt{2}$

C) $7\sqrt{3}$

D) 14

Here's How to Crack It

The perimeter of a square is $4s$. So, $28 = 4s$. Divide by 4 to find $s = 7$. The diagonal of a square divides the square into two 45°-45°-90° triangles, with sides in the ratio of $x:x:x\sqrt{2}$. If the side is 7, the diagonal is $7\sqrt{2}$. The answer is (B).

Polygons

Polygons are two-dimensional figures with three or more straight sides. Triangles and rectangles are both polygons. So are figures with five, six, seven, eight, or any greater number of sides. The most important fact to know about polygons is that any one of them can be divided into triangles. This means that you can always determine the sum of the measures of the interior angles of any polygon.

For example, the sum of the interior angles of any four-sided polygon (called a *quadrilateral*) is 360 degrees. Why? Because any quadrilateral can be divided into two triangles, and a triangle contains 180 degrees. Look at the following example:

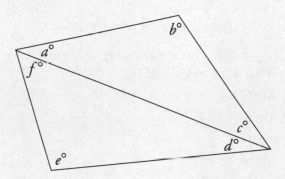

In this polygon, $a + b + c = 180$ degrees; so does $d + e + f$. That means that the sum of the interior angles of the quadrilateral must be 360 degrees ($a + b + c + d + e + f$).

A *parallelogram* is a quadrilateral whose opposite sides are parallel. In the following parallelogram, side AB is parallel to side DC, and AD is parallel to BC. Because a parallelogram is made of two sets of parallel lines that intersect each other, we know that the two big angles are equal, the two small angles are equal, and a big angle plus a small angle equals 180 degrees. In the figure below, big angles A and C are equal, and small angles B and D are equal. Also, because A is a big angle and D is a small angle, $A + D = 180$ degrees.

Need the Formula?

You may have learned the formula for this in math class. If so, you can use it: The sum of the degrees in an n-sided polygon is $180(n - 2)$. If you don't know the formula, don't worry about memorizing it. It doesn't come up much, and when it does come up, you can always break up the polygon into triangles.

Let's try an example:

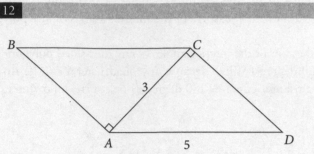

Note: Figure not drawn to scale.

In parallelogram *ABCD* above, *AC* = 3 and *AD* = 5.
What is the area of *ABCD* ?

A) 12

B) 15

C) 18

D) 20

Here's How to Crack It

The trick is to notice that this parallelogram is actually made of two equal triangles. By finding the area of the triangles, you can find the area of the parallelogram. The triangles are both right triangles, and the two sides given in the figure follow the 3-4-5 pattern. If you look at triangle *ACD* with $\overline{AC}$ as the base, the base is 3 and the height is 4. Now use the formula for area of a triangle:

$$A = \frac{1}{2} \times 3 \times 4 = 6$$

That means the parallelogram is 2 × 6 = 12.

Also, if you estimate the area, the base is 5 and the height is less than 3, so the area is less than 15. The only answer less than 15 is (A).

Volume

Volume questions on the SAT can seem intimidating at times. The test writers love to give you questions featuring unusual shapes such as pyramids and spheres. Luckily, at the beginning of the Math sections (and the beginning of this chapter), you're given a box with all the formulas you will ever need for volume questions on the SAT. Simply apply the Basic Approach using the given formulas and you'll be in good shape (pun entirely intended)!

Let's look at an example:

15

A sphere has a volume of 36π. What is the surface area of the sphere? (The surface area of a sphere is given by the formula $A = 4\pi r^2$.)

A) 3π

B) 9π

C) 27π

D) 36π

Here's How to Crack It

Start by writing down the formula for volume of a sphere from the beginning of the chapter: $V = \frac{4}{3}\pi r^3$. Put what you know into the equation: $36\pi = \frac{4}{3}\pi r^3$. From this you can solve for r. Divide both sides by π to get $36 = \frac{4}{3}r^3$. Multiply both sides by 3 to clear the fraction: $36(3) = 4r^3$. Note we left 36 as 36, because the next step is to divide both sides by 4, and 36 divided by 4 is 9, so $9(3) = r^3$ or $27 = r^3$. Take the cube root of both sides to get $r = 3$. Now that you have the radius, use the formula provided to find the surface area: $A = 4\pi(3)^2$, which comes out to 36π, which is (D).

Ballparking

You may be thinking, "Wait a second, isn't there an easier way?" By now, you should know that of course there is, and we're going to show you. On many SAT geometry problems, you won't have to calculate an exact answer. Instead, you can estimate an answer choice. We call this *Ballparking*, a strategy we discussed earlier in this book.

Ballparking is extremely useful on SAT geometry problems. At the very least, it will help you avoid careless mistakes by immediately eliminating answers that could not possibly be correct. In many problems, Ballparking will allow you to find the answer without even working out the problem at all.

For example, on many SAT geometry problems, you will be presented with a drawing in which some information is given and you will be asked to find some of the information that is missing. In most such problems, you're expected to apply some formula or perform some calculation, often an algebraic one. But you'll almost always be better off if you look at the drawing and make a rough estimate of the answer (based on the given information) before you try to work it out.

The basic principles you just learned (such as the number of degrees in a triangle and the fact that $\pi \approx 3$) will be enormously helpful to you in Ballparking on the SAT. You should also know the approximate values of several common square roots. Be sure to memorize them before moving on. Knowing them cold will help you solve problems and save time, especially when calculator use is not allowed.

Square Roots

$$\sqrt{1} = 1$$
$$\sqrt{2} \approx 1.4$$
$$\sqrt{3} \approx 1.7+$$
$$\sqrt{4} = 2$$

You will also find it very helpful if you have a good sense of how large certain common angles are. Study the following examples.

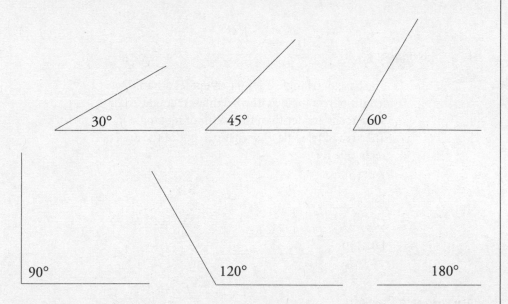

How High Is the Ceiling?

If your friend stood next to a wall in your living room and asked you how high the ceiling was, what would you do? Would you get out your trigonometry textbook and try to triangulate using the shadow cast by your pal? Of course not. You'd look at your friend and think something like this: "Dave's about 6 feet tall. The ceiling's a couple of feet higher than he is. It must be about 8 feet high."

Your Ballpark answer wouldn't be exact, but it would be close. If someone later claimed that the ceiling in the living room was 15 feet high, you'd be able to tell her with confidence that she was mistaken.

You'll be able to do the same thing on the SAT. Every geometry figure on your test will be drawn exactly to scale unless there is a note in that problem telling you otherwise. That means you can trust the proportions in the drawing. If line segment *A* has a length of 2 and line segment *B* is exactly half as long, then the length of line segment *B* is 1. All such problems are ideal for Ballparking.

The Correct Choice
Remember that the SAT is a multiple-choice test. This means that you don't always have to come up with an answer; you just have to identify the correct one from among the four choices provided.

Plugging In

As you learned already, Plugging In is a powerful technique for solving SAT algebra problems. It is also very useful on geometry problems. On some problems, you will be able to plug in ballpark values for missing information and then use the results either to find the answer directly or to eliminate answers that could not possibly be correct.

Here's an example:

20

The base of triangle T is 40 percent less than the length of rectangle R. The height of triangle T is 50 percent greater than the width of rectangle R. The area of triangle T is what percent of the area of rectangle R ?

A) 10

B) 45

C) 90

D) 110

Here's How to Crack It

This is a really hard problem. Don't worry—you'll still be able to find the right answer by sketching and plugging in.

When plugging in, always use numbers that are easy to work with. Let's say the length of the rectangle is 10; that means that the base of the triangle, which is 40 percent smaller, is 6. Now if we plug 4 in for the width of rectangle R, then the height of triangle T is 6. You should come up with two sketches that look like this:

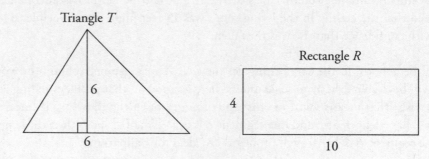

T has an area of $\frac{1}{2}bh$, or 18. R has an area of 40. Now set up the translation: $18 = \frac{x}{100}(40)$, where x represents what percent the triangle is of the rectangle.

Solve for x and you get 45. The correct answer is (B).

Geometry Drill 1: No Calculator Section

Work these Geometry questions with all your skills and knowledge, but without your calculator. Answers and explanations can be found on page 397.

2

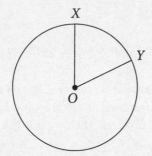

In the figure above, circle O has a radius of 8, and angle XOY measures $\dfrac{5}{16}\pi$ radians. What is the measure of minor arc XY?

A) $\dfrac{5}{16}\pi$

B) $\dfrac{5}{2}\pi$

C) 5π

D) 16π

3

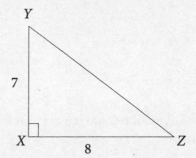

What is the value of $\tan \angle XZY$?

A) $\dfrac{7\sqrt{115}}{115}$

B) $\dfrac{8\sqrt{115}}{115}$

C) $\dfrac{7}{8}$

D) $\dfrac{8}{7}$

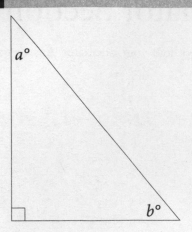

In the figure above, $\sin a = x$. What is the value of $\cos b$?

A) x

B) $\dfrac{1}{x}$

C) $|1-x|$

D) $\dfrac{90-x}{90}$

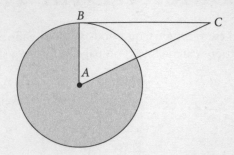

Note: Figure not drawn to scale.

The circle above with center A has an area of 21. BC is tangent to the circle with center A at point B. If $AC = 2AB$, then what is the area of the shaded region?

A) 3.5

B) 15.75

C) 17.5

D) 21

Geometry Drill 2: Calculator-Permitted Section

Calculator use is allowed on these questions, so use it to your best ability, but make sure to set them up on paper first. Answers and explanations can be found on page 397.

Answers and explanations can be found on page 397.

1

If a rectangular swimming pool has a volume of 16,500 cubic feet, a uniform depth of 10 feet, and a length of 75 feet, what is the width of the pool, in feet?

A) 22

B) 26

C) 32

D) 110

8

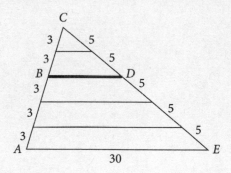

In the figure above, what is the length of $\overline{BD}$?

A) 8

B) 9

C) 12

D) 15

12

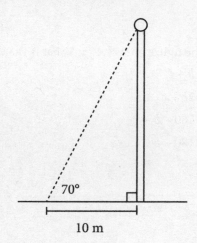

Martin wants to know how tall a certain flagpole is. Martin walks 10 meters from the flagpole, lies on the ground, and measures an angle of 70° from the ground to the base of the ball at the top of the flagpole. Approximately how tall is the flagpole from the ground to the base of the ball at the top of the flagpole?

A) 3 m

B) 9 m

C) 27 m

D) 29 m

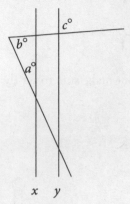

26

In the figure above, $x \parallel y$. What is the value of a?

A) $b + c$

B) $2b - c$

C) $180 - b + c$

D) $180 - b - c$

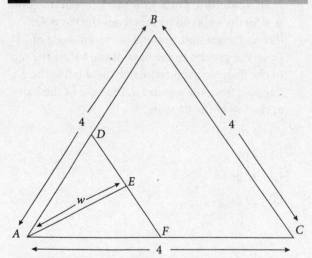

$\triangle ABC$ is equilateral and $\angle AEF$ is a right angle. D and F are the midpoints of AB and AC, respectively. What is the value of w?

A) 1

B) $\sqrt{3}$

C) 2

D) $2\sqrt{3}$

29

A toy pyramid (not shown) is made from poly(methyl methacrylate), better known by its trade term Lucite. The toy pyramid has a regular hexagonal base of 15 cm² and a height of 4 cm. In the base of the pyramid, there is a semispherical indentation 2 cm in diameter. If the pyramid weighs 21.129 g, then what is the density of Lucite? (Density equals mass divided by volume.)

A) 1.06 g/cm³

B) 1.18 g/cm³

C) 2.09 g/cm³

D) 6.51 g/cm³

CHAPTER DRILL ANSWERS AND EXPLANATIONS

Geometry Drill 1: No Calculator Section

2. **B** Because the question wants arc length and gives you the measure of the central angle in radians, you can use the formula $s = r\theta$ to find the arc length: $s = (8)\left(\dfrac{5}{16}\pi\right) = \dfrac{40}{16}\pi$, which reduces to $\dfrac{5}{2}\pi$, which is (B).

3. **C** Tangent is defined as $\dfrac{opposite}{adjacent}$. The side opposite angle XZY is 7, and the side adjacent to this angle is 8, so the tangent of $\angle XZY = \dfrac{7}{8}$, which is (C).

10. **A** You can plug in when you're dealing with a geometry problem with unknowns. When you're Plugging In for a right triangle, use one of the special right triangles to make your life easier. Use a 3-4-5 right triangle. Make the side opposite a 3, the side adjacent to a 4, and the hypotenuse 5. Because sine is $\dfrac{opposite}{hypotenuse}$, $\sin a = \dfrac{3}{5}$, so $x = \dfrac{3}{5}$. Cosine is $\dfrac{adjacent}{hypotenuse}$, so $\cos b = \dfrac{3}{5}$. This is your target; circle it. Make $x = \dfrac{3}{5}$ in each answer choice and look for the answer which equals $\dfrac{3}{5}$. Only (A) works.

15. **C** The trick is to recognize that $\triangle ABC$ is a 30°-60°-90° right triangle. $\angle ABC$ must equal 90° since a tangent line must be perpendicular to the radius of a circle drawn to the point of tangency. Only a 30°-60°-90° has a hypotenuse (AC) equal to double the length of one of the sides (AB). (You can also use the Pythagorean Theorem to show this.) This means that $\angle BAC = 60°$, so the shaded region has a central angle measure of $360° - 60° = 300°$. To get the area, use the proportion $\dfrac{Central\ Angle}{360°} = \dfrac{Sector\ Area}{Circle\ Area}$, or $\dfrac{300°}{360°} = \dfrac{s}{21}$. Reduce, cross-multiply, and solve to get $s = 17.5$. This matches (C).

Geometry Drill 2: Calculator-Permitted Section

1. **A** For this question, you need to know that volume equals *length* × *width* × *height*. You know that the volume is 16,500, the depth (or height) is 10, and the length is 75. Just put those numbers in the formula: $16,500 = 75 \times w \times 10$. Use your calculator to solve for w, which equals 22: Choice (A) is correct.

8. **C** The 5 equal lengths that make up the two sides of the largest triangle tell us that we are dealing with 5 similar triangles. The largest triangle has sides 15:25:30, and the sides of all 5 triangles will have an equivalent ratio. Reduced, the ratio is 3:5:6, which happens to be the dimensions of the smallest triangle. We want to find the length of *BD*, the base of a triangle with sides of 6 and 10. This is twice as big as the smallest triangle, so the base *BD* must be 6 × 2 =12, which is (C).

12. **C** Use SOHCAHTOA and your calculator to find the height of the flagpole. From the 70° angle, you know the adjacent side of the triangle, and you want to find the opposite side, so you need to use tangent. Tangent $= \dfrac{opposite}{adjacent}$, so $\tan 70° = \dfrac{x}{10\,\text{m}}$, where *x* is the height of the flagpole up to the ball. Isolate *x* by multiplying both sides by 10: $10 \tan 70° = x$. Use your calculator to find that $10 \tan 70° = 27.47$, which is closest to (C).

26. **D** Don't forget that you can plug in numbers on geometry questions. Let's make *b* = 70° and *a* = 30°. So the third angle in the triangle is 80°. You know that *c* would be 80°, because it is opposite an 80° angle. Your target answer is *a* = 30°, so plug in 80° and 70° to find it. The only possible answer is (D).

28. **B** There's a lot going on in this problem! But if we take it piece by piece, we'll crack it. Let's start filling in some information. The first thing the problem tells us is that triangle *ABC* is equilateral. Mark 60 degree angles on the figure. Next, we see that angle *AEF* is a right angle. Write that in as well. The problem also conveniently tells us that *D* and *F* are the midpoints of *AB* and *AC*, respectively. Therefore, *AD* and *AF* are 2. Finally, the last piece of information reveals that *E* is the midpoint of *DF*; mark *DE* and *EF* as equal.

Now, what do we have? Triangle *AEF* is a right triangle, with a hypotenuse of 2 and a leg of 1. Hmm, perhaps the good ol' Pythagorean Theorem can help us. Plug the numbers into the formula, and you'll find that the answer is (B).

You may have also noticed that triangle *ADE* is a 30°-60°-90° triangle with hypotenuse 2, which means that *DE* is 1 and *w*, opposite the 60°, is the square root of 3. In geometry questions on the SAT, there will often be multiple ways to get to the answer. On the day of the test, use whichever method you are most comfortable with.

29. **B** Work the problem in steps. You are given the mass, so to find density you need to find the volume of the pyramid. The formula at the beginning of the section tells you that, for a pyramid, $V = \dfrac{1}{3} Bh$, where *B* is the area of the base of the pyramid and *h* is the height. Therefore, the volume of the pyramid is $\dfrac{1}{3}(15)(4) = 20$. However, you need to subtract the volume of the semispherical indentation in the base. Once again, the reference sheet found beginning of the Math section tells you that

the volume of a sphere is given by the equation $V = \frac{4}{3}\pi r^3$. Because the diameter of the indentation is 2 cm, the radius of the hemisphere is 1 cm. If it were a whole sphere, the volume of the indentation would be $\frac{4}{3}\pi(1)^3 = 4.189$; you want only half, so dividing by 2 gives you 2.094 cm³ for the hemisphere. Subtracting 2.094 cm³ from the 20 cm³ of the pyramid gives you a total volume of $20 - 2.094 = 17.906$ cm³. Finally, you can find the density of Lucite by using the definition of density: Density $= \frac{21.129 \text{ g}}{17.906 \text{ cm}^3} \approx 1.18$ g/cm³, which is (B).

Summary

o Degrees and angles:

  - A circle contains 360 degrees.
  - When you think about angles, remember circles.
  - A line is a 180-degree angle.
  - When two lines intersect, four angles are formed; the sum of their measures is 360 degrees.
  - When two parallel lines are cut by a third line, the small angles are equal, the big angles are equal, and the sum of a big angle and a small angle is 180 degrees.

o Triangles:

  - Every triangle contains 180 degrees.
  - An isosceles triangle is one in which two of the sides are equal in length, and the two angles opposite the equal sides are equal in measure.
  - An equilateral triangle is one in which all three sides are equal in length, and all three angles are equal in measure (60 degrees).
  - The area of a triangle is $\frac{1}{2}bh$.
  - The height must form a right angle with the base.
  - The Pythagorean Theorem states that in a right triangle, the square of the hypotenuse equals the sum of the squares of the two legs. Remember ETS's favorite Pythagorean triplets (3-4-5 and 5-12-13).
  - Remember the other special right triangles: 45°-45°-90° and 30°-60°-90°.
  - Similar triangles have the same angles and their lengths are in proportion.

  - For trigonometry questions, remember SOHCAHTOA:

    - $\sin = \dfrac{opposite}{hypotenuse}$

    - $\cos = \dfrac{adjacent}{hypotenuse}$

    - $\tan = \dfrac{opposite}{adjacent}$

- o Circles:
  - The circumference of a circle is $2\pi r$ or πd, where r is the radius of the circle and d is the diameter.
  - The area of a circle is πr^2, where r is the radius of the circle.
  - A tangent touches a circle at one point; any radius that touches that tangent forms a 90-degree angle.
  - Arcs are proportional to the circumference based on the central angle: $\dfrac{central\ angle}{360°} = \dfrac{arc\ length}{2\pi r}$.
  - Sectors are proportional to the area based on the central angle: $\dfrac{central\ angle}{360°} = \dfrac{sector\ area}{\pi r^2}$.
  - If the central angle is given in radians, the measure of the arc is given by $s = r\theta$.

- o Rectangles and squares:
  - The perimeter of a rectangle is the sum of the lengths of its sides.
  - The area of a rectangle is *length × width*.
  - A square is a rectangle whose four sides are all equal in length.
  - Any polygon can be divided into triangles.
  - The volume of a rectangular solid is *length × width × height*. The formulas to compute the volumes of other three-dimensional figures are supplied in the instructions at the front of both Math sections.

- o When you encounter a geometry problem on the SAT, Ballpark the answer before trying to work it out.

- o You must be familiar with the size of certain common angles.

- o Most SAT geometry diagrams are drawn to scale. Use your eyes before you use your pencil. Try to eliminate impossible answers.

- o When a diagram is not drawn to scale, redraw it.

- o When no diagram is provided, make your own; when a provided diagram is incomplete, complete it.

- o When information is missing from a diagram, Ballpark and Plug In.

Chapter 17
Grid-Ins

On the SAT, 13 of the 58 Math questions will require you to produce your own answer. Although the format of these questions is different from that of the multiple-choice questions, the mathematical concepts tested aren't all that different. In this chapter, we will show you how to apply what you have learned in the previous chapters to these new questions.

WHAT IS A GRID-IN?

Both of the Math sections on your SAT will contain a group of problems without multiple-choice answers. There will be 5 of these in the No Calculator section and 8 in the Calculator section. ETS and the College Board call these problems "student-produced responses." We call them Grid-Ins because you have to mark your answers on a grid printed on your answer sheet. The grid looks like this:

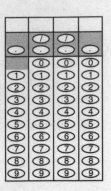

Despite their format, Grid-Ins are just like any other Math questions on the SAT, and many of the techniques that you've learned so far still apply. You can still use Plugging In and other great techniques, such as the Ratio Box and Average Pie. Your calculator will still help you out on many problems as well. So grid-ins are nothing to be scared of. In fact, many of these are simply regular SAT multiple-choice math problems with the answer choices lopped off. The only difference is that you have to arrive at your answer from scratch rather than choose from four possibilities.

You will need to be extra careful with answering Grid-In questions, however, because the grid format increases the likelihood of careless errors. It is vitally important that you understand how the Grid-In format works before you take the test. In particular, you'll need to memorize ETS's rules about which kinds of answers count and which do not. The instructions may look complicated, but we've boiled them down to a few rules for you to memorize and practice.

Take a look at the grid again. Because of the way it's arranged, the test writers can use only certain types of problems for Grid-Ins. For example, you'll never see variables in your answer (though there can be variables in the question) because the grids can accommodate only numbers. You will also never have a π, square root, or negative number in your answer. Most answers for Grid-Ins are integers.

This means that your calculator will be useful on several questions. As always, be careful to set up the problem on paper before you carefully punch the numbers into your calculator. Because you have to write in the answer on the grid yourself, you need to be more careful than ever to avoid careless mistakes.

Just as with the multiple-choice questions, there is no penalty for wrong answers on the Grid-Ins. An incorrect answer on one of these questions is no worse for your score than a question left blank. And, by the same token, a blank is just as costly as an error. Therefore, you *should be very aggressive in answering these questions.* Don't leave a question blank just because you're worried that the answer you've found may not be correct. ETS's scoring computers treat incorrect answers and blanks like they're exactly the same. If you have arrived at an answer, you have a shot at earning points; and if you have a shot at earning points, you should take it.

We're not saying you should guess blindly. But if you work a problem and are unsure of your answer, enter it anyway. There is no penalty for getting it wrong.

Order of Difficulty: Grid-Ins
As with the multiple-choice questions, Grid-Ins will be in a loose order of difficulty.

Take a Guess
Just like the multiple-choice questions, there is no penalty for wrong answers on the Grid-In questions.

THE INSTRUCTIONS

Here are the instructions for the Grid-In section as they will appear in Section 3 on the SAT. The instructions for Section 4 will look just like this, except they will start "For questions 31–38..."

DIRECTIONS

For questions 16-20, solve the problem and enter your answer in the grid, as described below, on the answer sheet.

1. Although not required, it is suggested that you write your answer in the boxes at the top of the columns to help you fill in the circles accurately. You will receive credit only if the circles are filled in correctly.

2. Mark no more than one circle in any column.

3. No question has a negative answer.

4. Some problems may have more than one correct answer. In such cases, grid only one answer.

5. **Mixed numbers** such as $3\frac{1}{2}$ must be gridded as 3.5 or 7/2. (If 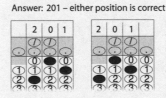 is entered into the grid, it will be interpreted as $\frac{31}{2}$, not as $3\frac{1}{2}$.)

6. **Decimal Answers:** If you obtain a decimal answer with more digits than the grid can accommodate, it may be either rounded or truncated, but it must fill the entire grid.

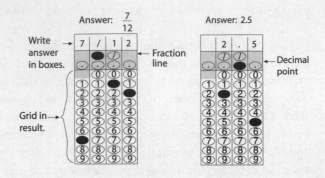

Answer: $\frac{7}{12}$ Answer: 2.5

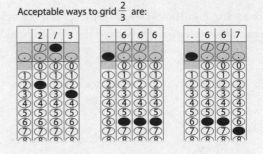

Acceptable ways to grid $\frac{2}{3}$ are:

Answer: 201 – either position is correct

NOTE: You may start your answers in any column, space permitting. Columns you don't need to use should be left blank.

What the Instructions Mean

Of all the instructions on the SAT, these are the most important to understand thoroughly before you take the test. Pity the unprepared student who takes the SAT cold and spends 10 minutes of potential point-scoring time reading and puzzling over the confusing instructions. We've translated these unnecessarily complicated instructions into a few important rules. Make sure you know them all well.

Fill In the Boxes

Always write your answer in the boxes at the top of the grid before you darken the ovals below. Your written answers won't affect the scoring of your test; if you write the correct answer in the boxes and grid in the wrong ovals, you won't get credit for your answer (and you won't be able to appeal to ETS and the College Board). However, writing in the answers first makes you less likely to make an error when you grid in, and it also makes it easier to check your work.

Fill In the Ovals Correctly

As we just pointed out, you receive no credit for writing in the answer at the top of the grid. The scoring computer cares only whether the ovals are filled in correctly. For every number you write into the grid, make sure that you fill in the corresponding oval.

Stay to the Left

Although you'll receive credit no matter where you put your answer on the grid, you should always begin writing your answer in the far left column of the grid. This ensures that you will have enough space for longer answers when necessary. You'll also cut down on careless errors if you always grid in your answers the same way.

FRACTIONS OR DECIMALS: YOUR CHOICE

You can grid in an answer in either fraction or decimal form. For example, if your answer to a question is $\frac{1}{2}$, you can either grid in $\frac{1}{2}$ *or* .5. It doesn't matter to ETS because $\frac{1}{2}$ equals .5; the computer will credit either form of the answer. That means you actually have a choice. If you like fractions, grid in your answers in fraction form. If you like decimals, you can grid in the decimal. If you have a fraction that doesn't fit in the grid, you can simply convert it to a decimal on your calculator or on paper and grid in the decimal.

Here's the bottom line: When gridding in fractions or decimals, use whichever form is easier and least likely to cause careless mistakes.

Watch Out
Negatives, π, and % cannot be gridded in! For a Grid-In question involving % or $, the SAT will tell you to ignore the % or $ symbol. But negative numbers, non-integer square roots, and π can't be gridded in, so they'll never be an answer for this type of problem.

Keep Left
No matter how many digits are in your answer, always start gridding in the left-most column. That way, you'll avoid omitting digits and losing points.

Decimal Places and Rounding

When you have a decimal answer of a value less than 1, such as .45 or .678, many teachers ask you to write a zero before the decimal point (for example, 0.45 or 0.678). On Grid-In questions, however, ETS doesn't want you to worry about the zero. In fact, there is no 0 in the first column of the grid. If your answer is a decimal less than 1, just write the decimal point in the first column of the grid and then continue from there.

You should also notice that if you put the decimal point in the first column of the grid, you have only three places left to write in numbers. But what if your decimal is longer than three places, such as .87689? In these cases, you will get credit if you round off the decimal so that it fits in the grid. But you'll *also* get credit if you just enter as much of the decimal as will fit.

For example, if you had to grid in .87689, you could just write .876 (which is all that will fit) and then stop. You need to grid in only whatever is necessary to receive credit for your answer. Don't bother with extra unnecessary steps. You don't have to round off decimals, so don't bother.

If you have a long or repeating decimal, however, be sure to fill up all the spaces in the grid. If your decimal is .666666, you *must* grid in .666. Just gridding in .6 or .66 is not good enough.

Note: Very long decimal answers are somewhat rare. Your answer should usually be integers or simple fractions.

Reducing Fractions

If you decide to grid in a fraction, ETS doesn't care if you reduce the fraction or not. For example, if your answer to a problem is $\frac{4}{6}$, you will get credit if you grid in $\frac{4}{6}$ or reduce it to $\frac{2}{3}$. So if you have to grid in a fraction, and the fraction fits in the grid, don't bother reducing it. Why give yourself more work (and another chance to make a careless error)?

The only time you might have to reduce a fraction is if it doesn't fit in the grid. If your answer to a question is $\frac{15}{25}$, it won't fit in the grid. You have two options: Either reduce the fraction to $\frac{3}{5}$ and grid that in, or use your calculator to convert the fraction to .6. Choose whichever process makes you the most comfortable when calculator use is allowed, and make sure you know how to reduce fractions for the No Calculator section.

Mixed Numbers

The scoring machine for the SAT does not recognize mixed numbers. If you try to grid in $2\frac{1}{2}$ by writing "2 1/2," the computer will read this number as $\frac{21}{2}$. You have to convert mixed numbers to fractions or decimals before you grid them in. To grid in $2\frac{1}{2}$, either convert it to $\frac{5}{2}$ or its decimal equivalent, which is 2.5. If you have to convert a mixed number to grid it in, be very careful not to change its value accidentally.

Don't Mix
Never grid in a mixed number. Change it into a top-heavy fraction or its decimal equivalent.

Don't Worry

The vast majority of Grid-In answers will not be difficult to enter in the grid. The test writers won't try to trick you by purposely writing questions that are confusing to grid in. Just pay attention to these guidelines and watch out for careless errors.

GRIDDING IN: A TEST DRIVE

To get a feel for this format, let's work through two examples. As you will see, Grid-In problems are just regular SAT Math problems.

16

If $a + 2 = 6$ and $b + 3 = 21$, what is the value of $\frac{b}{a}$?

Here's How to Crack It

You need to solve the first equation for a and the second equation for b. Start with the first equation, and solve for a. By subtracting 2 from both sides of the equation, you should see that $a = 4$.

Now move to the second equation, and solve for b. By subtracting 3 from both sides of the second equation, you should see that $b = 18$.

The question asked you to find the value of $\dfrac{b}{a}$. That's easy. The value of b is 18, and the value of a is 4. Therefore, the value of $\dfrac{b}{a}$ is $\dfrac{18}{4}$.

That's an ugly-looking fraction. How in the world do you grid it in? Ask yourself this question: "Does $\dfrac{18}{4}$ fit?" Yes! Grid in $\dfrac{18}{4}$.

Your math teacher wouldn't like it, but the scoring computer will. You shouldn't waste time reducing $\dfrac{18}{4}$ to a prettier fraction or converting it to a decimal. Spend that time on another problem instead. The fewer steps you take, the less likely you will be to make a careless mistake.

Here's another example. This one is quite a bit harder.

34

> Forty percent of the members of the sixth-grade class wore white socks. Twenty percent wore black socks. If twenty-five percent of the remaining students wore gray socks, what percent of the sixth-grade class wore socks that were not white, black, or gray? (Disregard the % when gridding your answer.)

Here's How to Crack It

The problem doesn't tell you how many students are in the class, so you can plug in any number you like. This is a percentage problem, so the easiest number to plug in is 100. Forty percent of 100 is 40; that means 40 students wore white socks. Twenty percent of 100 is 20. That means that 20 students wore black socks.

Your next piece of information says that 25 percent of the remaining students wore gray socks. How many students remain? Forty, because 60 students wore either white or black socks, and 100 − 60 = 40. Therefore, 25 percent of these 40—10 students—wore gray socks.

How many students are left? 30. Therefore, the percentage of students not wearing white, black, or gray socks is 30 out of 100, or 30 percent. Grid it in, and remember to forget about the percent sign.

ORDER OF DIFFICULTY

Like all other questions on the Math Test, Grid-In problems are arranged in a loose order of difficulty. Since this order is not strict, however, it is much more important to pay attention to your own strengths and weaknesses. Remember to focus on the questions you know how to answer first. Don't spend time on questions that you have no idea how to work.

Keep in mind, of course, that many of the math techniques that you've learned are still very effective on Grid-In questions. Plugging In worked very well on the previous question. If you're able to plug in or take an educated guess, go ahead and grid in that answer. Again, there is no penalty for getting it wrong.

Here's another difficult Grid-In question that you can answer effectively by using a technique you've learned before:

36

Grow-Up potting soil is made from only peat moss and compost in a ratio of 3 pounds of peat moss to 5 pounds of compost. If a bag of Grow-Up potting soil contains 12 pounds of potting soil, how many pounds of peat moss does it contain?

Here's How to Crack It
To solve this problem, set up a Ratio Box.

	Peat Moss	Compost	Whole
Ratio (parts)	3	5	8
Multiply By			
Actual Number			12 (lbs)

What do you multiply by 8 to get 12? If you don't know, divide 12 by 8 on your calculator. The answer is 1.5. Write 1.5 in each of the boxes on the *multiply by* row of your Ratio Box.

	Peat Moss	Compost	Whole
Ratio (parts)	3	5	8
Multiply By	1.5	1.5	1.5
Actual Number			12 (lbs)

The problem asks you how many pounds of peat moss are in a bag. To find out, multiply the numbers in the Peat Moss column. That is, multiply 3 × 1.5, and you get 4.5. ETS's answer is 4.5.

	Peat Moss	Compost	Whole
Ratio (parts)	3	5	8
Multiply By	1.5	1.5	1.5
Actual Number	4.5 (lbs)		12 (lbs)

Grid it in like this:

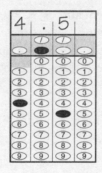

Careless Mistakes

On Grid-In questions, you obviously can't use Process of Elimination to get rid of bad answer choices, and techniques like Plugging In the Answers won't work either. In order to earn points on Grid-In questions, you're going to have to find the real answers, and you're going to have to be extremely careful when you enter your answers on your answer sheet. If you need to, double-check your work to make sure you have solved correctly. If you suspect that the question is a difficult one and you get an answer too easily, you may have made a careless mistake or fallen into a trap.

RANGE OF ANSWERS

More Than One

Some Grid-In questions have several possible correct answers. None is more correct than any other, so grid in the first one you find and move on.

Some Grid-In problems will have many possible correct answers. It won't matter which correct answer you choose, as long as the one you choose really is correct.

Here's an example:

───────────────────○───────────────────

| 17 |

If $4 < 3x + 2 < 5$, what is one possible value of x ?

Here's How to Crack It

With double inequalities or equations, don't try to do the entire problem at once. It's much easier to split this problem into two smaller problems:

$$4 < 3x + 2 \text{ and } 3x + 2 < 5$$

Solve each one. For the first inequality, start by subtracting 2 from both sides, leaving $2 < 3x$. Divide by 3, leaving (approximately) $0.666 < x$. For the other inequality, start, as before, by subtracting 2 from both sides, leaving $3x < 3$. Divide by 3 to get $x < 1$. Combining both inequalities back together, you'll get that x is between 0.666 and 1.

So, what do you enter as your answer? Anything between .666 and 1. Really. Anything. .8, .954, .667, .999, 5/6, 7/8, 9/10, whatever.

───────────────────○───────────────────

EXTENDED THINKING

Extended What?

The last two Grid-Ins will be a pair of questions based on the same information. They can cover any of the previous math content, and they are still worth just one point each. Use your knowledge of your own test-taking skills to decide which of these you want to try, if you do them at all.

The last two questions in Section 4 (calculator allowed) will be a pair of Grid-Ins that ETS and the College Board refer to as Extended Thinking questions. It claims that these questions, drawn from real-world contexts, will assess a student's ability to apply "complex cognitive skills." Don't panic, though. Aside from being paired and sometimes more difficult, they are not any different than other Grid-Ins. Many of the same strategies will apply to the Extended Thinking questions. They can be drawn from pretty much any mathematical content, from problem solving to functions, and they are only worth one point each.

Let's look at a set.

Questions 37 and 38 refer to the following information.

$$k = Ce^{\frac{-E_a}{RT}}$$

$$r = k[A]^2$$

$$\frac{1}{[A]_t} = kt + \frac{1}{[A]_0}$$

The kinetics of a chemical reaction can be described by the equations above, where e is a constant approximately equal to 2.718, k is the rate constant in L/mol-s, E_a is the activation energy in J/mol-K, T is temperature in Kelvin, r is the reaction rate in mol/s, and $[A]$ is the concentration of a species in mols/L, either initially as $[A]_0$, or at a given time of t as $[A]_t$. C is a constant equal to 4, and R is a constant of 8.314 J/mol.

37

If the reaction initially starts with 2 mol/L of species A, and the activation energy of the reaction is 10,082 J/mol, at 310 Kelvin, how many seconds will it take for the concentration of A to reach 0.4 mol/L?

38

If rate constant k triples for the reaction described in question 37, what is the concentration of species A after 50 seconds, in mol/L?

Most Extended Thinking
questions can be solved
independent of one
another, and one is often
easier than the other.
Consider doing the more
straightforward one and
skipping the more difficult
or time-consuming one.

Here's How to Crack It

As you can see, in order to have a chance at solving question 38, you first must solve question 37. In most cases, the two Extended Thinking questions will be more independent of each other. In that case, if one is easier than the other, maybe try that one and skip the other one. Only students aiming for a top score should attempt both Extended Thinking questions.

Let's start with question 37. There are three equations, so it is hard to know where to begin. Start by writing down the values for the variables you know. The question tells us that $[A]_0 = 2$ and $[A]_t = 0.4$. You want to find the time, t, so plug these values into the last equation to get $\dfrac{1}{0.4} = kt + \dfrac{1}{2}$. Simplify this equation to get $2.5 = kt + 0.5$, and $kt = 2$. To solve for t, you first need to figure out the value of k. You need to use the first equation to find the value of k, since the value of r in the second equation is never defined. According to the question, C and R are constants, where $C = 4$ and $R = 8.314$. Also according to the question, $E_a = 10,082$, and $T = 310$. Plug all of these values into the first equation to get $k = 4e^{\frac{-10,082}{(8.314)(310)}}$. Simplify the exponent to get $k = 4e^{-3.9118}$. Use your calculator to find that $k = 4(0.02) = 0.08$. Plug this value into the earlier equation $kt = 2$ to get $0.08t = 2$, and $t = 25$. The correct answer is 25. Grid it in!

Notice how the second equation was completely useless in solving this problem. That will happen occasionally on the SAT, so don't get distracted by the extraneous information.

Now that we have the value of rate constant k, let's crack question 38. In question 37, $k = 0.08$, so if k triples, the new value for k is $0.08 \times 3 = 0.24$. According to the information in question 37, $[A]_0 = 2$, and according to question 38, $t = 50$. Plug all of these values into the last equation, which has $[A]_t$ in it, to get $\frac{1}{[A]_t} = (0.24)(50) + \frac{1}{2}$. Simplify the right side of the equation to get $\frac{1}{[A]_t} = 12.5$. Multiply both sides by $[A]_t$ to get $1 = 12.5[A]_t$. Finally, divide both sides by 12.5 to get $0.08 = [A]_t$. The correct answer is 0.08.

Grid-In Drill 1: No Calculator Section

Work these Grid-Ins without your calculator using the skills you've learned so far. Answers and explanations can be found on page 423.

Answers and explanations can be found on page 423.

16

If $a^b = 4$, and $3b = 2$, what is the value of a ?

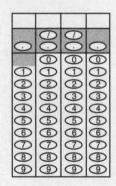

17

If $4x + 2y = 24$ and $\dfrac{7y}{2x} = 7$, what is the value of x ?

If $\dfrac{x^2 + x - 6}{x^2 - 8x + 12} = 4$, what is the value of x ?

If $-1 \le a \le 2$ and $-3 \le b \le 2$, what is the greatest possible value of $(a + b)(b - a)$?

Grid-In Drill 2: Calculator-Permitted Section

Work these Grid-Ins using your calculator as needed and applying the skills you've learned so far. Answers and explanations can be found on page 423.

Answers and explanations can be found on page 423.

32

$$n = 12 \times 2^{\frac{t}{3}}$$

The number of mice in a certain colony is shown by the formula above, such that n is the number of mice and t is the time, in months, since the start of the colony. If 2 *years* have passed since the start of the colony, how many mice does the colony contain now?

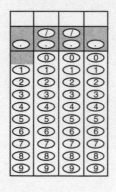

33

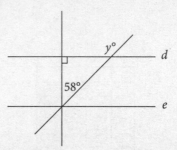

In the figure above, if d is parallel to e, what is the value of y ?

35

If Alexandra pays $56.65 for a table, and this amount includes a tax of 3% on the price of the table, what is the amount, in dollars, that she pays in tax? (Disregard the dollar sign when gridding your answer.)

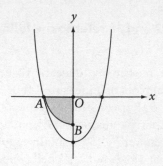

In the figure above, AB is the arc of the circle with center O. Point A lies on the graph of $y = x^2 - b$, where b is a constant. If the area of shaded region AOB is π, then what is the value of b ?

An unusually warm and wet month causes the monthly production of eggplants to double. What is the daily average number of eggplants produced in the garden during a 30-day month at the new rate?

Questions 37 and 38 refer to the following information.

A garden, measuring 10 feet by 12 feet, contains individual plots that measure 1 foot by 1 foot. 30% of the plots contain bell peppers, 30% contain cherry tomatoes, 25% contain squash, and the remaining 15% contain eggplants. Each bell pepper plot produces 2 bell peppers every 5 days, a tomato plot produces 4 cherry tomatoes every 6 days, a squash plot produces 1 squash every 15 days, and an eggplant plot produces 3 eggplants every 10 days.

37

In a 30-day month, how many vegetables are produced by the 10 × 12 foot garden?

CHAPTER DRILL ANSWERS AND EXPLANATIONS

Grid-In Drill 1: No Calculator Section

16. **8**   Using $3b = 2$, solve for b by dividing both sides by 3 to get $b = \dfrac{2}{3}$. That means $a^{\frac{2}{3}} = 4$. Fractional exponents tell you to use the denominator as the root and use the numerator as a regular exponent. So, $\sqrt[3]{a^2} = 4$. First, cube both sides to find $a^2 = 4^3 = 64$. Next, take the square root of both sides to find $a = 8$.

17. **3**   You can solve this question using simultaneous equations because you have two equations with two variables. First, you need to rearrange the equations a bit: $4x + 2y = 24$ divided by 2 on both sides becomes $2x + y = 12$. $\dfrac{7y}{2x} = 7$, multiplied by $2x$ on both sides, becomes $7y = 14x$. This, divided by 7 on both sides, becomes $y = 2x$, which can be manipulated into $2x - y = 0$. Now you can add the equations:

$$\begin{array}{r} 2x + y = 12 \\ +\ 2x - y = 0 \\ \hline 4x \quad\quad = 12 \end{array}$$

Therefore, $x = 3$.

18. **9**   Factor the numerator and the denominator into $\dfrac{(x-2)(x+3)}{(x-2)(x-6)} = 4$. The $(x - 2)$ cancels out of the top and bottom to leave $\dfrac{(x+3)}{(x-6)} = 4$. Multiply both sides by $(x - 6)$ to get $x + 3 = 4x - 24$. Subtract x from both sides: $3 = 3x - 24$. Add 24 to both sides: $27 = 3x$. Divide by 3 to get $x = 9$.

19. **9**   This looks suspiciously like a quadratic equation, and if you multiply it out, its equivalent is $b^2 - a^2$. You want to make this as large as possible, so you want b^2 to be large and a^2 to be small. If $b = -3$, $b^2 = 9$; if $a = 0$, $a^2 = 0$. So $b^2 - a^2$ can be as large as 9.

Grid-In Drill 2: Calculator-Permitted Section

32.   **3,072**

Because the t in $n = 12 \times 2^{\frac{t}{3}}$ represents the number of months, we cannot use the 2 *years* time frame given in the question in place of t. The colony has been growing for 24 months, which is evenly divisible by the 3 in the fractional exponent. The equation is much easier now that the fractional exponent is gone. $n = 12 \times 2^{\frac{24}{3}} = 12 \times 2^8 = 12 \times 256 = 3{,}072$.

33. **148** A line crossing two parallel lines creates big angles and small angles. The big angle that matches y is split by a line perpendicular to d and e. The big angle is $58 + 90 = 148$, which is also the value for y. Another way to solve this is to find the third angle of the triangle: $180 - 90 - 58 = 32$. The $32°$ angle and the $y°$ angle make up a straight line, so $180 - 32 = 148$.

35. **1.65** The best way to approach this problem is to set up an equation. There is some price such that if you add 3% of the price to the price itself, you get $56.65. This means that you can set up an equation: $x + 3\%$ of $x = 56.65$, or $x + 0.03x = 56.65$. Now you can just solve for x, and you get the original price, which was $55. Subtract this from $56.65 to get the tax $1.65.

36. **4** This question looks tough, so work it one step at a time, and start with what you know. Sector AOB is a quarter-circle (it covers an angle of 90 out of 360 degrees), so multiplying its area (π) by 4 gives you the area of the whole circle (4π). Plugging this into the equation for the area of a circle, $A = \pi r^2$, gives you $4\pi = \pi r^2$, and the radius must be a positive value, so $r = 2$. This means that the coordinates of point A must be $(-2, 0)$. Because A is on both the circle and the parabola, you can plug its x- and y-coordinates into the given equation of the parabola, $y = x^2 - b$. This becomes $0 = (-2)^2 - b$, so $b = 4$.

37. **1,374**

First, calculate the number of plots in the garden. Given that the garden measures 10 feet by 12 feet and each plot is one foot by one foot, there are $10 \times 12 = 120$ total plots. Next calculate the number of each type of vegetable plot as follows:

$120 \times 0.3 = 36$ bell pepper plots

$120 \times 0.3 = 36$ cherry tomato plots

$120 \times 0.25 = 30$ squash plots

$120 \times 0.15 = 18$ eggplant plots

According to the question, 2 bell peppers are grown every 5 days on each of the 36 pepper plots. That means that all the pepper plots together grow $2 \times 36 = 72$ peppers in 5 days. To determine how many peppers would grow in a month, set up a proportion.

$$\frac{72 \text{ peppers}}{5 \text{ days}} = \frac{x}{30 \text{ days}}$$

Cross-multiply, and then divide by 5 to find that the garden produces 432 peppers for the month. Repeat these steps with the other 3 vegetables. The 36 tomato plots produce 144 tomatoes every 6 days. Together, they produce 720 tomatoes in the month. The 30 squash plots produce 30 squash every 15 days, for a total of 60 squash in a month. Finally the 18 eggplant plots grow 54 eggplants every 10 days, which means during a 30-day period the garden will produce 162 eggplants. The total number of vegetables can be calculated as 432 bell peppers + 720 cherry tomatoes + 60 squash + 162 eggplants = 1,374 vegetables.

38. **10.8** During a normal month, each eggplant plot produces 3 eggplants every 10 days. Therefore, if the production were to double, each plot would produce 6 eggplants every 10 days. Given that the garden measures 10 feet by 12 feet and each plot is one foot by one foot, there are $10 \times 12 = 120$ total plots, 15% of which are eggplant plots. Therefore, there are $120 \times 0.15 = 18$ eggplant plots. Calculate the total number of eggplants produced in 10 days as $18 \times 6 = 108$. In a 30-day month, there are three 10-day periods, so the entire garden would produce $108 \times 3 = 324$ total eggplants. To find the daily average production, divide 324 by 30 to get an average of 10.8 eggplants each day.

Summary

- o Both of the Math sections on your SAT will contain a group of problems without multiple-choice answers. ETS and the College Board call these problems "student-produced responses." We call them Grid-Ins, because you have to mark your answers on a grid printed on your answer sheet.

- o Despite their format, Grid-Ins are really just like other Math questions on the SAT, and many of the same techniques that you have learned still apply.

- o The grid format increases the likelihood of careless errors. Know the instructions and check your work carefully.

- o Just like the rest of the exam, there is no guessing penalty for Grid-Ins, so you should always grid in your answer, even if you're not sure whether it's correct.

- o Always write the numbers in the boxes at the top of the grid before you (carefully) fill in the corresponding ovals.

- o Grid in your answer as far to the left as possible.

- o If the answer to a Grid-In question contains a fraction or a decimal, you can grid in the answer in either form. When gridding in fractions or decimals, use whichever form is easier and least likely to cause careless mistakes.

- o There's no need to round decimals, even though it is permitted.

- o If you have a long or repeating decimal, be sure to fill up all the spaces in the grid.

- o If a fraction fits in the grid, you don't have to reduce the fraction before gridding it in.

- o The scoring computer does not recognize mixed numbers. Convert mixed numbers to fractions or decimals before gridding them in.

- o Some Grid-In questions will have more than one correct answer. It doesn't matter which answer you grid in, as long as it's one of the possible answers.

o Like all other questions on the SAT Math Test, Grid-In problems are arranged in a loose order of difficulty. Use your knowledge of your own strengths and weaknesses to decide which ones to tackle first and which ones, if any, to skip.

o The last two Grid-Ins in Section 4 are Extended Thinking questions, a set of questions on the same information. Usually, they can be answered independently, and they are worth only 1 point each. Attempt both only if you are aiming for a top score.

o Negatives, π, square roots, %, and degree symbols cannot be gridded in.

Part V
How to Crack the Essay

Chapter 18
Reading and
Analyzing the
Essay Passage

The SAT includes an optional rhetorical analysis essay. Your job is to read a text (typically a speech or editorial of some sort) and discuss how the author effectively builds an argument. This might be a familiar task if you've done it in school. If not, don't worry. The format is straightforward, and with some practice, you can learn how to write a good SAT essay. In this chapter we'll look at two of the three tasks you will need to do for the essay—reading and analysis—and show you how to approach each task in the most effective way possible.

THE "OPTIONAL" ESSAY

The Essay section used to be a required part of the SAT, but not all colleges found this score to be helpful. This is why the essay is now "optional." Your essay score is now completely separate from your total score, so opting out of the essay will not have any effect on your 400–1600 score. Notice how we're using quotation marks whenever we say the essay is "optional," though? You should consider the essay to be optional for colleges, but *not* optional for you.

The problem is that some schools require the essay while others don't, and you can't do the essay independently of the rest of the SAT. That means if you opt out of the essay and later you realize you need it for your application, you can't simply redo just the essay: You have to redo the entire SAT. So go ahead and write the essay. You've already killed a Saturday morning, you're sitting in the testing room, and it's not ridiculously challenging to prepare for this essay. Just write it.

Writing the essay can make your college application look more attractive. Your essay score will appear on every score report you send to colleges, regardless of whether or not the school requires an essay. Every school to which you apply will see that you took the initiative to write the essay, which is a good thing.

YOUR ESSAY MISSION

In 50 minutes, you'll be required to read a text and write a logical, well-constructed analysis of the author's argument. The thing to remember here is that you are *not* being asked for your opinion on a topic or a text. Your essay will be an objective analysis of a speech or argument.

The prompt will be nearly the same every time, just with a different source text, and will be something like this:

As you read the passage below, consider how the author uses

- evidence, such as facts or examples, to support claims.
- reasoning to develop ideas and to connect claims and evidence.
- stylistic or persuasive elements, such as word choice or appeals to emotion, to add power to the ideas expressed.

Write an essay in which you explain how [the author] builds an argument to persuade [his/her] audience that [author's claim]. In your essay, analyze how [the author] uses one or more of the features listed above (or features of your own choice) to strengthen the logic and persuasiveness of [his/her] argument. Be sure that your analysis focuses on the most relevant aspects of the passage.

Your essay should not explain whether you agree with [the author's] claims, but rather explain how the author builds an argument to persuade [his/her] audience.

In the essay, you will:

- carefully read a text
- understand how an author appeals to a reader's logic, emotions, or morals
- write a logical analysis of an argument
- explain how style choices can affect an author's persuasiveness

In the essay, you will NOT:

- give your opinion about a text
- memorize examples from history or literature
- have previous experience with the text

Essay Scoring
Reading, Analysis, and Writing scores will be combined for a total score of 3–12. (Each category will receive a total score of 2–8, which is found by adding the individual 1–4 scores from your two readers.) Each task (Reading, Analysis, and Writing) is scored individually, so a high score in one does *not* guarantee a high score in another.

Two graders will read and score the essay on a 1–4 scale in three different categories: Reading, Analysis, and Writing.

> 4 = **Advanced**
>
> 3 = **Proficient**
>
> 2 = **Partial**
>
> 1 = **Inadequate**

The scores will be determined using the following rubric. There is a lot of information here. You don't need to memorize this, but it may help you understand the scoring a little more. We'll go through the first two tasks in this chapter, followed by the third task—Writing—in Chapter 19.

ETS's Essay Rubric			
Score of 4: Advanced	Score of 3: Proficient	Score of 2: Partial	Score of 1: Inadequate
Reading • Demonstrates thorough comprehension of the source text. • Shows an understanding of the text's central idea(s) and of most important details and how they interrelate, demonstrating a comprehensive understanding of the text. • Is free of errors of fact or interpretation with regard to the text. • Makes skillful use of textual evidence (quotations, paraphrases, or both), demonstrating a complete understanding of the source text.	• Demonstrates effective comprehension of the source text. • Shows an understanding of the text's central idea(s) and important details. • Is free of substantive errors of fact and interpretation with regard to the text. • Makes appropriate use of textual evidence (quotations, paraphrases, or both), demonstrating an understanding of the source text.	• Demonstrates some comprehension of the source text. • Shows an understanding of the text's central idea(s) but not of important details. • May contain errors of fact and/or interpretation with regard to the text. • Makes limited and/or haphazard use of textual evidence (quotations, paraphrases, or both), demonstrating some understanding of the source text.	• Demonstrates little or no comprehension of the source text. • Fails to show an understanding of the text's central idea(s), and may include only details without reference to central idea(s). • May contain numerous errors of fact and/or interpretation with regard to the text. • Makes little or no use of textual evidence (quotations, paraphrases, or both), demonstrating little or no understanding of the source text.
Analysis • Offers an insightful analysis of the source text and demonstrates a sophisticated understanding of the analytical task. • Offers a thorough, well-considered evaluation of the author's use of evidence, reasoning, and/or stylistic and persuasive elements, and/or feature(s) of the student's own choosing. • Contains relevant, sufficient, and strategically chosen support for claim(s) or point(s) made. • Focuses consistently on those features of the text that are most relevant to addressing the task.	• Offers an effective analysis of the source text and demonstrates an understanding of the analytical task. • Competently evaluates the author's use of evidence, reasoning, and/or stylistic and persuasive elements, and/or feature(s) of the student's own choosing. • Contains relevant and sufficient support for claim(s) or point(s) made. • Focuses primarily on those features of the text that are most relevant to addressing the task.	• Offers limited analysis of the source text and demonstrates only partial understanding of the analytical task. • Identifies and attempts to describe the author's use of evidence, reasoning, and/or stylistic and persuasive elements, and/or feature(s) of the student's own choosing, but merely asserts rather than explains their importance, or one or more aspects of the response's analysis are unwarranted based on the text. • Contains little or no support for claim(s) or point(s) made. • May lack a clear focus on those features of the text that are most relevant to addressing the task.	• Offers little or no analysis or ineffective analysis of the source text and demonstrates little or no understanding of the analytic task. • Identifies without explanation some aspects of the author's use of evidence, reasoning, and/or stylistic and persuasive elements, and/or feature(s) of the student's choosing. • Numerous aspects of the response's analysis are unwarranted based on the text. • Contains little or no support for claim(s) or point(s) made, or support is largely irrelevant. • May not focus on features of the text that are relevant to addressing the task or the response offers no discernible analysis (e.g., is largely or exclusively summary).

Writing	• Cohesive and demonstrates a highly effective use and command of language. • Includes a precise central claim. • Includes a skillful introduction and conclusion. The response demonstrates a deliberate and highly effective progression of ideas both within paragraphs and throughout the essay. • Wide variety in sentence structures. The response demonstrates a consistent use of precise word choice. The response maintains a formal style and objective tone. • Shows a strong command of the conventions of standard written English and is free or virtually free of errors.	• Mostly cohesive and demonstrates effective use and control of language. • Includes a central claim or implicit controlling idea. • Includes an effective introduction and conclusion. The response demonstrates a clear progression of ideas both within paragraphs and throughout the essay. • Variety in sentence structures. The response demonstrates some precise word choice. The response maintains a formal style and objective tone. • Shows a good control of the conventions of standard written English and is free of significant errors that detract from the quality of writing.	• Demonstrates little or no cohesion and limited skill in the use and control of language. • May lack a clear central claim or controlling idea or may deviate from the claim or idea over the course of the response. • May include an ineffective introduction and/or conclusion. The response may demonstrate some progression of ideas within paragraphs but not throughout the response. • Limited variety in sentence structures; sentence structures may be repetitive. • Demonstrates general or vague word choice; word choice may be repetitive. The response may deviate noticeably from a formal style and objective tone. • Shows a limited control of the conventions of standard written English and contains errors that detract from the quality of writing and may impede understanding.	• Demonstrates little or no cohesion and inadequate skill in the use and control of language. • May lack a clear central claim or controlling idea. • Lacks a recognizable introduction and conclusion. The response does not have a discernible progression of ideas. • Lacks variety in sentence structures; sentence structures may be repetitive. The response demonstrates general and vague word choice; word choice may be poor or inaccurate. The response may lack a formal style and objective tone. • Shows a weak control of the conventions of standard written English and may contain numerous errors that undermine the quality of writing.

TASK 1: READING

In order to write an essay that analyzes a source text, you must first read the text. Unlike with the Reading passages, there are no tricks to shorten your reading time or cut out pieces of the text. However, knowing what to look for as you read can help streamline the reading process and give you a good start on the second task of analysis.

According to ETS and the College Board, your Reading score on the essay will be based on your:

- comprehension of the source text
- understanding of central ideas, important details, and how these things are related
- accuracy in representation of the source text (i.e., no errors of fact or interpretation introduced)
- use of textual evidence (quotations, paraphrases, or both) to demonstrate understanding of the source text

When you start this task, the very first thing you have to do is read the text. Obvious, right? But reading for the essay is unlike leisure reading, when all you need to worry about is whether or not Katniss is going to make it to the end of the Games. As you read the essay prompt, you need to consider the central idea (SOAPS) and important details that support that idea (types of appeals and style elements).

SOAPS—Like in the Tub?

SOAPS is an acronym to help you remember the five things you need to look for in order to establish the central idea of a passage or argument.

Speaker
Occasion
Audience
Purpose
Subject

Plan Accordingly
Plan for 25–30 minutes for Reading and Analysis, and 20–25 minutes for Writing.

SOAPStone: Ever Hear of It?
You may have learned SOAPStone in your English class. It's almost the same thing as SOAPS.

Speaker

> Who is speaking or writing?

Knowing whose voice you are reading is very important for understanding the text thoroughly. It will help you understand their motivations as well as the reason(s) they are speaking or writing in the first place. As you read, ask what makes this person credible? What are the speaker's credentials?

- What gives a doctor the authority to speak about medical issues, or a politician the authority to speak about political issues? (Be specific.)

_____

_____

_____

For the doctor, you might mention medical school and many years studying medicine. Passing tests and acquiring hands-on experience give a doctor credibility on medical issues. The longer a doctor has been practicing medicine, the more experience he has, lending even more credibility. For the politician, you might mention experience working in government and policy. Many study political science in college. The politician may have run successful campaigns previously.

- Would you rather hear a stockbroker or an athlete speak about financial investing? Why?

_____

_____

_____

Probably the stockbroker! A stockbroker has experience in the field of investments and knows important information to help educate you. An athlete doesn't necessarily know the type of fiscal information you would want to hear.

So, remember! The speaker of the source text is very important. The next time you read an article online about the five foods you should never eat, consider the speaker or writer. Does that person have the credentials to give advice on nutrition? On the SAT Essay, you will not see a speaker unqualified to discuss the given topic.

Occasion

> What happened that requires this speech or text?

The event that caused the author to want to express her thoughts is an integral part of analyzing the work. It might be as simple as the type of event in which the speech was given. It might, however, be something larger such as a significant time in a war. You will need to think about the historical context of the text.

- What type of elements would you expect to hear in a coach's speech before a big game?

_____

_____

_____

You might expect elements such as motivational support (examples: "Go Team!"; "Keep your head in the game!"; "Victory will be ours!") and strategy (examples: "Remember that Wilkins is weak on his left side."; "Keep your eyes open for the gap in the line."; "Fake a pass to Jenkins.").

- What type of elements would you expect to hear in a politician's speech the day before Election Day?

_____

_____

_____

You might expect sweeping statements with few details, such as a reminder to "go out and vote" or a patriotic reminder about that politician's values. You might even hear a cheer of confidence meant to inspire.

- How might a minister's message at a wedding differ from her message at a funeral?

_____

_____

_____

At a wedding, a minister is likely to be optimistic and cheerful, while at a funeral, a minister is more likely to be solemn and comforting. In this case, since the speaker is the same, the occasion makes all the difference.

So, remember! Taking note of the occasion of the speech/writing will help you understand why the author uses a certain tone and some of his/her motivations.

Audience

> Who is the intended audience?

Considering your audience is critical when you are writing a speech. Therefore, it is critical that you consider who the author's audience is in order to understand the text. What do you know about them? What's the relationship between the speaker/author and the intended audience? What sort of values or prior ideas might the audience have? How might that affect their perception of the speaker/author?

- How might a politician's Election Eve speech to a conservative group differ from his speech to a liberal group?

_____

_____

_____

When speaking to groups that are very different, a politician is going to cater his speech to each group's values. To the conservatives, she will speak on conservative issues and to the liberals, the liberal issues. The politician likely has different goals for each.

- How would a principal's message to a group of new teachers be different from a message to a group of experienced teachers?

_____

_____

_____

A principal is more likely to be more informal in tone to experienced teachers and provide less detailed information. With new teachers, however, the principal will likely want to make a good impression as well as make sure the teachers understand her role as a supportive authority. With new teachers the principal will also need to give very clear information and perhaps repeat that information more than once and explain all the things the experienced teachers already know about the school.

So, remember: The audience can entirely change a work. When reading your source text for the essay, make sure to consider who the audience is and how that affected how the author built his or her argument.

Purpose

What is the author or speaker's intention?

Occasion, Subject, and Audience all contribute to Purpose. What is the author trying to accomplish with this work? Is it an attack? Defense? Persuasion? Does it aim to give praise or blame? Is its goal to teach, or something else?

Subject

What is the main idea?

Of course, you need to know what the work is about. What is the topic? What is the author's main point? What are the main lines of reasoning used?

Appeals

A rhetorical appeal is a persuasive strategy that an author or speaker uses to support his claims (or in a debate, to respond to opposing arguments). When a speaker or author wants to convince an audience of something, there are three main types of rhetorical appeals that can be used: appeal to credibility, appeal to emotion, and appeal to logic.

Appeal to Credibility: "Why Should I Believe You?"

This is the author's way of establishing trust with his audience. We tend to believe people whom we respect, and a good writer knows this! One of the central tasks of persuasion is to project an impression to the reader that the author is someone worth listening to, as well as someone who is likable and worthy of respect. Remember when we talked about the speaker in SOAPS and his credibility? This is how an author might use his own credentials to his benefit.

Consider the following:

- A doctor writes an article about health issues. What does she need to include in order to establish trust from her audience?

_____

_____

_____

How did you respond? She should probably include a brief biography about her practice and her medical experience, as well as information about whether she has been practicing for a long time, has done important research, or went to a top school.

- A speaker calls into a talk radio program about military strategy. What should he mention in order to establish credibility with other listeners?

_____

_____

_____

Here are some possibilities: any experience he has had (and how much) in the military or with military strategy, and what he has done to enable him to know what he is talking about. A 4-star general is more likely to be fairly listened to and believed than the soon-to-be Call of Duty tristate area champion.

Appeal to Emotion: "Gee, That Made Me Feel All Warm and Fuzzy."

This is when the author tries to appeal to the reader's emotions. This allows an author or speaker to connect with an audience by using fear, humor, happiness, disgust, and so on. Imagery and language choice are often big components of appeals to emotion.

- An article about world hunger runs in a magazine. What decisions could the magazine editor make to appeal to her readers' emotions?

_____

_____

_____

Pictures of starving children or visual charts showing how much food the average family throws away are two possible ways the editor could attempt to tug on heart strings.

- A motivational speaker wants to make an energetic entrance. What could he do (and why)?

_____

_____

_____

Some possibilities: Play upbeat music and run in, have certain people in the audience cheer ridiculously, have a cheesy announcer and balloons falling from the ceiling.

People get excited when other people get excited. Certain things, like balloons, confetti, and fireworks, trigger happiness in us, perhaps due to our childhood. If the speaker runs out with a huge smile on his face and dozens (hundreds?) of screaming fans, it is very likely going to excite his audience—or, at the very least, make them sit up a little straighter and be interested in what he will say next.

Appeal to Logic: "Well, This Just Makes Sense!"

This connects with an audience's reason or logic. This isn't logic like the formal logic in math, philosophy, or even computer science; it is the consistency and clarity of an argument as well as the logic of evidence and reasons.

Instead of simply saying, "This is a good idea," an author of a magazine article about environmental protection could convince her readers of her point by doing what?

_____

_____

_____

Some possibilities: Providing proof of some sort, in the form of data, statistics, expert opinions, testimonials, or other options.

- A salesman wants a husband and wife to buy a washer/dryer pair instead of a single appliance. How might he appeal to their logic?

_____

_____

_____

Discuss the cost benefits of buying two at once versus each one at a different time such as having two brand new appliances that won't need to be worried about for years, and benefits or discounts that apply only if they buy both the washer _and_ dryer, for example. He could also tell them about the money back guarantee to show that the appliances must be quality if the store is willing to refund their money if they aren't satisfied. All of these are examples of appeals to logic and reasoning. These are all things that make the couple think, "Well, gee, this just makes sense!"

Once you find all the SOAPS points and examples of appeals, you've got what you need for the Reading task. Remember, for the Reading task, the test writers want to see that you understand the text, can identify the central idea/theme of the text, and know how details and examples support that central idea.

SOAPS AND APPEALS DRILL

Read the following prompt and underline anything that references SOAPS points. There's a worksheet on pages 447–449 for you to track your notes, and you can check your answers on page 458.

As you read the passage below, consider how President John F. Kennedy uses

- evidence, such as facts or examples, to support claims.
- reasoning to develop ideas and to connect claims and evidence.
- stylistic or persuasive elements, such as word choice or appeals to emotion, to add power to the ideas expressed.

---

1   We set sail on this new sea because there is new knowledge to be gained, and new rights to be won, and they must be won and used for the progress of all people. For space science, like nuclear science and all technology, has no conscience of its own. Whether it will become a force for good or ill depends on man, and only if the United States occupies a position of pre-eminence can we help decide whether this new ocean will be a sea of peace or a new terrifying theater of war. I do not say that we should or will go unprotected against the hostile misuse of space any more than we go unprotected against the hostile use of land or sea, but I do say that space can be explored and mastered without feeding the fires of war, without repeating the mistakes that man has made in extending his writ around this globe of ours.

2   There is no strife, no prejudice, no national conflict in outer space as yet. Its hazards are hostile to us all. Its conquest deserves the best of all mankind, and its opportunity for peaceful cooperation many never come again. But why, some say, the moon? Why choose this as our goal? And they may well ask why climb the highest mountain? Why, 35 years ago, fly the Atlantic? Why does Rice play Texas?

3   We choose to go to the moon. We choose to go to the moon in this decade and do the other things, not because they are easy, but because they are hard, because that goal will serve to organize and measure the best of our energies and skills, because that challenge is one that we are willing to accept, one we are unwilling to postpone, and one which we intend to win, and the others, too.

4   It is for these reasons that I regard the decision last year to shift our efforts in space from low to high gear as among the most important decisions that will be made during my incumbency in the office of the Presidency…

5   To be sure, we are behind, and will be behind for some time in manned flight. But we do not intend to stay behind, and in this decade, we shall make up and move ahead.

6   The growth of our science and education will be enriched by new knowledge of our universe and environment, by new techniques of learning and mapping and observation, by new tools and computers for industry, medicine, the home as well as the school. Technical institutions, such as Rice, will reap the harvest of these gains.

7   And finally, the space effort itself, while still in its infancy, has already created a great number of new companies, and tens of thousands of new jobs. Space and related industries are generating new demands in investment and skilled personnel, and this city and this State, and this region, will share greatly in this growth. What was once the furthest outpost on the old frontier of the West will be the furthest outpost on the new frontier of science and space. Houston, your City of Houston, with its Manned Spacecraft Center, will become the heart of a large scientific and engineering community. During the next 5 years the National Aeronautics and Space Administration expects to double the number of scientists and engineers in this area, to increase its outlays for salaries and expenses to $60 million a year; to invest some $200 million in plant and laboratory facilities; and to direct or contract for new space efforts over $1 billion from this Center in this City…

8   Many years ago the great British explorer George Mallory, who was to die on Mount Everest, was asked why did he want to climb it. He said, "Because it is there."

9   Well, space is there, and we're going to climb it, and the moon and the planets are there, and new hopes for knowledge and peace are there. And, therefore, as we set sail we ask God's blessing on the most hazardous and dangerous and greatest adventure on which man has ever embarked.

Thank you.

(John F. Kennedy. September 12, 1962. Rice Stadium, Houston, TX)

Write an essay in which you explain how President Kennedy builds an argument to expand and move forward with the United States' space program. In your essay, analyze how Kennedy uses one or more of the features listed above (or features of your own choice) to strengthen the logic and persuasiveness of his argument. Be sure that your analysis focuses on the most relevant aspects of the passage.

Your essay should not explain whether you agree with Kennedy's claims, but rather explain how the author builds an argument to persuade his audience.

SOAPS:

1. **Speaker:** Who is speaking? What credentials does this person have to make his speech believable?

    _____

    _____

    _____

2. **Occasion:** What was the reason for President Kennedy to give this particular speech?

    _____

    _____

    _____

3. **Audience:** Who is the audience for this speech? What do you know about them?

    _____

    _____

    _____

    Can you figure anything out about their values based on how President Kennedy speaks to them and what he says?

    _____

    _____

    _____

4. **Purpose:** What is JFK's goal?

_____

_____

_____

5. **Subject:** What is the main idea of the speech?

_____

_____

_____

Appeals:

1. **Appeal to Emotion:** What does President Kennedy say to appeal to his audience's emotions?

_____

_____

_____

These words/phrases would appeal to which emotion(s)?

_____

_____

_____

2. **Appeal to Logic:** What does President Kennedy say to appeal to his audience's logic and reason?

_____

_____

_____

How might these words/phrases appeal to logic or reason?

_____

_____

_____

Awesome job! Now take a look at page 458 to see if your ideas can be found within ours and to grab some ideas of things you may have missed. Once you have the main points of the speech, it's time to start analyzing.

TASK 2: ANALYSIS

Remember: A good score on one task does not guarantee a good score on another. Doing a good job of explaining the main idea of the speech and the details that support that main idea will get you a good Reading score, but now we need to talk about Analysis.

For the Analysis task, you'll have to determine the pieces of evidence, stylistic elements, or logical reasoning the author uses to effectively achieve his or her objective.

According to ETS and the College Board, your Analysis score will be based on your ability to:

- analyze the source text and understand the analytical task
- evaluate the author's use of evidence, reasoning, and/or stylistic and persuasive elements, and/or features chosen by the student
- support claims or points made in the response
- focus on features of the text most relevant to addressing the task

For this task, you will need to explain the author's choice and use of specific elements in the essay. It's not enough to say, "The author uses a quote to appeal to the audience's reason." You have to explain *how* the quote appeals to the audience's reason. This task is all about the *how* and *why*. Look for facts, evidence, literary devices, persuasive elements, and other elements the author has used to form his or her argument.

Here are some common style elements that may show up in the text.

Style Detail	Definition	Example
Allusion	A brief reference to a person, thing, or idea from history, literature, politics, or something with cultural significance.	"Don't ask him for a donation; he's a total Scrooge." "Chocolate was her Kryptonite."
Comparison	Comparing two distinct things; the author/speaker makes a connection between them	"Juliet is the sun." "My love is like a red rose."
Diction	The author's choice of words.	"Skinny" instead of "slender" sounds less flattering. Slang or vernacular gives a text an informal feel, while a professional vocabulary makes a text feel more formal.
Hyperbole	Exaggeration not meant to be taken literally	"I'm so hungry I could eat a horse."

Imagery	Using language that appeals to our senses. Visual representation of an object or idea is a common perception of imagery, but imagery actually can create ideas that appeal to all five senses.	"The woman walked by, trailing a thick, cloying cloud of perfume." "The percussive thump of the large drums vibrated in her chest as the band marched by."
Juxtaposition	Placing two ideas side-by-side in order for the audience to make a comparison or contrast	"It was the best of times, it was the worst of times…"
Repetition	Deliberate repetition of a letter, word, or phrase to achieve a specific effect.	"We shall not flag or fail. We shall go on to the end. We shall fight in France, we shall fight on the seas and oceans, we shall fight with growing confidence and growing strength in the air…"
Statistics or quotes	A writer or speaker may add credibility to his or her argument by adding data or quotes from a respected/recognized source.	A quote from the American Academy of Pediatrics in a speech about best practices for carseat use.
Syntax	How words are put together to achieve a certain effect. First and last words of an idea can be particularly important.	An author who wants to convey a message quickly or urgently might choose to use short, direct sentences, while an author who wants to deliberately slow down a text may use longer, more convoluted sentences.
Tone	The attitude of the author/speaker toward the subject	Sarcastic, professional, critical

Note: These devices are deliberately used by the author/speaker for a specific purpose. You will need to know the purposes of the devices and their effects on a text, but you will not need to know the specific names.

Spot the Element

Let's read the following pieces of text and then identify the rhetorical device used in each.

> "…raised herself on one round elbow and looked out on a tiny river like a gleaming blue snake winding itself around a purple hill. Right below the house was a field white as snow with daisies, and the shadow of the huge maple tree that bent over the little house fell lacily across it. Far beyond it were the white crests of Four Winds Harbour and a long range of sunwashed dunes and red cliffs."
>
> —L.M. Montgomery, *The Road to Yesterday*

- Which of the five senses is appealed to most strongly in Mongomery's description of the setting?

_____

_____

_____

If you are thinking *vision*, then you are correct! Montgomery uses *imagery* (detailed descriptions) to allow the reader to "see" the setting.

- What literary device does Montgomery use to describe the river and the field of daisies?

_____

_____

_____

Comparisons! Montgomery compares the river to a "gleaming blue snake" and the daisies to a "field white as snow." These comparisons allow the reader to connect the images to something already in his mind to create more vibrant image.

"Well now, one winter it was so cold that all the geese flew backward and all the fish moved south and even the snow turned blue. **Late at night, it got so frigid that all spoken words froze solid afore they could be heard. People had to wait until sunup to find out what folks were talking about the night before.**"

- In this excerpt from a tall tale about Paul Bunyan, which literary device is used to great effect?

_____

_____

_____

If you are thinking *hyperbole,* then you are correct! Think about what the author's goal for using that particular device might be. Hyperbole helps the author communicate to the reader that it wasn't just plain old cold. It was *incredibly* cold. However, instead of just using italics like we just did, the author used the much more creative exaggeration of words freezing in midair to get his point across.

"Jackson pulled back the curtain to look at the rain. 'Better start building that Ark,' he said over his shoulder."

- What does Jackson mean?

_____

_____

_____

He means that it is raining really hard. How would you know that? Jackson says to start building an "ark," a reference to Noah's Ark, which he had to build to survive a great flood. What literary device is this? Allusion. An allusion is a reference to something (usually another great work, event, or person) without explicit mention of it.

LITERARY DEVICES DRILL

Now let's think back to the speech by President Kennedy. Go back and read for stylistic elements. Underline and annotate your passage. When you are done, turn to the next page to check your work.

Here are some examples of style devices and rhetorical elements you may have found in the speech.

- **Metaphor:** JFK uses the metaphor of space as the ocean when he says, "We set sail on this new sea" in the first paragraph. This metaphor is continued later in the paragraph with "whether this new ocean will be a sea of peace."

  In the seventh paragraph, JFK says that Houston will "become the heart" of a large scientific community.

  Rice will "reap the harvest" of the new advancements in technology.

  Imagery: JFK mentions "feeding the fires of war" which creates the image of war as a dangerous, uncontrollable element of nature.

- **Syntax**: JFK (who is widely remembered for his distinct syntax in his speeches) uses rhetorical questions such as "Why choose this as our goal?" He also uses repetition frequently. He asks several rhetorical questions in a row in the second paragraph. In the third paragraph he repeats the phrase "We choose to go to the moon."

- **Allusion:** JFK makes an allusion to Charles Lindbergh flying across from New York to Paris on his *Spirit of St. Louis* plane, completing the first solo crossing of the Atlantic with the words "Why, 35 years ago, fly the Atlantic?"

  JFK makes an allusion to Texas being "the furthest outpost on the old frontier of the West." This refers to the outer line of settlement in the United States moving steadily west and the fact that the location of his speech was, at one point, the furthest west that the country extended.

- **Statistics and Quotes**: JFK mentions specific figures for spending on the new space program such as "$60 million a year" for salaries and expenses, "$200 million" in plant and laboratory facilities, and "over $1 billion" to contract for new space efforts.

- **Diction**: We "choose" to go to the moon instead of "We are going to the moon."

  JFK describes the entire plan to go the moon as an "adventure" instead of "budget line item" or "task" or even "journey."

PUTTING IT ALL TOGETHER

Now that you have identified the parts of the speech, appeals, and the literary devices used in the passage on page 445, you have to figure out how those come together to create an effective argument.

This chapter ends with a drill that allows you to do just that. Reread President Kennedy's speech and look over your notes, and then answer the questions starting on page 456. When you're done, turn to page 460 to see how your answers compare with ours.

Reading and Analysis Drill

Answers and explanations can be found on page 460.

1. How did the president's appeals help make his speech more effective for his listeners? What would have been motivating for them, and why?

    _____

    _____

    _____

    _____

    _____

2. If he had been speaking to a different audience, would some of these strategies have been less effective? Explain.

    _____

    _____

    _____

    _____

    _____

3. What is the tone of the passage? How do you know?

    _____

    _____

    _____

    _____

4. What are some specific examples of word choice (diction), that make the speech convincing? Can you explain why? What word choices would have meant the same thing, but been less convincing?

_____

_____

_____

_____

_____

5. How does the structure of the speech impact his audience? Does the order in which the ideas are presented affect the argument? Why or why not?

_____

_____

_____

_____

6. What would you consider the three most effective parts of the speech? (These will be the basis for your essay body paragraphs.)

_____

_____

_____

_____

CHAPTER DRILL ANSWERS AND EXPLANATIONS

SOAPS and Appeals Drill

SOAPS

1. **Speaker:** *Who is speaking? What credentials does this person have to make his speech believable?*

   The speaker is the current (1962) President of the United States, John F. Kennedy. The job of the presidency alone carries enough weight for people to listen. However, Kennedy does mention his presidency in lines such as "during my incumbency in the office of the Presidency," probably to keep that authority in the minds of his listeners.

2. **Occasion:** *What was the reason for President Kennedy to give this particular speech?*

   JFK wanted to promote and rouse support for the United States' new space program. In paragraph 4 he says, "...I regard the decision to shift our efforts in space from low to high gear as among the most important decisions made..."

3. **Audience:** *Who is the audience for this speech? What do you know about them?*

   JFK mentions both Rice University and Houston in his speech, making several references that would be significant to those people. We know that they care about their university and their city, and we know they have school spirit! (In paragraph 2, JFK asks several questions including why climb a mountain, why fly across the Atlantic, and "Why does Rice play Texas?" You can almost imagine the listeners cheering at this reference.)

   Can you figure anything out about their values based on how President Kennedy speaks to them and what he says?

   We know they value their community because JFK makes several references to the good that this effort will do the locals such as more jobs and a better economy. We know they value education and the furthering of science because JFK discusses the benefit to the scientific community as well as the medical community. We know they value the idea of a God and his goodwill since JFK makes a point to "ask God's blessing" on his mission.

4. **Purpose:** *What is President Kennedy's goal?*

    JFK wants to garner support and excitement for the mission to put a man on the moon. He has come to Houston specifically to try to get the locals on board since they will be incredibly important to the entire effort. Evidence for this is right in the first paragraph.

5. **Subject:** *What is the main idea of the speech?*

    JFK's main idea is that putting a man on the moon will not only be positive for the local community, but also something America must do because Americans do not shy away from a challenge.

Appeals

1. **Appeal to Emotion:** *What does President Kennedy say to appeal to his audience's emotions?*

    -   JFK discusses how space science will become either a "force for good or ill," and the outcome depends on humanity. He mentions the need for America to "occupy a position of pre-eminence" so that we can steer the outcome, directly appealing to his audience's sense of responsibility and patriotism.

    -   JFK repeatedly discusses that "we choose to go to the moon" not because it is easy but because it is hard. He discusses that it will be "the most hazardous and dangerous and greatest adventure on which man has ever embarked."

    -   JFK uses words like "set sail" and "furthest outpost" and "old frontier of the West." These would appeal to the adventurous spirit.

    -   JFK tells his listeners that there is knowledge to be gained for "all people," and that space is "hostile to us all." That would effectively pull people together and inspire unity.

    -   JFK discusses "Rice play[ing] Texas" as an example of something that is hard, but is done anyway. (Here he is referring to their football teams competing since Texas historically has a good football team and Rice, not so much.) Pride! Go team!

    -   JFK asks for "God's blessing on the…adventure." Christian values.

2. **Appeal to Logic:** *What does President Kennedy say to appeal to his audience's logic and reason?*

    -   He makes a reference to "35 years ago, fly[ing] the Atlantic." This shows the audience that there have been things in the past that we felt were impossible and dangerous that are now commonplace to us. Flying across the Atlantic Ocean is a logical comparison to space travel.

    -   He discusses how "science and education will be enriched by new knowledge" as well as many other references to the benefits of space travel and space science including to Rice University specifically. By showing the benefits to the scientific community, he gives people an understanding that the benefits are worth the risks and costs. It also gives them a personal stake in the decision for any that work or attend Rice University in the science fields.

- He reassures the audience that we will not "go unprotected." This makes his audience feel as if it is not a hasty and unreasonably unsafe decision. Appeals to those that might be dubious towards the prospect of space exploration.

- He mentions how many jobs have already been created and how the region and the state will flourish as "the heart of a large scientific and engineering community." The long-term benefits to the Houston area are clearly positive outcomes.

Reading and Analysis Drill

Here are some possible answers to the previous questions. Yours may or may not match—these answers are *possible* answers, not the only correct ones.

1. The president's appeals to emotion fill his listeners with a sense of participation in the "adventure" that is putting a man on the moon. The listeners are not simply listening to a government official explain why he made a decision; they are made to feel pride, unity, control, and patriotism. The president's words make the listener feel as if he, as an American, is brave for taking this on. The listener feels like a pioneer who is doing what his ancestors before him did: exploring the unknown. The president's appeals to logic motivate the listeners to support the mission because of all the prosperity it will bring their community. First, the president helps them understand that goals that have seemed as impossible in the past have been accomplished to quell any doubters. Then, he details all of the wonderful things that will take place in Houston when the change takes place and for many years to come.

2. Had the president been speaking to a Portuguese audience, it is much less likely that they would have been excited about American patriotism or felt any nostalgia for the American pioneering heritage. Even if the president had simply been in another state, all of the details about how Houston will benefit would not have been as effective. What do the residents of Cheyenne, Wyoming, care about jobs in Houston?

3. The tone of this passage is inspiring and determined. The passage begins with the phrase "We set sail on this new sea," which conveys the idea of exploration and discovery, connecting the earliest explorers and founders of America. Although Kennedy acknowledges the uncertainty surrounding such a venture (exploring space), his tone is confident and self-assured: "I do say that space can be explored and mastered"; "We choose to go to the moon…and do other things, not because they are easy, but because they are hard…"; "…we shall make up and move ahead." Finally, he ends with a short anecdote about the British explorer George Mallory, who explained his reasons for climbing Mount Everest as such: "Because it is there." Kennedy's words are infused with an adventurous spirit, a perseverance in the face of challenges, that encapsulates the philosophical underpinnings of the United States.

4. When the president chose to use the word "choose" in the famous line "We choose to go to the moon," he was making a wise choice. Or perhaps it was the president's speechwriter—but either way, this word is more powerful than had he said something like "We probably should go to the moon" or "We can try to go to the moon." The word *choose* puts the power of choice in the listener. When people believe they are choosing something (even if a speaker tells them they are choosing it), they feel empowered. Another example of diction that made the speech convincing is the president's use of the word "adventure" in his concluding remarks. In describing his mission to put a man on the moon as an "adventure" he avoided the negative doubts of some listeners. "Adventure" is positive and exciting. He could have said "we ask God's blessing on the…most expensive decision on which man has embarked" or "on the…overwhelming task" both of which would leave the listener with a sense of cynicism or uncertainty. There are lots of great choices for convincing diction in this speech, so if you found another example, that's great!

5. The order of Kennedy's speech is carefully constructed to emotionally captivate the listener. This is a skill that political speechwriters must have, or they will probably not keep their jobs very long. Kennedy's opening brings the listeners in by making them feel as if space exploration is their responsibility (which makes them continue to listen earnestly). The middle of the speech addresses doubts and concerns, which reassures people and makes them feel as if Kennedy is forthright. The ending discusses the benefits that the listeners will reap and wraps up with a tie in to several previously mentioned points, which gives the speech a nice closure. In his last sentence, Kennedy entreats God for a blessing, which ends the speech on a humble note. All of these pieces fit together in exactly that order to ensure that the listener will feel all of those things. If Kennedy had begun humble and ended doubtful, the listeners would get the feeling that he wasn't very confident.

6. There is no correct response here as there are many possible answers. Here are three of the effective parts of the speech that you could write about. However, if you wrote a different set of three, that's fine. You should pick whichever three seemed the most effective to you.

    1. Nostalgia for the listener's pioneering heritage (Appeal to Emotion)

    2. Addressing the concern that America is already behind in the space race (Appeal to Logic)

    3. Pointing out the local benefits (Appeal to Logic)

Summary

o The SAT Essay may be "optional," but you should always opt to do it—especially if you're not sure whether the schools you're applying to require it. It's better to be safe than sorry—and to sit for an extra 50 minutes once rather than have to sit for the entire test a second time after finding out you need the essay to apply to your dream school!

o The essay is comprised of three separate tasks that will be scored individually: Reading, Analysis, and Writing.

o The essay does not require you to agree or disagree with a position or to write about a personal experience. Instead, you will have to read a passage and analyze how the author builds his or her argument.

o To score well on the Reading task, you will have to be able to identify (in your essay) the main idea and supporting details of the text. Think SOAPS:
  • **S**peaker
  • **O**ccasion
  • **A**udience
  • **P**urpose
  • **S**ubject

o To score well on the Analysis task, you will have to be able to explain (in your essay) how the author uses specific style elements and rhetorical devices to create an effective argument.

o While reading and analyzing the passage, you should also think about whether the author makes any kind of appeal (to credibility, emotion, or logic) to his or her audience.

Chapter 19
Writing the Essay

Alright! You've annotated, you've SOAPS'ed, you've made connections, and now you actually get to write the essay! In this chapter, we'll go through the basic parts of an effective essay and provide essay writing tips, a bunch of sample essays, and some feedback from our SAT experts.

TASK 3: WRITING

The previous chapter covered the first two tasks required to develop your essay: Reading and Analysis. Now we turn to the third and final task: writing the essay. According to ETS and the College Board, your Writing score will be based on whether you:

- make use of a central claim
- use effective organization and progression of ideas
- use varied sentence structures
- employ precise word choice
- maintain consistent, appropriate style and tone
- show command of the conventions of standard written English

This is also where you show your grader that you have read, understood, and analyzed the text.

SAT ESSAY TEMPLATE

Introduction

Your introduction needs to do three things:

1. **Describe the text.** This is where you'll bring in the SOAPS points. This can be done in one sentence.

2. **Paraphrase the argument.** This is where you'll show your grader that you understand the text by concisely summing up the main points and the overall message of the text. The Reading score comes from your demonstration of comprehension of the text.

3. **Introduce the examples you will be discussing in the body paragraphs.** You will establish a framework in your introduction that you should then follow for the rest of the essay.

Body Paragraphs

The body paragraphs will focus on different appeals or style elements the author uses to effectively communicate the argument. Each body paragraph will need to do the following:

1. Name and explain the rhetorical device or appeal.
   - Where is it in the text?
   - Use short, relevant quotes to show you understand the text and the rhetorical device, but do not rely on long excerpts from the passage. In order to get a high score, you need to use your words to explain what's going on.

2. Identify the effects of the author's rhetorical choices.
   - Explain the connection between the rhetorical device/appeal and the text, and your argument in general. Do not simply quote chunks of text and then briefly paraphrase. Your goal is to answer the question, "How does this contribute to the author's argument?"
   - For example, do not simply say, "This is an example of imagery." Explain *why* the imagery is effective. Perhaps the author's descriptions of the beautiful sunset effectively draw in the reader, creating an emotional connection between the author and her audience. This connection may make the audience more sympathetic to the author's subsequent points because there is an emotional connection now.
   - Explaining how the device or appeal works is how you show your grader your ability to analyze the text.

Conclusion

1. Restate the goal of the text and briefly paraphrase the elements you discussed in your essay.
2. Be concise and accurate.

SAT Essay Writing Tips

- Maintain formal style and objective tone. Avoid "I" and "you." Do not use slang.
- Use varied sentence structure.
- Write neatly.
- Use clear transitions.
- Use short, relevant quotes from the text.
- Don't worry about official terms for things. "Appeal to the emotions" is fine instead of specifically referencing "pathos," and "comparison of two things" can be used instead of referring to a metaphor. If you *do* know the official terms, though, feel free to use them!

Essay Writing on the SAT
Employing these techniques in your essay will help boost your score!

Note:
You can find blank essay answer sheets in your on-line tools that accompany this book. Just register your book (see "Register Your Book Online!" on page x) to unlock your Student Tools, and then download and print the forms. (For good measure, we've also included extra bubble sheets.)

SAMPLE ESSAYS

Let's take a look at a few final products for the prompt introduced in the previous chapter. (See page 445.) Be sure to notice what scores they received and why.

Sample Essay 1

In his eloquent speech at Rice Stadium, former-President Kennedy wields a vast array of oratory tools and constructs a case for investment in space exploration. Throughout his address, Kennedy makes use of evidence, reasoning, and stylistic elements that together form his argument for the decision that the United States should become a dominant force in the new field of space exploration, and attempt to reach the moon.

Kennedy begins his address with an analogy of space exploration as a "new sea," which he effectively continues by referring to the possible future of space as "whether this new ocean will be a sea of peace," and revisits in his final plea for divine blessing "as we set sail." The ocean is not the only natural analogy utilized by Kennedy in his speech, for he also makes use of references to mountaineering through the rhetorical question "why climb the highest mountain," as well as quoting George Mallory's stated reason for the expedition up Mount Everest: "Because it is there," and stating that "space is there, and we're going to climb it." Beyond natural analogies, Kennedy paints with colorful language, such as speaking of "the fires of war," "reap the harvest," the "infancy" of space exploration, and old Houston as "the furthest outpost on the old frontier." Kennedy also appeals to the locality in which he speaks by asking "Why does Rice play Texas?" and referencing "your City of Houston."

Kennedy's address makes use not only of creative language, but also of pieces of evidence. The primary evidence with which he appeals is a list of beneficial economic results of space exploration. He specifies that the area of Houston will see "double the number of scientists and engineers," bear an increase in "salaries and expenses to $60 million a year," receive investments of "some $200 million in plant and laboratory facilities," and be the source of funds "for new space efforts [of] over $1 billion." In addition to economic gains, Kennedy mentions a long list of educational boons such as "new knowledge of our universe and environment," "new techniques of learning and mapping and observation," and "new tools and computers for industry, medicine, the home as well as the school."

Mixed among the evidential and rhetorical components of Kennedy's address are threads of reasoning, which display the thought process by which Kennedy supports his appeal for national movement towards the exploration of space. Kennedy provides many reasons for the decision, including the universal appeal of "new knowledge to be gained, and new rights to be won." Some of the other explanations Kennedy provides for the decision include that "space science... has no conscience of its own," that the "opportunity for peaceful cooperation may never come again," and that space exploration is worth doing "because [it is] hard," which—while apparently paradoxical— Kennedy explains as well-reasoned since "that goal will serve to organize and measure the best of our energies and skills." He incorporates additional thoughtful elements as he discusses that while "we are behind,...we do not intend to stay behind, and in this decade we shall make up and move ahead."

Through these variable forms of evocative language, supportive evidence, and sound logic, former President Kennedy forges an appeal to his audience that is well-rounded and subtly sculpted into an address that exemplifies the oratory skill for which he was well known.

Score
Reading: 8
Analysis: 4
Writing: 8

SAT Experts Say: This essay contains a very impressive summary of the argument, but very little analysis. It is clear that this student can identify the stylistic elements, but he or she does not discuss their impact on the reader or why the author uses them.

A Perfect Score
As you read this sample essay, take note of how the student applies the writing tips from page 465.

Sample Essay 2

The powerful impact of President Kennedy's speech at Rice Stadium on the controversial decision to direct money of the United States towards building a preeminent space program lies in the eloquence and universality with which he weaves his appeal. Through analogies as well as acknowledging and addressing the concerns of those dubious towards the idea of space exploration, Kennedy crafts a persuasive argument, solidified by references to prior explorations and details of economic incentives.

Perhaps the most necessary element which distinguishes a well-formulated argument from a mere exercise of rhetoric is the proper use of supportive evidence, of which President Kennedy's address incorporates several examples. The first example he utilizes is subtle, but powerful. The United States had invested significantly in the development of nuclear technology, and part of the argument for that investment had been that nuclear technology could be used by the United States for its own benefit and protection, or against the United States by foreign nations who may intend harm. That argument translates clearly to space as well in Kennedy's words that "Whether [space science becomes] a force for good or ill depends on man, and only if the United States occupies a position of pre-eminence can we help decide [the future of space]." A further piece of evidence Kennedy uses to support his argument is the example of flight across the Atlantic. President Kennedy reminds his audience of this event in order to reference a previous accomplishment that had also once been seen as prohibitively difficult, much as practical exploration of space was seen by many in 1962. In his address, Kennedy also utilizes another evidentiary category, filling the second half of his speech with a lot of specific economic benefits for the area surrounding Houston from the newly bolstered space program as it develops, designed to overwhelm the listener with this positive side of investment.

Kennedy's mastery of persuasive rhetoric plays out not only in the evidence to which he refers, but also in the analogies woven through his address, which serve to evoke emotional responses in his listeners. The initial words of Kennedy's address provide the first of these analogies. Rooted in the history of exploration, Kennedy states that "We set sail on this new sea." A form of evidence in itself, this analogy serves to recall the listener's mind to a frontier that was once seen as unfathomably expansive and beyond human mastery. Kennedy continues the sea analogy by saying that space may become "a sea of peace or a new terrifying theater of war," calling to the listener's mind the unpredictable nature of the sea itself to be calm or horrifyingly volatile, as he suggests that the position of the United States in space exploration may decide the nature of this new frontier. Kennedy also reaches further back into the historical commonality of his listeners as he analogously describes Houston as "once the furthest outpost on the old frontier of the West" in order to call the listener's mind to the nature of change over time. The Houston in which Kennedy gave this speech looked essentially nothing like the Houston of the old West, and this analogy provokes the listener's imagination to project the possibilities for a new Houston, built on a strong space program. A third analogy with which Kennedy appeals to his listeners' emotions is the reference to their local sports team. As Kennedy asks "Why does Rice play Texas?" he seeks to raise the ubiquitous sense of pride many feel for their sports teams of preference, which he hopes may translate to a sense of national pride for the space program.

As most any well-crafted argument will do, Kennedy also acknowledges the arguments of those who may hold a counter perspective. By asking "But why, some say, the moon?" Kennedy introduces a potential counterargument that the goal of reaching the moon may be arbitrarily lofty. Rather than dismissing this point as irrelevant, Kennedy seeks to disarm it by embracing the lofty nature of reaching the moon and calling attention to other lofty goals deemed worthwhile, such as to "climb the highest mountain" and "fly the Atlantic." He continues to acknowledge the nature of this potential objection by saying that the goal has been chosen "because [it is] hard," and therefore will "serve to organize and measure the best of our energies and skills." Another possible counterargument Kennedy addresses is that "we are behind...in manned flight." Again, Kennedy could have easily attempted to dismiss this argument by protesting that the gap is small, but he instead chose again to affirm the objection by stating "we...will be behind for some time". Having fully acknowledged the strength of this potential problem, Kennedy then proceeds to describe the precise means by which the United States "shall make up and move ahead" through "new knowledge," "new techniques," and "new tools," which Kennedy seamlessly segues into economic benefits, as described above.

The difficulty of dissecting an address like that of President Kennedy at Rice Stadium is itself a final example of the persuasiveness of Kennedy's rhetoric. The power of Kennedy's address can be seen most clearly in the interwoven nature of all its elements. Through the marriage of these different elements, Kennedy's speech encourages, calms, and inspires.

Score
Reading: 8
Analysis: 8
Writing: 8

SAT Experts Say: This student shows a clear understanding of the text and writes a solid piece analyzing the author's argument. He or she indicates what Kennedy does (ex: "fill[s] the second half of his speech with a lot of specific economic benefits") and then tells us why Kennedy did it ("to overwhelm the listener with this positive side of investment.") This is the analysis that was lacking in Sample Essay 1 which, combined with good comprehension and solid writing skills, earned this essay a perfect score.

Sample Essay 3

Kenedy gave a speech about going to the moon. It's got a lot of stylistic elements in it. His whole speech is about how dangerous it is and how we should do it because it's dangerous. He says it's like Everest and that's hard and it killed a guy who tried to do it but we oughta do it anyway. At the beginning he said it was like going to sea and it would be dangerous because of hostile pirates or something. And that it's like Rice playing Texas. So maybe he could of meant we should do hard stuff even though you'll probably lose or die. Also he said it's like the Old West. I think maybe we like people trying do things that are dangerous, so maybe that's why people like this speech so much.

Score
Reading: 2
Analysis: 4
Writing: 2

SAT Experts Say: This student demonstrates practically no comprehension of the passage. The essay does not present an argument, but rather makes general statements about the essay that do not have any relevance to the prompt. In addition, the essay is sloppily written, including several spelling and grammatical errors——"Kenedy," "oughta," "could of," and so on. The tone is too informal ("because of hostile pirates or something," "we oughta do it anyway"), and the writing is disorganized; there is no logical progression of ideas. This essay would receive a low score.

Sample Essay 4

In 1962, President John F. Kennedy delivered a stirring, poetic speech at Rice Stadium. He structured his address using complex rhetorical devices that make it an exemplar for the ages. In particular, he spoke in a direct, simple manner that was very accessible to his audience, but layered that simple speech with complex rhetorical flourishes such as alliteration, anaphora, and epistrophe throughout. As a result, the address created a pleasing auditory effect that kept the audience engaged throughout the speech.

Beginning with his first words, and continuing throughout the address, President Kennedy used alliteration to capture the attention and the mood of his audience. In the first paragraph alone, Kennedy references setting sail on the new sea, feeding the fires of war, and the mistakes that man has made. Like a newspaper headline or song lyric, these phrases have a rhythm that make them catchy and memorable and demands the attention of the audience. At key lines the speech even settles into an iambic rhythm before returning to a blank prose style.

The pleasing rhythm of Kennedy's address is also significantly enhanced by his use of anaphora and epistrophe (also referred to as anadiplosis). Kennedy frequently employs anaphora—the repetition of beginning words in parallel phrases—at key points throughout his speech, and practically in every paragraph. In the first paragraph he repeats the phrase "I do"; in the second, rhetorical questions beginning with a repeated "why"; in the third, "we choose" repeated, followed by "because" repeated, followed by "one" repeated; and so on. And as he closes the speech, Kennedy uses epistrophe, the complementary device in which a word or phrase is repeated at the end of successive parallel clauses, noting that various things "are there". This repetition of phrases has a very powerful effect on the listener, because the phrases are so memorable when repeated, subconsciously leading the listener to conclude that the point being argued must be very important.

Through his use of evocative language, President Kennedy devised a speech that has a powerful effect on his audience. The combination of plain language with rhythm, repetition, and rhetoric evinces Kennedy's mastery of oratory and makes his address live on through the ages.

Score
Reading: 2
Analysis: 6
Writing: 6

SAT Experts Say: The main problem with this essay, as reflected in the scores above, is that the student fails to show whether he or she actually understood the speech and its central ideas. The essay lacks interpretation of the content of the speech itself, focusing only on its rhetorical devices. Although the essay does a good job of identifying these devices, the discussion does not point to the purpose of the essay; in other words, the student does not sufficiently explain how those devices are used to support Kennedy's specific claims. However, the essay demonstrates solid writing skills and offers a decent analysis of the stylistic devices and other technical elements.

Sample Essay 5

In 1962, John F. Kennedy gave an inspiring speech at Rice Stadium designed to convince his audience that space exploration was worth the risk, expense, and commitment that would be required. He employed a variety of rhetorical devices in composing a complex and powerful message.

One prominent feature of President Kennedy's speech was its use of simile and metaphor. In the first paragraph, Kennedy begins by comparing the mission to the moon to an ocean voyage, implicitly comparing space exploration to the discovery of America. He begins by stating that we "set sail on this new sea", and elaborates by emphasizing that the United States can use its power to help determine whether that "new ocean" will be a "sea of peace" or rather a dangerous mistake. He continues to make metaphorical comparisons by posing rhetorical questions about climbing a mountain and making a trans-Atlantic flight – past examples of once-impossible tasks that were undertaken and achieved through hard work and perseverance.

Another important feature of Kennedy's speech is his use of facts and supporting evidence to bolster his argument. Kennedy acknowledges that we "will be behind for some time in manned flight", but avers that we "shall make up and move ahead." He follows this claim with specific supporting evidence. He begins by discussing scientific advancements in knowledge and technology that he believes will allow the United States to achieve this goal. He then goes into detail about the positive economic effects that will be brought about by the investment in the space program, and ties these facts to the overall theme of the essay by analogizing space exploration to the settlement of the western United States: he describes Houston as "once the furthest outpost on the old frontier of the West" and imagines it as the heart of a new technological center.

A third device used by Kennedy is reference to local events, history, and pride as he speaks in Houston. By asking "Why does Rice play Texas?", Kennedy humorously plays on the long-time football rivalry between the football teams by putting it in the same category as the first trans-Atlantic flight. Later, he specifically describes plans to invest in advanced technology at Rice, as well as the city of Houston ("your City of Houston"), the region, and the state of Texas as a whole.

By using these techniques of analogy, supporting evidence, and reference to local facts and history, Kennedy created a very complex and interesting speech. While many of his other speeches may be better known, this speech is an excellent example of the depth of his rhetorical skill.

Score
Reading: 6
Analysis: 4
Writing: 6

SAT Experts Say: This is a solid essay that demonstrates sufficient comprehension of the speech, its central ideas, and important details, and that uses evidence from the speech to support its argument. In addition, the essay follows a clear, logical progression of ideas and shows effective use of language in writing. There is also a clear introduction and conclusion. However, this essay would lose points in the Analysis category, as the student doesn't go far enough in explaining the importance of the speech's features.

Sample Essay 6

This speech is about how we should go to the moon. He starts by talking about how it's like an ocean and it could be a hostile theater of war, so we should protect ourselves when we set sail in space.

In the next paragraph he says that space is like climbing a mountain or like Rice playing Texas. I guess he's trying to make a joke with the audience, because Rice always loses to Texas, but that's not a very smart thing to compare going to space to.

Next he's all like it will be so hard it will be to go to space. And we'll be behind for a long time and then ahead. Mr. Negative, right? That doesn't make me want to do it.

Then spends a lot of time talking about business industries and money stuff. Boring.

Finally, he says we should go to the moon because it's like trying climb a mountain. This makes no sense because he said earlier it was like sailing, and also because why would we want to be like the guy who died trying to climb a mountain? I guess it's a cool idea though so we should try to do it, but he should have just said that instead.

Score
Reading: 4
Analysis: 2
Writing: 4

SAT Experts Say: This is very weak essay. Though the essay shows a very basic understanding of the speech, it does not present a case, contain analysis, or respond to the prompt in any way. While the tone is very informal and even flippant, the writing (technically speaking) is mostly error-free, which might earn the essay a few Writing points. Overall, though, the essay is sloppy, lacks focus, and does not make any point.

Summary

o   Writing, the third and final task of the SAT Essay, is about putting all your ideas together in a coherent, well-written essay.

o   The essay will not require you to write about a personal experience or give your opinion on a certain topic. This essay is a technical analysis of an argument, not your opinion about that argument.

o   In order to get a good score for the Writing task, you should make a claim and be able to support it with evidence from the passage. You should also organize your thoughts in a coherent, logical manner, and show command of standard written English by varying your word choice and sentence structure.

o   Be sure that your essay has the three key parts: introduction, body paragraphs, and conclusion. Your introduction should describe the text and paraphrase the argument being made, as well as introduce the specific elements of the passage and argument that you will discuss in the essay. Your conclusion should restate the goal of the passage/argument and sum up the points you made.

o   Keep *analysis* in mind as you write your essay. You should not merely describe a text, but explain how that text is written and structured to accomplish a certain goal. And remember: cite evidence!

Part VI
Taking the SAT

THE SAT IS A WEEK AWAY. WHAT SHOULD YOU DO?

First of all, you should practice the techniques we've taught you on lots of practice tests. If you haven't done so already, take and score the practice tests in this book and online. You can also download a practice test from the College Board's website, **www.collegeboard.org**.

If you want more practice, pick up a copy of our very own *6 Practice Tests for the SAT* at your local bookstore or through our website, at **PrincetonReview.com/bookstore**.

Getting Psyched

The SAT is a big deal, but you don't want to let it scare you. Sometimes students get so nervous about doing well that they freeze up on the test and ruin their scores. The best thing to do is to think of the SAT as a game. It's a game you can get better at, and beating the test can be fun. When you go into the test center, just think about all those poor students who don't know how to Plug In when they see variables in the answer choices.

The best way to keep from getting nervous is to build confidence in yourself and in your ability to remember and use our techniques. When you take practice tests, time yourself exactly as you will be timed on the real SAT. Develop a sense of how long 35 minutes is, for example, and how much time you can afford to spend on cracking difficult problems. If you know ahead of time what to expect, you won't be as nervous.

Of course, taking a real SAT is much more nerve-racking than taking a practice test. Prepare yourself ahead of time for the fact that 35 minutes will seem to go by a lot faster on a real SAT than it did on your practice tests.

It's all right to be nervous; the point of being prepared is to keep from panicking.

Should You Sleep for 36 Hours?

Some guidance counselors tell their students to get a lot of sleep the night before the SAT. This probably isn't a good idea. If you aren't used to sleeping 12 hours a night, doing so will just make you groggy for the test. The same goes for going out all night: Tired people are not good test takers.

A much better idea is to get up early each morning for the entire week before the test and do your homework before school. This will get your brain accustomed to functioning at that hour of the morning. You want to be sharp at test time.

Before dinner the night before the test, spend an hour or so reviewing or doing a few practice problems. The goal here is to brush up on the material, not to exhaust yourself by over-cramming.

Furthermore...

Here are a few pointers for test day and beyond:

1. Eat a good breakfast before the test—your brain needs energy.
2. Work out a few SAT problems on the morning of the test to help dust off any cobwebs in your head and get you started thinking analytically.
3. Arrive at the test center early. Everyone is headed to the same place at the same time.
4. You must take acceptable identification to the test center on the day of the test. Acceptable identification must include a recognizable photograph and your name. Acceptable forms of ID include your driver's license, a school ID with a photo, or a valid passport. If you don't have an official piece of ID with your signature and your photo, you can have your school make an ID for you using a Student ID form provided by the College Board. Complete instructions for making such an ID are found on the College Board's website and in the *SAT Registration Bulletin*. According to ETS and the College Board, the following forms of ID are *unacceptable:* a birth certificate, a credit card, or a Social Security card. Make sure you read all of the rules in the *Registration Bulletin,* because conflicts with ETS are just not worth the headache. Your only concern on the day of the test should be beating the SAT. To avoid hassles and unnecessary stress, make *absolutely certain* that you take your admissions ticket and your ID with you on the day of the test.
5. The only outside materials you are allowed to use on the test are No. 2 pencils (wooden, NOT mechanical), a wristwatch (an absolute necessity), and a calculator. The latest rule is that mechanical pencils are not allowed. We're not sure why, but you should take lots of sharpened wooden pencils just to be safe. Digital watches are best, but if it has a beeper, make sure you turn it off. Proctors will confiscate pocket dictionaries, word lists, portable computers, and the like. Proctors have occasionally also confiscated stopwatches and travel clocks. Technically, you should be permitted to use these, but you can never tell with some proctors. Take a watch and avoid the hassles.
6. Some proctors allow students to bring food into the test room; others don't. Take some fruit (especially bananas) with you. Save them until your break and eat outside the test room.

#1: Eat Breakfast
You'll work better on a satisfied stomach.

#2: Try Some Problems
Get your mind moving.

#3: Show Up Early
Leave time for traffic.

#4: Take ID
A driver's license, a passport, or a school photo ID will do.

#5: Take Equipment
A few sharpened No. 2 pencils, a watch, and a calculator.

#6: Take Fruit or Other Energy Food
Grapes or oranges can give you an energy boost if you need it.

#7: Your Desk...
should be comfortable
and suited to your needs.

#8: Your Test...
should be printed
legibly in your booklet.

#9: Bubble with Care
A stray mark
can hurt your score.

#10: We're Here for You
The Princeton Review is
proud to advise students
who feel their exam was
not administered properly.

7. You are going to be sitting in the same place for more than three hours, so make sure your desk isn't broken or unusually uncomfortable. If you are left-handed, ask for a left-handed desk. (The center may not have one, but it won't hurt to ask.) If the sun is in your eyes, ask to move. If the room is too dark, ask someone to turn on the lights. Don't hesitate to speak up.

8. Make sure your booklet is printed legibly. Booklets sometimes contain printing errors that make some pages impossible to read. One year more than 10,000 students had to retake the SAT because of a printing error in their booklets. Also, check your answer sheet to make sure it isn't flawed.

9. Make sure you darken all your responses before the test is over. At the same time, erase any extraneous marks on the answer sheet. **A stray mark in the margin of your answer sheet can result in correct responses being marked as wrong.**

10. You deserve to take your SAT under good conditions. If you feel that your test was not administered properly (the high school band was practicing outside the window, or your proctor hovered over your shoulder during the test), don't hesitate to speak up.

Part VII
Practice Tests

Chapter 20
Practice Test 1

Reading Test

65 MINUTES, 52 QUESTIONS

Turn to Section 1 of your answer sheet to answer the questions in this section.

Questions 1-10 are based on the following passage.

The passage that follows is adapted from an 1859 novel that follows the lives of both English and French characters during the French Revolution.

"You were very sound, Sydney, in the matter of those crown witnesses today. Every question told."

"I always am sound; am I not?"

"I don't gainsay it. What has roughened your
5 temper? Put some punch to it and smooth it again."

With a deprecatory grunt, Carton complied.

"The old Sydney Carton of old Shrewsbury School," said Stryver, nodding his head over him as he reviewed him in the present and the past, "the old seesaw
10 Sydney. Up one minute and down the next; now in spirits and now in despondency!"

"Ah!" returned the other, sighing: "Yes! The same Sydney, with the same luck. Even then, I did exercises for other boys, and seldom did my own."

15 "And why not?"

"God knows. It was my way, I suppose."

"Carton," said his friend, squaring himself at him with a bullying air, as if the fire-grate had been the furnace in which sustained endeavour was forged, and
20 the one delicate thing to be done for the old Sydney Carton of old Shrewsbury School was to shoulder him into it, "your way is, and always was, a lame way. You summon no energy and purpose. Look at me."

"Oh, botheration!" returned Sydney, with a lighter
25 and more good-humoured laugh, "don't *you* be moral!"

"How have I done what I have done?" said Stryver; "how do I do what I do?"

"Partly through paying me to help you, I suppose. But it's not worth your while to apostrophise me, or
30 the air, about it; what you want to do, you do. You were always in the front rank, and I was always behind."

"I had to get into the front rank; I was not born there, was I?"

"I was not present at the ceremony; but my opinion
35 is you were," said Carton. At this, he laughed again, and they both laughed.

"Before Shrewsbury, and at Shrewsbury, and ever since Shrewsbury," pursued Carton, "you have fallen into your rank, and I have fallen into mine. You were
40 always somewhere, and I was always nowhere."

"And whose fault was that?"

"Upon my soul, I am not sure that it was not yours. You were always driving and shouldering and passing, to that restless degree that I had no chance for my life
45 but in rust and repose. It's a gloomy thing, however, to talk about one's own past, with the day breaking. Turn me in some other direction before I go."

"Well then! Pledge me to the pretty witness," said Stryver, holding up his glass. "Are you turned in a
50 pleasant direction?"

"Pretty witness," he muttered, looking down into his glass. "I have had enough of witnesses today and tonight; who's your pretty witness?"

"The picturesque doctor's daughter, Miss Manette."

55 "*She* pretty?"

"Is she not?"

"No."

CONTINUE

"Why, man alive, she was the admiration of the whole Court!"

60   "Rot the admiration of the whole Court! Who made the Old Bailey a judge of beauty? She was a golden-haired doll!"

"Do you know, Sydney," said Mr. Stryver, looking at him with sharp eyes, and slowly drawing a hand across
65 his florid face: "do you know, I rather thought, at the time, that you sympathized with the golden-haired doll, and were quick to see what happened to the golden-haired doll?"

"Quick to see what happened! If a girl, doll or no
70 doll, swoons within a yard or two of a man's nose, he can see it without a perspective-glass. I pledge you, but I deny the beauty. And now I'll have no more drink; I'll get to bed."

When his host followed him out on the staircase
75 with a candle, to light him down the stairs, the day was coldly looking in through its grimy windows. When he got out of the house, the air was cold and sad, the dull sky overcast, the river dark and dim, the whole scene like a lifeless desert. And wreaths of dust were spinning
80 round and round before the morning blast, as if the desert-sand had risen far away, and the first spray of it in its advance had begun to overwhelm the city.

Climbing to a high chamber in a well of houses, he threw himself down in his clothes on a neglected bed,
85 and its pillow was wet with wasted tears. Sadly, sadly, the sun rose; it rose upon no sadder sight than the man of good abilities and good emotions, incapable of their directed exercise, incapable of his own help and his own happiness, sensible of the blight on him, and
90 resigning himself to let it eat him away.

1

The primary purpose of the passage as a whole is to

A) describe the history between Carton and Stryver.

B) characterize life at the Shrewsbury School.

C) reveal Carton's character.

D) show that Stryver has been exploiting Carton.

2

Based on the information in the passage, Carton is best characterized as

A) unsound.

B) mercurial.

C) unlucky.

D) imperceptive.

3

Which choice provides the best evidence for the answer to the previous question?

A) Lines 10-11 ("Up . . . despondency")

B) Lines 13-14 ("Even . . . own")

C) Lines 35-36 ("At this . . . laughed")

D) Lines 45-46 ("It's a . . . breaking")

4

As used in line 11, "spirits" most nearly means

A) soul.

B) liquor.

C) essence.

D) jubilation.

5

Based on lines 17-22 ("squaring himself….shoulder him into it"), it can be reasonably inferred that

A) Stryver is frustrated with Carton's behavior.

B) Stryver is planning to push Carton into the fireplace.

C) Stryver believes Carton to be comparatively older.

D) Stryver wishes to bully Carton as he did at Shrewsbury.

CONTINUE ▶

6

The use of italics in line 55 primarily serves to emphasize Carton's

A) incredulity.

B) confusion.

C) annoyance.

D) affection.

7

The passage suggests which of the following about Stryver?

A) He is in love with Miss Manette.

B) He believes that Carton lacks the intelligence required to be successful.

C) He does not believe that Carton finds Miss Manette unattractive.

D) He was born into a wealthy family.

8

Which choice provides the best evidence for the answer to the previous question?

A) Lines 32-33 ("I had . . . was I")

B) Line 41 ("And whose . . . that")

C) Lines 58-59 ("Why . . . Court")

D) Lines 63-68 ("Do you . . . doll")

9

In context, "desert" in line 79 refers to

A) Styver's cold demeanor.

B) London's landscape.

C) Carton's windows.

D) sunlit dunes.

10

The "tears" referred to in line 85 are "wasted" because

A) Miss Manette will never love Carton.

B) Carton is unlikely to change his ways.

C) Carton's home is one of squalor.

D) Stryver will continue to exploit Carton's labor.

CONTINUE

No Test Material On This Page

Questions 11-21 are based on the following passage and supplementary material.

This passage is adapted from Priit Vesilind, *The Singing Revolution.* © 2008 by Sky Films Incorporated.

By the end of 1939 Soviet troops had forced their way into garrisons in the Baltic states of Estonia, Latvia, and Lithuania. In 1940 the Soviets forcibly annexed the three Baltic states into the USSR. But in 1941 Hitler double-crossed Stalin: he launched an attack on the Soviet Union. The Baltic nations were caught in the middle of the treachery. In 1945, when the war ended, Estonia remained occupied by the Soviets.

After nearly 50 years of Soviet occupation, when agitations for independence came in the late 1980s, the protestors pointed back to the Molotov-Ribbentrop Pact, a secret non-aggression treaty between the Soviet Union and Nazi Germany. If the Kremlin were to acknowledge the existence of this protocol, they reasoned, it would be admitting that the Baltic States had no legal "marriage" with Moscow, but that these nations were forcibly abducted with the collusion of the world's most heinous fascist regime. So the occupied nations had every right to ask for their freedom, and with no need for a legal "divorce."

The Baltic states had been morally supported with the firm stand taken in 1940 by the United States not to recognize the legality of the forceful annexation of Estonia, Latvia, and Lithuania. But politics were effective only if the Estonians had some other leverage. A nation of barely one million, burdened with half a million foreign settlers and 100,000 Soviet troops, could not threaten the Soviet Union militarily or economically, so it had to do it with the force of its culture. Estonia had always been a nation of singers. Its wealth of folk songs gave rhythm to village life and work, and its earnest anthems often invoked the longing for self-determination. Estonians had lived for centuries in servitude, and the themes of their music were often grim: sorrow, slavery, soil, blood, birch forests, and sacrifice. But there was always hope in their hearts.

Early in their national awakening, about 140 years ago, Estonians established a history of mass song festivals, held when money and politics allowed—celebrations that would kindle and fortify the courage to express their love of language and nation, and their reluctance to be absorbed by anyone. The festivals were a nationwide phenomenon, as were similar festivals held in Latvia and Lithuania.

In Tallinn the massive modern song stage held some 30,000 singers and the outdoor amphitheater could accommodate as many as 300,000. Often, 30 percent of all Estonians would be there—at a single concert. During the Soviet years the festivals were forced to pay tribute to Communist icons and the solidarity of the Soviet peoples. Choirs from other parts of the vast empire would come and all would whip up a rousing tribute to Stalin or Lenin. To these mandatory performances Estonians would introduce patriotic songs disguised as love songs or folk music. An unofficial national anthem, by the popular choir director Gustav Ernesaks, established itself in 1947, and survived the entire Soviet occupation despite a serious attempt by officials to eliminate it in 1969.

By the late 1980s the nation was simmering. A movement of young historians was already defying Soviet authority in speeches that laid history bare under the cover of Gorbachev's policy of glasnost, or "free speech." And the burden of protest songs had passed to rock-and-rollers, young men whose energized patriotic tunes blared from every radio.

Momentum built to a crescendo in the summer of 1988 when a rock concert in Tallinn's Old Town spilled into the Song Festival grounds and massive crowds gathered for six straight nights to lift arms, sway in unison, and sing patriotic songs. Emboldened, Estonians brought out forbidden blue-and-black-and-white national flags, some from attics and basements where they had been hidden since 1940. Shockingly, no one stopped them. For the finale of these "Night Song Festivals" more than 200,000 Estonians gathered.

This was the heart of "The Singing Revolution," a spontaneous, non-violent, but powerful political movement that united Estonians with poetry and music. After that there was no backing up. Sedition hung in the wind, waiting to be denied.

CONTINUE

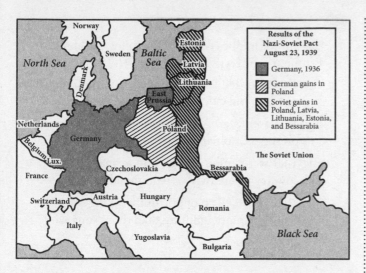

Diagram of Europe following the Nazi-Soviet Pact of 1939, also known as the Molotov-Ribbentrop Pact. Image adapted from CQ Researcher.

11

The point of view from which the passage is written is best described as

A) condemnatory of the Soviet Union's treacherous actions.

B) sympathetic to the Baltic states' struggle for freedom.

C) dismissive of the idea of non-violent revolution.

D) conflicted about the underlying cause of the revolution.

12

As used in line 18, "collusion" most nearly means

A) conspiracy.

B) impact.

C) separation.

D) danger.

13

In lines 33-36, the author draws a distinction between

A) the tone of Estonian songs and the people's true feelings.

B) the themes of Estonian folk songs and anthems.

C) the military strength of Estonia and that of the Soviet Union.

D) song festivals in Estonia and those in Latvia and Lithuania.

14

In the context of the passage, the phrase "their reluctance to be absorbed" suggests that Estonians

A) refused to speak Russian with the many foreigners settlers in Estonia.

B) wanted to have an independent nation.

C) worked to ensure their culture stayed distinct from those of the other Baltic states.

D) were unwilling to devote the amount of concentration to song festivals that the Soviets demanded.

15

The author includes statistics about the size of the song stage in Tallinn (lines 47-49) primarily to

A) provide a sense of how large the amphitheater is.

B) indicate the popularity of the tributes to Stalin and Lenin.

C) compare the size to that of similar stages in Latvia and Lithuania.

D) illustrate the wide appeal of the mass song festivals in Estonia.

CONTINUE →

16

As used in line 66, "burden" most nearly means

A) weight.

B) travail.

C) responsibility.

D) need.

17

The primary rhetorical effect of the last sentence of the passage is to

A) convey the sense of dread that hung over Estonia at the height of the Singing Revolution.

B) indicate the depth of disagreement between violent and non-violent revolutionaries.

C) show how crucial music and poetry were to Estonia's fight for independence.

D) communicate the sense of optimistic tension that Estonians felt after the Night Song Festivals.

18

Which of the following does the passage suggest about Estonia's relation to the Soviet Union?

A) Estonia had a richer cultural tradition of singing than the Soviet Union had.

B) Estonia had the political leverage necessary to free itself from the Soviet Union.

C) Estonia was smaller and weaker than the Soviet Union, making violent revolution impractical.

D) Estonia held song festivals during the Soviet occupation primarily to pay tribute to Communist icons.

19

The author implies which of the following about Estonian song festivals?

A) They afforded Estonians a medium through which national and cultural pride could be expressed.

B) They were started during the Soviet occupation to preserve Estonian culture and language.

C) They were unique in size and format to the country where they were founded.

D) They provided an opportunity to sing songs that were more uplifting than those sung while working.

20

Which choice provides the best evidence for the answer to the previous question?

A) Lines 19-21 ("So . . . 'divorce'")

B) Lines 44-46 ("The festivals . . . Lithuania")

C) Line 62 ("By the late . . . simmering")

D) Lines 79-82 ("This . . . music")

21

Which of the following claims is supported by the diagram?

A) In the 1939 pact, Germany gained the entirety of Poland.

B) The Soviet Union doubled in size after the pact.

C) Lithuania and Estonia are contiguous countries.

D) The Soviet Union's gains stretched from the Baltic Sea to the Black Sea.

CONTINUE

No Test Material On This Page

CONTINUE

Questions 22-31 are based on the following passage.

This passage is an excerpt adapted from a speech given in 1917 by American Senator Robert LaFollette. In the speech, LaFollette explains the special importance of free speech during times of war and the relation between free speech and democratic governance.

Since the declaration of war the triumphant war press has pursued those Senators and Representations who voted against war with malicious falsehood and
Line recklessly libelous attacks, going to the extreme limit of
5 charging them with treason against their country.

I have in my possession numerous affidavits establishing the fact that people are being unlawfully arrested, thrown into jail, held incommunicado for days, only to be eventually discharged without ever
10 having been taken into court, because they have committed no crime. Private residences are being invaded, loyal citizens of undoubted integrity and probity arrested, cross-examined, and the most sacred constitutional rights guaranteed to every American
15 citizen are being violated.

It appears to be the purpose of those conducting this campaign to throw the country into a state of terror, to coerce public opinion, to stifle criticism, and suppress discussion of the great issues involved in this
20 war.

I think all men recognize that in time of war the citizen must surrender some rights for the common good which he is entitled to enjoy in time of peace. But sir, the right to control their own Government
25 according to constitutional forms is not one of the rights that the citizens of this country are called upon to surrender in time of war.

Rather in time of war the citizen must be more alert to the preservation of his right to control his
30 Government. He must be most watchful of the encroachment of the military upon the civil power. He must beware of those precedents in support of arbitrary action by administrative officials, which excused on the plea of necessity in war time, become
35 the fixed rule when the necessity has passed and normal conditions have been restored.

More than all, the citizen and his representative in Congress in time of war must maintain his right of free speech. More than in times of peace it is necessary that
40 the channels for free public discussion of governmental policies shall be open and unclogged. I believe, Mr. President, that I am now touching upon the most

important question in this country today—and that is the right of the citizens of this country and their
45 representatives in Congress to discuss in an orderly way frankly and publicly and without fear, from the platform and through the press, every important phase of this war; its causes, the manner in which it should be conducted, and the terms upon which peace should
50 be made. I am contending, Mr. President, for the great fundamental right of the sovereign people of this country to make their voice heard and have that voice heeded upon the great questions arising out of this war, including not only how the war shall be prosecuted but
55 the conditions upon which it may be terminated with a due regard for the rights and the honor of this Nation and the interests of humanity.

I am contending for this right because the exercise of it is necessary to the welfare, to the existence, of this
60 Government to the successful conduct of this war, and to a peace which shall be enduring and for the best interest of this country.

Suppose success attends the attempt to stifle all discussion of the issues of this war, all discussion
65 of the terms upon which it should be concluded, all discussion of the objects and purposes to be accomplished by it, and concede the demand of the war-mad press and war extremists that they monopolize the right of public utterance upon these
70 questions unchallenged, what think you would be the consequences to this country not only during the war but after the war?

It is no answer to say that when the war is over the citizen may once more resume his rights and feel some
75 security in his liberty and his person. As I have already tried to point out, now is precisely the time when the country needs the counsel of all its citizens. In time of war even more than in time of peace, whether citizens happen to agree with the ruling administration or
80 not, these precious fundamental personal rights—free speech, free press, and right of assemblage so explicitly and emphatically guaranteed by the Constitution should be maintained inviolable.

CONTINUE ➡

22

The position that LaFollette takes is best described as

A) a law-maker suggesting a new piece of legislation.

B) an impartial observer arbitrating a legal issue.

C) a dissenter arguing for a cause.

D) a pacifist arguing against international conflicts.

23

In the passage, LaFollette draws a distinction between

A) rights that are appropriately and inappropriately sacrificed during war.

B) moments when free speech is and is not necessary.

C) just wars and wars sought for economic interest.

D) the interests of the Nation and the interests of humanity.

24

Which choice provides the best evidence for the answer to the previous question?

A) Lines 6-11 ("I have . . . crime")

B) Lines 21-27 ("I think . . . war")

C) Lines 30-31 ("He must . . . power")

D) Lines 50-57 ("I am . . . humanity")

25

As used in line 8, "incommunicado" most nearly means

A) justified.

B) sequestered.

C) luxuriously.

D) available.

26

Lines 32-36 suggest that

A) some rights are necessarily given up during war time.

B) restrictions on civil powers are always arbitrary.

C) the Government must be watchful of the military.

D) temporary restrictions may become permanent.

27

Based on the information in the passage, citizen governance is necessary in all of the following situations EXCEPT

A) electing legislators and executives.

B) negotiating a peace treaty.

C) declarations of war.

D) decisions about military strategy.

28

The principal rhetorical effect of the phrase in lines 48-50, ("its causes...peace should be made") is to

A) argue against granting free speech during war by emphasizing the difficulties faced by the military and the President.

B) suggest the numerous points at which citizens should exercise their free speech during times of war.

C) discuss three reasons why members of the press are currently unable to speak frankly without fear.

D) show that LaFollette believes that the citizens understand the dynamics of war far better than the President.

29

Which choice provides the best evidence for the answer to the previous question?

A) Lines 11-15 ("Private . . . violated")

B) Lines 16-20 ("It appears . . . war")

C) Lines 30-36 ("He must . . . restored")

D) Lines 37-41 ("More than . . . unclogged")

CONTINUE ➤

The author's attitude toward "the attempt to stifle" (line 63) can be described as

A) sympathetic.

B) apathetic.

C) frustrated.

D) morose.

As used in line 83, "inviolable" most nearly means

A) secretly.

B) freely.

C) unbreakable.

D) personally.

CONTINUE

No Test Material On This Page

Questions 32-41 are based on the following passage and supplementary material.

The following is from a passage about continental drift and plate tectonics from *Science World.*

By 1965, investigations led to the proposal that Earth's surface was broken into seven large plates and several smaller plates. It was further suggested that
Line these plates are rigid, and that their boundaries are
5 marked by earthquakes and volcanic activity. In recent years, satellite pictures have documented the existence of plate boundaries. An especially visible example is the San Andreas Fault in California.

Plates interact with one another at their boundaries
10 by moving toward, away, or alongside each other. Faults are examples of boundaries where two plates slide horizontally past each other. Mid-ocean ridges mark boundaries where plates are forced apart as new ocean floor is being created between them. Mountains,
15 volcanic-island arcs, and ocean trenches occur at the boundaries where plates are colliding, causing one plate to slide beneath the other. The network of crustal plates and the geologic activity caused by their movement is referred to as *plate tectonics.*
20 The original continental-drift theory suggested that continents plowed through the ocean floor like ships. Plate tectonics, on the other hand, holds that continents are carried along together with the surrounding seabed in huge plates—much like rafts
25 frozen into the ice on a flowing stream.

There are several major plates. The North American plate comprises North America and the western half of the North Atlantic seafloor. The South American plate includes South America east to the Mid-Atlantic Ridge.
30 The African plate contains Africa and its surrounding seafloor. The Antarctic plate has Antarctica and surrounding seafloor. The Eurasian plate includes Europe, Asia, and nearby seafloor. The Pacific plate underlies the Pacific Ocean. Recently, an international
35 team of geologists and other researchers analyzing seafloor measurements discovered that what was classified as the Indo-Australian plate may actually be two separate plates—one with the Indian subcontinent and the adjacent seabed, and the other with Australia
40 and surrounding waters.

Scientists believe that, in addition to the great, slow convection currents that carry plates about Earth, there are also smaller, rapidly rising *mantle plumes*, columns of hot material rising from deep within Earth. (Earth

45 is believed to be composed of an inner solid core, a middle mantle, and an outer crust.) These plumes of molten rock, often called *hot spots*, rise and erupt through the crust of a moving plate.

Most of the isolated mid-plate volcanoes, such as
50 those of Hawaii and Yellowstone, lie at one end of a line of extinct volcanoes that grow steadily older with distance from the active center. Hawaii's Mauna Loa is at the extreme southeastern end of the rest of the Hawaiian island chain. The volcanoes in this chain
55 become steadily older and less active to the northeast. Likewise, Yellowstone's hot springs and geysers are at the eastern end of a line of extinct volcanoes that extend into Idaho. Such a line of volcanoes suggests that the crust of Earth is passing over a hot spot, or hot
60 spots, in the deeper mantle. As the crustal plate moves, the hot spot "punches" up a line of volcanic and hot-spring activity.

Indeed, the motions of the Pacific plate are compatible with the direction of the Hawaiian chain
65 and the ages of its volcanic islands. Plate motion has slowly moved the volcanic islands away from the hot spot that created them. In other words, the Hawaiian island chain traces the motion of the Pacific plate.

As molten rock flows up along the mid-ocean
70 ridges to create new seafloor, the lava flows more abundantly in certain spots, producing volcanic islands. Scientists believe that these places of abundant lava flow may be hot spots that occur between two separating plates. Two such plates underlie the large,
75 highly volcanic island of Iceland, which straddles the Mid-Atlantic Ridge. On one side is the North American plate; on the other, the Eurasian plate. Similarly, ridges extend from the active volcanic island of Tristan da Cunha westward to South America and
80 eastward to Africa. Some geologists propose that, although such hot spots do not actually move plates, they may mark weak points in the mantle, which in turn help determine the lines along which plates fracture and separate.

85 Hot spots of volcanic activity often occur at the junction where plates collide. Examples are the volcanic Azores, which arise where the North American, Eurasian, and African plates meet. Another—Macquarie Island, south of New Zealand—
90 marks the meeting point for the Pacific, Antarctic, and Indo-Australian plates. These hot spots may be fueled in part by plate collision.

CONTINUE ➤

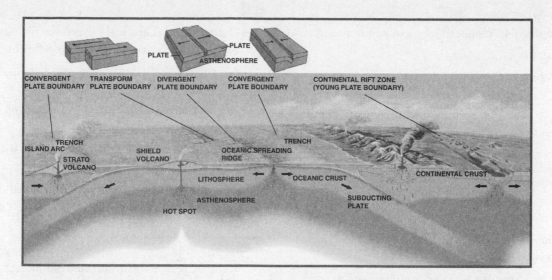

This image shows the three main types of plate boundaries: divergent, convergent, and transform. Image adapted from the U.S. Geological Survey.

32

Based on the information in the passage it can be reasonably inferred that

A) geological theories are only proven with the help of technological advances.

B) improvements in satellite technology advanced plate tectonics theory.

C) the plate tectonics theory was created in 1965.

D) the San Andreas Fault proved the veracity of plate tectonics theory.

33

In the third paragraph (lines 20-25), what is the distinction the author draws between continental-drift theory and plate tectonics?

A) Fluidity versus immobility

B) Drifting along versus pushing with purpose

C) Moving through versus moving with

D) Sailing on oceans versus rafting through streams

34

As used in line 42, "convection" most nearly means

A) liquefying.

B) melting.

C) mobilizing.

D) transferring.

35

In line 56, what is the most likely reason the author introduces Yellowstone's hot springs?

A) As an example of a mid-plate volcano

B) As proof that plates slide past each other

C) As support for an opposing theory

D) As an example of a mid-ocean ridge

36

Which choice provides the best evidence for the answer to the previous question?

A) Lines 3-5 ("It was . . . activity")

B) Lines 54-55 ("The volcanoes . . . northeast")

C) Lines 60-62 ("As the . . . activity")

D) Lines 65-67 ("Plate . . . them")

CONTINUE ➡

37

As used in line 64, "compatible" most nearly means

A) consistent.

B) adaptable.

C) opposed.

D) skewed.

38

What is the most likely reason the author mentions Iceland?

A) To offer an example of an island created at a mid-ocean ridge

B) To show a contrast between an island and a continent

C) To prove that an island can also be a volcano

D) To assert that the Mid-Atlantic Ridge connects two plates

39

Which choice provides the best evidence for the answer to the previous question?

A) Lines 9-12 ("Plates . . . other")

B) Lines 41-44 ("Scientists . . . Earth")

C) Lines 49-52 ("Most . . . center")

D) Lines 69-72 ("As . . . islands")

40

The principal rhetorical purpose of the phrase "Some geologists . . . separate" (lines 80-84) is to

A) suggest that scientists are still investigating plate tectonic theory.

B) emphasize the lack of data supporting how fractures separate.

C) reveal that some scientists disagree with the major tenets of plate tectonics.

D) expose a weakness in the continental-drift theory.

41

It can be reasonably inferred from information in the passage and the diagram that

A) continental rift zones always occur beside the ocean.

B) hot spots are molten plumes that travel through the lithosphere to the surface.

C) mid-ocean ridges are caused by the presence of subducting plates.

D) oceanic crust is more rigid than continental crust.

CONTINUE ▶

No Test Material On This Page

Questions 42-52 are based on the following passage.

Passage 1 is adapted from Theodore S. Melis, Ed., "Effects of Three High-Flow Experiments on the Colorado River Ecosystem Downstream from Glen Canyon Dam, Arizona," published in 2011 by the U.S. Geological Survey. Passage 2 is adapted from Paul E. Grams, "A Sand Budget for Marble Canyon, Arizona—Implications for Long-Term Monitoring of Sand Storage Change," published in 2013 by the U.S. Geological Survey.

Passage 1

At the time Glen Canyon Dam was constructed (1956–63), little consideration was given to how dam operations might affect downstream resources in Grand Canyon National Park. In fact, the dam was completed before enactment of the National Environmental Policy Act of 1969 and the Endangered Species Act of 1973. By the late 1950s, public values began to shift, and throughout the 1960s and 1970s recognition of the environmental consequences of Glen Canyon Dam and its operation grew. National Park Service and U.S. Geological Survey scientists and river recreationists observed the physical transformation of the river in Grand Canyon, including the loss of large beaches used for camping, narrowing of rapids so as to reduce navigability, and changes in the distribution and composition of riparian vegetation. The humpback chub and Colorado pikeminnow, species found only in the Colorado River Basin, were listed as endangered in 1967 by the U.S. Fish and Wildlife Service, which concluded in 1978 that the dam and its operation jeopardized the continued existence of humpback chub in Grand Canyon.

Annual spring snowmelt floods were the defining attribute of the pre-dam flow regime. Before the Colorado River was regulated by dams, streamflow gradually increased from mid-December to March, precipitously increased in April and May, and reached its peak in early June.

Pre-dam floods disturbed the aquatic ecosystem, and native fish species developed strategies to survive periods when the velocity in the main part of the channel was high and large amounts of suspended sediment were being transported. For example, several of the native fish species share unusual body shapes, including a large adult body size, small depressed skulls, large humps on their backs, and small eyes, which presumably developed as adaptations to life in a turbid and seasonally variable riverine environment. Sandbars, riverbanks, and their accompanying aquatic habitats were reshaped during floods. Additionally, the increased elevation of the river surface during floods provided water to native riparian vegetation otherwise principally dependent on precipitation.

Passage 2

Decline in the size and abundance of sandbars since the pre-Glen Canyon Dam era has been documented by analysis of old aerial and ground-level photographs and by topographic surveys that began in the mid-1970s. Scientists have estimated that sandbar area in the upstream 100 miles of Glen, Marble, and Grand Canyons was 25 percent less in 2000 than in average pre-dam years. This decline occurred because releases of water from Lake Powell are virtually free of sediment. The tributaries that enter the Colorado River downstream from the dam supply only a fraction of the pre-dam sand supply, and the capacity of the post-dam river to transport that sand greatly exceeds this limited supply. Normal dam operations, therefore, tend to erode, rather than build, sandbars.

By experimentation, scientists have learned that controlled floods, if released from the reservoir immediately following large inputs of sand from tributaries, can build sandbars. These sandbars are built during controlled floods when sand is carried from the riverbed and temporarily suspended at high concentration in the flow. The suspended sand is transported into eddies where it is then deposited in areas of low stream-flow velocity. Sandbars enlarged by this process provide larger camping beaches for river-rafting trips and create backwater habitats used by native fish. Newly deposited sandbars also provide areas for riparian vegetation to grow and are a source of windblown sand. Windblown sand carried upslope from sandbars helps to cover and potentially preserve some of the culturally significant archeological sites in Grand Canyon.

Scientists have also learned that controlled floods may erode sandbars if the concentration of suspended sand during a controlled flood is too low. The concentration of sand during a flood is directly proportional to the amount of the riverbed covered by sand and the size of that sand. Higher concentrations of suspended sand occur when the sand is relatively

CONTINUE →

fine and large amounts of the riverbed are covered by
85 sand. These findings are incorporated in the current
reservoir-release management strategy for Glen
Canyon Dam, which involves releasing controlled
floods— administratively referred to as High Flow
Experiments (HFEs)—whenever the Paria River
90 has recently delivered large amounts of sand to the
Colorado River. The magnitude and duration of the
controlled floods is adjusted to transport just the
amount of sand that has recently been delivered from
the Paria River.

42

The author of Passage 1 most likely believes that the
Glen Canyon Dam

A) is a useful tool for managing scarce water
   resources.

B) was built with a lack of foresight.

C) has decimated native fish populations.

D) has had a calming effect on the aquatic ecosystem.

43

Which choice provides the best evidence for the
answer to the previous question?

A) Lines 1-4 ("At the time . . . Park")

B) Lines 17-23 ("The humpback . . . Canyon")

C) Lines 24-25 ("Annual . . . regime")

D) Lines 30-34 ("Pre-dam floods . . . transported")

44

The author of Passage 1 mentions scientists and river
recreationists primarily to

A) provide support for the idea that the post-dam
   river looks drastically different.

B) draw a contrast between scientific observations
   and casual observations of river conditions.

C) emphasize the spirit of collaboration between the
   science community and the public in conservation
   efforts.

D) prove that the Glen Canyon Dam has had a
   ruinous effect on the river.

45

Passage 1 suggests that the humpback chub

A) is now extinct in the Grand Canyon.

B) has a small, depressed skull.

C) can survive in changing environments.

D) thrives in high velocity river channels.

46

As used in line 25, "regime" most nearly means

A) government.

B) tenure.

C) system.

D) management.

47

As used in line 65, "suspended" most nearly means

A) stopped.

B) mixed.

C) withheld.

D) hanging.

48

It is reasonable to conclude that controlled floods

A) successfully simulate pre-dam snowmelt floods.

B) contain large amounts of suspended sediment.

C) may be detrimental to the health of the Colorado
   River.

D) should be done during the months that snowmelt
   floods typically occur.

CONTINUE

49

Which choice provides the best evidence for the answer to the previous question?

A) Lines 58-59 ("Normal . . . sandbars")

B) Lines 66-68 ("The suspended . . . velocity")

C) Lines 71-73 ("Newly . . . sand")

D) Lines 77-79 ("Scientists . . . low")

50

The author of Passage 1 would most likely respond to the High Flow Experiments described in Passage 2 by

A) appreciating the efforts of scientists to maintain the sand supply below the dam.

B) warning of the calamity of interfering with the river ecosystem.

C) questioning the ability of controlled floods to build up sandbars.

D) worrying that reshaped habitats will harm native fish.

51

Which of the following best describes the structure of the two passages?

A) Passage 1 introduces a problem, and Passage 2 proposes a solution to the problem.

B) Passage 1 offers a historical discussion, and Passage 2 describes the implications of a scientific practice.

C) Passage 1 gives background information, and Passage 2 details recent changes.

D) Passage 1 describes an experiment, and Passage 2 offers suggestions for future action.

52

Which of the following statements is true of Passage 1, but not of Passage 2?

A) The passage gives details of scientific studies conducted on the river.

B) The passage offers documented evidence of topographic change in the river.

C) The passage indicates the importance of floods to the river ecosystem.

D) The passage gives specific examples of species affected by the dam.

STOP

If you finish before time is called, you may check your work on this section only.
Do not turn to any other section in the test.

No Test Material On This Page

CONTINUE

Writing and Language Test

35 MINUTES, 44 QUESTIONS

Turn to Section 2 of your answer sheet to answer the questions in this section.

DIRECTIONS

Each passage below is accompanied by a number of questions. For some questions, you will consider how the passage might be revised to improve the expression of ideas. For other questions, you will consider how the passage might be edited to correct errors in sentence structure, usage, or punctuation. A passage or a question may be accompanied by one or more graphics (such as a table or graph) that you will consider as you make revising and editing decisions.

Some questions will direct you to an underlined portion of a passage. Other questions will direct you to a location in a passage or ask you to think about the passage as a whole.

After reading each passage, choose the answer to each question that most effectively improves the quality of writing in the passage or that makes the passage conform to the conventions of standard written English. Many questions include a "NO CHANGE" option. Choose that option if you think the best choice is to leave the relevant portion of the passage as it is.

Questions 1–11 are based on the following passage.

And Justice for All

Her father got her the job. Amanda was between semesters at college, and her **1** work at the mall wouldn't do much for her when she got out of school. It was time to do something more serious, something that meant more to her. Many of her friends were getting internships in the city, working for this or that publishing house or TV studio. Amanda, however, wanted something different. She would start applying to law schools **2** soon and she wanted to know what the law looked like in action.

1
A) NO CHANGE
B) work, at the mall, wouldn't do much for her when
C) work at the mall wouldn't do much for her, when
D) work, at the mall, wouldn't do much for her, when

2
A) NO CHANGE
B) soon and,
C) soon, and
D) soon,

CONTINUE ➡

Fortunately, her dad knew someone from high school, a friend **3** named Ellen, who had then gone on to study at Duke University. It was a thankless job, and although the Department building itself covered almost one hundred acres (in New York City, there was an entire island devoted to it), no one paid the Department of Corrections much mind. Most people never come near a jail cell, so **4** it's easy for them to dismiss inmates as totally removed from society.

[1] At the Department, however, Amanda learned about prisoners' rights. [2] Or, by the same token, when was the use of force appropriate from the officers? [3] There is a clear provision in the Constitution that prohibits "cruel and unusual punishment." [4] The meaning of these four words **5** were nowhere more ambiguous than in prisons. [5] Everyone within these walls had been convicted of a crime and was now paying **6** they're debt to society, but how could a government ensure that the

---

3

Which of the following true statements contains information most in keeping with the main idea of this passage?

A) NO CHANGE

B) who had gone on to law school and now worked at the County Department of Corrections.

C) with whom he had not spoken in twenty-five years, though with whom he still felt very close.

D) DELETE the underlined portion.

4

Which of the following best concludes this paragraph by reinforcing ideas presented in this sentence and the preceding one?

A) NO CHANGE

B) people often know literally nothing about prison life, though they are endlessly fascinated.

C) movie studios are famous for their sordid but often wrong depictions of prison life.

D) incarceration rates in the United States are some of the highest in the world.

5

A) NO CHANGE

B) have been

C) are

D) is

6

A) NO CHANGE

B) their

C) there

D) his or her

place would deliver the "reform" in a reformatory or the "penitence" in a penitentiary? [6] Should inmates with, for example, mental illnesses be treated differently from others? 7

While Amanda did not gain any answers from her summer at the Department of Corrections, she 8 gathered together a whole new set of questions. She had uncovered questions and conundrums about the prison system itself, but she had begun to see prisoners' rights as central to the question of free rights as well. She began to wonder exactly what it was that a government owed its people and how much freedom was too much. Her internship that summer made her realize that politics and the law 9 was a living thing. As she applied to law schools the following fall, Amanda wrote passionately about what she had uncovered. "Although law has long been considered a profession of privilege and prestige," she concluded her essay, "I have seen firsthand how it affects the lives of all of us. We may believe that we never come into contact with the 10 law; however, it is written into everything around us, including how we see ourselves."

7

In the sequence of the paragraph, the best placement for sentence 2 would be

A) where it is now.

B) before sentence 1.

C) after sentence 3.

D) after sentence 6.

8

A) NO CHANGE

B) gathered up

C) collected up

D) gathered

9

A) NO CHANGE

B) were living things.

C) was a thing that was alive.

D) were things that were living.

10

A) NO CHANGE

B) law, however

C) law, however;

D) law, however,

11

Suppose the writer's goal had been to write an essay that criticizes the American justice system. Would this essay fulfill that goal?

A) Yes, because it refers to much of what Amanda learns as "conundrums."

B) Yes, because it shows that the U.S. justice system has some problems.

C) No, because it tells the story of one person becoming interested in the justice system.

D) No, because it suggests that working in the justice system inspired one person's entire career.

CONTINUE ➡

Questions 12–22 are based on the following passage and supplementary material.

Alexander's Empire of Culture

Alexander the Great is a name known to all, but not all know the extent of Alexander's accomplishments. Now that the study of the "classics" (mainly Roman and Greek civilizations) has **12** disappeared both from high-school and college curricula, Alexander the Great's legend is not on the tongue of every schoolboy, though his accomplishments have not **13** diminished for all that.

Alexander was born in Pella, Macedonia, in 356 BCE. His father, King Philip II, a strong military king **14** in his own write, believed that his son was born part man and part god. Alexander came to cultivate the image himself, bolstered by his keen intellect and learning, quickened in part by his tutor, the great Greek philosopher Aristotle. Pella was at that time a backwater of Greek culture, and **15** his arrival announced a new era of what historians would later call "enlightened monarchy," **16** even though that term is used much more to describe monarchies in the eighteenth century.

12

A) NO CHANGE
B) disappeared from both
C) disappeared both
D) from both disappeared

13

A) NO CHANGE
B) ameliorated
C) gone down
D) subsided

14

A) NO CHANGE
B) in his own right,
C) in his own rite,
D) by his own rite,

15

A) NO CHANGE
B) Aristotle's
C) their
D) the

16

Which of the following true statements would best conclude the paragraph by emphasizing the change that Alexander's rule brought to Macedonia?

A) NO CHANGE
B) although those who suffered defeat at Alexander's hands might not have seen it that way.
C) suggesting a style for the reigns of both Julius Caesar and Napoleon Bonaparte.
D) underlining further that Philip's former militaristic state was entering a new age.

Still, the age was not entirely new. Alexander spent nearly all his time abroad, first uniting the Greek kingdom that threatened to fall apart at Philip's death, then moving on to broader military conquests. **17** Alexander had conquered an incredible amount of land by the time of his death in 323 BCE, **18** as his empire stretched from Greece to modern-day India, some two million square miles. When his armies conquered Persia (now Iran and Iraq) once and for all, he took on the title by which he is still known today: King of Babylon, King of Asia, King of the Four Quarters of the World.

17

The author wants to insert an introductory phrase or clause at the beginning of this sentence that will emphasize the continuity Alexander's reign had with the previous one. Which of the following choices would most effectively give this emphasis?

A) In what must have been truly exhausting,

B) With great ambition,

C) As his father had before him,

D) Just as historians have noted,

18

Which of the following choices gives information consistent with the map shown below?

A) NO CHANGE

B) while he traveled on foot throughout most of modern-day Europe,

C) because he circled the entire Mediterranean Sea and much of the Indian Ocean,

D) as he conquered all of Italy hundreds of years before Caesar had done so,

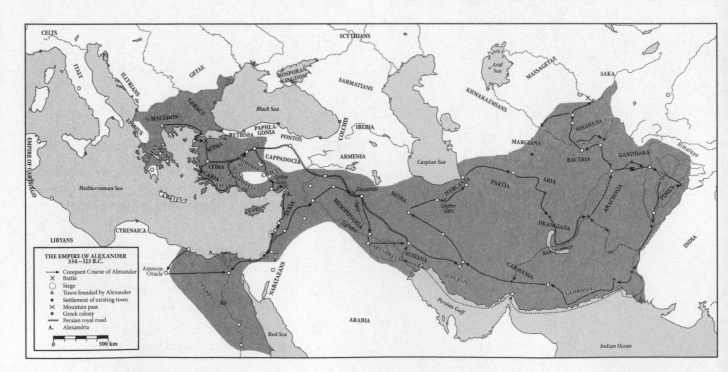

Extent of the empire of Alexander the Great

CONTINUE

Alexander's historical importance is not merely one of military might, however. [19] He moved to these different parts of the world, he brought Greek culture with him, and his reign marks [20] an unprecedented instance of contact between the ancient East and West. Over twenty cities throughout the empire bear his name. Alexandria, Egypt, perhaps the most famous of these cities, continues to [21] thrive. It is the second-largest city in the modern nation of Egypt.

Perhaps history is the wrong place to understand the accomplishments of Alexander the Great. Epic poetry seems more suitable. After all, Alexander's great teacher Aristotle showed him Homer's *Iliad* and *Odyssey*, and it seems that Alexander himself understood his life as a shuttling back and forth between man and god, the individual and the world, and the natural [22] and the unnatural.

[19]

A) NO CHANGE
B) As he
C) Although he
D) Moreover, he

[20]

Which of the following alternatives to the underlined portion would NOT be acceptable?

A) an unparalleled
B) a pioneering
C) an ahistorical
D) a never before seen

[21]

Which of the following is the most effective way to combine these two sentences?

A) thrive; it is
B) thrive, is
C) thrive. It's
D) thrive and is

[22]

A) NO CHANGE
B) versus
C) from
D) but

Questions 23–33 are based on the following passage.

Brother, Can You Spare a Dime?

   Although printed cheaply and for quick consumption, **23** today's experience of culture is largely shaped by dime novels. For much of the nineteenth century, Americans consumed fiction, poetry, and non-fiction by way of literary periodicals. Some of our best-known authors from this period, **24** though there were also some notable exceptions, published something close to their complete works between the pages of countless periodicals.

CONTINUE

23

A) NO CHANGE

B) we experience culture the way we do because of dime novels.

C) dime novels have shaped the way we experience culture today.

D) the shape of dime novels influences of cultural experiences.

24

Which of the following true phrases gives the most specific information in the context?

A) NO CHANGE

B) some of the best-known authors of all time,

C) and some who were not so well-known,

D) especially Edgar Allan Poe and Nathaniel Hawthorne,

Things started to change around the Civil War. Harriet Beecher Stowe's great **25** novel, *Uncle Tom's Cabin* had been an enormously popular serial novel in the abolitionist periodical *The National Era*. By the time the novel's forty-week run had concluded, however, publishers were clamoring for an actual book. **26** That book went on to become the first American bestseller. And it showed that Americans were willing to pay for books, which had, to that point, been too expensive to print and subsequently to buy. **27**

A) NO CHANGE

B) novel, *Uncle Tom's Cabin,*

C) novel *Uncle Tom's Cabin,*

D) novel *Uncle Tom's Cabin*

26

If the author were to remove the phrase "for an actual book" (ending the sentence at the word *clamoring*), the sentence would lose

A) specific information that clarifies the subject of the next sentence.

B) a description of the greed of publishers in the nineteenth century.

C) details that show how Stowe's work came to be so popular.

D) nothing, because this information is implied in the word "clamoring."

At this point, the writer is considering adding the following true statement:

> The average annual income for men in New England from 1820-1850 was a mere $323.25.

Should the writer make this addition here?

A) Yes, because it makes clear how expensive books must have been in the period.

B) Yes, because it shows that even those in New England could not afford books printed there.

C) No, because it strays from the paragraph's focus on the changes in book publishing.

D) No, because it suggests that people in New England were not wealthy enough to read.

In 1860, Irwin and Erastus Beadle published the first in a long series of what [28] would become known as Beadle's Dime Novels. The first was called *Malaeska, The Indian Wife of the White Hunter*. By the turn of the nineteenth century, dime novels were everywhere.

The [29] affects are difficult to chart, but we can actually see the influence of these dime novels everywhere. Much of the mythology of the Old West, for example, was concretized in these dime novels, and William Bonney and James Butler Hickok became the folk heroes Billy the Kid and Wild Bill Hickok as the dime novels charted their (largely imagined) adventures. [30]

28

A) NO CHANGE
B) becomes
C) is
D) would have become

29

A) NO CHANGE
B) effects
C) effect's
D) affect's

30

The author is considering deleting the names "Billy the Kid and Wild Bill Hickok" from the preceding sentence. Should the names be kept or deleted?

A) Kept, because they are specific names in a sentence that speaks in generalities.

B) Kept, because they demonstrate the transformation described in the sentence.

C) Deleted, because they are nicknames of people whose true names are already listed in the sentence.

D) Deleted, because they encourage the frontier behavior that made the Wild West such a violent place.

CONTINUE →

The new media of the twentieth-century—film, radio, and comic books—may have replaced the dime novel, but they did so with much they had **31** been taught from the dime novel's popularity. All three media, for instance, borrowed characters that had become popular in dime novels—characters such as Frank Reade and Nick Carter, Master Detective. Then, in comic books and radio, a new generation of superheroes—The Shadow, Superman, and Popeye—was created in the mold of the old swashbuckling romanciers of the dime-novel era.

So today, as we enjoy superhero action films or boy-wizard series of novels, we should be aware that there is nothing new under the sun. Indeed, **32** for our hopelessly mass-media universe, this now forgotten form laid the foundation, pushing the same books onto countless readers. Such a feat may be commonplace as films gross many billions of dollars at the box office, but in the nineteenth century, the dime novel brought a new **33** frame of reference and a belief that the small world was getting larger bit by bit.

31

A) NO CHANGE
B) got
C) learned
D) brought

32

If the punctuation is adjusted accordingly, the best placement for the underlined portion would be

A) where it is now.
B) after the word *form*.
C) after the word *foundation*.
D) at the end of the sentence.

33

Which of the following alternatives to the underlined portion would NOT be acceptable?

A) paradigm
B) integration
C) framework
D) context

Questions 34–44 are based on the following passage and supplementary material.

The Tiger Moth's Phantom Target

[1]

Bats have always seemed mysterious predators. While many other animal predators use methods **34** similar to human hunters, bats have evolved a series of unique methods of capturing prey. **35** The main curiosity among the bat's weaponry is its use of echolocation, or sonar.

[2]

Because bats hunt in the dark, they are not often able to see their prey. Instead, they use a process wherein they emit sounds and listen for the echoes. If **36** they are, say, standing atop a mountain and shout, you can figure out the distance across the canyon using the speed of sound waves and a series of precise calculations. Using its innate senses, a bat does these same **37** calculations instinctively. With extreme precision, a bat can identify its prey's location and size in the dark and capture its prey. While a bat does have relatively acute vision, **38** though not nearly as acute as some species of shrimp, its echolocation is what makes it such an effective predator.

34

A) NO CHANGE

B) similar to that of human hunters

C) similar to those of human hunters

D) like human hunters

35

A) NO CHANGE

B) The echolocation, sonar, of the bat's weaponry is its main curiosity.

C) The bat has a curious weaponry, main among which is its echolocation and sonar.

D) The bat's weaponry is mainly curious in its use of echolocation of sonar.

36

A) NO CHANGE

B) they're,

C) one is,

D) you are,

37

A) NO CHANGE

B) calculations by instinct.

C) calculations with its instincts.

D) calculations.

38

The writer intends to insert a phrase or clause that emphasizes a common misunderstanding about bats' vision. Which of the following would best suit that intention?

A) NO CHANGE

B) undermining the cliché "blind as a bat,"

C) despite the pitch darkness in which it hunts,

D) in addition to its incredible hearing,

CONTINUE ▶

[3]

However, scientists have recently discovered a species that can disrupt the bat's usually failsafe echolocation. The tiger moth, a victim of bat predation for over 50 million years, has figured out a way to "jam" **39** its system of echolocation. Most tiger moths can emit clicks that warn bats away from the moths, suggesting that the moths might be inedible toxic compounds. **40**

[4]

In the long history of bat research, scientists have never seen the like of these tiger moths. Although human methods of warfare have used sonic deception for as long as such warfare has existed, the tiger moth and **41** their sonar jamming provide one of the first instances of aural camouflage in the animal kingdom that scientists have discovered. It seems that no matter how ancient the conflict, bats and tiger moths continue to attack, **42** counterattack, and adapt in a war as old as time.

39

A) NO CHANGE
B) the bats'
C) the bat's
D) the bats

40

If the writer were to delete the words *inedible* and *toxic* from the preceding sentence, the sentence would primarily lose

A) an indication that the tiger moth is not consumed by any predators.
B) a specific description of the compound that prevents the bat from eating the tiger moth.
C) a detailed analysis of the mechanism of the clicks that produce this particular compound.
D) nothing, because the information is stated elsewhere in the passage.

41

A) NO CHANGE
B) it's
C) its
D) its'

42

A) NO CHANGE
B) counterattack, and, adapt
C) counterattack and adapt
D) counterattack and adapt,

[5]

One species, the tiger moth *Bertholdia trigona*, has done even better. This species emits a high-frequency clicking noise that throws off the bat's sonar altogether. While no one is certain exactly how these clicks camouflage the *B. trigona*, the clicks have been remarkably successful in defending the moths from bat attacks. Some suggest that the clicks force bats to misinterpret their sensory data, taking the moth clicks for their own echoes. As a result, bats **43** miss their prey at the moment of attempted capture, and the tiger moths flit away unharmed. **44**

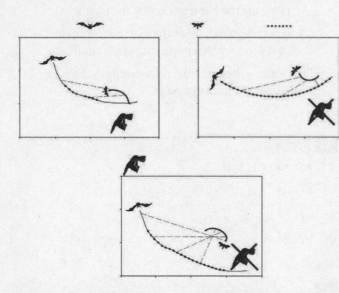

This image is adapted from the *Journal of Experimental Biology* © 2011.

43

Which of the following provides accurate information based on the diagrams?

A) NO CHANGE

B) attack other animals they find easier to detect,

C) fly after one another, bonking their heads together,

D) hear no sounds at all,

44

In the context of the passage as a whole, the best placement for paragraph 5 would be

A) where it is now.

B) after paragraph 1.

C) after paragraph 2.

D) after paragraph 3.

STOP
If you finish before time is called, you may check your work on this section only.
Do not turn to any other section in the test.

No Test Material On This Page

CONTINUE

Math Test – No Calculator

25 MINUTES, 20 QUESTIONS

Turn to Section 3 of your answer sheet to answer the questions in this section.

DIRECTIONS

For questions **1-15**, solve each problem, choose the best answer from the choices provided, and fill in the corresponding circle on your answer sheet. For questions **16-20**, solve the problem and enter your answer in the grid on the answer sheet. Please refer to the directions before question 16 on how to enter your answers in the grid. You may use any available space in your test booklet for scratch work.

NOTES

1. The use of a calculator **is not permitted**.
2. All variables and expressions used represent real numbers unless otherwise indicated.
3. Figures provided in this test are drawn to scale unless otherwise indicated.
4. All figures lie in a plane unless otherwise indicated.
5. Unless otherwise indicated, the domain of a given function f is the set of all real numbers x for which $f(x)$ is a real number.

REFERENCE

$A = \pi r^2$
$C = 2\pi r$

$A = \ell w$

$A = \frac{1}{2}bh$

$c^2 = a^2 + b^2$

Special Right Triangles

$V = \ell w h$

$V = \pi r^2 h$

$V = \frac{4}{3}\pi r^3$

$V = \frac{1}{3}\pi r^2 h$

$V = \frac{1}{3}\ell w h$

The number of degrees of arc in a circle is 360.
The number of radians of arc in a circle is 2π.
The sum of the measures in degrees of the angles of a triangle is 180.

CONTINUE

1

Which of the following equations has a vertex of $(3, -3)$?

A) $y = 5(x - 3)^2 - 3$

B) $y = 5(x + 3)^2 - 3$

C) $y = 5(x - 3)^2 + 3$

D) $y = 5(x + 3)^2 + 3$

2

A beverage store charges a base price of x dollars for one keg of root beer. A sales tax of a certain percentage is applied to the base price, and an untaxed deposit for the keg is added. If the total amount, in dollars, paid at the time of purchase for one keg is given by the expression $1.07x + 17$, then what is the sales tax, expressed as a percentage of the base price?

A) 0.07%

B) 1.07%

C) 7%

D) 17%

3

Syed took out a cash advance of d dollars from a financing company. The company deducts a fee of $\frac{1}{3}$ of the original advanced amount along with a wire transfer fee of $30.00. Which of the following represents the final advanced amount that Syed receives after all applied fees, in dollars?

A) $\frac{1}{3}d - 30$

B) $\frac{1}{3}(d - 30)$

C) $\frac{2}{3}(d - 30)$

D) $\frac{2}{3}d - 30$

4

What is the equation of a line that contains the point $(1, 6)$ and has a y-intercept of 4 ?

A) $y = \frac{1}{2}x + 4$

B) $y = x + 4$

C) $y = 2x + 4$

D) $y = 4x + 2$

5

The number of bonus points, $B(p)$, that a credit card holder receives is given by the function $B(p) = 4p + 7$, where p represents the number of purchases made. If the number of purchases is increased by 3, by how much does the number of bonus points increase?

A) 3

B) 4

C) 12

D) 19

6

Jeff tests how the total volume occupied by a fluid contained in a graduated cylinder changes when round marbles of various sizes are added. He found that the total volume occupied by the fluid, V, in cubic centimeters, can be found using the equation below, where x equals the number of identical marbles Jeff added, one at a time, to the cylinder, and r is the radius of one of the marbles.

$$V = 24\pi + x\left(\frac{4}{3}\pi r^3\right)$$

If the volume of the graduated cylinder is 96π cubic centimeters, then, what is the maximum number of marbles with a radius of 3 centimeters that Jeff can add without the volume of the fluid exceeding that of the graduated cylinder?

A) 1

B) 2

C) 3

D) 4

7

If b is two more than one-third of c, which of the following expresses the value of c in terms of b ?

A) $c = \dfrac{b-2}{3}$

B) $c = \dfrac{b+2}{3}$

C) $c = 3(b-2)$

D) $c = 3(b-6)$

8

The rotation rate of a mixing blade, in rotations per second, slows as a liquid is being added to the mixer. The blade rotates at 1,000 rotations per second when the mixer is empty. The rate at which the blade slows is four rotations per second less than three times the square of the height of the liquid. If h is the height of liquid in the mixer, which of the following represents $R(h)$, the rate of rotation?

A) $4 - 9h^2$

B) $1,000 - (4 - 3h)$

C) $1,000 - (9h - 4)$

D) $1,000 - (3h^2 - 4)$

CONTINUE

9

A dental hygiene company is creating a new 24-ounce tube of toothpaste by combining its most popular toothpastes, Cavity Crusher and Bad Breath Obliterator. Cavity Crusher contains 0.25% of sodium fluoride as its active ingredient, and Bad Breath Obliterator contains 0.30% of triclosan as its active ingredient for a total of 0.069 ounces of active ingredients in both toothpastes. Solving which of the following systems of equations yields the number of ounces of Cavity Crusher, c, and the number of ounces of Bad Breath Obliterator, b, that are in the new toothpaste?

A) $$c + b = 0.069$$
$$0.25c + 0.3b = 24$$

B) $$c + b = 24$$
$$0.0025c + 0.003b = 0.069$$

C) $$c + b = 24$$
$$0.025c + 0.03b = 0.069$$

D) $$c + b = 24$$
$$0.25c + 0.3b = 0.069$$

10

$$\frac{2d^2 - d - 10}{d^2 + 7d + 10} = \frac{d^2 - 4d + 3}{d^2 + 2d - 15}$$

In the equation above, what is the value of d ?

A) -4

B)   2

C)   4

D)   6

11

Which of the following is a possible equation for a circle that is tangent to both the x-axis and the line $x = 4$?

A) $(x + 2)^2 + (y + 2)^2 = 4$

B) $(x + 2)^2 + (y - 2)^2 = 4$

C) $(x - 2)^2 + (y + 4)^2 = 4$

D) $(x - 6)^2 + (y - 2)^2 = 4$

12

Reactant A is placed in a beaker, to which Reactant B will be added. Reactants A and B will not react unless B gets to a certain concentration. Once the reaction starts, both concentrations decrease until B has been consumed. Which of the following graphs, showing concentration in moles as a function of time in seconds, represents the reaction?

A)

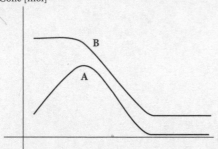

B)

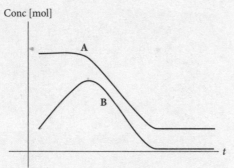

C)

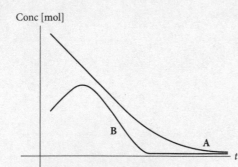

D)

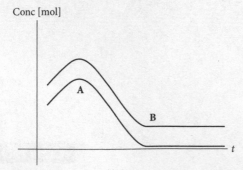

13

$$-2y \le 8$$
$$y - 3 \le x$$
$$-\frac{1}{3}y + 1 \ge x$$

Which of the following graphs shows the solution to the system of inequalities above?

A)

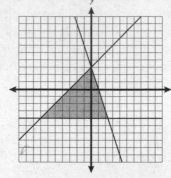

B)

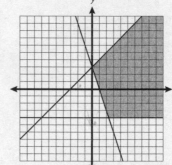

C)

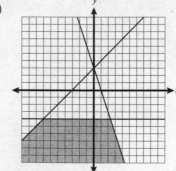

D)

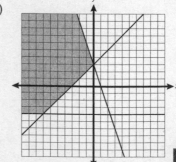

CONTINUE

14

If rectangle *ABCD* has an area of 48 and the tangent of ∠*BCA* (not shown) is $\frac{3}{4}$, then which of the following is the length of $\overline{BD}$ (not shown)?

A) 5

B) 10

C) 13

D) It cannot be determined from the given information.

15

Which of the following is equivalent to

$$\frac{2m + 6}{4} \times \frac{6m - 36}{3m + 9} \ ?$$

A) $\dfrac{12m^2 - 216}{12m + 36}$

B) $\dfrac{8m - 30}{3m + 13}$

C) $\dfrac{m - 6}{4}$

D) $m - 6$

CONTINUE

DIRECTIONS

For questions 16-20, solve the problem and enter your answer in the grid, as described below, on the answer sheet.

1. Although not required, it is suggested that you write your answer in the boxes at the top of the columns to help you fill in the circles accurately. You will receive credit only if the circles are filled in correctly.

2. Mark no more than one circle in any column.

3. No question has a negative answer.

4. Some problems may have more than one correct answer. In such cases, grid only one answer.

5. **Mixed numbers** such as $3\frac{1}{2}$ must be gridded as 3.5 or 7/2. (If  is entered into the grid, it will be interpreted as $\frac{31}{2}$, not as $3\frac{1}{2}$.)

6. **Decimal Answers:** If you obtain a decimal answer with more digits than the grid can accommodate, it may be either rounded or truncated, but it must fill the entire grid.

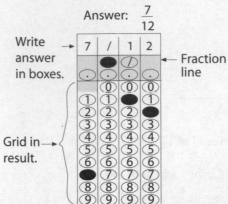

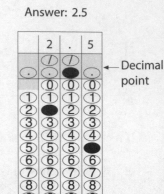

Acceptable ways to grid $\frac{2}{3}$ are:

Answer: 201 – either position is correct

NOTE: You may start your answers in any column, space permitting. Columns you don't need to use should be left blank.

CONTINUE ➤

16

A rectangular box has sides 3, 4, and x and a volume of 18. What is the value of x ?

17

Jeanne babysits Chuy one day each week. Jeanne charges a \$20 fee for the day, plus \$5.50 for every 30 minutes of babysitting. How much has Jeanne earned after three hours of babysitting? (Disregard the \$ sign when gridding your answer.)

18

The parabola $y = -x^2 + 5x + 6$ is intersected by the line $y = -\dfrac{1}{2}x + 12$. What is the y-coordinate of the intersection closest to the x-axis?

CONTINUE

19

$$13r + 8v = 47$$
$$22v = 63 - 17r$$

Based on the system of equations above, what is the sum of r and v ?

20

A gardener has a cultivated plot that measures 4 feet by 6 feet. Next year, she wants to double the area of her plot by increasing the length and width by x feet. What is the value of x ?

STOP
If you finish before time is called, you may check your work on this section only.
Do not turn to any other section in the test.

No Test Material On This Page

Math Test – Calculator

55 MINUTES, 38 QUESTIONS

Turn to Section 4 of your answer sheet to answer the questions in this section.

DIRECTIONS

For questions **1-30**, solve each problem, choose the best answer from the choices provided, and fill in the corresponding circle on your answer sheet. For questions **31-38**, solve the problem and enter your answer in the grid on the answer sheet. Please refer to the directions before question 31 on how to enter your answers in the grid. You may use any available space in your test booklet for scratch work.

NOTES

1. The use of a calculator **is permitted**.
2. All variables and expressions used represent real numbers unless otherwise indicated.
3. Figures provided in this test are drawn to scale unless otherwise indicated.
4. All figures lie in a plane unless otherwise indicated.
5. Unless otherwise indicated, the domain of a given function f is the set of all real numbers x for which $f(x)$ is a real number.

REFERENCE

$A = \pi r^2$
$C = 2\pi r$

$A = \ell w$

$A = \frac{1}{2} bh$

$c^2 = a^2 + b^2$

Special Right Triangles

$V = \ell wh$

$V = \pi r^2 h$

$V = \frac{4}{3}\pi r^3$

$V = \frac{1}{3}\pi r^2 h$

$V = \frac{1}{3}\ell wh$

The number of degrees of arc in a circle is 360.
The number of radians of arc in a circle is 2π.
The sum of the measures in degrees of the angles of a triangle is 180.

CONTINUE

1

The population, P, of Town Y since 1995 can be estimated by the equation $P = 1.0635x + 3,250$, where x is the number of years since 1995 and $0 \le x \le 20$. In the context of this equation, what does the number 1.0635 most likely represent?

A) The estimated population of town Y in 1995

B) The estimated population of town Y in 2015

C) The factor by which the population of town Y increased yearly

D) The factor by which the population of town Y decreased yearly

2

If $x^2 + 12x - 64$ and $x > 0$, what is the value of x?

A) 2

B) 4

C) 8

D) 16

3

Sai is ordering new shelving units for his store. Each unit is 7 feet in length and extends from floor to ceiling. The total length of the walls in Sai's store is 119 feet, which includes a length of 21 feet of windows along the walls. If the shelving units cannot be placed in front of the windows, which of the following inequalities includes all possible values of r, the number of shelving units that Sai could use?

A) $r \le \dfrac{119 - 21}{7}$

B) $r \ge \dfrac{119 + 21}{7}$

C) $r \le 119 - 21 + 7r$

D) $r \ge 119 + 21 - 7r$

4

Truffula Tree Fruit Weight

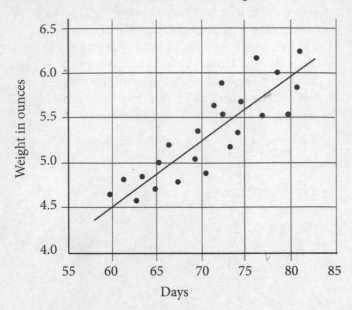

The scatterplot above shows the weight, in ounces, of the fruits on a certain truffula tree from days 55 to 85 after flowering. According to the line of best fit in the scatterplot above, which of the following is the closest approximation of the number of days after flowering of a truffula fruit that weighs 5.75 ounces?

A) 63

B) 65

C) 77

D) 81

5

Hannah placed an online order for shirts that cost $24.50 per shirt. A tax of 7% is added to the cost of the shirts, before a flat, untaxed shipping rate of $6 is charged. Which of the following represents Hannah's total cost for s shirts, in dollars?

A) $0.07(24.50s + 6)$

B) $1.07(24.50 + 6)s$

C) $1.07(24.50s) + 6$

D) $1.07(24.50 + s) + 6$

6

Once a certain plant begins to grow, its height increases at a linear rate. After six weeks, the plant is 54 centimeters tall. Which of the following functions best models the relationship between $h(w)$, the height, in centimeters, of the plant, and w, the number of weeks that the plant has been growing?

A) $h(w) = 6w$

B) $h(w) = 9w$

C) $h(w) = 54w$

D) $h(w) = 54 + w$

CONTINUE

7

Which of the following is equivalent to $(12x^2 + 4x + 5y)$ $+ (3x^2 - 2x + 3y)$?

A) $2x^2 - 2x + 8y$

B) $2x^2 + 15x + 8y$

C) $15x^2 - 2x + 8y$

D) $15x^2 + 2x + 8y$

8

An advertisement for Royal Rat Rations states: "7 out of 8 veterinarians recommend Royal Rat Rations for your fancy rat." No other information about the data is provided by the company.

Based on this data, which of the following inferences is most valid?

A) Royal Rat Rations provides the best nutrition for fancy rats.

B) If you do not feed your rat Royal Rat Rations, your rat will be unhealthy.

C) Only one veterinarian does not recommend Royal Rat Rations for your fancy rat.

D) Of the veterinarians surveyed by Royal Rat Rations, the majority recommend Royal Rat Rations for your fancy rat.

9

$$\frac{1}{2}t + 4 = \frac{3}{4}t - 5$$

In the equation above, what is the value of t ?

A) 4

B) 9

C) 18

D) 36

10

Dogs need 8.5 to 17 ounces of water each day for every 10 pounds of their weight. Everett has two dogs—Ringo is a 35-pound black lab mix, and Elvis is a 55-pound beagle. Which of the following ranges represents the approximate total number of ounces of water, w, that Elvis and Ringo need in a week?

A) $77 \leq w \leq 153$

B) $109 \leq w \leq 218$

C) $536 \leq w \leq 1,071$

D) $765 \leq w \leq 1,530$

CONTINUE

11

Priya is planning to send her favorite dry rub recipe to a friend who lives in France. Before sending the recipe, Priya wants to convert the American customary units in the instructions into metric units so that her friend will easily be able to understand the measurements. If the recipe calls for a ratio of four ounces of paprika to every seven ounces of chili powder, and if Priya's friend is planning to make a large batch of dry rub with 91 total ounces of chili powder, approximately how many total grams of paprika and chili powder will the recipe require? (1 ounce = 28.3 grams)

A) 4,047 grams

B) 4,521 grams

C) 4,925 grams

D) 5,149 grams

12

Luciano measured the amount of water that evaporated over a period of time from a container holding w ounces of water, where w is greater than 12. By the end of the first day, the cup had lost 2 ounces of water. By the end of the 7th day, the cup had lost an additional 8 ounces of water. By the end of the 11th day, the cup had lost half of the water that remained after the 7th day. Which of the following represents the remaining amount of water, in ounces, in Luciano's container at the end of the 11th day?

A) $\dfrac{w-2}{8}$

B) $\dfrac{w-2}{2} - 10$

C) $\dfrac{1}{2}w - 10$

D) $\dfrac{w-10}{2}$

CONTINUE

Questions 13 and 14 refer to the following information.

In the 1990s, the park rangers at Yellowstone National Park implemented a program aimed at increasing the dwindling coyote population in Montana. Results of studies of the coyote population in the park are shown in the scatterplot below.

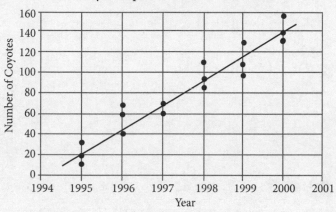

Coyote Population in Yellowstone Park

According to the data in the scatterplot, which of the following best represents the percent increase between the median of the results of the studies from 1995 and the median of the results of the studies from 1996 ?

A) 50%

B) 100%

C) 150%

D) 200%

13

Based on the line of best fit in the scatterplot above, which of the following is the closest to the average annual increase in coyotes in Yellowstone Park between 1995 and 2000 ?

A) 22

B) 24

C) 26

D) 28

15

Bailey's Boutique Clothing is having a 20% off sale during which shirts cost $30.00 and pants cost $60.00. On the day of the sale, Bailey's sells a total of 60 shirts and pants and earned a total of $2,250. On a regular day, Bailey's sells $\frac{2}{3}$ the number of shirts and pants sold during the sale and earns a total of $1,875. Solving which of the following systems of equations yields the number of shirts, s, and the number of pants, p, sold during a regular day?

A) $\quad s + p = 40$
$\quad 37.5s + 75p = 1,875$

B) $\quad s + p = 40$
$\quad 30s + 60p = 2,250$

C) $\quad s + p = 60$
$\quad 30s + 60p = 2,250$

D) $\quad s + p = 2,250$
$\quad 30s + 60p = 60$

16

Bryan, who works in a high-end jewelry store, earns a base pay of $10.00 per hour plus a certain percent commission on the sales that he helps to broker in the store. Bryan worked an average of 35 hours per week over the past two weeks and helped to broker sales of $5,000.00 worth of jewelry during that same two-week period. If Bryan's earnings for the two-week period were $850.00, what percent commission on sales does Bryan earn?

A) 1%

B) 2%

C) 3%

D) 4%

17

If $\dfrac{(C+x)}{x-3} = \dfrac{x+8}{3}$, which of the following could be an expression of C in terms of x ?

A) $3(1 + x)$

B) $x^2 + 2x - 24$

C) $\frac{1}{3}(x+6)(x-4)$

D) $\frac{1}{3}(x-3)(x+8)$

18

Lennon has 6 hours to spend in Ha Ha Tonka State Park. He plans to drive around the park at an average speed of 20 miles per hour, looking for a good trail to hike. Once he finds a trail he likes, he will spend the remainder of his time hiking it. He hopes to travel more than 60 miles total while in the park. If he hikes at an average speed of 1.5 miles per hour, which of the following systems of inequalities can be solved for the number of hours Lennon spends driving, d, and the number of hours he spends hiking, h, while he is at the park?

A) $1.5h + 20d > 60$
$\qquad h + d \le 6$

B) $1.5h + 20d > 60$
$\qquad h + d \ge 6$

C) $1.5h + 20d < 60$
$\qquad h + d \ge 360$

D) $20h + 1.5d > 6$
$\qquad h + d \le 60$

CONTINUE

19

In a certain sporting goods manufacturing company, a quality control expert tests a randomly selected group of 1,000 tennis balls in order to determine how many contain defects. If this quality control expert discovered that 13 of the randomly selected tennis balls were defective, which of the following inferences would be most supported?

A) 98.7% of the company's tennis balls are defective

B) 98.7% of the company's tennis balls are not defective

C) 9.87% of the company's tennis balls are defective

D) 9.87% of the company's tennis balls are not defective

20

If $-\dfrac{20}{7} < -3z + 6 < -\dfrac{11}{5}$, what is the greatest possible integer value of $9z - 18$?

A) 6

B) 7

C) 8

D) 9

21

$$-24 - 8j = 12k$$
$$3 + \frac{5}{3}k = -\frac{7}{6}j$$

Which of the following ordered pairs (j, k) is the solution to the system of equations above?

A) $(6, -6)$

B) $(3, 0)$

C) $(0, 2)$

D) $(-4, 1)$

CONTINUE

22

United States Investment in
Alternative Energy Sources

	Actual 2007 Investment	Projected 2017 Investment
Biofuels	0.31	0.34
Wind	0.40	0.32
Solar	0.27	0.30
Fuel Cells	0.02	0.04
Total	1.00	1.00

75   254

The table above shows the relative investment in
alternative energy sources in the United States by
type. One column shows the relative investment
in 2007 of $75 million total invested in alternative
energy. The other column shows the projected relative
investment in 2017 given current trends. The total
projected investment in alternative energy in 2017 is
$254 million. Suppose that a new source of alternative
energy, Cold Fusion, is perfected. It is projected that by
2017 that $57 million will be invested in Cold Fusion in
the United States, without any corresponding reduction
in investment for any other form of alternative energy.
What portion of the total investment of alternative
energy in the United States will be spent on biofuels?

A) 0.18

B) 0.22

C) 0.28

D) 0.34

23

$$(x - 2)^2 + y^2 = 36$$
$$y = -x + 2$$

The equations above represent a circle and a line that
intersects the circle across its diameter. What is the
point of intersection of the two equations that lies in
quadrant II?

A) $\left(-3\sqrt{2}, 3\sqrt{2}\right)$

B) $(-4, 2)$

C) $\left(2 + \sqrt{3}, 2\right)$

D) $\left(2 - 3\sqrt{2}, 3\sqrt{2}\right)$

CONTINUE

24

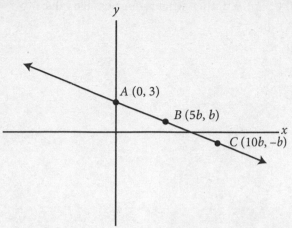

The graph of $f(x)$ is shown above in the xy-plane. The points $(0, 3)$, $(5b, b)$, and $(10b, -b)$ are on the line described by $f(x)$. If b is a positive constant, what are the coordinates of point C ?

A) $(5, 1)$

B) $(10, -1)$

C) $(15, -0.5)$

D) $(20, -2)$

25

Melanie puts $1,100 in an investment account that she expects will make 5% interest for each three-month period. However, after a year she realizes she was wrong about the interest rate and she has $50 less than she expected. Assuming the interest rate the account earns is constant, which of the following equations expresses the total amount of money, x, she will have after t years using the actual rate?

A) $x = 1,100(1.04)^{4t}$

B) $x = 1,100(1.05)^{4t-50}$

C) $x = 1,100(1.04)^{t/3}$

D) $x = 1,100(1.035)^{4t}$

26

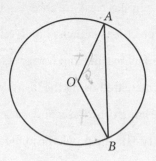

If the radius of the circle above is x, $\angle AOB = 120°$, and O is the center of the circle, what is the length of chord AB in terms of x ?

A) $\sqrt{2}x$

B) $\sqrt{3}x$

C) $\dfrac{x}{\sqrt{2}}$

D) $\dfrac{x}{\sqrt{3}}$

CONTINUE

27

Students in a physics class are studying how the angle at which a projectile is launched on level ground affects the projectile's hang time and horizontal range. Hang time can be calculated using the formula $t = \dfrac{2v \cdot \sin(\theta)}{g}$, where t is the hang time in seconds, v is the initial launch velocity, θ is the projectile angle with respect to level ground, and g is the acceleration due to gravity, defined as 9.8 m/s^2. Horizontal range can be calculated using the formula $R = \dfrac{v^2 \sin(2\theta)}{g}$, where R is the distance the projectile travels from the launch site, in feet. Which of the following gives the value of v, in terms of R, t, and θ?

A) $v = \dfrac{t \sin(\theta)}{2R \sin(\theta)}$

B) $v = \dfrac{2t \sin(\theta)}{R \sin(\theta)}$

C) $v = \dfrac{2R \sin(\theta)}{t \sin(2\theta)}$

D) $v = \dfrac{2R \sin(2\theta)}{t \sin(\theta)}$

28

If $(i^{413})(i^x) = 1$, then what is one possible value of x?

A) 0

B) 1

C) 2

D) 3

29

The function g is defined by $g(x) = 2x^2 - dx - 6$, where d is a constant. If one of the zeros of g is 6, what is the value of the other zero of g?

A) 2

B) $\dfrac{1}{2}$

C) $-\dfrac{1}{2}$

D) -2

CONTINUE

The flu shot for a flu season is created from four strains of the flu virus, named Strain A, B, C, and D, respectively. Medical researchers use the following data to determine the effectiveness of the vaccine over the flu season. Table 1 shows the effectiveness of the vaccine against each of these strains individually. The graph below the table shows the prevalence of each of these strains during each month of the flu season, represented as a percentage of the overall cases of flu that month.

Table 1

Strain	Effectiveness
A	35%
B	13%
C	76%
D	68%

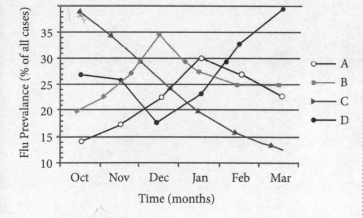

For the strain against which the flu shot was the most effective, approximately how effective was the shot overall during the month that strain was least prevalent?

A) 13%

B) 20%

C) 27%

D) 48%

DIRECTIONS

For questions 31-38, solve the problem and enter your answer in the grid, as described below, on the answer sheet.

1. Although not required, it is suggested that you write your answer in the boxes at the top of the columns to help you fill in the circles accurately. You will receive credit only if the circles are filled in correctly.

2. Mark no more than one circle in any column.

3. No question has a negative answer.

4. Some problems may have more than one correct answer. In such cases, grid only one answer.

5. **Mixed numbers** such as $3\frac{1}{2}$ must be gridded as 3.5 or 7/2. (If  is entered into the grid, it will be interpreted as $\frac{31}{2}$, not as $3\frac{1}{2}$.)

6. **Decimal Answers:** If you obtain a decimal answer with more digits than the grid can accommodate, it may be either rounded or truncated, but it must fill the entire grid.

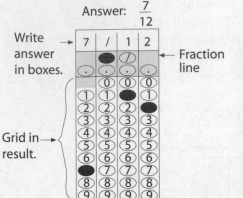

Acceptable ways to grid $\frac{2}{3}$ are:

Answer: 201 – either position is correct

NOTE: You may start your answers in any column, space permitting. Columns you don't need to use should be left blank.

CONTINUE

31

If $9 > 3v - 3$, what is the greatest possible integer value of v ?

32

In the expression $\dfrac{\frac{6}{5}}{\frac{12}{2y} - \frac{5}{y}} = 1$, what is the value of y ?

33

During a presidential election, a high school held its own mock election. Students had the option to vote for Candidate A, Candidate B, or several other candidates. They could also choose to spoil their ballot. The table below displays a summary of the election results.

	Candidate A	Candidate B	Other	Total
10th grade	0.32	0.58	0.10	1.00
11th grade	0.50	0.42	0.08	1.00
12th grade	0.63	0.32	0.05	1.00
Total	0.48	0.44	0.08	1.00

614 students voted for Candidate A. Approximately how many students attend the school?

34

If $\tan \theta = \dfrac{12}{5}$, then $\cos \theta =$

CONTINUE

35

Marcellus is traveling abroad in Ghana and using traveler's checks, which he has acquired from Easy Traveler's Savings Bank. Easy Traveler's Savings Bank charges a 7% fee on traveler's checks, which can then be used like cash at any location overseas at the same exchange rate, and any change will then be returned to Marcellus in local currency. For this trip, Marcellus bought a 651 Cedi traveler's check and paid a fee of 32.30 USD (United States dollars) for the check.

While in Ghana, Marcellus finds Leon's Pawnshop and Barter, which offers store credit for Marcellus's briefcase equal to its value in Cedis. If Marcellus's briefcase is worth 5,000 USD at the same exchange rate at which he bought his traveler's check, then how much store credit, to the closest Cedi, will Marcellus receive for the briefcase?

36

A square is inscribed in a circle. The area of the square is what percent of the area of the circle? (Disregard the percent symbol when gridding your answer.)

Questions 37 and 38 refer to the following information.

Professor Malingowski, a chemist and teacher at a community college, is organizing his graduated cylinders in the hopes of keeping his office tidy and setting a good example for his students. He has beakers with diameters, in inches, of $\frac{1}{2}, \frac{3}{4}, \frac{4}{5}, 1,$ and $\frac{5}{4}$.

37

Professor Malingowski notices one additional cylinder lying on the ground, and can recall certain facts about it, but not its actual diameter. If he knows that the value of the additional graduated cylinder's diameter, x, will not create any modes and will make the mean of the set equal to $\frac{5}{6}$, what is the value of the additional cylinder's diameter?

38

With his original five cylinders, Professor Malingowski realizes that he is missing a cylinder necessary for his upcoming lab demonstration for Thursday's class. He remembers that the cylinder he needs, when added to the original five, will create a median diameter value of $\frac{9}{10}$ for the set of six total cylinders. He also knows that the measure of the sixth cylinder will exceed the value of the range of the current five cylinders by a width of anywhere from $\frac{1}{4}$ inches to $\frac{1}{2}$ inches, inclusive. Based on the above data, what is one possible value of y, the diameter of this missing sixth cylinder?

STOP

If you finish before time is called, you may check your work on this section only.
Do not turn to any other section in the test.

SAT Essay

DIRECTIONS

The essay gives you an opportunity to show how effectively you can read and comprehend a passage and write an essay analyzing the passage. In your essay you should demonstrate that you have read the passage carefully, present a clear and logical analysis, and use language precisely.

Your essay must be written on the lines provided in your answer sheet booklet; except for the planning page of the answer booklet, you will receive no other paper on which to write. You will have enough space if you write on every line, avoid wide margins, and keep your handwriting to a reasonable size. Remember that people who are not familiar with your handwriting will read what you write. Try to write in print so that what you are writing is legible to those readers.

You have 50 minutes to read the passage and write an essay in response to the prompt provided inside this booklet.

REMINDER

— Do not write your essay in this booklet. Only what you write on the lined pages of your answer booklet will be evaluated.

— An off-topic essay will not be evaluated.

CONTINUE ➤

As you read the passage below, consider how the author uses

- evidence, such as facts or examples, to support claims.
- reasoning to develop ideas and to connect claims and evidence.
- stylistic or persuasive elements, such as word choice or appeals to emotion, to add power to the ideas expressed.

Excerpted from "Making A Brain Map That We Can Use" by Alva Noë. Originally published Janurary 16, 2015.

1   It is now conventional wisdom that the brain is the seat of the mind; it is alone through the brain's workings that we think and feel and know.

2   But what *is* a brain, anyway?

3   My thoughts turned to this question as I was reading a recent *New York Times* piece about Sebastian Seung's project to map the brain by tracing out each of the trillions of links between individual neurons. This undertaking to map the system of connections which make us what we are—to map what Seung called the connectome in his 2011 book—can seem, from a certain point of view, like a glorious and heroic step backward.

4   Trying to understand how the brain works by looking at the behavior of individual cells— so observed David Marr, one of modern cognitive science's foundational figures writing in the late 1970s—would be like trying to understand how a bird flies by examining the behavior of individual feathers. To understand flight, you need to understand aerodynamics; only once you get a handle on that can you ask how a structure of feathers, or any other physical system—such as a manufactured airship—can harness aerodynamics in the service of flight.

5   And so it is with the brain: Before we can understand how it works, it would seem that we need to understand what it's doing. But you can't read that off the action of individual cells. Just try!

6   Imagine you were to stumble one day upon a computer on the beach and imagine (very unrealistically) that you have never seen or heard of a computer before. How would you go about figuring out how it works? Well, one thing you could do would be to make a map of how all the detachable parts of the machine are connected. This piece of metal is soldered to this piece, which is stapled to this piece of plastic. And so on. Suppose you finished the job. Would you know what the thing is before you? Or how it works? Would your complicated, Rube-Goldberg-esque map of the connections between the parts even count as a model of the computer? Keep in mind that there are lots of different kinds of computers, made of lots of different materials, with lots of different types of parts and networks of connections. In fact, if Alan Turing was right (and Turing *was* right), the basic

CONTINUE

and essential job of a computer—the computing of computable functions—can be specified in entirely formal terms; the physical stuff of the computing machine is irrelevant to the question of what computations are being computed and, so, really, it is also irrelevant to the question of how this—or any other computer—works…

7   I'm raising both a practical point and a point of principle. The practical point is that we need some conception of what the whole *is for* before we have a ghost of a chance of figuring out how it works. This is Marr's point about feathers and flight. But there is also a matter of principle: When it comes to complex functional systems—like computers, for sure, and, probably, like brains—the laws and regularities and connections that matter are themselves *higher-level;* they don't bottom out in laws framed in terms of neuronal units any more than they do in laws framed in terms of quantum mechanical processes. The point is not just that it is hard to understand the brain's holistic operation in terms of what cells are doing but, instead, that it might be impossible—like trying to understand the stock market in terms of quantum mechanics. Surely, naturalism doesn't commit us to the view that it ought to be possible to frame a theory of the stock market in the terms of physics?

8   Gareth Cook, who wrote the recent *New York Times Magazine* article on Seung's quest, was wise to refer to Argentinian writer Jorge Luis Borges's cautionary tale, *On Exactitude In Science,* about a map being built as an exact, to-size replica of the domain being mapped. Such a map can't serve any explanatory purpose whatsoever. It won't be a useful map. My worry is that we already know that exactly the same thing is true of Seung's connectome.

Write an essay in which you explain how Noë builds an argument against the idea of cell-by-cell brain mapping. In your essay, analyze how Noë uses one or more of the features listed above (or features of your own choice) to strengthen the logic and persuasiveness of his argument. Be sure that your analysis focuses on the most relevant aspects of the passage.

Your essay should not explain whether you agree with Redford's claims, but rather explain how the author builds an argument to persuade his audience.

END OF TEST

DO NOT RETURN TO A PREVIOUS SECTION.

Completely darken bubbles with a No. 2 pencil. If you make a mistake, be sure to erase mark completely. Erase all stray marks.

1.

YOUR NAME: _____
(Print)
　　　Last　　　First　　　M.I.

SIGNATURE: _____　　DATE: __/__/__

HOME ADDRESS: _____
(Print)
　　　Number and Street

_____
　　　City　　　State　　　Zip Code

PHONE NO.: _____
(Print)

IMPORTANT: Please fill in these boxes exactly as shown on the back cover of your test book.

2. TEST FORM

3. TEST CODE

4. REGISTRATION NUMBER

5. YOUR NAME

First 4 letters of last name				FIRST INIT	MID INIT

6. DATE OF BIRTH

Month	Day		Year	
◯ JAN				
◯ FEB	⓪	⓪	⓪	⓪
◯ MAR	①	①	①	①
◯ APR	②	②	②	②
◯ MAY	③	③	③	③
◯ JUN		④	④	④
◯ JUL		⑤	⑤	⑤
◯ AUG		⑥	⑥	⑥
◯ SEP		⑦	⑦	⑦
◯ OCT		⑧	⑧	⑧
◯ NOV		⑨	⑨	⑨
◯ DEC				

7. SEX
◯ MALE
◯ FEMALE

The Princeton Review®

Test ①　Start with number 1 for each new section.
If a section has fewer questions than answer spaces, leave the extra answer spaces blank.

Section 1—Reading

1. Ⓐ Ⓑ Ⓒ Ⓓ
2. Ⓐ Ⓑ Ⓒ Ⓓ
3. Ⓐ Ⓑ Ⓒ Ⓓ
4. Ⓐ Ⓑ Ⓒ Ⓓ
5. Ⓐ Ⓑ Ⓒ Ⓓ
6. Ⓐ Ⓑ Ⓒ Ⓓ
7. Ⓐ Ⓑ Ⓒ Ⓓ
8. Ⓐ Ⓑ Ⓒ Ⓓ
9. Ⓐ Ⓑ Ⓒ Ⓓ
10. Ⓐ Ⓑ Ⓒ Ⓓ
11. Ⓐ Ⓑ Ⓒ Ⓓ
12. Ⓐ Ⓑ Ⓒ Ⓓ
13. Ⓐ Ⓑ Ⓒ Ⓓ
14. Ⓐ Ⓑ Ⓒ Ⓓ
15. Ⓐ Ⓑ Ⓒ Ⓓ
16. Ⓐ Ⓑ Ⓒ Ⓓ
17. Ⓐ Ⓑ Ⓒ Ⓓ
18. Ⓐ Ⓑ Ⓒ Ⓓ
19. Ⓐ Ⓑ Ⓒ Ⓓ
20. Ⓐ Ⓑ Ⓒ Ⓓ
21. Ⓐ Ⓑ Ⓒ Ⓓ
22. Ⓐ Ⓑ Ⓒ Ⓓ
23. Ⓐ Ⓑ Ⓒ Ⓓ
24. Ⓐ Ⓑ Ⓒ Ⓓ
25. Ⓐ Ⓑ Ⓒ Ⓓ
26. Ⓐ Ⓑ Ⓒ Ⓓ
27. Ⓐ Ⓑ Ⓒ Ⓓ
28. Ⓐ Ⓑ Ⓒ Ⓓ
29. Ⓐ Ⓑ Ⓒ Ⓓ
30. Ⓐ Ⓑ Ⓒ Ⓓ
31. Ⓐ Ⓑ Ⓒ Ⓓ
32. Ⓐ Ⓑ Ⓒ Ⓓ
33. Ⓐ Ⓑ Ⓒ Ⓓ
34. Ⓐ Ⓑ Ⓒ Ⓓ
35. Ⓐ Ⓑ Ⓒ Ⓓ
36. Ⓐ Ⓑ Ⓒ Ⓓ
37. Ⓐ Ⓑ Ⓒ Ⓓ
38. Ⓐ Ⓑ Ⓒ Ⓓ
39. Ⓐ Ⓑ Ⓒ Ⓓ
40. Ⓐ Ⓑ Ⓒ Ⓓ
41. Ⓐ Ⓑ Ⓒ Ⓓ
42. Ⓐ Ⓑ Ⓒ Ⓓ
43. Ⓐ Ⓑ Ⓒ Ⓓ
44. Ⓐ Ⓑ Ⓒ Ⓓ
45. Ⓐ Ⓑ Ⓒ Ⓓ
46. Ⓐ Ⓑ Ⓒ Ⓓ
47. Ⓐ Ⓑ Ⓒ Ⓓ
48. Ⓐ Ⓑ Ⓒ Ⓓ
49. Ⓐ Ⓑ Ⓒ Ⓓ
50. Ⓐ Ⓑ Ⓒ Ⓓ
51. Ⓐ Ⓑ Ⓒ Ⓓ
52. Ⓐ Ⓑ Ⓒ Ⓓ

Section 2—Writing and Language Skills

1. Ⓐ Ⓑ Ⓒ Ⓓ
2. Ⓐ Ⓑ Ⓒ Ⓓ
3. Ⓐ Ⓑ Ⓒ Ⓓ
4. Ⓐ Ⓑ Ⓒ Ⓓ
5. Ⓐ Ⓑ Ⓒ Ⓓ
6. Ⓐ Ⓑ Ⓒ Ⓓ
7. Ⓐ Ⓑ Ⓒ Ⓓ
8. Ⓐ Ⓑ Ⓒ Ⓓ
9. Ⓐ Ⓑ Ⓒ Ⓓ
10. Ⓐ Ⓑ Ⓒ Ⓓ
11. Ⓐ Ⓑ Ⓒ Ⓓ
12. Ⓐ Ⓑ Ⓒ Ⓓ
13. Ⓐ Ⓑ Ⓒ Ⓓ
14. Ⓐ Ⓑ Ⓒ Ⓓ
15. Ⓐ Ⓑ Ⓒ Ⓓ
16. Ⓐ Ⓑ Ⓒ Ⓓ
17. Ⓐ Ⓑ Ⓒ Ⓓ
18. Ⓐ Ⓑ Ⓒ Ⓓ
19. Ⓐ Ⓑ Ⓒ Ⓓ
20. Ⓐ Ⓑ Ⓒ Ⓓ
21. Ⓐ Ⓑ Ⓒ Ⓓ
22. Ⓐ Ⓑ Ⓒ Ⓓ
23. Ⓐ Ⓑ Ⓒ Ⓓ
24. Ⓐ Ⓑ Ⓒ Ⓓ
25. Ⓐ Ⓑ Ⓒ Ⓓ
26. Ⓐ Ⓑ Ⓒ Ⓓ
27. Ⓐ Ⓑ Ⓒ Ⓓ
28. Ⓐ Ⓑ Ⓒ Ⓓ
29. Ⓐ Ⓑ Ⓒ Ⓓ
30. Ⓐ Ⓑ Ⓒ Ⓓ
31. Ⓐ Ⓑ Ⓒ Ⓓ
32. Ⓐ Ⓑ Ⓒ Ⓓ
33. Ⓐ Ⓑ Ⓒ Ⓓ
34. Ⓐ Ⓑ Ⓒ Ⓓ
35. Ⓐ Ⓑ Ⓒ Ⓓ
36. Ⓐ Ⓑ Ⓒ Ⓓ
37. Ⓐ Ⓑ Ⓒ Ⓓ
38. Ⓐ Ⓑ Ⓒ Ⓓ
39. Ⓐ Ⓑ Ⓒ Ⓓ
40. Ⓐ Ⓑ Ⓒ Ⓓ
41. Ⓐ Ⓑ Ⓒ Ⓓ
42. Ⓐ Ⓑ Ⓒ Ⓓ
43. Ⓐ Ⓑ Ⓒ Ⓓ
44. Ⓐ Ⓑ Ⓒ Ⓓ

The Princeton Review

Test ❶ Start with number 1 for each new section.
If a section has fewer questions than answer spaces, leave the extra answer spaces blank.

Section 3—Mathematics: No Calculator

1. Ⓐ Ⓑ Ⓒ Ⓓ
2. Ⓐ Ⓑ Ⓒ Ⓓ
3. Ⓐ Ⓑ Ⓒ Ⓓ
4. Ⓐ Ⓑ Ⓒ Ⓓ
5. Ⓐ Ⓑ Ⓒ Ⓓ
6. Ⓐ Ⓑ Ⓒ Ⓓ
7. Ⓐ Ⓑ Ⓒ Ⓓ
8. Ⓐ Ⓑ Ⓒ Ⓓ
9. Ⓐ Ⓑ Ⓒ Ⓓ
10. Ⓐ Ⓑ Ⓒ Ⓓ
11. Ⓐ Ⓑ Ⓒ Ⓓ
12. Ⓐ Ⓑ Ⓒ Ⓓ
13. Ⓐ Ⓑ Ⓒ Ⓓ
14. Ⓐ Ⓑ Ⓒ Ⓓ
15. Ⓐ Ⓑ Ⓒ Ⓓ

16. 17. 18. 19. 20.

Section 4—Mathematics: Calculator

1. Ⓐ Ⓑ Ⓒ Ⓓ
2. Ⓐ Ⓑ Ⓒ Ⓓ
3. Ⓐ Ⓑ Ⓒ Ⓓ
4. Ⓐ Ⓑ Ⓒ Ⓓ
5. Ⓐ Ⓑ Ⓒ Ⓓ
6. Ⓐ Ⓑ Ⓒ Ⓓ
7. Ⓐ Ⓑ Ⓒ Ⓓ
8. Ⓐ Ⓑ Ⓒ Ⓓ
9. Ⓐ Ⓑ Ⓒ Ⓓ
10. Ⓐ Ⓑ Ⓒ Ⓓ
11. Ⓐ Ⓑ Ⓒ Ⓓ
12. Ⓐ Ⓑ Ⓒ Ⓓ
13. Ⓐ Ⓑ Ⓒ Ⓓ
14. Ⓐ Ⓑ Ⓒ Ⓓ
15. Ⓐ Ⓑ Ⓒ Ⓓ
16. Ⓐ Ⓑ Ⓒ Ⓓ
17. Ⓐ Ⓑ Ⓒ Ⓓ
18. Ⓐ Ⓑ Ⓒ Ⓓ
19. Ⓐ Ⓑ Ⓒ Ⓓ
20. Ⓐ Ⓑ Ⓒ Ⓓ
21. Ⓐ Ⓑ Ⓒ Ⓓ
22. Ⓐ Ⓑ Ⓒ Ⓓ
23. Ⓐ Ⓑ Ⓒ Ⓓ
24. Ⓐ Ⓑ Ⓒ Ⓓ
25. Ⓐ Ⓑ Ⓒ Ⓓ
26. Ⓐ Ⓑ Ⓒ Ⓓ
27. Ⓐ Ⓑ Ⓒ Ⓓ
28. Ⓐ Ⓑ Ⓒ Ⓓ
29. Ⓐ Ⓑ Ⓒ Ⓓ
30. Ⓐ Ⓑ Ⓒ Ⓓ

31. 32. 33. 34. 35.

36. 37. 38.

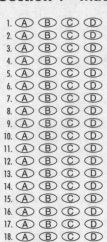

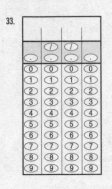
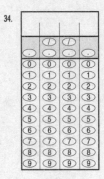

Chapter 21
Practice Test 1:
Answers and
Explanations

PRACTICE TEST 1 ANSWER KEY

Section 1:
Reading

1.	C	27.	A
2.	B	28.	B
3.	A	29.	D
4.	D	30.	C
5.	A	31.	C
6.	A	32.	B
7.	C	33.	C
8.	D	34.	D
9.	B	35.	A
10.	B	36.	C
11.	B	37.	A
12.	A	38.	A
13.	A	39.	D
14.	B	40.	A
15.	D	41.	B
16.	C	42.	B
17.	D	43.	A
18.	C	44.	A
19.	A	45.	C
20.	D	46.	C
21.	D	47.	B
22.	C	48.	C
23.	A	49.	D
24.	B	50.	A
25.	B	51.	B
26.	D	52.	D

Section 2:
Writing & Language

1.	A	23.	C
2.	C	24.	D
3.	B	25.	D
4.	A	26.	A
5.	D	27.	C
6.	D	28.	A
7.	D	29.	B
8.	D	30.	B
9.	B	31.	C
10.	A	32.	C
11.	C	33.	B
12.	B	34.	C
13.	A	35.	A
14.	B	36.	D
15.	B	37.	D
16.	D	38.	B
17.	C	39.	C
18.	A	40.	B
19.	B	41.	C
20.	C	42.	A
21.	D	43.	A
22.	A	44.	D

Section 3:
Math (No Calculator)

1.	A	11.	D
2.	C	12.	B
3.	D	13.	A
4.	C	14.	B
5.	C	15.	D
6.	B	16.	1.5 or $\frac{3}{2}$
7.	C		
8.	D		
9.	B		
10.	C		

17. 53

18. 10

19. $\frac{11}{3}$ or 3.66 or 3.67

20. 2

Section 4 :
Math (Calculator)

1.	C	20.	C
2.	B	21.	A
3.	A	22.	C
4.	C	23.	D
5.	C	24.	B
6.	B	25.	A
7.	D	26.	B
8.	D	27.	C
9.	D	28.	D
10.	C	29.	C
11.	A	30.	D
12.	D	31.	3
13.	B		
14.	D	32.	$\frac{5}{6}$ or 0.83
15.	A		
16.	C	33.	1,279
17.	C		
18.	A	34.	$\frac{5}{13}$ or 0.384 or 0.385
19.	B		

35. 7,054

36. 63.6 or 63.7

37. $\frac{7}{10}$ or 0.7

38. $1 \leq y \leq 1.25$

PRACTICE TEST 1 EXPLANATIONS

Section 1: Reading

1. **C**   The key to this question is the phrase *the passage as a whole*. Choice (A) describes the purpose of a section of a passage, but it is too specific and does not describe the purpose of the passage as a whole. Therefore, (A) is incorrect. Similarly, while the speakers briefly discuss the Shrewsbury School, the discussion occupies very little space, and is not the main point of the passage. Therefore, (B) is incorrect. Because the passage focuses on Carton, it is accurate to say that its purpose is to reveal his character. Therefore, (C) is correct. Because there is no evidence in the passage that Stryver has exploited Carton, (D) cannot be correct.

2. **B**   Because Stryver describes Carton as sound in the first paragraph, (A) is incorrect. *Mercurial* means "subject to sudden changes." Because Carton rapidly changes from growling to laughing to crying, (B) accurately describes him. Carton's luck is never described as bad, so (C) is incorrect. Because there is no indication that Carton does not notice the things occurring around him, (D) does not describe Carton. Choice (B) is the correct answer.

3. **A**   In the previous question, it is clear that Carton's personality and emotional state are somewhat easily changeable, so the correct answer for this question needs to reflect that theme. The quote in line 10, *Up one minute and down the next,* accurately illustrates the idea that Carton is *mercurial*; therefore, the answer must be (A). None of the other answer choices are relevant.

4. **D**   In the paragraph in question, *in spirits* describes Carton, and the paragraph says that carton is *up one minute and down the next*. Because *despondency* means "depression," *spirits* must mean the opposite of depression, like happiness. Choices (A), (B), and (C) all mean things other than happiness. Only *jubilation* is the opposite of *despondency*. Therefore, (D) is correct.

5. **A**   In the paragraph in question, Stryver calls Carton unmotivated and *lame*, so it is clear that Stryver dislikes Carton's behavior. Therefore, (A) is correct. Because Carton and Stryver are friends, it is clear that the description should not be taken literally; Stryver does not want to literally push Carton into the fireplace. Therefore, (B) is wrong. Similarly, the phrase *the old Sydney Carton* has nothing to do with Carton's actual age but rather is a term of endearment. Thus, (C) is incorrect. Because Stryver and Carton are presented as school friends, and there is no reason to believe Stryver ever bullied Sydney at school, (D) should be eliminated.

6. **A**   Two lines after the paragraph in question, Carton explicitly states that he does not find Miss Manette pretty. Because *incredulity* means "disbelief," (A) is a good description of Carton's attitude and the correct answer. Because Carton says that she is not attractive and Stryver says that she is attractive, Carton is not confused. He knows what he thinks and what Stryver thinks. Therefore, (B) is incorrect. Because there is no indication that Carton is annoyed by Stryver in the lines in

question, (C) should be eliminated. Because Carton thinks Miss Manette is not pretty, he does not feel affection towards her. Therefore, (D) is incorrect.

7. **C** While Stryver says that Miss Manette is pretty, to say that he is in love with her would be extreme. Therefore, (A) is incorrect. Though Carton is not successful, Stryver says that it is a lack of motivation that holds him back, not a lack of intelligence. Therefore, (B) is incorrect. In lines 63–68, Stryver says that it looked like Carton *sympathized* with Miss Manette, which indicates that Stryver believes Carton was paying attention to her and saw what happened to her at court. He was paying attention because she's attractive. Therefore, (C) is correct. Because Stryver and Carton never discuss either man's family, (D) cannot be correct.

8. **D** The answer to the previous question is that Stryver does not believe that Carton finds Miss Manette unattractive. Because the paragraphs indicated by (A) and (B) make no mention of Miss Manette, these choices are incorrect. Since the lines indicated by (C) state only that the court found Miss Manette attractive and makes no reference to Carton, this choice is incorrect. The paragraph indicated by (D) says that Carton *sympathized with* Miss Manette, which contradicts Carton's assertion that she is not attractive. Therefore, (D) provides support for the statement that Stryver does not believe that Carton finds Miss Manette unattractive, and is the correct answer.

9. **B** Because *lifeless desert* describes *the whole scene*, it refers to the physical landscape at which Carton is looking. Choices (A) and (C) do not describe a landscape, so both can be eliminated. Because Carton is looking at the city's landscape, not sand dunes, (D) should be eliminated, leaving (B), which is the correct answer.

10. **B** There is no indication of Miss Manette's feelings, positive or negative, toward Carton, so (A) is not correct. Since Carton is described as *incapable* and *resigned*, it is clear that he cannot change his behavior. Therefore, (B) is correct. The passage does not provide a physical description of Carton's apartment, so (C) is incorrect. There is no indication that Stryver is exploiting Carton, so eliminate (D).

11. **B** Use POE to find the answer choice that is consistent with the passage. Since the author is in support of the revolution, (B) is a good fit. Although the author doesn't seem to support the Soviet Union in the passage, (A) is still too extreme. Eliminate (C) and (D), since the author is neither conflicted nor dismissive. Choice (B) is correct.

12. **A** Use the context from earlier in the passage, in which *a secret non-aggression treaty between the Soviet Union and Nazi Germany* is discussed. Look for a word or phrase that matches this description, such as "scheme." Choice (A) is the best fit, and thus the correct answer.

13. **A** The author describes the songs as *grim*, but states that people had *hope in their hearts*. Choice (A) matches this contrast rather well. Choice (B) doesn't work because there is no distinction made between the themes of the songs and the anthems; rather, they are both categorized col-

lectively as having grim and sorrowful themes. The military of Estonia isn't discussed, so eliminate (C). Song festivals are mentioned in the following paragraph, so eliminate (D). You're left with (A), which is correct.

14. **B** Based on the information earlier in the passage, it's clear that Estonia wanted to be free from the Soviet Union, or to have a *legal "divorce,"* as stated at the end of the second paragraph. This phrase directly correlates with this desire. Choice (B) is a good fit. Eliminate (A) because there is no mention of speaking Russian. Choice (C) is incorrect because it's never stated that Estonia wanted to be culturally separate from other Baltic nations. Eliminate (D) because the passage implies the opposite: Estonians took the festivals very seriously and put a lot of effort and time into them. Choice (B) is correct.

15. **D** Based on the tone of the entire passage, the size of the amphitheater is used to show how much support this revolution had. Choice (D) matches this tone well. Choice (A) is incorrect because the question asks for the purpose of this fact, and this answer does not address the purpose of including this statistic. Choice (B) is also incorrect because the author is not trying to show the popularity of the Soviet Union and its leaders. You can eliminate (C) because no comparison is made to other theaters in the passage. The correct answer is (D).

16. **C** Cross out the word *burden* and replace it with your own word that is consistent with the text. The paragraph begins by stating that *historians* were *defying "free speech,"* but that later it was musicians who needed to do this. So a good replacement for *burden* would be "authority" or "leadership." Choice (C) is the best match and therefore the correct answer.

17. **D** The final paragraph states that the revolution was *powerful* and that *sedition hung in the wind*, so find an answer choice consistent with these descriptions. Choice (A) is incorrect, as *dread* is too extreme, and there were positive outcomes from the revolution. Eliminate (B) because disagreement among revolutionaries is discussed in the passage. Choice (C) is incorrect because *music and poetry* is too broad. It was specifically these festivals that included *music and poetry* that were vital. Therefore, (D) is the answer.

18. **C** Use POE to find an answer that is supported by information in the passage. The passage does not discuss the Soviet Union's singing traditions, so eliminate (A). Choices (B) and (D) are directly contradicted by the passage, so get rid of those choices as well. Choice (C) is supported by the third paragraph, which states that Estonia *could not threaten the Soviet Union militarily*. Choice (C) is correct.

19. **A** Use POE to find an answer that is supported by information in the passage. Choice (A) is a good match because lines 39–46 discuss the impact of the song festivals. Choice (B) is incorrect because the festival started over 100 years ago, not during the Soviet occupation. Eliminate (C), as it's not stated that the song festivals were unique. Choice (D) is incorrect because the passage doesn't discuss whether these songs were sung while working. Therefore, the answer is (A).

20. **D**   The festivals were a means of demonstrating national and cultural pride; use POE to find the answer that best exemplifies this. Choice (D) is the best fit because the festivals *united Estonians with poetry and music.* Choices (A) and (C) are irrelevant to the festivals. Choice (B) discusses the festivals but does not mention anything about national or cultural pride. Thus, (D) is correct.

21. **D**   According to the diagram, the Soviet Union acquired Estonia, Latvia, Lithuania, Bessarabia, and part of Poland in the pact. This land mass stretches from the Baltic Sea to the Black Sea; therefore, (D) is the correct answer. Although Germany did receive a portion of Poland, the Soviet Union also received a significant chunk. Therefore, (A) is incorrect. As depicted in the diagram, the Soviet Union is much larger than the part of Poland it acquired; eliminate (B). And *contiguous* means sharing a common border; Lithuania and Estonia are separated by Latvia, so they are not contiguous, so eliminate (C).

22. **C**   The fourth paragraph states, *But sir, the right to control their own Government is not one of the rights that the citizens of this country are called upon to surrender in time of war.* The author is objecting to the restrictions placed on those who have protested the war, and only (C) captures the author's dissenting views. While it is true that LaFollette is a lawmaker, no legislation is proposed, so eliminate (A). Since LaFollette argues for a single point of view throughout the text, eliminate (B). While it is true that LaFollette was dissenting against the war, this is not his primary purpose, so eliminate (D).

23. **A**   The fourth paragraph states, *…all men recognize that in time of war the citizen must surrender some … But sir, the right to control their own Government according to constitutional forms is not one of the rights...* Therefore, LaFollette believes that some rights are appropriately given up and some are not. Only (A) describes this distinction. LaFollette describes free speech as a fundamental personal right and never describes a moment in which it might be unnecessary, so eliminate (B). LaFollette never discusses what would and would not justify a war, so eliminate (C). LaFollette does mention the interests of humanity (how wars are ended) and the interests of this country (enduring peace), but does not draw a distinction between them, so eliminate (D). Choice (A) is correct.

24. **B**   The answer to the previous question states that LaFollette draws a distinction between rights that are appropriately and inappropriately given up in times of war. Neither this distinction nor any other distinction is mentioned in (A), so it can be eliminated. The aforementioned distinction is mentioned in the lines referenced in (B), which is the correct answer. Neither this distinction nor any other distinction is mentioned in (C) or (D), so they can be eliminated.

25. **B**   The passage states that *people are being unlawfully arrested, thrown into jail…only to be eventually discharged without ever having been taken into court.* A good way to describe these individuals would be *detained* and *separated.* The only answer choice that means something similar to this is (B), *sequestered.* Thus, (B) is the correct answer.

26. **D** The passage states that *citizens must beware of those precedents in support of arbitrary action by administrative officials, which excused on the plea of necessity in war time, become the fixed rule when the necessity has passed and normal conditions have been restored.* Thus, LaFollette is concerned that officials may restrict free speech during times of war but then fail to remove those restrictions when wartime has passed. More simply, LaFollette is worried that exceptions may become rules. Choice (D) matches this idea most closely. LaFollette does grant that *the citizen must surrender some rights,* but this is mentioned in paragraph 4. Thus, (A) can be eliminated. While LaFollette does say that some restrictions are arbitrary, paragraph 4 explicitly denies that all restrictions are arbitrary. Thus, (B) can be eliminated. While LaFollette does seem to be concerned with military action, (C) is never mentioned in the passage and can be eliminated. Choice (D) is correct.

27. **A** The passage states that *the right of the citizens…to discuss…every important phase of this war; its causes, the manner in which it should be conducted, and the terms upon which peace should be made.* In this paragraph, LaFollette explicitly mentions declaring war, which is referenced in (C); how to conduct war, (D); and how to end a war, (B). Thus, each of these can be eliminated. While LaFollette probably believes that citizens ought to elect legislators and executives, it is never mentioned in the passage. Thus, (A) is correct.

28. **B** The beginning of the sentence in question states that it is *the right of the citizens…to discuss… every important phase of this war.* The list that follows serves as examples of the important phases of a war in which citizen oversight might be necessary. Choice (B) best matches this description and is the correct answer. LaFollette's main point in the passage is to argue against the restriction of free speech during war, so (A) can be eliminated. LaFollette does offer reasons why the press might be afraid to speak out, but not in the referenced paragraph; eliminate (C). LaFollette does not believe that citizens understand wars better than the president, only that the country needs the counsel of all citizens, so (D) can be eliminated.

29. **D** The answer to the previous question states that LaFollette believes that free speech is necessary for the conduct of war. Choice (D) introduces this idea explicitly. The lines in (A) reference reasons that people are currently afraid to publicly discuss the issues in question, but do not provide reasons why speech is necessary and can be eliminated. The lines in (B) explain why some are attempting to restrict speech and can be eliminated. The lines in (C) give reasons why we should be concerned by the attempts to restrict free speech, but they provide no explicit mention of why free speech is necessary during times of war; eliminate (C). Choice (D) is the correct answer.

30. **C** The last paragraph of the passage states that *now is precisely the time when the country needs counsel of all its citizens.* Therefore, LaFollette believes that attempts to stifle discussion about *issues of war* are highly undesirable and contrary to the major goals of American democracy. Only (C) expresses an attitude that matches this position. LaFollette does not offer any sympathetic explanations for suppressing free speech, so (A) can be eliminated. LaFollette clearly cares about the suppression of free speech, so (B) can be eliminated. Choice (D), *morose,* is a

negative attitude, but it is overly negative and too passive for the tone of the passage. LaFollette is displeased with the suppression of free speech, but he is not sad or depressed about it.

31. **C** The first sentence of the last paragraph states that *It is no answer to say that when the war is over the citizen may once more resume his rights....* Thus, LaFollette rejects even the idea of a temporary restriction of free speech, a right that he calls *precious* and *fundamental*. LaFollette thinks that free speech should never be withheld but instead should be maintained *without interruption* or *restriction*. Choice (C) best matches this meaning and is the correct answer.

32. **B** Choice (B) is the correct answer, as satellite photos gave evidence of the fault lines at the edges of the earth's plates. Choice (A) is incorrect because it's too extreme. Choice (C) is also wrong because it says that the theory was created in 1965, whereas the passage indicates that there had been investigations of the theory before then. Choice (D) is too narrow; the San Andreas Fault is used as an example, but it alone doesn't prove that plate tectonics is a valid theory.

33. **C** The author states in paragraph 3 that continental-drift theory described the continents as mobile chunks that moved *through* the ocean floor, while plate tectonics has the continents moving *with* the surrounding seabed. Therefore, (C) is correct. Choice (A) is too extreme because the continents don't flow or stay immobile in either theory, nor do they move with or without purpose in either theory, as (B) states. Choice (D) looks very similar to the metaphor given, but the actual distinction is the idea of *plowing through* versus *moving in conjunction with*. Thus, (D) is also incorrect.

34. **D** The convection currents transfer or diffuse heat from the molten rock, and this leads to the plate movements. Thus, (D) is correct. Choices (A) and (B) are incorrect because the word *convection* doesn't mean to liquefy or melt. Choice (C) is incorrect because, while the plates are moving, *convection* doesn't mean to move as in a military endeavor.

35. **A** The author introduces Yellowstone's hot springs as an example of how volcanoes can exist mid-plate when hot spots push lava up through the plate, so (A) is the correct answer. Choice (B) is incorrect because it is too extreme—one example doesn't prove anything. Choice (C) is incorrect because Yellowstone isn't used in this passage to support an opposing theory. Choice (D) is incorrect because it's referring to a mid-ocean ridge, which occurs at the borders of plates.

36. **C** The passage says that *These plumes of molten rock, often called hot spots, rise and erupt through the crust of a moving plate*, which suggests the hot spots are punching up through a complete piece of the crust to create volcanoes, as there's no fracture for it to flow through. Thus, (C), *As the crustal plate moves, the hot spot "punches" up a line of volcanic and hot-spring activity,* is correct, and you can eliminate (A), (B), and (D).

37. **A** The Hawaiian Islands are consistent or on a line with the movement of the Pacific plate, so (C) and (D), which state the opposite, are incorrect. The islands are created as the plate moves, but then the plate moves on and the islands don't change to suit it, so (B) is incorrect. Choice (A) is the answer.

38.   **A**   Choice (A) is correct because it matches the passage, which states that Iceland was created by lava flow that bubbled up from between two tectonic plates at a mid-ocean ridge. Choice (B) contrasts an island and a continent, which the passage does not, while (C) states that the author mentions Iceland to prove that an island can be a volcano. The author never says that an island can't be a volcano, so (C) is incorrect. Choice (D) is true, but it doesn't answer the question. Iceland does straddle the mid-Atlantic ridge, but the reason that the author mentions Iceland is to give an example of an island that was created by lava flow at a hot spot.

39.   **D**   The passage says that *the lava flows more abundantly in certain spots, producing volcanic islands* (lines 70–72) and *underlie the large, highly volcanic island of Iceland, which straddles the Mid-Atlantic Ridge* (lines 75–76). Thus, (D) is correct. Choices (A), (B), and (C) do not coordinate with any answer choices in the previous questions.

40.   **A**   The author uses the phrase *Some geologists propose* to show that plate tectonics are a theory, and there are still things about it that scientists don't know and want to learn. Thus, (A) is correct. The passage never mentions a lack of data, so (B) can be eliminated, while (C) implies that the phrase is introducing an opposing viewpoint, which it does not. Choice (D) refers to the continental-drift theory, which is not part of the logic of this paragraph, so it is incorrect.

41.   **B**   The passages states that *plumes of molten rock, often called hot spots, rise and erupt through the crust of a moving plate.* The diagram depicts this process with a line traveling up through the lithosphere to the surface. Therefore, (B) is correct. While the diagram does depict a continental rift zone by the ocean, there is no evidence in the graph or the passage that this is always the case. Therefore, (A) is incorrect. The passage states that *mid-ocean ridges mark boundaries where plates are forced apart as new ocean floor is being created between them;* thus, (C) can be eliminated. There is no mention in either the passage or the diagram of the relative rigidity of oceanic and continental crust, so (D) can be eliminated as well.

42.   **B**   The author's main point in the first paragraph is that the construction of the Glen Canyon Dam did *affect downstream resources*, including *the loss of large beaches used for camping* and the addition of several animals to the endangered species list. Choice (B) matches the context of this passage, so keep it. Eliminate (A), as no mention is made of maintaining water resources. According to the passage, the fish were adapted to the pre-dam era, so (C) doesn't work because *decimated* is too extreme. Choice (D) is the opposite of what the first paragraph suggests, so eliminate it. Choice (B) is the answer.

43.   **A**   The correct answer to the previous question was that the dam was *built with a lack of foresight*. This is shown best with (A), since it's mentioned that *little consideration was given to how dam operations might affect downstream resources*. Choices (B) and (D) both show consequences but don't necessarily match the phrase *little consideration*, so eliminate them. Choice (C) isn't negative at all, so get rid of it. The correct answer is (A).

44. **A** The passage states that the scientists and recreationists *observed the physical transformation of the river in Grand Canyon*, so the correct answer should match this information. Choice (A) is a good fit, so keep it. Eliminate (B), as no mention is made of casual observation, as well as (C) because the passage never hints at collaboration between scientists and the public. Choice (D) is too extreme because the passage never proves anything. Choice (A) is correct.

45. **C** The first paragraph of Passage 1 discusses the humpback chub and mentions that it has been listed as endangered, as well as that *the dam and its operation jeopardized the continued existence of humpback chub in Grand Canyon*. Choice (A) is incorrect because it's too extreme. The chub is endangered, not extinct. Choice (B) refers to the fish later in the passage instead of the chub, so eliminate it. Choice (D) is never mentioned, so eliminate this choice as well. This leaves (C), which is correct; it can be inferred the chub can survive a variety of environments because it's still alive.

46. **C** Go to the first sentence of the second paragraph in Passage 1 and cross out the word *regime*. Replace it with your own word using the context of the paragraph. A good replacement would be "process," so find a word in the answer choices that matches this meaning. Choice (C) fits, so keep it for now. Choice (A) is a dictionary definition of *regime*, so eliminate it. Choices (B) and (D) are not related to "process" in any way, so get rid of them as well. Choice (C) is therefore correct.

47. **B** Go to the second sentence of the second paragraph in Passage 2 and cross out the word *suspended*. Replace it with your own word using the context of the paragraph. The paragraph mentions that sand is included *at high concentration in the flow*, so a good replacement would be "combined." Choice (B) is the best match and therefore the correct answer.

48. **C** Use POE to find an answer consistent with the passage. *Controlled floods* are discussed in the final two paragraphs, so this should be the reference window. Choices (A) and (D) are incorrect because snowmelt is mentioned only in the first passage. While controlled floods sometimes lead to the higher concentrations of suspended sand, this is not always the case. Therefore, (B) can be eliminated. Choice (C) works because the first sentence of the final paragraph states that the floods *may erode sandbars if the concentration of suspended sand during a controlled flood is too low*. Therefore, (C) is correct.

49. **D** The correct answer to the previous question deals with the negative effects of controlled flooding on the health of the river, so the answer to this question should reflect this theme. The lines referenced in (D) describe sandbar erosion, which would certainly qualify as something "detrimental"; therefore, (D) is the correct answer. The lines from the passage referenced by the other answer choices do not illustrate any negative effects on the river.

50. **A** The High Flow Experiments mentioned in Passage 2 refer to controlled floods used to increase sandbars. Therefore, the author of Passage 1 would have a positive attitude towards these floods because *Sandbars, riverbanks, and their accompanying aquatic habitats were reshaped*, which is

ultimately beneficial to the ecosystem. Choice (A) is a good match for this information. Eliminate (B), (C), and (D) because they are too negative.

51. **B** Passage 1 is mostly interested in the geologic history of the Glen Canyon Dam, whereas Passage 2 primarily discusses the use of controlled floods. Use POE to find the answer. Eliminate (A); even though a problem is presented in Passage 1, Passage 2 doesn't address the same problem or solution. Choice (B) is a good fit, so keep it for now. Choice (C) is pretty vague, and it's not clear whether the changes in Passage 2 are recent, so eliminate it. No experiment is discussed in Passage 1 with any specifics, so eliminate (D). Choice (B) is correct.

52. **D** Use POE to find an answer that is applicable to both passages. Eliminate (A) and (B) because neither passage discusses a scientific experiment or topographic changes. Choice (C) is true of both passages, so eliminate it as well. This leaves (D), which is correct: Passage 2 never discusses any specific species, whereas Passage 1 mentions *the humpback chub and Colorado pikeminnow*.

Section 2: Writing and Language

And Justice for All

1. **A** If you can't cite a reason to use a comma, don't use one. In this case, commas are not necessary because the fact that she works at the mall is important as a contrast to *more serious*. Therefore, the answer is (A).

2. **C** The idea before the punctuation (*She would start applying to law schools soon*) is complete. The idea after the comma and conjunction (*she wanted to know what the law looked like in action*) is also complete. Remember the STOP punctuation rules. Choices (A) and (D) can be eliminated because two complete ideas cannot be joined with just a conjunction or just a comma; both are needed. The comma in (B) is in the wrong place, so the answer is (C).

3. **B** Notice the question! It asks which statement is most in keeping with the main idea. The passage centers on the Department of Corrections, and the only choice that introduces this information is (B). The next sentence doesn't even make sense without the specific information in (B).

4. **A** Notice the question! It asks for a statement that reinforces ideas in this sentence as well as the preceding sentence. The ideas in these sentences are about no one paying much attention to the Department of Corrections. Choice (B) contradicts this idea. Choices (C) and (D) contain the wrong focus. Therefore, (A) is the answer.

5. **D** The subject of this sentence is *meaning*, which is singular. Eliminate the choices with plural verbs—(A), (B), and (C)—because they are inconsistent. The correct answer is (D).

6.   **D**   The underlined pronoun refers to *Everyone,* which is singular. Choice (D) is the only possible answer because it is consistent in number.

7.   **D**   The sentence should come after another question about the treatment of inmates in order to make sense of the phrase *by the same token.* This question appears in Sentence 6, so this sentence should go after Sentence 6, as (D) suggests.

8.   **D**   Choices (A), (B), (C), and (D) all say essentially the same thing, but (D) does so in the most concise way possible. Therefore, (D) is correct.

9.   **B**   The subject of this verb is *politics and the law,* which is plural, thus eliminating (A) and (C). Choice (B) is the correct answer because it is more concise than (D).

10.   **A**   The idea before the conjunction (*We may believe that we never come into contact with the law*) is complete, and the idea after the conjunction (*it is written into everything...ourselves*) is also complete. When a conjunctive adverb connects two complete ideas in one sentence, it is preceded by a semicolon and followed by a comma. Therefore, (A) is correct.

11.   **C**   This essay focuses on Amanda's personal discoveries about the law; it does not the justice system. Eliminate (A) and (B). Choice (D) is incorrect because the passage doesn't discuss her entire career, just the summer before she applied to law schools. Choice (C) is correct.

Alexander's Empire of Culture

12.   **B**   The correct idiom is *disappear from.* The sentence as written implies two things have disappeared when it should be just the *study of the classics.* Eliminate (A). Choices (C) and (D) are not the correct form of the idiom. Choice (B) is the correct answer.

13.   **A**   This sentence is correct as written. Although the phrase *for all that* might sound foreign, it is being used correctly here. Choice (B) does not make sense. Choices (C) and (D) are basically the same as (A), and remember: If there is no grammatical reason to change the original, don't. Therefore, (A) is correct.

14.   **B**   The correct idiom uses the words *in* and *right,* so (A), (C), and (D) can be eliminated. Choice (B) is correct.

15.   **B**   The correct answer will feature words or phrases that are as precise as possible. The sentence as written does not make clear to whom the pronoun is referring: Alexander or Aristotle. Choice (B) clears up this pronoun ambiguity. Choice (C) can be eliminated because Alexander was born in Pella, and his arrival as a newborn would not have announced an enlightened era, nor is it likely they arrived together.

16.   **D**   Notice the question! It asks for a concluding statement that emphasizes the change brought about by Alexander's rule. Choices (A), (B), and (C) do not address the change from militaristic Philip to enlightened Alexander. Only (D) has the correct emphasis.

17.   **C**   Notice the question! It asks for an introductory phrase that emphasizes continuity from the previous rule. The only choice that refers to the previous rule and explains how the second sentence connects to the first in the paragraph is (C).

18.   **A**   Check the answer choices against the map, and make sure that the information is consistent with the figure. Choices (B) and (D) contain information that cannot be gleaned from the map, while (C) contains information that contradicts the map. Choice (A) is consistent with the map, so it is the correct answer.

19.   **B**   As written, the first part of the sentence creates a comma splice, wherein a comma separates two complete ideas. Choice (A) can be eliminated. Choice (B) is the best of the remaining answer choices because it is the most concise. A conjunction such as *although* or *moreover* is not needed due to the *however* in the preceding sentence. This sentence's purpose is to explain the preceding sentence.

20.   **C**   *Unprecedented* means "never done or known before." Choices (A), (B), and (D) have the same definition, so they can be eliminated—the question asks for what would NOT be acceptable. Choice (C) means "lacking historical context" and is not an acceptable alternative.

21.   **D**   The idea before the period (*Alexandria, Egypt, perhaps the most...continues to thrive*) is a complete idea. The idea after the period (*It is the second...of Egypt*) is also a complete idea. Therefore, the two cannot be joined together with only a comma. (Remember your STOP punctuation rules.) Eliminate (B). Of the remaining answer choices, (D) is the most effective way to combine the two sentences because it eliminates the need to repeat the subject, which makes the sentence flow better. Therefore, (D) is correct.

22.   **A**   The sentence as written is consistent in structure with *between man and god* and *the individual and the world,* both of which use the conjunction *and.* As the last item in this list, *and* should be used between *the natural and the unnatural.* All other choices are not consistent and change the meaning. Therefore, (A) is the answer.

Brother, Can You Spare a Dime?

23.   **C**   The correct answer will contain phrases that are as precise as possible. It is the dime novel that was *printed cheaply and for quick consumption,* so the words *dime novel* need to be placed immediately next to the modifier phrase. Choices (A), (B), and (D) all include this misplaced modifier. Only (C) makes the sentence precise.

24.   **D**   Notice the question! It asks for the phrase that gives the most specific information. Choice (D) provides specific names of authors who wrote by way of literary periodicals. Choices (A), (B), and (C) refer to the authors only in vague terms.

25. **D** The title of Stowe's book is necessary information, which means we do not want to surround it in commas, so eliminate (B). Choices (A) and (C) have other unnecessary commas. The correct answer is (D) because it contains no commas at all.

26. **A** The correct answer will support the passage while being as precise as possible. The next sentence begins with the subject *That book*, and without the phrase *the publishers were clamoring for an actual book*, the reader wouldn't know what *that book* is. This reasoning is summed up in (A). Choice (B) is incorrect because there is no support for publishers being greedy. Choice (C) is incorrect because the passage says Stowe's work was already popular as a periodical series.

27. **C** The average annual income of a man in this period is not in line with the main idea of the paragraph, which discusses the shift from periodicals to novels. To add this statement would be inconsistent with the paragraph's focus, which is stated in (C).

28. **A** Choices (B) and (D) use the wrong verb tense. Choice (C) is not in line with the focus of the paragraph. Additionally, since we do not know if the series is still known this way, (A) is the correct answer.

29. **B** *Effect* is generally a noun, while *affect* is a verb except in certain unusual circumstances. The underlined portion needs to be a noun, so *affects* is incorrect. Eliminate (A) and (D). The sentence discusses multiple effects, not something belonging to the effects, so the plural form of the verb is needed, not the possessive form. Eliminate (C). This leaves (B), which is the correct answer.

30. **B** The correct answer will feature words or phrases that make the passage as precise as possible. Without the actual names, the phrase *William Bonney and James Butler Hickcock became the folk heroes* does not make sense. We need the names of transformed folk heroes in order to make sense of the sentence. Eliminate (C) and (D). Choice (A) is incorrect because the rest of sentence does not speak in generalities; it provides two names already. Choice (B) is correct.

31. **C** The correct idiom is *learned from*, not *taught from*, so eliminate (A). The new media has not brought anything from the dime novel's popularity because it is something entirely new, so eliminate (D). *Learned* is more precise than *got*, so the correct answer is (C).

32. **C** As written, the sentence is unclear for whom or what the foundation is being laid, so eliminate (A). The underlined portion needs to follow the word *foundation* in order to clarify this. The correct answer will make the passage as precise as possible. This is (C).

33. **B** A *frame of reference* is a set of criteria or stated values in relation to which measurements or judgments can be made. *Integration*, (B), is the intermixing of people or groups that were previously segregated. Since this does not serve as an acceptable alternative to *frame of reference*, it is the correct answer.

The Tiger Moth's Phantom Target

34. **C** Be sure to compare similar things to maintain consistency and precision. The sentence as written compares *methods* to *humans*. Compare methods to methods, or change the construction of the sentence. Eliminate (A) and (D) because both make the same mistake. Choice (B) uses the singular pronoun *that* to refer to the plural *methods,* so eliminate it. Choice (C) uses the correct comparison and the plural pronoun, so it is correct.

35. **A** All four choices use similar words. Choose the one that expresses the idea most clearly. In this case, the clearest choice is (A). Choice (B) is passive and contains unnecessary commas. Choice (C) contains the awkward phrase *main among which is its*. Choice (D) uses *curious* as an adjective instead of a noun, implying that the weaponry is curious about something instead of being a curiosity itself.

36. **D** This sentence does not refer to the bats (bats cannot shout). Eliminate (A) and (B). The sentence uses the word *you* later, so this underlined portion should be consistent with the rest of the sentence. Eliminate (C). Choice (D) correctly replaces *they* with *you*.

37. **D** All four choices use similar words. Choose the one that expresses the idea most clearly and concisely. In this case, the answer is (D). *Instincts* does not need to be repeated because the word *innate* was already used.

38. **B** Notice the question! The question asks for a phrase that emphasizes a common misunderstanding about bats' vision. Choice (A) compares bats' vision to shrimp, which is not a common misunderstanding. Choices (C) and (D) describe aspects of bats' hunting but do not emphasize a common misunderstanding. Only (B) discusses the common thought (or cliché) about bats being blind.

39. **C** The pronoun *its* is ambiguous, as it is unclear whether it refers to the tiger moth or the bat. The correct choice features words that are as precise as possible, so eliminate (A). The other choices clear up the ambiguity, but only (C) has the correct possessive singular pronoun needed. Choice (B) uses a plural pronoun, but since only a single system of echolocation is referred to, the singular *bat's* is appropriate.

40. **B** The words *inedible* and *toxic* specifically explain why the warning would result in the bats not going after the moths. This is best summarized in (B). Choice (A) is incorrect because we do not know about *any* predators, just bats. Choice (C) is incorrect because *inedible* and *toxic* do not give any information about the mechanism of the clicks. Choice (D) is incorrect because the information is not stated elsewhere. The answer is (B).

41. **C** The pronoun refers to *the tiger moth,* which is the name of a species and therefore a collective noun. Collective nouns are singular, so eliminate (A) because it is inconsistent. When dealing with pronouns, remember that possessives do not use apostrophes, while contractions do use apostrophes. Choice (B) contains a contraction. It would not make sense to say *the tiger moth*

and it is sonar jamming, so eliminate (B). There is no such word as *its',* so eliminate (D). The sonar jamming belongs to the tiger moth, so a possessive pronoun is needed, as in (C).

42. **A** All of the commas are correct as written. There should be a comma after each item in a list. A comma is needed after *counterattack,* but not after *and* or *adapt.* Choices (B), (C), and (D) contain unnecessary commas, so the answer is (A).

43. **A** Check the answer choices against the figures. Only (A) can be supported by the diagram. There is no indication of other animals, as in (B); what sounds are or are not heard, as in (D); or bats running into each other, as in (C).

44. **D** Paragraph 5 does not fit as a conclusion, so eliminate (A). This paragraph should come after the discussion of the tiger moth and its tactics and before the conclusion of the essay. This indicates the best placement is after the third paragraph, so (D) is the answer.

Section 3: Math (No Calculator)

1. **A** The vertex form of a parabola is $y = a(x - h)^2 + k$, where (h, k) denotes the vertex. Plug in the point $(3, -3)$ into the vertex form to get $y = a(x - 3)^2 - 3$. The correct answer is (A).

2. **C** You can plug in to make sense of this equation. Say that $x = \$100$. The amount of the keg would then be $\$107 + \$17$. The $\$17$ must be the untaxed deposit since it is a flat fee rather than percentage based. Therefore, the tax is $\$7$, which is 7% of the original $\$100$ base price. The answer is (C).

3. **D** Whenever there are variables in the question, plug in. Be sure to plug in a number that is divisible by 3. Let $d = 300$. $\frac{1}{3}$ of the original amount of $\$300$ is $\$100$, and that is deducted by the company, leaving Syed with $\$200$. Then, subtract the wire transfer fee to get $\$200 - \$30 = \$170$, which is the target number. Plug in 300 for d in the answer choices to see which one is equal to the target number of 170. In (A), $\frac{1}{3}(300) - 30 = 70$. This is not the target number, so eliminate (A). Likewise in (B), $\frac{1}{3}(300 - 30) = 90$, and in (C), $\frac{2}{3}(300 - 30) = 180$. Neither of these is the target number, so eliminate (B) and (C). In (D), $\frac{2}{3}(300) - 30 = 170$, which is the target number. The correct answer is (D).

4. **C** All of the answers are written in the slope-intercept form $y = mx + b$, where b is the y-intercept and x and y are points on the line. Eliminate (D) because the y-intercept in that equation is 2. For the remaining answer choices, plug in the x- and y-values to determine which equation

works. If $x = 1$ and $y = 6$, (A) becomes $6 = \dfrac{1}{2}(1) + 4$. Solve both sides of the equation to get $6 = 4\dfrac{1}{2}$. Eliminate (A). Choice (B) becomes $6 = 1 + 4$, so eliminate (B). Choice (C) becomes $6 = 2(1) + 4$, or $6 = 6$. Therefore, the correct answer is (C).

5. **C**   Whenever there are variables in the question and the answer choices, think Plugging In. If 2 purchases were made, then $p = 2$, and the number of bonus points can be calculated as $4(2) + 7 = 8 + 7 = 15$. If the number of purchases were then increased by 3, the new p equals 5 and the number of bonus points can be calculated as $4(5) + 7 = 27$. The bonus points increased by $27 - 15 = 12$. The correct answer is (C).

6. **B**   This is a good Plug In the Answers problem. Start with (B) and plug in 2 for x and 3 for r in the equation to get $V = 24\pi + 2\left(\dfrac{4}{3}\pi 3^3\right)$, which is equal to the target amount of 96π, so (B) is correct.

7. **C**   Whenever there are variables in the question and in the answers, think Plugging In. Let $c = 30$. Therefore, $b = 2 + \dfrac{1}{3}(30) = 2 + 10 = 12$. Plug 12 in for b in the answers to see which answer equals the target number of 30. Choice (A) becomes $\dfrac{12 - 2}{3} = \dfrac{10}{3} = 3.\overline{3}$. Eliminate (A), since it does not equal the target number. Choice (B) becomes $\dfrac{12 + 2}{3} = \dfrac{14}{3} = 4.\overline{6}$. Eliminate (B). Choice (C) becomes $3(12 - 2) = 3(10) = 30$. Keep (C), but check (D) just in case it also works. Choice (D) becomes $3(12 - 6) = 3(6) = 18$. Eliminate (D). The correct answer is (C).

8. **D**   Treat this question as a translation problem. According to the question, $R(h) =$ four rotations per second less than three times the square of the height of the liquid. The height of the liquid is represented by h. Therefore, three times the square of the height of the liquid $= 3h^2$. Four less than this amount is $3h^2 - 4$. Since the original speed was 1,000, subtract this value from 1,000 to get the current rate of rotation. The correct answer is (D).

9. **B**   Start with the easier equation and use Process of Elimination. The easier equation is related to the total number of ounces, $c + b$, in the tube. According to the question, the tube has 24 ounces, so $c + b = 24$. Eliminate (A), since it does not include this equation. The other equation in the set is related to the amount of active ingredients. According to the question, c includes 0.25% of sodium fluoride and b contains 0.30% triclosan. $0.25\% = 0.0025$ and $0.30\% = 0.003$. Therefore, in the correct equation, c should be associated with 0.0025 and b should be associated with 0.003. Eliminate (C) and (D) because both of these equations get the percentages wrong. The correct answer is (B).

10. **C** Whenever the question includes variables and the answer choices are numbers, think

Plugging In the Answers. In (A), $d = -4$, and the equation becomes

$\dfrac{2(-4)^2 - (-4) - 10}{(-4)^2 + 7(-4) + 10} = \dfrac{(-4)^2 - 4(-4) + 3}{(-4)^2 + 2(-4) - 15}$. Solve both sides of the equation to get

$\dfrac{2(16) + 4 - 10}{16 - 28 + 10} = \dfrac{16 + 16 + 3}{16 - 8 - 15}$, or $\dfrac{26}{-2} = \dfrac{35}{-7}$. Reduce both fractions to get $-13 = -5$. This is

not true, so eliminate (A). In (B), $d = 2$, and the equation becomes

$\dfrac{2(2)^2 - 2 - 10}{2^2 + 7(2) + 10} = \dfrac{2^2 - 4(2) + 3}{2^2 + 2(2) - 15}$. Solve both sides of the equation to get

$\dfrac{2(4) - 2 - 10}{4 + 14 + 10} = \dfrac{4 - 8 + 3}{4 + 4 - 15}$, or $\dfrac{-4}{28} = \dfrac{-1}{-7}$. Reduce both fractions to get $\dfrac{-1}{7} = \dfrac{1}{7}$. Eliminate

(B). In (C), $d = 4$ and the equation becomes $\dfrac{2(4)^2 - 4 - 10}{4^2 + 7(4) + 10} = \dfrac{4^2 - 4(4) + 3}{4^2 + 2(4) - 15}$. Solve both

sides of the equation to get $\dfrac{2(16) - 4 - 10}{16 + 28 + 10} = \dfrac{16 - 16 + 3}{16 + 8 - 15}$, or $\dfrac{18}{54} = \dfrac{3}{9}$. Reduce both fractions

to get $\dfrac{1}{3} = \dfrac{1}{3}$. The correct answer is (C).

11. **D** All the answer choices are equal to 4 (which is r^2, making $r = 2$), so you need to focus on where the center of the circle lies. If the circle is tangent to both the x-axis (which is equivalent to the line $y = 0$) and the line $x = 4$, then the center must be 2 units from $y = 0$ and 2 units from $x = 4$. Choices (A) and (B) both have centers with an x value of -2 (remember the standard form of the circle equation is $(x - h)^2 + (y - k)^2 = r^2$, where (h, k) is the center and r is the radius), which is 6 units from $x = 4$. Eliminate (A) and (B). Choice (C) has a center at $(2, -4)$. The x-value is 2 units from $x = 4$; however, the y-value is 4 units from $y = 0$. Eliminate (C) and choose (D).

12. **B** According to the question, Reactant A does not react unless B gets to a certain concentration. Therefore, the correct answer will have an initial flat line for A while the line for B is rising. Only graph (B) shows this initial relationship. Therefore, the correct answer is (B).

13. **A** All of the answer choices have the same lines graphed, so this question is really about the shading. Plugging In is probably the easiest way to approach this problem. Start with $(0, 0)$ because this is an easy value to check. This works in all three equations since $0 \le 8$, $-3 \le 0$, and $1 \ge 0$. Therefore, this value needs to be shaded as a possible answer. Eliminate (B), (C), and (D) because they do not include this point. The correct answer is (A).

14. **B** The question says that tan $\angle BCA$ is $\frac{3}{4}$, so draw segment CA. Since tan $= \frac{opp}{adj}$, $\frac{AB}{BC} = \frac{3}{4}$. Let $AB = 3x$ and $BC = 4x$. The question says that the area of the rectangle is 48. The formula for the area of the rectangle is $A = lw$. Plug in $A = 48$, $l = 3x$, and $w = 4x$ into the formula to get $48 = (3x)(4x)$. Simplify the right side to get $48 = 12x^2$. Divide both sides by 12 to get $4 = x^2$. Then take the square root of both sides to get $x = 2$. Therefore, $AB = 3x = 3(2) = 6$, and $BC = 4x = 4(2) = 8$. The question asks for the length of $\overline{BD}$, which is the diagonal of the rectangle and equal to diagonal AC. The diagonal of the rectangle is the hypotenuse of a right triangle. Since the two legs are 6 and 8, this is 6-8-10 right triangle, so the hypotenuse is 10. The answer is (B).

15. **D** Whenever there are variables in the question and answers, think Plugging In. If $m = 2$, the expression becomes $\frac{2(2)+6}{4} \times \frac{6(2)-36}{3(2)+9} = \frac{4+6}{4} \times \frac{12-36}{6+9} = \frac{-24}{15} = \frac{10}{4} \times \frac{-240}{60} = -4$.

Plug 2 in for m in the answer choices to see which one equals the target number of -4. Choice (A) becomes $\frac{12(2)^2 - 216}{12(2)+36} = \frac{12(4)-216}{24+36} = \frac{48-216}{60} = \frac{-168}{60} = -2.8$. This does not match the target number, so eliminate (A). Choice (B) becomes $\frac{8(2)-30}{3(2)+13} = \frac{16-30}{6+13} = \frac{-14}{19}$. Eliminate (B). Choice (C) becomes $\frac{2-6}{4} = \frac{-4}{4} = -1$. Eliminate (C). Choice (D) becomes $m - 6 = 2 - 6 = -4$. The correct answer is (D).

16. **1.5** or $\frac{3}{2}$

Plug the given values into the equation: $18 = (3)(4)(x)$. Multiply the right side of the equation to find that $18 = 12x$. Divide both sides by 12 to find that $x = \frac{18}{12}$. Both 18 and 12 are divisible by 6, so this fraction reduces to $\frac{3}{2}$.

17. **53** Jean charges $5.50 \times 2 = \$11$ per hour for babysitting. Therefore, her entire earnings for three hours can be calculated as $(3 \times 11) + 20 = 53$. The correct answer is 53.

18. **10** To solve the problem without a graphing calculator, set the two equations equal to each other: $-x^2 + 5x + 6 = -\dfrac{1}{2}x + 12$. Multiply the entire equation by 2 to get $-2x^2 + 10x + 12 = -x + 24$. Rewrite the equation to equal 0, so it becomes $-2x^2 + 11x - 12 = 0$. Multiply the entire equation by -1 to get $2x^2 - 11x + 12 = 0$. Then factor the quadratic to get $(2x - 3)(x - 4) = 0$. Solve for the two possible values of x: If $2x - 3 = 0$, then $x = \dfrac{3}{2}$, and if $x - 4 = 0$, then $x = 4$. Because the slope of the line is negative, the x-value of the point that is farthest to the right along the x-axis must also be closer to the x-axis. Plug 4 in for x in the second equation to get $y = -\dfrac{1}{2}(4) + 12 = -2 + 12 = 10$. The correct answer is 10.

19. $\dfrac{11}{3}$ or **3.66** or **3.67**

    Whenever there are two equations with the same two variables, the equations can be solved simultaneously by adding or subtracting them. Take the second equation and rewrite it so that the variables are on the left side of the equation: $17r + 22v = 63$. Stack the equations and add them together.

$$
\begin{array}{r}
13r + 8v = 47 \\
\underline{17r + 22v = 63} \\
30r + 30v = 110
\end{array}
$$

Divide the entire equation by 30 to get $r + v = \dfrac{110}{30}$. This is too big to grid in, so reduce it to $\dfrac{11}{3}$.

20. **2** The area of the current plot is $4 \times 6 = 24$ square feet, so the new plot will be $24 \times 2 = 48$ square feet. According to the question, x feet will be added to each side to obtain the new area of 48 feet. Since the length is only 2 feet more than the width, you need two factors of 48 that differ by 2. You may recognize that these factors are 6 and 8. So, the increase was 2 feet in each direction. Alternatively, you can write a quadratic: $(4 + x)(6 + x) = 48$. Expand the right side of the equation to get $x^2 + 10x + 24 = 48$. Set the equation to 0 by subtracting 48 from both sides to get $x^2 + 10x - 24 = 0$. Factor the equation to get $(x + 12)(x - 2) = 0$. Therefore, $x = -12$ or $x = 2$. Since lengths can never be negative the only possible value is $x = 2$. The correct answer is 2.

Section 4: Math (Calculator)

1. **C** Use Process of Elimination. According to the question, P represents the population, so the outcome of the entire equation has something to do with the population. Therefore, eliminate both (A) and (B) because 1.0635 can't represent the population if P does. In the given equation, the only operations are multiplication and addition, which means that over time the population would increase. Therefore, eliminate (D). The correct answer is (C).

2. **B** To solve the quadratic equation, first set the equation equal to 0. The equation becomes $x^2 + 12x - 64 = 0$. Next, factor the equation to get $(x + 16)(x - 4) = 0$. Therefore, the two possible solutions for the quadratic equation are $x + 16 = 0$ and $x - 4 = 0$, so $x = -16$ or 4. Since the question states that $x > 0$, $x = 4$ is the only possible solution. Another way to approach this question is to plug in the answers. Start with (B), $x = 4$. Plug 4 into the equation to get $4^2 + 12(4) = 64$. Solve the left side of the equation to get $16 + 48 = 64$, or $64 = 64$. Since this is a true statement, the correct answer is (B).

3. **A** To figure out the total number of shelving units Sai could use, find the total available wall space and divide by the length of the units. The total amount of wall space can be calculated as $119 - 21$. Because the length of each unit is 7 feet, the maximum number of units Sai could put up can be calculated as $\dfrac{119 - 21}{7}$. Because this is the maximum number of units Sai could put up, r has to be less than or equal to this number. Therefore, the correct answer is (A).

4. **C** Weight is shown on the vertical axis of the graph, given in ounces. Make your own mark indicating 5.75 on this axis; then draw a horizontal line from that mark to the line of best fit. Once you hit it, draw a vertical line straight down to the horizontal axis. It should hit between 75 and 80 days, slightly closer to the mark for 75. This makes (C) the correct answer. Draw your lines carefully, using your answer sheet as a straightedge if necessary.

5. **C** Whenever the question includes variables, plug in. If $s = 2$, the shirts cost $2(\$24.50) = \$49$. The tax on the shirts is $0.07(\$49) = \$3.43$. So, the shirts with tax and the $6 shipping fee cost $\$49 + \$3.43 + \$6 = \$58.43$. Plug in 2 for s in the answers to see which answer equals the target number of $58.43. In (A), $0.07[24.50(2) + 6] = 3.85$. This is not the target number, so eliminate (A). In (B), $1.07(24.50 + 6)(2) = 65.25$. Again, this is not the target number, so eliminate (B). In (C), $1.07[24.50(2)] + 6 = 58.43$. This is the target number, so keep it, but be sure to check the remaining answer choice. In (D), $1.07(24.50 + 2) + 6 = 34.355$, which is not the target number. Therefore, the correct answer is (C).

6. **B** The question states that after 6 weeks the plant is 54 centimeters tall. Therefore, when $w = 6$, $h(w) = 54$. Plug in 6 for w in the answer choices to see in which one equals the target number of 54. In (A), $h(w) = 6(6) = 36$. Eliminate (A). In (B), $h(w) = 9(6) = 54$. The correct answer is (B).

7. **D** Because the operation between the parentheses is addition, the parentheses can be removed, and the resulting expression becomes $12x^2 + 4x + 5y + 3x^2 - 2x + 3y$. Reorder the terms so that like terms are next to each other: $12x^2 + 3x^2 + 4x - 2x + 5y + 3y$. Combine like terms to get $15x^2 + 2x + 8y$. The correct answer is (D).

8. **D** You do not know how the survey is conducted, nor do you know how many veterinarians were surveyed (it may be the case that only 8 were surveyed). Therefore, you cannot infer that the survey accurately measures all veterinarians' beliefs about Royal Rat Rations. Choice (A) is not supported. First, you do not know what veterinarians believe in general, and second, veterinarians may be recommending Royal Rat Rations for a reason other than its nutrition. Choice (B) is similarly not supported: Besides not knowing veterinarians' beliefs, this choice assumes that no other rat food is acceptable. Choice (C) is not supported because you do not know the sample size of the survey, nor is there any indication that there is only one veterinarian who does not recommend Royal Rat Rations. Choice (D) is the correct answer: You know the opinions only of the veterinarians surveyed by Royal Rat Rations.

9. **D** Use a calculator to translate the fractions into decimals. $\frac{1}{2}t + 4 = \frac{3}{4}t - 5$ becomes $0.5t + 4 = 0.75t - 5$. Subtract $0.5t$ from both sides to get $4 = 0.25t - 5$, and then add 5 to both sides. This results in $9 = 0.25t$. Use a calculator to divide! $t = 36$; therefore, the correct answer is (D).

10. **C** Taking the two dogs together, Everett has $35 + 55 = 90$ pounds of dog. Set up the following proportion to determine the lowest amount of water the dogs need per day: $\frac{8.5 \text{ ounces}}{10 \text{ lbs}} = \frac{x}{90 \text{ lbs}}$. Cross-multiply to get $10x = 765$, so $x = 76.5$. Multiply by 7 days to get the weekly amount of water the dogs need: $76.5 \times 7 = 535.5$ ounces, or approximately 536 ounces. Only (C) includes 536 as the low-end amount. Therefore, the correct answer is (C).

11. **A** In order to answer this question, you need to deal with the ratio as well as the unit conversion. For the large batch of dry rub, Priya's friend is planning to use 91 ounces of chili powder. Since the paprika and the chili powder must be used in a ratio of 4 to 7, you can set up a proportion to determine how much paprika is needed: $\frac{4}{7} = \frac{x}{91}$. Cross-multiply and solve for x to determine that x (i.e., paprika) = 52 ounces. So you have 52 ounces of paprika and 91 ounces

of chili powder for a total of 143 ounces. Multiply that by your conversion number, 28.3, to determine that this is equivalent to 4,046.9 grams, which is closest to (A).

12. **D** Whenever there are variables in the problem and in the answer choices, plug in. If $w = 20$, then Luciano's cup has $20 - 2 = 18$ ounces at the end of day 1. At the end of 7 days, Luciano's cup would have $18 - 8 = 10$ ounces. After 11 days, Luciano's cup would hold $10 - 5 = 5$ ounces. Plug in 20 for w in the answer choices to see which answer is equal to the target number of 5. Choice (A) becomes $\dfrac{20 - 2}{8} = \dfrac{18}{8} = 2.25$. This does not match the target number of 5, so eliminate (A). Choice (B) becomes $\dfrac{20 - 2}{2} - 10 = \dfrac{18}{2} - 10 = 9 - 10 = -1$. Eliminate (B). Choice (C) becomes $\left(\dfrac{1}{2}\right)(20) - 10 = 10 - 10 = 0$. Eliminate (C). Choice (D) becomes $\dfrac{20 - 10}{2} = \dfrac{10}{2} = 5$. This matches the target number; therefore, the correct answer is (D).

13. **B** According to the line of best fit, in 1995 there were 20 coyotes in the park. In 2000, there were 140 coyotes in the park. This is an increase of 120 coyotes over a period of 5 years, so $\dfrac{120}{5}$ = an average increase of 24 coyotes per year, which is (B).

14. **D** The median number of coyotes in the park in 1995 was 20, and the median number of coyotes in the park in 1996 was 60. (Be careful to RTFQ; the question wants the median, not the line of best fit!) In order to calculate the percent increase, it is necessary to use the percent change formula: $\dfrac{difference}{original} \times 100$. The calculation here will be $\dfrac{60 - 20}{20} \times 100 = \dfrac{40}{20} \times 100 = 2 \times 100$ $= 200\%$, which is (D).

15. **A** Start with the easier equation and use Process of Elimination. The easier equation is related to the total number of shirts and pants, $s + p$, sold on a regular day. The question states that on a regular day Bailey's sells $\dfrac{2}{3}$ the number of pants and shirts sold during a sale. $\dfrac{2}{3}(60) = 40$. Therefore, one of the equations in the correct answer will be $s + p = 40$. Eliminate (C) and (D) since neither includes this equation. The other equation is related to the money Bailey's earns on a regular day. According to the question, Bailey's earns a total of $1,875 on a regular day,

so the equation must equal $1,875. Eliminate (B) because the total in the money equation is incorrect. The correct answer is (A).

16. **C** There are a few different ways to approach this question. In any approach, the best first step is to figure out how much income Bryan earned during the two-week period without the commission. Since he worked an average of 35 hours per week for two weeks, he worked a total of 70 hours. At a rate of $10.00 per hour base pay, this would add up to $700.00 ($70 \times 10 = 700$). Since Bryan's earnings were actually $850.00, that means he must have earned $150.00 of commission ($850 - 700 = 150$). At this point, you can calculate the percent commission algebraically or simply work backwards from the answer choices. Algebraically, you know that $150.00 is equal to a certain percent of $5,000.00 in sales, which can be represented as follows: $150 = \dfrac{x}{100}(5,000)$. Solve for x, and you get 3, which is (C). If instead you wish to work backwards from the answer choices, you can take each choice and calculate what 1%, 2%, etc. of $5,000.00 would be, and then add that back to $700.00 to see which choice matches your target of $850.00: (C).

17. **C** Cross-multiply to get $3(C + x) = (x - 3)(x + 8)$. Expand the right side of the equation to get $3(C + x) = x^2 + 5x - 24$. Distribute the 3 to get $3C + 3x = x^2 + 5x - 24$. Subtract $3x$ from both sides of the equation to get $3C = x^2 + 2x - 24$. Factor the right side of the equation to get $3C = (x + 6)(x - 4)$. Divide both sides by 3 to get $C = \dfrac{(x + 6)(x - 4)}{3} = \dfrac{1}{3}(x + 6)(x - 4)$. The correct answer is (C). Alternatively, you can plug in for x to get a target value for C, and then use Process of Elimination.

18. **A** Start with the easiest piece of information first, and use Process of Elimination. Since h is the number of hours spent hiking and d is the number of hours driving, the total number of hours Lennon spends in the park can be calculated as $h + d$. The question states that Lennon has up to 6 hours to spend in the park—"up to" means ≤. So, $h + d \leq 6$. Eliminate (B), (C), and (D). The correct answer is (A).

19. **B** The quality control expert discovered that 13 out of 1,000 randomly selected tennis balls were defective. $\dfrac{13}{1000} = 0.013$, which is equivalent to 1.3%. This means that $100 - 1.3 = 98.7\%$ of tennis balls tested were not defective, and this data most supports (B), which is the correct answer.

20. **C**   When solving inequalities, the natural impulse is to isolate the variable. In this case, though, look at what the question is asking. The question doesn't want you to find just the the value of z but rather the value of $9z - 18$. To get from the value of $-3z + 6$ given in the inequality to this new value, the original inequality must be multiplied by -3. Just multiply the entire inequality by this value, making sure to flip the inequality signs when multiplying by a negative number. The equation becomes $-3\left(-\dfrac{20}{7}\right) > -3(-3z + 6) > -3\left(-\dfrac{11}{5}\right)$ or $\dfrac{60}{7} > 9z - 18 > \dfrac{33}{5}$. The question asks for the greatest possible integer value, so focus on the high end of the given values. The value at that end, $\dfrac{60}{7}$, equals 8.57, so the greatest integer less than that is 8. The answer is (C).

21. **A**   Whenever there are variables in the question and numbers in the answer choices, think Plugging In the Answers. In (A), $j = 6$, and $k = -6$. Plug these two values into the first equation to get $-24 - 8(6) = 12(-6)$. Solve for both sides of the equation to get $-24 - 48 = -72$, or $-72 = -72$. Therefore, the values work for the first equation. Plug the values into the second equation to get $3 + \dfrac{5}{3}(-6) = -\dfrac{7}{6}(6)$. Solve both sides of the equation to get $3 + (-10) = -7$, or $-7 = -7$. Since the values given in (A) work in both equations, the correct answer is (A).

22. **C**   You know the new proportion must be less than the current 0.34 for biofuels (because the total amount spent on alternative energy is increasing, but the amount spent on biofuels is remaining the same), so you can eliminate (D). Next, determine the amount that will be spent on biofuels in 2017 by multiplying 0.34 by the total of $254 million: $0.34 \times 254 = \$86.36$ million. Because 57 million new dollars will be spent on alternative energy, the new total will be $254 + 57 = \$311$ million. Divide $86.36 million by $311 million to get the new proportion: $\dfrac{86.38}{311} = 0.28$, which is (C).

23. **D**   In quadrant II, the x-coordinate is negative, and the y-coordinate is positive. Therefore, eliminate (C). Whenever the question includes variables and the answer choices are numbers, think Plugging In the Answers. Of the remaining choices, (B) is easiest to work with. In (B), the x-value is -4 and the y-value is 2. Plug these values into the second equation to get $-4 = -2 + 2$. Since this is not a true statement, eliminate (B). Try the values in (A) in the second equation to get $3\sqrt{2} = -(-3\sqrt{2}) + 2$. This is also not true, so the correct answer is (D).

24. **B** Right away, (A) can be eliminated, since point C has a negative y-coordinate. Given any two points, the slope of the line can be determined using the equation $\dfrac{y_2 - y_1}{x_2 - x_1}$. Use this formula to find the value of b by setting the slope of $\overline{AB}$ equal to the slope of $\overline{BC}$. Use points $(0, 3)$ and $(5b, b)$ in the left side of the equation and points $(5b, b)$ and $(10b, -b)$ in the right side of the equation to get $\dfrac{3 - b}{0 - 5b} = \dfrac{-b - b}{10b - 5b}$. Simplify both sides of the equation to get $\dfrac{3 - b}{-5b} = \dfrac{-2b}{5b}$, or $\dfrac{3 - b}{-5b} = \dfrac{-2}{5}$. Cross-multiply to get $5(3 - b) = 10b$. Divide both sides by 5 get $3 - b = 2b$, then $3 = 3b$, and finally $b = 1$. Plug in $b = 1$ for point C to get $[10(1), -(1)]$, or $(10, -1)$. Therefore, the correct answer is (B).

25. **A** The formula for compound interest is $A = P(1 + r)^t$, where P is the starting principle, r is the rate expressed as a decimal, and t is the number of times the interest is compounded. Melanie received less than 5% interest, so you can eliminate (B) because $1.05 = 1 + 0.05$, which indicates that she was receiving 5% interest. You can also eliminate (C) because over the course of a year the interest is compounded 4 times, not $\dfrac{1}{3}$ of a time. Because Melanie invested $1,100 at what she thought was 5% compounded 4 times (12 months in a year ÷ 3 months per period), she expected $1,100(1 + 0.05)^4 = \$1,337.06$ after a year. Instead, she has $1,337.06 - 50 = \$1,287.06$ after one year. Because t is in years in the answer choices, make $t = 1$ in (A) and (D) and eliminate any choice that does not equal 1,287.06. Only (A) works.

26. **B** You can start by Plugging In a value for x; try $x = 4$. Because angle AOB is 120° and the triangle is isosceles, angles A and B are each 30°. Cut triangle AOB in half to make two 30-60-90 triangles with a hypotenuse of 4 and legs of 2 and $2\sqrt{3}$. The leg with length $2\sqrt{3}$ lies on chord AB. Double it to get the total length: $4\sqrt{3}$ or just $\sqrt{3}x$, which is (B) when you put $x = 4$ into the answer choices.

27. **C** Whenever there are variables in the question and in the answer choices, think Plugging In.

   The question states the value of g, but it is a constant and a weird one at that. Pick numbers for all the variables that will make the math more straightforward. If $v = 4$ and $g = 2$, then

   $$t = \dfrac{2(4) \cdot \sin(\theta)}{2} = \dfrac{8 \cdot \sin(\theta)}{2} = 4 \cdot \sin(\theta), \quad \text{and } R = \dfrac{4^2 \cdot \sin(2\theta)}{2} = \dfrac{16 \cdot \sin(2\theta)}{2} = 8 \cdot \sin(2\theta).$$

Plug these values into the answer choices to see which equation works. Choice (A) becomes

$$4 = \frac{4 \cdot \sin(\theta) \cdot \sin(\theta)}{2[8\sin(2\theta)\sin(\theta)]}.$$ Simplify the right side of the equation to get $4 = \frac{4 \cdot \sin(\theta) \cdot \sin(\theta)}{16\sin(2\theta)\sin(\theta)}$,

or $4 = \frac{\sin(\theta)}{4\sin(2\theta)}$. This will not simplify further, so eliminate (A). Choice (B) becomes

$$4 = \frac{2[4\sin(\theta)]\sin(\theta)}{8\sin(2\theta)(\sin(\theta))}.$$ Simplify the right side of the equation to get $4 = \frac{8\sin(\theta)(\sin(\theta))}{8\sin(2\theta)(\sin(\theta))}$ or

$4 = \frac{\sin(\theta)}{\sin(2\theta)}$. Eliminate (B). Choice (C) becomes $4 = \frac{2[8\sin(2\theta)]\sin(\theta)}{(4\sin(2\theta))(\sin(2\theta))}$. Distribute the 2 to

get $4 = \frac{16\sin(2\theta)\sin(\theta)}{(4\sin(\theta))(\sin(2\theta))}$. Reduce the equation to get $4 = \frac{16}{4}$ or $4 = 4$. The correct answer

is (C).

28. **D** $i^a = 1$ when a is a multiple of 4. Using your exponents rules, $413 + x$ must also be a multiple of 4. Plug in the answers and look for what makes $413 + x$ a multiple of 4. Only (D) works.

29. **C**   The zero of g is the value of the variable, in this case x, when the equation is set to 0. This is also called the root or solution of an equation. Set the equation to 0 to get $0 = 2x^2 - dx - 6$. Plug 6 in for x to get $0 = 2(6^2) - d(6) - 6$. Simplify the equation to get $0 = 72 - 6d - 6$, or $0 = 66 - 6d$. Solve for d to get $-66 = -6d$, so $11 = d$. Plug 11 in for d and set the quadratic to 0 to get $0 = 2x^2 - 11x - 6$. Factor the equation to get $0 = (x - 6)(2x + 1)$. The other zero of the equation is when $2x + 1 = 0$. Solve for x to get $2x = -1$, or $x = \frac{-1}{2}$. The correct answer is (C).

30. **D**   The flu shot is most effective against Strain C, which is least prevalent in March. To determine the overall efficacy of the flu shot at this time, multiply the prevalence of each strain of flu by the efficacy of the flu shot against that strain, and then add those products to get a weighted average of the efficacy of the shot: $(0.23 \times 0.35) + (0.25 \times 0.13) + (0.13 \times 0.76) + (0.39 \times 0.68) = 0.477 = 47.7\%$, which is closest to (D).

31. **3**   Solve the equation for v. Take $9 > 3v - 3$ and add 3 to both sides to get $12 > 3v$. Now divide both sides by 3 to find that $4 > v$. Therefore, the largest integer that v could be is 3. Grid in 3.

32. $\dfrac{5}{6}$ or **0.83**

Start by multiplying the second fraction in the denominator of the equation by $\dfrac{2}{2}$ to get

$\dfrac{\dfrac{6}{5}}{\dfrac{12}{2y}-\dfrac{10}{2y}}=1$. Combine the fractions in the denominator to get $\dfrac{\dfrac{6}{5}}{\dfrac{2}{2y}}=1$. Reduce the fraction in

the denominator to get $\dfrac{\dfrac{6}{5}}{\dfrac{1}{y}}=1$. Dividing by a number is the same as multiplying by its reciprocal,

so the equation becomes $\dfrac{6}{5}\times y=1$. Multiply both sides of the equation by $\dfrac{5}{6}$ to get $y=\dfrac{5}{6}$. The

correct answer is $\dfrac{5}{6}$.

33. **1,279** 614 students voting for Candidate A represents 0.48 of the population out of 1. Set up a pro-

portion: $\dfrac{0.48}{1.00}=\dfrac{614}{x}$, where x is the total number of students in the school. Cross-multiply:

$0.48x = 614$. Divide both sides by 0.48 and you get approximately 1,279.

34. $\dfrac{5}{13}$ or **0.384** or **0.385**

Draw a right triangle and label a non-right angle θ. SOHCAHTOA tells you that tangent

is $\dfrac{\text{opposite}}{\text{adjacent}}$, so the leg opposite θ is 12 and the leg adjacent to θ is 5. Cosine is $\dfrac{\text{adjacent}}{\text{hypotenuse}}$,

so you need to find the hypotenuse of the triangle. You can use the Pythagorean Theorem, or you

can recognize this as a 5-12-13 Pythagorean triplet. The hypotenuse is therefore 13. The leg adja-

cent to θ is still 5, so $\cos\theta = \dfrac{5}{13}$.

35. **7,054** First, you need to determine the current exchange rate. The 7% fee is the same (relative to the ex-

change rate), whether it was applied to the Cedi or USD. Therefore, 7% of 651 Cedi is equal to 32.30

USD. Translate English to math: 0.07(651) = 32.30, or 45.57 Cedi = 32.30 USD. Next, you want

the value of an item worth 5,000 USD in Cedi, so set up a proportion: $\dfrac{45.57 \text{ Cedi}}{32.30 \text{ USD}}=\dfrac{x \text{ Cedi}}{5,000 \text{ USD}}$.

Cross-multiply: (45.57)(5,000) = 32.30x, or 227,850 = 32.30x. Divide both sides by 32.30 and you

get x = 7,054.18 USD, which rounds to 7,054.

36. **63.6 or 63.7**

First, draw a square inscribed in a circle. Because the diameter of the circle is equal to the diagonal of the square, you can plug in a number like $2\sqrt{2}$ for the length of the diameter. Because the diameter forms a 45°-45°-90° triangle, each side of the square has a length of 2. Using the area formula for a square ($A = s^2$), plug in 2 for the s to get $A = 2^2$, which simplifies to $A = 4$. The area of the square is 4. To find the area of the circle, use the formula $A = \pi r^2$. Because the diameter of the circle is $2\sqrt{2}$, $r = \sqrt{2}$. Plug that into the area formula to see that $A = \pi(\sqrt{2})^2$, which simplifies to $A = 2\pi$. To find the solution, translate the question from English into math. The area of the square is what percent of the area of the circle becomes: $4 = \frac{x}{100} \cdot 2\pi$. Solve for x: First, divide each side by 2π, and then multiply each side by 100. The answer is a non-repeating decimal beginning 63.66197…. When entering your answer, simply cut off the decimal (do not round) so it takes up four spaces. You should enter 63.6.

37. $\frac{7}{10}$ or **0.7**

If the mean of the new set is $\frac{5}{6}$, then the sum of the diameters of the cylinders divided by the number of cylinders must equal $\frac{5}{6}$. Set up the equation: $\frac{5}{6} = \dfrac{\frac{1}{2} + \frac{3}{4} + \frac{4}{5} + 1 + \frac{5}{4} + x}{6}$, where x is the unknown cylinder. Multiply both sides by 6 to simplify: $5 = \frac{1}{2} + \frac{3}{4} + \frac{4}{5} + 1 + \frac{5}{4} + x$.

Combine like terms (use your calculator, but be careful with parentheses!): $5 = \frac{43}{10} + x$. Subtract $\frac{43}{10}$ from both sides and you get $\frac{7}{10}$.

38. $1 \le y \le 1.25$

A set with an even number of elements will have as its median the average of the middle two terms. In the current set, $\frac{4}{5}$ and 1 have an average of $\frac{9}{10}$, so the new cylinder must be equal to or greater than 1, so the median will be the average of $\frac{4}{5}$ and 1. The range of the set of five cylinders is the greatest minus the least: $\frac{5}{4} - \frac{1}{2} = \frac{3}{4}$. Because the new cylinder must be $\frac{1}{4}$ inches to $\frac{1}{2}$ greater than $\frac{3}{4}$, the cylinder must be between 1 and $\frac{5}{4}$ inches in diameter.

RAW SCORE CONVERSION TABLE SECTION AND TEST SCORES

Raw Score (# of correct answers)	Math Section Score	Reading Test Score	Writing and Language Test Score	Raw Score (# of correct answers)	Math Section Score	Reading Test Score	Writing and Language Test Score
0	200	10	10	30	530	28	29
1	200	10	10	31	540	28	30
2	210	10	10	32	550	29	30
3	230	11	10	33	560	29	31
4	240	12	11	34	560	30	32
5	260	13	12	35	570	30	32
6	280	14	13	36	580	31	33
7	290	15	13	37	590	31	34
8	310	15	14	38	600	32	34
9	320	16	15	39	600	32	35
10	330	17	16	40	610	33	36
11	340	17	16	41	620	33	37
12	360	18	17	42	630	34	38
13	370	19	18	43	640	35	39
14	380	19	19	44	650	35	40
15	390	20	19	45	660	36	
16	410	20	20	46	670	37	
17	420	21	21	47	670	37	
18	430	21	21	48	680	38	
19	440	22	22	49	690	38	
20	450	22	23	50	700	39	
21	460	23	23	51	710	40	
22	470	23	24	52	730	40	
23	480	24	25	53	740		
24	480	24	25	54	750		
25	490	25	26	55	760		
26	500	25	26	56	780		
27	510	26	27	57	790		
28	520	26	28	58	800		
29	520	27	28				

Please note that the numbers in the table may shift slightly depending on the SAT's scale from test to test; however, you can still use this table to get an idea of how your performance on the practice tests will translate to the actual SAT.

CONVERSION EQUATION SECTION AND TEST SCORES

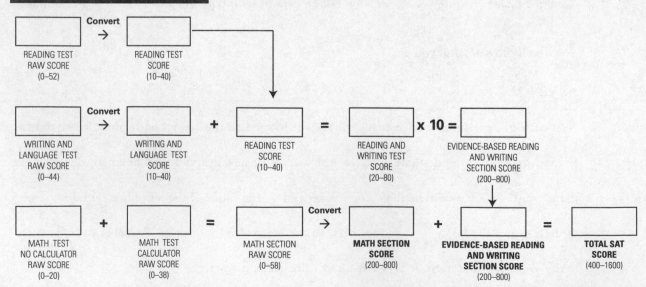

Chapter 22
Practice Test 2

Reading Test

65 MINUTES, 52 QUESTIONS

Turn to Section 1 of your answer sheet to answer the questions in this section.

Each passage or pair of passages below is followed by a number of questions. After reading each passage or pair, choose the best answer to each question based on what is stated or implied in the passage or passages and in any accompanying graphics (such as a table or graph).

Questions 1-10 are based on the following passage.

This passage is adapted from *Jane Eyre,* a nineteenth-century English novel by Charlotte Brontë.

    While he spoke my very conscience and reason turned traitors against me, and charged me with crime in resisting him. They spoke almost as loud as Feeling:
Line and that clamored wildly. "Oh, comply!" it said.
5 "Think of his misery; think of his danger—look at his state when left alone; remember his headlong nature; consider the recklessness following on despair—soothe him; save him; love him; tell him you love him and will be his. Who in the world cares for you or who will be
10 injured by what you do?"
    Still indomitable was the reply—"I care for myself. The more solitary, the more friendless, the more unsustained I am, the more I will respect myself. I will keep the law given by God; sanctioned by man. I will
15 hold to the principles received by me when I was sane, and not mad—as I am now. Laws and principles are not for the times when there is no temptation: they are for such moments as this, when body and soul rise in mutiny against their rigor; stringent are they; inviolate
20 they shall be. If at my individual convenience I might break them, what would be their worth? They have a worth—so I have always believed; and if I cannot believe it now, it is because I am insane—quite insane: with my veins running fire, and my heart beating faster
25 than I can count its throbs. Preconceived opinions, foregone determinations, are all I have at this hour to stand by: there I plant my foot."

I did. Mr. Rochester, reading my countenance, saw I had done so. His fury was wrought to the highest:
30 he must yield to it for a moment, whatever followed; he crossed the floor and seized my arm and grasped my waist. He seemed to devour me with his flaming glance: physically, I felt, at the moment, powerless as stubble exposed to the draught and glow of a furnace:
35 mentally, I still possessed my soul, and with it the certainty of ultimate safety. The soul, fortunately, has an interpreter—often an unconscious, but still a truthful interpreter—in the eye. My eye rose to his; and while I looked in his fierce face I gave an involuntary
40 sigh; his gripe was painful, and my over-taxed strength almost exhausted.
    "Never," said he, as he ground his teeth, "never was anything at once so frail and so indomitable. A mere reed she feels in my hand!" And he shook me with
45 the force of his hold. "I could bend her with my finger and thumb: and what good would it do if I bent, if I uptore, if I crushed her? Consider that eye: consider the resolute, wild, free thing looking out of it, defying me, with more than courage—with a stern triumph.
50 Whatever I do with its cage, I cannot get at it—the savage, beautiful creature! If I tear, if I rend the slight prison, my outrage will only let the captive loose. Conqueror I might be of the house; but the inmate would escape to heaven before I could call myself
55 possessor of its clay dwelling-place. And it is you, spirit—with will and energy, and virtue and purity— that I want: not alone your brittle frame. Of yourself

CONTINUE →

you could come with soft flight and nestle against my
heart, if you would: seized against your will, you will
60 elude the grasp like an essence—you will vanish ere I
inhale your fragrance. Oh! Come, Jane, come!"

As he said this, he released me from his clutch, and
only looked at me. The look was far worse to resist
than the frantic strain: only an idiot, however, would
65 have succumbed now. I had dared and baffled his fury;
I must elude his sorrow: I retired to the door.

"You are going, Jane?"

"I am going, sir."

"You are leaving me?"

70 "Yes."

"You will not come? You will not be my comforter,
my rescuer? My deep love, my wild woe, my frantic
prayer, are all nothing to you?"

What unutterable pathos was in his voice! How
75 hard it was to reiterate firmly, "I am going."

1

Jane's attitude toward Mr. Rochester is best
characterized as

A) sympathetic.

B) uncaring.

C) despising.

D) reckless.

2

Based on the information in the passage, it can
be inferred that Jane refuses Rochester's advances
because

A) she does not love him as much as he loves her.

B) it would violate her personal ideals.

C) he thinks that she is weak and frail.

D) she wishes to cause him injury.

3

Which choice provides the best evidence for the
answer to the previous question?

A) Lines 1-3 ("While . . . him")

B) Lines 13-16 ("I will . . . now")

C) Lines 36-38 ("The soul . . . eye")

D) Lines 50-51 ("Whatever . . . creature")

4

In context, the phrase "I am insane—quite insane"
in line 23 refers chiefly to

A) a severe mental illness that Jane suffers from.

B) a mental state brought on by God's law.

C) a feeling that currently urges Jane to reject
Rochester.

D) a reduction of judgment due to emotion.

5

As used in line 29, "wrought" most nearly means

A) hammered.

B) made.

C) excited.

D) wrung.

6

The fourth paragraph (lines 42-61) provides a contrast
between

A) Jane's body and her will.

B) Rochester's love and anger toward Jane.

C) a bird and its cage.

D) Jane's purity and impurity.

7

The inmate Rochester mentions in line 53 refers to

A) a criminal locked away in jail.

B) Rochester trapped in his emotions.

C) Jane stuck in the traditions of her time.

D) the possible behavior of Jane's spirit.

CONTINUE

8

Which choice provides the best evidence for the answer to the previous question?

A) Lines 38-41 ("My eye . . . exhausted")

B) Lines 45-47 ("I could . . . her")

C) Lines 55-57 ("And it . . . frame")

D) Lines 63-65 ("The look . . . now")

9

As used in line 63, "worse" most nearly means

A) less desirable.

B) more difficult.

C) of lower quality.

D) unskillful.

10

Based on the information in the final paragraph, it can be reasonably inferred that Jane values

A) her emotions over her reason.

B) freedom over social convention.

C) her principles over her feelings.

D) true love above all else.

CONTINUE

No Test Material On This Page

Questions 11-21 are based on the following passage and supplementary material.

This passage is adapted from Hillary Clinton's remarks to the U.N. Fourth World Conference on Women Plenary Session in 1995 in Beijing, China.

There are some who question the reason for this conference. Let them listen to the voices of women in their homes, neighborhoods, and workplaces. There
Line are some who wonder whether the lives of women and
5　girls matter to economic and political progress around the globe. Let them look at the women gathered here and at Huairou— the homemakers and nurses, the teachers and lawyers, the policymakers and women who run their own businesses. It is conferences like
10　this that compel governments and peoples everywhere to listen, look, and face the world's most pressing problems. Wasn't it after all—after the women's conference in Nairobi ten years ago that the world focused for the first time on the crisis of domestic
15　violence?

The great challenge of this conference is to give voice to women everywhere whose experiences go unnoticed, whose words go unheard. Women comprise more than half the world's population, 70 percent of
20　the world's poor, and two-thirds of those who are not taught to read and write. We are the primary caretakers for most of the world's children and elderly. Yet much of the work we do is not valued—not by economists, not by historians, not by popular culture, not by
25　government leaders.

At this very moment, as we sit here, women around the world are giving birth, raising children, cooking meals, washing clothes, cleaning houses, planting crops, working on assembly lines, running
30　companies, and running countries. Women also are dying from diseases that should have been prevented or treated. They are watching their children succumb to malnutrition caused by poverty and economic deprivation. They are being denied the right to go to
35　school by their own fathers and brothers. They are being forced into prostitution, and they are being barred from the bank lending offices and banned from the ballot box.

Those of us who have the opportunity to be here
40　have the responsibility to speak for those who could not. As an American, I want to speak for those women in my own country, women who are raising children on the minimum wage, women who can't afford health

care or child care, women whose lives are threatened
45　by violence, including violence in their own homes.

Speaking to you today, I speak for them, just as each of us speaks for women around the world who are denied the chance to go to school, or see a doctor, or own property, or have a say about the direction of their
50　lives, simply because they are women. The truth is that most women around the world work both inside and outside the home, usually by necessity.

We need to understand there is no one formula for how women should lead their lives. That is why
55　we must respect the choices that each woman makes for herself and her family. Every woman deserves the chance to realize her own God-given potential. But we must recognize that women will never gain full dignity until their human rights are respected and protected.

60　Tragically, women are most often the ones whose human rights are violated. Even now, in the late twentieth-century, the rape of women continues to be used as an instrument of armed conflict. Women and children make up a large majority of the world's
65　refugees. And when women are excluded from the political process, they become even more vulnerable to abuse. I believe that now, on the eve of a new millennium, it is time to break the silence. It is time for us to say for the world to hear that it is no longer
70　acceptable to discuss women's rights as separate from human rights.

If there is one message that echoes forth from this conference, let it be that human rights are women's rights and women's rights are human rights once and
75　for all. Let us not forget that among those rights are the right to speak freely—and the right to be heard.

Women must enjoy the rights to participate fully in the social and political lives of their countries, if we want freedom and democracy to thrive and endure. It
80　is indefensible that many women in nongovernmental organizations who wished to participate in this conference have not been able to attend—or have been prohibited from fully taking part.

As long as discrimination and inequities remain
85　so commonplace everywhere in the world, as long as girls and women are valued less, fed less, fed last, overworked, underpaid, not schooled, subjected to violence in and outside their homes—the potential of the human family to create a peaceful, prosperous
90　world will not be realized.

CONTINUE ➡

Poverty Rates by Age and Gender: 2012
(in percent)

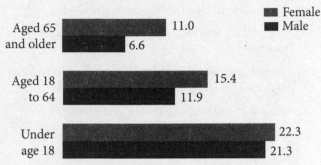

Poverty rates in the United States, divided by age and gender. Image courtesy the U.S. Census Bureau.

11

The position that Clinton takes in her speech can best be described as that of

A) a critic countering a series of arguments.

B) a scholar analyzing social phenomena.

C) an advocate seeking a particular outcome.

D) a mediator seeking a fair compromise.

12

As used in line 23, "valued" most nearly means

A) increased.

B) considered.

C) bought.

D) insured.

13

In lines 12-13, what is the most likely reason that Clinton mentions the prior "women's conference in Nairobi"?

A) To provide an example of a previous, failed attempt to solve the problem of domestic violence

B) To disagree with those who question the reason for the current conference

C) To contend that a great number of women and their experiences have gone unnoticed

D) To offer evidence for the claim that conferences compel people to address problems

14

Which choice provides the best evidence for the answer to the previous question?

A) Lines 1-2 ("There are . . . conference")

B) Lines 9-12 ("It is . . . problems")

C) Lines 21-22 ("We are . . . elderly")

D) Lines 30-32 ("Women . . . treated")

15

In lines 39-45, Clinton draws a distinction between

A) those who work at schools and hospitals.

B) people who can and cannot speak out.

C) employed and unemployed women.

D) women who can and cannot vote.

16

Based on the information in the passage, women face each of the following challenges EXCEPT

A) lack of access to health care.

B) violence in their homes.

C) limited financial resources.

D) widespread unemployment.

17

As used in line 40, "speak" most nearly means

A) talk aloud.

B) scold.

C) advocate.

D) gossip.

CONTINUE

The principal rhetorical effect of the phrase in lines 73-75 ("let it be that...once and for all") is to

A) argue against attempts to understand women's rights as distinct from other rights.

B) show that many women who should be at the conference are unable to attend.

C) emphasize the special nature of women's rights as they relate to human rights at large.

D) suggest that the need to focus on the specific problems of women is now past.

Which choice provides the best evidence for the answer to the previous question?

A) Lines 57-59 ("But we . . . protected")

B) Lines 68-71 ("It is . . . rights")

C) Lines 75-76 ("Let us . . . heard")

D) Lines 79-83 ("It is . . . part")

Based on the information presented in Clinton's speech, it can be inferred that some of those who have important positions of authority in the world

A) are actively working against the prosperity of women.

B) do not consider the labor done by women to be of serious import.

C) are ready to ensure that men and women have equal legal rights.

D) have made it unacceptable to discuss women's right.

Using information in the graph and the passage, it can be reasonably inferred that

A) in America and across the world the greatest gender disparity in poverty rates is among those 65 and older.

B) women 18 to 64 comprise 15.4 percent of the world's poor.

C) while a high percentage of children are poor in America, the opposite is true worldwide.

D) poverty rates in America are in line with a worldwide gender disparity.

CONTINUE

No Test Material On This Page

Questions 22-31 are based on the following passage.

Passage 1 is adapted from *Gardner's Art Through the Ages.* © 1991 by Harcourt Brace Jovanovich, Inc. Passage 2 is adapted from John Boardman, "The Parthenon Frieze—Another View." © 1977 by John Boardman. Both passages discuss the Parthenon Frieze, a band of sculpture that once encircled all four walls of the Parthenon, a temple to the goddess Athena. The naos is the inner sanctuary of the temple.

Passage 1

The inner Ionic frieze of figures was seen from below in reflected light against a colored ground. It enriched the plain wall and directed attention
Line toward the entrance to the temple. Though its subject
5 is still a matter of scholarly dispute ("the riddle of the Parthenon frieze"), it probably represents the Panathenaic procession that took place every four years when the citizens of Athens gathered in the marketplace and carried the *peplos*, or robe, for the
10 statue of Athena to the Parthenon. The robe was not for Phidias' ivory and gold statue, but for an older, archaic one, kept, ultimately, in the Erechtheion of the Acropolis. This is the first known representation of a nonmythological subject in Greek temple reliefs.
15 The Panathenaic frieze is unique in the ancient world for its careful creation of the impression of the passage of time, albeit a brief fragment of time. The effect is achieved by the use of a sequence of figures posed to present a gradation of motion. In the part of
20 the frieze that decorated the western side of the naos, the viewer can see the procession forming: youths are lacing their sandals and holding or mounting their horses; they are guided by marshals who stand at intervals, and particularly at the corners, to slow
25 movement and guide the horsemen at the turn. In the friezes of the two long sides of the naos, the procession moves in parallel lines, a cavalcade of spirited youths, chariots, elders, jar carriers, and animals for sacrifice. Seen throughout the procession
30 is that balance of the monumentally simple and the actual, of the tactile and the optical, of the "ideal" and the "real," of the permanent and the momentary that is characteristically Greek and the perfect exemplification of the "inner concord of opposites" that Heraclitus,
35 the philosopher, wrote of in the sixth century B.C. The movement of the procession becomes slower and more solemn as it nears the eastern side of the naos, when, after turning the corner, it approaches the seated divinities, who appear to be guests of Athena at her
40 great festival. Standing figures face against the general movement at ever-closer intervals, slowing the forward motion of the procession.

Passage 2

There are many representations of festival or sacrifice in classical Greek art but it is unparalleled to
45 find them attended by a number of guest deities, let alone the complete pantheon. And here we see Athena herself in their number; and they seem to be ignoring the handling of the peplos, which is the nearest we get to the culminating act of the procession. Finally,
50 there is the choice of subject. In Lawrence's words, "Never before has a contemporary subject been treated on a religious building and no subsequent Greek instance is known, with the doubtful exception of the Erechtheum. The flagrant breach with tradition
55 requires explanation."
It is unthinkable that a classical Athenian, looking up at the frieze, could have said to himself "there I go", or even more vaguely "there we go". The subject must be, in some respect, more than mortal and
60 the explanation must lie in the frieze itself and in knowledge of the background to its carving and the building on which it was placed. Moreover the explanation must have been apparent to the classical Athenian who knew this background. We cannot
65 exempt the frieze from the conventions of classical art.
We must rule out, then, the explanation that it is a contemporary or generic statement of the Panathenaic procession conducted by the citizens of Periclean Athens.
70 In classical Athens of these years there was one group of mortal Athenian citizens who, by their actions, had acquired the right to depiction on public buildings and in the company of the gods: these are the men who fought at Marathon.
75 Pausanias tells us that the people of Marathon worshipped the Athenian men who died as heroes, and a Hellenic inscription records that young Athenian men lay wreaths at their tomb. The heroising of the dead at Marathon is a fact which cannot be called
80 into dispute, and it was appropriate that they should have been celebrated on the Parthenon, in a position secondary to that of the purely divine and heroic subjects.

CONTINUE

My suggestion is that the frieze shows the fighters
85 of Marathon celebrating the prime festival of the
goddess Athena, on the temple dedicated to her as a
thanksgiving for her aid at Marathon and afterwards,
and in a manner which indicates the heroic status of
those who fell there.

22

The author of Passage 1 references a quote from
Heraclitus (lines 29-35) primarily to

A) reinforce the sense of the passage of time present
in the frieze.

B) suggest that opposing qualities of the carving
present a sense of overall balance.

C) prove that the style of the frieze is
characteristically Greek.

D) emphasize the contrast between the men in the
procession and the goddess Athena at its end.

23

Which of the following best describes the structure of
Passage 1?

A) A purpose for the frieze is proposed, and then a
description is given.

B) An interpretation of the frieze is questioned and a
new solution is offered.

C) The frieze is described in detail, with emphasis on
its unique qualities.

D) A historical overview is given that helps explain
the layout of the frieze.

24

As used in line 44, "unparalleled" most nearly means

A) crooked.

B) normal.

C) unsurpassed.

D) unprecedented.

25

The first two paragraphs of Passage 2 primarily serve
to

A) reject the idea that the frieze depicts the
Panathenaic procession.

B) argue against the idea that the frieze represents the
passage of time.

C) suggest that the frieze represents the heroes of
Marathon.

D) outline problems in the traditional interpretation
of the frieze.

26

As used in line 59, "mortal" most nearly means

A) human.

B) deadly.

C) terrible.

D) common.

27

In the context of the passage, the author's use of the
phrase "there I go" (lines 57-58) is primarily meant to
convey the idea that

A) figures in the frieze were not meant to be portraits
of individual citizens.

B) the frieze cannot be a representation of a human
event.

C) the citizens of Athens did not participate in the
Panathenaic procession.

D) the subject of the frieze should be obvious to
modern viewers.

CONTINUE

28

Which choice provides the best evidence for the answer to the previous question?

A) Lines 46-49 ("And here . . . the procession")

B) Lines 54-55 ("The flagrant . . . explanation")

C) Lines 62-64 ("Moreover . . . background")

D) Lines 66-69 ("We must . . . Athens")

29

The author of Passage 2 would most likely argue that the "youths" (line 21) described in Passage 1 are

A) citizens of Athens from around the time the Parthenon was built.

B) Athenian men who died in battle at Marathon.

C) people of Marathon who were worshipped as heroes in Athens.

D) purely divine participants in the celebration of a festival of Athena.

30

Passage 2 differs from Passage 1 in that Passage 1

A) focuses on determining the subject of the frieze.

B) gives a detailed description of the figures in the frieze.

C) considers how Greek citizens might have viewed the frieze.

D) entirely rejects the traditional interpretation of the frieze.

31

Which choice provides the best evidence for the answer to the previous question?

A) Lines 4-10 ("Though its subject . . . Parthenon")

B) Lines 13-14 ("This is the . . . reliefs")

C) Lines 15-17 ("The Panathenaic frieze . . . time")

D) Lines 19-25 ("In the part . . . turn")

CONTINUE

No Test Material On This Page

CONTINUE

Questions 32-42 are based on the following passage.

The following is an excerpt from "A Strange Tale of a New Species of Lizard" by Carl Zimmer in *The New York Times*. Originally published December 14, 2014.

Each year, scientists publish roughly 17,000 detailed descriptions of newly discovered animals. Recently, in the journal Breviora, researchers described yet another,
Line a new species of lizard called *Aspidoscelis neavesi*.
5   At first glance, this seems to be a run-of-the mill lizard: a small, slender creature with spots along its back and a bluish tail. In fact, *Aspidoscelis neavesi* is quite exceptional. The lizard was produced in the laboratory by mating two other species, and its
10 creation defies conventional ideas about how new species evolve.

The evolution of a new animal species is usually a drawn-out affair. Typically, an existing animal population is somehow divided, and the newly isolated
15 populations reproduce only among themselves. Over thousands of generations, the animals may become genetically distinct and can no longer interbreed.

Of course, scientists have long known that some related species sometimes interbreed. But the hybrid
20 progeny generally were thought to be evolutionary dead-ends—sterile mules, for instance. In recent decades, however, researchers have learned that these hybrids may represent new species.

Some of the most striking examples occur among
25 whiptail lizards, which live in the southwestern United States. In the 1960s, scientists noticed that some whiptail lizard species had a strange genetic makeup. They have two copies of each chromosome, just as we do, but each copy is very different from its counterpart.
30 The genes look as if they come from different species. Perhaps stranger, many species produce no males. The eggs of the females hatch healthy female clones, a process known as parthenogenesis.

Normally, unfertilized animal eggs have only
35 one set of chromosomes. But parthenogenic female whiptail lizards can duplicate the chromosomes in their offspring without males.

These findings led scientists to a hypothesis for how these strange species came about: Sometimes
40 individuals from two different species of whiptail lizards interbreed, and their hybrid offspring carry two different sets of chromosomes.

Somehow, this triggers a switch to parthenogenesis. The female hybrids start to produce clones distinct
45 from either parental species. In other words, they instantly become a new species of their own.

Dr. Neaves didn't follow up on this finding, instead pursuing a career researching fertility and stem cells. But at a dinner in 2002, he mentioned the whiptail
50 lizards to Peter Baumann, a molecular biologist at Stowers Institute for Medical Research, where Dr. Neaves served as president.

Dr. Baumann decided it was high time to use new scientific tools to study whiptail lizards, and he and
55 Dr. Neaves started making road trips to New Mexico to catch them and take them back to Stowers. As they came to understand the biology of the lizards better, they and their colleagues began to bring different species together to see if they could hybridize. Most of
60 the time, their experiments failed.

In 2008, the scientists tried to recreate the hybrid with four sets of chromosomes. They put female *Aspidoscelis exsanguis* (the parthenogenic species with three sets of chromosomes) and male *Aspidoscelis*
65 *inornata* in the same containers. In short order, the lizards started mating, and the females laid eggs. When the eggs hatched, the scientists examined the genes of the baby lizards and found four sets of chromosomes.

Four of the new hybrids were females. To the
70 delight of the scientists, the females could clone themselves—and the offspring could produce clones of their own. Today, the scientists have a colony of 200 of these lizards.

32

The author mentions "sterile mules" (line 21) primarily in order to

A) delineate one of the only instances of an occurrence.

B) contradict the opinion presented in the passage.

C) provide evidence that supports scientists' beliefs.

D) reiterate that the lizard is an unusual creature.

CONTINUE

33

As used in line 24, "striking" most nearly means

A) beautiful.

B) conspicuous.

C) aggressive.

D) remarkable.

34

The passage suggests that the relationship between Dr. Neaves and Dr. Baumann is best characterized as which of the following?

A) A scientific effort to understand parthenogenesis

B) A competitive rivalry to breed *Aspidoscelis exsanguis* first

C) A joint labor to disprove the theories of Stowers

D) A friendship based on a shared interest in whiptail lizards

35

The third paragraph (lines 12-17) most strongly suggests that evolution

A) can happen only over thousands of generations.

B) depends on the separation of individuals of one species.

C) customarily takes many years to occur.

D) isolates populations so they can't interbreed.

36

Which choice provides the best evidence for the answer to the previous question?

A) Lines 12-13 ("The evolution . . . affair")

B) Lines 13-15 ("Typically . . . themselves")

C) Lines 15-17 ("Over . . . interbreed")

D) Lines 21-23 ("In recent . . . species")

37

As used in line 53, "high time" most nearly means

A) a festival.

B) an hour late.

C) an opportune moment.

D) a lofty ideal.

38

According to the passage, parthenogenesis in whiptail lizards is characterized by each of the following EXCEPT

A) female individuals that can duplicate chromosomes without males.

B) stem cells from the male *Aspidoscelis inornata*.

C) clones that are different from the parental species.

D) offspring with two sets of chromosomes.

39

The passage suggests that whiptail lizards

A) have two identical sets of chromosomes.

B) were first discovered in the 1960s.

C) require a male and a female to breed.

D) create only female clones.

40

Which choice provides the best evidence for the answer to the previous question?

A) Lines 32-33 ("The eggs . . . parthenogenesis")

B) Lines 44-45 ("The female . . . species")

C) Lines 61-62 ("In . . . chromosomes")

D) Lines 66-68 ("When . . . chromosomes")

CONTINUE ➡

41

Which of the following, if true, would most weaken the author's argument in lines 8-11?

A) Scientists don't always consider animal breeds created in labs to be new species.

B) Evolution is a complex process that can't be manipulated by humans.

C) The two animals used in the process are not considered different species by some scientists.

D) Researchers have proven that all lizards have the ability to clone themselves, but they only clone in captivity.

42

As used in line 43, the sentence "Somehow, this triggers a switch to parthenogenesis," suggests that

A) scientists are still looking for the switch that causes cloning.

B) hybridization is a complex, but manageable process.

C) scientists are unclear as to how female whiptails can clone themselves.

D) no one knows why female whiptails choose cloning over mating.

CONTINUE

No Test Material On This Page

Questions 43-52 are based on the following passage and supplementary material.

This passage is adapted from David P. Hill, Roy A. Bailey, James W. Hendley II, Peter H. Stauffer, Mae Marcaida, "California's Restless Giant: The Long Valley Caldera." © 2014 by U.S. Geological Survey.

About 760,000 years ago a cataclysmic volcanic eruption in the Long Valley area of eastern California blew out 150 cubic miles—600 cubic kilometers
Line (km^3)—of magma (molten rock) from a depth of about
5 4 miles (6 km) beneath the Earth's surface. Rapid flows of glowing hot ash (pyroclastic flows) covered much of east-central California, and airborne ash fell as far east as Nebraska. The Earth's surface sank more than 1 mile (1.6 km) into the space vacated by the erupted magma,
10 forming a large volcanic depression that geologists call a caldera.

Long Valley Caldera is part of a large volcanic system in eastern California that also includes the Mono-Inyo Craters chain. This chain extends from
15 Mammoth Mountain at the southwest rim of the caldera northward 25 miles (40 km) to Mono Lake. Eruptions along this chain began 400,000 years ago, and Mammoth Mountain was formed by a series of eruptions ending 58,000 years ago. The volcanic
20 system is still active—eruptions occurred in both the Inyo Craters and Mono Craters parts of the volcanic chain as recently as 600 years ago, and small eruptions occurred in Mono Lake sometime between the mid-1700s and mid-1800s.

25 Although no volcanic eruptions are known to have occurred in eastern California since those in Mono Lake, earthquakes occur frequently. These are caused by movement along faults and by the pressure of magma rising beneath the surface, two closely
30 related geologic processes. In 1872, a magnitude 7.4 earthquake centered 80 miles (125 km) south of Long Valley was felt throughout most of California, and moderate (magnitude 5 to 6) earthquakes have shaken the Long Valley area since 1978.

35 In 1978, a magnitude 5.4 earthquake struck 6 miles southeast of the caldera, heralding a period of geologic unrest in the Long Valley area that is still ongoing. That temblor ended two decades of low quake activity in eastern California. The area has since experienced
40 numerous swarms of earthquakes, especially in the southern part of the caldera and the adjacent Sierra Nevada.

The most intense of these swarms began in May 1980 and included four strong magnitude 6 shocks,
45 three on the same day. Following these shocks, scientists from the U.S. Geological Survey (USGS) began a reexamination of the Long Valley area, and they soon detected other evidence of unrest—a dome-like uplift within the caldera. Measurements showed
50 that the center of the caldera had risen almost a foot (30 centimeters) since the summer of 1979—after decades of stability. This swelling, which by 2014 totaled more than 2.5 feet (75 centimeters) and affected more than 100 square miles (250 km^2), is caused by
55 new magma rising beneath the caldera.

In response to this increased unrest, USGS intensified its monitoring in the Long Valley region. Today, a state-of-the-art network of seismometers and geodetic equipment closely monitors earthquake
60 activity and the swelling in the caldera. Data from these instruments help scientists to assess the volcanic hazard in the Long Valley area and to recognize early signs of possible eruptions.

During the early 1990s, trees began dying at several
65 places on Mammoth Mountain on the southwest edge of Long Valley Caldera. Studies conducted by USGS and U.S. Forest Service scientists showed that the trees are being killed by large amounts of carbon dioxide (CO_2) gas seeping up through the soil from magma
70 deep beneath Mammoth Mountain. Such emissions of volcanic gas, as well as earthquake swarms and ground swelling, commonly precede volcanic eruptions. When they precede an eruption of a "central vent" volcano, such as Mount St. Helens, Washington, they normally
75 last only a few weeks or months. However, symptoms of volcanic unrest may persist for decades or centuries at large calderas, such as Long Valley Caldera. Studies indicate that only about one in six such episodes of unrest at large calderas worldwide actually culminates
80 in an eruption.

Over the past 4,000 years, small to moderate eruptions have occurred somewhere along the Mono-Inyo volcanic chain every few hundred years, and the possibility remains that the geologic unrest in the
85 Long Valley area could take only weeks to escalate to an eruption. Nonetheless, geologists think that the chances of an eruption in the area in any given year are quite small.

CONTINUE ▶

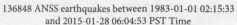

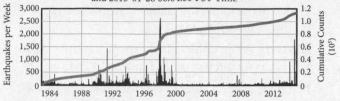

Long Valley Caldera cumulative earthquakes between 1983 and 2015, USGS.
The vertical bars on the graphs above correspond with the left-side *y*-axis and represent the number of earthquakes per week. The thicker gray line indicates the cumulative number of earthquakes and corresponds with the right-side *y*-axis.

43

As used in line 10, "depression" most nearly means

A) dejection.

B) decrease.

C) crater.

D) trouble.

44

The authors use the phrase "as recently as 600 years ago" (line 22) primarily to

A) suggest that there will be another eruption this century.

B) convey a sense of the magnitude of geologic time.

C) communicate irony, because 600 years ago is not recent.

D) indicate that the word 'recently' is a relative term.

45

As used in line 38, "temblor" most nearly means

A) drum.

B) earthquake.

C) eruption.

D) caldera.

46

What is the reason geologists have increased their monitoring of the Long Valley Caldera?

A) It has been more than 150 years since the last eruption.

B) Eruptions happen frequently in volcanic chains of such size.

C) The area is experiencing geologic activity indicative of an impending eruption.

D) The swelling of the caldera may damage the sensitive geodetic equipment.

47

Which choice provide the best evidence for the answer to the previous question?

A) Lines 19-24 ("The volcanic . . . mid-1800s")

B) Lines 38-39 ("That temblor . . . California")

C) Lines 58-60 ("Today, . . . caldera")

D) Lines 70-72 ("Such emissions . . . eruptions")

48

In the context of the passage as a whole, what is the primary purpose of the last paragraph?

A) To suggest that geologists believe danger from an eruption is not imminent

B) To explain how quickly geologic unrest can turn into a catastrophic eruption

C) To warn of the dire impact of another eruption like Mount St. Helens

D) To emphasize the impact of the earthquakes discussed earlier in the passage

CONTINUE

49

It can be inferred from the passage that Mammoth Mountain

A) erupted most recently around 600 years ago.

B) is an active volcano that the USGS is monitoring for early signs of eruption.

C) shows signs that the larger volcanic system to which it belongs is still active.

D) was formed 760,000 years ago by pyroclastic flows from a volcanic eruption.

50

Which choice provides the best evidence for the answer to the previous question?

A) Lines 1-5 ("About 760,000 . . . surface.")

B) Lines 19-24 ("The volcanic system . . . mid-1800s)

C) Lines 25-27 ("Although no . . . frequently.)

D) Lines 75-77 ("However, symptoms . . . Caldera")

51

Which of the following situations is most analogous to the recent swelling of the Long Valley Caldera?

A) Many small tremors along a particular fault precede a large, magnitude 8 earthquake.

B) A scientist discovers a new species of insect by chance while observing snakes in the Amazon rainforest.

C) Bad road conditions cause a collision between two cars, and poor visibility contributes to a multi-car pile-up.

D) A doctor is unable to give a definitive diagnosis to a patient after assessing symptoms typical of a particular disease.

52

Which of the following claims is supported by information in the graph?

A) Long Valley Caldera had experienced more than 120,000 cumulative earthquakes by 2015.

B) Long Valley Caldera experienced roughly 30,000 earthquakes per week in 1990.

C) By 2012, Long Valley Caldera had experienced 1.0 cumulative earthquakes.

D) By 1988, Long Valley Caldera had experienced over 2,500 cumulative earthquakes.

STOP
If you finish before time is called, you may check your work on this section only.
Do not turn to any other section in the test.

No Test Material On This Page

Writing and Language Test

35 MINUTES, 44 QUESTIONS

Turn to Section 2 of your answer sheet to answer the questions in this section.

DIRECTIONS

Each passage below is accompanied by a number of questions. For some questions, you will consider how the passage might be revised to improve the expression of ideas. For other questions, you will consider how the passage might be edited to correct errors in sentence structure, usage, or punctuation. A passage or a question may be accompanied by one or more graphics (such as a table or graph) that you will consider as you make revising and editing decisions.

Some questions will direct you to an underlined portion of a passage. Other questions will direct you to a location in a passage or ask you to think about the passage as a whole.

After reading each passage, choose the answer to each question that most effectively improves the quality of writing in the passage or that makes the passage conform to the conventions of standard written English. Many questions include a "NO CHANGE" option. Choose that option if you think the best choice is to leave the relevant portion of the passage as it is.

Questions 1–11 are based on the following passage and supplementary material.

Park Rangers, Naturally

Of the many parks that are part of the American heritage, the National Park **1** Service (NPS) is easily the most majestic. From the moment of the first European settlements in the fifteenth and sixteenth centuries, visitors and residents alike have marveled at the natural beauty and diversity of **2** the American landscape's attractiveness. As part of a commitment to preserving these national treasures against the forward movement of industrialization, the National Park Service was founded in 1916 during the presidency of Woodrow Wilson.

1

Which of the following alternatives to the underlined portion would NOT be acceptable?

A) Service, NPS,

B) Service NPS

C) Service—NPS—

D) Service, abbreviated NPS,

2

A) NO CHANGE

B) the pulchritudinous American landscape.

C) the pretty American landscape.

D) the American landscape.

CONTINUE

Today, there are over 400 parks in the service, and these parks are run and overseen by the Department of the Interior. The day-to-day operations, **3** including maintenance and tours, are the work of park rangers. These park rangers are responsible for the upkeep of the **4** parks, their main responsibility is to maintain the balance between the wildlife and plant species and the human visitors that come to the parks every day.

5 Without park rangers, the parks would be overrun with pollution. Some are scientists who revel in the ecological aspects of maintaining the parts. Some are educators **6** helping visitors to understand the unique aspects and historical significance of the parks. Still others come from law enforcement and firefighting, given that their posts are often very far indeed from the municipal bodies that typically provide **7** them.

3

The writer wants to include a detail that will clarify the phrase "day-to-day operations." Which of the following would best fulfill this goal?

A) NO CHANGE

B) and some that are more long-term,

C) often repetitive tasks,

D) not the political decisionmaking,

4

A) NO CHANGE

B) parks their

C) parks—their

D) parks, their—

5

Which of the following would best introduce the topic of this paragraph?

A) NO CHANGE

B) Park rangers can come from all walks of life.

C) Many millions visit the National Parks every year.

D) The most successful park rangers usually have some background in ecology.

6

A) NO CHANGE

B) that are helping

C) who are helping

D) who help

7

A) NO CHANGE

B) these services.

C) those.

D) it.

CONTINUE

There are nearly 4,000 park rangers in service with the NPS today. [8] Visitors are on the rise, poising that number for growth. [9] Although park visitation numbers peaked in 1987, the general trend has been a steady rise. The numbers continue to be high, with over 270 million visitors in 2013. It seems that as economic conditions in the country as uncertain, more and more people turn to parks for economical, educational, and enlightening alternatives to the more costly tourist activities and trips. Now, too, that climate science has [10] foretold difficult times, the NPS is seen to be protecting the last vestiges of our green world before it slips away.

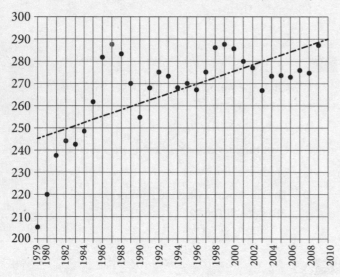

Visitors to America's National Parks, 1979–2009 (in millions)

8

A) NO CHANGE

B) Visitation numbers are poised on the rise for significant growth.

C) That number is poised to grow, as visitation numbers are on the rise.

D) Poised on the rise, visitation numbers are growing.

9

Which of the following gives accurate information based on the graph?

A) NO CHANGE

B) Park visitation peaked in the mid-1980s and has tapered off since then.

C) Park visitation reached record highs in 2009.

D) Park visitation has risen in a linear progression since the late 1970s.

10

Which of the following alternatives to the underlined portion would be LEAST acceptable?

A) predicted

B) stated

C) anticipated

D) forecast

CONTINUE

11 The park-ranger workforce is so diverse, there are actually a few common attributes among park rangers. Park rangers need at least a two-year degree and some experience working in parks. Many seasonal park workers and volunteers go on to become park rangers. Ultimately, attaining work as a park ranger is less about a skill-set than a particular mindset. Park rangers must honor and revere the natural world: they spend their entire careers learning about and living in the places they work. Park rangers have special jobs, so it naturally takes a group of special people to do those jobs.

11

A) NO CHANGE
B) Truly, the park-ranger
C) Because the park-ranger
D) Although the park-ranger

CONTINUE

Questions 12–22 are based on the following passage and supplementary material.

The Ferry Godfather

[1] For much of the early part of American history, Pennsylvania and Virginia, two major early colonies and states, shared a border. [2] This part of Virginia became the modern state of West Virginia on June 20, 1863. [3] Then came the Civil War. [4] Amid the furor of secession and conflict, President Abraham Lincoln granted a special provision for that part of Virginia that was loyal to the Union. **12**

Although this region is not in the news quite so often today, in America's early history one part of it was on the tip of everyone's tongue. The town of Harpers Ferry played a crucial role in pre-Civil War era. George Washington proposed that the United States station one of **13** their two major armories there, and by 1799, Harpers Ferry became **14** one of the major industrial towns, in the United States. Its position about 60 miles from Washington, D.C., and Baltimore put it close enough to major cities, but its place **15** in the hills at the meeting of the Potomac and Shenandoah Rivers made it difficult to access and easy to defend.

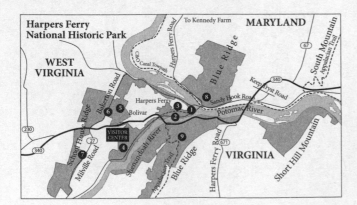

12

For the sake of the logic and coherence of this paragraph, sentence 2 should be placed

A) where it is now.

B) before sentence 1.

C) after sentence 3.

D) after sentence 4.

13

A) NO CHANGE

B) they're

C) its

D) it's

14

A) NO CHANGE

B) one, of the major industrial towns, in the United States.

C) one, of the major industrial towns in the United States.

D) one of the major industrial towns in the United States.

15

Which of the following gives accurate information based on the map?

A) NO CHANGE

B) approximately 20 miles northeast of the town of Bolivar

C) across the Shenandoah River from Maryland

D) at the foot of the Adirondack Mountains

CONTINUE

Because it was situated on the borderline between the Union and the Confederacy, and because its armory was full of the weapons being manufactured to fight the Civil War, **16** the Confederacy took it four times and the Union did also, and both sides saw it as a pivotal strategic base.

In the popular imagination today, Harpers Ferry is still seen as a crucial **17** place of great importance during the Civil War but mainly for events that occurred there before the war had even started. In 1859, radical abolitionist John Brown led a raid on Harpers Ferry, seeking to free slaves and begin a guerilla campaign to free slaves all over the country. While Brown's raid was ultimately a dismal failure and Brown was executed for treason, **18** his raid began a national conversation.

16

A) NO CHANGE

B) the war saw Harpers Ferry change hands eight times,

C) Harpers Ferry changed hands eight times during the war,

D) eight was the number of times Harpers Ferry changed hands,

17

A) NO CHANGE

B) place

C) place that was important

D) place where a great deal happened

18

The writer wants to include an idea here that shows that Brown's raid still had major importance. Which of the following true ideas would best fulfill this goal?

A) NO CHANGE

B) Hermann Melville's poem about John Brown is very well-known.

C) the raid was based on some earlier well-known slave revolts.

D) he could not have chosen a more central location.

CONTINUE

Abolitionists in the North saw him as a hero and a freedom fighter while those in the South saw him as a [19] filthy terrorist. [20] The Civil War and the nation's movement towards it used John Brown's name as both sides' rallying cry.

Today, Harpers Ferry is a sleepy town in the mountains of West Virginia. Much of its heritage remains [21] intact. Historical tours run every day. Above all, Harpers Ferry is a living reminder that the crucial events in history are not limited to the big places and the major players. Without the catalyzing effect of this small [22] town: American history as we know it might have been much different.

19

A) NO CHANGE

B) heroic

C) janky

D) vile

20

A) NO CHANGE

B) Brown's name became a rallying cry for both sides as the nation moved toward Civil War.

C) Brown's cry was the rally that both sides named as the Civil War moved in on the nation.

D) both sides used Brown's name as the nation's Civil War was moving toward it.

21

A) NO CHANGE

B) intact, historical

C) intact historical

D) intact; and historical

22

A) NO CHANGE

B) town; American

C) town. American

D) town, American

CONTINUE

Questions 23–33 are based on the following passage.

Stefan Zweig's Return

Stefan Zweig's name has been showing up a lot lately. In addition to a 23 large amount of recently republished works, Wes Anderson cites Zweig as the major influence on Anderson's recent film *The Grand Budapest Hotel* (2014). It seems that Zweig has suddenly become 24 revelant again after nearly 75 years of obscurity. Why this sudden interest? What can he offer that our culture seems to need?

23

Which of the following alternatives to the underlined portion would be LEAST acceptable?

A) bevy

B) mass

C) multitude

D) volume

24

A) NO CHANGE

B) relevant

C) irrelevant

D) irrevelant

CONTINUE

Stefan Zweig was born in 1881. [25] His parents were part of the Jewish cultural elite in Vienna at the time. Stefan was afforded every possible luxury and privilege. By 1904, Zweig had earned a doctoral degree from the University of Vienna, and he formed the connections that would allow his entry into the [26] city's cultural elite. Zweig went on to publish a near infinitude of works of fiction, drama, journalism, and biography, and enjoyed a period of major celebrity in the 1920s and 1930s. [27]

The author would like to combine the two sentences reproduced below:

His parents were part of the Jewish cultural elite in Vienna at the time. Stefan was afforded every possible luxury and privilege.

Which of the following gives the best combination of the two sentences?

A) His parents were part of the Jewish cultural elite in Vienna at the time; Stefan was afforded every possible luxury and privilege.

B) Zweig was afforded every possible luxury and privilege because his parents were part of the Jewish cultural elite in Vienna at the time.

C) Born to parents who were part of Vienna's Jewish cultural elite, Stefan was afforded every possible luxury and privilege.

D) His parents were part of the Jewish cultural elite in Vienna at the time, and so Stefan benefited from their eliteness with luxury.

A) NO CHANGE

B) cities

C) citie's

D) cities'

The writer is considering deleting the phrase "of fiction, drama, journalism, and biography" and placing a comma after the word *works*. Should the phrase be kept or deleted?

A) Kept, because it shows that Zweig had no problem finding work after he left Vienna.

B) Kept, because it demonstrates the range of Zweig's talents.

C) Deleted, because it is implausible that a single writer could work well in so many forms.

D) Deleted, because it presents information given in numerous places throughout the essay.

CONTINUE

Still, Zweig's relationship with his homeland was always tenuous. While he did support the German side in World War I, Zweig remained a committed pacifist and participated only in the Archives of the Ministry of War. By the second war, **28** however, Zweig's pacifism was no longer looked on with such understanding. Zweig and his wife fled Nazi Germany in 1939 and spent their remaining years in the Americas. Only a few short years after their escape, Zweig and his wife took their own lives out of despair over what had become of Europe. Zweig's ancestral home, **29** which, you'll recall, was in Vienna, insisted on tearing itself apart, and Jewish men like himself were being slaughtered by the millions.

For many years, cultural critics saw Zweig's work as a historical curiosity. His decision to flee Europe was seen as an act of quaint pacifism, and his ultimate decision to end his own life was seen as the act of a privileged man for **30** which everyday realities were simply too much to bear. Much more popular in the post-WWII era were more traditionally "masculine" figures, who not only went to war but treated writing, painting, and filmmaking **31** like competitive sports.

28

A) NO CHANGE

B) indeed,

C) on the one hand,

D) although,

29

Which of the following choices would best emphasize the personal stake that Zweig had in the conflict in Europe?

A) NO CHANGE

B) not the Americas to which he had moved,

C) in which he had such pride,

D) the land of Goethe and Beethoven,

30

A) NO CHANGE

B) who

C) whose

D) whom

31

Which of the following conclusions to this sentence would best support the idea presented at the beginning in the sentence?

A) NO CHANGE

B) with a pacifist bent.

C) like proper gentlemen.

D) as the province of veterans.

CONTINUE

Today, however, Zweig's sensibility makes a good deal more sense. Like Zweig, many of us were alive and aware before the great catastrophes of [32] his own age, and our longing for a "simpler time" is not pure nostalgia. We know that things cannot be as they once were, but we [33] have sensed the injustice in the world being so complicated, and in the power just a few people have to take it all away from us.

[32]

A) NO CHANGE

B) their

C) her

D) our

[33]

A) NO CHANGE

B) are sensing

C) sense

D) sensed

CONTINUE

Questions 34–44 are based on the following passage.

For Figs? The Chimps Aren't Chumps

Sometimes as you fall asleep, you're thinking about what to eat for breakfast the next morning. "When I get up, I'll go to the fridge. I'll have an egg, [34] a piece of toast, and a few strips of bacon while I'm making coffee." Even though you may know where your food is coming from, you plan breakfast as a way to plan the day.

Our species may have been doing this kind of breakfast planning long before refrigerators, long before our species was even our species. A team of researchers recently followed groups of chimpanzees through three periods of fruit scarcity in West Africa. [35] For a chimpanzee, every day during a fruit-poor season can be like Black Friday, where all the "shoppers" want the same hot item.

---

[34]

A) NO CHANGE

B) a piece of toast, and a few strips of bacon,

C) a piece, of toast, and a few strips, of bacon,

D) a piece of toast and a few strips of bacon

---

[35]

At this point, the author wants to add a sentence that accurately summarizes the scientists' research in a way that is consistent with other information in the passage. Which sentence would most effectively achieve that goal?

A) They wanted to see whether the chimps would prefer new, high-yield fruits like figs to their traditional diet of bananas.

B) They wanted to discover where chimps spent the time between waking and sleep.

C) They wanted to know how the chimps acquired highly sought-after fruits, like figs, when the trees that bear these fruits are depleted so quickly.

D) They wanted to uncover the secrets of human evolution and how chimps would operate in a retail environment.

CONTINUE

36 Why does everyone freak out during Black Friday when the deals aren't even that good? If you want to be sure to get the new, say, plasma TV, what do you have to do? Camp out in front of the store! Well, that's exactly what the researchers found the chimpanzees to do with the coveted fruits. In fruit-poor seasons, **37** the nomadic chimpanzees set up their campsites within striking distance of the ripe fruits. When the fruits were **38** "_____," or quick to disappear, the female chimpanzees set up their sleeping nests more pointedly in the direction of the fruit **39** than the fruit was plentiful. Moreover, in order to ensure that the fruit supply would not be **40** gobbled by the time the chimps got there, they woke up early, often before sunrise, when the forests were still dark.

36

Which of the following would provide the best transition from the previous paragraph and introduction to this paragraph?

A) NO CHANGE

B) The similarity to Black Friday shoppers goes even a bit further than this.

C) For a monkey, every day of the year is like Black Friday, but without Thanksgiving.

D) Black Friday is the day after the American Thanksgiving, and it is often characterized by heavy retail traffic.

37

A) NO CHANGE

B) the nomadic chimpanzee sets up their

C) the nomadic chimpanzee sets up its

D) the nomadic chimpanzees set up its

38

Which of the following provides the most precise word given the definition that immediately follows?

A) lively

B) desiccated

C) ephemeral

D) eternal

39

A) NO CHANGE

B) then the

C) than if the

D) than when the

40

A) NO CHANGE

B) depleted

C) chomped

D) ate

CONTINUE ➔

The findings about the chimp [41] has led scientists to reopen a number of heated questions. The first has to do with animals' existence outside the present moment: how much do they remember, and how much do they plan? In other words, is "consciousness" really only [42] the province of humans? The other set of questions has to do with the lines of evolution. It has been firmly established that chimpanzees are our evolutionary ancestors, but now we have to wonder if we've inherited even more [43] than we thought from them initially. Have the lives of chimpanzees conditioned the small, day-to-day patterns of our own lives?

While such questions may seem purely academic and conceptual, they actually have a good deal to do with our lived experience. We learn more and more about what we share with other animals—and with each discovery, we learn a new way to relate to the world around us.

41

A) NO CHANGE
B) have lead
C) have led
D) has lead

42

A) NO CHANGE
B) the providence of humans?
C) the provenance of humans?
D) providential for humans?

43

A) NO CHANGE
B) from them than we initially thought.
C) then initially thought.
D) than we had been thinking from them initially.

44

Suppose the author's goal had been to present an argument that suggests Black Friday shopping is an animalistic behavior. Would the information in this essay support that argument?

A) Yes, this essay establishes a parallel between humans and chimpanzees and explores it in detail.
B) Yes, this essay suggests that chimps have adapted Black Friday behavior easily.
C) No, this essay suggests that chimpanzees are more advanced than most Black Friday shoppers.
D) No, this essay is more concerned with describing a behavior of chimpanzees than in passing judgment on humans.

STOP
**If you finish before time is called, you may check your work on this section only.
Do not turn to any other section in the test.**

Math Test – No Calculator
25 MINUTES, 20 QUESTIONS

Turn to Section 3 of your answer sheet to answer the questions in this section.

DIRECTIONS

For questions **1-15**, solve each problem, choose the best answer from the choices provided, and fill in the corresponding circle on your answer sheet. For questions **16-20**, solve the problem and enter your answer in the grid on the answer sheet. Please refer to the directions before question 16 on how to enter your answers in the grid. You may use any available space in your test booklet for scratch work.

NOTES

1. The use of a calculator **is not permitted**.
2. All variables and expressions used represent real numbers unless otherwise indicated.
3. Figures provided in this test are drawn to scale unless otherwise indicated.
4. All figures lie in a plane unless otherwise indicated.
5. Unless otherwise indicated, the domain of a given function f is the set of all real numbers x for which $f(x)$ is a real number.

REFERENCE

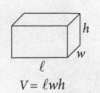

$A = \pi r^2$
$C = 2\pi r$

$A = \ell w$

$A = \frac{1}{2} bh$

$c^2 = a^2 + b^2$

Special Right Triangles

$V = \ell wh$

$V = \pi r^2 h$

$V = \frac{4}{3} \pi r^3$

$V = \frac{1}{3} \pi r^2 h$

$V = \frac{1}{3} \ell wh$

The number of degrees of arc in a circle is 360.
The number of radians of arc in a circle is 2π.
The sum of the measures in degrees of the angles of a triangle is 180.

CONTINUE

1

If two times a number is equal to that number minus 4, what is the number?

A) −7

B) −6

C) −4

D) −3

2

The number of soil samples, s, that Sonal needs for an experiment must be greater than 6 but less than or equal to 13. Which of the following represents an acceptable number of soil samples for Sonal's experiment?

A) $6 < s < 13$

B) $6 \leq s < 13$

C) $6 < s \leq 13$

D) $6 \leq s \leq 13$

3

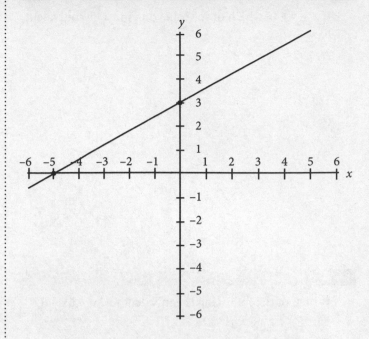

In the figure above, the graph of $y = f(x)$ is shown. Which of the following could be the equation of $f(x)$?

A) $f(x) = -\dfrac{3}{5}x + 3$

B) $f(x) = -\dfrac{3}{5}x - 3$

C) $f(x) = \dfrac{3}{5}x - 3$

D) $f(x) = \dfrac{3}{5}x + 3$

CONTINUE

4

If $x + y = 0$, which of the following must be equivalent to $x - y$?

A) $-2y$

B) $\dfrac{x}{y}$

C) x

D) x^2

5

Which of the following is equivalent to $2x^2 - 6x - 8$?

A) $2(x - 4)(x + 1)$

B) $3(x + 4)(x - 1)$

C) $2(x - 3)(x + 2)$

D) $3(x - 4)(x - 2)$

6

Ryan and Allison build a ramp to help their elderly cat, Simms, walk up to their bed. They need the ramp to make a 35° angle with their bedroom floor. How long must the ramp be to reach the top of their bed that is exactly three feet off the ground?

A) $\dfrac{\sin 35°}{3}$

B) $\dfrac{\sin 55°}{3}$

C) $\dfrac{3}{\sin 55°}$

D) $\dfrac{3}{\sin 35°}$

7

If $3a + 2b = 24$ and $4a + 5b = 53$, what is the value of $a + b$?

A) 2

B) 7

C) 9

D) 11

CONTINUE

8

Given the equation $y = 3x^2 + 4$, what is the function of the coefficient of 3 ?

A) It moves the graph of $y = 3x^2 + 4$ three units higher than the graph of $y = x^2 + 4$.

B) It moves the graph of $y = 3x^2 + 4$ three units lower than the graph of $y = x^2 + 4$.

C) It makes the graph of $y = 3x^2 + 4$ wider than the graph of $y = x^2 + 4$.

D) It makes the graph of $y = 3x^2 + 4$ narrower than the graph of $y = x^2 + 4$.

9

Steven needs to buy t theme park tickets for himself and his family. Each ticket costs \$80, and the number of tickets he needs to buy can be modeled by the expression $t^2 - 4t - 90 = 6$ when $t > 0$. What is the total cost of the theme park tickets that Steven purchased?

A) \$640

B) \$800

C) \$960

D) \$1,120

10

$$2c + 3d = 17$$
$$6c + 5d = 39$$

In the system of linear equations above, what is the value of $4c - 4d$?

A) −4

B) 1

C) 4

D) 13

11

If $x^2 + 2xy + y^2 = 64$ and $y - x = 12$, which of the following could be the value of x ?

A) −10

B) −4

C) 2

D) 10

CONTINUE

12

Samantha offers two different packages of yoga classes at her yoga studio. She offers two hot yoga sessions and three zero gravity yoga sessions at a total cost of $400. She also offers four hot yoga sessions and two zero gravity sessions at a price of $440. Samantha wants to offer a larger package for long-time clients in which the cost must exceed $800. If Samantha does not wish to include more than 13 sessions for the long-time client package, will she be able to create this package for her clients?

A) No, because the closest package that she can offer consists of three hot yoga and three zero gravity yoga sessions.

B) No, because the closest package that she can offer consists of four hot yoga and four zero gravity yoga sessions.

C) Yes, because she can offer five hot yoga and five zero gravity yoga sessions.

D) Yes, because she can offer six hot yoga and six zero gravity yoga sessions.

13

Cuthbert is conducting a chemistry experiment that calls for a number of chemicals to be mixed in various quantities. The one amount of which he is unsure is grams of potassium, p. If Cuthbert is certain that $(3p^2 + 14p + 24) - 2(p^2 + 7p + 20) = 0$, what is one possible value of $3p + 6$, the exact number of grams of potassium that Cuthbert would like to use for this experiment?

A) 20

B) 18

C) 12

D) 10

14

What is the value of $(2 + 8i)(1 - 4i) - (3 - 2i)(6 + 4i)$? (Note: $i = \sqrt{-1}$)

A) 8

B) 26

C) 34

D) 50

15

If $2\sqrt{x} = x - 3$, which of the following is the solution set for x?

A) $\{-1, 9\}$

B) $\{1, -9\}$

C) $\{9\}$

D) $\{1, 9\}$

CONTINUE

DIRECTIONS

For questions 16–20, solve the problem and enter your answer in the grid, as described below, on the answer sheet.

1. Although not required, it is suggested that you write your answer in the boxes at the top of the columns to help you fill in the circles accurately. You will receive credit only if the circles are filled in correctly.

2. Mark no more than one circle in any column.

3. No question has a negative answer.

4. Some problems may have more than one correct answer. In such cases, grid only one answer.

5. **Mixed numbers** such as $3\frac{1}{2}$ must be gridded as 3.5 or 7/2. (If $\boxed{3\ 1\ /\ 2}$ is entered into the grid, it will be interpreted as $\frac{31}{2}$, not as $3\frac{1}{2}$.)

6. **Decimal Answers:** If you obtain a decimal answer with more digits than the grid can accommodate, it may be either rounded or truncated, but it must fill the entire grid.

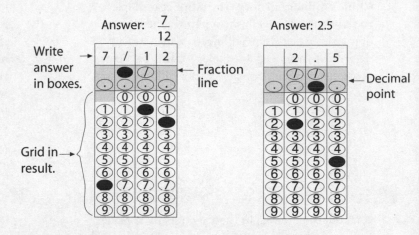

Answer: $\frac{7}{12}$ Answer: 2.5

Write answer in boxes. Fraction line. Grid in result. Decimal point.

Acceptable ways to grid $\frac{2}{3}$ are:

Answer: 201 – either position is correct

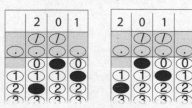

NOTE: You may start your answers in any column, space permitting. Columns you don't need to use should be left blank.

16

A group of students at Omega High School are using staples and popsicle sticks to build a scale model of the Great Wall of China as part of a project detailing China's military history. The number of staples the students will need is three times the number of popsicle sticks they will need. If the students determine they need 84 staples for this particular project, how many popsicle sticks will they need?

17

A standard parabola in the *x,y*-coordinate plane intersects the *x*-axis at (5, 0) and (–5, 0). What is the value of the *x*-coordinate of this parabola's line of symmetry?

18

Danielle is a civil engineer for Dastis Dynamic Construction, Inc. She must create blueprints for a wheelchair accessible ramp leading up to the entrance of a mall that she and her group are building. The ramp must be exactly 100 meters in length and make a 20° angle with the level ground. What is the horizontal distance, in meters, from the start of the ramp to the point level with the start of the ramp immediately below the entrance of the mall, rounded to the nearest meter? (Disregard units when inputting your answer.)

(Note: sin 20° ≈ 0.324, cos 20° ≈ 0.939, tan 20° ≈ 0.364)

19

If twice a number is equal to that number minus five, what is three times that number plus seventeen minus that number?

CONTINUE

20

Given that the equation $3x^2 + 2x - 8 = 0$ has two distinct solutions, what is the value of the smaller solution subtracted from the larger solution?

STOP
If you finish before time is called, you may check your work on this section only.
Do not turn to any other section in the test.

Math Test – Calculator

55 MINUTES, 38 QUESTIONS

Turn to Section 4 of your answer sheet to answer the questions in this section.

DIRECTIONS

For questions **1-30**, solve each problem, choose the best answer from the choices provided, and fill in the corresponding circle on your answer sheet. For questions **31-38**, solve the problem and enter your answer in the grid on the answer sheet. Please refer to the directions before question 31 on how to enter your answers in the grid. You may use any available space in your test booklet for scratch work.

NOTES

1. The use of a calculator **is permitted**.
2. All variables and expressions used represent real numbers unless otherwise indicated.
3. Figures provided in this test are drawn to scale unless otherwise indicated.
4. All figures lie in a plane unless otherwise indicated.
5. Unless otherwise indicated, the domain of a given function f is the set of all real numbers x for which $f(x)$ is a real number.

REFERENCE

$A = \pi r^2$
$C = 2\pi r$

$A = \ell w$

$A = \frac{1}{2} bh$

$c^2 = a^2 + b^2$

Special Right Triangles

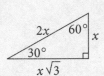

$V = \ell wh$

$V = \pi r^2 h$

$V = \frac{4}{3}\pi r^3$

$V = \frac{1}{3}\pi r^2 h$

$V = \frac{1}{3}\ell wh$

The number of degrees of arc in a circle is 360.
The number of radians of arc in a circle is 2π.
The sum of the measures in degrees of the angles of a triangle is 180.

CONTINUE

1

If $3y = y + 2$, what is the value of $2y$?

A) 1

B) 2

C) 3

D) 4

2

Merry joined an online community that charges a monthly fee of $15. A one-time enrollment fee of $50 was charged when she joined. Which of the following represents the total amount of fees that Merry has paid to the community organizers after m months, in dollars?

A) $15m + 50$

B) $15 + 50m$

C) $15m - 50$

D) $(15 + 50)m$

3

Rob has his favorite guitar tuned up and ready to bring to a performance by his cover band at a local venue Saturday. He decides at the last minute to bring x additional guitars, just in case his favorite guitar has an issue. If the total number of guitars that Robert brings to the performance can be modeled as $x + 1$, what does the "+ 1" account for in the expression?

A) It accounts for an additional guitar that Rob returns to his house and picks up in the middle of the performance.

B) It accounts for his favorite guitar, which Rob was bringing from the beginning.

C) It accounts for the number of additional guitars that Rob decided to bring.

D) It accounts for an additional non-guitar musical instrument that Rob decided to bring.

4

A group of 24 students was polled as to whether they enjoy biology class, chemistry class, both, or neither. The results are shown in the table below:

	Biology	Chemistry
Enjoy	14	18
Don't Enjoy	10	6

Given the above data, which of the following conclusions is true?

A) The ratio of those who enjoy biology class to those who enjoy chemistry class is 7:8.

B) The ratio of those who enjoy chemistry class to those who don't enjoy chemistry class is 9:4.

C) The ratio of those who enjoy biology class to those who don't enjoy chemistry class is 7:2.

D) The ratio of those who don't enjoy biology class to those who enjoy chemistry class is 5:9.

CONTINUE

5

Dr. Goldberg, a noted dietician, mixes different solutions as part of her research into sugar substitutes. By weight, she mixes 40% of a sample of substitute A and 70% of a sample of substitute B to create substitute C. If Dr. Goldberg initially had 60 grams of substitute A and 110 grams of substitute B, then what would be the weight, in grams, of substitute C ?

A) 24

B) 77

C) 101

D) 170

6

Which of the following is equivalent to the expression $x^4 - x^3 - x^2$?

A) $x(x^2 - x - 1)$

B) $x(x - x^2 - x^3)$

C) $x(x^3 - x^2)$

D) $x^2(x^2 - x - 1)$

7

Officer Blake drives his squad car 1 mile per minute while patrolling local highways during his shift. If he has driven 480 miles by the end of his shift, how many total hours did he drive his car at the above rate?

A) 8

B) 12

C) 16

D) 20

8

In the inequality $37 \le -2x + 1$, what is the appropriate order of steps needed to solve the inequality for x ?

A) Add 1 to both sides, divide both sides by 2, and flip the inequality sign to $\ge$.

B) Subtract 1 from both sides, divide both sides by -2, and flip the inequality sign to $\ge$.

C) Add 1 to both sides, divide both sides by -2, and keep the original inequality sign.

D) Subtract 1 from both sides, divide both sides by 2, and keep the original inequality sign.

CONTINUE

9

What is the value of $(2x^2 + 4x + 8) - (2x^2 - 4x + 7)$?

A) $4x^2 + 8x + 15$

B) $2x^2 + x + 1$

C) $8x + 1$

D) $8x + 15$

10

As part of a project for his cartography elective, Adam climbs several hills to create a relief map for the woods surrounding his house. He records the vertical heights of the five hills he climbed at 55 feet, 42 feet, 38 feet, 50 feet, and 48 feet. For his project, Adam must convert his measurements to inches. If 1 foot = 12 inches, what is the measurement, in inches, of the *tallest* hill Adam will have on his map?

A) 660

B) 600

C) 576

D) 456

11

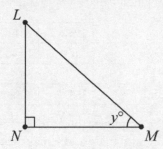

In the figure above, if $y = 40$ and $\overline{LN} = 8$, which of the following most closely approximates the length of $\overline{MN}$?

A) 0.10

B) 9.53

C) 10.44

D) 12.45

12

McCoy Max Speed, Inc. makes custom skateboards for its customers. Two wooden skateboards and three composite skateboards cost $650. Three wooden skateboards and one composite skateboard cost $450. How much would McCoy Max Speed charge a customer who purchases five wooden skateboards and four composite skateboards?

A) $500

B) $600

C) $1,000

D) $1,100

CONTINUE

13

The chart below shows data about the number of employees at Cuda Cola, a popular beverage company.

	2012	2013	2014
Total Employees	1,670	1,890	2,110
Percent Male	65%	60%	55%
Percent Female	35%	40%	45%

Assuming the employee total grows at the same rate each year, and male and female percentages continue to decrease and increase by 5%, respectively, approximately how many male employees will work at Cuda Cola in 2015 ?

A) 1,515

B) 1,398

C) 1,282

D) 1,165

14

John Croxley, the mayor of Black Rock, NY, is counting the number of restaurants that have opened in his town per month for the last seven months. He compiles the seven numbers into Set F, which contains the elements 4, 5, 11, 13, 16, 18, and x. If both the median and average (arithmetic mean) of Set F equal 11, what must be the value of x, the unknown number of restaurants that opened in Mayor Croxley's town last month?

A) 9

B) 10

C) 11

D) 12

15

$$17s + 20t = 59$$
$$30s + 40t = 110$$

In the system of equations above, what is the value of t in terms of s ?

A) $\dfrac{2s}{5}$

B) $\dfrac{s}{5}$

C) $\dfrac{5}{2s}$

D) $\dfrac{5}{s}$

CONTINUE

16

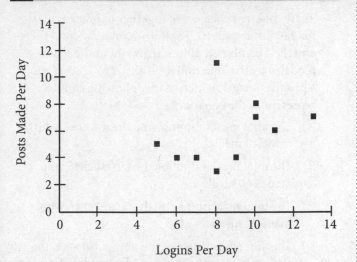

Given the scatterplot graph above, ten students at Welton Academy were polled at random about their usage of the school's new physics-centered social media app, E = MC Shared. The app was developed to encourage students to discuss physics curricula and concepts in ways that mirrored social media trends in 2013. Students were asked how many times they logged into the app each day as well as how many posts they actually made using the app. With the given data, what conclusions can be drawn about this group of students?

A) The majority of students polled logged in more times per day than they posted.

B) The majority of students polled posted more times per day than they logged in.

C) The majority of students polled logged in and posted an equal number of times.

D) No relationship can be drawn between logins per day and posts per day.

17

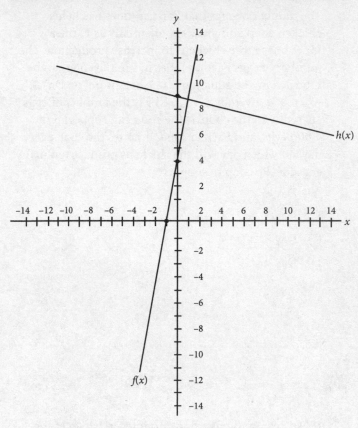

Two graphs, $f(x)$ and $h(x)$, are shown above. If $f(x) = 3x + 4$ and $f(x)$ and $h(x)$ are perpendicular, which of the following could be the equation of $h(x)$?

A) $h(x) = \dfrac{1}{3}x + 9$

B) $h(x) = -\dfrac{1}{3}x + 9$

C) $h(x) = 3x + 9$

D) $h(x) = -3x + 9$

CONTINUE

18

The number of eggs that Farmer Jones has in his chicken coop will grow exponentially as Farmer Jones buys more chickens to increase production. The number of eggs Farmer Jones has in the coop can be modeled by the equation $y = 3^x$ beginning on Day 1, where x is given by $x = 1$, and y is the number of eggs currently in the coop. If the coop can support only 4,000 eggs, and Farmer Jones empties the coop every day, on which day will the chickens produce too many eggs for the coop to support?

A) Day 6

B) Day 7

C) Day 8

D) Day 9

19

If $a = \dfrac{4a^2}{16}$ and a is a nonzero integer, which of the following is equivalent to a ?

A) $4a$

B) $4\sqrt{a}$

C) $\sqrt{2a}$

D) $2\sqrt{a}$

20

Three different chefs work together to prepare meals for 280 dinner guests. Each works at a different speed, and their combined output throughout the night is modeled by the equation $8x + 4x + 2x = 280$. If x is a positive integer, which of the following could $8x$ represent in the equation?

A) The total meal output by the slowest chef, who made 40 meals.

B) The total meal output by the fastest chef, who made 160 meals.

C) The total meal output by the fastest chef, who made 80 meals.

D) The difference between the output between the slowest and fastest chef, which would be 120 meals.

CONTINUE

21

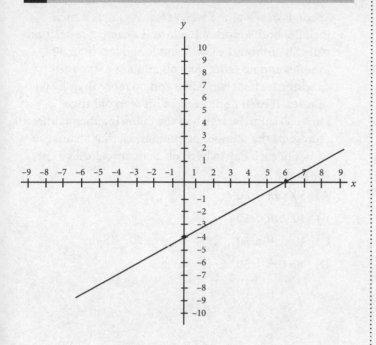

The graph, $y = f(x)$, shown above models the performance of a certain crop, where x is the nutrients subtracted or added to the soil and y is the gain or loss of pieces of fruit added to the total harvest. A more powerful fertilizer that is used causes the graph $y = f(x)$ to be reflected over the line $y = x$. Which of the following best describes the behavior of the crop with the new fertilizer?

A) For every three nutrients added to the soil, the crop loses two additional fruits for the total harvest.

B) For every two nutrients added to the soil, the crop loses two additional fruits for the total harvest.

C) For every three nutrients added to the soil, the crop adds two additional fruits to the total harvest.

D) For every two nutrients added to the soil, the crop adds three additional fruits to the total harvest.

22

George and Joe both interview the same 20 fellow students regarding their interest in their school's new Model UN Club. George asked the students to respond with Interested, Sort of Interested, and Not Interested. Joe asked the students to rate their interest on a scale of 1 to 5. The results of the polls are below.

George's Poll

Response	Number of Students
Interested	8
Sort of Interested	5
Not Interested	7

Joe's Poll

Rating	Number of Students
1	5
2	4
3	3
4	4
5	4

After reviewing the data, the Model UN advisors determine that Joe neglected to include whether a 1 or 5 was the best rating in his report. What additional piece of information would most help the advisor determine whether a 1 or 5 was the best rating?

A) Requesting that George redo his poll with the same rating system as Joe's poll.

B) Requesting that Joe redo his poll with the same rating system as George's poll.

C) Polling all of the students who said "Interested" in George's Poll and asking them to choose between "Extremely Interested" and "Very Interested."

D) Polling all of the students who gave a "1" rating in Joe's poll and ask them if they are interested in Model UN.

CONTINUE ▶

23

Each winter, Captain Dan's Ski Lodge rents both pairs of skis and snowboards to its guests for a flat daily rate per pair of skis and a flat daily rate per snowboard. Five pairs of skis and two snowboards will cost a family $370. Three pairs of skis and four snowboards will cost a family $390. During a particularly slow season, Captain Dan announces a 10% discount on all skis and snowboards. What would be the cost of renting two pairs of skis and two snowboards if they were rented during this discount period?

A) $99

B) $110

C) $198

D) $220

24

If $8x + 8y = 18$ and $x^2 - y^2 = -\dfrac{3}{8}$, what is the value of $2x - 2y$?

A) $-\dfrac{1}{3}$

B) $-\dfrac{1}{6}$

C) $\dfrac{1}{3}$

D) $\dfrac{1}{6}$

25

Shaun is developing a weight loss regimen, which includes both a workout plan and a calorie-restriction plan. Shaun wants to work out for no less than 30 minutes and no more than 60 minutes a day and consume no less than 2,000 and no more than 2,500 calories. If each minute, m, of his workout time burns 50 calories, which of the following inequalities represents the number of minutes, m, that Shaun can work out each day to burn off as many calories as he consumes?

A) $30 \le m \le 60$

B) $30 \le m \le 50$

C) $40 \le m < 50$

D) $40 \le m \le 50$

26

A professional baseball team wishes to average 45,500 ticket purchases per game for the entire 162-game season. Through the first 60 games of the season, the team has averaged 43,000 ticket purchases per game. Which of the following most closely approximates how many ticket purchases per game the team must average for the remainder of the season in order to hit its overall goal of an average of 45,500 ticket purchases per game for the season?

A)   46,970

B)   47,880

C)   48,000

D)   48,220

CONTINUE

27

A certain polynomial, *P*, has a degree of 2. Polynomial *P* has zeros of 2 and –3, and *a* > 0 when the function of polynomial *P* is written in the form of $y = ax^2 + bx + c$. Given this information, which of the following could be the graph of polynomial *P* ?

A)

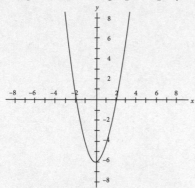

B)

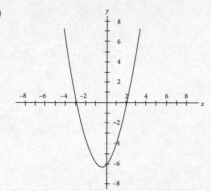

C)

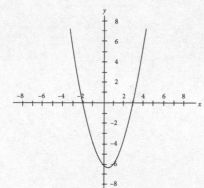

D)

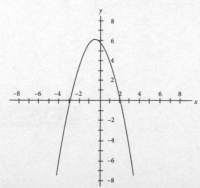

28

Circle *O* (not shown) is divided into three sectors. Points *P*, *Q*, and *R* are on the circumference of the circle. Sector *POR* has an area of 8π, and sector *ROQ* has an area of 6π. If the radius of circle *O* is 4, what is the measure of the central angle of sector *QOP*, in degrees?

A) 45

B) 90

C) 135

D) 180

29

Medical residents at Lakewood Hospital are choosing their individual specialties. Among them, 40% choose cardiology, 16% choose oncology, 34% choose endocrinology, and the remaining *x*% choose hematology. Once the doctors pick their first specialty, they are then each asked to choose a second specialty from the previous four options in case their original specialty is already filled. They may not pick their original specialty again. 20% of those who originally picked cardiology choose oncology as their second choice. If no other field chooses oncology as their second choice, and the hospital boasts 200 medical residents, then what is the total number of residents who named oncology as either their first or second choice, in terms of *x* ?

A) $8x - 128$

B) $8x - 144$

C) $x^2 + 24x - 188$

D) $x^2 - 24x + 188$

CONTINUE

30

Mr. Lastorka's science class is running experiments with an energy-efficient model electric car. As the initial rate of energy delivered to the car, measured in watts, increases, the number of millimeters moved by the car from its starting position increases exponentially. The results of several trial runs are shown on the scatterplot graph below.

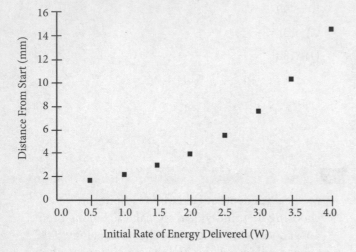

Based on the data, the students in Mr. Lastorka's class determine the exact equation involving Watts, x, and total distance from start, y. They call the function $y = f(x)$. Mr. Lastorka then instructs his class to reflect $y = f(x)$ over the x-axis. He challenges each student to determine the new function and what it would mean from a physics perspective. Four student pairs gave their answers below. Who is correct, and for what reasons?

A) Charles and Shannon, who identify the new equation as $y = -2^x$ and explain that the new graph indicates that the car is still moving forward at the same rate as before.

B) Michael and Lauren, who identify the new equation as $y = -2^x$ and explain that the new graph indicates the car is now moving in reverse at the same rate as before.

C) Matthew and Karen, who identify the new equation as $y = 2^{-x}$ and explain that the new graph indicates that the car is now moving forward more rapidly than before.

D) Andy and Joanie, who identify the new equation as $y = 2^{-x}$ and explain that the new graph indicates that the car is no longer moving in any direction.

CONTINUE

DIRECTIONS

For questions 31-38, solve the problem and enter your answer in the grid, as described below, on the answer sheet.

1. Although not required, it is suggested that you write your answer in the boxes at the top of the columns to help you fill in the circles accurately. You will receive credit only if the circles are filled in correctly.

2. Mark no more than one circle in any column.

3. No question has a negative answer.

4. Some problems may have more than one correct answer. In such cases, grid only one answer.

5. **Mixed numbers** such as $3\frac{1}{2}$ must be gridded as 3.5 or 7/2. (If 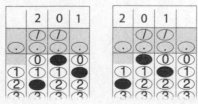 is entered into the grid, it will be interpreted as $\frac{31}{2}$, not as $3\frac{1}{2}$.)

6. **Decimal Answers:** If you obtain a decimal answer with more digits than the grid can accommodate, it may be either rounded or truncated, but it must fill the entire grid.

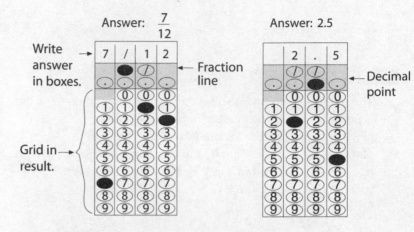

Acceptable ways to grid $\frac{2}{3}$ are:

Answer: 201 – either position is correct

NOTE: You may start your answers in any column, space permitting. Columns you don't need to use should be left blank.

31

What number divided by two is equal to that same number minus 15 ?

32

The number of hours Robert spends in his game room is proportional to the number of hours he spends playing *Call of Destiny IV: Modern Battlefield*. If he plays *Call of Destiny IV* for 6 hours, he will spend 8 hours in his game room. How many hours will Robert spend in his game room if he plays *Call of Destiny IV* for only 3 hours?

33

Twelve Smooth-Glide pens and eight Easy-Write pencils cost exactly $16.00 at Office World. Six Smooth-Glide pens and ten Easy-Write pencils cost $11.00 at the same location. How much will nine Smooth-Glide pens and nine Easy-Write pencils cost at Office World? (Disregard the dollar sign when gridding your answer.)

34

In the equation $3x^2 - 16x = -20$, what is one possible value of x ?

CONTINUE

35

In a certain ancient farming community, anthropologists determine that new dwellings were constructed monthly as modeled by the function $f(x) = 2x + 100$, where x is the current month of the year and $f(x)$ is the number of dwellings constructed by the end of that month. Additionally, they determine that the population grew exponentially each month, thanks to the discovery of more fertile land for farming. This growth is modeled by the equation $g(x) = 3^x$, where $g(x)$ represents the current population at the end of a given month. What is the smallest integer value of x, with 1 representing the end of January and 12 representing the end of December, at which the population surpasses the number of dwellings built?

36

In a school-wide competition held at Saul C. Tigh Memorial High School, Olympiad teams are challenged to come up with different circuits involving both real and imaginary currents. Imaginary currents exist in spots where the electrical energy encounters zero resistance, such as through a coil or wire. Real currents exist only where the electrical energy headed through the circuit encounters resistance, such as when a light bulb "resists" the current and takes up some of the energy carried throughout the circuit.

The members of Team Charlie develop a circuit in which the total current, real and imaginary, can be measured at $50 + 12i$ amps. They then add the current together with the current produced by Team Delta's circuit, $40 - 9i$ amps. Finally, they decide to multiply the resulting current, in amps, by Team Epsilon's total current, $60 - 2i$ amps. What is the final current, in amps, after the entire process is completed?

Questions 37 and 38 refer to the following information.

The chart below shows the population distribution for the 2,400 occupants of the city of Centre Hill.

	Adult Male	Adult Female	Child
% Living in Uptown	9	8	6
% Living in Midtown	22	20	15
% Living in Downtown	21	22	12
% Living in Suburbs	48	50	67

37

If there are an equal number of adults and children, and adult females outnumber adult males by 200, what is the sum of the women living uptown and the children living in the suburbs of Centre Hill?

38

Centre Hill plans to annex the area around a nearby lake. This new part of Centre Hill will be called, appropriately, The Annex. The Annex will add to the current population of Centre Hill. The percent of adult males living in Uptown will decrease to 6% after incorporating The Annex into Centre Hill. If the information from Part 1 holds true for the original four districts of the city of Centre Hill, then how many adult males live in The Annex?

STOP
If you finish before time is called, you may check your work on this section only.
Do not turn to any other section in the test.

SAT Essay

DIRECTIONS

The essay gives you an opportunity to show how effectively you can read and comprehend a passage and write an essay analyzing the passage. In your essay you should demonstrate that you have read the passage carefully, present a clear and logical analysis, and use language precisely.

Your essay must be written on the lines provided in your answer sheet booklet; except for the planning page of the answer booklet, you will receive no other paper on which to write. You will have enough space if you write on every line, avoid wide margins, and keep your handwriting to a reasonable size. Remember that people who are not familiar with your handwriting will read what you write. Try to write in print so that what you are writing is legible to those readers.

You have 50 minutes to read the passage and write an essay in response to the prompt provided inside this booklet.

REMINDER

— Do not write your essay in this booklet. Only what you write on the lined pages of your answer booklet will be evaluated.

— An off-topic essay will not be evaluated.

CONTINUE →

As you read the passage below, consider how the author uses

- evidence, such as facts or examples, to support claims.
- reasoning to develop ideas and to connect claims and evidence.
- stylistic or persuasive elements, such as word choice or appeals to emotion, to add power to the ideas expressed.

"Robert Redford: Protect Our Wild Horses" by Robert Redford, published in *USA Today,* November 3, 2014.

1   Horses and I have had a shared existence, personal and professional, for as long as I can remember. And while I carry a strong passion for all horses, my tenacious support for the preservation of habitat for wildlife and the American mustangs derives from their symbolic representation of our national heritage and freedom.

2   Any infringement on their legally protected right to live freely is an assault on America's principles. The varied and subjective interpretation of laws intended to protect these animals on our public lands, continues to leave wild horses under attack.

3   Recent "stand-offs" between ranchers and the federal government are reminiscent of old westerns. But this American tragedy does not have a hero riding in to save the day, and wild horses have become the victim in the controversies over our public land resources.

4   In 1971, as a result of concern for America's dwindling wild horse populations, the US Congress passed the Wild Free Roaming Horse and Burro Act. The act mandated that the Bureau of Land Management (BLM), protect free roaming wild horses and burros, under a multiple use management policy, on designated areas of our public lands.

5   The BLM manages 245 million acres of our public lands, with livestock grazing permits on 155 million acres. Wild horses are designated to share a mere 26.9 million acres. That means only 17 percent of BLM-managed public land is made available to wild horses. Wild horse populations vary between 32,000 and 50,000, while livestock grazing allocations accommodate numbers in the millions. Yes, in the millions.

6   Advocates are only asking that the horses be treated fairly. Wild horses are consistently targeted as the primary cause of negative impact to grazing lands resulting from decades of propaganda that ignores math, science and solutions that can be implemented today.

7   Ranchers hold nearly 18,000 grazing lease permits on BLM land alone. Grazing costs on BLM land go for $1.35 per cow and calf pair, well below the market rate of $16. This price disparity derived from BLM's current permit policy establishes an uneven playing field on grazing economies. Understandably, ranchers have a vested interest in maintaining the status quo.

CONTINUE

8   Although less than 3 percent of America's beef is produced on federal land, this subsidized grazing program costs the taxpayer more than $123 million dollars a year, and more than $500 million when indirect costs are accounted for.

9   The long-term economic success of public lands lies in maintaining a bio-diverse ecosystem within its boundaries. However, understanding the need for a preservation balance in thriving agricultural communities often becomes sidelined.

10   The BLM needs to comply with its original "multiple use" principle in managing wild horses and burros. In light of the inequitable share of livestock on BLM land, the ongoing persecution of wild horses and those that value them is unacceptable and threatens the very spirit of the American West. I urge Congress to stand up for much needed reform of the BLM's wild horse and burro program and livestock grazing on federal lands.

11   Now is not the time to repudiate environmental balance, but rather it is the time for all of us to work together—politician, advocate, rancher, scientist, and citizen. Only by doing this will the United States move forward and be a leader in environmental issues and ensure sustainability to our delicate ecosystem.

Write an essay in which you explain how Robert Redford builds an argument to convince Congress to do more to protect wild horses. In your essay, analyze how Redford uses one or more of the features listed above (or features of your own choice) to strengthen the logic and persuasiveness of his argument. Be sure that your analysis focuses on the most relevant aspects of the passage.

Your essay should not explain whether you agree with Redford's claims, but rather explain how the author builds an argument to persuade his audience.

END OF TEST

DO NOT RETURN TO A PREVIOUS SECTION.

Completely darken bubbles with a No. 2 pencil. If you make a mistake, be sure to erase mark completely. Erase all stray marks.

1.

YOUR NAME: _____
(Print)
           Last   First   M.I.

SIGNATURE: _____   DATE: ___ / ___ / ___

HOME ADDRESS: _____
(Print)
           Number and Street

_____
   City   State   Zip Code

PHONE NO.: _____
(Print)

5. YOUR NAME

First 4 letters of last name				FIRST INIT	MID INIT

(Bubbles A–Z for each column)

IMPORTANT: Please fill in these boxes exactly as shown on the back cover of your test book.

2. TEST FORM

3. TEST CODE

4. REGISTRATION NUMBER

6. DATE OF BIRTH

Month	Day	Year
○ JAN		
○ FEB	0 0	0 0
○ MAR	1 1	1 1
○ APR	2 2	2 2
○ MAY	3 3	3 3
○ JUN	4	4 4
○ JUL	5	5 5
○ AUG	6	6 6
○ SEP	7	7 7
○ OCT	8	8 8
○ NOV	9	9 9
○ DEC		

7. SEX
○ MALE
○ FEMALE

The **Princeton Review**®

**Test ② ** Start with number 1 for each new section.
If a section has fewer questions than answer spaces, leave the extra answer spaces blank.

Section 1—Reading

1. A B C D
2. A B C D
3. A B C D
4. A B C D
5. A B C D
6. A B C D
7. A B C D
8. A B C D
9. A B C D
10. A B C D
11. A B C D
12. A B C D
13. A B C D
14. A B C D
15. A B C D
16. A B C D
17. A B C D
18. A B C D
19. A B C D
20. A B C D
21. A B C D
22. A B C D
23. A B C D
24. A B C D
25. A B C D
26. A B C D

27. A B C D
28. A B C D
29. A B C D
30. A B C D
31. A B C D
32. A B C D
33. A B C D
34. A B C D
35. A B C D
36. A B C D
37. A B C D
38. A B C D
39. A B C D
40. A B C D
41. A B C D
42. A B C D
43. A B C D
44. A B C D
45. A B C D
46. A B C D
47. A B C D
48. A B C D
49. A B C D
50. A B C D
51. A B C D
52. A B C D

Section 2—Writing and Language Skills

1. A B C D
2. A B C D
3. A B C D
4. A B C D
5. A B C D
6. A B C D
7. A B C D
8. A B C D
9. A B C D
10. A B C D
11. A B C D
12. A B C D
13. A B C D
14. A B C D
15. A B C D
16. A B C D
17. A B C D
18. A B C D
19. A B C D
20. A B C D
21. A B C D
22. A B C D

23. A B C D
24. A B C D
25. A B C D
26. A B C D
27. A B C D
28. A B C D
29. A B C D
30. A B C D
31. A B C D
32. A B C D
33. A B C D
34. A B C D
35. A B C D
36. A B C D
37. A B C D
38. A B C D
39. A B C D
40. A B C D
41. A B C D
42. A B C D
43. A B C D
44. A B C D

Test ❷ Start with number 1 for each new section.
If a section has fewer questions than answer spaces, leave the extra answer spaces blank.

Section 3—Mathematics: No Calculator

1. Ⓐ Ⓑ Ⓒ Ⓓ
2. Ⓐ Ⓑ Ⓒ Ⓓ
3. Ⓐ Ⓑ Ⓒ Ⓓ
4. Ⓐ Ⓑ Ⓒ Ⓓ
5. Ⓐ Ⓑ Ⓒ Ⓓ
6. Ⓐ Ⓑ Ⓒ Ⓓ
7. Ⓐ Ⓑ Ⓒ Ⓓ
8. Ⓐ Ⓑ Ⓒ Ⓓ
9. Ⓐ Ⓑ Ⓒ Ⓓ
10. Ⓐ Ⓑ Ⓒ Ⓓ
11. Ⓐ Ⓑ Ⓒ Ⓓ
12. Ⓐ Ⓑ Ⓒ Ⓓ
13. Ⓐ Ⓑ Ⓒ Ⓓ
14. Ⓐ Ⓑ Ⓒ Ⓓ
15. Ⓐ Ⓑ Ⓒ Ⓓ

16. 17. 18. 19. 20.

Section 4—Mathematics: Calculator

1. Ⓐ Ⓑ Ⓒ Ⓓ
2. Ⓐ Ⓑ Ⓒ Ⓓ
3. Ⓐ Ⓑ Ⓒ Ⓓ
4. Ⓐ Ⓑ Ⓒ Ⓓ
5. Ⓐ Ⓑ Ⓒ Ⓓ
6. Ⓐ Ⓑ Ⓒ Ⓓ
7. Ⓐ Ⓑ Ⓒ Ⓓ
8. Ⓐ Ⓑ Ⓒ Ⓓ
9. Ⓐ Ⓑ Ⓒ Ⓓ
10. Ⓐ Ⓑ Ⓒ Ⓓ
11. Ⓐ Ⓑ Ⓒ Ⓓ
12. Ⓐ Ⓑ Ⓒ Ⓓ
13. Ⓐ Ⓑ Ⓒ Ⓓ
14. Ⓐ Ⓑ Ⓒ Ⓓ
15. Ⓐ Ⓑ Ⓒ Ⓓ
16. Ⓐ Ⓑ Ⓒ Ⓓ
17. Ⓐ Ⓑ Ⓒ Ⓓ
18. Ⓐ Ⓑ Ⓒ Ⓓ
19. Ⓐ Ⓑ Ⓒ Ⓓ
20. Ⓐ Ⓑ Ⓒ Ⓓ
21. Ⓐ Ⓑ Ⓒ Ⓓ
22. Ⓐ Ⓑ Ⓒ Ⓓ
23. Ⓐ Ⓑ Ⓒ Ⓓ
24. Ⓐ Ⓑ Ⓒ Ⓓ
25. Ⓐ Ⓑ Ⓒ Ⓓ
26. Ⓐ Ⓑ Ⓒ Ⓓ
27. Ⓐ Ⓑ Ⓒ Ⓓ
28. Ⓐ Ⓑ Ⓒ Ⓓ
29. Ⓐ Ⓑ Ⓒ Ⓓ
30. Ⓐ Ⓑ Ⓒ Ⓓ

31. 32. 33. 34. 35.

36. 37. 38.

Chapter 23
Practice Test 2:
Answers and
Explanations

PRACTICE TEST 2 ANSWER KEY

Section 1: Reading

1.	A	27.	B
2.	B	28.	D
3.	B	29.	B
4.	D	30.	B
5.	C	31.	D
6.	A	32.	C
7.	D	33.	D
8.	C	34.	A
9.	B	35.	C
10.	C	36.	A
11.	C	37.	C
12.	B	38.	B
13.	D	39.	D
14.	B	40.	A
15.	B	41.	D
16.	D	42.	C
17.	C	43.	C
18.	A	44.	B
19.	B	45.	B
20.	B	46.	C
21.	D	47.	D
22.	B	48.	A
23.	A	49.	C
24.	D	50.	D
25.	D	51.	D
26.	A	52.	A

Section 2: Writing & Language

1.	B	23.	D
2.	D	24.	B
3.	A	25.	C
4.	C	26.	A
5.	B	27.	B
6.	D	28.	A
7.	B	29.	C
8.	C	30.	D
9.	A	31.	A
10.	B	32.	D
11.	D	33.	C
12.	D	34.	A
13.	C	35.	C
14.	D	36.	B
15.	A	37.	A
16.	C	38.	C
17.	B	39.	D
18.	A	40.	B
19.	D	41.	C
20.	B	42.	A
21.	A	43.	B
22.	D	44.	D

Section 3: Math (No Calculator)

1.	C	11.	A
2.	C	12.	D
3.	D	13.	B
4.	A	14.	A
5.	A	15.	C
6.	D	16.	28
7.	D	17.	0
8.	D	18.	94
9.	C	19.	7
10.	C	20.	$\frac{10}{3}$

Section 4: Math (Calculator)

1.	B	18.	C
2.	A	19.	D
3.	B	20.	B
4.	D	21.	D
5.	C	22.	D
6.	D	23.	C
7.	A	24.	A
8.	B	25.	D
9.	C	26.	A
10.	A	27.	B
11.	B	28.	A
12.	D	29.	D
13.	D	30.	B
14.	B	31.	30
15.	C	32.	4
16.	A	33.	13.5
17.	B	34.	2 or $\frac{10}{3}$
		35.	5
		36.	5,406
		37.	860
		38.	250

PRACTICE TEST 2 EXPLANATIONS

Section 1: Reading

1. **A** Although Jane resists Mr. Rochester, the first sentence of the passage indicates that her conscience and emotions are actually favorably inclined toward Mr. Rochester. Because she has positive feelings toward him, (A) is an accurate description of her attitude. While Mr. Rochester perceives Jane to be uncaring, (B) is incorrect because the narration indicates that she does care but resists her own feelings. Similarly, (C) is incorrect because the first sentence tells us she has positive feelings for Rochester. Because Jane acts calmly, ignoring her emotions, she cannot accurately be described as reckless. Therefore, (D) is also incorrect, and (A) is the correct answer.

2. **B** Because questions 2 and 3 are general paired questions, consider question 2 and the textual evidence given in question 3 at the same time. Question 2 asks for the reason Jane refused Rochester's advances. Consider the lines referenced in question 3's answer choices and whether they support any of the answers in question 2. Choices (A), (C), and (D) of question 3 do not support any of the answer choices in question 2, so they can be eliminated. Choice (B) of question 3 (*I will hold to the principles received by me when I was sane, and not mad—as I am now*) provides support only for (B) in question 2, so (B) must be the answer to both question 2 and question 3. These answers make sense because they indicate that Jane resists Rochester because she wishes to hold to her principles.

3. **B** See the explanation for question 2. As noted above, (B) of question 3 (*I will hold to the principles received by me when I was sane, and not mad—as I am now*) provides support only for (B) in question 2, so (B) must be the answer to both question 2 and question 3. These answers make sense because they indicate that Jane resists Rochester because she wishes to hold to her principles.

4. **D** There is no evidence that Jane is literally insane. Rather, she is speaking metaphorically about the conflict between her reason and her desires. Therefore, (A) is wrong. Because Jane says the law (not her mental state) has been given by God, (B) is incorrect. Jane says that her insanity tempts her to disregard the worth of her principles, and it is her principles that are preventing her from giving in to Mr. Rochester, so her insanity is tempting her to give in to Rochester. Therefore, (C) is wrong; her insanity does not urge her to reject Rochester, but rather to accept his advances. Choice (D) is correct because her feeling of insanity is directly related to her emotions, as evidenced by the phrase *with my veins running fire, and my heart beating faster than I can count its throbs*, which Jane provides to explain why she feels insane.

5. **C** Because *wrought* describes Mr. Rochester's fury, and the passage says that his fury has reached its highest, *wrought* must mean something like "increased." Because *hammered* has nothing to do with increasing fury, (A) is incorrect. Choice (B) also does not have anything to do with "increased," so eliminate it. Because *excited* could mean "increased" when applied to someone's emotions, (C)

accurately describes the passage's use of *wrought*. Since *wrung* means *squeezed and twisted*, (D) does not describe the passage's use of *wrought*. The correct answer is (C).

6. **A** Choice (A) is correct because Mr. Rochester describes Jane's soul as strong and her body as weak in paragraph 5. While paragraph 1 states that Rochester loves Jane, and paragraph 4 states that he is angry with her for refusing his advances, Rochester is angry for the entirety of paragraph 5. Therefore, it does not contrast his love with his anger, and (B) is incorrect. Though Rochester speaks of a cage, he never actually mentions a bird; eliminate (C). Similarly, Rochester only refers to Jane's purity. Because he never calls Jane impure, (D) is not correct.

7. **D** Rochester is speaking metaphorically, not about a literal convict, so (A) is incorrect. Because he is talking about Jane, not himself, (B) cannot be correct. When Rochester refers to breaking the prison and Jane's body, you can tell that the inmate's prison refers to Jane's body, not the ideals of the time. Therefore, (C) is incorrect. The inmate refers to Jane's soul, so (D) accurately describes Rochester's use of *inmate* and is the correct answer.

8. **C** Think about the evidence in the passage that helped you answer the previous question: Rochester is using the word *inmate* to refer to Jane's soul trapped in her body. Because (A) mentions neither soul nor body, (A) is incorrect. Choice (B) refers only to Jane's body, so it cannot be correct. Choice (C) mentions both Jane's spirit and body (her *brittle frame*), providing good support for the answer to the previous question. Choice (D) makes no mention of either soul or body, so it is incorrect. The correct answer is (C).

9. **B** Because Jane is having a harder time resisting Rochester now that he is sad, *worse* means something close to *harder*. Because *less desirable*, *of lower quality*, and *unskillful* all mean things other than *harder*, you can eliminate (A), (C), and (D). Because *harder* matches *more difficult*, (B) accurately describes the passage's use of *worse* and is the correct answer.

10. **C** *Pathos* refers to Jane's emotions, so the paragraph depicts Jane overcoming her emotions. Therefore, (A) cannot be correct. Jane makes no allusion to social conventions, which makes (B) incorrect. However, because the paragraph depicts Jane overcoming her emotions, (C) is a good description of Jane's values. Since Jane battles to overcome her feelings, (D) is not an accurate description of her values. Choice (C) is the answer.

11. **C** Clinton's speech speaks out against gender inequality all over the world and advocates in favor of these injustices being amended. Choice (C) best reflects this idea. Although Clinton criticizes how women are treated worldwide, she does not counter any arguments, so eliminate (A). She does not take a scholarly approach to analyze women's place in society, so eliminate (B). Clinton is not mediating between two parties, so eliminate (D).

12. **B** Although women play different roles in society, many of these roles are not appreciated. Choice (B) most accurately reflects this meaning. Choices (A), (C), and (D) have meanings that are related to the word *valued* but are not used in the context of the word's use in the passage.

13. **D** Clinton discusses the importance of conferences in compelling people to consider important issues. She then mentions the conference in Nairobi as helping to bring to light the crisis of domestic violence. Therefore, (D) is the correct answer. The passage does not claim that the crisis of domestic violence was not solved, so eliminate (A). The passage does not discuss anyone questioning the reason for holding the current conference, so eliminate (B). Although Clinton mentions the fact that the experiences of women tend to go unnoticed, this is not her reason for mentioning the conference in Nairobi. Eliminate (C).

14. **B** Think about the evidence in the passage that helped you answer the previous question: *It is conferences like this that compel governments and peoples everywhere to listen, look, and face the world's most pressing problems.* She then mentions the conference in Nairobi as helping to bring to light the crisis of domestic violence. Choice (B) provides the most support for why Clinton mentions the conference in Nairobi. The current conference was not held because of the conference in Nairobi, so eliminate (A). Women being the primary caretakers of the world is not the reason for mentioning the conference in Nairobi, so eliminate (C). Women dying from preventable diseases is not the reason for mentioning the conference in Nairobi, so eliminate (D).

15. **B** Clinton discusses how some women are able to attend a conference that speaks out against the inequalities against women, while others are not able to do so. Choice (B) most accurately reflects this idea. Clinton does not differentiate between people who work in schools and hospitals, so eliminate (A). Clinton does not mention employed women, unemployed women, or women who can or cannot vote, so eliminate (C) and (D).

16. **D** Choices (A), (B), and (C) are each discussed in paragraph 4, so eliminate them. The passage does not discuss women suffering from widespread unemployment, so (D) is the correct answer.

17. **C** In paragraph 4, Clinton discusses women who have a voice standing up for women who are unable to stand up for themselves. Choice (C) most accurately reflects this idea. Choices (A), (B), and (D) have meanings that are related to the word *speak* but are not used in the same context as this word is used in the passage.

18. **A** In paragraph 8, Clinton argues that women's rights are also human rights, which matches (A). Women's attendance at the conference is not discussed in this paragraph, so eliminate (B). Clinton does not claim that women's rights have a special nature, just that these rights are the same as human rights, so eliminate (C). Clinton does not suggest that we no longer need to focus on women's problems; this is the opposite of what is discussed in the passage, so eliminate (D).

19. **B** Think about the evidence in the passage that helped you answer the previous question: In paragraph 8, Clinton argues that women's rights are also human rights. Choice (B) provides the most support for the rhetorical effect of the phrase discussed in the previous question. Although Clinton discusses the respect and protection of women's rights, this is not the phrase that best supports the rhetorical effect of the discussed phrase, so eliminate (A). Giving examples of the specific rights

in question does not provide the best support for the rhetorical effect of the discussed phrase, so eliminate (C). The attendance of women at the conference is not related to the discussed phrase, so eliminate (D).

20. **B**   In paragraph 2, Clinton discusses the experiences of women throughout the world: *Yet much of the work we do is not valued—not by economists, not by historians, not by popular culture, not by government leaders.* Choice (B) most accurately reflects this idea. Clinton does not state that these leaders are purposely working against the prosperity of women, so eliminate (A). Choice (C) is contradicted by what the passage states, so eliminate this choice. Although these leaders may not value the work of women, the passage does not state that these leaders have made it unacceptable to discuss women's rights, so eliminate (D).

21. **D**   The graphic shows poverty rates in America divided by gender and age. Across all age groups, women experience higher rates of poverty than their male counterparts. This falls in line with the passage's assertion that women comprise 70 percent of the world's poor. Therefore, (D) is correct. Choice (A) is incorrect because, while the graphic shows a high gender disparity among those 65 and older, it refers only to American poverty rates. The graphic actually states that 15.4 percent of American women 18 to 65 are impoverished, not that they make up that percentage of the world's poor. Therefore, (B) is incorrect. And there is no mention of how many children are impoverished worldwide in either the graphic or the passage, so (C) is incorrect.

22. **B**   The next-to-last sentence of the passage states that *Seen throughout the procession is that balance of the monumentally simple and the actual,* and goes on to list several more types of balance, *that Heraclitus, the philosopher, wrote of in the sixth century B.C.* This is support for (B). While the author does discuss the representation of the passage of time in the frieze, this idea is not connected to Heraclitus, so (A) can be eliminated. The mention of Heraclitus also does not support the idea that the frieze is *characteristically Greek,* so (C) is incorrect. Choice (D) is tempting, if the entirety of the sentence mentioning Heraclitus isn't included; however, the balance mentioned isn't between mortals and the goddess Athena.

23. **A**   In the first paragraph of Passage 1, the author proposes his idea of what the frieze *probably represents.* In the second paragraph, he describes the frieze. This matches (A). Choice (B) may seem close at first because the author does indicate that the subject of the frieze *is still a matter of scholarly dispute.* However, he does not question someone else's interpretation, so (B) is incorrect. Choice (C) falls into the category of "too narrow": The author does describe the frieze, but only in paragraph 2. Choice (C) doesn't take paragraph 1 into account. Since no *historical overview* is given, (D) is also incorrect.

24. **D**   By using the word *unparalleled,* the author is saying that it is unusual to see a representation of a festival in classical Greek art that shows deities in attendance. Choices (A), (B), and (C) do not match the meaning of "unusual," and (D) does. Therefore, (D) is the answer.

25. **D** Passage 2 begins with the first paragraph describing ways that the particular piece of art in question is unusual in the world of classical Greek art: It shows deities attending a festival, including Athena, and they are ignoring the peplos. This represents a *flagrant breach with tradition* that *requires explanation*. Paragraph 2 continues with an explanation of what it cannot represent. Since the author does not say that the frieze cannot depict the Panathenaic procession, (A) is incorrect. The author also does not discuss the passage of time, so (B) is incorrect. While the author goes on to describe the *heroes of Marathon*, the question is asking about the purpose of the first two paragraphs, so (C) is a tempting trap answer but must be eliminated. Choice (D) comes the closest to what the author is doing in the first two paragraphs, describing *problems in the traditional interpretation of the frieze.*

26. **A** Paragraph 2 begins by discussing what a *classical Athenian,* or resident of Athens, would not have thought as he looked at the frieze, that is, that it was a representation of himself. In the second sentence, *mortal* could be replaced by *classical Athenian,* because the subject must be something greater than a resident of Athens. Therefore, (B), (C), and (D) do not fit, and (A) is the correct answer.

27. **B** Paragraph 2 begins by discussing what a *classical Athenian,* or resident of Athens, would not have thought as he looked at the frieze: *"there I go"* or even more vaguely *"there we go."* The next sentence tells us that the subject of the frieze must be *more than mortal,* or more than about the *classical Athenian* looking at it. Putting these together, we can surmise that when the author says that the *classical Athenian* wouldn't say *"there I go,"* he means that the frieze is not about the *classical Athenian.* Paragraph 3 confirms this idea by saying *we must rule out…that it is a contemporary or generic statement of the Panathenaic procession conducted by the citizens….* Since there was never a discussion of the figures themselves and whether they represented *individual citizens,* (A) is incorrect. Choice (B) does match pretty closely, so keep it. Choice (C) has more to do with who participated in the procession rather than the subject of the frieze, so eliminate (C). Choice (D) goes too far because the author never says that the *subject of the frieze should be obvious to modern viewers.* Choice (B) is the correct answer.

28. **D** Think about the evidence in the passage that helped you answer the previous question: Support for (B) in question 7 comes from paragraph 2 and paragraph 3, so (A) and (B) can be eliminated. While it may be true that *the explanation must have been apparent to the classical Athenian who knew this background,* this does not support the idea that the frieze cannot represent a human event, so eliminate (C). Choice (D) directly supports (B) in question 27, and is therefore the correct answer.

29. **B** The author of Passage 2 proposes that the frieze *shows the fighters of Marathon celebrating the prime festival of the goddess Athena…as a thanksgiving for her aid at Marathon and afterwards.* This ties into (B), *Athenian men who died in battle at Marathon.* There is no indication that the author believes the *youths* were *from around the time the Parthenon was built,* so eliminate (A). Choice (C) is too broad because it includes all *people of Marathon who were worshipped as heroes,* whereas the author specifies the fighters of Marathon, so eliminate (C). Choice (D) contradicts the author's description that the frieze is a representation of the fighters, not *purely divine participants,* so eliminate it. Choice (B) is the answer.

30. **B**   Passage 1 does not *focus on determining the subject of the frieze*—that's only in the first paragraph. Eliminate (A). Passage 2 considers *how Greek citizens might have viewed the frieze,* but Passage 1 does not. Eliminate (C). Passage 1 also does not *entirely reject* the traditional perspective, so eliminate (D). Passage 1 does give *a detailed description of the figures* in the second paragraph, so (B) is the correct answer.

31. **D**   Think about the evidence in the passage that helped you answer the previous question: Passage 1 gives a *detailed description of the figures* in the frieze in the second paragraph. Only (D) references lines that give a detailed description of figures in the frieze, so (D) is the correct answer.

32. **C**   Choice (A) is incorrect because the mules are not unusual. They are an example familiar to many people to help readers understand what the author is describing. Choice (B) is incorrect because the mules are not part of a counterargument. Choice (D) is partially true in that sterile mules are part of the larger argument that the whiptails are unusual; however, the specific purpose of mentioning the sterile mules at that point in the passage is to give an example of why scientists believe that hybrids are sterile. Thus, (C) is correct.

33. **D**   The lizards are unusual to the point of being remarkable, so (D) is correct. They are not especially *beautiful,* (A), or *conspicuous,* (B). Choice (C) is a trap because *aggressive* is related to *striking* but not contextually correct in this instance.

34. **A**   The scientists do seem to be friends, as stated in (D), but the best description of their relationship in this article is as a team of scientists working on parthenogenesis, so (A) is correct. They are not rivals, so (B) is incorrect. Stowers is an institute where Dr. Neaves served as president, so they were not trying to disprove theories from Stowers, which makes (C) incorrect.

35. **C**   Choices (A) and (B) are too extreme, so they are incorrect. Choice (D) refers to something that often happens in evolution, but evolution itself doesn't isolate populations. Choice (C) mirrors what is said in the passage and is the correct answer.

36. **A**   Think about the evidence in the passage that helped you answer the previous question. Choice (A) is correct, since the line *The evolution of a new animal species is usually a drawn-out affair* supports the idea that evolution usually takes many years to happen. Choices (B), (C), and (D) do not support this and are therefore incorrect.

37. **C**   The Doctor thought it was a good time to move forward due to the new technology available, so it was an opportune moment, (C). The passage implies that it's taken a long time, but an hour late, (B), is too short a time. It's not a festival, so (A) is incorrect, nor is it a lofty ideal, making (D) incorrect.

38. **B**   Choices (A), (C), and (D) are mentioned in the passage and are aspects of parthenogenesis. Choice (B) is mentioned, but only the female lizards can clone themselves, so any cells from a male whiptail would be useless for parthenogenesis. Therefore, (B) is the answer.

39. **D** Choice (A) is the opposite of what the passage says, so it's incorrect. The lizards have different sets of chromosomes. The whiptails weren't discovered in the 1960s; their genetic makeup was found to be strange, so (B) is wrong. The lizards don't require a male and female, (C), but the clones come only from female whiptails, so the clones must be female. Thus, (D) is correct.

40. **A** Think about the evidence in the passage that helped you answer the previous question: Choice (A) clarifies that the clones come only from female whiptails, so the clones must be female. Choices (B), (C), and (D) do not support this and are therefore incorrect.

41. **D** Choices (A) and (C) aren't definitive enough and (B) is too general, making them all incorrect. Choice (D) addresses the author's argument that mating animals in captivity defies ideas about how species evolve. If lizards never clone themselves in the wild, then species outside of the lab don't evolve through cloning. Thus, (D) is correct.

42. **C** The word *somehow* implies that scientists still don't understand how female whiptails clone themselves, so (C) is correct. Choice (A) is incorrect because it uses the word *switch* in an incorrect and misleading way, while (B) is too vague and doesn't answer the question. Choice (D) addresses why the whiptails clone, but the sentence is referring to how they do it, so (D) is incorrect.

43. **C** Look earlier in the sentence for the phrase the *Earth's surface sank more than 1 mile*. Go through the answer choices to find the one that matches this description. Choice (C) is correct because a *crater* is a "large, bowl-shaped cavity in the earth." Eliminate (A), (B), and (D), as none of them match this physical description.

44. **B** The second paragraph primarily discusses the extensive time range of volcanic eruptions, starting *as far back as 400,000 years ago* and *as recently as 600 years ago*. Use POE to find the answer choice that matches this information. There is no evidence of another eruption this century based on the passage, so eliminate (A). Choice (B) works because it shows the large range of time in geologic terms. Choice (C) almost works, but the author is not just trying to be ironic. The information is not relevant to the paragraph, so eliminate (C). Choice (D) is incorrect because a relative term doesn't fit; *recently* isn't being compared to any other variables. Choice (B) is the answer.

45. **B** The pronoun *that* precedes *temblor*, so it must refer to something earlier in the previous sentence. The first sentence discusses *a magnitude 5.4 earthquake struck 6 miles southeast of the caldera*, so (B) is correct because the *temblor ended two decades of low quake activity*.

46. **C** The third sentence in paragraph 7 states that the geologists studied trees that were dying on Mammoth Mountain from carbon dioxide, and that this would often *precede volcanic eruptions*. This information suggests the possibility of a volcanic eruption. Choice (C) is a good match for this information. There is no evidence to support (A) and (B), so eliminate them. There is no mention of geodetic equipment in this paragraph, so eliminate (D) as well. Choice (C) is the answer.

47. **D**   Think about the evidence in the passage that helped you answer the previous question: The geologists are monitoring the caldera to try to predict a future eruption. Use POE to find the best reference from the passage to the previous question. Eliminate (A) because that sentence refers to eruptions from centuries ago. Choice (B) does not reference geologist activity at all, so get rid of it. Eliminate (C) because it discusses the equipment, not the geologists. Choice (D) works because it details studies from the USGS regarding forms of evidence that often *precede volcanic eruptions.*

48. **A**   The final sentence in the last paragraph states that *geologists think that the chances of an eruption in the area in any given year are quite small.* This contradicts the information in (B) and (C), so eliminate them. Earthquakes are only a small part of the overall passage, so eliminate (D) because it is too limited. Choice (A) is correct.

49. **C**   Use POE to find the answer choice that is best supported by the passage. Choice (A) is incorrect since it was *both the Inyo Craters and Mono Craters* that erupted 600 years ago. Choice (B) almost works, but the passage never suggests that Mammoth Mountain is actually active, as opposed to the larger chain—the Long Valley Caldera—it's part of. Choice (C) is a good fit because the seventh paragraph states that *symptoms of volcanic unrest may persist for decades or centuries at large calderas, such as Long Valley Caldera.* The information in (D) is mentioned in the first paragraph, but there is no evidence that refers to Mammoth Mountain, so eliminate it. Choice (C) is correct.

50. **D**   Think about the evidence in the passage that helped you answer the previous question: The seventh paragraph states that *symptoms of volcanic unrest may persist for decades or centuries at large calderas, such as Long Valley Caldera.* This sentence is referenced by (D), while the other choices do not relate to the correct answer to the previous question. Therefore, (D) is the answer.

51. **D**   The last few sentences of the seventh paragraph state that *symptoms of volcanic unrest may persist for decades or centuries at large calderas, such as Long Valley Caldera. Studies indicate that only about one in six such episodes of unrest at large calderas worldwide actually culminates in an eruption.* The swelling of the Long Valley Caldera is part of these symptoms, so this basically says that there is no definitive outcome that results from them. Choice (D) is a good analogy for this information and therefore the correct answer.

52. **A**   2015 is at the far right end of the graph, at which point the line indicating the number of cumulative earthquakes hits above the 1.2 line. However, each number on the right y-axis needs to be multiplied by 10^5, so the number of cumulative earthquakes is actually greater than 120,000. Therefore, (A) is the correct answer. Choice (B) is incorrect for the same reason; earthquakes per week are tracked on the right axis, not the left. Choice (C) is incorrect because 1.2 needs to be multiplied by 10^5. Choice (D) is incorrect because cumulative earthquakes are tracked on the right y-axis, not the left.

Section 2: Writing and Language

Park Rangers, Naturally

1. **B** This question asks for the answer choice that would NOT be acceptable, so the underlined portion is correct as it stands. Choice (B) is the correct response because the other answer choices match the underlined portion—they set off the abbreviation *NPS* from its official name of *National Park Services*.

2. **D** Use POE here, since there doesn't seem to be a common thread being tested on this question. Eliminate (B) and (C) because *pulchritudinous* and *pretty* basically mean the same thing, making these choices interchangeable and impossible to choose between. Go back to the passage and notice that it already uses the phrase *marveled at the natural beauty*, so using another word to describe its beauty again would be redundant. Therefore, eliminate (A). Choice (D) is the most concise response, and therefore the correct answer.

3. **A** Notice the question! You're asked for a choice that will include detail to clarify *day-to-day operations*. Look at the next sentence, which describes the activities of the *park rangers*. It states that they are in charge of the park's *upkeep* and *maintain the balance between the wildlife and plant species and the human visitors*. Both of these correspond with the underlined portion of *maintenance and tours*. Nothing is stated about the length of the tasks, whether or not they are repetitive, or the political aspects of them, so eliminate (B), (C), and (D). Choice (A) provides the detail the question asks for and is the correct answer.

4. **C** The idea before the punctuation, *These park rangers are responsible for the upkeep of the parks*, is a complete idea, as is the clause, *their main responsibility is to maintain the balance between the wildlife and plant species and the human visitors that come to the parks every day*, that follows it. Therefore, a comma alone cannot separate two complete ideas, so eliminate (A) and (D). Eliminate (B) as well, because punctuation is needed to separate two complete ideas. Choice (C) is the correct answer because a dash (HALF-STOP punctuation) can be used to separate these complete ideas.

5. **B** The paragraph describes the *park rangers* as *scientists*, *educators*, and professionals with backgrounds in *law enforcement* and *firefighting*. Look for the answer choice that is consistent with this type of diversity. Eliminate (A) because *pollution* is not talked about in the paragraph, as well as (C) because the paragraph is not interested in the *visitors* to the park. *Ecology* is too limited for (D), so eliminate it. You're left with (B), which is the correct answer.

6. **D** Look to the previous sentence, which describes some of the park rangers, and notice the phrase *Some are scientists who revel*. Since the next sentence is also describing the park rangers, it needs to be consistent and parallel with the previous sentence, so it should be *Some are educators who help*. Choice (D) is the correct response.

7. **B** Notice that the answer choices are pronouns, so look at the current sentence to determine what the pronoun *them* refers to; this might be unclear because both *posts* and *municipal services* are used in the sentence. Eliminate (A) and (C), which are ambiguous, and (D) because it's singular and ambiguous. Choice (B) is the clearest, most precise choice and is therefore correct.

8. **C** Use POE to find the clearest and most concise response. Choice (A) is awkward because *visitors are on the rise* doesn't necessarily refer to their numbers, so eliminate it. Choice (B) is incorrect, as *poised on the rise* is an idiom error and should be *poised to rise*. Choice (D) is awkward, unclear, and redundant, as *poised on the rise* seems to be referring to the *numbers*, which are also described as *growing*. Choice (C) is the answer.

9. **A** Check the underlined portion of this sentence, which states that the *visitation numbers peaked in 1987*, and compare it with the chart. This information is true, as is the second phrase, *the general trend has been on a steady rise*, so keep (A). Eliminate (B) because 1987 isn't really the *mid-1980s* and has not *tapered off*. Choice (C) is simply incorrect, and (D) can be eliminated because the growth has been somewhat erratic and not *linear*. Choice (A) is correct.

10. **B** The question asks for the LEAST acceptable response to the underlined portion, so the underlined word is correct. Use POE to eliminate answer choices that are similar in meaning to *foretold*. Choice (B) is the odd man out because *stated* just means "to express or declare," whereas the other choices mean "to predict." Therefore, (B) is the correct answer.

11. **D** The idea before the punctuation, *The park-ranger workforce is so diverse*, is a complete idea, as is the clause that follows it, *there are actually a few common attributes among park rangers*. A comma cannot separate two complete ideas, so eliminate (A). Look at (C) and (D), since the transition words *because* and *although* are exact opposites, and then refer back to the sentence to see if the two ideas are complimentary or contrasting. The words used in the sentence are *diverse* and *a few common*, so pick the transition word that indicates a contrast. Choice (D) is the answer.

The Ferry Godfather

12. **D** Sentence 2 begins with the phrase *this part*. Because a pronoun is used, go back and find the noun it refers to. Sentence 4 states that *Lincoln granted a special provision for that part of Virginia*, so the pronoun *this* refers to the *part of Virginia*. Therefore, Sentence 2 should go after Sentence 4, and (D) is the correct answer.

13. **C** The answer choices here suggest that this question is testing pronouns. Go back earlier in the sentence to find what the pronoun refers to. It's *the United States*, which is a collective noun and therefore singular. Eliminate (A) and (B). Eliminate (D) as well because a contraction is not necessary here. Choice (C) is the correct answer.

14. **D**   This question is testing comma usage, so check to see if the comma is separating two complete ideas or if it's necessary to break up the incomplete ideas. Neither appears to be the case, and this sentence does not need a break. Choice (D) is correct.

15. **A**   Use POE to determine whether the information in the map is consistent with the answer choices. Choice (A) seems like a good choice because Harpers Ferry is directly at the meeting point of the Shenandoah and Potomac Rivers, so keep it. Eliminate (B) because there is not enough information to support the 20-mile northeast approximation from Bolivar to Harpers Ferry. Choice (C) is also unsupported because Harpers Ferry is across the Shenandoah from Virginia, not Maryland, so eliminate (C). Choice (D) is incorrect because the Adirondack Mountains are not even on the map (they are actually in upstate New York). Choice (A) is correct.

16. **C**   Use POE for this question, as there doesn't seem to be a specific rule being tested. Eliminate (A) because *it* is an ambiguous pronoun that could refer to either the *armory* or *the Civil War*. Choice (B) is incorrect because *war* should not be the subject of this phrase as though it *saw Harpers Ferry* literally *change hands*. Same goes for (D), as *eight* should not be the subject of the phrase. Choice (C) makes it clear that it was *Harpers Ferry* that *changed hands*, making it the most precise answer choice and the correct answer.

17. **B**   If you look at the answer choices, you may notice that there isn't a huge difference between them; watch out for redundancy and try to be concise. The sentence uses the word *crucial* already, so eliminate (A), (C), and (D), which mean the same thing as *crucial*. The answer is (B).

18. **A**   Notice the question! Use POE to find an answer choice that is consistent with the *major importance* of Brown's raid. *A national discussion* started because of the raid, so keep (A). Choice (B) suggests the raid's importance, but *Herman Melville* is not mentioned anywhere else in the passage, so eliminate (B). Eliminate (C) and (D) because neither deals with the impact of the raid after the fact. Choice (A) is the answer.

19. **D**   The correct answer to this question needs to contrast the positive terms of *hero* and *freedom fighter*, so eliminate (B), which is also positive. Eliminate (A) because, taken literally, *filthy* means "unclean" and doesn't really contrast *hero*. Choice (C) is slang, and therefore incorrect. Choice (D) works because *vile* is consistent with *terrorist* and contrasts the positive tone of *hero*.

20. **B**   Use POE to find the clearest and most concise answer choice. Eliminate (A) and (D) because both use the ambiguous pronoun *it*. Choice (C) is incorrect because it's unclear how *Brown's rally* was named. This would change the overall meaning of the sentence. Choice (B) is the clearest and most concise, and therefore the correct answer.

21. **A**   The underlined portion uses a period, so check for complete and incomplete ideas. The period here separates two complete ideas, so the period is STOP punctuation that is being used correctly. Eliminate (D) because the transition *and* is used after the semicolon, turning the complete idea into an incomplete one. Choice (A) is correct.

22. **D** The underlined portion uses HALF-STOP punctuation (a colon) to separate the two ideas, so the first idea must be complete in order for the colon to work. The first idea is incomplete, so eliminate (A). Also eliminate (B) and (C), as STOP punctuation can be used only between two complete ideas. Choice (D) is the answer.

Stefan Zweig's Return

23. **D** Notice the question! When a question asks for the LEAST acceptable alternative, we can assume that the underlined portion, *large amount,* is correct. Choices (A), (B), and (C) can each be defined as a significant quantity of something, whereas (D) is associated with space, making it the LEAST acceptable answer and therefore the correct answer.

24. **B** In the following sentence, the author wonders about the *sudden interest* in Zweig's work after its *obscurity,* so an acceptable alternative to the underlined word would be something similar to *important. Relevant* is the best match, so (B) is the correct answer.

25. **C** Notice the question! The best way to combine these two sentences would be to turn it into one concise sentence. Choice (A) can be eliminated because the only difference is the semicolon, which basically serves the same purpose as a period. Choice (D) is awkward because *eliteness* is an improper form of the word *elite.* Therefore, (C) is the answer because it's grammatically correct and concise.

26. **A** This question is testing the use of apostrophes, and since the phrase *city's cultural elite* indicates possession, check to see whether or not the noun is singular or plural. Since *city* is singular, then the *'s* is correct, and (A) is the correct answer.

27. **B** The passage states that Zweig *published a near infinitude of works* and then goes on to list what the works are. Therefore, the examples of those works are necessary to the sentence. Eliminate (C) and (D). Also get rid of (A) since the examples are not for other types of work Zweig could get. Choice (B) is the correct answer.

28. **A** The paragraph opens by describing Zweig's relationship with Vienna as *tenuous* and then goes on to describe him as a *committed pacifist.* The next sentence states that his *pacifism was no longer looked on with such understanding,* which means that the conjunction must show a contrast. Eliminate (B) and (C). Choice (A) is correct because *however* shows a clear shift to a new idea.

29. **C** The answer to this question needs to address Zweig's personal stake in the European conflict, so eliminate (A) and (D), as neither choice addresses Zweig himself. Also eliminate (B) because the passage never states that he moved to America. Choice (C) is correct because it states Zweig has such *pride* in his home country of Vienna.

30. **D** Based on the answer choices, this question is testing pronoun uses. Since the pronoun in the sentence refers to the *privileged man,* eliminate (A); *which* cannot be used to refer to a person. The

correct answer will be an object pronoun, so eliminate (B) because it's a subject pronoun, and (C) because it's possessive. Choice (D) is the answer.

31. **A** Notice that the question asks for the choice that best supports the idea presented at the beginning of the sentence, which emphasizes more *"masculine" figures. Competitive sports* might be something that is traditionally considered *"masculine."* Therefore, the sentence seems to make sense as is, and (A) is the correct answer. The other choices can be eliminated because none of them refer to *masculine* behavior or activities.

32. **D** Based on the answer choices, this question is testing pronouns. Be careful, however, because the underlined portion is not addressing Zweig, but rather *many of us.* You can eliminate (A) and (C) because those are singular pronouns and therefore inconsistent. The next phrase states *our longing,* so the use of *our* in (D) creates consistency.

33. **C** Check out the answer choices, which show that verb tense is the concept being tested here. Look at the earlier part of the sentence that states *We know that things cannot be* and select the choice that is consistent with the verb *know.* Choice (C) is consistent and is therefore the best response.

For Figs? The Chimps Aren't Chumps

34. **A** Based on the answer choices, the question is testing comma usage. In a list of items, a comma must be used after each item in the list and before *and,* so eliminate (D). Also, (B) and (C) use unnecessary commas after *bacon* and *strips,* and there is no reason to slow down the flow of ideas in this sentence. Choice (A) is correct.

35. **C** Notice the question and use POE. Although the passage is ultimately concerned with *chimpanzees* seeking *fruit,* there is no information that suggests the *banana* was its *traditional diet.* Eliminate (A). The *chimpanzees waking and sleeping* habits are never discussed in the passage, so get rid of (B). Choice (C) works because the following paragraph discusses how *the nomadic chimpanzees set up their campsites within striking distance of the ripe fruits.* Therefore, keep (C) because it's consistent with this paragraph. *Human evolution* isn't discussed anywhere in the passage, so eliminate (D). The correct answer is (C).

36. **B** Notice the question! Look for the choice that serves as a transition and introduction. The previous paragraph ends with *for a chimpanzee, every day during a fruit-poor season can be like Black Friday where all the "shoppers" want the same hot item.* Use POE to find the choice that correlates with this statement. Eliminate (A) because the value of the *deals* is irrelevant. Eliminate (C) and (D) because *Thanksgiving* isn't necessary for the comparison between how *chimpanzees* get food and *Black Friday.* Choice (B) is the answer.

37. **A** Look out for the pronoun changes in the answer choices, specifically *its* and *their.* The subject of the sentence is *chimpanzees,* a plural noun. Eliminate (C) and (D) because *its* is singular. Eliminate (B) because the verb *sets* is singular and is not consistent with the plural subject *chimpanzees.* Choice (A) is correct.

38. **C** The definition in the sentence is *quick to disappear*, so use POE to find the word that most directly matches the meaning. Eliminate (B) and (D) because *desiccated* means to "dry up" and *eternal* would be the opposite of *quick to disappear*. *Ephemeral* means "brief" or "fleeting," so it's a good match, making (C) the correct answer.

39. **D** The word *than*, a comparison word, is used several times in the answer choices. Figure out what is being compared and eliminate answer choices that don't match. The sentence begins with *when the fruits were*, so the answer is going to have to compare to a time period. Only (D) does this, so it's the correct answer.

40. **B** Use POE to find a word that is consistent with the paragraph, which is a lack of food. *Gobbled*, *ate*, and *chomped* all refer to the consumption of food, but not necessarily a lack of food, so eliminate (A), (C), and (D). *Depleted* would fit because it means to "use up completely." Choice (B) is correct.

41. **C** The answer choices split between the verbs *have* and *has*, so find the subject and pick the verb that is consistent. The subject in this case is *findings*, which is plural, so eliminate (A) and (D), since *has* is singular. Eliminate (B) because the verb *lead* is present tense, but *have* is present perfect and a simple past tense verb is needed. The answer is (C).

42. **A** This question is testing diction, so find the word that is consistent with the context of the sentence. *Province*, (A), means "type of learning," which would fit well with the previous sentence, so keep it. *Providence* means "goodwill from a higher power," so it doesn't fit; eliminate (B). Choice (C) can be eliminated because *provenance* means "origin." Finally, eliminate (D) since *providential* means "lucky." Choice (A) is the answer.

43. **B** The answer choices don't seem to indicate that a clear grammatical rule is being tested here, so use POE. Choice (A) seems to change the intended meaning, since the adverb *initially* comes after what it's supposed to be modifying instead of before, which it should; eliminate (A). Choice (D) makes the same mistake, so eliminate it as well. Choice (B) is much clearer and more concise, so hold onto it. Choice (C) uses *then*, which is the wrong word choice (it indicates time) and should therefore be eliminated. Choice (B) is correct.

44. **D** This question asks whether this essay successfully relates the activities of *chimpanzees* to *Black Friday shoppers*. Humans are discussed very briefly in this passage, so the answer to the question is no. Eliminate (A) and (B). Eliminate (C) as well since *Black Friday shoppers* and *chimpanzees* are never directly compared. The correct answer is (D).

Section 3: Math (No Calculator)

1. **C** Translate the question into an equation. Let x equal the number, and then $2x = x - 4$. Solving for x, we find that $x = -4$. This is (C).

2. **C** Sonal needs s soil samples. If according to the question, he must have more than 6 samples, then $s > 6$. Also according to the question, he may have no more than 13 samples, so $s \leq 13$. Combining these two expressions, we find that $6 < s \leq 13$. This is (C).

3. **D** The graph of $f(x)$ has a y-intercept at $y = 3$. Because of this, we know that when $y = 3$, $x = 0$. $f(x)$ must then satisfy the condition that $f(0) = 3$. This is true only for (A) and (B). Alternatively, by recognizing that each equation is in the slope-intercept form: $f(x) = y = mx + b$, where b is the y-intercept, we can reach the same conclusion. Next, notice that the slope of the line is positive. That is, as the value of x increases, so too does y. Returning to the slope-intercept form, m gives the slope of the line. Only (D) has a positive coefficient (m). Choice (D), then, is the correct function.

4. **A** If $x + y = 0$, then $x = -y$. Using this relationship and substituting into the expression $x - y$, we find that $x - y = -y - y = -2y$. This is (A).

5. **A** This question requires factoring the expression $2x^2 - 6x - 8$. Begin by factoring 2 from the expression: $2(x^2 - 3x - 4)$. This expression is further factorable, giving $2(x - 4)(x + 1)$, which is (A).

6. **D** The question describes a ramp that forms a triangle, the length of which is the hypotenuse of the triangle. The height of the ramp (3 feet) is the length of the side of the triangle opposite the 35° angle. In general for some angle θ, $\sin\theta = \dfrac{opposite}{hypotenuse}$. In the question, this corresponds to $\sin 35° = \dfrac{opposite}{hypotenuse} = \dfrac{3}{length\ of\ ramp} \Rightarrow length\ of\ ramp = \dfrac{3}{\sin 35°}$. This is (D).

7. **D** This question requires evaluating both equations to determine the values of a and b. You can begin by solving either of the two equations for a or b, and then substituting the solution into the other equation. But note that the question asks for the value of $a + b$, so check to see if there's a faster way: Can you stack and add (or subtract) the equations? If you stack and add the equations, you get $7a + 7b = 77$. Now divide both sides of the equation by 7, resulting in $a + b = 11$. This is (D).

8. **D** When a function $f(x)$ is transformed into a function of the form $f(ax)$, where a is a constant, if $a > 0$, the function will be compressed horizontally by a factor of a. Here, $y = x^2 + 4$ can be represented as the parent function, and $y = 3x^2 + 4$ as the transformed function compressed horizontally versus the parent function, and thus narrower, by a factor of 3. This is (D). If you're not sure, try plugging values into each equation to construct a rough graph of each equation and compare them.

9. **C** Rearranging and factoring the expression provided in the question, we have $t^2 - 4t - 90 = 6 \Rightarrow t^2 - 4t - 96 = 0 \Rightarrow (t - 12)(t + 8) = 0$. Therefore, $t - 12 = 0$ and $t + 8 = 0$. t must then equal 12 or -8. If t represents the number of tickets Steven buys, then only $t = 12$ is consistent with the context of the question. If each ticket costs \$80, Steven must have spent \$80 × 12 = \$960. This is (C).

10. **C** We must find values of c and d by solving the system of equations in order to determine the value of $4c - 4d$. There are several ways to go about this. One way is to multiply the terms of the equation $2c + 3d = 17$ by -3 to get $-6c - 9d = -51$. If you stack and add this equation with the second equation, the result is $-4d = -12$, which solves to $d = 3$. Plug this value for d into the equation $6c + 5d = 39$ to get $6c + 15 = 39$, so $6c = 24$ and $c = 4$. Therefore, $4c - 4d = 4(4) - 4(3) = 16 - 12 = 4$. This is (C).

11. **A** Factoring the left side of the equation $x^2 + 2xy + y^2 = 64$ gives $(x + y)^2 = 64$. Taking the square root of both sides of the equation, we find that $x + y = 8$ or -8. The other equation provides that $y - x = 12$, so $y = x + 12$. Substitute this value of y into the first equation: either $x + (x + 12) = 8$, so $2x + 12 = 8$, $2x = -4$, and $x = -2$, or else or $x + (x + 12) = -8$, so $2x + 12 = -8$, so $2x = -20$, and $x = -10$. Therefore, x could be either -2 or -10, and only -10 is an option in the answers, so (A) is correct.

12. **D** Translate from English to math in bite-sized pieces. Make the price of a hot yoga lesson h and the price of a zero gravity yoga session z. If she offers 2 hot yoga and 3 zero gravity yoga sessions for \$400, then $2h + 3z = 400$. Similarly, if 4 hot yoga and 2 zero gravity yoga sessions are \$440, then $4h + 2z = 440$. Now, be sure to Read the Full Question: You want to know whether Samantha can create a package that's greater than \$800 but has fewer than 13 sessions. If you stack the two equations and then add them together, you get $6h + 5z = 880$. In other words, she can offer 6 hot yoga and 5 zero gravity yoga sessions (11 total sessions) for \$880. This satisfies her requirements, so you know the answer is "Yes"; eliminate (A) and (B). For (C), because you don't know the price of each lesson individually, you don't know yet whether 5 hot yoga and 5 zero gravity yoga sessions will be over \$800; leave (C) for now. For (D), if 6 hot yoga and 5 zero gravity yoga sessions were over \$800, then adding a zero gravity yoga session will still be over \$800. Given what you already know, (D) must be true; choose (D).

13. **B** Begin by simplifying the equation given. $(3p^2 + 14p + 24) - 2(p^2 + 7p + 20) = 3p^2 + 14p + 24 - 2p^2 - 14p - 40 = p^2 - 16 = 0$. Factoring the left side of the simplified equation, we find that $(p - 4)(p + 4) = 16$. Solving for p, we find that $p = \pm 4$. The value of $3p + 6$ must then be either $3(-4) + 6 = -6$ or $3(4) + 6 = 18$. The latter value is (B).

14. **A** Taking note that $i = \sqrt{-1}$, the expression $(2 + 8i)(1 - 4i) - (3 - 2i)(6 + 4i)$ becomes $(2 + 8\sqrt{-1})(1 - 4\sqrt{-1}) - (3 - 2\sqrt{-1})(6 + 4\sqrt{-1})$. Expanding, this becomes $2 - 8\sqrt{-1} + 8\sqrt{-1} - 32(\sqrt{-1})^2 - (18 + 12\sqrt{-1} - 12\sqrt{-1} - 8(\sqrt{-1})^2) = 2 - 32(\sqrt{-1})^2 - 18 + 8(\sqrt{-1})^2 = 8(\sqrt{-1})^2 - 32(\sqrt{-1})^2 - 16$. This further simplifies to $-8 + 32 - 16 = 8$. This is (A).

15. **C**   Plug In the Answers! The answer choices aren't in any particular order, and some numbers appear more than once, so you don't need to start in the middle. Instead, start with 9 because it is in three of the four choices. If $x = 9$, then $2\sqrt{9} = 9 - 3$. $\sqrt{9} = 3$, so the left side of the equation is $2 \times 3 = 6$, and the right side of the equation is $9 - 3 = 6$. This works, so 9 is part of the solution set; eliminate (B) because it doesn't include 9. Next, try $x = 1$: $2\sqrt{1} = 1 - 3$, which solves to $2 = -2$. This isn't true, so 1 is not part of the solution set; eliminate (D). Lastly, try $x = -1$: $2\sqrt{-1} = -1 - 3$. You cannot take the square root of a negative number, so this doesn't work. Eliminate (A) and choose (C).

16. **28**   Let s equal the number of staples required by the students and let p be the number of popsicle sticks required. If the number of staples the students will need is three times the number of popsicle sticks they will need, then $s = 3p$. If the students need 84 staples for this project, then $s = 84$. Substitute 84 for s to get $84 = 3p$. Divide both sides by 3 to get $28 = p$. The students will need 28 popsicle sticks.

17. **0**   If a parabola intersects the x-axis at the points $(5, 0)$ and $(-5, 0)$, it must be symmetric about the x-axis and centered at $x = 0$. The x-coordinate of its vertical axis of symmetry must then be 0.

18. **94**   The question describes a 100-meter ramp that forms a triangle. The length of this ramp corresponds to the hypotenuse of a triangle. The height of the ramp is the length of the side of the triangle opposite the 20° angle; the horizontal distance from the start of the ramp immediately below the entrance of the mall is the side of the triangle adjacent to the 20° angle. The function that relates adjacent and hypotenuse is cosine: $\cos\theta = \dfrac{adjacent}{hypotenuse}$. In this problem, $\cos 20° = \dfrac{x}{100}$, where x is the horizontal distance. Solve by multiplying both sides by 100: $\cos 20° = x$. Next, replace $\cos 20°$ with the value given in the problem, 0.939: $100(0.939) = x$. Multiply 100 by 0.939 to get $x = 93.9$, which rounds to 94.

19. **7**   Let x equal the number. Then, $2x = x - 5 \Rightarrow x = -5$. Three times that number plus seventeen minus that number is $3(-5) + 17 - (-5) = 7$.

20. $\dfrac{10}{3}$ $3x^2 + 2x - 8 = (x + 2)(3x - 4) = 0$. Solving $x + 2 = 0$ and $3x - 4 = 0$ for x, we find that the two solutions for x are -2 and $\dfrac{4}{3}$. The question asks us to subtract the value of the smaller solution from the larger solution. This difference is $\dfrac{4}{3} - (-2) = \dfrac{4}{3} + \dfrac{6}{3} = \dfrac{10}{3}$.

Section 4: Math (Calculator)

1. **B** To solve this question, simply subtract y from both sides of the equation to get $2y = 2$, which is (B).

2. **A** Whenever the question includes variables, plug in. If $m = 2$, then Merry would pay the one-time enrollment fee plus 2 months' worth of monthly fees, which is $50 + 15(2) = 80$. Plug in 2 for m in the answer choices to see which answer equals the target number of 80. In (A), $15(2) + 50 = 80$. This is the target number, so leave this answer, but be sure to check the other choices just in case. In (B), $15 + 50(2) = 115$. In (C), $15(2) - 50 = -20$, and in (D), $(15 + 50)(2) = 130$. Since none of the other answer choices equals the target number, the correct answer is (A).

3. **B** Since the question states that Rob is planning to bring his favorite guitar plus x additional guitars, he will have a total of $x + 1$ guitars. The question states that the variable x represents the number of additional guitars, so the number 1 must represent Rob's favorite guitar, which is (B).

4. **D** The best way to approach this question is through POE. According to the data in the table, the ratio of those who enjoy biology to those who enjoy chemistry is 14 to 18, which can be reduced to a ratio of 7 to 9; eliminate (A). The ratio of those who enjoy chemistry to those who don't enjoy chemistry is 18 to 6, which can be reduced to a ratio of 3 to 1; eliminate (B). The ratio of those who enjoy biology to those who don't enjoy chemistry is 14 to 6, which can be reduced to a ratio of 7 to 3; eliminate (C). The ratio of those who don't enjoy biology to those who enjoy chemistry is 10 to 18, which can be reduced to a ratio of 5 to 9; this matches (D).

5. **C** Dr. Goldberg takes 40% of substitute A, which consists of 60 grams. Mathematically, this can be expressed as $\frac{40}{100}(60)$ or $(0.4)(60) = 24$ grams. She takes 70% of substitute B, which consists of 110 grams. Mathematically, this can be expressed as $\frac{70}{100}(110)$ or $(0.7)(110) = 77$ grams. Substitute C will therefore consist of 24 grams + 77 grams = 101 grams, which is (C).

6. **D** To solve this question, simply factor out the largest value that fits within each of the terms in the expression provided. In this case, x^4, x^3, and x^2 are all divisible by x^2, so that is what you will want to factor out. Doing so will leave you with $x^2(x^2 - x - 1)$, which is (D).

7. **A** Since Officer Blake drives 480 miles at a rate of 1 mile per minute, his total drive time was 480 minutes. The question asks for Officer Blake's driving time in hours, so you need to convert those minutes into hours. Since there are 60 minutes in 1 hour, you can divide 480 minutes by 60 to determine that Officer Blake drove for 8 hours, which is (A).

8. **B** The goal here is to isolate x. Since the right-hand side of the equation is $-2x + 1$, you will want to subtract 1 from both sides, so eliminate (A) and (C). To get x by itself, you will want to divide by -2, not 2, so eliminate (D) and choose (B). Remember that when you multiply or divide across an

inequality sign using a negative number, you need to flip the inequality sign in the opposite direction, as reflected in (B).

9. **C** To solve this question, rearrange the expressions $(2x^2 + 4x + 8)$ and $(2x^2 - 4x + 7)$ in order to place the similar terms next to each other. Doing so will give you $2x^2 - 2x^2 + 4x - (-4x) + 8 - 7$ (remember to distribute the negative sign for each of the terms in the second expression). Simplifying this new expression will yield $0 + 8x + 1$, or $8x + 1$, (C). Another way to approach this question would be to plug in a simple number for x, such as $x = 2$, and match your target value with the values in the answer choices.

10. **A** The tallest hill that Adam measures is 55 feet high. Since 1 foot is equivalent to 12 inches, simply multiply $55 \times 12 = 660$ inches, (A).

11. **B** Triangle legs LN and MN are opposite and adjacent, respectively, to $\angle y$. Therefore, from SOHCAHTOA, we need to use the tangent trigonometric function. Plugging in the values that the question gives us into the equation for tangent, we get $\tan 40° = \dfrac{8}{MN}$. Now, use your calculator to determine that the length of MN most closely approximates 9.53, which is (B).

12. **D** If you represent the wooden skateboards with a w and the composite skateboards with a c, you can write two equations based on the information given in the question: $2w + 3c = 650$ and $3w + c = 450$. It is possible to isolate one of the variables and solve these two equations by substitution, but in this case it is easier simply to stack the equations on top of each other and add them together as follows:

$$\begin{array}{r} 2w + 3c = 650 \\ + 3w + c = 450 \\ \hline 5w + 4c = 1{,}100 \end{array}$$

Since the question asks for the price of five wooden skateboards and four composite skateboards, the answer is (D).

13. **D** The question states that the number of employees increases at the same rate per year, so you can determine this numerical increase by subtracting one year's total from the next year's total. Subtracting the 2013 total from the 2014 total gives $2{,}110 - 1{,}890 = 220$. To find the total in 2015, add 220 to the 2014 total: $2{,}110 + 220 = 2{,}330$. The question also states that the male percentages continue to decrease at the same rate, which, based on the data in the table, is 5% per year. The percent male in 2014 was 55%, so the percent male in 2015 will be 50%. 50% of 2,330 can be expressed as $\dfrac{50}{100}(2330)$ or $(0.5)(2330) = 1{,}165$, which is (D).

14. **B** The formula for determining an average can be expressed by $Average = \dfrac{Total}{\# \, of \, things}$. Plug the

values provided into the equation as follows: $11 = \dfrac{4+5+11+13+16+18+x}{7}$, or $11 = \dfrac{67+x}{7}$.

Multiply both sides by 7 to get $77 = 67 + x$. Subtract 67 from both sides to get $x = 10$, which is (B).

15. **C** There are a variety of ways to approach this question. You could solve one equation for s or t and substitute it into the other equation, but look to see if you can do it more simply by stacking and adding (or subtracting) the equations. If you double the first equation to get $34s + 40t = 118$, you can then stack and subtract the equations to eliminate t and solve for s, as follows:

$$
\begin{array}{r}
34s + 40t = 118 \\
-\ (30s + 40t = 110) \\
\hline
4s \qquad\quad = 8
\end{array}
$$

So, $4s = 8$ and therefore $s = 2$. Now plug in 2 for the value of s in one of the equations: $30(2) + 40t = 110$, so $40t = 110 - 60$, so $40t = 50$ and $t = \dfrac{5}{4} = 1.25$. Next, plug $s = 2$ into the answer

choices to determine which one matches your target of 1.25: (C), $\dfrac{5}{2s} = \dfrac{5}{2(2)} = \dfrac{5}{4} = 1.25$.

16. **A** The best way to approach this question is through POE. Choice (A) states that the majority of students polled logged in more times than they posted. The values along the x-axis of the graph are, for most of the data points, higher than the values along the y-axis of the graph, and thus (A) is true according to the data provided. This same data contradicts (B) and (C). You can eliminate (D) because the data does, in fact, allow you to draw a conclusion about the relationship between the variables.

17. **B** Don't get too thrown off by the graph. All you need to know to solve this question is that perpendicular lines have slopes that are the negative reciprocals of each other. Since the standard equation for a line is $y = mx + b$, the slope of the $f(x)$ line is 3. The slope of the $h(x)$ line must therefore be $-\dfrac{1}{3}$. The only answer choice that matches is (B).

18. **C** The best way to deal with this question is to Plug in the Answers (PITA), starting with (A). If $x = 6$, then $y = 3^6 = 729$. This is less than 4,000, so eliminate (A) and move to the next answer choice. If $x = 7$, then $y = 3^7 = 2{,}187$. This is still less than 4,000, so eliminate (B). If $x = 8$, then $y = 3^8 = 6{,}561$. This is greater than 4,000, so (C) must be the correct answer.

19. **D** The first step here is to simplify the equation and solve for a. Start by multiplying both sides by 16 to get $16a = 4a^2$. Divide both sides by 4 to get $4a = a^2$. Divide both sides by a to get $4 = a$. This is now your target answer. Plug $a = 4$ into the values of a in the answer choices to determine which one matches 4. Choice (D) is the answer, since $2\sqrt{a} = 2\sqrt{4} = 2(2) = 4$.

20. **B**   Since work = rate × time, the 280 in the equation must represent the total number of meals (i.e. the "work"). All three chefs are working together, so they work for the same amount of time, and x must represent that time. The coefficients 8, 4, and 2 must therefore represent the chefs' respective rates, or how many meals each prepares in a set amount of time. Since 8 is the greatest of these three coefficients, $8x$ must be the meal output of the fastest chef, either (B) or (C). Now you need to solve the equation: $8x + 4x + 2x = 280$. Combining like terms gives you $14x = 280$. Divide both sides by 14 to determine that $x = 20$. This number represents the amount of time that the chefs worked, so the actual number of meals prepared by the fastest chef would be $8 \times 20 = 160$ meals, which is (B).

21. **D**   Start by finding the slope of the line provided on the graph using the points $(0, -4)$ and $(6, 0)$ and the point-slope formula: $\dfrac{y_2 - y_1}{x_2 - x_1} = \dfrac{0 - (-4)}{6 - 0} = \dfrac{4}{6} = \dfrac{2}{3}$. When this line is reflected across the line $y = x$, the x and y values switch, so the new slope would be the reciprocal of the original slope. Since our original slope was $\dfrac{2}{3}$, our new slope will be $\dfrac{3}{2}$. The numerator here reflects the gain or loss of pieces of fruit in the harvest, and the denominator reflects the nutrients subtracted or added. This means that for every two nutrients added, there will be a harvest gain of three pieces of fruit, which is (D).

22. **D**   The issue that needs clarification here is whether the students polled by Joe thought that a score of 1 or a score of 5 was good. Since (A) and (C) deal with George's poll, they would do nothing to help clarify this ambiguity. Choice (B) might help us to figure out which of the students Joe polled were interested in the Model UN Club; it would not help to determine whether 1 or 5 was the best rating. Choice (D) is correct.

23. **C**   In order to determine the normal cost for renting skis and snowboards, you need to write two equations and then manipulate and solve those equations. If you call skis x and snowboards y, your two equations will be $5x + 2y = 370$ and $3x + 4y = 390$. Look for a way to stack and add the equations to eliminate one of the variables. For instance, multiply the first equation by 2 to get $10x + 4y = 740$, and then stack and subtract the equations, as follows:

$$
\begin{array}{r}
10x + 4y = 740 \\
-\ (3x + 4y = 390) \\
\hline
7x \qquad\quad = 350
\end{array}
$$

So, $7x = 350$ and $x = 50$, so the price of a pair of skis is \$50. Plug this number back into either equation to find the cost of a snowboard: $10(50) + 4y = 740$, so $4y = 740 - 500$ and $4y = 240$. Therefore, $y = 60$, the cost of a snowboard. So, the cost of two pairs of skis and two snowboards would normally be $2(50) + 2(60) = 100 + 120 = 220$. Finally, remember that prices are discounted by 10%, so multiply the price of $220 by 10% to get $22, and subtract $22 from the price. The final cost of two pairs of skis and two snowboards is $220 - 22 = 198$, which is (C).

24. **A** Start by simplifying $8x + 8y = 18$ by dividing each term by 8: $x + y = \frac{18}{8}$ or $: x + y = \frac{9}{4}$. The second equation provided in the question can be factored: $x^2 - y^2$ is the same as $(x + y)(x - y)$, so the second equation can also be written $(x + y)(x - y) = -\frac{3}{8}$. Since you know that $x + y = \frac{9}{4}$, you can rewrite the second equation as $\frac{9}{4}(x - y) = -\frac{3}{8}$. Multiply both sides by $\frac{4}{9}$: $x - y = -\frac{3}{8}\left(\frac{4}{9}\right)$ or $x - y = -\frac{1}{6}$. Since the question asks for the value of $2x - 2y$, simply multiply everything by 2: $2(x - y) = 2\left(-\frac{1}{6}\right) = -\frac{1}{3}$, which is (A).

25. **D** If each minute of his workout time burns 50 calories, and he wants to consume no fewer than 2,000 calories, Shaun must work out for a minimum of $\frac{2,000}{50} = 40$ minutes. If he wants to consume no more than 2,500 calories, Shaun must work out for a maximum of $\frac{2,500}{50} = 50$ minutes. Since the question asks for the inequality that represents the number of minutes for which Shaun will burn off as many calories as he consumes, (D) is correct, as it includes both the minimum (40 minutes) and maximum (50 minutes) amount of time that he can work out. Choice (C) is incorrect because the answer should include 50 (he can work out for a "maximum" of 50 minutes, so he could work out for 50 minutes), but the lesser than sign ("<") excludes 50.

26. **A** There are 162 games in the season, so the team needs a total of $162 \times 45,500 = 7,371,000$ ticket purchases to have a mean of 45,500 ticket purchases per game for the season. The 60 games with an average total ticket purchase of 43,000 gives a total of 2,580,000 ticket purchases, leaving 4,791,000 ticket purchases left for the team to reach its goal. Dividing 4,791,000 by 102 makes (A) the closest value to the average of 46,971 ticket purchases per game the team needs to make.

27. **B** The best way to deal with this question is through POE. If the polynomial has zeroes of 2 and –3, then that means you have two points: (2, 0) and (–3, 0)—eliminate (A) and (C). Since it is given in the question that $a > 0$ when the parabola is in the form $y = ax^2 + bx + c$, the parabola must be pointed upwards—eliminate (D) and choose (B).

28. **A** Since the radius of the circle is 4, the area of the entire circle is $\pi r^2 = \pi(4^2) = 16\pi$. Sector *POR* has an area of 8π and sector *ROQ* has an area of 6π, so the remaining sector (*QOP*) has an area of $16\pi - 8\pi - 6\pi = 2\pi$. You can set up a proportion to determine the associated angle using the following formula: $\dfrac{sector\ area}{total\ area} = \dfrac{sector\ angle}{360°}$. Using the numbers you now have, your calculation will look like this: $\dfrac{2\pi}{16\pi} = \dfrac{sector\ angle}{360°}$ or $\dfrac{1}{8} = \dfrac{sector\ angle}{360}$. Multiply both sides of the equation by 360 to determine that the sector angle is 45°, which is (A).

29. **D** 16% of the 200 medical residents named oncology as their first choice: $\dfrac{16}{100}(200)$ or $(0.16)(200) = 32$ residents. 40% of the 200 medical residents named cardiology as their first choice: $\dfrac{40}{100}(200)$ or $(0.4)(200) = 80$ residents. Of these 80 residents, 20% chose oncology as their second choice: $\dfrac{20}{100}(80)$ or $(0.2)(80) = 16$ residents. The total number of residents who named oncology as either their first or second choice was therefore $32 + 16 = 48$ residents. To find the value of x, you need to subtract the percentages given in the question from the total, 100%: $100 - 40 - 16 - 34 = x = 10\%$. Now, plug $x = 10$ into the answer choices in order to determine which one matches your target of 48 residents. Only (D) works: $x^2 - 24x + 188 = 100 - 24(10) + 188 = 100 - 240 + 188 = 48$.

30. **B** If the original graph is reflected across the x-axis, the x-values will remain the same but the y-values will switch signs. Since the y-axis represents distance from start, negative y-values means that the car is now going in reverse. The only answer that matches this information is (B).

31. **30** Translate English to math. "What number divided by two is equal to that same number minus 15?" can be written as an equation, with x representing the missing number: $\dfrac{x}{2} = x - 15$. Add 15 to both sides of the equation to get $\dfrac{x}{2} + 15 = x$. Subtract $\dfrac{x}{2}$ from both sides to get $15 = \dfrac{x}{2}$. Multiply both sides by 2 to get $x = 30$.

32. **4** When dealing with values that are directly proportional, you can use the equation $\dfrac{x_1}{y_1} = \dfrac{x_2}{y_2}$. For this question, you can call the number of hours spent playing *Call of Destiny* x and the number of hours spent in the game room y. Your equation will then look like this: $\dfrac{6}{8} = \dfrac{3}{y_2}$. Cross-multiply to get $6y_2 = 3(8)$ or $6y_2 = 24$. Divide both sides of the equation by 6 to get $y_2 = 4$.

33. **13.5** Start by translating English to math. Make s the price of Smooth-Glide pens and e the price of Easy-Write pencils. If 12 pens and 8 pencils cost \$16, then $12s + 8e = 16$. Similarly, if 6 pens and 10 pencils cost \$11, then $6s + 10e = 11$. Remember to Read the Full Question! The question wants the price of 9 pens and 9 pencils. If you stack the equations and add, you get $18s + 18e = 27$. This is exactly double the number of pens and pencils you want, so divide the entire equation by 2 to get $9s + 9e = 13.5$.

34. **2 or $\dfrac{10}{3}$**

There are a few different ways to approach this question. Since the calculator is permitted

on this section of the test, you can put the equation into the standard $ax^2 + bx + c = 0$ form

and plug that equation into the "$y =$" button on your graphing calculator. The equation, once

rearranged, is $3x^2 - 16x + 20 = 0$. You can trace the graph or use the "calc" feature to calcu-

late the zeroes, which are the same as the values of x. Doing so will yield values of $x = 2$ and

$x = 3.33$. Alternatively, you can factor the equation the long way or use the quadratic formula,

$\dfrac{-b \pm \sqrt{b^2 - 4ac}}{2a}$. In this equation, $a = 3$, $b = -16$, and $c = 20$. Plugging those values into the

equation, you get $\dfrac{-(-16) \pm \sqrt{(-16)^2 - 4(3)(20)}}{2(3)} = \dfrac{16 \pm \sqrt{16}}{6} = \dfrac{16 \pm 4}{6}$. Therefore, the

solutions are $\dfrac{16 + 4}{6} = \dfrac{20}{6} = \dfrac{10}{3}$ and $\dfrac{16 - 4}{6} = \dfrac{12}{6} = 2$. Either value ($\dfrac{10}{3}$ or 2) is a valid answer.

35. **5** Since you are looking for the value of x for which the population surpassed the number of dwell-ings, you can set up an inequality: $3^x > 2x + 100$. Now, simply plug in values for x starting with $x = 1$ until the left-hand side of the inequality is larger than the right-hand side. Using the values $x = 1$, $x = 2$, $x = 3$, and $x = 4$, you will find that the left-hand side of the inequality is less than the right-hand side. Using $x = 5$, $3^5 = 243$, and $2(5) + 100 = 110$, making the left-hand of the inequality greater than the right-hand side. Therefore, the answer is 5.

36. **5,406** The first step here is to add Team Charlie's and Team Delta's total currents together as follows:

$$
\begin{array}{r}
50 + 12i \\
+\ \ 40 - 9i \\
\hline
90 + 3i
\end{array}
$$

Next, use FOIL to multiply this value by the total current from Team Epsilon: $(90 + 3i)$ $(60 - 2i) = 5,400 - 90(2i) + 60(3i) - 2i(3i) = 5400 - 180i + 180i - 6i^2 = 5,400 - 6i^2$. Since

$i^2 = -1$, this is equivalent to $5,400 - 6(-1) = 5,400 + 6 = 5,406$. If you have a calculator that is able to deal with imaginary numbers, you can simply type the expressions into your calculator, which will solve everything for you.

37. **860** The question states that there are 2,400 total inhabitants of Centre Hill, so if there are an equal number of adults and children, then there are 1,200 of each. Since there are 200 more adult females than adult males, you can set up two equations: $f + m = 1,200$ and $f = m + 200$. You can rewrite the second equation by subtracting m from both sides: $f - m = 200$. Next, stack and add the two equations as follows:

$$
\begin{array}{rl}
f + m = & 1,200 \\
+ \quad f - m = & \underline{\quad 200} \\
2f \quad = & 1,400
\end{array}
$$

Divide both sides of the equation by 2 to determine that $f = 700$. The number of women living uptown is therefore 8% of 700: $\dfrac{8}{100}(700)$ or $(0.08)(700) = 56$. The number of children living in the suburbs is 67% of 1,200: $\dfrac{67}{100}(1,200)$ or $(0.67)(1,200) = 804$. The sum of these two figures is $56 + 804 = 860$.

38. **250** Using your information from question 37, you can determine that the total number of adult males prior to the addition of the annex is $1,200 - 700 = 500$. The original percentage of adult males living Uptown is 9% of 500: $\dfrac{9}{100}(500)$ or $(0.09)(500) = 45$. Since the question states that the percentage of adult males living Uptown decreases to 6%, you can conclude that the 45 adult males living Uptown after the annexation constitute 6% of the total adult male population: $45 = \dfrac{6}{100}(x)$ or $45 = (0.06)x$. Divide both sides of the equation by 0.06 to determine that $x = 750$. Since the original number of adult males was 500, $750 - 500 = 250$ additional adult males live in The Annex.

RAW SCORE CONVERSION TABLE — SECTION AND TEST SCORES

Raw Score (# of correct answers)	Math Section Score	Reading Test Score	Writing and Language Test Score
0	200	10	10
1	200	10	10
2	210	10	10
3	230	11	10
4	240	12	11
5	260	13	12
6	280	14	13
7	290	15	13
8	310	15	14
9	320	16	15
10	330	17	16
11	340	17	16
12	360	18	17
13	370	19	18
14	380	19	19
15	390	20	19
16	410	20	20
17	420	21	21
18	430	21	21
19	440	22	22
20	450	22	23
21	460	23	23
22	470	23	24
23	480	24	25
24	480	24	25
25	490	25	26
26	500	25	26
27	510	26	27
28	520	26	28
29	520	27	28
30	530	28	29
31	540	28	30
32	550	29	30
33	560	29	31
34	560	30	32
35	570	30	32
36	580	31	33
37	590	31	34
38	600	32	34
39	600	32	35
40	610	33	36
41	620	33	37
42	630	34	38
43	640	35	39
44	650	35	40
45	660	36	
46	670	37	
47	670	37	
48	680	38	
49	690	38	
50	700	39	
51	710	40	
52	730	40	
53	740		
54	750		
55	760		
56	780		
57	790		
58	800		

Please note that the numbers in the table may shift slightly depending on the SAT's scale from test to test; however, you can still use this table to get an idea of how your performance on the practice tests will translate to the actual SAT.

CONVERSION EQUATION — SECTION AND TEST SCORES

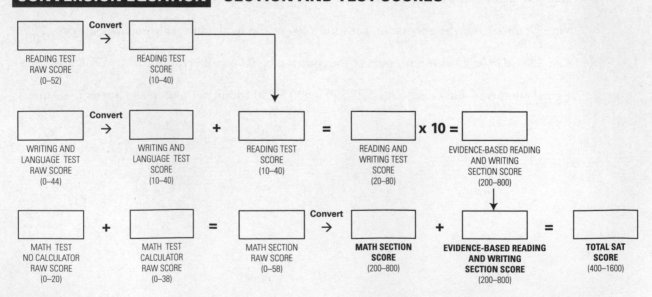

Chapter 24
Practice Test 3

Reading Test

65 MINUTES, 52 QUESTIONS

Turn to Section 1 of your answer sheet to answer the questions in this section.

Questions 1-10 are based on the following passage.

The passage that follows is adapted from a 1907 novel that follows the actions of an English baronet who, using a secret identity, leads a group of wealthy Englishmen in daring rescues of members of the French aristocracy during the Reign of Terror.

Sir Andrew's face had become almost transfigured. His eyes shone with enthusiasm; hero-worship, love, admiration for his leader seemed literally to glow upon
Line his face. "The Scarlet Pimpernel, Mademoiselle," he
5 said at last "is the name of a humble English wayside flower; but it is also the name chosen to hide the identity of the best and bravest man in all the world, so that he may better succeed in accomplishing the noble task he has set himself to do."
10 "Ah, yes," here interposed Comtesse's son, "I have heard speak of this Scarlet Pimpernel. They say in Paris that every time a royalist escapes to England that devil, the Public Prosecutor, receives a paper with that little flower designated in red upon it. . . . Yes?"
15 "Yes, that is so," assented Lord Antony.
"Then he will have received one such paper to-day?"
"Undoubtedly."
"Oh! I wonder what he will say!" said Suzanne,
20 merrily. "I have heard that the picture of that little red flower is the only thing that frightens him."
"Ah, monsieur," sighed the Comtesse, "it all sounds like a romance, and I cannot understand it all."
"Why should you try, Madame?"
25 "But, tell me, why should you and your leader spend your money and risk your lives when you set

foot in France, all for us French men and women, who are nothing to you?"
"Sport, Madame la Comtesse, sport," asserted Lord
30 Antony, with his jovial, loud and pleasant voice; "we are a nation of sportsmen, you know, and just now it is the fashion to pull the hare from between the teeth of the hound."
"Ah, no, no, not sport only, Monsieur . . . you have
35 a more noble motive, I am sure, for the good work you do."
"Faith, Madame, I would like you to find it then . . . as for me, I vow, I love the game, for this is the finest sport I have yet encountered.—Hair-breadth escapes . . .
40 the devil's own risks!—Tally ho!—and away we go!"
But the Comtesse shook her head, still incredulously. To her it seemed preposterous that these young men and their great leader, all of them rich, probably wellborn, and young, should for
45 no other motive than sport, run the terrible risks, which she knew they were constantly doing. Their nationality, once they had set foot in France, would be no safeguard to them. Anyone found harboring or assisting suspected royalists would be ruthlessly
50 condemned and summarily executed, whatever his nationality. And this band of young Englishmen had, to her own knowledge, bearded the implacable and bloodthirsty tribunal of the Revolution, within the very walls of Paris itself, and had snatched away condemned
55 victims, almost from the very foot of the guillotine. With a shudder, she recalled the events of the last few

CONTINUE ▶

days, her escape from Paris with her two children, all three of them hidden beneath the hood of a rickety cart, and lying amidst a heap of turnips and cabbages,
60 not daring to breathe, whilst the mob howled outside.

It had all occurred in such a miraculous way; she and her husband had been placed on the list of "suspected persons," which meant that their trial and death were but a matter of days—of hours, perhaps.

65 Then came the hope of salvation; the mysterious epistle, signed with the enigmatical scarlet device; the clear, peremptory directions; the parting from the Comte de Tournay, which had torn the poor wife's heart in two; the hope of reunion; the flight with her
70 two children; the covered cart; that awful hag driving it, who looked like some horrible demon, with the ghastly trophy on her whip handle!

The Comtesse looked round at the quaint, old-fashioned English inn, the peace of this land of civil
75 and religious liberty. She closed her eyes to shut out the haunting vision of that West Barricade, and of the mob retreating panic-stricken when the old hag spoke of the plague.

Every moment under that cart she expected
80 recognition, arrest, herself and her children tried and condemned, and these young Englishmen, under the guidance of their brave and mysterious leader, had risked their lives to save them all.

And all only for sport? The Comtesse's eyes as she
85 sought those of Sir Andrew plainly told him that she thought that *he* at any rate rescued his fellowmen from terrible and unmerited death, through a higher and nobler motive than his friend would have her believe.

1

The passage as a whole is primarily concerned with

A) considering the reasons behind a set of exploits.

B) examining the causes of a revolution.

C) comparing the self-confidence of two different men.

D) questioning the ruthlessness of a government.

2

Based on the information in the passage, it can be inferred that the when the Comtesse escaped, the people in the nearby crowd did not approach her cart because

A) the cart was moving too quickly.

B) they feared arrest and death by guillotine.

C) the woman driving the cart was known to be violent.

D) they were afraid of contracting a disease.

3

Which choice provides the best evidence for the answer to the previous question?

A) Lines 51-55 ("And this . . . guillotine")

B) Lines 65-70 ("Then came . . . children")

C) Lines 70-72 ("the covered . . . handle")

D) Lines 75-78 ("She . . . plague")

4

As used in line 14, "designated" most nearly means

A) budgeted.

B) chosen.

C) classed.

D) illustrated.

5

In context, the phrase "pull the hare from between the teeth of the hound" (lines 32-33) refers chiefly to

A) dangerous English hunting customs.

B) plans to avenge the deaths of innocent Englishmen.

C) delivering members of the French aristocracy from harm.

D) the cruelty of French nobles toward revolutionaries.

CONTINUE

6

Which choice provides the best evidence for the answer to the previous question?

A) Lines 37-40 ("Faith . . . go")

B) Lines 46-48 ("Their nationality . . . them")

C) Lines 48-51 ("Anyone . . . nationality")

D) Lines 61-64 ("It had . . . perhaps")

7

In lines 41-46, the Comtesse is best described as

A) critical.

B) anxious.

C) relieved.

D) perplexed.

8

As used in line 52, "bearded" most nearly means

A) camouflaged.

B) braved.

C) embellished.

D) masked.

9

Lines 73-78 provide a contrast between

A) tranquility and turmoil.

B) traditionalism and modernity.

C) freedom and ignorance.

D) austerity and hysteria.

10

The use of italics in line 86 primarily serves to emphasize a perceived distinction between

A) the reasons behind one man's actions and those behind his companions' actions.

B) the effectiveness of two different methods of carrying out the same plan.

C) honest, noble motivations for rescue and rescue for monetary gain.

D) a desire for adventure and a desire for public admiration and praise.

CONTINUE

No Test Material On This Page

Questions 11-21 are based on the following passage and supplementary material.

This passage is adapted from Daniel J. Boorstin, *The Creators: A History of Heroes of the Imagination.* © 1992 by Daniel J. Boorstin.

The great works of Greek temple architecture were made to be viewed from the outside, not to be experienced from within. In one of the grand revisions
Line of the creative imagination, the Romans would change
5 all this. They built an architecture of interiors, of vast enclosed spaces. And this was a new kind of space—within arches, vaults, and domes, in omnipresent dominating curves, where walls became ceilings, and ceilings reached up to the heavens. The artificial world,
10 the world of interiors that architects would make for man, was transformed into a new curvesomeness. The classic Greeks had gathered out in the open air. Roman architecture brought people indoors to share their public and exchange their private concerns.

15 This grand Roman innovation in architecture would be accomplished in two centuries as the essential ingredient, concrete, was perfected gradually by trial and error.

The Roman Empire had brought cities into being
20 and created a far-flung urban culture with common needs. And the new architectural creations arose from the needs of these Roman cities. While the glory of classic Greek architecture was in its temples to gods and civic deities, the grandeur of Roman architecture
25 began in the public baths. How and why Romans acquired their mania for public baths remains a mystery. But its signs were everywhere.

Some of the earliest were the grand Stabian baths of the second century B.C. at Pompeii, with elegant
30 arches and a soaring conical dome topped by a central opening that anticipated one of the most appealing features of the Pantheon three centuries later. Grand public bath buildings sanitized and enriched urban life all across the Roman provinces. Besides the
35 *balneum,* or private bath, found in the town houses and country villas of wealthy Romans, there were the *thermae,* or public baths. Some historians count these among "the fairest creations of the Roman Empire." During the second century B.C. they multiplied at a
40 great rate in Rome. It became common for a public-spirited citizen to make a gift of a public bath building to his neighborhood. Others were built commercially by contractors who hoped to make a profit from

admission fees. Agrippa's census (33 B.C.) counted 170
45 such establishments in Rome, and a century later Pliny the Elder (23 A.D.–79 A.D.) had to give up counting. Soon there were nearly a thousand. When Pliny the Younger arrived for a brief stay at his country villa near Ostia, and did not want to fuel his own furnaces, he
50 found "a great convenience" in the three public baths in the neighboring village.

The essentials of a public bath were quite the same everywhere—a changing room, a sweating room heated by hot-air passages under the floor or
55 in the walls, a large vaulted hall gently heated with intermediate temperatures, an unheated frigidarium partly open to the sky with a cold plunge, and a rotunda heated by circulating vapor, open at the top to admit sunlight at noon and in the afternoon. In
60 addition, there were swimming pools. Nearby areas provided for strolling, for conversation, for sunning, for exercise, for various kinds of handball, hoop-rolling, and wrestling. Attached were concert halls, libraries, and gardens. The baths at their best were
65 public art museums and museums of contemporary art. To them we owe the preservation of some of our best copies of Greek sculpture and our great treasures of Roman sculpture.

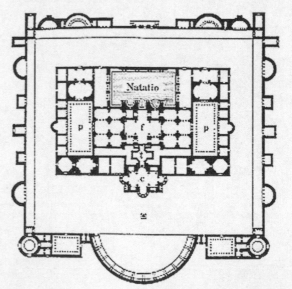

p Palestra f Frigidarium t Tepidarium c Caldarium

Rome, Baths of Diocletian

CONTINUE

11

Which of the following best expresses the main idea of the passage?

A) Public baths in Roman society provided not only sanitary facilities but also social and cultural gathering places.

B) Roman architecture rejected the exterior-based Greek traditions in favor of large, public, interior spaces.

C) The large curved spaces that concrete made possible in Roman architecture were more appropriate for civic than for religious functions.

D) A combination of civic need and innovation in building materials led Romans to great architectural innovation.

12

In the first paragraph (lines 1-14), what is the most likely reason the author mentions Greek temple architecture?

A) To show how Roman architectural innovations improved upon the earlier Greek traditions

B) To locate the new trends in architecture developed by the Romans within architectural history

C) To prove that Roman architects were more creative in their imagining of interior space than Greek architects

D) To argue that the new interior spaces created by Romans were better suited to religious architecture than Greek temples were

13

As used in line 7, "omnipresent" most nearly means

A) large.

B) pervasive.

C) eternal.

D) imposing.

14

The author implies that which of the following was critical to Roman architectural developments?

A) The need for large, interior spaces where urban culture could be expressed

B) The convenience of public baths to people of all social strata

C) The development over time of construction techniques using concrete

D) The rapid expansion of baths into community and cultural centers

15

Which choice provides the best evidence for the answer to the previous question?

A) Lines 5-6 ("They . . . spaces")

B) Lines 15-18 ("This . . . error")

C) Lines 22-27 ("While . . . mystery")

D) Lines 42-47 ("Others . . . thousand")

16

What is the primary purpose of the third paragraph (lines 19-27) in relation to the structure of the passage as a whole?

A) To introduce a need that gave rise to innovations described elsewhere in the passage

B) To reinforce a contrast mentioned in the first paragraph and provide additional detail

C) To emphasize the mysterious nature of the innovations discussed in the passage

D) To dismiss an earlier thesis in favor of the one described in the following paragraphs

CONTINUE

17

As used in line 31, "anticipated" most nearly means

A) foreshadowed.

B) expected.

C) prevented.

D) enjoyed.

18

It can be inferred from the description of public baths in the last paragraph that

A) a visit to the bath might be quite different from a visit to a modern bath.

B) they were much like modern gyms; patrons would first exercise, then bathe.

C) Romans believed in the benefits of exposing oneself to a variety of temperatures.

D) the convenience of having so many activities in one location is unparalleled in history.

19

The author believes that the most exemplary Roman baths provided

A) a venue for architectural experimentation.

B) important sanitary facilities for citizens.

C) fine arts enrichment to the public.

D) community gathering spaces.

20

Which choice provides the best evidence for the answer to the previous question?

A) Lines 15-18 ("This grand . . . error")

B) Lines 21-22 ("And the new . . . cities")

C) Lines 32-34 ("Grand public . . . provinces")

D) Lines 64-66 ("The baths . . . art")

21

Which of the following is supported by information in both the passage and the diagram?

A) Roman baths usually included frigidariums.

B) The palestrae were located on opposite sides of the building.

C) Commercial contractors always built public baths in a rectangular shape.

D) The natatio was often used for wrestling and hoop-rolling.

CONTINUE

No Test Material On This Page

Questions 22-31 are based on the following passage.

This passage is adapted from a speech delivered by Rafael Palma of the Philippines on November 22, 1919, as a senator for the country's fourth district. In the passage, Palma discusses the reasons that women should be allowed to vote. Palma's speech was delivered in the context of the first session of the fifth Filipino legislature, which was preparing to vote on the question of female suffrage.

I have seldom felt so proud of being a
representative of the people as now, when it gives me
an opportunity to advocate a cause which cannot be
Line represented or defended in this chamber by those
5 directly and particularly affected by it, owing to the
leaven of prejudice that the beliefs and ideas of the
past have left in the mind of modern man. The cause
of female suffrage is one sure to strike a sympathetic
chord in every unprejudiced man, because it represents
10 the cause of the weak who, deprived of the means to
defend themselves, are compelled to throw themselves
upon the mercy of the strong.

But it is not on this account alone that this cause
has my sympathy and appeals to me. It has, besides,
15 the irresistible attraction of truth and justice, which
no open and liberal mind can deny. If our action as
legislators must be inspired by the eternal sources of
right, if the laws passed here must comply with the
divine precept to give everybody his due, then we
20 cannot deny woman the right to vote, because to do
otherwise would be to prove false to all the precepts
and achievements of democracy and liberty which
have made this century what may be properly called
the century of vindication.

25 Female suffrage is a reform demanded by the
social conditions of our times, by the high culture of
woman, and by the aspiration of all classes of society
to organize and work for the interests they have in
common. We cannot detain the celestial bodies in
30 their course; neither can we check any of those moral
movements that gravitate with irresistible force
towards their center of attraction: Justice. The moral
world is governed by the same laws as the physical
world, and all the power of man being impotent to
35 suppress a single molecule of the spaces required for
the gravitation of the universe, it is still less able to
prevent the generation of the ideas that take shape in
the mind and strive to attain to fruition in the field of
life and reality.

40 It is an interesting phenomenon that whenever
an attempt is made to introduce a social reform, in
accordance with modern ideas and tendencies and in
contradiction with old beliefs and prejudices, there is
never a lack of opposition, based on the maintenance
45 of the *statu quo*, which it is desired to preserve at
any cost. As was to be expected, the eternal calamity
howlers and false prophets of evil raise their voices on
this present occasion, in protest against female suffrage,
invoking the sanctity of the home and the necessity of
50 perpetuating customs that have been observed for many
years.

Frankly speaking, I have no patience with people
who voice such objections. If this country had not been
one of the few privileged places on our planet where
55 the experiment of a sudden change of institutions
and ideals has been carried on most successfully,
without paralyzation, retrogression, disorganization or
destruction, I would say that the apprehension and fears
of those who oppose this innovation might be justified.

60 However, in less than a generation our country,
shaken to its very foundations by the great social
upheavals known as revolutions, has seen its old
institutions crumble to pieces and other, entirely new
institutions rise in their place; it has seen theories,
65 beliefs, and codes of ethics, theretofore looked upon
as immovable, give way to different principles and
methods based upon democracy and liberty, and despite
all those upheavals and changes which have brought
about a radical modification in its social and political
70 structure, or rather in consequence of the same, our
people has become a people with modern thoughts and
modern ideals, with a constitution sufficiently robust
and strong to withstand the ravages of the struggle for
existence, instead of remaining a sickly and atrophied
75 organism, afraid of everything new and opposed to
material struggles from fear of the wrath of Heaven and
from a passive desire to live in an ideal state of peace
and well-being.

In view of the fruitful results which those
80 institutions of liberty and democracy have brought
to our country; and considering the marked progress
made by us, thanks to these same institutions, in all the
orders of national life, in spite of a few reactionists and
ultra-conservatives, who hold opinions to the contrary

CONTINUE

85 and regret the past, I do not and cannot, understand
how there still are serious people who seriously object
to the granting of female suffrage, one of the most
vivid aspirations now agitating modern society.

22

In this speech, the role that Palma plays can best be
described as that of

A) an analyst discussing the advantages of each side
of an issue.

B) a traditionalist cautioning against the dangers of
reform.

C) an idealist arguing for a social change.

D) a politician rousing support for his party.

23

Based on the information in lines 1-7, it can be
inferred that at the time that Palma gave his speech
women were

A) Palma's primary supporters.

B) not allowed to speak before the Filipino
legislature.

C) not represented by any other Filipino leaders.

D) not viewed with sympathy by the members of the
Filipino legislature.

24

As used in line 30, "check" most nearly means

A) certify.

B) inspect.

C) advise.

D) stop.

25

Based on the information presented in Palma's
speech, it can be inferred that some of those who
oppose the bill to give women the right to vote

A) believe that trying to give women the right to vote
would be equivalent to trying to check the sun
and moon in their course.

B) are prejudiced against the causes of modern men
and women and do not support liberal democracy.

C) claim that doing so will be damaging to home life
and may disrupt long-established traditions.

D) assert that any sudden changes to the country's
civic institutions might permanently paralyze the
country.

26

Which choice provides the best evidence for the
answer to the previous question?

A) Lines 25-29 ("Female suffrage . . . common")

B) Lines 46-51 ("As was to . . . years")

C) Lines 64-67 ("It has seen . . . liberty")

D) Lines 79-88 ("In view . . . society")

27

The principal rhetorical effect of the phrase
"paralyzation, retrogression, disorganization, or
destruction" in lines 57-58 is to

A) highlight with increasing force how changes in
ideals and institutions can damage a society.

B) emphasize the number of ways in which
past changes have not negatively affected the
Philippines.

C) show that the Philippines became disabled, after
which it reversed its social progress, became
disorganized, and was nearly destroyed.

D) suggest four methods by which the legislature
could halt the progress of radical social upheavals.

CONTINUE

28

Palma refers to "great social upheavals" in order to

A) use an analogy to show that allowing women to vote would not permanently weaken the nation.

B) argue that giving women more rights would cause the nation to crumble in less than a generation.

C) demonstrate that the theories, beliefs, and codes of ethics of the peoples of the Philippines are unchangeable.

D) contrast the old institutions of the country, which upheld liberal democracy, with the new institutions, which support more radical ideas.

29

Which choice provides the best evidence for the answer to the previous question?

A) Lines 7-12 ("The cause . . . strong")

B) Lines 40-46 ("It is an . . . cost")

C) Lines 67-74 ("Despite all . . . existence")

D) Lines 85-88 ("I do not . . . society")

30

As used in the passage, "marked" in line 81 most nearly means

A) fixed.

B) targeted.

C) significant.

D) underlined.

31

In the final paragraph of the passage (lines 79-88), Palma's attitude toward those who oppose female suffrage can best be described as

A) perplexed and mournful.

B) academic and unbiased.

C) deferential and hopeful.

D) bewildered and dissenting.

CONTINUE

No Test Material On This Page

Questions 32-41 are based on the following passage and supplementary material.

This passage is adapted from "Yellowstone Wolf Project: Annual Report, 2012."

Although wolf packs once roamed from the Arctic tundra to Mexico, they were regarded as dangerous predators, and gradual loss of habitat and
Line deliberate extermination programs led to their demise
5 throughout most of the United States. By 1926, when the National Park Service (NPS) ended its predator control efforts, there were no gray wolf (*Canis lupus*) packs left in Yellowstone National Park (YNP).

In the decades that followed, the importance of
10 the wolf as part of a naturally functioning ecosystem came to be better understood, and the gray wolf was eventually listed as an endangered species in all of its traditional range except Alaska. Where possible, NPS policy calls for restoring native species that have been
15 eliminated as a result of human activity. Because of its large size and abundant prey, the greater Yellowstone area was identified in the recovery plan as one of three areas where the recovery of wolves had a good chance of succeeding.

20 At the end of 2012, at least 83 wolves in 10 packs (6 breeding pairs) occupied YNP. This is approximately a 15% decline from the previous three years when numbers had stabilized at around 100 wolves. Breeding pairs declined slightly from eight the previous year.
25 Wolf numbers in YNP have declined by about 50% since 2007, mostly because of a smaller elk population, the main food of wolves in YNP. State-managed wolf hunts harvested 12 wolves that lived primarily in YNP when these animals moved into Montana and
30 Wyoming. The number of wolves living in the park interior has declined less, probably because they supplement their diet with bison. The severity of mange continued to decline in 2012, although some packs still showed signs of the mite. There was no
35 evidence that distemper was a mortality factor in 2012 as it was in 1999, 2005, and 2008. Pack size ranged from 4 (Blacktail and Snake River) to 11 (Lamar Canyon, Cougar, and Yellowstone Delta) and averaged 10, which is the long-term average. Seven of 11 (64%)
40 packs had pups.

The number of wolves observed spending most of their time in the park was significantly fewer than the parkwide peak of 174 in 2003, a decline that was brought about by disease and food stress, and suggests

45 a long-term lower equilibrium for wolves living in YNP, especially on the northern range. Northern range wolves have declined 60% since 2007 compared to only 23% for interior wolves during the same period. Northern range wolves are more dependent on elk as
50 a food source, and elk have declined 60% since 2007. Wolf packs in the interior also prey on bison, which were still widely available in 2012. Disease impacts have also likely played a larger role in the wolf decline on the northern range because of higher canid density
55 (wolves, coyotes, and foxes) than in the interior where density was lower.

Wolf–prey relationships were documented by observing wolf predation directly and by recording the characteristics of prey at kill sites. Wolf packs
60 were monitored for two winter-study sessions in 2012 during which wolves were intensively radio-tracked and observed for 30-day periods in March and from mid-November to mid-December. The Blacktail, Agate Creek, and Lamar Canyon packs were the main study
65 packs monitored by three-person ground teams and aircraft during the March session, with the Junction Butte pack replacing the Agate Creek pack for the November–December session. Additionally, other park packs (Canyon, Cougar Creek, Mary Mountain,
70 Mollie's, Quadrant, 8-mile) were monitored from only aircraft. The Delta pack was monitored less intensively because of logistical constraints and the Bechler pack (no radio collars) was unable to be located. Data from downloadable GPS collars was also utilized to
75 detect predation events for wolves from the Agate Creek, Blacktail, Lamar Canyon, and Junction Butte packs during winter studies and also during a spring–summer (May–July) monitoring period. During these established predation studies, and opportunistically
80 throughout the year, project staff recorded behavioral interactions between wolves and prey, kill rates, total time wolves fed on carcasses, percent consumption of kills by scavengers, characteristics of wolf prey (e.g., sex, species, nutritional condition), and characteristics
85 of kill sites.

Given the controversy surrounding wolf impacts on ungulate populations, wolf and elk interactions continue to be a primary focus of predation studies in YNP. The northern Yellowstone elk population
90 has declined since wolf reintroduction. In addition

CONTINUE

to wolves, factors affecting elk population dynamics include other predators, management of elk outside the park, and weather patterns (e.g. drought, weather severity). Weather patterns influence forage quality
95 and availability, ultimately impacting elk nutritional condition. Consequently, changes in prey selection and kill rates through time result from complex interactions among these factors.

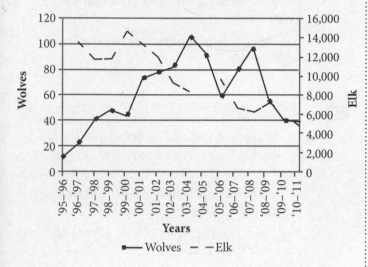

Yellowstone National Park northern range elk-wolf populations, 1995–2010.

32

The passage suggests that which of the following previous beliefs about wolf packs may be inaccurate?

A) The sizes of elk populations and wolf populations are related to one another.

B) Wolves are part of the naturally functioning ecosystem.

C) Predator control efforts can be extremely effective.

D) Wolf packs are too dangerous to be left alive.

33

As used in line 14, "native" most nearly means

A) inborn.

B) constitutional.

C) indigenous.

D) canine.

34

As used in line 28, "harvested" most nearly means

A) gathered.

B) killed.

C) acquired.

D) grown.

35

Which of the following, if true, would most weaken the author's argument in lines 30-32?

A) Predation studies on Delta and Bechler packs done by a separate research group show their diet to consist almost entirely of elk.

B) Northern packs that occasionally roam into the park's interior have more stable populations than other northern packs.

C) In 2013 a pack of coyotes infected with mange migrated into the park and wolf populations soon declined.

D) Studies of bison populations are incomplete and are known to over-estimate the number of bison living in YNP.

36

The fifth paragraph (lines 57-85) most strongly suggests which of the following about the predation data gathered in 2012?

A) The wolves are primarily responsible for the drops in the elk population.

B) The predation data is incomplete.

C) Most of the packs were observed by ground teams.

D) Researchers documented characteristics of only wolf prey.

CONTINUE

37

Which choice provides the best evidence for the answer to the previous question?

A) Lines 59-63 ("Wolf packs . . . mid-December")

B) Lines 63-68 ("The Blacktail . . . session")

C) Lines 71-73 ("The Delta . . . located")

D) Lines 78-85 ("During . . . sites")

38

The passage suggests that the relationship between elk and wolf populations is best characterized as which of the following?

A) The size of the northern wolf packs is the major limiting factor on elk populations.

B) The superior hunting tactics that wolves possess are one of many factors that affect elk populations.

C) The sizes of wolf and elk populations affect one another.

D) The size of the elk population is the major limiting factor on the wolf packs.

39

Which choice provides the best evidence for the answer to the previous question?

A) Lines 25-27 ("Wolf numbers . . . YNP")

B) Lines 51-52 ("Wolf packs . . . 2012")

C) Lines 57-59 ("Wolf-prey . . . sites")

D) Lines 90-94 ("In addition . . . severity")

40

The author references weather (lines 94-96) primarily in order to

A) illustrate one possible logistical difficulty in tracking wolves in YNP.

B) provide a reason for the improved quality of elk food.

C) argue for the design of a new predation study in YNP.

D) provide additional information relevant to the decline of elk.

41

Which claim about wolf and elk populations studied by the National Park Service is supported by the graph?

A) Currently, elk populations out-number wolf populations in YNP.

B) Since wolf reintroduction in YNP, elk populations have only decreased.

C) Wolf populations are highest when elk populations are lowest.

D) Currently, elk populations and wolf populations are about the same.

CONTINUE

No Test Material On This Page

CONTINUE

Questions 42-52 are based on the following passage.

This first passage is adapted from an article from Imperial College London published in 2010, and the second is adapted from an article from Reuters published in 2013. Both discuss the different factors that may have contributed to the extinction of the dinosaurs.

Passage 1: Asteroid killed off the dinosaurs, says international scientific panel

A panel of 41 international experts reviewed 20 years' worth of research to determine the cause of the Cretaceous-Tertiary (KT) extinction, which happened around 65 million years ago. The extinction wiped out *(5)* more than half of all species on the planet, including the dinosaurs, bird-like pterosaurs and large marine reptiles, clearing the way for mammals to become the dominant species on Earth.

The new review of the evidence shows that the *(10)* extinction was caused by a massive asteroid slamming into Earth at Chicxulub (pronounced chick-shoo-loob) in Mexico. The asteroid, which was around 15 kilometers wide, is believed to have hit Earth with a force one billion times more powerful than the atomic *(15)* bomb at Hiroshima. It would have blasted material at high velocity into the atmosphere, triggering a chain of events that caused a global winter, wiping out much of life on Earth in a matter of days.

Scientists have previously argued about whether the *(20)* extinction was caused by the asteroid or by volcanic activity in the Deccan Traps in India, where there were a series of super volcanic eruptions that lasted approximately 1.5 million years. These eruptions spewed 1,100,000 km³ of basalt lava across the Deccan *(25)* Traps, which would have been enough to fill the Black Sea twice, and were thought to have caused a cooling of the atmosphere and acid rain on a global scale.

In the new study, scientists analyzed the work of paleontologists, geochemists, climate modelers, *(30)* geophysicists and sedimentologists who have been collecting evidence about the KT extinction over the last 20 years. Geological records show that the event that triggered the extinction destroyed marine and land ecosystems rapidly, according to the researchers, *(35)* who conclude that the Chicxulub asteroid impact is the only plausible explanation for this.

Dr. Joanna Morgan, co-author of the review from the Department of Earth Science and Engineering at Imperial College London, said: "We now have great *(40)* confidence that an asteroid was the cause of the KT extinction. This triggered large-scale fires, earthquakes measuring more than 10 on the Richter scale, and continental landslides, which created tsunamis. However, the final nail in the coffin for the dinosaurs *(45)* happened when blasted material was ejected at high velocity into the atmosphere. This shrouded the planet in darkness and caused a global winter, killing off many species that couldn't adapt to this hellish environment."

(50) Ironically, while this hellish day signaled the end of the 160-million-year reign of the dinosaurs, it turned out to be a great day for mammals, who had lived in the shadow of the dinosaurs prior to this event. The KT extinction was a pivotal moment in Earth's history, *(55)* which ultimately paved the way for humans to become the dominant species on Earth.

Passage 2: Asteroid may have killed dinosaurs more quickly than scientists thought

Dinosaurs died off about 33,000 years after an asteroid hit the Earth, much sooner than scientists had believed, and the asteroid may not have been the *(60)* sole cause of extinction, according to a study released Thursday. Earth's climate may have been at a tipping point when a massive asteroid smashed into what is now Mexico's Yucatan Peninsula and triggered cooling temperatures that wiped out the dinosaurs, researchers *(65)* said. The time between the asteroid's arrival, marked by a 110-mile-(180-km-) wide crater near Chicxulub, Mexico, and the dinosaurs' demise was believed to be as long as 300,000 years. The study, based on high-precision radiometric dating techniques, said the *(70)* events occurred within 33,000 years of each other.

Other scientists had questioned whether dinosaurs died before the asteroid impact. "Our work basically puts a nail in that coffin," geologist Paul Renne of the University of California Berkeley said. The theory that *(75)* the dinosaurs' extinction about 66 million years ago was linked to an asteroid impact was first proposed in 1980. The biggest piece of evidence was the so-called Chicxulub crater off the Yucatan coast in Mexico.

It is believed to have been formed by a six-mile- *(80)* (9.6-km-) wide object that melted rock as it slammed into the ground, filling the atmosphere with debris that eventually rained down on the planet. Glassy spheres known as tektites, shocked quartz and a layer of iridium-rich dust are still found around the world *(85)* today.

CONTINUE

Renne and colleagues reanalyzed both the dinosaur extinction date and the crater formation event and found they occurred within a much tighter window in time than previously known. The study looked at
90 tektites from Haiti, tied to the asteroid impact site, and volcanic ash from the Hell Creek Formation in Montana, a source of many dinosaur fossils. "The previous data that we had ... actually said that they (the tektites and the ash) were different in age, that
95 they differed by about 180,000 years and that the extinction happened before the impact, which would totally preclude there being a causal relationship," said Renne, who studies ties between mass extinctions and volcanism.
100 The study, published in *Science,* resolves existing uncertainty about the relative timing of the events, notes Heiko Pälike of the Center for Marine Environmental Sciences at the University of Bremen, Germany. Renne, for one, does not believe the
105 asteroid impact was the sole reason for the dinosaurs' demise. He says ecosystems already were in a state of deterioration due to a major volcanic eruption in India when the asteroid struck. "The Chicxulub impact then provided a decisive blow to ecosystems," Renne and his
110 co-authors wrote in *Science.*

42

In the first paragraph of Passage 1, the author suggests that mammals

A) were the only species that survived the KT extinction.

B) were very rare until 65 million years ago.

C) were not the dominant species on earth before the asteroid hit.

D) were wiped out after an asteroid hit the earth.

43

Which choice provides the best evidence for the answer to the previous question?

A) Lines 1-4 ("A panel . . . ago")

B) Lines 4-8 ("The extinction . . . Earth")

C) Lines 9-12 ("The new . . . Mexico")

D) Lines 53-56 ("The KT . . . Earth")

44

As used in line 24, "spewed" most nearly means

A) conflagrated.

B) disgorged.

C) exhumed.

D) siphoned.

45

Based on the information in Passage 1, it can be reasonably inferred that

A) fires, earthquakes, and tsunamis killed most of the dinosaurs.

B) lowered temperatures decimated many species.

C) the impact of the asteroid caused volcanoes to erupt.

D) there is no consensus on what caused the KT extinction.

46

As used in line 44 and line 73, the phrases "final nail in the coffin," and "nail in that coffin" in both passages refer to

A) a profound deduction.

B) a deadly result.

C) a gruesome metaphor.

D) a terminating event.

47

The author's reference to the "high-precision radiometric dating techniques" in lines 68-69 primarily serves to

A) propose a new theory.

B) validate the study's data.

C) prove the conclusion right.

D) counter the assumption.

48

As used in line 97, "preclude" most nearly means

A) cause.

B) limit.

C) bar.

D) tap.

49

The author of Passage 2 mentions tektites (line 83) primarily in order to

A) explore another cause for the KT extinction.

B) diminish the role of the asteroid in the demise of the dinosaurs.

C) substantiate that the volcanoes caused the most damage.

D) contrast with volcanic ash in order to support the new theory.

50

Which choice provides the best evidence for the answer to the previous question?

A) Lines 19-23 ("Scientists have previously . . . years")

B) Lines 61-65 ("Earth's climate may . . . said")

C) Lines 92-97 ("The previous data . . . relationship")

D) Lines 106-108 ("He says ecosystems . . . struck")

51

The passages differ in that Passage 1

A) describes the size of the asteroid, while Passage 2 only mentions its impact.

B) concludes that the extinction happened before the asteroid hit, while Passage 2 says the extinction happened after the asteroid hit.

C) explains how mammals were affected by the KT extinction, while Passage 2 does not.

D) contradicts the previous theory concerning the KT extinction, while Passage 2 supports it.

52

Is the main conclusion of the study described in Passage 2 consistent with the panel's conclusion, as described in Passage 1?

A) Yes, since the asteroid caused earthquakes and volcano eruptions that shrouded the earth in debris.

B) Yes, since the asteroid is considered the primary cause of the KT extinction by both parties.

C) No, since the study in Passage 2 conveys doubt about the timing of the asteroid impact.

D) No, since Passage 1 concludes that the asteroid impact led to the growth of mammal populations.

STOP

If you finish before time is called, you may check your work on this section only.
Do not turn to any other section in the test.

No Test Material On This Page

Writing and Language Test

35 MINUTES, 44 QUESTIONS

Turn to Section 2 of your answer sheet to answer the questions in this section.

DIRECTIONS

Each passage below is accompanied by a number of questions. For some questions, you will consider how the passage might be revised to improve the expression of ideas. For other questions, you will consider how the passage might be edited to correct errors in sentence structure, usage, or punctuation. A passage or a question may be accompanied by one or more graphics (such as a table or graph) that you will consider as you make revising and editing decisions.

Some questions will direct you to an underlined portion of a passage. Other questions will direct you to a location in a passage or ask you to think about the passage as a whole.

After reading each passage, choose the answer to each question that most effectively improves the quality of writing in the passage or that makes the passage conform to the conventions of standard written English. Many questions include a "NO CHANGE" option. Choose that option if you think the best choice is to leave the relevant portion of the passage as it is.

Questions 1–11 are based on the following passage and supplementary material.

SLP, OMG!

[1] While a large number of people believe that social media are fads that will soon die out, a new trend shows that such a belief may be false. It's true that most younger people write to one another (via Twitter, Facebook, or text) more than [2] speaking to one another (who uses a phone to talk anymore?), but the spoken word is as important as ever. This importance is nowhere clearer than in the rise of speech-language pathologists (SLPs).

1

Which of the following would best introduce the main subject of this paragraph?

A) NO CHANGE

B) Although many believe that society is moving away from the spoken word altogether,

C) Even though some believe that kids today can't write or spell,

D) Because a new batch of research has been performed on the belief,

2

A) NO CHANGE

B) spoken

C) they speak

D) have spoken

CONTINUE

The Bureau of Labor Statistics projects that the SLP profession will grow by 19% between 2012 and 2022. Alongside this growth, the nature of the profession is changing as well: while **3** SLPs overwhelmingly work in hospitals, there has been a notable rise in recent years in private-practice SLPs.

The name "speech-language pathologist" is actually a bit of an understatement. **4** Some SLPs do work with communication disorders, stemming from speech impediments to disabilities relating to oral, written, or graphical language. An SLP who specializes in speech may work on articulation or phonation, though some of these specialists will also work with attention and **5** memory. In particular, they work with the components of those practices that deal with language. Some are more concerned with the mechanical side of speech, addressing **6** their respiratory aspects, particularly as related to volume, breathiness, or rasp.

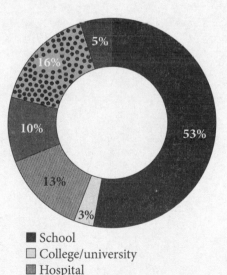

- ■ School
- ☐ College/university
- ■ Hospital
- ■ Residential health care facility
- ▓ Non-residential health care facility
- ■ Other

Image modified from *ASHA Leader*.

3

Which choice gives information consistent with the graph?

A) NO CHANGE

B) currently about half of all SLPs work in schools,

C) there are only about 5,300 SLPs at work in schools,

D) colleges and universities devote only about 3% of their budgets to SLPs,

4

The writer is considering replacing the words *an understatement* with the words *a misnomer*. Should the writer make the change or keep the sentence as is?

A) Make the change, because the word *misnomer* is more common in social science.

B) Make the change, because the paragraph goes on to say that "speech-language pathologist" is the wrong name for the profession.

C) Keep the sentence as is, because *understatement* is longer and therefore more formal.

D) Keep the sentence as is, because the name is not incorrect, merely insufficient to represent the range of duties.

5

Which of the following gives the best way to combine these two sentences?

A) NO CHANGE

B) memory; they work in particular with the components

C) memory. Particularly the components

D) memory, particularly the components

6

A) NO CHANGE

B) one's

C) its

D) it's

CONTINUE →

Although communication disorders are SLPs' most common targets, some specialists will work more with swallowing disorders. If an infant is struggling to feed, for instance, an SLP might work in tandem with a medical doctor to clear the esophageal function to get it back into **7** good working order. An SLP can **8** lead a regimen of swallowing therapies and advise dietary changes that might make swallowing more comfortable.

A) NO CHANGE

B) ship shape.

C) gravy.

D) good times.

Which of the following would best maintain this sentence's focus on the actions an SLP might take to address a swallowing disorder?

A) NO CHANGE

B) handle many patients at once

C) work in a school or hospital

D) keep detailed paperwork on a patient's progress

CONTINUE

In most cases, a speech-language pathologist will work interdisciplinarily, often with other SLP specialists or medical doctors. Along with the increased involvement of SLPs, research continues **9** to show that the mechanisms, of the mouth and respiratory system, are central, to an understanding, of the body as a whole. Speech-language pathology also offers an interesting intersection of the social and medical. Speech is after all not merely a biological **10** function, it's also a major means of socialization, and the range of things that might render a patient speechless is vast. Although the digital age has changed many facets of our lives, the rise of the SLP reminds us that there are some basics that no machine can fix or replace for **11** itself.

9

A) NO CHANGE

B) to show that the mechanisms, of the mouth and respiratory, system are central to an understanding

C) to show that the mechanisms of the mouth and respiratory system are central to an understanding

D) to show that the mechanisms of the mouth and respiratory system are central, to an understanding,

10

A) NO CHANGE

B) function; it's

C) function, but it's

D) function it's

11

A) NO CHANGE

B) it.

C) them.

D) us.

CONTINUE

Questions 12–22 are based on the following passage.

The Other Steel City

[1]

[12] Set on the banks of Monocacy Creek, the area that is now Bethlehem, PA, was inhabited by a rich [13] diversity of indigenous peoples. [A] By the time of that contact, the area was primarily one of the Algonquian-speaking Lenape tribe and its various divisions. [14] They traded with many settlers in the mid-Atlantic region.

12

Which of the following best introduces the historical tone of this essay?

A) NO CHANGE

B) Home to over 700,000 people,

C) Long before European contact,

D) About 50 miles north of Philadelphia,

13

Which of the following alternatives to the underlined portion would be LEAST acceptable?

A) variety

B) arrangement

C) assortment

D) multiplicity

14

A) NO CHANGE

B) It

C) Some

D) These groups

CONTINUE

[2]

While many groups in other regions were systematically exterminated and relegated to smaller plots of land, the Lenape **15** went on to continue to be a contributing factor to the landscape of the early region. Even after the initial European settlement on Christmas **16** Eve in 1741, the Lenape trading continued, though the written history primarily follows the progress of white settlers.

[3]

These settlers, a group of Moravians led by David Nitschman and Count Nicolas von Zinzendorf, called the region Bethlehem, after the birthplace of Jesus Christ. The Moravians set up missions to convert the Lenape and non-English-speaking Christians to the tenets of Moravianism, **17** a practice widely criticized for its ignorance of local traditions. [B] Although the group was relatively small and its religious influence did not reach as far as **18** other groups, the Moravians had a lasting cultural influence on the shape of the early United States. With their strong ties to Germany and musical bent, the annual Moravian Bach festival was one of the first places for people to hear the music from overseas that would become so internationally influential. [C]

15

A) NO CHANGE
B) continued going on
C) went on
D) continued

16

A) NO CHANGE
B) Eve in 1741 the Lenape trading continued
C) Eve in 1741 the Lenape trading continued,
D) Eve, in 1741, the Lenape trading continued,

17

Which of the following true choices helps to maintain the focus on the way the Moravian settlers have been characterized throughout the essay?

A) NO CHANGE
B) using diplomacy rather than force.
C) a cornerstone of European colonizing missions in Africa and Asia.
D) which helped to bring European literacy and economics to many outside of Europe.

18

A) NO CHANGE
B) some other
C) those other
D) that of some other

CONTINUE

[4]

In the twentieth century, Bethlehem became known all over for the world for something much different: steel. Bethlehem Steel was founded in 1857 amid the industrial revolution, and by the 1940s, **19** its factory was providing substantial amounts of armor and steel for troops in World War II, in addition to providing the metalwork for bridges and structures all over the country. The plant ceased operations in 1995, but its blast furnaces, those reminders of past industrial glory, **20** remains.

[5]

Some cities might have been laid low by the death of a major industry, but Bethlehem has emerged seemingly unscathed. Although locals know it as the "Christmas City," for the many decorations and activities there in December, Bethlehem is also a significant culture center for the region, and its former steel mill has been repurposed to host all variety of events. [D] The contributions of Bethlehem have changed from century to century, so it should be no surprise that the twenty-first century should bring to the city something **21** no one's ever seen the like of.

19
A) NO CHANGE
B) their
C) they're
D) it's

20
A) NO CHANGE
B) is remaining.
C) remain.
D) are remaining.

21

Which of the following would best conclude the essay by preserving its style and tone?
A) NO CHANGE
B) to *steel* its reputation as a real *blast*!
C) it hasn't seen before.
D) everyone pretty much expects by now.

22

Upon reviewing this essay and concluding that some information has been left out, the writer composes the following sentence:

> After these many years of education, Bethlehem became a Moravian stronghold, with the Moravian Academy and College still a nucleus of intellectual life in the region.

The best placement for this sentence would be at point
A) [A] in paragraph 1.
B) [B] in paragraph 3.
C) [C] in paragraph 3.
D) [D] in paragraph 5.

CONTINUE

Questions 23–33 are based on the following passage.

Look It Up!

[1] Imagine you're texting someone, and the two of you get into a heated debate. [2] They correct our spelling. [3] Finally, to prove your point once and for all, you write a voluminous, paragraph-long text, only to see that your interlocutor has responded, "TL; DR." [4] Now, you might know that this means "too long, didn't read," but what if you don't? `23` [5] Well, Urban Dictionary can save the day. [6] Just type the phrase into Google and see what turns `24` down. [7] Dictionaries have a way of showing up in every facet of our digital lives. [8]They translate pages in foreign languages. [9] They define words that we think we know and those we've never heard of. [10] Dictionaries are everywhere. `25`

`23`

The writer is considering deleting the phrase *what if you don't?*, and adjusting the punctuation accordingly. Should this phrase be kept or deleted?

A) Kept, because it adds variety to a paragraph full of declarative sentences.

B) Kept, because it poses a question that is answered in the following sentence.

C) Deleted, because it is a rhetorical question to which the answer is already implied.

D) Deleted, because no part of the paragraph goes on to answer it.

`24`

A) NO CHANGE

B) in.

C) back.

D) up.

`25`

The best placement for sentence 2 would be

A) where it is now.

B) at the beginning of the paragraph.

C) after sentence 5.

D) after sentence 8.

CONTINUE

In fact, dictionaries are so prevalent that it's easy to forget that they [26] have not always existed. The word "dictionary" was in fact not coined until John of Garland published his *Dictionarius* in 1220 to help readers with their Latin *diction*. [27] Furthermore, [28] numerous dictionaries appeared throughout the Middle Ages and the Early Modern period, the first noteworthy English dictionary came from Samuel Johnson, whose *Dictionary of the English Language* was published first in 1755. Johnson's opus remains the first modern dictionary, containing consistent spellings, variant definitions, textual [29] usages, and alphabetical, arrangements. Johnson's dictionary was the law of the lexicon until 1884, when the Oxford English Dictionary (OED) began its reign, which continues today.

26

A) NO CHANGE
B) were not
C) did not
D) did not have

27

The writer is considering replacing the word *diction* with *pronunciation*. Should the writer make the change or keep the sentence as is?

A) Make the change, because *pronunciation* is the more commonly used word.
B) Make the change, because *diction* has an imprecise meaning in the sentence.
C) Keep the sentence as is, because *diction* helps to explain the term given earlier in the sentence.
D) Keep the sentence as is, because *pronunciation* means something contrary to *diction*.

28

A) NO CHANGE
B) indeed, numerous dictionaries
C) a number of dictionaries
D) while numerous dictionaries

29

A) NO CHANGE
B) usages, and, alphabetical
C) usages, and alphabetical
D) usages and alphabetical,

CONTINUE

Johnson's American counterpart was Noah Webster, who published his first dictionary in 1806. Webster's best-known **30** work *An American Dictionary of the English Language*, was published in 1828. The text was based in large part on Johnson's dictionary, though it included 12,000 **31** words that had not appeared in previous dictionaries. In addition, Webster was a spelling reformer who thought English spellings were overly ornate and complex. As a result, when Americans write "color" and "gray" where the English write **32** other things, Americans have Noah Webster to thank.

33 What is interesting about these two dictionaries, and about the history of dictionaries in general, is how clearly they show the different directions that language can be pulled. On the one hand, a new dictionary should solidify the language in a new way—it should settle old disputes and give definitive definitions. On the other hand, each dictionary update shows that language is fluid and that no printed word can contain the varieties of language as it is actually used. After all, the OED may have told the world that "selfie" was the word of the year in 2013, but didn't the world know that already?

30

A) NO CHANGE

B) work, *An American Dictionary of the English Language*

C) work, *An American Dictionary of the English Language*,

D) work *An American Dictionary of the English Language*

31

Which of the following true statements would best emphasize the unique achievement of Webster's dictionary?

A) NO CHANGE

B) words that drew from languages varying from Old English to Sanskrit.

C) words, which is a heck of a lot of words.

D) words from many sources, including books and speeches.

32

A) NO CHANGE

B) "colour" and "grey,"

C) differently,

D) DELETE the underlined portion, placing the comma after the word *write*.

33

A) NO CHANGE

B) Both what is interesting about these two dictionaries and what is interesting about dictionaries in general,

C) About the history of dictionaries in general, but in particular about these two,

D) These two dictionaries are interesting, but so is the history of dictionaries in general,

---

CONTINUE ➤

Questions 34–44 are based on the following passage.

Goodnight, sleep tight...

[1]

They are the horror of every city-dweller and international traveler. You can't see them. You only see their aftermath, usually in the form that becomes more uncomfortable as the day **34** of an itchy welt goes on. Bed bugs are the silent feeders: they come out at night and disappear with the light of morning. They hide in the unseen places in the mattress or in the cracks of the floor. Like the most annoying vampires in the world, **35** human blood is the food of bed bugs.

[2]

Interest in bed bugs seems to be nearly as old as written history itself. **36** They were not the nuisance then that they have since become. Remember, previous ages believed in the medicinal value of leeches and blood-letting, and bed bugs were seen as helping to extract the toxins that came from snake bites or ear infections **37** by removing them.

34

The best placement for the underlined portion would be

A) where it is now.

B) after the word *aftermath* (and before the comma).

C) after the word *form*.

D) after the word *uncomfortable*.

35

A) NO CHANGE

B) bed bugs feed on human blood.

C) a typical meal for bed bugs is one of human blood.

D) human blood is what bed bugs need to live.

36

The writer wants to insert a piece of evidence that will support the previous sentence ("Bed bugs . . . itself"). Which of the following true statements would offer that support?

A) Some Greek writers mention them as early as 400 BC.

B) Written history is thought to have begun around the 4th century BCE.

C) Bed bugs typically live for approximately 6-12 months.

D) In the United States, bed bugs are typically associated with the East Coast.

37

A) NO CHANGE

B) by assisting in their removal.

C) getting them out of there.

D) DELETE the underlined portion.

CONTINUE

[3]

By the twentieth century, however, bed bugs were seen to be the nuisance that [38] they are. This was in part due to [39] there prevalence: in 1933, the UK Ministry of Health reported that *all* the houses in many areas of the country had some bed-bug infestation. Military bases during World War II had significant problems with bed-bug infestation as the bugs appeared all over Europe.

[4]

With increased public awareness and some advances in pesticides, bed bugs were nearly eradicated from the United States in the 1940s, though they reemerged as an urban menace in the 1980s. [40] No one is entirely clear on the reason, though scientists hypothesize that the resurgence of bed bugs is due to increased pesticide [41] resistants and international travel. The nuisance is now treated [42] locally. Though the lifespan and long dormancy of the bed bugs have led many to believe that the problem may be a permanent one.

38

A) NO CHANGE

B) it is.

C) some can be.

D) they are known to be.

39

A) NO CHANGE

B) they're

C) their

D) the

40

With the preceding sentence, the writer intended to introduce this paragraph in a way that established continuity with the previous paragraph. Has the writer achieved this goal?

A) Yes, because the previous paragraph addresses the resurgence of bed bugs in the later part of the century.

B) Yes, because the previous paragraph suggests an earlier moment chronologically.

C) No, because there is no mention of the 1940s or the 1980s in the previous paragraph.

D) No, because this paragraph doesn't mention anything about military bases or wartime incidences.

41

A) NO CHANGE

B) resistance

C) resistivity

D) resisting

42

A) NO CHANGE

B) locally; though

C) locally, and

D) locally, though

CONTINUE

[5]

Today, bed bugs are still mainly considered a nuisance. They cost renters and owners millions of dollars each year in exterminator fees and infested furniture replacement. But a recent study has shown that we may have a new reason to worry about the bugs. Now, some research has shown that bed bugs can transmit disease, a practice of which they were long believed incapable. A study documented in the *American Journal of Tropical Medicine and Hygiene* showed that bed bugs could transmit Chagas disease between mice, **43** which many objected to as being inhumane.

[6]

If these findings are true, then bed bugs may be a more significant public health threat than was previously believed. Like mosquitoes in malaria-ridden countries, bed bugs may be redefined as a true menace, rather than just an itchy nuisance. **44**

43

Which of the following true choices would best maintain the focus of this sentence and paragraph?

A) NO CHANGE

B) which are often used in laboratory tests.

C) though not in rats, whom they haven't tested.

D) which is really startling.

44

The best placement for paragraph 6 would be

A) where it is now.

B) after paragraph 2.

C) after paragraph 3.

D) after paragraph 4.

STOP

**If you finish before time is called, you may check your work on this section only.
Do not turn to any other section in the test.**

No Test Material On This Page

Math Test – No Calculator

25 MINUTES, 20 QUESTIONS

Turn to Section 3 of your answer sheet to answer the questions in this section.

DIRECTIONS

For questions **1-15**, solve each problem, choose the best answer from the choices provided, and fill in the corresponding circle on your answer sheet. For questions **16-20**, solve the problem and enter your answer in the grid on the answer sheet. Please refer to the directions before question 16 on how to enter your answers in the grid. You may use any available space in your test booklet for scratch work.

NOTES

1. The use of a calculator **is not permitted**.
2. All variables and expressions used represent real numbers unless otherwise indicated.
3. Figures provided in this test are drawn to scale unless otherwise indicated.
4. All figures lie in a plane unless otherwise indicated.
5. Unless otherwise indicated, the domain of a given function f is the set of all real numbers x for which $f(x)$ is a real number.

REFERENCE

$A = \pi r^2$
$C = 2\pi r$

$A = lw$

$A = \frac{1}{2}bh$

$c^2 = a^2 + b^2$

Special Right Triangles

$V = lwh$

$V = \pi r^2 h$

$V = \frac{4}{3}\pi r^3$

$V = \frac{1}{3}\pi r^2 h$

$V = \frac{1}{3}\ell wh$

The number of degrees of arc in a circle is 360.
The number of radians of arc in a circle is 2π.
The sum of the measures in degrees of the angles of a triangle is 180.

CONTINUE

1

Marco is ordering salt, which is only sold in 30-pound bags. He currently has 75 pounds of salt, and he needs to have a minimum of 200 pounds. Which of the following inequalities shows all possible values for the number of bags, b, that Marco needs to order to meet his minimum requirement?

A) $b \geq 4$

B) $b \geq 5$

C) $b \geq 6$

D) $b \geq 7$

2

A website hopes to sign up 100,000 subscribers. So far, the website has signed up an average of 500 subscribers per day for d days. Which of the following represents the number of additional subscribers, W, the website must sign up to reach its goal?

A) $W = 500d$

B) $W = 99,500d$

C) $W = 100,000 - 500d$

D) $W = 100,000 + 500d$

3

If f is a function and $f(4) = 5$, which of the following CANNOT be the definition of f?

A) $f(x) = x + 1$

B) $f(x) = 2x - 3$

C) $f(x) = 3x - 2$

D) $f(x) = 4x - 11$

4

Which of the following is equivalent to the expression $\dfrac{x^3 + x^2}{x^4 + x^3}$?

A) $\dfrac{x^5}{x^7}$

B) $\dfrac{2}{x}$

C) $\dfrac{5x}{7x}$

D) x^{-1}

CONTINUE

5

Régine is measuring how many solutions from Batch x and Batch y are acidic. She measured a total of 100 solutions from both batches. 40% of the solutions from Batch x and 70% of the solutions from Batch y were acidic, for a total of 48 acidic solutions. Solving which of the following systems of equations yields the number of solutions in Batch x and Batch y ?

A) $x + y = 100$
     $0.4x + 0.7y = 48$

B) $x + y = 48$
     $0.4x + 0.7y = 100$

C) $x + y = 100 \times 2$
     $0.4x + 0.7y = 48$

D) $x + y = 100$
     $40x + 70y = 48$

6

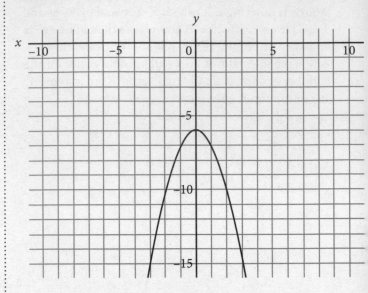

Which of the following equations best describes the figure above?

A) $y = -x^4 + 6$

B) $y = -(x^2 + 6)$

C) $y = -x^2 + 6$

D) $y = x^4 + 6$

CONTINUE

7

The price of an item that cost $43 in 2010 always increases by $3 per year. The current price in dollars, P, of the item can be represented by the equation $P = 3t + 10$, where t is the number of years since the item was first manufactured. Which of the following best explains the meaning of the number 10 in the equation?

A) It is the price of the item in 1999.

B) It is the price of the item in 2000.

C) It is the price of the item in 2001.

D) It is the annual increase in the price of the item.

8

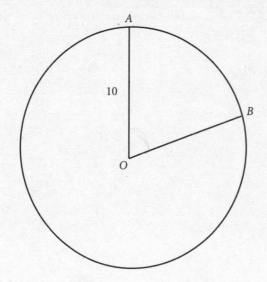

In the circle with center O and radius 10 shown above, $\angle AOB = \dfrac{2\pi}{5}$. What is the length of minor arc AB ?

A) π

B) 2π

C) 4π

D) 20π

9

Clark's Rule is a formula used to determine the correct dosage of adult over-the-counter medicine a child can receive. The child's weight, in pounds, is divided by 150, and the result is multiplied by the adult dose of the medicine. A mother needs to give her daughter acetaminophen, which has an adult dose of 1,000 milligrams. She does not know her daughter's exact weight, but she knows the weight is between 75 and 90 pounds. Which of the following gives the range of correct dosage, d, in milligrams of acetaminophen the daughter could receive?

A) $50 < d < 60$

B) $500 < d < 600$

C) $1{,}000 < d < 1{,}200$

D) $1{,}600 < d < 2{,}000$

10

Ohm's Law, which can be written as $IR = V$, relates the current I in amperes that flows through a conductive material with resistance R ohms to the voltage V between the two ends. The power P in watts can be related to I and R by the equation $I = \sqrt{\dfrac{P}{R}}$. Which of the following gives P in terms of V and R ?

A) $P = \dfrac{R}{V^2}$

B) $P = \dfrac{V}{R}$

C) $P = \dfrac{V^2}{R}$

D) $P = V^2 R^3$

11

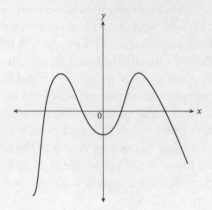

The figure above shows the graph in the *xy*-plane of the function *g*. How many distinct real roots does *g* have?

A) 1

B) 2

C) 3

D) 4

12

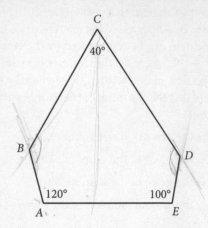

Note: Figure not drawn to scale.

In the figure above, $\angle ABC \cong \angle CDE$. Which of the following is true?

A) $\overline{AB} \parallel \overline{CD}$

B) $\overline{BC} \parallel \overline{AE}$

C) $\overline{CD} \parallel \overline{AE}$

D) $\overline{BC} \cong \overline{AE}$

CONTINUE

13

For which of the following values of w does

$$\sqrt[4]{16w^3 x^{\frac{9}{w}}} = (2)\left(3^{\frac{3}{4}}\right)\left(x^{\frac{3}{4}}\right)?$$

A) 2

B) 3

C) 4

D) 6

14

If $r = (\frac{1}{2}a + b)^2$ and $s = -4ab + 3b$, what is $r - 2s$ in terms of a and b ?

A) $\frac{1}{4}a^2 + b^2 - 7ab - 6b$

B) $\frac{1}{4}a^2 + b^2 - 7ab + 6b$

C) $\frac{1}{4}a^2 + b^2 + 9ab - 6b$

D) $\frac{1}{2}a^2 + b^2 + 9ab - 6b$

15

Which of the following lines contains all points equidistant from the points $(0, 4)$ and $(8, 0)$ in the xy-plane?

A) $2y = -x + 8$

B) $2y = x$

C) $y = 2x - 6$

D) $y = -2x$

CONTINUE

DIRECTIONS

For questions 16-20, solve the problem and enter your answer in the grid, as described below, on the answer sheet.

1. Although not required, it is suggested that you write your answer in the boxes at the top of the columns to help you fill in the circles accurately. You will receive credit only if the circles are filled in correctly.

2. Mark no more than one circle in any column.

3. No question has a negative answer.

4. Some problems may have more than one correct answer. In such cases, grid only one answer.

5. **Mixed numbers** such as $3\frac{1}{2}$ must be gridded as 3.5 or 7/2. (If $\boxed{3\ 1\ /\ 2}$ is entered into

   the grid, it will be interpreted as $\frac{31}{2}$, not as

   $3\frac{1}{2}$.)

6. **Decimal Answers:** If you obtain a decimal answer with more digits than the grid can accommodate, it may be either rounded or truncated, but it must fill the entire grid.

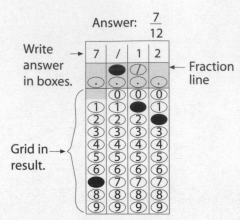

Answer: $\frac{7}{12}$ — Write answer in boxes. Fraction line. Grid in result.

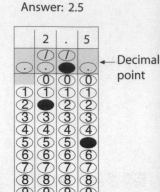

Answer: 2.5 — Decimal point

Acceptable ways to grid $\frac{2}{3}$ are:

Answer: 201 – either position is correct

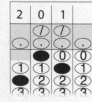

NOTE: You may start your answers in any column, space permitting. Columns you don't need to use should be left blank.

CONTINUE ▶

16

$$\frac{p}{3} + \frac{q}{2} = 1$$

$$p - 3q = 1$$

Based on the system of equations above, what is the value of p ?

17

$$y = x$$
$$(y - 2)^2 - 4 = -x$$

The system of equations above intersects at two points. What is the sum of the coordinates of the point of intersection in quadrant I?

18

$$1 < (c - 1)^2 < 36$$

What is the greatest integer solution to the inequality above?

19

$$2y - x \leq 4$$
$$-2x + y \geq -4$$

If s is the sum of the x- and y-coordinates of any point in the solution to the system of inequalities above as graphed in the xy-plane, what is the greatest possible value of s ?

CONTINUE

20

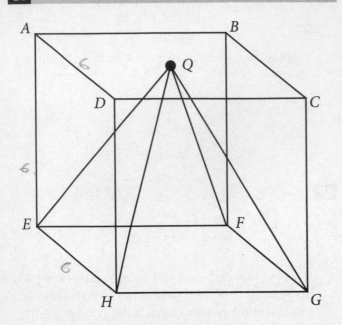

A cube with side length 6 is shown in the figure above. If point *Q* lies on square *ABCD* and is equidistant from points *A*, *B*, *C*, and *D*, what is the volume of pyramid *EFGHQ*?

STOP

If you finish before time is called, you may check your work on this section only. Do not turn to any other section in the test.

No Test Material On This Page

Math Test – Calculator

55 MINUTES, 38 QUESTIONS

Turn to Section 4 of your answer sheet to answer the questions in this section.

DIRECTIONS

For questions **1-30**, solve each problem, choose the best answer from the choices provided, and fill in the corresponding circle on your answer sheet. For questions **31-38**, solve the problem and enter your answer in the grid on the answer sheet. Please refer to the directions before question 31 on how to enter your answers in the grid. You may use any available space in your test booklet for scratch work.

NOTES

1. The use of a calculator **is permitted**.
2. All variables and expressions used represent real numbers unless otherwise indicated.
3. Figures provided in this test are drawn to scale unless otherwise indicated.
4. All figures lie in a plane unless otherwise indicated.
5. Unless otherwise indicated, the domain of a given function f is the set of all real numbers x for which $f(x)$ is a real number.

REFERENCE

$A = \pi r^2$
$C = 2\pi r$

$A = lw$

$A = \frac{1}{2}bh$

$c^2 = a^2 + b^2$

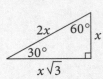

Special Right Triangles

$V = lwh$

$V = \pi r^2 h$

$V = \frac{4}{3}\pi r^3$

$V = \frac{1}{3}\pi r^2 h$

$V = \frac{1}{3}lwh$

The number of degrees of arc in a circle is 360.
The number of radians of arc in a circle is 2π.
The sum of the measures in degrees of the angles of a triangle is 180.

CONTINUE

1

An air pump at a gas station dispenses 90 pounds of air for $0.25. Which of the following expressions gives the number of pounds of air dispensed, P, for d dollars?

A) $P = d + 90$

B) $P = d + 360$

C) $P = 90d$

D) $P = 360d$

2

Taylor is 6 feet tall. If 1 foot is equal to approximately 0.3 meters, then which of the following is closest to Taylor's height in meters?

A) 1.8

B) 2

C) 18

D) 20

3

A developer is creating a plan for a 44-acre park that includes a 4-acre lake that cannot be developed. If 8 to 10 acres, inclusive, must be reserved for soccer fields, which of the following inequalities shows all possible values for p, the amount of land that within the park that is available for development?

A) $26 \leq p \leq 40$

B) $30 \leq p \leq 32$

C) $34 \leq p \leq 36$

D) $36 \leq p \leq 40$

CONTINUE

4

Fuel Efficiency by Vehicle Weight

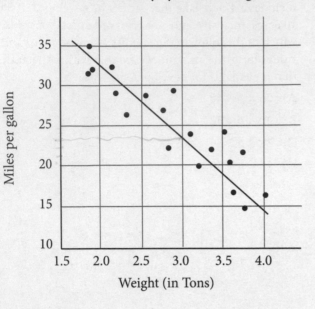

The scatterplot above shows the fuel efficiency, in miles per gallon, of a variety of vehicles weighing between 1.5 and 4 tons. Based on the line of best fit to the data represented, which of the following is the closest to the expected miles per gallon of a vehicle that weighs 3 tons?

A) 20

B) 24

C) 27

D) 28

5

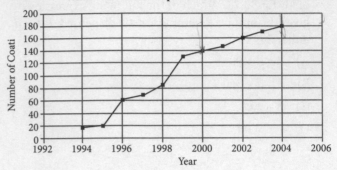

As part of a recent wildlife conservation effort in Guatemala, park rangers in Tikal National Park have tracked the growing number of white-nosed coati living within a certain protected region over the period 1994-2004.

According to the data above, if the population of coati in the protected region of Tikal National Park increased at the same rate from 2004-2006 as it did from 2000-2004, then what was the number of coati in the park in 2006 ?

A) 180

B) 190

C) 200

D) 210

CONTINUE

6

$$\frac{8d + 10 - d}{3} = \frac{d(3 + 4) + a}{3}$$

If the equation above has infinitely many solutions for d, what is the value of a ?

A) −10

B) 10

C) 15

D) 20

7

Maggie's and Glenn's Distances from Home During Jog

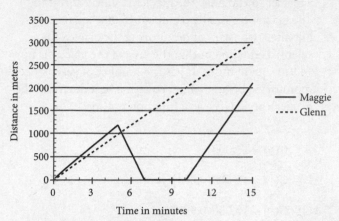

Maggie and Glenn both leave from the same house to go for a jog along a trail. Shortly after leaving, Maggie realizes she forgot her iPod and returns home to find it before heading back out onto the same trail. The graph above shows how far each of them is from home for the first fifteen minutes of their jogs.

What is Glenn's approximate average speed in meters per second for the portion of his jog shown?

A) 3.3

B) 15

C) 200

D) 12,000

CONTINUE

8

Environmentalists have been monitoring the area of a glacier in Canada. The glacier is slowly shrinking. The glacier originally occupied 15,000 square miles, but after two years of monitoring the glacier, the scientists document that the area of the glacier is now 14,910 square miles. If y is the number of years since monitoring began, which equation best describes the glacier's area, $G(y)$, as a function of time?

A) $G(y) = 15,000 \dfrac{1}{y}$

B) $G(y) = 15,000(0.003)^y$

C) $G(y) = 15,000(0.997)^y$

D) $G(y) = 0.997^y$

9

Mike consumes an average of 1,680 calories per day. Each day he has finals, Mike consumes 12% more calories per day than he usually does. During the last day of finals, he celebrates by consuming an additional 900 calories. Which of the following represents the total number of calories Mike consumes during d days of finals?

A) $1.12(1,680d + 900)$

B) $1.12(1,680d) + 900$

C) $1.12(1,680 + 900)d$

D) $(1,680 + 0.12d) + 900$

10

The varsity swim team at Northwest High is planning a team trip and needs to choose between Austin, TX, and Pensacola, FL. The team takes a vote and the results of the vote are shown in the table below.

	Juniors	Seniors
Austin, TX	14	19
Pensacola, FL	7	23

Given the information shown above, which of the following statements is true?

A) The number of juniors that prefer Pensacola, FL, is twice the number of juniors that prefer Austin, TX.

B) The seniors are more than three times as likely to prefer Pensacola, FL, than are the juniors.

C) The number of seniors that prefer Austin, TX, is 5% more than the number of juniors that prefer Austin.

D) One-third of the juniors prefer Pensacola, FL.

CONTINUE

11

The 2013 U.S. Census recorded the highest educational attainment of all adults aged 25 years or older in county T, one of the most educated parts of the country. The results are given in the two-way table below.

	Men	Women	Total
High School Diploma	7,535	7,234	14,769
Bachelor's Degree	17,170	23,455	40,625
Master's Degree	45,105	41,078	86,183
Professional Degree	23,501	23,405	46,906
Doctoral Degree	16,232	15,817	32,049
Total	109,543	110,989	220,532

According to the data presented in the table above, if you were to choose a person at random out of the entire population aged 25 years or older in county T, what is the approximate probability that the person you chose is a man with a doctoral degree (given as a percent)?

A) 2%

B) 7%

C) 28%

D) 51%

12

The cost in dollars, C, of producing a custom-made T-shirt with a team logo is given by the formula $C = 110 + \dfrac{x}{2}$, where x is the number of T-shirts produced. When every T-shirt produced is sold, the revenue from selling the customized T-shirts is given by $R = 15x - \dfrac{x^2}{10}$. Which one of the following would be the formula for the profit from producing and selling x T-shirts?

(Profit = Revenue – Cost)

A) $-\dfrac{x^2}{10} - \dfrac{31}{2}x + 110$

B) $-\dfrac{x^2}{10} - \dfrac{29}{2}x + 110$

C) $-\dfrac{x^2}{10} + \dfrac{29}{2}x - 110$

D) $-\dfrac{x^2}{10} + \dfrac{31}{2}x - 110$

13

While on vacation in Morocco, Erik decided to splurge on a fancy hotel that cost 2,000 Moroccan dirhams per night. If he stayed in that particular hotel for three nights, but his bank only lets him withdraw $200 at a time, how many visits to the ATM must Erik have made in order to cover the cost of his hotel stay?

(Note: 1 Moroccan dirham = $0.11)

A) 1

B) 2

C) 3

D) 4

CONTINUE

14

Peter's Petrol Station is selling regular unleaded gas for $3.49 a gallon and premium gas for $3.79 a gallon. If a car wash is purchased, then a discount of $0.10 per gallon is applied. During one morning, a total of 850 gallons of gas was sold, and 100 gallons were sold at the discounted rate. The total collected in sales was $3,016.50. Solving which of the following systems of equations yields the number of regular unleaded gallons of gas, u, and the number of premium gallons of gas, p, that were sold during that morning?

A) $u + p = 850$
    $3.49u + 3.79p = 301.65$

B) $u + p = 850$
    $3.49u + 3.79p = 3,016.50$

C) $u + p = 850$
    $3.49u + 3.79p = 3,026.50$

D) $u + p = 3,016.50$
    $3.49u + 3.79p = 850$

15

Of the 784 juniors and seniors at Abingdon High School, 319 are currently enrolled in one or more Advanced Placement (AP) courses. Of these AP students, 75 are enrolled in AP Biology, 58 are enrolled in AP U.S. History, and 22 are enrolled in both AP Biology and AP U.S. History. Approximately what percent of the juniors and seniors at Abingdon High School are enrolled in AP courses other than Biology and U.S. History?

A) 17%

B) 27%

C) 37%

D) 47%

16

To receive a B in his chemistry class, Mateo needs to earn an average score from 80 to 89, inclusive. His grade is based only on 3 tests. The highest possible score on each of these tests is 100 points. He scored 79 on his first test and 95 on his second test. If y represents his score on the third test, which of the inequalities below shows all values of y that would earn Mateo a B in his chemistry class?

A) $66 \leq y \leq 93$

B) $66 \leq y \leq 100$

C) $80 \leq y \leq 89$

D) $80 \leq y \leq 93$

17

$$Y = \frac{A}{A + W}$$

A gardener prepares a mixture of fertilizer with concentration, by volume, equal to Y. It is prepared by mixing a volume of fertilizer given by A with a volume of water given by W. The expression above represents the mixture described. What physical quantity does the term $A + W$ represent in the equation above?

A) The volume of the mixture

B) The mass of fertilizer added

C) The volume of the fertilizer in the mixture

D) The concentration of the fertilizer

CONTINUE

18

Two groups of subjects are combined in a psychological research experiment. The mode score for group A is 7 and the mode score for group B is 6. Which of the following conclusions can be made?

A) The mode for the whole group is 6.

B) The mode for the whole group is between 6 and 7.

C) The mode for the whole group is 7.

D) The mode cannot be determined from the given information.

19

The map below shows the layout of streets in a city and the location of several places. Each horizontal or vertical line between two adjacent streets represents a city block, and each city block represents 0.6 miles.

Josh needs to drive from Kelly's Kitchen to Gary's Grocery. If Josh drives the shortest distance possible on the roads shown above at a constant speed of 30 miles per hour, how long does it take him to make the trip from Kelly's Kitchen to Gary's Grocery?

A) 6 minutes

B) 10 minutes

C) 12 minutes

D) 20 minutes

20

$$2s - \frac{1}{3}t = 10$$
$$5s = t + 12 - s$$

Which of the following is a true statement about the system of equations above?

A) There are infinitely many solutions to the system of equations.

B) When the system is solved for s, the result is 5.

C) When the system is solved for t, the result is 6.

D) There are no solutions to the system of equations.

21

The student council at Shermer High School wants to use student opinion to decide on one of three possible homecoming themes for the year. President Peterson thinks that the best way to determine popular opinion is for each of the 10 members of the student council to poll 10 of their friends and select the theme that receives the most votes. Vice President Vaidya wants to go to the cafeteria during lunch and poll 100 students to determine the winner. Treasurer Thompson says the best method would be to assign numbers to each of the 1,000 students in the school, randomly select 100 of them to poll, and select the winner based on the results. Secretary Stephens argues that they must poll each of the 250 members of the senior class to find the most popular theme. Whose method is most likely to accurately determine overall student opinion regarding the most popular homecoming theme?

A) President Peterson

B) Secretary Stephens

C) Treasurer Thompson

D) Vice-President Vaidya

CONTINUE

22

Is the point (–2, –2) located inside, on, or outside the circle with equation $(x + 3)^2 + (y – 1)^2 = 9$?

A) Inside the circle

B) On the circle

C) Outside the circle

D) It cannot be determined from the given information.

23

If the expression $\dfrac{x-12}{\sqrt{8}}$ is most nearly equal to $\dfrac{x\sqrt{2}}{4}-C$, then what is the value of C ?

A) –3

B) $-\sqrt{3}$

C) 2

D) $3\sqrt{2}$

24

A survey was conducted among a randomly chosen sample of full-time salaried workers about satisfaction in their current jobs. The table below shows a summary of the survey results.

Reported Job Satisfaction by Education Level (in thousands)

Highest Level of Education	Satisfied	Not Satisfied	No Response	Total
High School Diploma	17,880	12,053	2,575	32,508
Bachelor's Degree	24,236	8,496	3,442	36,174
Master's Degree	17,605	5,324	1,861	24,790
Doctoral Degree	12,210	2,081	972	15,263
Total	71,931	27,954	8,850	108,735

Of the people whose highest level of education was a bachelor's degree who reported job satisfaction, 1,000 people were randomly selected to complete a follow-up survey in which they were asked about their salary satisfaction. There were 658 people in this follow-up sample who said that they were satisfied with their salaries, and the other 342 people were not satisfied. Using the data from both the initial survey and the follow-up survey, which of the following statements is most likely true?

A) Approximately 16 million people with bachelor's degrees and who are satisfied with their jobs would report salary satisfaction.

B) Approximately 24 million people with bachelor's degrees would report salary satisfaction.

C) Approximately 47 million people with bachelor's degrees would report salary satisfaction.

D) Approximately 72 million people with bachelor's degrees would report salary satisfaction.

CONTINUE

25

Line d has a slope of $\frac{4}{5}$ and passes through the point $(1, 1)$. Line e is parallel to line d and has a y-intercept 3 times that of line d. Which of the following is the equation of line e ?

A) $5y - 4x = 3$

B) $5y - x = 4$

C) $10y - 8x = 30$

D) $20y + 25x = 12$

26

$$\frac{q^2 - q - 42}{q + 6} = \sqrt{q - 5}$$

The equation above can be solved for two solutions, one of which is extraneous. What is the value of the extraneous solution?

A) 5

B) 6

C) 8

D) 9

27

A gaming company conducted a study to find out what age groups preferred which types of games. The table below outlines the survey results.

Age Group	First Person Shooters	Sports Games	Adventure Games	Total
9- to 13-year olds	16,000,000	9,000,000	25,000,000	50,000,000
14- to 18-year olds	48,000,000	13,000,000	31,000,000	82,000,000
19- to 22-year olds	38,000,000	27,000,000	19,000,000	84,000,000
23- to 60-year olds	8,000,000	3,000,000	10,000,000	21,000,000

According to the information provided in the table, the gaming company concludes that if they can double the number of 19- to 22-year olds playing sports games, and increase the number of sports gamers in the 9- to 13-year old age group, they will have equal total numbers of players for each game type if they double the number of players of adventure games in which age group?

A) 23- to 60-year olds

B) 19- to 22-year olds

C) 14- to 18-year olds

D) 9- to 13-year olds

28

$$V(t) = at + k$$

At a certain manufacturing plant, the total number of vacation days, $V(t)$, an employee has accrued is given by the function above, where t is the number of years the employee has worked at the plant, and a and k are constants. If Martin has accrued 9 more vacation days than Emilio has, how many more years has Martin worked than Emilio?

A) $\dfrac{9}{a}$

B) $9 - a$

C) $9 + a$

D) $9a$

29

In the figure above, $\sin x° = \dfrac{2\sqrt{29}}{29}$. What is the perimeter of the figure?

A) $10 + \dfrac{2\sqrt{29}}{29}$

B) $7 + \sqrt{29}$

C) $14 + 2\sqrt{29}$

D) $39 + 2\sqrt{29}$

30

At Santa Monica High School, the ratio of juniors to seniors is 4 to 3, the ratio of seniors to sophomores is 5 to 4, and the ratio of freshmen to sophomores is 7 to 6. What is the ratio of freshmen to seniors?

A) $\dfrac{7}{3}$

B) $\dfrac{5}{3}$

C) $\dfrac{9}{7}$

D) $\dfrac{14}{15}$

CONTINUE

DIRECTIONS

For questions 31-38, solve the problem and enter your answer in the grid, as described below, on the answer sheet.

1. Although not required, it is suggested that you write your answer in the boxes at the top of the columns to help you fill in the circles accurately. You will receive credit only if the circles are filled in correctly.

2. Mark no more than one circle in any column.

3. No question has a negative answer.

4. Some problems may have more than one correct answer. In such cases, grid only one answer.

5. **Mixed numbers** such as $3\frac{1}{2}$ must be gridded as 3.5 or 7/2. (If $\begin{array}{|c|c|c|c|}\hline 3 & 1 & / & 2 \\\hline\end{array}$ is entered into the grid, it will be interpreted as $\frac{31}{2}$, not as $3\frac{1}{2}$.)

6. **Decimal Answers:** If you obtain a decimal answer with more digits than the grid can accommodate, it may be either rounded or truncated, but it must fill the entire grid.

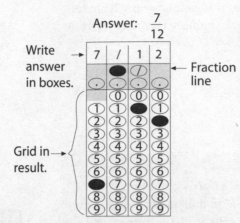

Answer: $\frac{7}{12}$ → Write answer in boxes. ← Fraction line Grid in result.

Answer: 2.5 ← Decimal point

Acceptable ways to grid $\frac{2}{3}$ are:

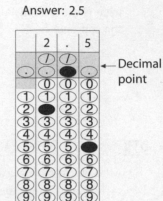

Answer: 201 – either position is correct

NOTE: You may start your answers in any column, space permitting. Columns you don't need to use should be left blank.

31

Hayoung is competing in a triathlon comprised of swimming, running, and biking. She starts by swimming m miles. Next, she runs 11 times the distance that she swims. Finally, she bikes 18 times the distance that she swims. If Hayoung swims 2.5 miles, what is the total distance, in miles, Hayoung travels as she competes?

32

At the local mall, Casey's Card Cart sells cards à la carte. Casey's revenue R, in dollars, for x days is given by the function $R(x) = 250x - 20$. If Casey earned $1,230, how many days has she sold cards?

33

Marty is planning which crops to plant on his farm for the upcoming season. He has enough seed to plant 4 acres of wheat and 7 acres of soybeans, but the total area of farmland he owns is only 9 acres. He earns $90 per acre for every acre of wheat planted and $120 for every acre of soybeans planted, and he must pay a 10% tax on all money he earns from selling his crops. What is the maximum profit, in dollars, that Marty can earn from planting wheat and soybeans this season?

34

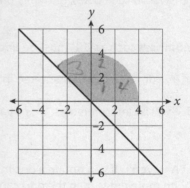

What is the area of the shaded region of the circle, bound by the x-axis and the line $y = -x$, rounded to the nearest whole number?

CONTINUE ▶

35

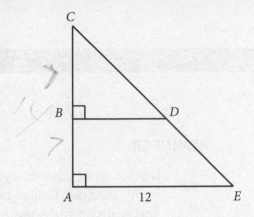

In the figure, $\overline{AC}$ is bisected by $\overline{BD}$. If $\overline{BC}$ is 7, then what is the length of $\overline{BD}$?

36

The daily recommended serving of protein is 50 grams. A nutritional bar contains 32% of the daily recommended serving of protein and 10% of the daily recommended serving of fat. If the nutritional bar contains 700% more grams of protein than grams of fat, what is the daily recommended serving of fat, in grams? (Disregard units when gridding your answer.)

Questions 37 and 38 refer to the following information.

Set R consists of all the one-digit prime numbers. Set S contains all of the elements of Set R, as well as an additional positive integer, x.

37

If the sum of all of the elements of Set S is 30, what is the value of $x^2 - 11x - 25$?

38

Michael wants to change the value of x so that the mean of Set S is equal to the median of Set S and for Set S to have no mode. What value of x would accomplish his goal?

STOP
If you finish before time is called, you may check your work on this section only.
Do not turn to any other section in the test.

SAT Essay

DIRECTIONS

The essay gives you an opportunity to show how effectively you can read and comprehend a passage and write an essay analyzing the passage. In your essay you should demonstrate that you have read the passage carefully, present a clear and logical analysis, and use language precisely.

Your essay must be written on the lines provided in your answer sheet booklet; except for the planning page of the answer booklet, you will receive no other paper on which to write. You will have enough space if you write on every line, avoid wide margins, and keep your handwriting to a reasonable size. Remember that people who are not familiar with your handwriting will read what you write. Try to write in print so that what you are writing is legible to those readers.

You have 50 minutes to read the passage and write an essay in response to the prompt provided inside this booklet.

REMINDER

— Do not write your essay in this booklet. Only what you write on the lined pages of your answer booklet will be evaluated.

— An off-topic essay will not be evaluated.

CONTINUE →

As you read the passage below, consider how the author uses

- evidence, such as facts or examples, to support claims.
- reasoning to develop ideas and to connect claims and evidence.
- stylistic or persuasive elements, such as word choice or appeals to emotion, to add power to the ideas expressed.

Helen Keller's Address before the New York Association for the Blind, January 15, 1907

1   It is a great pleasure to me to speak in New York about the blind. For New York is great because of the open hand with which it responds to the needs of the weak and the poor. The men and women for whom I speak are poor and weak in that they lack one of the chief weapons with which the human being fights his battle. But they must not on that account be sent to the rear. Much less must they be pensioned like disabled soldiers. They must be kept in the fight for their own sake, and for the sake of the strong. It is a blessing to the strong to give help to the weak. Otherwise there would be no excuse for having the poor always with us…

2   For it is the community where the blind man lives that ultimately determines his success or his failure. The State can teach him to work, supply him with raw materials and capital to start his business. But his fellow-citizens must furnish the market for his products and give him the encouragement without which no blind man can make headway…

3   It is not helpful, in the long run it is harmful, to buy worthless articles of the blind. For many years kind-hearted people have bought futile and childish things because the blind made them. Quantities of beadwork that can appeal to no eye, save the eye of pity, have passed as specimens of the work of the blind. If beadwork had been studied in the schools for the blind and supervised by competent seeing persons, it could have been made a profitable industry for the sightless. I have examined beautiful beadwork in the shops, purses, bags, belts, lamp-shades and dress-trimmings, some of it very expensive, imported from France and Germany. Under proper supervision this beadwork could be made by the blind…

4   In Boston, in a fashionable shopping district, the Massachusetts commission has opened a salesroom where the best handicraft of all the sightless in the State may be exhibited and sold. There are hand-woven curtains, table-covers, bed-spreads, sofa-pillows, linen suits, rugs; and the articles are of good design and workmanship. People buy them not out of pity for the maker, but out of admiration for the thing. Orders have already come from Minnesota, from England, from Egypt. So the blind of the New World have sent light into Egyptian darkness!

CONTINUE

5   …Nay, I can tell you of blind men who of their own accord enter the sharp competition of business and put their hands zealously to the tools of trade. It is our part to train them in business, to teach them to use their tools skillfully. Before this association was thought of, blind men had given examples of energy and industry, and with such examples shining in the dark other blind men will not be content to be numbered among those who will not, or cannot, carry burden on shoulder or tool in hand—those who know not the honour of hard-won independence.

6   The new movement for the blind rests on a foundation of common sense. It is not the baseless fabric of a sentimentalist's dream. We do not believe that the blind should be segregated from the seeing, gathered together in a sort of Zion City, as has been done in Roumania and attempted in Iowa. We have no queen to preside over such a city. America is a democracy, a multi-monarchy, and the city of the blind is everywhere. Each community should take care of its own blind, provide employment for them, and enable them to work side by side with the seeing. We do not expect to find among the blind a disproportionate number of geniuses. Education does not develop in them remarkable talent. Like the seeing man, the blind man may be a philosopher, a mathematician, a linguist, a seer, a poet, a prophet.

7   But believe me, if the light of genius burns within him, it will burn despite his infirmity, and not because of it...

8   I appeal to you, give the blind man the assistance that shall secure for him complete or partial independence. He is blind and falters. Therefore go a little more than halfway to meet him. Remember, however brave and self-reliant he is, he will always need a guiding hand in his.

Write an essay in which you explain how Helen Keller develops her argument about the necessity of industries for the blind. In your essay, analyze how Keller uses one or more of the features listed above (or features of your own choice) to strengthen the logic and persuasiveness of her argument. Be sure that your analysis focuses on the most relevant aspects of the passage.

Your essay should not explain whether you agree with Keller's claims, but rather explain how the author builds an argument to persuade her audience.

END OF TEST

DO NOT RETURN TO A PREVIOUS SECTION.

The Princeton Review®

Completely darken bubbles with a No. 2 pencil. If you make a mistake, be sure to erase mark completely. Erase all stray marks.

1.

YOUR NAME: _____
(Print)
        Last   First   M.I.

SIGNATURE: _____   DATE: __ / __ / __

HOME ADDRESS: _____
(Print)
        Number and Street

_____
    City   State   Zip Code

PHONE NO.: _____
(Print)

IMPORTANT: Please fill in these boxes exactly as shown on the back cover of your test book.

2. TEST FORM

3. TEST CODE

4. REGISTRATION NUMBER

5. YOUR NAME

First 4 letters of last name | FIRST INIT | MID INIT

(Bubble grids for letters A–Z and numbers 0–9 as shown)

6. DATE OF BIRTH

Month	Day	Year
JAN		
FEB	0 0	0 0
MAR	1 1	1 1
APR	2 2	2 2
MAY	3 3	3 3
JUN	4 4	4
JUL	5 5	5
AUG	6 6	6
SEP	7 7	7
OCT	8 8	8
NOV	9 9	9
DEC		

7. SEX
- MALE
- FEMALE

The Princeton Review®

Test ③ Start with number 1 for each new section.
If a section has fewer questions than answer spaces, leave the extra answer spaces blank.

Section 1—Reading

1. A B C D
2. A B C D
3. A B C D
4. A B C D
5. A B C D
6. A B C D
7. A B C D
8. A B C D
9. A B C D
10. A B C D
11. A B C D
12. A B C D
13. A B C D
14. A B C D
15. A B C D
16. A B C D
17. A B C D
18. A B C D
19. A B C D
20. A B C D
21. A B C D
22. A B C D
23. A B C D
24. A B C D
25. A B C D
26. A B C D

27. A B C D
28. A B C D
29. A B C D
30. A B C D
31. A B C D
32. A B C D
33. A B C D
34. A B C D
35. A B C D
36. A B C D
37. A B C D
38. A B C D
39. A B C D
40. A B C D
41. A B C D
42. A B C D
43. A B C D
44. A B C D
45. A B C D
46. A B C D
47. A B C D
48. A B C D
49. A B C D
50. A B C D
51. A B C D
52. A B C D

Section 2—Writing and Language Skills

1. A B C D
2. A B C D
3. A B C D
4. A B C D
5. A B C D
6. A B C D
7. A B C D
8. A B C D
9. A B C D
10. A B C D
11. A B C D
12. A B C D
13. A B C D
14. A B C D
15. A B C D
16. A B C D
17. A B C D
18. A B C D
19. A B C D
20. A B C D
21. A B C D
22. A B C D

23. A B C D
24. A B C D
25. A B C D
26. A B C D
27. A B C D
28. A B C D
29. A B C D
30. A B C D
31. A B C D
32. A B C D
33. A B C D
34. A B C D
35. A B C D
36. A B C D
37. A B C D
38. A B C D
39. A B C D
40. A B C D
41. A B C D
42. A B C D
43. A B C D
44. A B C D

Test ❸ Start with number 1 for each new section.
If a section has fewer questions than answer spaces, leave the extra answer spaces blank.

Section 3—Mathematics: No Calculator

1. Ⓐ Ⓑ Ⓒ Ⓓ
2. Ⓐ Ⓑ Ⓒ Ⓓ
3. Ⓐ Ⓑ Ⓒ Ⓓ
4. Ⓐ Ⓑ Ⓒ Ⓓ
5. Ⓐ Ⓑ Ⓒ Ⓓ
6. Ⓐ Ⓑ Ⓒ Ⓓ
7. Ⓐ Ⓑ Ⓒ Ⓓ
8. Ⓐ Ⓑ Ⓒ Ⓓ
9. Ⓐ Ⓑ Ⓒ Ⓓ
10. Ⓐ Ⓑ Ⓒ Ⓓ
11. Ⓐ Ⓑ Ⓒ Ⓓ
12. Ⓐ Ⓑ Ⓒ Ⓓ
13. Ⓐ Ⓑ Ⓒ Ⓓ
14. Ⓐ Ⓑ Ⓒ Ⓓ
15. Ⓐ Ⓑ Ⓒ Ⓓ

16. [grid-in answer space]
17. [grid-in answer space]
18. [grid-in answer space]
19. [grid-in answer space]
20. [grid-in answer space]

Section 4—Mathematics: Calculator

1. Ⓐ Ⓑ Ⓒ Ⓓ
2. Ⓐ Ⓑ Ⓒ Ⓓ
3. Ⓐ Ⓑ Ⓒ Ⓓ
4. Ⓐ Ⓑ Ⓒ Ⓓ
5. Ⓐ Ⓑ Ⓒ Ⓓ
6. Ⓐ Ⓑ Ⓒ Ⓓ
7. Ⓐ Ⓑ Ⓒ Ⓓ
8. Ⓐ Ⓑ Ⓒ Ⓓ
9. Ⓐ Ⓑ Ⓒ Ⓓ
10. Ⓐ Ⓑ Ⓒ Ⓓ
11. Ⓐ Ⓑ Ⓒ Ⓓ
12. Ⓐ Ⓑ Ⓒ Ⓓ
13. Ⓐ Ⓑ Ⓒ Ⓓ
14. Ⓐ Ⓑ Ⓒ Ⓓ
15. Ⓐ Ⓑ Ⓒ Ⓓ
16. Ⓐ Ⓑ Ⓒ Ⓓ
17. Ⓐ Ⓑ Ⓒ Ⓓ
18. Ⓐ Ⓑ Ⓒ Ⓓ
19. Ⓐ Ⓑ Ⓒ Ⓓ
20. Ⓐ Ⓑ Ⓒ Ⓓ
21. Ⓐ Ⓑ Ⓒ Ⓓ
22. Ⓐ Ⓑ Ⓒ Ⓓ
23. Ⓐ Ⓑ Ⓒ Ⓓ
24. Ⓐ Ⓑ Ⓒ Ⓓ
25. Ⓐ Ⓑ Ⓒ Ⓓ
26. Ⓐ Ⓑ Ⓒ Ⓓ
27. Ⓐ Ⓑ Ⓒ Ⓓ
28. Ⓐ Ⓑ Ⓒ Ⓓ
29. Ⓐ Ⓑ Ⓒ Ⓓ
30. Ⓐ Ⓑ Ⓒ Ⓓ

31. [grid-in answer space]
32. [grid-in answer space]
33. [grid-in answer space]
34. [grid-in answer space]
35. [grid-in answer space]
36. [grid-in answer space]
37. [grid-in answer space]
38. [grid-in answer space]

Chapter 25
Practice Test 3:
Answers and
Explanations

PRACTICE TEST 3 ANSWER KEY

	Section 1: Reading				Section 2: Writing & Language				Section 3: Math (No Calculator)				Section 4: Math (Calculator)	

Section 1: Reading

1.	A	27.	B
2.	D	28.	A
3.	D	29.	C
4.	D	30.	C
5.	C	31.	D
6.	C	32.	D
7.	D	33.	C
8.	B	34.	B
9.	A	35.	A
10.	A	36.	B
11.	D	37.	C
12.	B	38.	C
13.	B	39.	A
14.	C	40.	D
15.	B	41.	A
16.	A	42.	C
17.	A	43.	B
18.	C	44.	B
19.	C	45.	B
20.	D	46.	D
21.	A	47.	B
22.	C	48.	C
23.	B	49.	D
24.	D	50.	C
25.	C	51.	C
26.	B	52.	B

Section 2: Writing & Language

1.	B	23.	B
2.	C	24.	D
3.	B	25.	D
4.	D	26.	A
5.	D	27.	C
6.	C	28.	D
7.	A	29.	C
8.	A	30.	C
9.	C	31.	A
10.	B	32.	B
11.	D	33.	A
12.	C	34.	C
13.	B	35.	B
14.	D	36.	A
15.	D	37.	D
16.	A	38.	A
17.	B	39.	C
18.	D	40.	B
19.	A	41.	B
20.	C	42.	D
21.	C	43.	D
22.	B	44.	A

Section 3: Math (No Calculator)

1.	B
2.	C
3.	C
4.	D
5.	A
6.	B
7.	A
8.	C
9.	B
10.	C

11.	D
12.	A
13.	B
14.	C
15.	C
16.	$\frac{7}{3}$ or 2.33
17.	6
18.	6
19.	8
20.	72

Section 4: Math (Calculator)

1.	D
2.	A
3.	B
4.	B
5.	C
6.	B
7.	A
8.	C
9.	B
10.	D
11.	B
12.	C
13.	D
14.	C
15.	B
16.	A
17.	A

18.	D
19.	C
20.	D
21.	C
22.	C
23.	D
24.	A
25.	A
26.	B
27.	D
28.	A
29.	C
30.	D
31.	75
32.	5
33.	918
34.	19
35.	6
36.	20
37.	1
38.	8

PRACTICE TEST 3 EXPLANATIONS

Section 1: Reading

1. **A** The main idea of the passage is that the Scarlet Pimpernel rescues French nobles because it is fun. Choice (A) is correct because that is the reason behind the Pimpernel's actions. The characters never discuss the cause of the French Revolution, so (B) cannot be the answer. Because the young man is a member of the Scarlet Pimpernel's team, and both are self-confident, (C) is incorrect. Both characters presumably disagree with the French government, and neither ever questions that the government is ruthless. Therefore, (D) is incorrect.

2. **D** Because there is no indication that the cart is moving quickly, (A) is incorrect. Since the Comtesse is herself escaping arrest, (B) is incorrect; the mob would not be punished for catching a fugitive. Choice (C) is wrong, as we do not know that the woman driving the cart is violent, only frightening. In the sixteenth paragraph, the driver causes the mob to retreat by mentioning the plague. Therefore, (D) is correct.

3. **D** The answer to the previous question is that the crowd did not approach the Comtesse's cart because they were afraid of contracting a disease. Choice (D) is correct because it is the only answer choice that mentions disease or plague.

4. **D** In this sentence, the flower is drawn in red. Therefore, *designated* must mean something like "drawn." Only *illustrated* has this meaning. Therefore, (D) is correct.

5. **C** In the passage, Lord Antony explains that the Scarlet Pimpernel and his companions save French aristocrats because it is exciting, like pulling the hare from between the teeth of the hound. Choice (A) is too literal, and Lord Antony speaks metaphorically. In the passage, there is no mention of dead Englishmen, so eliminate (B). Choice (C) is an accurate characterization of Lord Antony's use of the phrase in question: In Lord Antony's metaphor, the French aristocracy is the hare, and the harm is the teeth of the hound. Because the passage concerns the cruelty of French revolutionaries toward nobles, (D) contradicts the passage and is incorrect.

6. **C** The answer to the previous question is that Lord Antony uses the phrase in question to describe the sensation of delivering French nobles from harm. Choice (A) does not mention either the aristocrats or the danger they are in, so it is incorrect. Choice (B) is incorrect because it describes the danger to the Pimpernel and his companions, not the French nobles. Choice (D) describes only the danger that the Comtesse has found herself in, so (D) can be eliminated. Choice (C) is correct because it describes the Pimpernel's men delivering French nobles from harm.

7. **D** In the sentence in question, the Comtesse is described as *incredulous*, which means that she has trouble believing the reason given to explain why the Pimpernel and his companions have gone to France to rescue aristocrats. She is not *critical;* therefore, (A) is incorrect. She is not *anxious*, so eliminate (B). While the Comtesse may be relieved that she has been rescued, the sentence in question describes her as *incredulous*. Therefore, (C) is incorrect. *Perplexed* means "puzzled"; because the Comtesse finds the given explanation inadequate to explain the behavior, she is puzzled. Choice (D) is correct.

8. **B** *Bearded* describes the Pimpernel's men, who we know are courageous for rescuing the Comtesse. Therefore, *bearded* must mean something like "faced with courage." Of the four answer choices, only (B) captures their courage and is correct.

9. **A** The two sentences in question draw a contrast between the peace of England and the chaos of France. *Tranquility* means "peace" and *turmoil* means "chaos." Therefore, (A) is correct. Choice (B) is also incorrect: Although the inn is old-fashioned, there is no indication that France should be thought of as modern. While the Comtesse is free, that fact is not mentioned in the description of the inn or England, nor does she actually ever describe the mob as ignorant. (In fact, fleeing the plague seems a very intelligent thing to do.) Therefore, (C) is incorrect. Because *austerity* means "extreme simplicity," (D) does not accurately describe the contrast between England and France.

10. **A** In the paragraph in question, the Comtesse compares her perception of Sir Antony's motives with those of Sir Andrew. Therefore, (A) is a good description of the distinction emphasized by the italics. There is never any indication that Sir Antony's *methods* are different from Sir Andrew's, so (B) is incorrect. While the Comtesse feels there is a distinction between Sir Andrew's motivations and those of Sir Antony, (C) is incorrect: Antony is motivated by excitement, not money. And while the Comtesse sees a distinction between Antony's motivations (a love of adventure) and Sir Andrew's motive (one that is *higher and nobler*), (D) is incorrect because there is no indication that Andrew is seeking admiration and praise (which seems unlikely to be the *higher* motive she implies).

11. **D** The passage is primarily concerned with descriptions of Roman baths, how they came into being, and their significance. Choice (A) is incorrect because very little is discussed in the passage regarding sanitation. Choice (B) is too limited in scope, and (C) is incorrect because religion is never discussed in the passage. Choice (D) best expresses the overall idea of the passage and is the correct answer.

12. **B** The first sentence draws a contrast between Greek and Roman architecture, so use POE to find an answer choice that reflects this. Eliminate (A) because the passage doesn't suggest that Roman architecture improved upon Greek architecture. Choice (B) works because *new trends* shows how Roman architecture differed from Greek architecture; keep it. Choice (C) is too extreme because nothing is proven, so eliminate it. Choice (D) is incorrect because religion is not discussed much in the passage, so eliminate (D). Choice (B) is correct.

13. **B** Cross out *omnipresent* and use the context to find an acceptable replacement. The curves are also described as *dominating*, and later in the paragraph the world the architects created is described as one that *was transformed into a new curvesomeness*. This suggests that the curves are a characterizing feature, so find the choice that matches these descriptions. Choice (B) is a match, since *pervasive* means "everywhere." Choice (A) is too limited, and (C) is a trap because the ceilings, not the curves, *reached up to the heavens*. Choice (D) is incorrect because *imposing* means "impressive in appearance." Choice (B) is correct.

14. **C** The second paragraph states that this *grand Roman innovation in architecture would be accomplished in two centuries as the essential ingredient, concrete, was perfected gradually by trial and error*. Choice (C) matches this information. The other answer choices pertain to the passage, but since the question is asking for the *critical* component, (C) is the correct answer.

15. **B** Lines 15–18 identify concrete as the *essential* ingredient in Roman innovation and state that it was *perfected gradually by trial and error*. Choice (B) is correct.

16. **A** The third paragraph states that *the new architectural creations arose from the needs of these Roman cities*, so the correct answer will reflect this idea. Choice (A) is a good match because the needs of the new Roman cities are what prompted the differences between Greek and Roman architecture discussed in the first paragraph. Choice (B) doesn't work because the passage does not reinforce this contrast but rather explains it. Choice (C) is alluded to at the end of the paragraph, but it is hardly the primary purpose. The author does not dismiss anything, so (D) is incorrect as well. Choice (A) is the correct answer.

17. **A** The first sentence of this paragraph describes the *grand Stabian baths* and how some of their features would show up in the *Pantheon three centuries later*. Therefore, replace *anticipated* with something that means "indicated" or "suggested." Choice (A) is the closest to this meaning and the correct answer.

18. **C** Use POE to find an answer choice consistent with what is in the last paragraph. The paragraph details the variously heated and cooled spaces within the baths, which supports (C), as the baths were a critical part of Roman life and offered the opportunity to experience different temperatures. Eliminate (A) because there is no comparison with modern baths, and eliminate (B) because gyms are not mentioned. Choice (D) is incorrect because *unparalleled in history* goes too far. Choice (C) is correct.

19. **C** The second-to-last sentence in the last paragraph states that the *baths at their best were public art museums and museums of contemporary art*. Choice (C) reflects this idea and is the correct answer. The other answer choices have some relevance to the passage, but the phrase "most exemplary" in the question makes (C) correct.

20. **D** The previous answer is best supported by the sentence *the baths at their best were public art museums and museums of contemporary art*. Therefore, (D) is correct.

21. **A**　The passage states that most public baths had an *unheated frigidarium partly open to the sky.* The graphic also includes a frigidarium in the center of the structure. Therefore, (A) is supported by both the passage and the diagram. Choice (B) is supported by the graphic, but there is no mention of palestrae in the passage. Therefore, (B) is incorrect. While the passage mentions that commercial contractors built public baths and the graphic shows a rectangular structure, there is no evidence that contractors *always* built baths in this shape; (C) is incorrect. And the passage never mentions natatio, so there is no evidence that this is where hoop-rolling and wrestling occurred, so (D) is incorrect. The answer is (A).

22. **C**　Palma argues that women should be allowed to vote, so he is not discussing both sides of the issue; he is focusing specifically on the arguments in support of one side of the issue. Thus, (A) is incorrect. Palma is arguing in favor of a reform—the right for women to vote—not cautioning against reform, so (B) is incorrect. Giving women the right to vote is a social change. Palma argues for this change, so (C) accurately describes Palma's role when giving the speech. Palma is a politician, but his focus is on rousing support for a bill that will give women the right to vote, not gaining support for his party. Therefore, (D) is incorrect. Choice (C) is the answer.

23. **B**　The passage does not provide any information about those who supported Palma, so (A) is incorrect. In the first paragraph, Palma states that he is advocating a cause that *cannot be represented or defended in this chamber*—that is, in the chamber of the legislature—*by those directly and particularly affected by it.* Those *directly and particularly affected* would be women. Palma is saying that women could not defend their own cause in the legislature, which supports the idea that women were not allowed to speak before the Filipino legislature at that time; thus, (B) is correct. Palma does not discuss whether other Filipino leaders of his time supported female suffrage, so (C) is incorrect. The passage does not discuss how members of the legislature viewed women, so (D) is also incorrect.

24. **D**　In the sentence in question, Palma says that we *cannot detain the celestial bodies in their course; neither can we check any of those moral movements.* A good replacement word for *check* is something like "detain," so go to the answer choices to find one that has a meaning like "detain." *Certify, inspect,* and *advise* all have meanings that are different from the meaning of the word *detain*, while *stop* has a similar meaning, so the correct answer is (D).

25. **C**　Palma states that *we cannot detain the celestial bodies in their course.* However, right before that he states that *female suffrage is a reform demanded by the social conditions of our times.* Immediately after he discusses the movements of celestial bodies, he also says *neither can we check any of those moral movements that gravitate with irresistible force toward their center of attraction: Justice.* Thus, he discusses the difficulty of halting the stars, or celestial bodies, in order to show that female suffrage is inevitable. This does not relate to the claims of those who oppose female suffrage, so eliminate (A). Palma does not say that those who oppose the bill are prejudiced against the causes of modern men and women in general, only that they are prejudiced against the cause of female suffrage. Thus, (B) is incorrect. In lines 46–51, Palma states that *the eternal calamity howlers and false*

prophets of evil raise their voices on this present occasion, in protest against female suffrage, invoking the sanctity of the home and the necessity of perpetuating customs that have been observed for many years. In other words, many who oppose the bill do so because they claim that giving women the right to vote may threaten *the sanctity of the home* and disrupt *customs that have been observed for many years.* Therefore, (C) is supported by the passage and is the correct answer. Choice (D) focuses on civic rather than social institutions and is too extreme, stating that giving women the right to vote will *permanently paralyze the country.* Those who oppose the bill do not make such extreme claims, so (D) is incorrect.

26. **B** As determined in the previous question, the opponents claim that women's suffrage will damage home life and perhaps disrupt long-established customs. Choice (A) mentions female suffrage, but only as something *the times demand* and without listing negative consequences. Choice (C) does mention that things *theretofore looked upon as immovable* have given way, but this sentence describes only what the country experienced during previous revolutions, not what is forecast. Choice (D) mentions *a few reactionists and ultra-conservatives* but does not detail their objections; (D) is incorrect. Choice (B) fully supports the answer for question 25 by naming the objections of those who oppose woman's suffrage. Choice (B) is the correct answer.

27. **B** Palma says that sudden changes have been *carried on most successfully, without paralyzation, retrogression, disorganization, or destruction.* Therefore, he is not showing how these things can damage a society, so (A) is incorrect. However, he uses this list to show how social changes can occur without paralyzing a nation or causing it to regress, become disorganized, or be destroyed. Therefore, (B) is the correct answer. Since Palma says that the Philippines experienced change without any of the negative consequences he lists, (C) does not agree with the information in the passage, and is therefore incorrect. Palma does not suggest that the nation should be paralyzed, regress, become disorganized, or be destroyed, so you can eliminate (D).

28. **A** In the sentence in question, Palma indicates that the great social upheavals have caused old institutions to *crumble to pieces.* However, later in that same sentence, he states that *despite all those upheavals…our people has become a people with modern thoughts and ideals…robust and strong.* In the next paragraph, he goes on to say that *in view of the fruitful results which those institutions of liberty and democracy have brought to our country…I do not and cannot, understand how there still are serious people who seriously object to the granting of female suffrage.* These quotes indicate that he introduces the social upheavals of the past in order to show that the country will survive any upheavals caused by giving women the right to vote. Thus, he uses an analogy to show that allowing women to vote would not permanently weaken the nation, making (A) the correct answer. Choice (B) is the opposite of what Palma is attempting prove—he does not believe that giving women more rights would cause the nation to crumble—so (B) is incorrect. Palma does mention *theories, beliefs, and codes of ethics,* but while he says that they were *looked upon as immovable,* he goes on to say that he has seen them *give way to different principles and methods based upon democracy and liberty.* Thus, while they appeared unchangeable, they did in fact change, so (C) is incorrect. Because Palma states that the old institutions gave *way to principles and methods*

based upon democracy and liberty, the new, not the old, institutions are the ones that uphold liberal democracy. Thus, (D) is incorrect.

29. **C** Palma discusses the country's previous social upheavals in lines 61–62 in order to demonstrate (in the lines that follow) that the country will be able to survive any social upheaval brought about by female suffrage, just as it survived turmoil in the past. Choices (A), (B), and (D) do not directly address the idea that the country has faced and survived upheaval before, so they do not sufficiently support the answer to question 28. Choice (C) clearly supports Palma's point by noting that *despite all those upheavals and changes*, the country has emerged with a *robust and strong* constitution and *a people with modern thoughts and modern ideals*. Therefore, (C) is correct.

30. **C** In the final paragraph of the passage, Palma discusses the *fruitful results* of the country's new institutions, and discusses the *marked progress* that these institutions have brought to *all the orders of national life*. Therefore, a good word to describe that progress might be "serious" or "noticeable." Of the answer choices, only *significant* is close in meaning to "serious" or "noticeable," so (C) is the correct answer. There is no evidence that the country's progress is fixed or guaranteed to continue, so (A) and (B) are incorrect. Choice (D), *underlined*, relates to the literal meaning of *marked*, but does not match the meaning intended by the context of the passage.

31. **D** Although the passage suggests that Palma is perplexed by those who oppose female suffrage, it does not indicate that his attitude toward them is mournful, so (A) incorrect. Palma supports the cause of female suffrage throughout his speech, so he is not unbiased or viewing the matter academically; (B) is incorrect. He is not deferential, or submissive, toward those who oppose female suffrage, so (C) is incorrect. In lines 85–87, Palma says, *I do not and cannot, understand how there still are serious people who seriously object to the granting of female suffrage*. These lines suggest that his attitude is one of bewilderment and dissent. Therefore, (D) is the correct answer.

32. **D** The third paragraph states that the size of elk populations and wolf populations could be related, so (A) is incorrect. The first sentence of the second paragraph states that wolves are part of a naturally functioning ecosystem, so (B) is incorrect. The first paragraph mentions that predator control efforts eradicated the gray wolf from Yellowstone, so (C) is incorrect. In the first paragraph, the passage mentions that wolves were regarded as dangerous and were deliberately exterminated. However, the rest of the passage focuses on how wolves have been restored to their natural habitat. Therefore, (D) is correct.

33. **C** The passage uses the word *native* to describe species that had existed in particular places until human interference affected their populations; therefore, the word is being used to describe animals that originated in or had long inhabited an area. Although (A) might sound like it could have such a meaning, *inborn* actually describes factors or traits present at birth, so (A) is incorrect. Choice (B), *constitutional*, is used to refer to someone's physical or mental condition and is also incorrect. Choice (C), *indigenous*, means originating in a specific area, making it the correct answer. Choice (D), *canine*, can be used to refer to animals of the dog family, which includes wolves; however, *canine* is not a synonym for *native*, so (D) is incorrect.

34. **B** The passage mentions that the wolf hunts *harvested* the wolves. The word *hunt* suggests that the wolves were trapped or killed. The next sentence reinforces this idea by noting that the number of wolves in the interior *declined less,* and the paragraph as a whole discusses the declining wolf population. Therefore, the only answer choice that makes sense is (B), *killed.*

35. **A** The author's argument in lines 30–32 is that the wolves in Yellowstone have a more stable population because they eat bison in addition to elk. Choice (A) proposes that the Delta and Bechler packs survived without eating much bison, which undermines the author's theory that eating bison is what prevented the wolf populations from declining as dramatically within the park as without. Therefore, (A) is correct. Choice (B) indicates that wolves entering the park have more stable populations, which agrees with the author's point that wolves in the park have a more stable population. Choice (C) says that the population of wolves in Yellowstone has declined, but the author acknowledges that the population declined; his point is that the population has declined less in the park than elsewhere. Therefore, (C) is incorrect. Because (D) does not mention wolves, it cannot be correct.

36. **B** The paragraph explains how data on wolf-prey relationships was gathered but makes no claims regarding what patterns that data revealed, so (A) is not supported by the paragraph and is incorrect. Because the paragraph mentions a wolf pack for which predation data could not be gathered, (B) is strongly supported by the content of the fifth paragraph. The paragraph notes that some of the packs were monitored by radio-tracking, ground teams, and aircraft, while others were monitored by only aircraft or not monitored at all, so there is no indication that most of the packs were monitored by ground teams, and (C) is incorrect. Because it is noted that researchers also documented things like percent consumption by scavengers, (D) is incorrect. Choice (B) is the correct answer.

37. **C** The answer to the previous question is that the predation data is incomplete. Choices (A) and (B) describe the method of gathering data but do not mention gaps in the data collected. Therefore, both are incorrect. Choice (C) mentions two packs that were not monitored fully, which supports the idea that the predation data is incomplete. Therefore, (C) is correct. Choice (D) describes some of the data gathered without alluding to any gaps in the data. Therefore, (D) is incorrect.

38. **C** Choice (A) is extreme; while the size of wolf packs is a limiting factor, there is no evidence in the passage to suggest that it is *the major* limiting factor. And though the passage discusses how wolves and other factors affect the elk population, it does not mention the *superior hunting tactics of wolves*, so (B) is incorrect. Because the passage discusses the effect of wolf populations and elk populations on one another, (C) accurately describes the relationship between elk and wolf populations. Choice (D) is also extreme; while the size of elk packs affects wolf populations, there is no evidence to suggest it is *the major* limiting factor. Therefore, the correct answer is (C).

39. **A** The answer to the previous question is that the sizes of wolf and elk populations affect one another. Choice (A) notes that wolf population numbers in YNP have declined *mostly because of a smaller elk population.* Because wolves primarily prey on elk in YNP, their population must affect the elk

population; the explicit statement here that the smaller elk population affected the number of wolves shows that the elk population also affects the wolf population. Choice (B) discusses bison, so it is not relevant as evidence about the elk and wolf populations. Choice (C) notes that wolf-prey relationships were studied does not give any specific information about those relationships. Choice (D) offers support for the claim that the wolf population affects the elk population but lacks support for the reverse relationship. Thus, (B), (C), and (D) are incorrect, and (A) is the correct answer.

40. **D** The sentence states that weather affects the ability of elk to forage. This has nothing to do with tracking wolves in Yellowstone. Therefore, (A) is incorrect. There is no evidence that the quality of the food has improved, so (B) is incorrect. Choice (C) is also incorrect; while the paragraph mentions predation studies, it does not argue for them. Because *weather patterns influence forage quality and availability* and forage quality and availability in turn affect the elk population, the reference to the weather does provide additional information about a cause of the decline of elk in Yellowstone. Therefore, (D) is correct.

41. **A** The graph shows that the wolf population in 2010–2011 was about 40, while the elk population was about 4,500. The wolf population has never reached as many as 120 during the time reflected in the graph, while the elk population had not dipped below the mid-4,000s in 2011; therefore, the graph supports the claim that elk populations currently outnumber wolf populations in YNP, and (A) is supported by the graph. Because elk populations increased from 1998 to 2000 and in other years, (B) is incorrect. Elk populations were at their lowest in 2010–2011, but wolf populations were at their highest in 2003–2004, so (C) is incorrect. Because there are about 40 wolves and 4,500 elk in Yellowstone as of 2011, (D) is incorrect. If you answered (D) or eliminated (A), you likely did not notice that the wolf population is on the left axis of the graph and the elk population is on the right.

42. **C** The question asks what the author suggests about mammals in the first paragraph of Passage 1. Choice (A) is incorrect because the paragraph states that *more than half of all species* were wiped out in the KT extinction, so species other than mammals must also have survived. Choice (B) sounds good, since mammals were not dominant, but the author doesn't say that they were very rare; eliminate (B). While many species were wiped out, many mammals survived, so (D) is too extreme. The passage states that mammals became dominant after the KT extinction, so (C) is the correct answer.

43. **B** As determined in the previous question, mammals were not dominant on Earth until after the asteroid hit. Since question 42 asks specifically about the first paragraph, the first paragraph is probably the best place to find support for a claim made in that paragraph. Choice (A) is from the first paragraph but simply states that experts reviewed the research. Choice (B) is also from the first paragraph and explicitly states that *the extinction wiped out more than half of all species on the planet, thus clearing the way for mammals to become the dominant species on Earth,* so (B) is the correct answer. While (C) comes immediately after the first paragraph and could comment upon it, the lines do not address mammals or their dominance. Choice (D) is from the sixth paragraph, and while it

does support the idea that *humans* were not dominant until after the KT extinction, the fact that humans were not dominant does not in and of itself indicate that no mammals were dominant. Choice (D) is not better than (B).

44. **B** The word *spewed* is used in the passage to describe the process of volcanic eruptions releasing vast amounts of lava that spread across the land. Thus, *spewed* must means something like "to release or expel substances out." Choice (B) is correct, as it means "to eject something." Choice (A) means "to set fire," and although lava is hot and burns what it touches, the correct answer needs to address the issue of releasing the lava. Choice (C) means "to dig out of the earth," and (D) means "to draw off or convey liquid." Neither reflects the sense that the lava is being pushed out of the volcano, and so neither choice is better than (B).

45. **B** Passage 1 states that the asteroid caused fires, earthquakes, and tsunamis, but it isn't clear that those are what killed most of the dinosaurs. In fact, the passage argues that it was the dust cloud that shielded the sun that dealt the final blow. So, (A) is incorrect. Choice (C) makes a causal link between the asteroid and the volcanoes, but this relationship is never put forward in the passage, so (C) is incorrect. The passage states that *scientists have previously argued* about the cause of the extinction, but this does not mean they are still in complete disagreement, particularly given the agreement surrounding the new study; (D) is incorrect. The correct answer is (B).

46. **D** Both passages use the saying *nail in the coffin* to state that something came to a clear end. Choice (D) is the correct answer because the saying refers to an event that caused something to end, that is, a terminating event. Choice (A) is incorrect, as the saying is not a deduction. Choice (B) is tempting because the *nail in that coffin* in Passage 1 is the asteroid that ended the reign of the dinosaurs, but in Passage 2, the *nail in the coffin* is the end of the belief that the dinosaurs could have died before the asteroid's impact. Choice (C) looks good because the saying is a metaphor, but the question asks what the passages are using the metaphor to refer to, not what type of literary device is being used.

47. **B** The reason the author mentions the high-precision radiometric dating techniques is to justify the study's claims that the time span between the asteroid hitting earth and the extinction of the dinosaurs was shorter than had been previously thought. Thus, (B) is correct. The data, not the techniques, was used to propose a new theory. Similarly, the author doesn't mention the techniques in order to prove the conclusion correct. The author wants to make sure that people understand that the data was better than before, so (A) and (C) are not correct. Choice (D) can be mistaken for meaning that the new data counters the old assumption, but the purpose of mentioning the device is to lend authority to the claim.

48. **C** The word *preclude* is used to describe what would happen to a causal relationship between the asteroid and the dinosaur extinction if the previous data was correct. The scientist who uses the word explains that the previous data showed the extinction to have occurred before the asteroid hit, and that would completely undermine any claims that the asteroid had caused the extinction. Therefore, *preclude* must means something like "prevent from happening." Choice (B) is close to

this meaning, but (C) is the correct answer because to bar means to stop something completely, rather than just limit it. Choice (A) does not make sense; no matter what the older data showed, the data could not cause a relationship between the asteroid and the extinction; it could only confirm or disprove hypotheses about the relationship. Choice (D) means "to strike with light blows" and does not make sense in the context of the sentence.

49. **D**   The author of Passage 2 mentions tektites because they represent residue from the asteroid, while volcanic ash provides information about the timing of the large-scale volcanoes that erupted. The aging of these samples affected the theories that were set forth. Thus, (D) is correct. The tektites don't suggest another cause, (A); they definitely don't diminish the role of the asteroid in the demise of the dinosaurs, (B); and they don't substantiate that the volcanoes caused the most damage, (C), since that's too vague and unsupported by the passage.

50. **C**   Think about the evidence from the passage that helped you answer the previous question: Tektites were mentioned because they helped prove that there was not a causal relationship between the impact and the extinction. Only (C) works, and it's the correct answer.

51. **C**   The correct answer is (C), as Passage 1 mentions mammals and their rise to dominance and Passage 2 does not. Both passages described the size of the asteroid, so (A) is incorrect. Both passages say that the primary cause of the extinction was an asteroid that hit before the extinction took place, so (B) is incorrect. Both passages indicate that previous theories have been reconsidered and adjusted in light of an evaluation of evidence, so (D) is incorrect.

52. **B**   The main difference between the passages is that Passage 2 puts forth the idea that the ecosystems were already in decline when the asteroid hit, while Passage 1 doesn't mention that possibility when it discusses the volcanoes. Otherwise, both passages ultimately ascribe the KT extinction to the asteroid. Thus, (B) is correct. Choice (A) is incorrect because the asteroid didn't cause the volcanic eruptions. Choice (C) is incorrect because Passage 2 clarifies the timing of the impact and states that past estimates were inaccurate. Passage 2 doesn't discuss mammals at all, so (D) is incorrect.

Section 2: Writing and Language

SLP, OMG!

1. **B**   Notice the question! It asks for a choice that would *best introduce the main subject*. The rest of the paragraph is about the spoken word, so (B) is correct. The other answer choices do not introduce this paragraph's discussion of the spoken word.

2. **C**   Keep the verb tense in this sentence consistent. The other verbs are *is* and *write*. Choice (C) is the only choice that uses the present tense (*speak*) and matches the parallel structure set up by the comparison: *most younger people write…more than they speak….* Therefore, (C) is the correct answer.

3. **B** Check the answer choices against the graphs. Choice (A) can be eliminated because SLPs do not *overwhelmingly work in hospitals*; the percentages for non-residential health-care facilities and schools are both higher than for hospitals. Choice (B) is correct because 53% is *about half*. Choice (C) can also be eliminated because the number of SLPs working in schools cannot be determined from the graph provided. 53% of SLPs work in schools, but we don't know the total that 53% is out of. Choice (D) can be eliminated because the percentages provided don't represent budget amounts.

4. **D** *Understatement* is the more appropriate choice because the rest of the passage details the wide range of duties that a speech-language pathologist could undertake; therefore, the sentence should be kept as is for the reason stated in (D).

5. **D** Notice the question! Choices (A) and (C) do not combine the sentences together. Also, (C) has a period separating a complete idea and an incomplete idea, which is incorrect. Choice (B) flows essentially the same way as (A) by inserting a semicolon in place of the period, so you can eliminate (B). Choice (D) incorporates the two ideas together in one fluid sentence, connecting the incomplete idea (*particularly the components…*) to the phrase it describes (*attention and memory*). Therefore, (D) offers the best combination and is the correct answer.

6. **C** Possessive pronouns do not use apostrophes, while contractions do. Choices (B) and (D), therefore, are both contractions for *one is* and *it is* respectively. Since a possessive pronoun is needed in this sentence, eliminate (B) and (D). The respiratory aspects belong to *speech*, which is singular. Thus, (C) is correct because *its* is the singular possessive form.

7. **A** The correct phrase should convey that the SLP and medical doctor working together could restore an infant's esophageal function to proper working order. Choices (C) and (D) do not convey this idea. Choice (B) is an idiom that *could* express this idea but could also simply mean that something is neat and tidy, which wouldn't express the intended meaning. Choice (A) clearly conveys the right meaning, so the sentence is correct as written.

8. **A** Notice the question! It asks for a choice that would *best maintain this sentence's focus on the actions an SLP might take to address a swallowing disorder*. Only (A) details a specific action an SLP might take, while the others are either off topic or do not mention an action that an SLP might take to address a swallowing disorder.

9. **C** If you cannot cite a reason to use a comma, don't use one! Commas are not needed for any reason in this sentence, so the correct answer is (C).

10. **B** Notice what changes in the answer choices: punctuation! Choice (A) creates a comma splice, and (D) creates a run-on sentence, so both choices can be eliminated. Choices (B) and (C) both use correct STOP punctuation; the only difference is the use of *but,* which creates a contrast. There is a contrast in the sentence; however, it is already set up in the first half of the sentence by the phrase *after all not merely*. Thus, *but* is not needed in the second half, and you can eliminate (C) and choose (B).

11. **D**   Notice that pronoun use is changing in the answer choices. Use POE. Choice (A) can be eliminated because the machine (what *itself* would refer back to) is not being fixed or replaced. Choices (B) and (C) can also be eliminated because *it* could suggest that the pronoun refers back to *machine, the rise,* or *the digital age,* whereas *them* could refer back to *basics* or *facets.* In either case, the pronoun is not precise. Choice (D) is correct because the pronoun needed should refer back to people in general (notice *our lives* and *us* used in the sentence). The sentence means that there are some basics that no machine can replace or fix *for us* even though the digital age has changed many facets of our lives.

The Other Steel City

12. **C**   Notice the question! It asks for a choice that *best introduces the historical tone of this essay.* Only (C) contains a historical reference. The other answer choices mention information related to its location or population, and information about those topics does not fulfill the stated purpose of the question.

13. **B**   Notice the question! The question asks which is the *least* acceptable. The original sentence uses *diversity* to convey the vast range of indigenous people who once inhabited Bethlehem. Only (B) changes the meaning (the sentence isn't discussing how the inhabitants were ordered or grouped) and is therefore the *least* acceptable.

14. **D**   Choice (D) provides the most clarity by indicating who specifically traded with the settlers. You may have been tempted to choose (A), but (A) is incorrect because it includes the potentially ambiguous *they*.

15. **D**   All four choices mean essentially the same thing, so choose the one that is most concise and makes sense in context. In this case, that is (D), *continued*.

16. **A**   The phrase at the beginning of the sentence is an introductory idea (*Even after the initial European settlement on Christmas Eve in 1741*) and should have a comma following *1741*, so eliminate (B) and (C). The phrase *in 1741* is necessary in order to know which Christmas Eve is being discussed, so (D) can be eliminated because commas before and after the phrase would indicate that the phrase is unnecessary. Thus, the sentence is correct as written, making (A) the answer.

17. **B**   Notice the question! It asks for a choice that *helps to maintain the focus on the way the Moravian settlers have been characterized throughout the essay.* Use POE. Choices (C) and (D) do not maintain the focus on the Moravian settlers, as both choices are about European influence. Choice (A) does not present information that is consistent with how the Moravian settlers have been characterized throughout the essay; the remainder of the third paragraph presents the Moravian influence in a positive light, which leaves (B) as the correct answer.

18. **D** Choices (A), (B), and (C) all say essentially the same thing. Unlike the other choices, however, (D) contains *that of.* The *as* in the original sentence indicates a comparison is being made, which, in this sentence, is *its* (the Moravian) *religious influence* to *other groups.* However, the comparison should be consistent in structure, so (D) is correct because the pronoun *that* (referring to the religious influence) is used to make the second part of the comparison consistent with the first part so that the comparison is influence to influence rather than influence to groups.

19. **A** Remember: Possessive pronouns do not use apostrophes, while contractions do use apostrophes. Choice (C) is the contraction for *they are,* and (D) is the contraction for *it is.* Neither is correct in this case because a possessive pronoun is needed to indicate whose factory was providing armor and steel. The factory belongs to Bethlehem, which is singular. Eliminate (B) because *their* is plural. Therefore, the sentence is correct as written, so (A) is the answer.

20. **C** Notice that the answer choices all contain verbs (some plural and some singular) and check for subject/verb consistency. The subject for the second clause is *furnaces,* which is plural. Eliminate (A) and (B) because both are singular. Next, check the verb tense. Since the *furnaces* presently stand and will continue to stand (their presence appears to be permanent), the simple present tense (*remain*) is needed, so (C) is correct. Choice (D) is not correct because it uses the wrong verb tense and would change the meaning of the sentence.

21. **C** Notice the question! It asks for a choice that *would best conclude the essay by preserving its style and tone.* The style and tone of this essay is informative and formal, so (C) is most appropriate. The rest of the choices are all too conversational in tone, which is not consistent with the essay as a whole.

22. **B** Use POE. The sentence should be added to the paragraph that talks about the Moravians, so eliminate (A) and (D). The proposed insertion does not contain information that should conclude paragraph 3. The final sentence of the third paragraph is primarily talking about a music festival, so to double back and make a broad point about *intellectual life* after such a narrow example would be awkward. Eliminate (C). Also, the sentence before (B) uses the phrase *set up missions to convert the Lenape and non-English-speaking Christians to the tenets of Moravianism,* which is consistent with the new sentence's use of *After years of teaching....* Thus, (B) is the best placement for the sentence and the correct answer.

Look It Up!

23. **B** Without the phrase *what if you don't?,* the next sentence (*Well, Urban Dictionary can save the day.*) does not make sense. Therefore, the phrase should be kept, and eliminate (C) and (D). Because the sentence following the phrase answers the question being asked, the correct answer is (B).

24. **D** The correct idiomatic expression to use when looking for (or trying to discover) someone or something is *turn up.* All the other choices could follow *turn* in other circumstances (*turn down* the volume, *turn in* your homework, *turn back* before it's too late). However, in this sentence, the reader

is instructed to look for something in a Google search. What the reader finds would be what the reader *turns up*, making (D) the correct answer.

25. **D** The correct choice will feature words that are as precise as possible. Where Sentence 2 is currently placed, it is unclear what *they* is referring back to, so eliminate (A). There would be nothing for *they* to refer back to if Sentence 2 were placed at the beginning of the paragraph, so eliminate (B). In placing Sentence 2 after Sentence 5, *they* seems to be referring back to *Urban Dictionary*, which is singular. *They* is plural and, therefore, inconsistent, so (C) is also incorrect. Choice (D) is correct because the construction is consistent with Sentences 8 and 9, and *they* is appropriately placed so that *they* refers back to the plural noun *dictionaries*.

26. **A** The verb in the underlined portion should be consistent with the rest of the verb phrase: *were not*, *did not*, and *did not have* can't come before *existed*, so (B), (C), and (D) are incorrect. The verb phrase *have not…existed* is therefore correct as written. Choice (A) is correct.

27. **C** The word *pronunciation* may be more common, but that does not make it more relevant in the circumstances, so (A) is incorrect. *Diction* does have a precise meaning (that is, the choice and use of words or phrases in speech and writing), so (B) is incorrect. Choice (D) is incorrect because the two words do not have radically different definitions. Since the beginning of the sentence mentions the term *dictionary* and when this word was *coined*, the phrase should be kept for the reason stated in (C).

28. **D** The sentence already contains *furthermore*, which is not underlined, so using *indeed* would be redundant. Eliminate (B). Both (A) and (C) mean the same thing, but (A) is more concise; eliminate (C). However, you can have a comma between two complete ideas only when it accompanies a FANBOYS; therefore, eliminate (A) as well. The first idea (*Furthermore…Modern period*) needs to be incomplete because the idea following the comma is complete. By adding *while* before *numerous dictionaries*, the first idea is incomplete, making (D) the correct answer.

29. **C** There should be a comma after every item in a list—in this case, *consistent spellings, variant definitions, textual usages, and alphabetical arrangements*. This eliminates (D). Choice (B) is incorrect because a comma is not needed after *and*. The phrase *alphabetical arrangements* needs to be together, so there should not be a comma separating those two words, which means (A) is incorrect and (C) is the answer.

30. **C** If the phrase *An American Dictionary of the English Language* were removed, the meaning and completeness of the sentence would not change. Even though it is the title of the book, the rest of the sentence indicates this work was Webster's best-known and when it was published, so this phrase is not essential to the meaning of the sentence. Commas should go before and after unnecessary information such as this, as (C) indicates. The correct answer is (C).

31. **A** Notice the question! It asks for a choice that would *best emphasize the unique achievement of Webster's dictionary*. Only (A) notes what he did that was unique. The other choices fail to indicate how Webster's dictionary was different from previously published dictionaries.

32. **B** The sentence sets up a contrast between the way Americans write two specific words and the way English write them. Only (B) completes that contrast, giving the clearest sense of how the English spell those words, and is the correct answer.

33. **A** The entire underlined phrase is serving as the subject of this sentence and cannot be a complete idea, so eliminate (D). Choice (C) leaves out the phrase *what is interesting,* which is what the second half of the sentence explains. Choice (B) creates a plural subject with the phrase *both what is interesting about these two dictionaries and…dictionaries in general,* which is not consistent with the non-underlined, singular verb *is.* Therefore, the sentence is correct as written and (A) is the answer.

Goodnight, sleep tight...

34. **C** Use POE, testing the underlined portion in each place suggested by the answer choices. The best placement for the underlined portion is after the word *form,* (C), because the *aftermath* of a bed bug bite takes the *form of an itchy welt.* Placement of the underlined portion in any other place would not convey this intended meaning.

35. **B** The sentence begins with a comparison (*Like the most annoying vampire…*), so the word after the comma should complete the comparison. Since the author is comparing *vampires* to *bed bugs,* (B) is the only option. The two parts of the comparison should match, which is why the remaining answers are incorrect. Choices (A) and (D) are comparing *vampires* to *human blood,* and (C) is comparing *vampires* to *a typical meal.*

36. **A** The previous sentence states *Interest in bed bugs seems to be nearly as old as written history itself,* so the correct answer will provide support for this statement (that is, bed bugs have been around for a long time). Use POE. Choices (C) and (D) can be eliminated because they do not mention the presence of bed bugs throughout history. While (B) contains a reference to history, it does not support the previous sentence (again, no mention that bed bugs have been around for a *really* long time). Choice (A) contains the needed support and is the correct answer.

37. **D** Since (D) provides the option to delete, look to see if the variation of the underlined phrase is even needed, especially since the other three choices all say essentially the same thing. The phrase isn't needed because earlier in the second clause the bed bugs are mentioned as *helping to extract the toxins,* which makes the options in (A), (B), and (C) redundant and unnecessary to the sentence. Choice (D) is correct.

38. **A** Choice (B) can be eliminated because the singular pronoun *it* would be referring to *bed bugs* which is plural. Choice (C) changes the meaning of the sentence by indicating that *some* bed bugs are a nuisance, whereas the original sentence is suggesting that bed bugs as a whole are a nuisance. Choices (A) and (D) are similar in meaning; however, (D) is wordy while (A) maintains the simple present tense, which is needed, so no change should be made to the sentence. Choice (A) is correct.

39. **C** Notice what is changing in the choices. When dealing with pronouns, possessives use NO apostrophes, but contractions do use apostrophes. So, *they're* is the contraction for *they are*. *Their* shows plural possession. *There* is used to refer to location. Eliminate (A) and (B) because the sentence needs a possessive pronoun: It is the *bed bugs'* prevalence that is being discussed. Choice (D) is incorrect because the use of *the* would provide no ownership of *prevalence* and would not be precise. Thus, (C) is correct.

40. **B** Notice the question! It asks whether or not the author has achieved the goal of providing continuity between the two paragraphs. The third paragraph describes the significant problem bed bugs were during the *twentieth century* because of their prevalence and lists events in *1933* and *during World War II* for support. The fourth paragraph continues this timeline of events by mentioning the efforts of the United States in the *1940s* and the reappearance of bed bugs in the *1980s*. Thus, the goal for continuity between paragraphs has been achieved for the reason stated in (B).

41. **B** The author is explaining that the resurgence of bed bugs is due to two causes: *pesticide _____* and *international travel*. The part of speech needed is a noun to be consistent with the other noun used (*international travel*), so eliminate (A), (C), and (D). Choice (B) is correct, as it uses the correct noun to convey the intended meaning.

42. **D** Notice what is changing in the answer choices: punctuation! Periods and semicolons can be used only to separate complete ideas. In this sentence there is a complete idea before the punctuation and an incomplete idea after the punctuation, so neither (A) nor (B) is correct. Choice (C) is incorrect because *and* does not reflect the contrast between two ideas in the sentence. Choice (D) is correct because it ties the two ideas together with a comma and *though,* which accurately reflects the way the second statement qualifies the first.

43. **D** Notice the question! It asks for a choice that *would best maintain the focus of this sentence and paragraph*. The focus of this paragraph is on the unexpected discovery that bed bugs can transmit disease. The only option that does this is (D), as the paragraph references a *new reason* and *worry*. Choices (A), (B), and (C) bring up irrelevant points about mice or rats in the context of this paragraph and are not consistent with the focus of the sentence or paragraph.

44. **A** Use the first phrase in the sixth paragraph (*If these findings are true*) to help. The phrase *these findings* is referring back to the study that was discussed at the end of the fifth paragraph. Therefore, the only logical place for the sixth paragraph is where it is currently, which is (A). Otherwise, the flow of the passage would be disrupted and inconsistent because *these findings* would not be referring back to the study.

Section 3: Math (No Calculator)

1. **B** Because Marco already has 75 pounds of salt, he needs $200 - 75 = 125$ additional pounds. Estimate the number of bags he needs. 125 is close to 120, and $120 \div 30 = 4$, so he must need more than 4 bags (because 125 is more than 120). This means that Marco needs at least 5 more bags. Therefore, the correct answer is (B).

2. **C** Whenever there are variables in the question and in the answers, think Plugging In. Let $d = 2$. The number of subscribers the website has signed up so far can be calculated as $500(2) = 1,000$. Therefore, the website needs to sign up $100,000 - 1,000 = 99,000$ additional subscribers. Plug 2 in for w in the answers to see which answer equals the target number of 99,000. Choice (A) becomes $W = 500(2) = 1,000$. This doesn't match the target number, so eliminate (A). Choice (B) becomes $W = 99,500(2) = 199,000$. Eliminate (B). Choice (C) becomes $W = 100,000 - 500(2) = 100,000 - 1,000 = 99,000$. Keep (C), but check (D) just in case it also works. Choice (D) becomes $W = 100,000 + 500(2) = 100,000 + 1,000 = 101,000$. Eliminate (D). The correct answer is (C).

3. **C** Since the question states $f(4) = 5$, then when $x = 4$, the result should be 5. Plug in $x = 4$ into each answer choice to see which equation does NOT equal 5. Choice (A) becomes $f(4) = 4 + 1 = 5$. This works, so eliminate (A). Choice (B) becomes $f(4) = 2(4) - 3 = 8 - 3 = 5$. Eliminate (B). Choice (C) becomes $f(4) = 3(4) - 2 = 12 - 2 = 10$. The correct answer is (C).

4. **D** Factor the expression to get $\dfrac{x^2(x+1)}{x^3(x+1)}$. Reduce the fraction to get $\dfrac{x^2}{x^3}$, or $\dfrac{1}{x}$. Another way of writing $\dfrac{1}{x}$ is x^{-1}. Therefore, the correct answer is (D).

5. **A** Start with the easier equation first and use Process of Elimination. The easier equation has to do with the total number of solutions. According to the question, Régine measures a total of 100 solutions. This information can be expressed as $x + y = 100$. Eliminate (B) and (C) because neither of these includes this equation. Remember that percentage means divided by 100. Therefore, $40\% = 0.4$ and $70\% = 0.7$. Given this information, x should be associated with 0.4 and y should be associated with 0.7. On this basis, eliminate (D). The correct answer is (A).

6. **B** The graph shown is a regular parabola that has been turned upside down and moved down 6. The equation of a regular parabola that points upward is $y = x^2$. Therefore, the graph of a parabola that points downwards is $y = -x^2$. Eliminate (D) because that answer is missing the negative sign. To move a parabola down 6 units, a 6 must be subtracted from the equation of the parabola. Eliminate (A) and (C), which add 6 instead. Choice (B) can be rewritten as $y = -x^2 - 6$. The correct answer is (B).

7. **A**   Start by labeling the equation with the information in the question. The question says that P is the price of the item and t is the time in years, so label these. The question also states that the price increases by \$3 per year, so the 3 in the equation is the price increase. Now look at the answer choices, which are about the number 10 in the equation, and see what can be eliminated. Choice (D) refers to the price increase, which is 3, so eliminate (D). The other answer choices refer to the year. Plug in the price given in the question, \$43, to solve for t. The equation becomes $43 = 3t + 10$, so $3t = 33$, and $t = 11$. That represents the number of years from when the item was manufactured until the year 2010, the year of the given price. Subtract 11 years from 2010 to get 1999, which is (A).

8. **C**   Use the formula arc $= r\theta$, where r is the radius and θ is the measure of the central angle in radians. Because the angle is already in radians, you just need to plug in 10 for the radius and the angle $\dfrac{2\pi}{5}$ into the formula. You then get $s = (10)\dfrac{2\pi}{5}$ or 4π, which is (C).

9. **B**   Start by calculating the least amount of acetaminophen the child needs. If the child is 75 pounds, then the amount of acetaminophen needed can be calculated as $\dfrac{75}{150} \times 1{,}000 = \dfrac{1}{2} \times 1{,}000 = 500$. Since only (B) gives 500 as the low-end value, the correct answer is (B).

10. **C**   Whenever there are variables in the question and in the answer choices, think Plugging In, picking numbers that ensure that I is an integer. If $P = 18$ and $R = 2$, then $I = \sqrt{\dfrac{P}{R}} = \sqrt{\dfrac{18}{2}} = \sqrt{9} = 3$. Because $V = IR$, $V = 3 \times 2 = 6$. Plug $P = 18$, $R = 2$, and $V = 6$ into the answers to see which answer works. Choice (A) becomes $18 = \dfrac{2}{6^2}$. Solve the right side of the equation to get $18 = \dfrac{2}{36}$. This statement is not true, so eliminate (A). Choice (B) becomes $18 = \dfrac{6}{2}$. This statement is not true, so eliminate (B). Choice (C) becomes $18 = \dfrac{6^2}{2}$. Solve the left side of the equation to get $18 = \dfrac{36}{2}$. This statement is true, so keep (C), but check the remaining answer just in case. Choice (D) becomes $18 = (6^2)(2^3)$ or $18 = 36 \times 8$. This statement is not true, so eliminate (D). The correct answer is (C).

11. **D**   A root of the equation is the same as an x-intercept. In the graph, the function crosses the x-axis at 4 points. Therefore, the correct answer is (D).

12. **A** Label the congruent angles, $\angle ABC$ and $\angle CDE$, as such. In order to find the measure of those angles, use the formula $180(n-2)$, where n is the number of sides, to determine the sum of the interior angles of the figure. Because the figure has five sides, plug 5 in for n to get $180(5-2)$, or $180(3)$, which equals 540. Subtract 120 to get 420. Subtract 100 to get 320. Subtract 40 to get 280. Since the two remaining angles are congruent, divide by 2 to find that the two unlabeled angles are both equal to 140. Because $\angle ABC$ and $\angle BCD$ have a combined measure of 180, $\overline{AB}$ and $\overline{CD}$ are parallel. Therefore, (A) accurately describes the relationships in the figure.

13. **B** Taking the 4th root of a number is the same as taking the number to the $\frac{1}{4}$ power. Therefore, the equation can be rewritten as $2w^{\frac{3}{4}}x^{\frac{9}{4w}} = 2\left(3^{\frac{3}{4}}\right)\left(x^{\frac{3}{4}}\right)$. Divide both sides by 2 to get $w^{\frac{3}{4}}x^{\frac{9}{4w}} = \left(3^{\frac{3}{4}}\right)\left(x^{\frac{3}{4}}\right)$. Therefore, in the equation $w^{\frac{3}{4}} = 3^{\frac{3}{4}}$ and $x^{\frac{9}{4w}} = x^{\frac{3}{4}}$, so $w = 3$. The correct answer is (B).

14. **C** Whenever there are variables in the question and in the answers, think Plugging In. If $a = 2$ and $b = 3$, $r = [\frac{1}{2}(2) + 3]^2 = (1 + 3)^2 = 16$, and $s = -4(2)(3) + 3(3) = -24 + 9 = -15$. The expression $r - 2s$ becomes $16 - 2(-15) = 16 + 30 = 46$. Plug 2 in for a and 3 in for b in each of the answers to see which answer equals the target number of 46. Choice (A) becomes $\frac{1}{4}(2^2) + 3^2 - 7(2)(3) - 6(3) = 1 + 9 - 42 - 18 = -50$. This does not match the target number, so eliminate (A). Choice (B) becomes $\frac{1}{4}(2^2) + 3^2 - 7(2)(3) + 6(3) = 1 + 9 - 42 + 18 = -14$. Eliminate (B). Choice (C) becomes $\frac{1}{4}(2^2) + 3^2 + 9(2)(3) - 6(3) = 1 + 9 + 54 - 18 = 46$. Keep (C), but check (D) just in case it also works. Choice (D) is the same as (C) except for the coefficient on the a^2 term, so it can't equal 46. Eliminate (D). The correct answer is (C).

15. **C** First, start with a sketch of the two points to see what the line in question might look like.

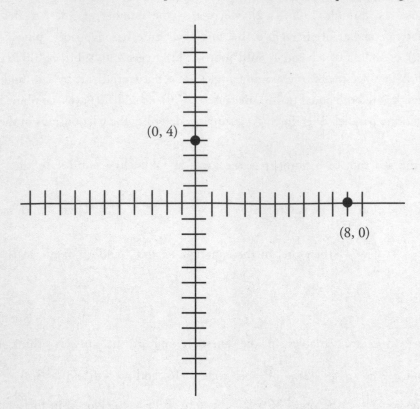

The point directly between the two points will definitely be on the line, so find the midpoint of

the two points. Midpoint $=\left(\dfrac{x_1+x_2}{2}, \dfrac{y_1+y_2}{2}\right)=\left(\dfrac{0+8}{2}, \dfrac{4+0}{2}\right)=(4,2)$. Check this point in the

answer choices and eliminate any that do not contain it. Choice (A) becomes $2(2) = -4 + 8$ or

$4 = 4$, which is true. Choice (B) becomes $2(2) = 4$, and (C) becomes $2 = 2(4) - 6$ or $2 = 8 - 6$.

These are also true, but (D) becomes $2 = -2(4)$, which is false. Eliminate (D). To sketch the re-

maining equations, rewrite them in slope-intercept form of the equation $y = mx + b$, where m

is the slope and b is the y-intercept. Choice (A) becomes $y = -\dfrac{1}{2}x + 4$, (B) becomes $y = \dfrac{1}{2}x$,

and (C) is already in the right form. Now sketch the graphs of each of these on the xy-plane.

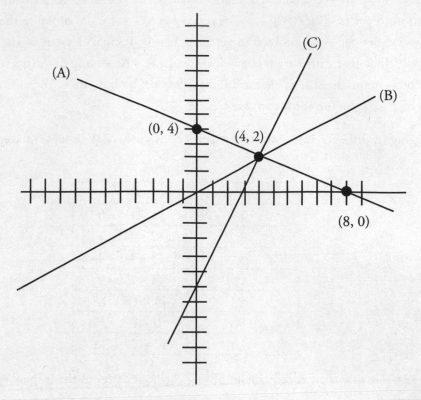

The line in (A) contains both the given points, but all the points to the left of (0, 4) are closer to that point and all those to the right of (8, 0) are closer to it. So eliminate (A). Many points on line (B) are also clearly closer to one or the other of the given points, so eliminate (B). Line (C) appears to be perpendicular to the line formed by the two given points, and this is in fact what will make all the points on a line equidistant from 2 given points. Therefore, the correct answer is (C).

16. $\dfrac{7}{3}$ or **2.33**

Get rid of the fractions in the first equation by multiplying the entire equation by 6, to get $2p + 3q = 6$. Whenever there are two equations with the same two variables, they can be solved simultaneously by adding or subtracting them. The key is to get one variable to disappear. Stack the equations and add them.

$$
\begin{array}{r}
2p + 3q = 6 \\
\underline{p - 3q = 1} \\
3p = 7
\end{array}
$$

Therefore, $p = \dfrac{7}{3}$.

17. **6** Substitute x for y in the second equation to get $(x-2)^2 - 4 = -x$. Expand the left side of the equation to get $(x-2)(x-2) - 4 = -x$ or $x^2 - 4x + 4 - 4 = -x$. Simplify the equation to get $x^2 - 4x = -x$. Set the equation to 0 to get $x^2 - 3x = 0$. Factor an x out of the equation to get $x(x-3) = 0$. Therefore, either $x = 0$ or $x - 3 = 0$, and $x = 3$. According to the question, the point of intersection is in quadrant I, where the x and y values are both positive. Therefore, $x = 3$ and $y = 3$. The sum of $3 + 3 = 6$. The correct answer is 6.

18. **6** Try Plugging In different values of c to see which ones work. Make a table to keep track of all the numbers.

$c =$	$(c-1)^2 =$
1	$(1-1)^2 = 0$
2	$(2-1)^2 = 1$
3	$(3-1)^2 = 4$
4	$(4-1)^2 = 9$
5	$(5-1)^2 = 16$
6	$(6-1)^2 = 25$
7	$(7-1)^2 = 36$

The largest value of c that works without hitting the boundaries of the inequality is 6, so the correct answer is 6.

19. **8** When no picture is provided, it helps to draw one. First, rewrite each equation so that it is in the slope-intercept form of a line, which is $y = mx + b$, where m is the slope and b is the y-intercept of the line. The first equation becomes $2y \le x + 4$, or $y \le \frac{1}{2}x + 2$. The second equation becomes $y \ge 2x - 4$. The resulting graph looks as follows:

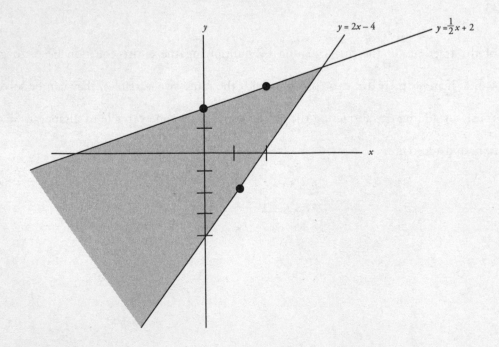

As the graph shows, the greatest $x + y$ is the point at which the two lines intersect. Set the equations of the two lines, $y = \frac{1}{2}x + 2$ and $y = 2x - 4$, equal to each other and solve for x. The resulting equation is $\frac{1}{2}x + 2 = 2x - 4$. Solve for x to get $-\frac{3}{2}x + 2 = -4$ or $-\frac{3}{2}x = -6$, so $x = 4$. Next, plug 4 into one of the two equations to solve for y. Therefore, $y = 2(4) - 4 = 4$ and $x + y = 4 + 4 = 8$. The correct answer is 8.

20. **72**   The formula for the volume of a pyramid, given at the start of each math section, is $V = \frac{1}{3}lwh$, where l is the length of the base, w is the width of the base, and h is the height. Since the cube has side 6, the length and width of the base are both 6. The height of the pyramid is also the height of the cube, which is also 6. Plug these into the formula to get $V = \frac{1}{3}(6)(6)(6) = 72$.

Section 4: Math (Calculator)

1. **D**   Whenever there are variables in the question and in the answers, think Plugging In. Let $d = 2$. For $1 the air pump dispenses $90 \times 4 = 360$ pounds of air. Therefore, for $2 the air pump will dispense $360 \times 2 = 720$ pounds of air. Plug in 2 for d in the answer choices to see which answer equals 720. Choice (A) becomes $P = 2 + 90 = 92$. Eliminate (A). Choice (B) becomes $P = 2 + 360 = 362$. Eliminate (B). Choice (C) becomes $P = 90(2) = 180$. Eliminate (C). Choice (D) becomes $P = 360(2) = 720$. Therefore, the correct answer is (D).

2. **A**   Set up a proportion: $\dfrac{1 \text{ foot}}{0.30 \text{ meters}} = \dfrac{6 \text{ feet}}{x \text{ meters}}$. Cross-multiply to get $x = 6 \times 0.30 = 1.8$ meters. Therefore, the correct answer is (A).

3. **B**   In order to find the undeveloped area, take the entire area of the park and subtract the area of the developed portions. Subtract the 4 acre lake to get $44 - 4 = 40$ undeveloped acres. Next, subtract the largest and smallest possible soccer field area: $40 - 10 = 30$, and $40 - 8 = 32$. Therefore, the correct answer is (B).

4. **B**   Weight is shown on the horizontal axis of the graph, given in tons. Look for the mark indicating 3 on this axis; then draw a vertical line from that mark to the line of best fit. Once you hit it, draw a horizontal line over to the vertical axis. It should hit between 20 and 25 miles per gallon, slightly closer to the mark for 25. This makes (B) the correct answer. Draw your lines carefully, using your answer sheet as a straightedge if necessary, to avoid trap answers like the close-but-not-quite (C).

5. **C**   You can see from the graph that from 2000 to 2002, the number of coati increased from 140 to 160. From 2002 to 2004, the number increased from 160 to 180. Therefore, the number of coati is increasing at a rate of 20 every 2 years. In 2006, if the rate of increase remains the same, the number of coati should be $180 + 20 = 200$, which is (C).

6. **B** The question states that there are infinitely many solutions to the equation. That means any real number should work for d. Plug in an easy number like 0 for every d in the equation to get $\dfrac{0+10-0}{3} = \dfrac{0+a}{3}$. Simplify the equation to $\dfrac{10}{3} = \dfrac{a}{3}$, so $a = 10$, which is (B).

7. **A** First, convert the minutes shown in the graph to seconds. Multiply 15 minutes by 60 seconds to get 900 seconds. Then, since speed is distance divided by time, simply divide 3,000 meters by 900 seconds. The answer is 3.3 m/s, which is (A).

8. **C** Plug 2 in for y in the answers to see which function most closely equals the area of 14,910. Choice (A) becomes $15,000\left(\dfrac{1}{2}\right) = 7,500$. This does not match the target number, so eliminate (A). Choice (B) becomes $15,000(0.003)^2 = 0.135$. Eliminate (B). Choice (C) becomes $15,000(0.997)^2 \approx 14,910$. The correct answer is (C).

9. **B** First, calculate what Mike's daily calorie consumption is during finals. 12% of 1,680 is $0.12 \times 1,680 = 201.6$. During finals Mike consumes $1,680 + 201.6 = 1,881.6$ calories per day. Whenever the question includes variables, Plug in. Let $d = 2$. Over 2 days Mike consumes $2 \times 1,881.6 = 3,763.2$ calories. He also adds 900 calories at the end of finals. His total consumption over the entire finals period is $3,763.2 + 900 = 4,663.2$ calories, so 4,663.2 is the target number. Plug in 2 for d in each of the answer choices. In (A), $1.12[1,680(2) + 900] = 4,771.2$, which is not the target number. Eliminate (A). In (B), $1.12[1,680(2)] + 900 = 4,663.2$, which is the target. Leave (B), but check the other answer choices just in case. In (C), $1.12(1,680 + 900)(2) = 5,779.2$, and in (D), $[1,680 + (0.12)(2)] + 900 = 2,580.24$. Eliminate both (C) and (D). The correct answer is (B).

10. **D** Use Process of Elimination on this question. Choice (A) cannot be correct because more juniors prefer Austin to Pensacola. Choice (B) sounds appealing, but "more than three times as likely" means the seniors as a whole need to prefer Pensacola more than three times as much as the juniors do as a whole. Seniors prefer Pensacola 23 out of 42, or 55%. Juniors prefer it 7 out of 21, or 33%. So, seniors do not prefer Pensacola more than three times as much as juniors do. You can also eliminate (C) because more than half of all juniors prefer Austin, while less than half of all seniors prefer Austin. The statement in (D) is correct because 7 is one-third of the total of 21 juniors.

11. **B** We are looking for the probability that a randomly selected person is a man with a doctoral degree. There are 16,232 men with doctoral degrees, and 220,532 total adults aged 25 years or older. So the probability that a randomly selected person fits the category we are looking for is $\dfrac{16,232}{220,532} = 0.07 = 7\%$, which is (B).

12. **C** Whenever there are variables in the question and in the answers, think Plugging In. If

$x = 10$, then $C = 110 + \dfrac{10}{2} = 110 + 5 = 115$ and $R = 15(10) - \dfrac{10^2}{10} = 150 - \dfrac{100}{10} = 150 - 10 = 140$.

Therefore, the profit can be calculated as $140 - 115 = 25$. Plug 10 in for x in the an-

swers to see which answer equals the target number of 25. Choice (A) becomes

$-\dfrac{10^2}{10} - \dfrac{31}{2}(10) + 110 = -\dfrac{100}{10} - 31(5) + 110 = -10 - 155 + 110 = -55$. This doesn't match the tar-

get number, so eliminate (A). Choice (B) becomes $-\dfrac{10^2}{10} - \dfrac{29}{2}(10) + 110 = -\dfrac{100}{10} - 29(5) + 110 =$

$-10 - 145 + 110 = -45$. Eliminate (B). Choice (C) becomes $-\dfrac{10^2}{10} + \dfrac{29}{2}(10) - 110 = -\dfrac{100}{10} + 29(5)$

$- 110 = -10 + 145 - 110 = 25$. Keep (C), but check (D) just in case it also works. Choice (D)

becomes $-\dfrac{10^2}{10} + \dfrac{31}{2}(10) - 110 = -\dfrac{100}{10} + 31(5) - 110 = -10 + 155 - 110 = 35$. Eliminate (D) and

choose (C).

13. **D** To stay at his fancy hotel for three nights at 2,000 Moroccan dirhams per night, Erik will need 6,000 dirhams. Using the currency conversion rate of 1 dirham = $0.11, we can multiply 6,000 × 0.11 to determine that Erik's hotel stay will cost $660. Since his bank allows him to withdraw only $200 at a time, Erik must go to the ATM four times: (D).

14. **C** Start with the easier equation first and use Process of Elimination. The easier equation involves the total amount of gas sold. According to the question, 850 gallons of gasoline were sold, which can be expressed as $u + p = 850$. Eliminate (D) since it does not include this equation. The other equation in the answers is related to the amount of money collected. According to the question, $3,016.50 was collected; however, this sum included a discount of $0.10 per gallon for 100 of the gallons that were purchased or $0.10 × 100 = $10. Without the discount unleaded gas costs $3.49 and premium gas costs $3.79 a gallon, and the amount of money collected would have been $3,016.50 + $10 = $3,026.50. Only (C) provides the correct total. Therefore, the correct answer is (C).

15. **B** First, let's figure out how many students are enrolled in AP courses other than Biology and U.S. History. We know that 319 students are enrolled in at least one AP course, and of those, 75 + 58 = 133 are enrolled in Biology and U.S. History. However, since 22 students are enrolled in both of those courses, we need to subtract 22 from 133 (so as not to double-count the students taking both courses). That leaves us with $133 - 22 = 111$ total students who are taking AP Biology and

AP U.S. History. Of the 319 students taking AP courses, that means there are 319 − 111 = 208 students taking AP courses other than Biology and U.S. History. We know that there are 784 juniors and seniors total, so $\frac{208}{784}$ = 0.265, or approximately 27% of all juniors and seniors, which is (B).

16. **A** Total score = average score × the number of tests. In order for Mateo to receive a B, he needs his total score over the 3 tests to be between 3 × 80 = 240 points and 3 × 89 = 267 points. On his first and second tests, Mateo scored a total of 79 + 95 = 174 points. Therefore, on his third test Mateo must score between 240 − 174 = 66 and 267 − 174 = 93 points in order to receive a B. The correct answer is (A).

17. **A** Use Process of Elimination to solve this question. Choice (A) is possible so leave it. Choice (B) discusses the mass of the fertilizer, but no reference to mass is made in the question. Eliminate (B). According to the question, the quantity described in (C) is represented by A, so eliminate (C). According to the question, the quantity described in (D) is represented by Y, so eliminate (D). The correct answer is (A).

18. **D** The mode of the combined groups cannot be determined without knowing exactly what scores each group received. To illustrate this, plug in! Let's say that the scores of Group A were {1, 1, 7, 7, 7}, and the scores for Group B were {1, 1, 6, 6, 6}. The scores of the whole group would, therefore, be {1, 1, 1, 1, 6, 6, 6, 7, 7, 7}. This set has a mode of 1, so eliminate (A), (B), and (C) and choose (D).

19. **C** First, count the number of blocks that Josh needs to drive. He needs to drive 4 blocks north and 6 blocks east for a total of 10 blocks. You need to convert this into miles, which can be done with the following proportion: $\frac{10 \text{ blocks}}{x \text{ miles}} = \frac{1 \text{ block}}{.6 \text{ miles}}$. The drive is a total of 6 miles. Since Josh drives at 30 miles per hour, you can set up a second proportion: $\frac{30 \text{ miles}}{1 \text{ hour}} = \frac{6 \text{ miles}}{x \text{ hours}}$. Cross-multiply and solve to get that $x = \frac{6}{30}$ or $\frac{1}{5}$ of an hour. This equals 12 minutes in (C).

20. **D** The first step is to rewrite the bottom equation so that it is in the same format as the first equation. Move all of the variables in the bottom equation to the left side of the equation to get $6s − t = 12$. If the answer is (A) and there are infinitely many solutions to the system of equations, then the two equations must be the same equation. To determine whether this is the case, multiply the top equation through by 3 to get $6s − t = 30$. Since it cannot be the case that the equation $6s − t$ equals both 12 and 30, the correct answer is (D). There are no solutions to the system of equations.

21. **C** Two factors are important in determining how to poll a group: the size of the sample and how that sample is selected. Secretary Stephens's plan has the largest sample with 250 students, but all those students belong to the senior class. Perhaps the senior class would prefer a theme that the other three classes would not. The sample is skewed and not necessarily representative of the entire student body, so eliminate (B). The other three plans all poll 100 students, so the manner in which those students are selected becomes more important. President Peterson's plan is also skewed specifically to friends

of the student council members, whose opinions might not reflect the majority, so eliminate (A). Vice President Vaiyda's plan has more potential for a varied sample, but it is still not as good as Treasurer Thompson's plan, which guarantees that a random assortment of people will be chosen for the poll. Eliminate (D), and choose (C).

22. **C** Since x and y are points on the circle, plug in the point $(-2, -2)$ into the left side of the equation. This gives you $(-2 + 3)^2 + (-2 - 1)^2$, which equals $1^2 + (-3)^2$. Simplifying, you get 10. Because 10 is greater than r^2 (which is 9), the point must be outside the circle, which is (C).

23. **D** Whenever the question includes variables, think Plugging In. According to the question, $\frac{x-12}{\sqrt{8}} = \frac{x\sqrt{2}}{4} - C$. Plug in 12 for x to get $\frac{12-12}{\sqrt{8}} = \frac{12\sqrt{2}}{4} - C$, or $\frac{0}{\sqrt{8}} = \frac{12\sqrt{2}}{4} - C$. Solve for C to get $0 = \frac{12\sqrt{2}}{4} - C$, then $0 = 3\sqrt{2} - C$, and finally $3\sqrt{2} = C$. The correct answer is (D).

24. **A** All of the answer choices refer to the number of salary-satisfied bachelor's-degree-holders, so you must use the follow-up survey results to calculate that number. First, find the percent of bachelor's-degree-holders who reported also being salary-satisfied in the follow-up survey. This number was 658 out of the 1,000 people, so divide 658 by 1,000 and then multiply by 100 to get the percent. The result is 65.8% salary-satisfied bachelor's-degree-holders for the follow-up survey. Since the people in the follow-up were randomly selected, you can assume that they are generally representative of the bachelor's-degree-holding population at large. Therefore, the 65.8% of salary-satisfied individuals should be true of all 24,236,000 job-satisfied bachelor's-degree-holders. Watch the units on charts—this one is in the thousands, so there are 24,236,000 not 24,236 job-satisfied bachelor's-degree-holders. Multiply 65.8%, or .658, by the total number of job-satisfied bachelor's-degree-holders, 24,236,000, to find that there should be 15,947,288 salary-satisfied, job-satisfied bachelor's-degree-holders. Choice (A) is the closest to this and is the correct answer .

25. **A** The equation of a line expressed in slope-intercept form is $y = mx + b$, where m is the slope and b is the y-intercept. One way to find the y-intercept of line d is to plug in the slope and given point and solve for b. The equation $y = mx + b$ becomes $1 = \frac{4}{5}(1) + b$. Subtract $\frac{4}{5}$ from both sides to get $b = \frac{1}{5}$. The y-intercept of line e is 3 times $\frac{1}{5}$, so the y-intercept of line e is $\frac{3}{5}$. Additionally, parallel lines have slopes that are equal to each other. Therefore, line e will also have a slope equal to $\frac{4}{5}$. Therefore, the equation of line e is $y = \frac{4}{5}x + \frac{3}{5}$. Rewrite this in a form that looks more like the answer choices by multiplying everything by 5 to get $5y = 4x + 3$. Subtract $4x$ from both sides to get $5y - 4x = 3$. Therefore, the correct answer is (A).

26. **B** An extraneous solution is an answer that when plugged back into the equation causes the equa-

tion to be false. Begin by factoring and reducing the fraction on the left side of the equation

to get $\dfrac{(q-7)(q+6)}{q+6} = \sqrt{q-5}$ or $q-7 = \sqrt{q-5}$. Square both sides of the equation to get

$q^2 - 14q + 49 = q - 5$. Set the equation to 0 to get $q^2 - 15q + 54 = 0$. Factor the quadratic

to get $(q-9)(q-6) = 0$. Therefore, $q = 9$ or $q = 6$. Eliminate (A) and (C) because neither of

these answers is a possible solution for q. Plug 6 in for q in the equation to see if this value of

q works. The equation becomes $\dfrac{6^2 - 6 - 42}{6+6} = \sqrt{6-5}$. Solve both sides of the equation to get

$\dfrac{-12}{12} = 1$. Since this statement is not true, 6 is the extraneous solution. The correct answer

is (B).

27. **D** First, determine the total number of gamers in each game type by adding up the columns. There are 110,000,000 gamers preferring first person shooters, 52,000,000 preferring sports games, and 85,000,000 preferring adventure games. You don't know by how much the 9- to 13-year old group will increase in sport game preference, but presumably the increase will be made to match the currently largest group, first person shooters. Therefore, in order to raise adventure games to the level of first person shooters, you need to add 110,000,000 − 85,000,000 = 25,000,000 gamers to the adventure games group. If you are going to do so by doubling one of the age groups, then 25,000,000 is equal to the size of the current group. 9- to 13-year olds currently have 25,000,000 preferring adventure games, so (D) is the answer.

28. **A** Whenever there are variables in the question and in the answers, think Plugging In. Let's say

that for Emilio $a = 2$, $t = 4$, and $k = 10$. Then Emilio's accrued vacation days can be calculated as

$V(t) = 2(4) + 10 = 18$. This means that Martin has accrued $18 + 9 = 27$ vacation days. Because a

and k are constants, their values do not change. The number of years that Martin has worked at

the manufacturing plant can therefore be calculated as $27 = 2t + 10$. Solve for t to get $17 = 2t$ or

$t = \dfrac{17}{2} = 8.5$. Therefore, Martin has worked $8.5 − 4 = 4.5$ more years than Emilio. Plug 2 in for a

in the answers to see which answer equals 4.5. Choice (A) becomes $\dfrac{9}{2} = 4.5$. Keep (A) but check

the remaining answers just in case. Choice (B) becomes $9 − 2 = 7$, (C) becomes $9 + 2 = 11$, and (D)

becomes $9(2) = 19$. Eliminate (B), (C), and (D). The correct answer is (A).

29. **C** SOHCAHTOA tells you that sine is $\dfrac{\text{opposite}}{\text{hypotenuse}}$, so if the side opposite the angle with mea-

sure $x°$ is O and the hypotenuse is H, then $\dfrac{O}{H} = \dfrac{2\sqrt{29}}{29}$. Solve for O, and you get $O = \dfrac{2H\sqrt{29}}{29}$.

Now, you can use the Pythagorean Theorem with the given side and substituting $\dfrac{2H\sqrt{29}}{29}$ for

O in order to solve for H: $10^2 + \left(\dfrac{2H\sqrt{29}}{29}\right)^2 = H^2$. Solve the exponents, and then reduce the

fraction: $100 + \dfrac{116H^2}{841} = H^2$; $100 + \dfrac{4H^2}{29} = H^2$. Subtract $\dfrac{4H^2}{29}$ from both sides: $100 = \dfrac{25H^2}{29}$.

Divide both sides by $\dfrac{25}{29}$, so $116 = H^2$. Square root both sides, and you find that $H = 2\sqrt{29}$.

Using $O = \dfrac{2H\sqrt{29}}{29}$ from above, you can solve for O: $O = \dfrac{2\left(2\sqrt{29}\right)\sqrt{29}}{29} = 4$. Add the sides and

you get $14 + 2\sqrt{29}$, which is (C).

30. **D** A good approach to this question would be to plug in some numbers. Start with the number

of juniors and plug in a number that is easy to deal with, such as 200. Then you can set up

a proportion using the ratio given in the question stem: $\dfrac{\text{juniors}}{\text{seniors}} = \dfrac{4}{3} = \dfrac{200}{x}$. Cross-multiply

and solve for x to determine that the number of seniors would be 150. Next, use the relation-

ship $\dfrac{\text{seniors}}{\text{sophomores}} = \dfrac{5}{4}$. Using 150 for seniors, you get $\dfrac{\text{seniors}}{\text{sophomores}} = \dfrac{5}{4} = \dfrac{150}{x}$. Cross-multiply

and solve for x to determine that the number of sophomores would be 120. Next, use the re-

lationship $\dfrac{\text{freshmen}}{\text{sophomores}} = \dfrac{7}{6}$. Using 120 for sophomores, you get $\dfrac{\text{freshmen}}{\text{sophomores}} = \dfrac{7}{6} = \dfrac{x}{120}$.

Cross-multiply and solve for x to determine that the number of freshmen would be 140. The ratio

of freshmen to seniors, therefore, would be $\dfrac{\text{freshmen}}{\text{seniors}} = \dfrac{140}{150} = \dfrac{14}{15}$, which is (D).

31. **75** Hayoung swims 2.5 miles. She runs $11 \times 2.5 = 27.5$ miles, and she bikes $18 \times 2.5 = 45$ miles. Her total triathlon mileage $= 2.5 + 27.5 + 45 = 75$ miles. The correct answer is 75.

32. **5** Plug 1,230 in for the value of the function to get $1,230 = 250x - 20$. Solve for x to get $1,250 = 250x$ and $x = 5$. The correct answer is 5.

33. **918** In order to find the greatest profit, maximize the number of acres of soybeans Marty plants, since soybeans bring in more money per acre than does wheat. At most, Marty can plant 7 acres of soybeans. Therefore, the most money he can make on soybeans is $7 \times 120 = 840$. He then has $9 - 7 = 2$ acres left on which to plant wheat. The money he makes from this wheat is $2 \times 90 = 180$. The total amount Marty makes before taxes is therefore $840 + 180 = 1,020$. The tax on this money

equals 1,020 × 0.10 = 102. Subtract the amount Marty pays in taxes to get 1,020 − 102 = 918 profit. The correct answer is 918.

34. **19** The formula for the area of a circle is $A = \pi r^2$. If a full circle were shown, its radius would be 4, so the area of the full circle would be $A = \pi 4^2 = 16\pi$. The interior angle of the fraction of the circle shown can be calculated as 90 + 45 = 135 degrees. Therefore, the figure shown is $\dfrac{135}{360}$ of the area of a full circle. The area of the figure can be calculated as $\dfrac{135}{360}(16\pi) = 0.375(16\pi) = 6\pi \approx 18.8 \approx 19$. The correct answer is 19.

35. **6** The two triangles share three angles; thus they are similar. $\overline{AC}$ is twice the length of $\overline{BC}$ because it is bisected by $\overline{BD}$. This relationship is constant between the two similar triangles. Therefore, $\overline{BD}$ is half of $\overline{AE}$: 12 ÷ 2 = 6.

36. **20** First, determine the grams of protein in the bar. If the bar contains 32% of the daily recommended serving of protein, and the daily recommended serving of protein is 50 grams, then the bar contains 0.32 × 50 = 16 grams of protein. Next, determine the grams of fat in the bar by using the percent change equation: percent change = $\dfrac{\text{difference}}{\text{original}} \times 100$. The percent change is 700, and the original is the grams of fat (because percent more means the original is the smaller number), which means $700 = \dfrac{16 - x}{x} \times 100$. Divide both sides by 100: $7 = \dfrac{16 - x}{x}$. Multiply both sides by x to get $7x = 16 - x$. Add x to both sides to get $8x = 16$. Divide both sides by 8 and you find $x = 2$. That is the number of grams of fat in the bar. To find the daily recommended serving of fat, translate English to math. 2 is 10% of the daily recommended serving, so if the daily recommended serving is y, 2 = 0.10y. Divide both sides by 0.10, and you find that the daily recommended serving of fat is 20.

37. **1** First, you need to determine the content of Set R. If Set R consists of all the one-digit prime numbers, then $R = \{2, 3, 5, 7\}$. The sum of the elements of Set S would therefore be 2 + 3 + 5 + 7 + x = 30. Combine like terms: 17 + x = 30. Subtract 17 from both sides, and you find x = 13. Plug x = 13 into the equation and solve: $(13)^2 - 11(13) - 25 = 1$.

38. **8** The additional positive integer x cannot equal 2, 3, 5, or 7 (otherwise there would be a mode). Next, determine what the median could be for various ranges of x. If x is less than 2, then the set would be, in consecutive order, $\{x, 2, 3, 5, 7\}$, making the median 3. Try this set. If the median equals the mean, then the sum of the elements divided by 5 (the number of elements) must equal 3: $\dfrac{x+2+3+5+7}{5}=3$. Multiply both sides by 5 and combine like terms: $x + 17 = 15$. Subtract 17 from both sides, and you find $x = -2$. However, x must be a positive integer, so this doesn't work. Try a new median. If $x = 4$, then the set is $\{2, 3, 4\ (x), 5, 7\}$, with a median of 4. However, the mean is $\dfrac{2+3+4+5+7}{5}=5.25$, not 4, so this doesn't work. If x is 6 or greater, the set would either be $\{2, 3, 5, 6\ (x), 7\}$ or $\{2, 3, 5, 7, x\}$. In either case, the median is 5. Set up the average equal to the median of 5: $\dfrac{2+3+5+7+x}{5}=5$. Multiply both sides by 5 and combine like terms: $17 + x = 25$. Subtract 17 from both sides, and you find that $x = 8$.

Raw Score (# of correct answers)	Math Section Score	Reading Test Score	Writing and Language Test Score
0	200	10	10
1	200	10	10
2	210	10	10
3	230	11	10
4	240	12	11
5	260	13	12
6	280	14	13
7	290	15	13
8	310	15	14
9	320	16	15
10	330	17	16
11	340	17	16
12	360	18	17
13	370	19	18
14	380	19	19
15	390	20	19
16	410	20	20
17	420	21	21
18	430	21	21
19	440	22	22
20	450	22	23
21	460	23	23
22	470	23	24
23	480	24	25
24	480	24	25
25	490	25	26
26	500	25	26
27	510	26	27
28	520	26	28
29	520	27	28

Raw Score (# of correct answers)	Math Section Score	Reading Test Score	Writing and Language Test Score
30	530	28	29
31	540	28	30
32	550	29	30
33	560	29	31
34	560	30	32
35	570	30	32
36	580	31	33
37	590	31	34
38	600	32	34
39	600	32	35
40	610	33	36
41	620	33	37
42	630	34	38
43	640	35	39
44	650	35	40
45	660	36	
46	670	37	
47	670	37	
48	680	38	
49	690	38	
50	700	39	
51	710	40	
52	730	40	
53	740		
54	750		
55	760		
56	780		
57	790		
58	800		

Please note that the numbers in the table may shift slightly depending on the SAT's scale from test to test; however, you can still use this table to get an idea of how your performance on the practice tests will translate to the actual SAT.

CONVERSION EQUATION SECTION AND TEST SCORES

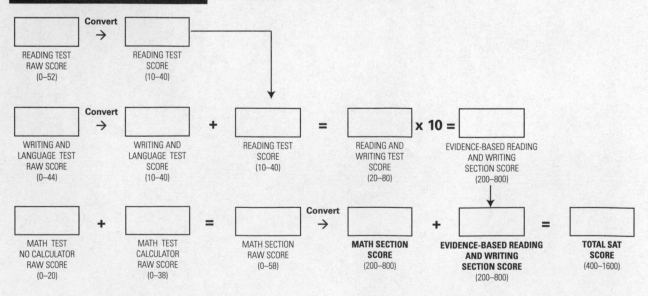

NOTES

NOTES

NOTES

NOTES

NOTES

NOTES

China (Beijing)
1501 Building A,
Disanji Creative Zone,
No.66 West Section of North 4th Ring Road Beijing
Tel: +86-10-62684481/2/3
Email: tprkor01@chol.com
Website: www.tprbeijing.com

China (Shanghai)
1010 Kaixuan Road
Building B, 5/F
Changning District, Shanghai, China 200052
Sara Beattie, Owner: Email: sbeattie@sarabeattie.com
Tel: +86-21-5108-2798
Fax: +86-21-6386-1039
Website: www.princetonreviewshanghai.com

Hong Kong
5th Floor, Yardley Commercial Building
1-6 Connaught Road West, Sheung Wan, Hong Kong
(MTR Exit C)
Sara Beattie, Owner: Email: sbeattie@sarabeattie.com
Tel: +852-2507-9380
Fax: +852-2827-4630
Website: www.princetonreviewhk.com

India (Mumbai)
Score Plus Academy
Office No.15, Fifth Floor
Manek Mahal 90
Veer Nariman Road
Next to Hotel Ambassador
Churchgate, Mumbai 400020
Maharashtra, India
Ritu Kalwani: Email: director@score-plus.com
Tel: + 91 22 22846801 / 39 / 41
Website: www.score-plus.com

India (New Delhi)
South Extension
K-16, Upper Ground Floor
South Extension Part–1,
New Delhi-110049
Aradhana Mahna: aradhana@manyagroup.com
Monisha Banerjee: monisha@manyagroup.com
Ruchi Tomar: ruchi.tomar@manyagroup.com
Rishi Josan: Rishi.josan@manyagroup.com
Vishal Goswamy: vishal.goswamy@manyagroup.com
Tel: +91-11-64501603/ 4, +91-11-65028379
Website: www.manyagroup.com

Lebanon
463 Bliss Street
AlFarra Building - 2nd floor
Ras Beirut
Beirut, Lebanon
Hassan Coudsi: Email: hassan.coudsi@review.com
Tel: +961-1-367-688
Website: www.princetonreviewlebanon.com

Korea
945-25 Young Shin Building
25 Daechi-Dong, Kangnam-gu
Seoul, Korea 135-280
Yong-Hoon Lee: Email: TPRKor01@chollian.net
In-Woo Kim: Email: iwkim@tpr.co.kr
Tel: + 82-2-554-7762
Fax: +82-2-453-9466
Website: www.tpr.co.kr

Kuwait
ScorePlus Learning Center
Salmiyah Block 3, Street 2 Building 14
Post Box: 559, Zip 1306, Safat, Kuwait
Email: infokuwait@score-plus.com
Tel: +965-25-75-48-02 / 8
Fax: +965-25-75-46-02
Website: www.scorepluseducation.com

Malaysia
Sara Beattie MDC Sdn Bhd
Suites 18E & 18F
18th Floor
Gurney Tower, Persiaran Gurney
Penang, Malaysia
Email: tprkl.my@sarabeattie.com
Sara Beattie, Owner: Email: sbeattie@sarabeattie.com
Tel: +604-2104 333
Fax: +604-2104 330
Website: www.princetonreviewKL.com

Mexico
TPR México
Guanajuato No. 242 Piso 1 Interior 1
Col. Roma Norte
México D.F., C.P.06700
registro@princetonreviewmexico.com
Tel: +52-55-5255-4495
+52-55-5255-4440
+52-55-5255-4442
Website: www.princetonreviewmexico.com

Qatar
Score Plus
Office No: 1A, Al Kuwari (Damas)
Building near Merweb Hotel, Al Saad
Post Box: 2408, Doha, Qatar
Email: infoqatar@score-plus.com
Tel: +974 44 36 8580, +974 526 5032
Fax: +974 44 13 1995
Website: www.scorepluseducation.com

Taiwan
The Princeton Review Taiwan
2F, 169 Zhong Xiao East Road, Section 4
Taipei, Taiwan 10690
Lisa Bartle (Owner): lbartle@princetonreview.com.tw
Tel: +886-2-2751-1293
Fax: +886-2-2776-3201
Website: www.PrincetonReview.com.tw

Thailand
The Princeton Review Thailand
Sathorn Nakorn Tower, 28th floor
100 North Sathorn Road
Bangkok, Thailand 10500
Thavida Bijayendrayodhin (Chairman)
Email: thavida@princetonreviewthailand.com
Mitsara Bijayendrayodhin (Managing Director)
Email: mitsara@princetonreviewthailand.com
Tel: +662-636-6770
Fax: +662-636-6776
Website: www.princetonreviewthailand.com

Turkey
Yeni Sülün Sokak No. 28
Levent, Istanbul, 34330, Turkey
Nuri Ozgur: nuri@tprturkey.com
Rona Ozgur: rona@tprturkey.com
Iren Ozgur: iren@tprturkey.com
Tel: +90-212-324-4747
Fax: +90-212-324-3347
Website: www.tprturkey.com

UAE
Emirates Score Plus
Office No: 506, Fifth Floor
Sultan Business Center
Near Lamcy Plaza, 21 Oud Metha Road
Post Box: 44098, Dubai
United Arab Emirates
Hukumat Kalwani: skoreplus@gmail.com
Ritu Kalwani: director@score-plus.com
Email: info@score-plus.com
Tel: +971-4-334-0004
Fax: +971-4-334-0222
Website: www.princetonreviewuae.com

Our International Partners

The Princeton Review also runs courses with a variety of
partners in Africa, Asia, Europe, and South America.

Georgia
LEAF American-Georgian Education Center
www.leaf.ge

Mongolia
English Academy of Mongolia
www.nyescm.org

Nigeria
The Know Place
www.knowplace.com.ng

Panama
Academia Interamericana de Panama
http://aip.edu.pa/

Switzerland
Institut Le Rosey
http://www.rosey.ch/

All other inquiries, please email us at
internationalsupport@review.com